Dan Heimbach has provided a highly reac
in society together with a thorough presentation of the potentially society-changing perspective of true biblical sexual morality. I have never seen anywhere this kind of compelling analysis. This may be the most important book written in our generation.

—PAIGE PATTERSON, President,
Southwestern Baptist Theological Seminary

I've known Dan Heimbach for many years, so I'm not surprised that *True Sexual Morality: Recovering Biblical Standards for a Culture in Crisis* is such an extraordinary book. It's unlike anything you've read on the subject, and I mean that as the highest of compliments. With biblical sexual morality as his standard, he examines the sexual chaos that devastates so many and cripples our culture. Dan takes on the toughest and broadest question of all, the one often dodged: what must be the Christian approach to sexuality? And he answers it fully and persuasively. He doesn't flinch or equivocate. This work is comprehensive and scholarly, yet practical and highly readable. It's written for pastors and laypersons—for all of us. What a breathtaking achievement!

—FRED BARNES, Co-Founder and Executive Editor,
The Weekly Standard, and Co-Host of FOX News Channel's
"The Beltway Boys"

A very thorough study of biblical sexual morality and how it is twisted by the world.

—ELISABETH ELLIOT GREN

Postmodern America has entered a period of such deep and sustained sexual rebellion, recovery seems a dim prospect indeed. Having rejected the clear and objective teachings of God's Word, and thus the Creator's pattern for human sexuality, modern individuals now demand the right to craft their own sexual morality, gender, and pattern of intimate relations. Now comes Dan Heimbach's book, *True Sexual Morality.* Here at long last is a strong, biblical, prophetic, and courageous corrective to the sexual anarchy reigning in our culture. Dan Heimbach combines intellectual rigor with a deep understanding of sexual patterns prevalent in our society today. His corrective is firmly established in the Bible and the rich tradition of Christian moral teaching. This book should help frame debate and equip thinking Christians to join the battle for moral sanity—and for our souls.

—R. ALBERT MOHLER, JR., President,
The Southern Baptist Theological Seminary

Dan Heimbach presents biblical sexual morality in a way that upholds high standards of holiness, purity, beauty, and joy in clear contrast to the bankrupt, destructive immorality flooding our culture today. Here is a clearly written and much needed challenge to Christians and non-Christians alike!

—WAYNE GRUDEM, Research Professor of Bible and Theology,
Phoenix Seminary

Here is an uncompromising explanation of the Bible's clear and explicit teaching concerning God's design for our sexuality and why He gave us the gift of gender. All Christians owe a tremendous debt of gratitude to Dan Heimbach for providing an enormously effective weapon against the pagan sexuality emerging in our culture.

—RICHARD LAND, President,
The Southern Baptist Convention's Ethics and
Religious Liberty Commission

In this important work, Dan Heimbach has rendered an invaluable service to the church of the Lord Jesus. It is comprehensive, thorough, and most importantly biblically and theologically sound. It definitely fills a void in current discussion concerning sexual morality. It should become a standard text and resource for serious Christian study in the years ahead.

—DANIEL AKIN, President,
Southeastern Baptist Theological Seminary

What should Christians do in light of the massive sexual revolution currently underway in Western culture? Dan Heimbach answers that question in *True Sexual Morality*. The insights he brings are filled with biblical truth which will help equip the Christian to stand firm on the shifting sands of moral decay and corruption. This work will prove to be a classic Christian critique of our age. It will also be a sharp arrow in the Christian's quiver of essential weapons for spiritual warfare. Here is a *tour de force* for biblical truth and practice.

—PHIL ROBERTS, President,
Midwestern Baptist Theological Seminary

Dan Heimbach's *True Sexual Morality* sets the record straight! Based on wide research and careful analysis, the dangers of radical feminism and libertine sexuality are shown for what they really are: directly and vehemently opposed to Scripture and its glorious vision of true sexual morality. And what a vision this is, as Heimbach turns to commend the wise and good plan God had in mind in making us male and female. All who care about the true good of men and women, and the upholding of truth and Scriptural teaching, will find in this book enormous instruction, insight, vision, and encouragement.

—BRUCE WARE, Senior Associate Dean,
School of Theology, The Southern Baptist Theological Seminary

TRUE SEXUAL MORALITY

TRUE SEXUAL MORALITY

Recovering Biblical Standards for a Culture in Crisis

DANIEL R. HEIMBACH

CROSSWAY BOOKS
WHEATON, ILLINOIS

True Sexual Morality: Recovering Biblical Standards for a Culture in Crisis

Published by Crossway Books
a publishing ministry of Good News Publishers
1300 Crescent Street
Wheaton, Illinois 60187

Cover design: David LaPlaca

Cover photo: PhotoDisc

First printing 2004

Printed in the United States of America

Library of Congress Cataloging-in-Publication Data
Heimbach, Daniel R., 1950-
True sexual morality : recovering biblical standards for a culture in crisis / Daniel R. Heimbach.
p. cm.
Includes bibliographical references and index.
ISBN 13: 978-1-58134-485-1 (trade pbk. : alk. paper)
ISBN 10: 1-58134-485-6
1.Sex—Religious aspects—Christianity. 2. Sexual ethics. 3. Sex—Biblical teaching. 4. Sexual ethics—Biblical teaching. I. Title.
BT708.H45 2004
241'.66—dc22 2004006697

CH 18 17 16 15 14 13 12 11 10 09 08
15 14 13 12 11 10 9 8 7 6 5 4 3 2

To Anna:

"An excellent wife who can find? She is far more precious than jewels. . . . Many women have done excellently, but you surpass them all" (Prov. 31:10, 29).

To Jonathan and Joel:

May you "be blameless and innocent children of God without blemish in the midst of a crooked and twisted generation, among whom you shine as lights in the world, holding fast to the word of life, so that in the day of Christ I may be proud that I did not run in vain or labor in vain" (Phil. 2:15-16).

Contents

APPENDICES:

ACKNOWLEDGMENTS

IT HAS TAKEN MORE than six years to complete this work, and I have received advice, support, encouragement, and assistance from many sources. I am especially grateful to the following:

To Phyllis Jackson and Alana Adams, who provided expert secretarial assistance under sometimes arduous circumstances. I could not have had better assistants.

To Paige Patterson, who had faith in me and believed in this project from the start, who has been a constant source of encouragement, and whose own bold example served to inspire me throughout.

To James Dobson, whose dedication to honoring and preserving marriage and family life in the face of cultural erosion and mounting spiritual-moral attack has fired many others to join the cause, including myself.

To colleagues and friends, who read portions of this work at various stages and provided many invaluable suggestions. I especially wish to recognize contributions from Jerry Gramckow, Os Guinness, John Yates, Henry and Madelin Barratt, Wayne Grudem, David Black, David Lanier, Mark Liederbach, David Jones, Ken Coley, John and Patricia Boozer, and members of a seminary class who read a draft manuscript during the Fall 2003 semester. I am indebted to many for improving the result. Of course, any errors are my own.

To Jim Dyer and Jerry Cooper, who have held me accountable and have been to me like Aaron and Hur to Moses at the battle of Rephidim (Ex. 17:12).

To Marvin Padgett, Jill Carter, and Bill Deckard of Crossway Books, who made publication easy, because they approach what they do as a matter of calling and spiritual mission far beyond what is merely required of professionals.

To C. S. Lewis and Francis A. Schaeffer, whose work in theology and ethics inspires my own, and who have been examples to me for how prophetic witness can be expressed in common ways without being shallow or holding back on the deepest and best God has to offer.

To my mother and father, who were and still are the greatest earthly teachers I have known. Nowhere is this more true than regarding the subject of this book.

To Anna, Jonathan, and Joel—my wife and sons—who have faithfully prayed for "the book" from start to finish. To them I owe a debt beyond measure. If what I have written affects no one else, it will be enough if it affects them.

Above all, I am grateful to the one who called me to this task, upon whose Word I have relied, for whose sake I have persisted, and to whom I am solely accountable. In the end, what matters is not what I say or think of God but only what God says or thinks of me.

Now to him who is able to keep you from stumbling and
to present you blameless before the presence of his glory
with great joy, to the only God, our Savior,
through Jesus Christ our Lord, be glory, majesty, dominion,
and authority, before all time and now and forever. Amen.
(JUDE 24-25)

FOREWORD

SCARCELY A DAY PASSES without a front-page story of sex scandal, rape, abuse, kidnapping, or some other sordid event disgusting to some and titillating to others. We live in a time defined by its fascination with obscenity. Politicians stumble from office, athletes have promising careers "slam-dunked," religious denominations and churches are shaken to their foundations and see their credibility damaged for generations to come as a result of escapades of the clergy.

In 1989, Ted Bundy, just weeks before being executed for multiple sex-related murders, confessed that his savage actions began with an addiction to pornography. Bundy's warnings to the American public notwithstanding, multiplied billions of dollars are now spent every year on the sex industry in America. As a result, homes are fractured, and sexuality, a unique creation of God meant profoundly to satisfy and comfort, is metamorphosed from incomparable blessing to incomparable curse in the lives of millions.

Voices raised against this Epicurean madness are dismissed by post-modern society as "prudish" or "puritan" or "legalistic." Indeed, Christians have sometimes failed to address sexual issues in a thoughtful and helpful fashion, giving instead the impression that Christian living is an endless series of prohibitions aimed at preventing any enjoyment in life. A number of presentations on sexual issues from a biblical perspective have made it to the bookstores in recent years, and these have doubtless had a positive effect in our churches. But the secular community has never been seriously challenged to reflect on the claims of Christ and the Bible about the purpose, function, and success of human sexuality. Most simply have no idea what the true basis and purpose of Christian sexual morality is all about.

Daniel Heimbach, professor of Christian ethics at Southeastern Baptist Theological Seminary in Wake Forest, North Carolina, has provided a compelling monograph with multiple virtues. In *True Sexual Morality,* Professor Heimbach provides a highly readable, even scintillating review of the current ferment in society together with a thorough presentation of the potentially society-changing perspective of true biblical sexual morality.

Heimbach, a popular classroom lecturer, had just started work on this volume when he was asked by Focus on the Family to help develop a project on sexual morality. This led to formulating *The Colorado Statement on Biblical Sexual Morality,* a work on which Heimbach devoted much energy. That labor of love is closely related to the present book. It is, I believe, the most thorough and extensive presentation on this subject ever written and may be the most important book written in our generation

The siren songs of contemporary sexual appeal are denominated in this book as "counterfeits." These include romantic sexual morality, playboy sexual morality, therapeutic sexual morality, and pagan sexual morality. Heimbach's assessment of these perspectives and the litany of tragically disrupted lives left in the wake of such ideologies is worth the price of the book. I have not seen anywhere this kind of compelling analysis.

However, Heimbach's presentation of biblical principles for sexual behavior, anchored in the holiness of God and in God's intense desire to provide the very best for the human family, is where the book achieves its most profound contribution. Juxtaposing the world's failures and frustrations against the ideals God revealed in the text of scripture, Heimbach builds a case for biblical moral action which, even if rejected by secularists, will, I am persuaded, provide an apologetic that cannot be ignored.

One of the unique features of this volume is the wide appeal it is certain to have. Heimbach's naval career, buttressed by years serving as an advisor to President George H. W. Bush (father of George W. Bush), working with interdenominational ministries like Focus on the Family and the Council of Biblical Manhood and Womanhood, and now teaching in a seminary, make it possible for this book to be read profitably by any Christian sitting in the pew. At the same time, this book should be an invaluable resource for pastors guiding their congregations. Finally, the volume will doubtless be employed as a text in university and seminary classes on sexual ethics, married life, the family, and relational counseling in the area of human sexuality.

Churches and the academy have desperately needed a resource like this. With thanksgiving to our God for his longsuffering patience with America and gratitude to him for placing this burden on Daniel Heimbach, I commend this work to all who love our Lord Jesus Christ and take their Christian witness seriously.

PAIGE PATTERSON, President
Southwestern Baptist Theological Seminary

PREFACE

THE NATION'S FIRST Museum of Sex opened in New York on Saturday, September 27, 2002, for the purpose of celebrating how New Yorkers have led the nation introducing prostitution, strip shows, pornography, and open approval of homosexual behavior. On Tuesday, October 8, 2002, Miss America 2002, Erika Harold, upset officials of the Miss America Pageant by announcing she would campaign for sexual chastity. Though rocked by sex scandals on a regular basis, officials felt it was too controversial to have the reigning Miss America associated with urging teens to abstain from sex outside of marriage. Then on Wednesday, November 14, 2002, Anna Nicole Smith, of "The Anna Nicole Smith Show," told interviewers she was disappointed there was "no nudeness" on her show. She complained, "I don't mind being nude. I don't think I am being exploited at all. And if I am, so what? At least I am being paid for it."[1] Stories like these, appearing in the news at about the same time illustrate how rapidly Americans are changing in terms of what they view as acceptable sexual behavior.

This book is written because it is desperately needed. Americans are facing a moral-spiritual crisis as catastrophic as thermonuclear war, and of the challenges we face, none is more consequential or demanding than the moral conflict over sex. While this conflict does not use weapons of material mass destruction, it does use massively destructive moral ideas—ideas so deadly they threaten the survival of our civilization. And yet because it concerns morality, not munitions, most evangelicals seem oblivious to how serious this crisis has become. Something must be done to better address what I now believe is the most serious spiritual-moral crisis to arise in the history of Christianity and Western culture.

Addressing sexual morality could not be more controversial. It is the "mother of all controversial issues." It is not a safe topic, and is all the more dangerous if one opposes prevailing opinion by upholding biblical standards when just about everyone is racing to reject them. But there is a silver lining. All this controversy also shows how terribly relevant moral instruction on sexual behavior is just now, and how necessary it is that Christians offer a compelling witness for what is in fact true sexual morality.

This book does not fit categories typical for contemporary writing, either Christian or non-Christian. Instead it takes an approach more like writers of the past, and I am grateful that Crossway Books has understood and encouraged this approach. Here then are six ways readers of this book are not getting the usual fare.

1. *This book is different from a lot of contemporary writing because it addresses a need, not a niche.* It was not conceived to exploit a market. Of course I hope readers will be interested and affected. However, what motivated my writing was not a sense of economic opportunity but a strong sense of God's call to address something readers need to hear whether anyone realizes it ahead of time or not.

As was true of the prophet Jeremiah, "there has been in my heart as it were a burning fire shut up in my bones" (Jer. 20:9). Like Jeremiah, I have been compelled to speak and apply God's Word at a critical turning point for my culture, hoping others will listen, will be affected, and will use it to rescue the perishing and strengthen resolve against a tide of sexual immorality sweeping the culture and much of the church toward destruction.

This sense of need has percolated for more than three decades. Being a son of missionaries, I was not raised in the United States, and, arriving in this country as a teen at the height of the 1960s sexual revolution, I was keenly aware that deep differences were dividing contemporary culture from traditional-biblical sexual morality. Among evangelicals, it was taken for granted that everyone understood biblical standards, but I also had the impression that most knew little of what we were up against.

Later, in the Navy, I saw how prostitution and adultery devastate even Christian marriages if a husband lets down his guard just one evening during eight months far from home. Those who failed could only blame themselves. But I also wondered if churches might have done a better job preparing them to resist temptation in the real world.

After that, as a member of Senator Richard Lugar's staff, I faced conflicting moral agendas on sex education, and then at the White House and the Pentagon I resisted a ceaseless stream of homosexual pressure to remove barriers based on traditional moral standards in education, the workplace, immigration, health care, and military recruiting and discipline.

Nothing today generates more stress in public life than conflict over opposing views on sex, and the war over sex is now a tool being used to collapse moral foundations of major public institutions like the federal justice system, the public education system, and the American military services. Yet, while I resisted the onslaught of the sexual revolution in public policy, it seemed evangelicals were as a whole hardly aware of, much less alarmed by, this growing crisis. That may have been due, in part, to uncertainty regarding Christians expressing moral views on political subjects. But I wondered then, as now, if it was not also because many were simply out of touch with the sexual moral crisis sweeping our nation.

Countless Christians have written to affirm traditional sexual standards, but most have failed to address the actual challenge we face these days. Most address its effects and say little to nothing of its causes or of strategic resources for withstanding the attack. Philip Yancey therefore is right to say, "I know of no greater failure among Christians than in presenting a persuasive approach to sexuality."[2] This book is written to address that need.

2. *This book is different from a lot of scholarly writing in biblical ethics because it goes beyond analyzing and applying previous material.* This book offers new insight on the structure God uses for sexual morality in the Bible and how it is challenged today. It is a work of constructive moral theology and not just a compilation or application of what has been thought or taught before. It defends historic biblical standards, but does so in a way that goes beyond what others have addressed.

This is not to say that what is here constructed is unrelated to previous work, for I have relied much on the work of both C. S. Lewis and Francis A. Schaeffer. Readers also will notice that, in discussing counterfeit views, I have extrapolated from categories identified in *Ethics for a Brave New World*, by John Feinberg and Paul Feinberg.[3] But while I have built on these predecessors, I also have attempted something more. No one has yet constructed a full biblical theology of sexual morality, no one has yet analyzed the whole sexual moral crisis challenging contemporary American culture and, while the Feinbergs identified two counterfeit views (the natural impulse view and the affection view), I identify four (the romantic, playboy, therapeutic, and pagan views).

It may interest readers to know that, while they appear later, the chapters on counterfeit views were written before I addressed the structure of biblical sexual morality. This was to meet obligations with Focus on the Family. But that order of analysis resulted in giving me a real, though unplanned, advantage. Having studied the various ways sexual morality is being perverted, I was equipped to see more clearly what the biblical prohibitions are in fact protecting. It helped me see what biblical sexual morality is for, and what is at stake when God's rules are violated.

3. *This book is different because, though it involves original theological construction, it also rejects influences on sexual morality from sources out-*

side the Bible. What is constructed, though original, depends on the biblical record taken on its own terms. I have tried to understand the moral structure in God's original revelation and to limit analytical construction to explaining what has been there all along.

I admit to including some speculative discussion—places where I have guessed beyond solid biblical evidence—and, where that is so, readers are alerted lest anyone confuse speculation with reliable revelation. Even so, I am well aware of my own limitations and invite readers to think for themselves and to hold all they read accountable to the Word of God. I have no interest in originality for its own sake and desire only to lead myself and others toward greater understanding of God's true revelation.

4. *This book is different from much other contemporary writing in ethics, religion, and culture because I assume that universal moral truth can be known and applied.* I believe objective moral truth on sexual behavior does exist and does apply to everyone all the time regardless of culture, experience, or choice. That is, I believe in what Francis Schaeffer called "true truth," and in this book I have examined what that is for sexual morality. Of course, as a Christian I think the only reliable source of true moral truth on sex is our Creator—the one who gave us the gift of sexuality in the first place.

5. *This book is different from many other books on sexual morality because it combines exposition and analysis with warning and exhortation.* I hope to awaken and provision the church to meet the greatest challenge of our day. For this reason, I have written in a way that I trust is not only substantive and analytical but is also prophetic and evangelistic. I have written for hearts and minds together, and have taken this approach because I believe that, unless passion is linked with understanding and unless understanding is linked with passion, Christians in our generation will fail the most critical challenge ever to arise in the history of the church.

6. *This book is different from most other contemporary Christian writing because it addresses two completely different audiences together.* One is academic readers—pastors, teachers, seminarians, and scholars who must be equipped to handle intellectual challenges in a sound biblical manner. The other is nonacademic readers—parents, Sunday school teachers, young adults, and teens who need to understand how what they believe applies in everyday life.

I believe there are times both audiences must hear the same message the same way at the same time, and the contemporary crisis over sexual morality is such a time. We are confronting a challenge all Christians must face together and, unless we do face it together, we will certainly fail together.

Academic readers must be stirred by the prophetic relevance of the intellectual challenge, and nonacademic readers must understand the power of ideas leading people to do what they do. Opposition to biblical sexual morality in the culture is not just a matter of taste. It is driven by ideas changing how people think and behave. The surrounding culture is rejecting traditional-biblical sexual morality because more and more people are accepting ideas that redefine biblical moral standards as *evil, corrupt,* or *harmful.*

The challenge we confront today calls for more than repeating (one more time, with new illustrations) the same old litany of biblical requirements. It demands instead a far deeper examination of: (1) what goes into God's approach to sexual morality; (2) what makes God's approach so wonderful and good; (3) what ideas are deceiving friends and neighbors into thinking biblical standards are bad; (4) what is wrong with the ideas that are destroying respect for traditional-biblical standards; and (5) what is at stake in all of this for the future of our culture and of the church.

A book addressing these elements together will not reach enough people if addressed only to scholars, and it will not carry enough impact if addressed only to non-scholars. It must have substance and relevance together, and it must reach both audiences together. With this in mind, I have prepared a full meal—a meal of meat and potatoes as well as appetizer and desert. But all has been served in a way I hope will be appetizing and nourishing to scholars and non-scholars alike.

Readers will note, I have used the term *sexual morality* rather than *sexual ethics.* That is because the focus of this book is limited to evaluating, explaining, and applying standards of sexual behavior (moral rules on sex) and does not include presenting a full theology of sexual identity (a whole sexual ethic). Sexual *ethics* covers more ground than sexual *morality,* and a volume on sexual ethics would not be complete if it did not include theological foundations for sexual identity. Naturally, doing so is very important, but that is a project for another day.

Of course, in real life sexual identity and sexual behavior are never actually separated. So, while this book does not present a full theology of sexual identity, it does in places express one. Where that is the case, readers will see I take the historic Christian view. Thus, for example, on gender roles, I take what is called the "complementarian" position, which is nothing other than what Christians have believed and taught throughout history.

I pray that what is written will affect readers as much as it has affected me. I pray that it touches hearts as well as minds. I pray that it reaches parents as well as pastors, teens as well as teachers, Sunday school members as well as scholars. I pray that those who know the truth will be moved to cherish it all the more, and I pray that those being swept toward destruction by a tide of cultural pressure will be saved before it is too late. Finally, I pray that all who read this book will heed the biblical warning to,

> *Look carefully then how you walk, not as unwise but as wise, making the best use of the time, because the days are evil (Eph. 5:15-16).*

Daniel R. Heimbach
Wake Forest, North Carolina
October 2004

LIST OF CHARTS

LIST OF DIAGRAMS

PART ONE

SEXUAL CHAOS IN THE CULTURE

1

SEX AT THE CENTER OF THE MORAL CRISIS

SOMETHING ENORMOUS IS COMING

I had the privilege in February 1991 of bringing my wife and sons, one five and the other two, to meet the first President Bush in the Oval Office. Needless to say it was a once-in-a-life-time opportunity. It was a farewell privilege for serving on the President's White House staff, and though I had served two years I had never before met personally with the President in his office. It was a place of tremendous dignity, where people met with the leader of the free world by invitation only.

Since we were coming as a family with two young boys, we were very concerned to avoid embarrassment. My wife and I dressed our boys better than ever before, and we carefully instructed them how to behave. But since they were only five and two, there was only so much we could do. We arrived—anxious parents with children—and were ushered into what is perhaps the most dignified office on earth. We felt terribly vulnerable! To our great relief, the president sensed how we felt and, opening a side door, ushered in Ranger, one of the first-family dogs. The boys were delighted, as were we! They with meeting a dog, and we with a gentleman as concerned with preserving our dignity as with his own.

Four years later, Bill Clinton, the next President of the United States, hid from security cameras behind that same door, where he engaged in acts of immoral sex with a White House intern named Monica Lewinsky. The nation was shocked, and many at first refused to believe what they heard. At the start, Hilary Clinton herself said that, if it were true, her husband should resign to preserve the dignity of the presidency.

Sadly, it was true. President Clinton did actually commit acts of flagrant sexual immorality in the most dignified office in the land. But he never resigned, and Hillary, Congress, the media, and most Americans instead changed their minds on sexual morality. After getting over the initial shock, most simply decided that what Bill Clinton did sexually, even in the Oval Office, was not all that important. Some decided it might not even have been immoral. And even if it was, perhaps sexual morality was such a private thing that others should not believe it affects public dignity no matter what a president does, or where he may choose to do it.

By excusing his behavior and refusing to resign, President Clinton affected moral attitudes on sex in the culture, moving many further along in a permissive direction. Many who before thought such behavior was shocking, decided it was their own shocked reaction, not Clinton's behavior, that was wrong. But while Clinton's self-justification and refusal to resign affected many, it was in reality a small part of something much larger. Sexual morality in America has been changing dramatically for decades, and what some called *the Clinton factor* was itself more a symptom than a cause.

Something enormous affecting sex has been changing American culture, and the cause is something far more powerful and significant than any president, movie, law, political party, celebrity, book, CD, magazine, or video. Like the ripples in the water glass in the opening scene of Jurassic Park, shivers in the moral ground on which Americans stand signal the approach of something enormous. Like tremors rising from deep underground, something seismic is affecting the foundations of our culture. Since we became a nation, nothing so divisive has threatened common life in America, and never have the stakes been so high. In just one generation, we have witnessed a total revolution in the way most people think of sex, and this in turn is creating a demand for monumental revisions affecting every social institution at almost every level.

Pornography in print, celluloid, and electronic forms is exploding, and what shocked our parents is considered standard for entertainment and advertising today. Same-sex relationships are considered normal, and restricting sex to marriage is considered abnormal. Behavior once thought shameful is flaunted now with pride, and praised as daring and courageous. Marriage has never been so uncertain. Sexual identity has never been more confused,[1] and manners expected between men and women have never been more conflicted. Not just the idea of saving sex for marriage but now even marriage itself is under attack, and everything related to sex, gender, and family, whether in law, politics, defense, education, entertainment, health, business, or religion, is being shaken to the core.

The United States Census in 2000 showed that two-parent families now represent less than 25 percent of all households in America, down from 45 percent as recently as 1960. Over the same forty-year period, the percentage of single-parent families tripled, the divorce rate doubled, the percentage of people getting married at all dropped lower than ever before, cohabitation increased 1000 percent (by a factor of 10), and the rate of illegitimacy (births to unmarried women) rose by more than 500 percent (by a factor of 5).[2] But while this rise in illegitimate births is terrible, the actual rise in illegitimate pregnancy has been at least two or three times higher, because 80 percent of abortions in America (which are not counted in the illegitimacy rate) are performed on women who are not married. No one keeps statistics on the rate of sexual promiscuity, but indications like these show that the rise in promiscuity must be epidemic as well.

Yet impersonal statistics like these tell only part of the story. To understand the whole story we must look past raw numbers and consider how these changes are affecting real people in real life.

First, consider the way *changing views on sexual morality are straining the military services.* In 1991, a few months after I arrived at the Pentagon as Deputy Assistant Secretary of the Navy for Manpower, we were shocked by the shameful behavior of Naval aviators attending a professional conference called Tailhook. This annual event had become known for sexual entertainment, which was bad enough. But as the problem unfolded, I was soon more amazed by reactions in official Washington than with what originally took place at Tailhook.

Most politicians and members of the media were not particularly concerned about the rampant promiscuity, marital infidelity, or failure of officers to set an example of virtue. Instead, I found that what shocked and concerned most others around me was the idea that men aroused by sexual entertainment could not at the same time respect the dignity of female colleagues. For most of my colleagues in Washington, it seemed that the problem was not sexual entertainment for military officers but failing to distinguish the entertainers from colleagues while feeling aroused. We had totally different views about moral responsibility concerning sex, and clearly my way of thinking was no longer the majority position.

Or, consider the way *changing views on sexual morality are affecting students.* Cohabitation among unmarried college students is now considered so normal that Yale University, in 1997, could not imagine why anyone would need to be excused from a university housing policy assigning unmarried male and female students to the same dormitory, on the same floor, where they were expected to use the toilet and shower facilities together at the same time.

This went beyond tolerating promiscuity to demanding that even modest students live immodestly.

Four orthodox Jewish students asked to be exempt from Yale's housing policy because, they explained, it went against their religious tradition and individual moral conscience. But Yale refused.[3] To the university, denying the relevance of gender differences in the most intimate situations was far more important than respecting scruples based on religion, tradition, or conscience. When Yale denied their request, these students filed a suit in court. But the court favored Yale and ruled against the students as well.[4]

Or, consider the way *changing views on sexual morality are threatening the freedom of private groups to continue teaching and applying traditional standards.* Homosexual behavior is now so widely accepted that the courts are under enormous pressure to move beyond tolerance and to actually deny the rights of groups still convinced that homosexual behavior is wrong. In 2000 a deeply divided U.S. Supreme Court, on a 5-4 vote, denied that the federal government should punish private organizations like the Boys Scouts that teach and apply traditional sexual standards. Although the Court did not change its view of the Constitution this time, it very nearly did. From the way it handled this case, we know the highest court in our land is just one vote away from revolutionizing sexual norms throughout American law.

Or, consider the way *changing views on sexual morality are affecting the business world.* Top business leaders are moving rapidly to be seen as supportive of the radical effort to redefine what it means to be an officially recognized, morally legitimate member of a *family.* Businesses are abandoning the idea that being in a *family* requires either marriage or responsibility for children, and are replacing it with the radical new idea that anyone living in a sexual relationship is a perfectly legitimate *family member* regardless of marriage or children. As a result, most major corporations, including IBM, AT&T, Sprint, Hewlett-Packard, Xerox, Time-Warner, Microsoft, Kodak, and Disney have been revising company policies on who qualifies to receive employee family benefits. Most major companies in America are now supporting policies that deny any basis for distinguishing between heterosexual marriage and family relationships and all kinds of nonmarital *domestic partnerships* involving same-sex couples, live-in-lovers, or even just good friends.

Or, finally, consider the way *changing views on sexual morality are provoking conflict over sex education.* Jane Fonda has become the main spokesperson for a media crusade funded by Durex, the world's largest producer of condoms, which is aimed at saving America from the danger of government-sponsored programs promoting abstinence. This former anti-America protester, who made Vietcong propaganda films and played a sex kitten in the movie *Barbarella,* is outraged that American tax dollars are being used to support the view that sex without marriage is *not* perfectly normal or safe. In Fonda's words, "Abstinence until marriage is based on an unreal world that isn't there." And she thinks most people would be shocked to discover "their tax money is being used for that."[5]

These are just a few of many examples illustrating the way thinking on sexual morality is changing the culture. But however much change there is in the culture at large, nowhere is conflict over sex raising more trouble than among Christians in the church. Opposing factions are tearing churches and whole denominations apart. Sexual standards long thought essential are being denounced as un-Christian, and top officials in the church are in some cases themselves claiming that the church will die if Christians do not learn to reject the Bible and take a new, more sensual approach on sex.

I actually believe that never in history has the church been torn by more serious, widespread controversy. Never has there been such ferment—so many articles and books; so many denominational reports; so many battles at convention, or presbytery, or general assembly; so many pronouncements; so many statements; so many major shifts in official policy—over such critically important areas of doctrine. In fact, never has there been such opposition to the authority and relevance of scripture, such demand for revising everything Christian, or such deep and bitter division between crusading factions as now being caused by conflict over sex—not when the church was invaded by gnosticism in the first century, not when the church split between East and West in the sixth century, not when the church divided over the Protestant Reformation in the sixteenth century, not when German higher criticism infiltrated the church in the nineteenth and early-twentieth century, and not even during recent battles dividing churches, denominations, and Christian organizations over the issue of biblical inerrancy.

There simply has been nothing comparable in the entire history of the church, no other time when turmoil has risen so high or reached so far. The stakes in the current conflict over sex are more critical, more central, and more essential than in any controversy the church has ever known. This is a momentous statement, but I make it soberly, without exaggeration. Conflict over sex these days is not just challenging tradition, orthodoxy, and respect for authority in areas such as ordination, marriage, and gender roles. And it does not just affect critically important doctrines like the sanctity of human life, the authority and trustworthiness of scripture, the Trinity, and the incarnation of Christ. Rather, war over sex among Christians is now raging over absolutely essential matters of faith without which no one can truly be a Christian in the first place—matters such as sin, salvation, the gospel, and the identity of God himself. These are not marginal issues! What is approaching us truly is enormous.

A Different Force Is Rising

In 1971 astronomers discovered the presence of a very different, previously unknown phenomenon called a *black hole,* after noticing that matter and light were acting strangely in some regions of space. Black holes have such enormous gravitational pull that even light cannot escape, which means they cannot be seen. But they have a tremendous effect on everything nearby. They bend space. They bend light. They draw planets, stars, and galaxies into orbit.

Not only is something enormous approaching in American culture concerning sex, but a new and different force is rising that is giving tremendous new power to those attacking traditional morality. And, just as astronomers discovered black holes in space after noticing strange new effects on other heavenly bodies, we can observe sexual morality changing in strange new ways that indicate the presence of something new in the culture—something with enormous pull. Changes affecting sexual morality are occurring these days that cannot be explained on the basis of natural lust and youthful rebellion. They are coming from a source that is far more significant and powerful. There is indeed a dark new spiritual presence in the culture that, like a black hole, is bending morality in a new direction and pulling everything close into its orbit.

A different view on sexual morality, involving a strange new force linking spirituality with what has traditionally been considered sexual sin, was evident in the movie *Titanic.* James Cameron, the director, told viewers the movie was not the usual romance story because it had a morally inspiring religious message. But what sort of *religion* inspiring what sort of *morality?* Rose, the heroine, in the opening scene credits Jack, a fellow-passenger, not only with saving her physically when the ocean liner sank, but with saving her in a spiritual sense as well. In her words, "he saved me in every way that a person can be saved."

From the story she tells, it is clear that Rose's inclusion of spiritual *salvation* relates to premarital sex she had with Jack just hours before the ship went down. The claim means that she was saved *spiritually*—reached a higher dimension of spirituality—through what the Bible calls sexual sin. So, the religion James Cameron recommends is a religion promising salvation through sex, and the morality he thinks inspiring is a morality that treats sexual sin as if it were heroic and salvific.

This very different view of sexual morality—this different view involving a strange new force linking spirituality with sexual sin—was also displayed at a high school graduation ceremony in Vermont in 1998. During the ceremony, a member of the graduating class, Kate Logan, started delivering a speech. But as she spoke, Kate Logan stunned her classmates, their parents, and the visiting dignitaries by taking off her clothes and finishing the speech naked. Afterwards she said it was an effort to express the *spirituality* of graduation.[6] She explained that "When I was up there, it felt natural. It didn't feel like I was doing anything crazy." She was not pulling a prank and did not think she had done anything wrong. Rather, she believed it made perfect sense and deserved special praise. Why? Because what she did came from a new and different way of thinking about sex and spirituality. To Kate Logan, disrobing in front of everyone at graduation made sense because she believed unrestrained sex is the one true path to spiritual life.

This different view on sexual morality, involving a strange new force linking spirituality with sexual sin, is also seen at the Burning Man festival held annually at Black Rock Desert, Nevada.[7] This festival of the new counterculture is named for the closing ceremony, in which a large wooden dummy is set on fire. It started on Baker Beach, near San Francisco, in 1986, and then moved to Nevada when the event outgrew the original location. Now more than twenty-four thousand participants attend each year, some from other countries but most from places around central California like the San Francisco Bay area and Silicon Valley.

These are not drifters looking for handouts but are for the most part well-educated, middle-class professionals trying to go beyond conventions and enhance their lives in exciting new ways. Burning Man is a festival for and by a new breed of young, urban professionals whom *Time* magazine has described as "bright young pagans: the computer-programming, anthropologically aware polymaths who have popularized the imaginative role-playing bulletin boards of cyberspace."[8]

Larry Harvey, who began the festival, says, "It's about sacred space," and others say it is about "radical self-expression" or "power to create and direct your destiny." But however they describe it, attendees all seem to be searching for meaning and trying to either find or enhance spirituality by overcoming conventional barriers like limiting sex to marriage and keeping it separate from spiritual worship. The attendees say, "We are all gods and goddesses here," and think spiritual answers will be discovered if you just "trust your soul to understand everything it experiences."[9] As reported in 1999, one young woman explained she had come because there at the Burning Man festival "I can be free, I can be naked, I can be fat, I can be gay. You can just be whatever it is you need to be, today."[10]

The festival lasts a week and includes events like a daily "drag" race (men in dresses riding bicycles), a Friday afternoon Critical Bike Ride (hundreds of topless women riding bicycles in a circle around cheering spectators), and a Saturday morning Massive Nude Photograph (thousands of naked people lying around together while photographers take pictures). People take off their clothes, paint their bodies wild colors, and dance. They also wander around visiting theme camps like the "Sisters of Perpetual Indulgence" (homosexual men dressed like nuns), "Wimminbago" (topless lesbians in a Winnebago), and the "Temple of Ishtar" (women giving lectures on the evils of Christianity and turning into goddesses for periods of sexual worship).[11] Clearly the major theme at Burning Man seems to be searching for the best way to enhance spirituality through sex.

This different view on sexual morality involving a strange new force linking spirituality with sexual sin is also seen in a program promoting permissive sex in churches under the guise of sex education. The Sexuality Information and Education Council of the United States (SIECUS), founded in 1964 to provide leadership for the sexual revolution, has since grown to be the leading proponent in America for permissive sex education in public schools. Until 1998, the group considered itself secular and avoided religion. But starting in 1998, SIECUS has focused on churches, hoping to change what Christians think and teach about sexual morality. (Note: A full discussion of SIECUS, in a special report by Focus on the Family, is reproduced in Appendix C.)

The new SIECUS thrust linking permissive sex with spirituality began when the organization launched what it called the Religion Initiative. This represents a new strategy in which SIECUS plans to infiltrate churches with sex education materials that take a permissive view on sexual morality, justifying it in terms of nonbiblical spirituality. Basic principles guiding this new approach were released two years later in a document titled a *Religious Declaration on Sexual Morality, Justice, and Healing*. (Note: A copy of this declaration is included in Appendix B.) The declaration described sexual activity as "integral to our spirituality" and suggested that restricting sex risks "loss of meaning." At the time, Debra Haffner, president of SIECUS, told reporters her organization believed churches needed a new approach on religion and sex because, "For too long the only voices in the public square on religion and sexuality have been the anti-sexuality pronouncements of the religious right."[12] She was saying that the biblical approach on sexual morality was too repressive and that SIECUS was therefore promoting a different approach for churches—one that affirms spirituality in ways that never deny sexual desire.

Finally, this different view on sexual morality, involving linking spirituality with sexual sin, has been growing among a rising number of celebrities, social critics, scholars, and theologians who are leading the feminist and homosexual revolutions and who see themselves on the cutting edge of philosophy, religion, and culture. Because we will discuss many of these people in the next three chapters, they will not be covered separately here except to note that what they are saying, writing, and doing is having a tremendous effect.

Biblical Standards at the Flash Point

Different approaches on sexual morality are splitting the culture and the church into opposing factions. The traditional approach to sexual morality, based on scripture and long believed essential to American society, holds that sex is for moral purposes beyond the experience of sex itself—moral purposes that serve to support and fulfill marriage and family duties. These purposes are fixed. They never change, and are the same for everyone regardless of what a person thinks, feels, or chooses. Sex is for husbands and wives, who then become fathers and mothers responsible for raising children to be productive members of society. Sex is not allowed except in marriage. Marriage justifies sex; sex does not justify marriage. Serving the family legitimizes happiness; happiness does not legitimize serving the family. Sex is not for everyone, but is a privilege saved for people who promise God, the community, and each other to use sex only in the right way and for the right reasons.

With the rise of modernism, an opposing, permissive approach to sexual morality rose to usurp the traditional approach in American culture. Under modernism, which denies spiritual life, sex has no necessary purpose or significance. Individuals use sex however they choose, and what they choose does not matter to anyone else. Sex is strictly a personal choice, and the only thing everyone must accept is that everyone must have sex regardless of whether or not he or she is married. Sex justifies marriage; marriage does not justify sex. Families depend on being happy, and no one is compelled to stay in the family if he or she is unhappy. According to this *non-spiritual* version of the permissive approach, sex is actually nothing special. It is just a commodity one consumes without creating or assuming anything beyond the immediate experience.

Starting in the 1990s, however, postmodernism has generated a new version of the permissive approach. Former proponents of the modernist, nonspiritual version decided they could no longer tolerate acting as if sex were nothing special. But neither did they wish to give up permissive sex. Thus a new postmodern version has evolved, one that affirms spirituality while justifying sensuality. According to this version, sex is again profound and deeply meaningful because it enhances spirituality. Sex is not ultimately for love, marriage, or family relationships. Rather it is for connecting yourself with spiritual power running the universe. Sex involves cosmic power without sacrificing human independence. The spirituality of sex is not limited by anything beyond sex, but rather is more like electricity, with everyone controlling a switch.[13]

Living to please God while engaging the surrounding culture requires knowing how that culture affects you. Real truth as revealed by God never changes. It is the same yesterday, today, and forever. But the ways real truth is attacked by human culture change all the time, and Jesus severely rebuked those who studied scripture but did not think it important to understand how the surrounding culture of their time was attacking real truth. He said,

> When it is evening, you say, "It will be fair weather, for the sky is red." And in the morning, "It will be stormy today, for the sky is red and threatening." You know how to interpret the appearance of the sky, but you cannot interpret the signs of the times (Matt. 16:2-3).

It is important that we know not only what God says in scripture but also how that truth is coming under attack in the culture around us. When we are attacked, we cannot stand firmly on the side of truth if we do not know where the enemy is aiming or from where he is firing. That is what Jesus meant by criticizing religious contemporaries for failing to "interpret the signs of the times."

Considering what is happening today, the one development (or sign) attacking truth in American culture more severely than anything else is permissive sexual morality energized by nonbiblical spirituality. In other words, the greatest single moral-spiritual threat to truth in our culture these days is a rising fascination with paganism that defines morality as anything spiritual and then reduces it to anything sexual. Richard Land, president of the

Southern Baptist Ethics and Religious Liberty Commission, was right in 1998 to observe,

> The number one battle line now, and for the next decade, for the soul and conscience of America is the struggle over sexuality. The issues are clear and compelling. We must either reassert Judeo-Christian sexual values or be submerged in a polluted sea of pagan sexuality.[14]

Sexual morality is the most important moral-spiritual issue of our time because it is the pivot on which the foundations of American culture as a whole are being turned from genuine moral-spiritual truth to the complete reverse. And because the future of social and religious life in America, and perhaps even the survival of America herself, is at stake, powerful forces are battling in opposite directions—one using sexual revolution to shift American cultural foundations in a pagan direction, and one resisting sexual revolution to keep the order we have from crumbling.

Sexual Morality as Pivot Point for the Moral Crisis

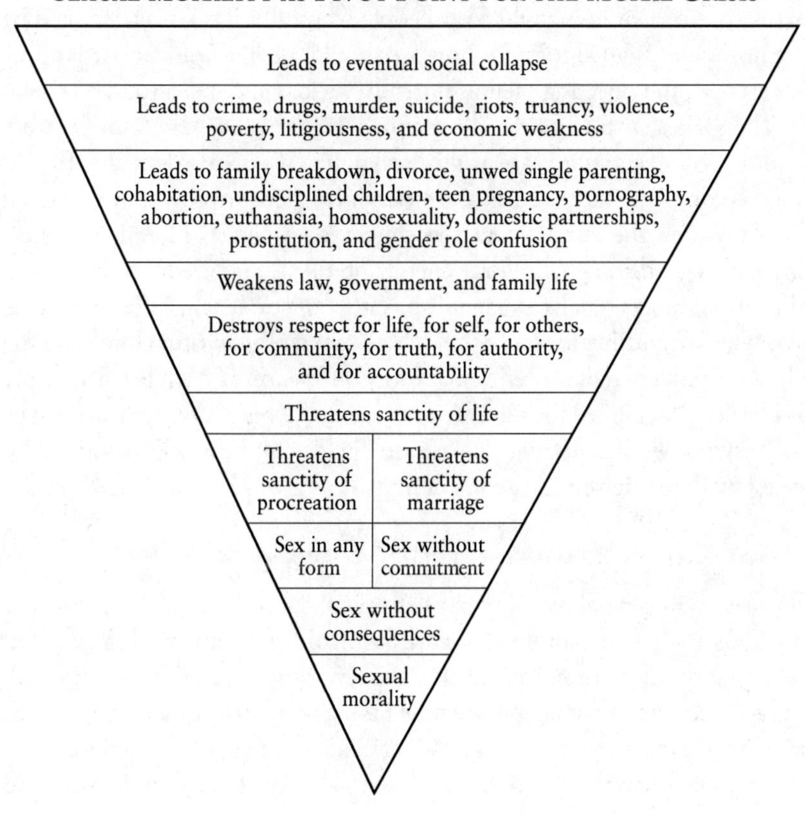

Evangelicals must understand that total sexual revolution in America is not coincidental but is a carefully planned strategy called *deconstruction* that is being developed by those wanting to redefine, redesign, and reconstruct every institution in America (marriage, family, law, politics, business, defense, entertainment, education, and religion) from top to bottom.[15] They know and understand that once sexual morality changes, the whole social system has to be completely redefined. And the main power energizing this movement is shifting from the mere promise of free sex to sexual indulgence justified as spiritual and cosmic. Like switching from low-test to high-octane fuel, the movement is shifting from natural-lust to natural-lust-energized-by-crusading-spirituality.

Of course this has been generating tremendous conflict in many areas, and everywhere controversy arises it ultimately has to do with whether biblical truth on sex is indeed true. Is the traditional approach to sexual morality, originally found in scripture, unchangingly true for everyone? Or is it a product of human imagination and nothing more? If the traditional approach was made up by men, then it makes perfect sense to reject everything it restricts in favor of doing whatever people want. But if sex was designed by a creator who assigned rules for how we should use it, those standards apply to everyone, and rejecting them is horribly wicked and dangerous.

The stakes in this battle are growing higher every day, and in every instance biblical standards are at the flash point. We do not deny that the situation is complex, but evangelicals must realize there are now only two main forces dividing the culture and the church over sexual morality. Biblical Christianity is the one main force energizing those who are battling for sexual restraint, and sexualized paganism is now the one main force energizing those who are battling for sensuality. These two moral-spiritual forces are the only ones with enough power to make any difference, and while Christianity has up till now enjoyed the advantage of being the only contestant with spiritual answers, we are entering a new season in the culture in which both major contestants are offering spiritual solutions.

Seismic Shifts Resulting from Modernism

Attitudes about sexual morality have changed dramatically in America since the 1960s sexual revolution. Naturally this did not happen in a day, but change has occurred rapidly. And even though some have stood their ground, no one denies that most people are now taking a radically different approach to sex from even a generation ago. What change we have seen in the culture has actually taken place in two stages, with the first led by modernism and the second by postmodernism. While the influence of modernism on sexual morality has taken different directions—depending on whether people focus on affection, enjoyment, or a sense of fulfillment—the main emphasis of modernists has always been denying spiritual life, arguing that morality is a matter of private taste and therefore biblical standards on sex have to be kept from influencing public life.

Modernism has produced major changes in the way most Americans think about sexual morality, and these include the following:

1. There has been a shift from thinking sex should fit moral standards, to thinking moral standards should fit sex.
2. There has been a shift from thinking sexual morality depends on something greater than sex, to thinking sexual morality depends on nothing but sex.
3. There has been a shift from thinking sexual morality is beyond individual choice, to thinking sexual morality all depends on individual choice.
4. There has been a shift from thinking sexual morality is the same for all regardless of how anyone feels, to thinking sexual morality is different for each person depending on how each person feels.
5. There has been a shift from thinking sexual standards never change, to thinking sexual standards change all the time.
6. There has been a shift from thinking sexual standards are public and sexual behavior ought to be private, to thinking sexual standards are private and sexual behavior is public.
7. There has been a shift from thinking sexual discipline is a moral solution, to thinking sexual discipline is a moral problem.
8. There has been a shift from thinking desires for sex should never be trusted, to thinking desires for sex should never be questioned.
9. There has been a shift from thinking sex involves interconnecting dimensions (emotional, physical, psychological, and spiritual) that cannot be separated, to thinking sex can be limited to one dimension without affecting other dimensions.
10. There has been a shift from thinking sex is something personal that necessarily creates a relationship, to thinking sex is nothing personal and therefore has nothing necessarily to do with relationships.
11. There has been a shift from thinking marriage is necessary for sex, to thinking sex is necessary for marriage.
12. There has been a shift from thinking sex is a privilege reserved for people committed to certain goals, to thinking everyone is entitled to sex unrelated to commitment or goals.

Seismic Shifts Resulting from Postmodernism

Since the 1990s, sexual attitudes in the culture have been moving past modernism into a new, postmodern direction. The main difference is that, while modernism denied spiritual life, postmodernism affirms it, and nowhere more strongly than in relation to sex. But the sort of spirituality affirmed is pagan, not Christian. It approaches spirituality in a way that views it, not as something *beyond* but rather as something *under* human control, and this makes sexual morality even more radically permissive. And even though postmodern paganism is radically permissive, its affirmation of spirituality is causing it to infiltrate parts of the church even more swiftly than it infiltrates the broader culture.

The influence of postmodern paganism on sexual morality in both the church and the culture is causing radical new changes in the way many people think, including the following:

1. There is a shift from theologies of sex, to sexual theologies. In other words, there is a shift from addressing sex in terms of Christian faith and doctrine, to addressing Christian faith and doctrine in terms of sex.
2. There is a shift from thinking sexual passion is best experienced by satisfying God, to thinking God is best experienced by satisfying sexual passion. In other words, there is a shift from thinking a relationship with God affects sex, to thinking a relationship with God is experienced through sex.
3. There is a shift from making sure that sexual experience is consistent with the character of God, to making sure that the character of God is consistent with sexual experience. In other words, there is a shift from measuring sex by God, to measuring God by sex.
4. There is a shift from restricting sexual behavior to keep sex holy, to releasing sexual experience because nothing ever makes sex unholy. In other words, there is a shift from thinking sex is easily corrupted, to thinking sex is impossible to corrupt.
5. There is a shift from thinking salvation frees sinners *from* what the Bible calls sexual sin, to thinking salvation frees men and women *to indulge in* what the Bible calls sexual sin. In other words, there is a shift from thinking salvation overcomes bondage to sexual immorality, to thinking salvation overcomes the fear that sex is ever immoral.
6. There is a shift from interpreting sex according to the Bible, to interpreting the Bible according to sex. In other words, there is a shift from applying scripture to interpreting sex and toward applying sex to interpreting scripture.

7. There is a shift from viewing sexual sin as an indulging of desires that alienates a person from God, to viewing sexual sin as a denying of desires that alienates a person from self. In other words, there is a shift from fear of opposing God, to fear of opposing self.
8. There is a shift from thinking sexual desires need to be disciplined because human nature is fallen, to thinking sexual desires should be unrestrained because there is nothing wrong with human nature. In other words, there is a shift from perfecting human nature by denying the flesh, to perfecting human nature by indulging the flesh.
9. There is a shift from viewing the church as a community of people who submit to God and give up trying to justify themselves, to viewing the church as a community of people who submit to no one and justify themselves by affirming sexual desires. In other words, there is a shift from thinking the church consists of repentant sinners, to thinking the church consists of people who deny having any sin for which they must repent.
10. There is a shift from sex being part of living life for God, to God being part of living life for sex. In other words, there is a shift from sexual life being spiritual, to spiritual life being sexual.
11. There is a shift from the rule of God over sex, to ruling God by sex. In other words, there is a shift from trusting the power of God to control sex, to trusting the power of sex to control God.
12. There is a shift from worshiping a God who became flesh, to worshiping flesh that becomes God. In other words, there is a shift from worshiping God out of gratitude for sex, to worshiping God *as* sex.

We Have Been Warned of This

Although paganism's merging of promiscuity with spirituality is new in the West today, it is not new in other parts of the world nor is it new even in our own history. In fact, sensuality energized by religion has been more typical in human culture over time than the restraining of sexual desires mandated by our Creator. Sexual paganism has not been a force in the West since the rise of Christianity. But now, as the culture rejects morality rooted in scripture and supported by centuries of Christian tradition, nothing remains to restrain the powerful attraction of justifying sensuality in spiritual terms.

So, even though sexual paganism might feel novel and exciting to contemporary Americans, it really is nothing of the sort. Sexual paganism is a very old challenge to Christian morality that in fact never went away. It has been there all along, waiting in the wings for a time when the culture would tire of sexual restraint, lose respect for biblical standards, and seek something else to replace Christian answers to our need. Evangelical leaders in the past have tried to alert Christians to this danger lurking in the culture, and have warned what to expect should the church lose confidence in God's moral revelation, or should the culture lose respect for its Christian heritage.

Abraham Kuyper (1837–1920)

In 1898, the Dutch statesman-theologian Abraham Kuyper spoke at Princeton Seminary, where he told students and faculty the ultimate opponent of Christianity is, and has always been, paganism. He went on to alert Christians that paganism was on the move and would again become a major challenge to Christianity in the West. More than a hundred years ago, Kuyper was warning Christians in America that "*pagan* thought, *pagan* aspirations, *pagan* ideals are gaining ground even among us and penetrating to the very heart of the rising generation." And he was especially concerned that Christians "not forget that the fundamental contrast has always been, still is, and will be until the end: *Christianity* and *Paganism.*"[16]

According to Kuyper, the greatest problem we have as finite creatures is relating with the infinite. The ultimate dilemma we have as creatures living in material bodies in a material world is how to gain meaning and significance beyond material existence. In scripture we learn that God has already solved the problem. The Creator, who stands over creation, has made a way for us to connect with him on a personal basis that neither sacrifices his transcendence nor compromises his holiness. But, Kuyper pointed out, the main opposition to this amazing answer is "*paganism,* which in its most general form is known by the fact that it surmises, assumes and worships God *in the creature.*"[17] The difference between the two solutions—one offered by Christianity and the other by paganism—is that, while Christianity solves the problem of human significance by linking us with the infinite on God's terms, paganism claims the problem can be solved by reaching the infinite on our own terms without depending on or submitting to anyone else.

Kuyper feared that, because modernism was leading the culture to reject Christianity, Western culture would again succumb to paganism. And he observed, "Ever since it entered its 'mystical' period, modernism . . . in Europe and America, has acknowledged the necessity of carving out a new form for the religious life of our time." In place of Christianity, he saw that,

> a kind of hollow piety is again exercising its enticing charms, and every day it is becoming more fashionable to take a plunge into the warm stream of mysticism. With an almost sensual delight this modern mysti-

> cism quaffs its intoxicating draught from the nectar-cup of some intangible infinite.[18]

Thus Kuyper over a century ago warned there would be a major conflict dividing the culture, with the major contestants being "Christian faith . . . against renewed paganism [which is now] collecting its forces and gaining day by day."[19] Kuyper's warning was general and did not especially address sexual morality. But he knew there would be enormous consequences, and conflict over sexual morality was certainly included when he spoke about renewed paganism offering "intoxicating draughts" of "sensual delight."

C. S. Lewis (1898–1963)

Fifty years after Kuyper spoke at Princeton, C. S. Lewis warned Christians of much the same thing. He also was concerned that, although Christianity had been the dominant moral-spiritual force in Western culture for centuries, we could not assume that paganism was gone or that it would not return as soon as people lost respect for Christian faith and morality. Rather than *paganism,* Lewis spoke of *pantheism,* which he saw becoming ever more popular in the elite intellectual circles of his time. But Lewis was, in fact, addressing the same thing as Kuyper because Lewis's *pantheism* included what he called "Nature religions" that "sanctify . . . our whole biological life" and therefore worship the natural "Life-force" by engaging in rituals like sex "with real women in the temple of the fertility goddess."[20]

In 1947 Lewis already knew that modern philosophy and modern science were both "quite powerless to curb the human impulse toward pantheism [paganism]," and he believed the growing influence of pagan pantheism was already "nearly as strong today as it was in ancient India or in ancient Rome."[21] According to Lewis, people in elite circles who thought what they were doing was new and enlightening were wrong because,

> Pantheism [paganism] is in fact the permanent natural bent of the human mind; the permanent ordinary level below which man sometimes sinks, under the influence of priestcraft and superstition, but above which his own unaided efforts can never raise him for very long. . . . It is the attitude into which the human mind automatically falls when left to itself. . . . If "religion" means simply what man says about God, and not what God does about man, then Pantheism [paganism] almost *is* religion. And "religion" in that sense has, in the long run, only one really formidable opponent—namely Christianity.[22]

Like Kuyper, Lewis believed that paganism-pantheism was Christianity's ultimate opponent and that, should the influence of Christianity weaken, it would assure the immediate return of paganism-pantheism in Western culture. Without Christianity, modern culture would not be able to resist the lure of sensual spirituality. And, while Lewis also remained general and did not address sexual morality in specific terms, the brief reference he made to sexual worship shows that Lewis was aware that sex would have to play a major role in the conflict ahead.

Francis A. Schaeffer (1912–1984)

In 1970, Francis Schaeffer said that he saw America heading toward a "revolution with repression" aimed especially at removing the influence of Bible-believing Christians in the culture. He urged,

> the church today should be getting ready and talking about issues of tomorrow and not about issues of 20 and 30 years ago, because the church is going to be squeezed in a wringer. If we found it tough in these last few years, what are we going to do when we are faced with the real changes that are ahead?[23]

And then in 1984, just before he died, Schaeffer again warned evangelicals:

> The titanic freedoms which we once enjoyed have been cut loose from their Christian restraints and are becoming a force of destruction leading to chaos. And when this happens, there really are very few alternatives. All morality becomes relative, law becomes arbitrary, and society moves toward disintegration.[24]

The reason for the crisis he saw emerging was that modernism was generating a moral-spiritual vacuum that people would not be able to tolerate very long. He said,

> modern man does in fact assume—wittingly or unwittingly—that the universe and man can be explained by the impersonal plus time plus chance.... But man has aspirations; he has what I call mannishness. He desires that love be more than being in bed with a woman, that moral motions be more than merely sociological something-or-others, that his significance lie in being more than one more cog in a vast machine. . . . On the basis of modern thought, however, all of these would simply be an illusion. And since there are aspirations which separate man from his impersonal universe, man then faces at the heart of his being a terrible, cosmic, final alienation. He drowns in cosmic alienation, for there is nothing in the universe to fulfill him.[25]

Schaeffer understood that, by denying any real basis for significance or morality or law, modernism was leaving the culture in a state that people would not be able to endure very long. Something cosmic (i.e., spiritual) would need to fill the void left by modernism, and there were only two options. If it was not filled on God's terms on the basis of biblical truth, then it would have to be filled on man's terms by something completely opposed to biblical faith and practice. The void, he said, would eventually be filled by some spiritual "ism" promising to satisfy the human need for cosmic significance and resulting in a very different approach to morality. And, when that happened, there would be a terrible "battle going on—not just a heavenly battle, but a life-and-death struggle over what will happen to men and women and children in both this life and the next."[26]

Schaeffer saw that what Kuyper and Lewis anticipated decades earlier was actually starting to take place in the 1970s and 80s. For Schaeffer, the crisis was not future but already starting, and he did not think it would be long until the culture was in a state of full-scale moral-spiritual revolution. He said in 1970, "I believe when my grandchildren grow to maturity, they will face a culture that has little similarity to ours."[27] He saw that modernism had already created the vacuum demanding revolution, and he believed the culture would either not survive or would be completely reconstructed morally and spiritually within two generations.

Schaeffer's warning to Christians was therefore marked with a sense of urgency beyond the warnings of Kuyper and Lewis. In 1984 he asked,

> Sixty years ago could we have imagined that unborn children would be killed by the millions here in our own country? . . . Or that every form of sexual perversion would be promoted by the entertainment media? Or that marriage, raising children, and family life would be objects of attack?[28]

Of course, he expected a negative answer. Kuyper and Lewis had both warned what was coming. But few paid attention, so most evangelicals in America were caught by surprise and had no idea why such radical changes were happening in the culture.

In warning evangelicals of the crisis sweeping their way, Schaeffer did not say it would involve conflict with a force called *paganism,* nor did he say it would focus especially on sex. But he did understand that the battle forming in the culture was in fact "cosmic," and he knew the other side was promoting "every form of sexual perversion."

The Post-Christian, Postmodern Battle to Fill the Void Left by Modernism

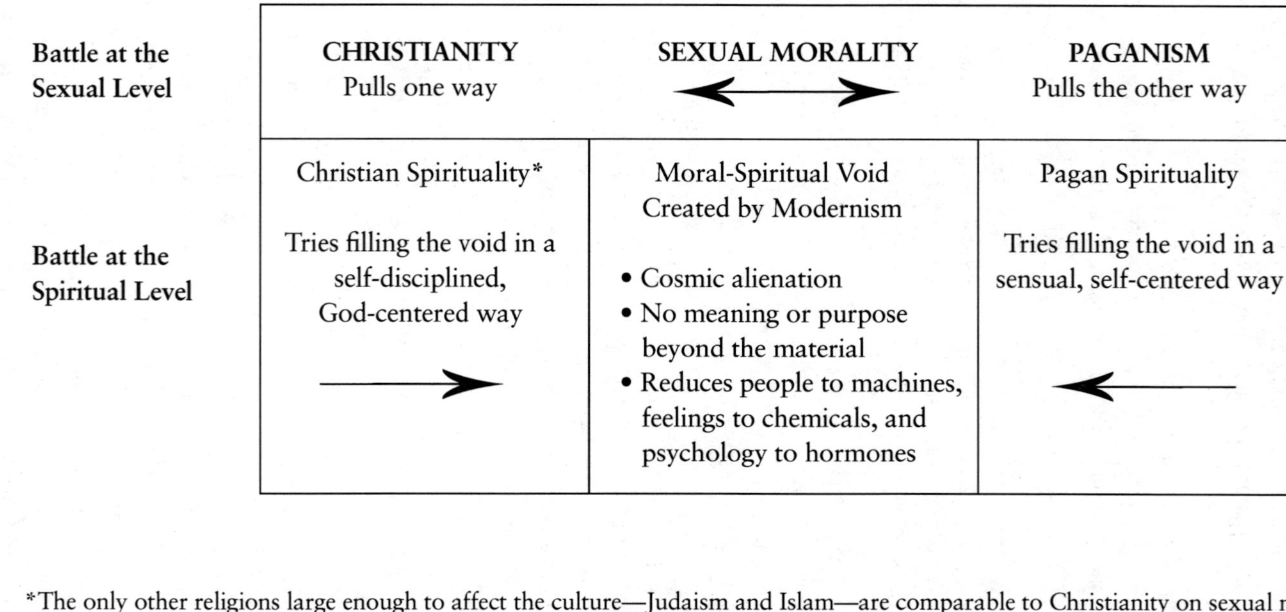

Battle at the Sexual Level	**CHRISTIANITY** Pulls one way	**SEXUAL MORALITY** ⟵⟶	**PAGANISM** Pulls the other way
Battle at the Spiritual Level	Christian Spirituality* Tries filling the void in a self-disciplined, God-centered way ⟶	Moral-Spiritual Void Created by Modernism • Cosmic alienation • No meaning or purpose beyond the material • Reduces people to machines, feelings to chemicals, and psychology to hormones	Pagan Spirituality Tries filling the void in a sensual, self-centered way ⟵

*The only other religions large enough to affect the culture—Judaism and Islam—are comparable to Christianity on sexual morality.

In his final hours, Schaeffer urged evangelicals to wake up and take the emerging challenge seriously. He said,

> we must ask where we as evangelicals have been in the battle for truth and morality in our culture. Have we as evangelicals been on the front lines contending for the faith and confronting the moral breakdown over the last forty to sixty years?[29]

Sadly, he observed, "Most of the evangelical world has not been active in the battle, or even been able to see that we are in a battle."[30] And Schaeffer died believing that the diminished confidence in the Bible and accommodation precisely at points where the culture opposed biblical truth was what he reluctantly called *the great evangelical disaster.*

Carl F. H. Henry (1913–2003)

Schaeffer may not have used the term *paganism* for the force rising to challenge the moral-spiritual influence of Christianity in American culture, but Carl F. H. Henry did. A contemporary who responded with Schaeffer to the same crisis, Henry saw the situation the way Kuyper had a century before. The force Henry saw rising to oppose Christianity—the new spirituality toward which the post-Christian, postmodern culture was turning for meaning and purpose and morality—was *paganism,* or what Henry called *neo-paganism.*[31]

So, while Schaeffer urged evangelicals to engage the culture in a battle for truth and morality on a cosmic scale, Henry alerted evangelicals to battle a barbarian invasion aimed at revolutionizing the moral-spiritual foundations on which American culture was built. "Our generation," he said, is now "lost to the truth of God, to the reality of divine revelation, to the content of God's will, to the power of His redemption, and to the authority of His Word." And for this loss, he said, the culture "is paying dearly in a swift relapse to paganism."[32]

Instead of following objective moral truth as revealed in scripture and confirmed in nature, Henry said, the new barbarians were returning to pagan ideas, answering the human need for meaning in ways that put man in charge of running the universe and reduced morality to sensuality. He said,

> A half-generation ago, the pagans were still largely threatening at the gates of Western culture; now the barbarians are plunging into the . . . mainstream. As they seek to reverse the inherited intellectual and moral heritage of the Bible, the Christian world-life view and the secular world-life view

> engage as never before in rival conflict for the mind, the conscience, the will, the spirit, the very selfhood of contemporary man. Not since the apostolic age has the Christian vanguard faced so formidable a foe in its claims for the created rationality and morality of mankind.[33]

Like Schaeffer, Henry believed the culture was already in a state of moral-spiritual crisis. Paganism was already challenging the influence of Christianity, and the conflict already was causing "a striking shift in sexual behavior that welcomes not only divorce and infidelity but devious alternatives to monogamous marriage as well."[34]

Henry also, like Schaeffer, warned American evangelicals to engage the moral-spiritual crisis rising in the culture. But even in 1988 he feared time was running out. He felt that,

> Unless evangelical Christians break out of their cultural isolation, unless we find new momentum in the modern world, we may just find ourselves so much on the margin of the mainstream movements of modern history that soon ours will be virtually a Dead Sea Caves community. Our supposed spiritual vitalities will be known only to ourselves, and publicly we will be laughed at as a quaint but obsolescent remnant from the past.[35]

What is flooding the culture now is indeed enormous. The moral-spiritual crisis we are facing centers on sexual morality and is strategically bent on replacing biblical moral standards with something quite different. This rising moral revolution allows people to reject Christianity while continuing to affirm that sex and life have meaning and purpose beyond the material dimension. We are living now in a post-Christian, postmodern culture in which Christianity and paganism are warring over the moral-spiritual void left by modernism. And the center of this battle, the strategic ground that will decide who wins (at least for now, before Christ comes back) is sexual morality. So, if evangelicals plan to be engaged in this conflict with any intelligence, we must try to understand what the other side is doing.

2

THE RETURN OF SEXUAL PAGANISM

TO MANY, A CALL TO resist paganism sounds either ancient or foreign, and Christians today might be tempted to ignore such a call. Many certainly have so far. We have had warnings over the years from respected leaders like Abraham Kuyper, C. S. Lewis, Francis Schaeffer, and Carl F. H. Henry. But few have taken these warnings seriously, and hardly anyone acts as though paganism is much of a challenge. How can paganism be a relevant concern in the twenty-first century? How can it really be significant in America today? But ignoring the growing presence, relevance, and power of paganism in the culture today is truly a terrible mistake.

In the 1980s, Margot Adler said, "feminists and pagans are both coming from the same source without realizing it, and heading toward the same goal without realizing it, and the two are now beginning to interlace."[1] Now, a generation later, feminists and pagans do both realize exactly what they are doing, and what began as separate movements—the feminist movement and the neo-pagan movement—has become a single movement with a common cause. The union of feminism and paganism is now very intentional, and fellow-travelers are falling in line, including homosexuals, most of the entertainment industry, sex education advocates, and liberal theologians. Paganism is infiltrating twenty-first-century American culture rapidly through cartoon programming; popular television programs like "Hercules," "Sinbad," and "Xenia"; blockbuster movies like *Star Wars* and *Titanic;* games like Dungeons and Dragons and Ouija boards; the new academic field of women's studies; intense concentration on spirituality by leading feminists and homosexuals[2]; a new emphasis on spirituality in marketing promiscuous sex education materials; neo-pagan festivals like Burning Man; religious themes appearing at Renaissance fairs; New Age art depicting the spirituality of Nature; celebrity popularization of Eastern religions; efforts to justify sexual sin among Christians; sexual worship retreats and seminars based on Tantric Buddhism; theological conferences featuring goddess worship; and a veritable explosion of interest in reviving pre-Christian pagan cults.

REDUCING SPIRITUAL LIFE TO SEX

While paganism comes in different forms, all variations are based on a common belief system that defines spirituality in material terms. Pagans believe spiritual and material life are not different things but are one thing, and so they reduce spiritual life to experiencing physical and emotional sensations in the material world. They believe that what people see, hear, and feel in material ways is also in fact the spiritual power running the universe. David Wells says,

> To the pagan mind, nature was alive with divine presences, linked to them in rhythms that were cosmic and supernatural. The seasons of sowing and harvesting, the rhythms of spring, summer, fall, and winter, of the dying and regeneration of nature—all these were as much supernatural as natural. . . . All things terrestrial were the shadows of things celestial. By the same token, things terrestrial were alive with the powers of celestial beings. All the powers of nature—thunderstorm, lightning, drought, famine, earthquake—were personified, and the people saw themselves as inescapably a part of the pulsating rhythms of the cosmos. And if one were in contact with the gods and goddesses through these rhythms, then every act . . . "in some way participates in the sacred." . . . every act had divine significance.[3]

C. S. Lewis explains that, while Christians believe God is everywhere, pagans (or pantheists, to use his terminology) believe God is everything. In other words, they think God is the stuff of which everything consists and therefore they deny that anything exists that is not part of this One-Ultimate-Supreme-Being. As Lewis says, pagan pantheists see God as "a universal medium rather than a concrete entity"[4]—a way of thinking sometimes indicated by capitalizing the word *Nature*. Because of this, pagans all think ordinary men and women already are, or can make themselves, gods and goddesses, and for this same reason they also say there is nothing and no one in all reality greater than ourselves. Of course, this also means they deny the existence of any God with power and authority over us, and it also leads them to believe we should all try very hard to act like deities (gods and goddesses) running the universe.

Naturally this has enormous implications. First, it results in thinking spiritual life is something we should be able to control by manipulating material things. To pagans with faith in Nature, religious life does not require submission to God's authority but instead depends on material sensations. C. S. Lewis calls this approach *popular religion* and, as we have noted, claims it is "the permanent natural bent of the human mind," because it has been the most common form of religion practiced through history.[5] And no wonder! Paganism promises ordinary human beings that they can be gods and goddesses running the universe, doing whatever they please.

Second, it produces a form of worship that consists of doing material things in hope of gaining spiritual life or power. For pagans, spiritual power is something to manipulate and control, not something to obey. So, whereas Christian worship requires putting ourselves under God's authority, pagan worship never involves submission and always involves trying to get spiritual power under human control.

Third, it means the pagan concept of *truth* is subjective rather than objective. Truth, to the pagan, is something known not by reason but rather through *body-acts* (something that you claim to feel for yourself and that no one else can verify). Pagan truth is not rational but sensual; and it is not something that remains fixed and applies to all the same way, but rather is something that changes and never applies the same to all.

Fourth, paganism ends up affecting morality—especially sexual morality—in very serious ways. The sort of effect it has, however, depends on which of two approaches pagans take with regard to Nature. C. S. Lewis separates pagan pantheists into two camps. First are those who affirm Nature the way it is and who therefore believe spiritual life is run by *indulging* natural desires. Second are those who oppose Nature the way it is and who therefore believe spiritual life involves *denying* natural desires. C. S. Lewis criticizes both of these approaches:

> The Christian doctrine does neither of these things. If any man approaches it [material life] with the idea that because Jahweh is the God of fertility our lasciviousness is going to be authorised or that the Selectiveness and Vicariousness of God's method will excuse us for imitating (as "Heroes," "Supermen" or social parasites) the lower Selectiveness and Vicariousness of Nature, he will be stunned and repelled by the inflexible Christian demand for chastity, humility, mercy and justice. On the other hand if we come to it [material life] regarding the death which precedes every re-birth, or the fact of inequality, or our dependence on others and their dependence on us, as the mere odious necessities of an evil cosmos, and hoping to be

> delivered into transparent and "enlightened" spirituality where all these things vanish, we shall be equally disappointed. . . . we find (as we do not find either in the Nature religions or in the religions that deny Nature) a real illumination: Nature is being lit up by a light from beyond Nature. Someone is speaking who knows more about her than can be known from inside her.[6]

The difference between these pagan approaches explains why, even though most pagans are very indulgent, some are actually extremely ascetic, denying the value of everything we experience in natural life. Both approaches are based, however, on the same belief system. They both reduce spirituality to what people experience in the material world, and both assume that spiritual life is controlled on human terms, through sensation. Nature-indulging pagans and Nature-opposing pagans both believe that morality follows experience, not the other way around. Neither believes that morality exists beyond human control, and neither believes that anyone must obey any rules they have not chosen for themselves.

All pagans also think morality is something that matters only in the illusionary-material world, and that it is completely irrelevant in what they see as the real-spiritual world. They believe that truly *spiritual* people do not have to be moral. After all, gods and goddesses do whatever they want. For them, nothing is off-limits. Because, if everything is part of the One-Ultimate-Supreme-Being (the pantheist view of God), there can be no ultimate difference between good and bad. Good and bad is all the same at the highest level of spiritual existence. And so, pagans believe, the more spiritual a person becomes, the less moral that person needs to be. Morality applies only to unspiritual people. Spirituality transcends morality.

Of course, this affects what pagans think about morality and sex, with Nature-opposing pagans saying spiritual life comes from always denying sexual desires (whatever they may be) and Nature-indulging pagans saying it comes from always indulging sexual desires (whatever they may be). For obvious reasons, the Nature-indulging approach of *sexual paganism* has always been a lot more popular than the Nature-opposing approach, and therefore pagan sexual morality has nearly always been very sensual and promiscuous. So, from here on we will no longer mention this distinction in pagan approaches to sex. From here on, all references to *paganism* will assume we are addressing the Nature-indulging (not the Nature-opposing) variety of pantheistic paganism, and all references to *pagan sexual morality* will assume we are addressing sexual (not anti-sexual) paganism.

SEEKING SALVATION THROUGH SEX

As paganism spreads through American culture, it is important to realize we are dealing with a particular version of paganism—sexual paganism—that believes *salvation* is something men and women do for themselves through sex. In the first chapter we saw how this idea of salvation through sex is already spreading through the culture. It appeared in the movie *Titanic.* It is why Kate Logan disrobed at her graduation in Vermont. It is why priestesses of Ishtar are conducting sexual worship at the Burning Man festival in Nevada. And it is driving the SIECUS Religion Initiative. These expressions of sexual paganism are not appearing at the same time by accident. Proponents of pagan salvation through sex are spreading their faith with zeal.

Michel Foucault, the French philosopher revered now in university programs dealing with human sexuality, claims sex has replaced the role of traditional Christian preaching and is now the main way through which people in the West are finding meaning and purpose for life. According to Foucault, "a great sexual sermon . . . has swept through our societies over the last decades," one in which people are being told that meaning and purpose in life does not come from becoming reconciled to God but from exploring and indulging sexual desire.[7]

Mary Daly, a former Catholic theologian turned pagan feminist, claims that women can reach spiritual salvation on their own terms through *pure lust.* Daly claims that women need to pursue pure lust in order to escape their present "state of bondage" and reach "cosmic harmony."[8]

Thomas Moore, a former Catholic monk who now promotes pagan sexuality, says "the highest levels of spirituality are made accessible through sex," and claims that, "wherever eros stirs, the soul comes to life" and, "whenever we put a lid on eros, the soul feels deprived of breath and life."[9]

Eugene Rogers, who teaches theology at the University of Virginia, claims, "if there is no bodily [sexual] desire to assume, there is nothing to redeem" because "the body is the way of the creature into the triune God." He believes that, unless homosexuals satisfy their sexual desires, God will have "nothing by which to redeem them, no hook in the flesh by which to capture them and pull them up" into "life with God."[10]

And Chris Glaser, who leads a Presbyterian ministry in Los Angeles, claims that sexual "lovemaking serves many of us as a means of grace." He therefore urges homosexuals to "make love with God" because, he says, they must "find physical, soulful ways to relate to God" through sex.[11]

They say it in different ways, but these and others are promoting the same thing. They all advocate the sexual pagan idea of salvation achieved on human terms through sex. That is, of course totally contrary to the Bible, which offers salvation as a work of God beyond human control. Biblical salvation is not something we do for ourselves. God saves us on his own, and we do nothing at all to earn it, deserve it, or control it. Biblical salvation is free. It is an act of grace, not of works, and to receive it we must agree that God is right about sin. We must accept God's salvation on his terms alone, without setting limits or conditions. According to the Bible,

> the grace of God has appeared, bringing salvation for all people, training us to renounce ungodliness and worldly passions, and to live self-controlled, upright, and godly lives in the present age (Titus 2:11-12).

In contrast to this, sexual pagans believe that unrestrained sex puts them in contact with spiritual powers running the universe. It is what makes them gods or goddesses. And they believe that experiencing sexual ecstasy gives spiritual power they can use however they wish. That is what Daly means by escaping "the state of bondage" and reaching "cosmic harmony." That is at least part of what Moore calls reaching "the highest levels of spirituality." That is why Rogers calls sex the "hook in the flesh" by which people get pulled into "life with God." And that is why Glaser calls sex "a means of grace."

By offering salvation through sex, paganism reverses God's offer of salvation through Jesus Christ. Whereas the Bible reveals that we are sinners who need to be saved *from* sexual sin, pagans claim that we are sinless gods or goddesses who can have spiritual life by saving ourselves *through* sexual sin. And whereas the Bible insists that sexual sin is part of the *problem* from which we need to be saved, pagans make sexual sin the ultimate *purpose* for which people must try saving themselves. Peter Jones summarizes the way sexual pagans pervert salvation, saying, "when beds become altars, altars quickly become beds."[12]

Sexual Worship Leads to Human Sacrifice

Pagan spirituality promises sex without limits. But it comes at a price. Justifying promiscuous sex on spiritual terms also justifies and eventually leads to human sacrifice, because there is in fact a direct connection between denying moral boundaries guarding the sanctity of sex and denying moral boundaries guarding the sanctity of human life. They come as a package.

Spiritualizing sex on pagan terms destroys the sanctity of marriage and family life, and spiritualizing death on pagan terms destroys the sanctity of human life. By reducing spiritual life to material experiences, and basing morality on passions of the flesh, paganism frees people to indulge sexual lust however they like. Then, because death is the ultimate material experience and experiencing death is the ultimate sensation, paganism also justifies and sometimes even demands human sacrifice.

According to sexual paganism advocates Monica Sjoo and Barbara Mor, pagans like themselves have always linked sex with human sacrifice. These women explain that, in pagan thinking, life and death form a single circle of existence. They are not two things, but one thing. According to them, life produces death and death produces life—one leads to the other—and neither exists unless caused by the other. Therefore Sjoo and Mor say that pagans have always believed,

> What was taken from her [Nature as divine being] by humans in the form of harvest had to be returned in human or animal sacrifice. . . . Blood sacrifice and sexual rites were interwoven with mourning the dead, ploughing the fields, harvesting crops—all to aid the rebirth of the seed and the dead body, through a ritual renewal of the Great Mother [Nature as divine being] through the mingling of blood, sex, and spirit.[13]

Moreover, they explain, pagans link sex with human sacrifice because,

> From the beginning there was a primary human [pagan] perception that our living was sustained by death. . . . There was a kind of ontological [physically experienced] pain in this perception that can be resolved only through ritual, which is a fusion of fertility and death, of life through death and vice versa. . . . [Harmonizing life with death] was always a major concern of [pagan] religion.[14]

So, because pagans believe that death produces life and that spiritual-and-material-existence-is-all-the-same, they do not think that death is the end of life or that killing someone is actually *taking* a person's life. Instead, when a person dies physically, pagans think that person continues living in the natural world, only at a higher, more powerful level. Seen in this way, the killing of innocent people no longer seems bad. And, in fact, some pagan cultures have even thought that being selected to be a human sacrifice was a great honor—something for which victims should be grateful.

But, of course, the Bible shows that this really is a terrible lie. For it is, in fact, the same lie Satan used to deceive Eve in the Garden of Eden. It is the lie he used when he urged Eve to disobey God because, "You will not surely die" (Gen. 3:4). Pagans who deny the reality of death—who say death is not real, or killing someone is not taking that person's life—are perpetuating the same lie. They still believe the same deception by which Satan led the human race to sin in the first place.

In the logic of sexual paganism, justifying unlimited sex on spiritual terms and sacrificing innocent human life are not separate things but rather are two sides of a single coin. Pagan sex and pagan sacrifice do not exist separately. One always produces the other. They are opposite sides of a single belief system in which people try saving themselves and controlling spiritual life through sensuality. They are complementary sides of a single strategy to supplant God on human terms. We shall consider recent, real-life evidence of this connection when we discuss the pagan-feminist view of abortion later in this chapter.

SEXUAL PAGANS DESPISE THE CHRISTIAN GOD

Reemerging paganism in American culture covers a wide spectrum. But each variation (including children's cartoons) is highly sexual, and everyone seriously promoting pagan revival (interested in something more than entertainment) is openly hostile toward the God of the Bible.

Roy Maynard, who covered Burning Man in 1999, reported what took place at a temple of Ishtar theme camp. Maynard described nightly ceremonies of sexual worship in which priestesses claiming to embody the goddess selected consorts for divine initiation. But before pairing up, prospects had to sit through lectures "all about the holiness of self, the neglected female deities of the ancient world, and of course the evils of Christianity."[15] The neo-pagan priestesses of Ishtar at Burning Man were not just excusing promiscuous sex but were attacking Christian faith and practice. They were not satisfied with luring men to have sex, but were also spreading hatred for the biblical view of God.

Attacking God openly is part of the program for sexual pagans these days. It is not unusual but rather is so regular it must be taken as characteristic. Robin Morgan, who first popularized paganism among leaders of the feminist movement,[16] says the reason she attacks Christianity and Christians is because we "cast the cosmos itself—the life force, energy, matter, and miracle—into the form of a male god."[17] In other words, it is because she hates the view of God given in the Bible.

In fact, some contemporary pagans ridicule God so pornographically that we cannot repeat what they say.[18] But evidence of their scorn (without the pornography) is expressed by Monica Sjoo and Barbara Mor:

> Yahweh is called the jealous God. [But] What was Yahweh jealous of? Of the Goddess, and her lover, of their sacred-sexual relation itself, and of its domination over the minds and hearts and bodies of generations of Neolithic people. That is why the God and religion of the Bible are identified so clearly from all other preceding gods and religions: The Bible God and his religion are based on a violently asexual, or antisexual morality never before seen on earth. Sex—the source of life and pleasure of love—becomes the enemy of God.[19]

Ginette Paris, who advocates sexual paganism, also attacks Christian morality and by inference the Christian God. She claims biblical moral standards are "cruel," "disastrous," and "sadistic,"[20] and says "Christianity, Judaism, Islam are murderous religions" that should be condemned by a "world court . . . as we denounce other human rights abuses."[21] For Paris, paganism offers better morality than Christianity and it is time "to point an accusatory finger at the other camp [biblical Christianity] and denounce its own immorality."[22]

Thomas Moore, the former Catholic monk turned promoter of pagan sexuality, is more subtle. While still claiming to be Catholic, he nevertheless attacks the source of biblical religion. He believes that Christians "have special trouble with sex" because "any religion or philosophy that defines itself against the values of paganism" has to "find sex challenging."[23] Thus, according to Moore, Christian opposition to paganism is to blame for wounding Western society with

> a deep-seated masochism, which finds distorted satisfaction in the suppression of desire. . . . [So,] instead of giving in to our passions, allowing emotion to course through our bodies and psyches, and generously offering ourselves to intimacy, we surrender our joy in life to . . . authorities [who then] . . . condemn us for our longings and pleasures.[24]

Although Moore focuses mainly on promoting the appeal of pagan sexuality, he cannot resist attacking biblical opposition to paganism which of course comes directly from the biblical revelation of God.

John Shelby Spong, former Episcopal Bishop of Newark (now retired), is even more hateful than Moore. I do not think Spong has become entirely pagan in a classical sense; he does not advocate sacramental sex or goddess worship. But he does reduce spirituality to sensuality, and he attacks God as viciously as any pagan. Though Spong has held a senior office in the church and still exerts enormous influence as a Christian teacher, he openly claims to be deeply offended by the Apostles' Creed, which addresses God as "Father Almighty." Spong says that phrase "repel[s] me" and "I do not care to worship a God defined by masculinity."[25] He also refuses to believe in "a record-keeping deity before whom I shall appear on the day of judgment to have my eternal destiny announced." According to Spong, "my heart will never worship that which my mind has rejected."[26] He says that Christians must,

> recognize the ogre into which they have turned God. A human father who would nail his son to a cross for any purpose would be arrested for child abuse. . . . I would choose to loathe rather than worship a deity who required the sacrifice of his son.[27]

Naomi Goldenberg, a sexual pagan feminist with psychological training, also frankly hates God because biblical religion has "denied women the [pagan] experience of seeing themselves as divine beings."[28] Goldenberg claims that "God is going to change" and believes "We women are going to bring an end to God." This she finds "most satisfying" because,

> I had no great tie to God anyway. He never seemed to be relevant to me at all. Reflection on His cultural demise left me with no sense of loss. . . . there was a magnificence attached to the idea of watching Him go.[29]

Goldenberg despises the biblical God so much, she labels him "a death god" and says that she hopes, "as we watch Christ and Yahweh tumble to the ground, we will [soon] completely outgrow the need for an external god."[30]

Finally Mary Daly, the former Catholic theologian now sexual pagan, despises God so much she calls him "the he-goddess" who displays "the hubris of the he-man's religious fantasy."[31] Daly considers the God of the Bible a "false God" who "represents the necrophilia [death-love] of patriarchy, whereas [the pagan concept of] *Goddess* affirms the life-loving being of women and nature."[32] And she claims that Christians worship a

> divine patriarch [who] castrates women as long as he is allowed to live on in the human imagination. . . . [and who] functions to legitimize the existing social, economic, and political status quo, in which women and other victimized groups are subordinate.[33]

But Daly not only hates God in general, she especially hates Jesus Christ.

Daly calls Jesus "a male pseudo-goddess" or "plastic goddess," by which she means to say Jesus is nothing more than a fake imitation of pagan reality.[34] She calls worshiping Jesus "Christolotry," a form of idolatry that "functions to mandate and legitimate intolerance, self-hatred, hatred and scapegoating of others, inquisitions, sadomasochism, [and] pornography."[35] And, while Daly is shocking, she is at least honest enough to admit that,

> the women's movement *does* point to, seek, and constitute the primordial, always present, and future Antichrist.
>
> . . . The Antichrist dreaded by the patriarchs may be the surge of consciousness, the spiritual awakening, that can bring us beyond Christolotry into a fuller stage of conscious participation in the *living* God.[36]

The reason for reviewing these statements is to show that, despite variations, those who are seriously working to revive sexual paganism in American culture are not only justifying promiscuous sex but are openly attacking God as well. The movement reviving sexual paganism is not only renouncing biblical standards but is aimed at destroying faith in God and respect for his moral character.

Worshiping Pure Lust

Of those promoting sexual paganism these days, the grande dame is Mary Daly. Daly was raised in a Catholic family, attended Catholic schools, and received training in Catholic theology. But she grew hostile to Christianity, and renounced it in 1971 during a sermon delivered at Harvard's Memorial Church.[37] Reflecting on that sermon, she says it was "a radical departure," a "clarion call . . . to abandon patriarchal religion." Within a year Daly also embraced lesbianism, and says,

> From that moment nothing was ever the same again. . . . the transformation was permanent. . . . Enormous forces were unleashed. . . . I had broken. . . . what I would later name the *terrible taboo*.[38]

As that was happening, Daly also led the effort to make women's studies a new academic field. In the same year she renounced Christianity, she also chaired the group that gave women's studies a permanent place in the American Academy of Religion. And because she was embracing anti-Christian sexual paganism, her role in developing the field ensured that women's studies was deeply marked by anti-Christian, pro-lesbian, pro-pagan sentiment from the start. Because of Mary Daly's role, as programs in women's studies have spread from school to school across the United States, they have also in nearly every case promoted sexual paganism as well.

Understanding that role, it is no small thing that Mary Daly calls herself a "wicked/wiccan woman." It is no small thing that she says to "those who think I have gone overboard," their "assessment is correct, [and] probably beyond their wildest imagination."[39] And it was no small thing that, in 1973 (two years after she renounced Christianity, one year after she was "transformed" by lesbian sex, and while she was in the midst of launching the field of women's studies), Daly said,

> To put it rather bluntly, I propose that Christianity itself should be castrated by cutting away the products of supermale arrogance: the myths of sin and salvation that are simply two diverse symptoms of the same disease.[40]

Evangelicals unfamiliar with Daly may think her remarks bizarre but essentially harmless. But Daly's views are not easily dismissed because she has been so influential. Daly has been an enormously important figure shaping the philosophy of the feminist movement in America through the 1970s, 80s, and 90s. And, in a sense, she summarized her impact on American feminism when she said,

> Ever since childhood, I have been honing my skills for living a life of a radical feminist pirate and cultivating the courage to sin. . . . [Because] "to be" in the fullest sense is "to sin."[41]

When Daly renounced Christianity, she did not lose interest in spirituality. She did not become modernist and deny the reality and importance of spiritual life. Rather she became postmodern. She shifted her view on spiritual life, replacing God's revelation in the Bible with sensual experience—which, of course, made her pagan. Daly decided the "biblical and popular image of God as a great patriarch in heaven" had to be replaced by what she called "Being" or "Goddess the Verb,"[42] terms that meant she no longer believed anyone exists in the universe greater than herself and so she would now worship her own existence. It was Daly's version of the ancient pagan idea that men and women either are, or can be, gods and goddesses running the cosmos. In redefining God, she declared,

> The new wave of feminism . . . [must be] not only multifaceted but cosmic and ultimately religious in its vision. This means reaching outward and inward toward the god beyond and beneath the gods [like the Christian God] who have stolen our [ultimately divine] identity.[43]

Upon becoming pagan, Daly started working to reverse biblical good and evil. What God called good, Daly called evil; and what God called evil, Daly called good. She explained that "racy [sexual pagan] women reason from a perspective that is other than that which accepts patriarchal [biblical] meanings/myths of good and evil."[44] Her method was "reversing the reversals inherent in Christian dogma." And she believed that this reversal was necessary because, she claimed, biblical thinking is "inside out and upside down." For Daly, biblical morality is the world of "mirrordom," and to solve this problem, everything Christian had to be reversed.[45]

Daly therefore says, "rather than confessing the [Christian] creeds . . . which implies eternal confessions of guilt," women should be "lusty." Which, she says, means they must "sin in the most major way." They must "sin in the most colossal and cosmic way." They must "conjure the courage to sin" in order "to realize being"[46] (by which she means, in order to discover their own natural divinity). And when she urges women to sin, Daly is not offering something she thinks women *may choose if they like.* Rather, it is something she seriously believes every woman *must do* in order to be truly herself, truly free, truly spiritual, truly *cosmic.* She argues that sinning is both good and necessary because,

> To sin is to trust intuitions [desires of the flesh] and the reasoning rooted in them. To sin is to come into the fullness of our [pagan] powers, confronting now newly understood dimensions of the battles of principalities and powers. To sin is to move deeper into the archespheres [powers running the cosmos], overcoming the ghosts of sado-sublimation [respect for biblical teaching], realizing elemental potency [reaching ultimate spiritual power on pagan terms].[47]

And, since Daly reverses biblical morality and promotes sin, sexual sin ends up having an especially important role in her overall view of spiritual life. She starts by claiming,

> It is only by . . . the sin of reuniting her passion and intellect [only by letting her mind accept whatever her flesh desires] that a woman can realize her [spiritual] powers.[48]

Daly then argues that sex between women is "the seat of a tremendous power which is transmissible to other women by [sexual] contact." And so, she finally concludes, "it is essential to know that precisely by breaking the taboo [against lesbian sex], women can connect with our elemental powers."[49] Step-by-step Daly reveals that, in fact, she is saying sexual sin is the only real path by which men or women can be saved, can have real spiritual life. In her words,

> The soul that touches, breaths, loves, lusts. . . . is in touch with air, earth, fire and waters. She is in contact, communion. . . . Her flights are etheric, aerial [divine]. She is aura, force-field, glowing with gynergy [goddess power]. Her expanses [ability to manipulate spiritual forces] are astral, her contacts cosmic. The female soul is sensate, lusty, inspired/fired [energized by natural passion]. She is ethereal, material [a goddess in the flesh].[50]

Daly's faith in salvation through sexual sin makes her scorn the biblical view of salvation through Jesus Christ, which she calls "the ghoulish gift of fallacious faith."[51] It also leads her to claim that biblical morality robs women of "our selves, our souls, our home" and to attack opposition to lesbian sex, saying it "skins women alive."[52] Because Daly thinks women must sin sexually to have spiritual life, she believes denying sexual sin mutilates a woman's soul, which is why she thinks biblical sexual morality "skins women alive."

All this naturally makes lust the highest virtue in Daly's ethic. She says,

> There are many bright virtues in archaic time/space [the pagan worldview], but the greatest of these is lust, ontological lust. . . . Ontological lust is a cardinal virtue. . . . All other virtues of wild [pagan] women hinge on ontological lust, which is the hinge of the door to freedom [from biblical restrictions], to the possibility of breaking out [becoming independent from God].[53]

Daly defines her hope of spiritual life in sensual terms and calls it *pure lust.* Indeed, nothing more clearly expresses Daly's sexual paganism than her description of the vision to which she trusts the ultimate destiny of her soul. Though she trained to be a Catholic theologian, Daly has become a sexual pagan who now believes,

> Pure lust names the high humor, hope, and cosmic accord/harmony of those women who choose to escape, to follow our heart's deepest desire

> and bound out of the state of bondage [biblical morality], wander-lusting and wonder-lusting with the elements, connecting with the auras of animals and plants, moving in planetary communion with the farthest stars. This lust is in its essence astral [divinely cosmic]. It is pure passion: unadulterated, absolute, simple sheer striving for abundance of being [trying to deify yourself]. It is unlimited, unlimiting desire/fire [unrestrained indulging of sensual passions]. One moved by its magic is musing/remembering [connecting with cosmic powers]. Choosing to leave the dismembered state [ordinary existence in the natural world], she casts her lot, life, with the trees and the winds, the sands and the tides, the mountains and the moors [she commits her destiny to paganism rather than accept the one true God revealed in scripture].[54]

Whatever else we say about Mary Daly, no one can fault her for deception. She likes to be shocking but has always been bluntly honest about what she believes and intends. Having embraced sexual paganism, she has never since claimed to be Christian. Daly honestly hates God, honestly despises Jesus Christ, and is honestly working to paganize the culture by reversing the influence of biblical sexual morality. But while her influence has been enormous and she remains a central figure in feminism, Daly is no longer cutting-edge. The feminist movement is now overrun with sexual pagans, and new leaders have emerged who are looking past Daly's promotion of sexual sin in order to revive interest in human sacrifice.

Making Abortion a Human Sacrifice

Earlier we claimed that, in theory, the pagan worldview, by justifying unrestricted sex, also ends up justifying and eventually demanding the sacrifice of innocent human life. Now we will see that this is in fact happening in American culture today. Lulled by unparalleled prosperity and unchallenged military might, Americans are losing traditional respect for Judeo-Christian discipline and are succumbing to the lure of unrestrained sex justified on spiritual terms. Human sacrifice lies down this path. And just as ancient pagans linked sex with human sacrifice, so also neo-pagans today are claiming god-like power over death—in the same way that they have already claimed god-like power over generating life through sex.

Ginette Paris, Monica Sjoo, and Barbara Mor represent a new edge among sexual pagans trying to revive the practice of human sacrifice by making abortion a *sacrament*. Paris says, "abortion is a sacred act," and therefore she thinks "our culture needs new rituals as well as laws to restore to abortion its sacred dimension." And to bring this about she urges women to make abortion "a sacrifice to [the pagan goddess] Artemis."[55] Sjoo and Mor head the same way, saying,

> all women—on a global scale—have got to regain our ancient ontological power—and intuitive skill—for making life-and-death decisions.[56]

Why? Because, they say,

> abortion . . . is indeed a participation ritual, in which a woman participates heavily and unforgettably in her own death . . . in the death of a potential child.[57]

These women acknowledge that the life in the womb is sacred like their own. But they also believe its sacred value is created by—and therefore is entirely dependent upon—a mother's sovereign choice. Paris therefore recommends, if a mother plans to abort her child, she should make up "a ritual that is well adapted to the circumstance," and she describes several examples. Paris mentions how she has,

> heard women address their fetus directly . . . [to] explain why it is necessary to separate now. Others write a letter of farewell and read it to a friend, a spouse, or indeed to their whole family. Still others invent their own farewell ritual, inspired perhaps by rituals from other cultures, like offering a little doll to a divinity as a symbol of the aborted fetus.[58]

Similarly Sjoo and Mor recommend that women planning abortions try going into trances in which they might speak "to the fetus as one sacred being to another: *This is not the right time or space for us to be together. Please leave now. At the right time, we will meet again.*"[59]

Between them, Paris, Sjoo, and Mor offer two reasons for making abortion a sacrament—one practical and one cosmic. First, Paris explains that rituals affirming the *sacred dimension* of abortion are needed because having an abortion provokes "an important *spiritual* crisis in women and within couples, a crisis that goes beyond the purview of the medical process."[60] In other words, she argues that making abortion a sacrament, an act of religious worship, will help mothers stop feeling guilty about killing their children.

The second, more important reason these pagan feminists give for making abortion a sacrament is that they believe it is time that women assert divine sovereignty over death as well as life. Paris thinks a woman "cannot function properly if she does not also possess full power, namely, the power over death as well as life."[61] And Sjoo and Mor say,

> women . . . have got to regain our ancient ontological power—and intuitive skill—for making life-and-death decisions. For they are always linked: Life-and-death-are-linked. To decide *at the root* about life—about what life is, and could be—women must also know how to decide *at the root* about death; about what death is, what death is for, what death means to Life. . . . that is how females regain the evolutionary memory and habit of being cosmic women once again. . . . This is the real challenge presented by feminist issues, including abortion rights.[62]

They explain,

> When women begin to define our own lives, including being ontologically responsible for each life we choose to bring—or not bring—into the world, then women will become fully functioning *definers of the world.* And we will be fully responsible for the kind of world, the spiritual and physical quality of world, into which we bring new life.[63]

These women argue that if, to justify unlimited sex, women claim godlike power over *creating* human life, they must also at the same time claim sovereign power over *killing* human life. Sovereignty over life entails sovereignty over death as well. Sexual pagans leading the postmodern feminist movement understand this connection and are using it to argue that affirming their own divinity gives women a *duty* to assert power over death as well as life. Then, if they truly have such authority over life and death, they can claim both the *ability* and the *responsibility* for creating a new world. But the sort of world those women envision is one in which "psychic abortion [abortion as a human sacrifice] can not only occur, but will predominate."[64] That is, they envision creating a new world in which practicing human sacrifice by means of abortion will not only be allowed but will be the way things are done most of the time.

Those who began paganizing feminism in America at first avoided resurrecting ancient names for pagan deities. So, even though Mary Daly is completely pagan, she never refers to divinity except as "Being," or "Goddess the Verb." But the next generation of pagan feminists, those now pushing to make abortion a form of human sacrifice, is urging that women also revive ancient goddess cults by name.

Thus in justifying human sacrifice by abortion, Paris wants to revive the ancient cult of Artemis:

> It is time to call back the image of Artemis, the wild one, who despite her beauty refuses marriage and chooses to belong only to herself. . . . When the Artemis myth manifests itself in our lives, it can be recognized by a sense of no longer belonging to a group, a couple, or a family . . . the most extreme example of fusion [the most important duty Artemis frees women from] being the connection between a mother and her young children.[65]

She selects Artemis to receive aborted babies as human sacrifices because, she says, "Artemis had a reputation for liking bloody sacrifices, including human ones." Then Paris goes on to say,

> The fierceness displayed by Artemis . . . is symbolic of the fact that certain values must absolutely not be betrayed or else our soul is violated. . . . Abortion always has been and continues to be another way of choosing death over life. . . . [Artemis] who has the strength to support women as they give birth does not falter when, with her swift arrow, she provides a quick death.[66]

Resurrecting a goddess who likes "bloody sacrifices, including human ones" makes sense only if you already favor the idea of sacrificing innocent human victims. But there is more for which we must prepare, and Christians must also look past neo-pagan interest in human sacrifice to also consider the particular goddess Paris is resurrecting for this purpose.

The goddess Paris resurrects is one the Greeks called Artemis and the Romans called Diana. Sjoo and Mor describe this goddess:

> Diana-Artemis, Goddess of Witches, was the Great Goddess of the legendary Amazons. . . . She was Queen of Heaven. . . . She was a Lesbian, scornful of men. . . . As the Moon, she rides the clouds, very cool, untouched by man, filling the nights with psychic brilliance. . . . [She was also] Artemis, the orgiastic and many breasted Mother of All; in this form she was honored at the Temple of Artemis at Ephesus. . . . [She was the] Dark Goddess of the Night Sky, giver of plagues and sudden death. . . . To the Christians, Diana the Moon was the Devil incarnate. . . . Long into the Renaissance, she was imagined as a terrible demon. . . . [and some even claimed] the devil "Lucifer" . . . was . . . Diana's twin brother.[67]

Thus, the goddess Paris is reviving to receive abortions as "bloody" human sacrifices is none other than the original witch, the great opponent of family duties within God's order of creation, the goddess early Christians associated directly with the devil, the goddess in whose name the citizens of Ephesus rioted against Christian evangelism, shouting, "Great is Artemis of the Ephesians! . . . Great is Artemis of the Ephesians!" (Acts 19:28, 34).

As paganism infiltrates American society, it is the lure of indulgent pagan sexuality that first opens the door. But pagan sacrifice is following close behind. God alone is sovereign over life and death. So, if men and women usurp God's sovereignty over life through sex, we should not be surprised when it leads them to assert sovereignty over death as well.

3

PAGANIZING "CHRISTIAN" SEXUAL MORALITY

THE RISING OF A DIFFERENT GOSPEL

Of course, we should expect Christian theologians, based on faith in the inerrant authority of the Bible, to always affirm and teach that sexual promiscuity, gender role confusion, and homosexual behavior are sinful, immoral, and destructive. Indeed, we should expect Christian theologians to defend biblical standards with as much vigor as non-Christian sexual pagans display attacking traditional Christian moral boundaries. But in fact sexual paganism is flooding into church life in America through teachers who are supposed to provide instruction in Christian sexual morality.

Sexual paganism not only is challenging the influence of Christian sexual morality in the culture outside the church but is affecting faith and practice inside the church, and this is happening because a growing number of Christian teachers are actually deserting to the other side. Teachers responsible for Christian moral training are accepting *pagan* sexual morality based on *pagan* spirituality, and are then using their authority as teachers to lead people in the church into sexual paganism. That is, a growing number of those responsible for teaching at "Christian" colleges or seminaries, or for teaching "Christian" doctrine at universities, or for leading "Christian" ministries, or for writing for "Christian" publications are in fact trying to change what people in churches believe about sex, and are trying to make them think and act more like pagans than like faithful followers of biblical revelation. In this chapter we will examine the work of six teachers—three women and three men—to demonstrate what really is a significant movement affecting major segments of the church.

The individuals reviewed in this chapter all hold positions either related to or intended to affect Christian education. Each is not so much trying to *compete* with as to *transform* Christian sexual morality into something different. This certainly is extreme, but then extremely nonbiblical teaching is hardly unusual in the church these days. True understanding of Christian morality, and even Christianity itself, is being tested not only outside but also inside the church.

If instructors teaching *Christian* sexual morality in the church treat sexual paganism as a new, improved version of *Christianity,* and if they persuade *Christians* to replace biblical with pagan sexual morality, the resulting witness given by the church will be severed from the true gospel of Jesus Christ. It will be a totally different gospel that changes the way people understand every dimension of Christian life. It will be a new gospel so radically different that it turns the witness of the church completely upside down.

Paul rebuked first-century Christians in Galatia for turning to a different gospel, and we should be as concerned now as we face the same thing in our day. Paul said,

> I am astonished that you are so quickly deserting him who called you in the grace of Christ and are turning to a different gospel (Gal. 1:6).

And he continued,

> But even if we or an angel from heaven should preach to you a gospel contrary to the one we preached to you, let him be accursed. As we have said before, so now I say again: If anyone is preaching to you a gospel contrary to the one you received, let him be accursed (vv. 8-9).

We have seen that Naomi Goldenberg is on the other side of this struggle. But she is nevertheless correct about what is at stake. She says,

> The feminist movement in Western culture is engaged in the slow execution of Christ and Yahweh. Yet very few of the women and men now working . . . [to change sexual morality] within Christianity and Judaism realize the extent of their heresy. . . . they understand themselves to be improving the practice of their religions. . . . I do not agree. . . . The reforms that Christian and Jewish women are proposing are major departures from tradition. When feminists succeed in changing the position of women in Christianity and Judaism they will shake these religions to their roots.[1]

Goldenberg then adds,

> There will of course be nothing to prevent people who practice new [pagan] religions from calling themselves Christians or Jews. Undoubtedly, many followers of new faiths will still cling to old labels. But a mere semantic veneer of tradition ought not to hide the fact that very nontraditional faiths will be practiced. Those of us who fancy ourselves scholars of religion will perceive what is happening more clearly if we do not pretend that we are watching minor metamorphoses occurring within the Jewish and Christian traditions.[2]

Sexual paganism is being injected into the bloodstream of the church, and the teachers covered in this chapter are just a few of many promoting this viewpoint. We covered Mary Daly in chapter 2 because she no longer claims to be teaching Christian sexual morality. But she did continue teaching at a Catholic school for over thirty years, and for that reason might be included in this chapter as well. The only significant difference separating Daly from teachers covered in this chapter is that, while Daly rejects Christian sexual morality and urges people to leave the church, those covered here still claim they are teaching Christian sexual morality and want those who believe them to remain in the church, even though what these teachers believe is really no less pagan than what Daly teaches.

The Sexual Goddess

For twenty-two years, Rosemary Radford Ruether trained future ministers at Garrett-Evangelical Theological Seminary near Chicago, and she is now doing the same at the Pacific School of Religion in Berkeley, California. Unlike Mary Daly, who openly renounced Christianity, Ruether remains a member of the Catholic church and is deeply concerned with preparing future leaders for the church, even though she openly admits preferring pagan sources to scripture.

While Ruether claims she is a *Christian* theologian, she has spent her whole career trying to make Christians think and act like pagans.[3] She has explained that she is skeptical of "Christians who see the biblical tradition as totally superior to . . . paganism," saying, "I reject absolutist views of biblical religion," and, "Scripture is not enough to create the content of Christian identity."[4]

Ruether began favoring pagan sources over scripture while still a student at Claremont Graduate School. She reports:

> I was influenced by two brilliant classicists, Robert Palmer and Philip Merlan at Claremont. Both of these men preferred the culture and philos-

> ophy of Greco-Roman antiquity to Christianity. Their perspective transformed my stance toward Christianity. I learned . . . the superiority of Yahwism [biblical faith] to Ba'alism [Canaanite faith], Christianity to paganism were no longer possible.[5]

Ruether also admits,

> I have a great deal of sympathy with . . . the [pagan] goddess religion. . . . the many goddesses of the Mediterranean world: Ishtar, Anath, Isis, as well as the Greek poetic rendition of these figures as Athena, Hera, Aphrodite, and Artemis. . . . I retain a fondness for the ancient mother. . . . I have no objection to people finding religious nurture through theophanies of the divine outside the biblical or Christian traditions.[6]

So even though Ruether still claims she is teaching *Christian* theology, she obviously favors the ancient pagan goddess Isis, also known as Artemis, or Diana—the one pre-Christian pagans worshiped through sex with temple prostitutes—the one Ginette Paris says loves human sacrifices—the one Sjoo and Mor call the "Goddess of Witches."[7] Ruether knows this very well but still thinks favoring the ancient goddess is compatible with her vision for a new (so-called) *Christianity* that will "not fall back on biblical exclusivism over against paganism" but rather will "embrace both non-Christian and Christian traditions."[8]

Ruether's strategy for paganizing Christianity depends on getting Christian women to think they require a different idea of God than that given in the Bible. She agrees with feminists who say the view of "God the Father" in the Bible must be rejected in favor of pagan goddess religion.[9] "God," she says, "is not a Christian and does not prefer Christians to the rest of humanity." For Ruether, "God is not a Christian or Jew rather than a pagan."[10] To replace the biblical view of God, Ruether tells women to form a new, non-biblical view of the Christian "God" reconceived as a pagan goddess, to take a new pagan approach to worship in the church, and to base these both on sexual experiences unique to their lives as women.[11]

Of course this leads Ruether to a nonbiblical, pagan view of sin and salvation. She rejects "the classical [biblical] notion that the human soul is radically fallen, alienated from God, and unable to make any move to reconcile itself with God," and decides that, "redemption cannot be done by one person [Jesus Christ] for everyone else."[12] Instead, she believes,

> redemption happens whenever we . . . taste the joys of. . . . mutual well-being, [when] every act of sustaining life becomes a sacrament of God's

> presence, whether this is . . . sexual pleasure between lovers . . . or giving birth to a baby.[13]

Because Ruether defines God, sin, and salvation in pagan terms, she also takes a completely unrestricted pagan approach toward sex and sexual morality. Ruether gives Christian women a set of worship liturgies, many of which are highly sensual, including practices borrowed from the occult. She suggests women go through *Christian* baptism naked: "if a pool is available, the initiate descends unclothed into it"; offers a ritual celebrating menstruation in which groups of women bathe together naked—"shedding their clothes, the women now move to a pool of water"; includes a ritual honoring persecuted witches—"We have chosen to make this a time of remembrance . . . of women that were killed as witches"[14]; and proposes several "self-blessing" rituals affirming different sorts of immoral sex including a rite for women committing themselves to a lesbian lifestyle, a "covenant celebration" for same-sex marriages, and a "puberty rite" for women claiming power over choosing when to have sex regardless of marriage:[15]

> [You must] decide for yourself what is right and what is wrong. . . . your body is becoming able to conceive and bear. . . . choose to use it when you decide that you are ready. . . . You are the decision maker. You must decide when you are ready to use your body for love.[16]

In short, Rosemary Radford Ruether, a feminist theologian trained in classical pagan literature, is urging *Christians* openly and specifically to paganize *Christian* worship and replace *biblical* with *pagan* sexual morality within the church itself. If Ruether has her way, sensual pagan celebrations will replace biblical worship and *Christian* sexual standards will be changed to conform with *pagan,* not *biblical,* faith and practice.

A Sinless Self

Virginia Ramey Mollenkott, who grew up in a Plymouth Brethren family, took undergraduate training at Bob Jones University, and later earned a Ph.D. in English from New York University, has spent a career promoting religious feminism. She began teaching at evangelical Christian schools, and even served as an English language consultant to the New International Version Bible translation committee. But, while starting with evangelicals, Mollenkott has wandered far from those roots and like Daly and Ruether is also working to paganize the church.

Though raised by evangelical Christians, Virginia Mollenkott now denies that Jesus Christ is the only way of salvation, justifies lesbian sex, prefers "sensuous spirituality" to biblical revelation, holds a pantheistic pagan view of God, relies on a "Spirit Guide,"[17] claims to be "a sinless self traveling through eternity and temporarily having human experiences in a body known as Virginia Ramey Mollenkott,"[18] and even says that she is "God herself."[19]

Although Mollenkott remains active in church life and still claims to be "evangelical," she now asserts that she has been "authentically lesbian for as long as I can remember" and that all her "special people are feminist lesbian women and gay men."[20] She has also adopted a thoroughly nonbiblical, pagan view of God that ends up deifying herself. She says, "my self is a consciousness within the all-embracing consciousness I call by the name of God. Her consciousness is in mine, and mine in hers." Mollenkott believes "the ultimate, the sacred, God herself is everywhere at the core of everything and everyone (including me)" and prays "that God's self" will be manifested "*as* my self."[21] In other words, Mollenkott has abandoned the biblical revelation of God and now takes a completely pantheistic, pagan view instead.

Along with justifying lesbian sex, pantheistic self-worship, and sensuous spirituality, Mollenkott also denies the reality of sin—especially sexual sin—and the possibility of ever having to face judgment for sin.[22] Therefore, having denied the reality of sin, Mollenkott believes she can have sex however she wishes without fearing that God will someday judge sin, including sexual sin.

Mollenkott even goes so far now as to say Christians should take lessons on sexual morality from witches, and should accept joining a witch's coven as a valid way for women to integrate sexuality with spirituality. In particular, she suggests: that bringing "witchcraft's egalitarian male-female polarity into the context of a typical Sunday morning worship service" would be a good way to help Christians "recognize our terrific need for . . . reforms"; that Christians "might perhaps learn [from pagan goddess worshipers] the importance of stressing . . . God's immanence as opposed to . . . God's transcendence"[23]; and that,

> The integration and honoring of both sexuality and spirituality can be achieved . . . through starting or joining an alternative spirituality group such as a witches' coven.[24]

In 1992 at a conference for women in theology, Mollenkott proclaimed she believes that Christianity needs to become "interreligious," and that women must lead the way by denying the uniqueness of Jesus Christ and introducing goddess worship in their churches. This, she said, will "modify" sexual morality among Christians until what Christians believe on sex will be "fused" with pagan sexual morality.[25] And her whole effort is a strategy to persuade Christians to drop biblical sexual morality in favor of the sort of sexual morality practiced by pagan shamans.[26]

What Mollenkott believes and writes on sexual morality, sexual spirituality, and goddess worship is virtually identical to Ruether, or even Daly. But what makes Mollenkott unique is that she not only claims to be *Christian* (like Ruether) but also insists she still is an *evangelical* Christian. For example, the article in which Mollenkott recommends Christians take lessons on sexual morality from witches is titled "An Evangelical Feminist Confronts the Goddess."

But if Mollenkott has abandoned scripture and truly believes that lesbian sex is not sinful, that "sensual" spirituality is better than trusting the Bible, and that witches know more about sexual morality than Christians, and if she worships her "self" as a pantheistic pagan goddess, why then does Mollenkott not leave the church and renounce Christianity as did Mary Daly? And why especially, despite her pagan beliefs, does she still insist on calling herself an *evangelical* Christian? The answer is to be found in Mollenkott's "call to subversion," issued first in 1999.[27] Mollenkott remains in the church and still calls herself evangelical because she is trying to "subvert" what evangelical Christians believe and teach about sex.

For Mollenkott, subverting sexual morality among evangelical Christians is justified because, "in occupied territory, subversion is necessary for two reasons: to survive and to move society toward justice."[28] That is, by calling herself *evangelical* Mollenkott is subverting Christian sexual morality, first to give pagans a voice *within* the evangelical Christian community, and second (if possible) to influence evangelical Christians toward accepting pagan sexual morality.

Amazingly, Mollenkott thinks she can actually persuade evangelical Christians (at least some) to replace biblical with pagan sexual morality merely by switching labels. She is counting on finding at least some evangelicals gullible enough to give up faith in biblical moral truth merely because she takes *paganism* and labels it *evangelical.*

Veneration of Jezebel

Tina Pippin graduated with a Ph.D. in theology from the Southern Baptist Theological Seminary in Louisville, Kentucky, in 1987, and now teaches at

Agnes Scott College—a Presbyterian school for women whose catalog assures parents that Judeo-Christian values "are central" to the life of the school. But while the college at which she teaches promises education that remains faithful to Christian principles, Pippin is urging students to reject biblical revelation in favor of paganism.

Specifically, Pippin is working to replace biblical with pagan sexual morality among women in her classes. In fact she has made this so clear that some of her students have complained, "it's not okay to be Christian on this campus anymore, but it's okay to be homosexual."[29] Pippin takes such complaining as a sign of progress, for she is part of an "affinity group" within the American Academy of Religion that is working to promote moral acceptance of homosexual behavior within religious education. So, while she is responsible for teaching *Christian* sexual morality to *Christian* women at a *Christian* college, Pippin is nevertheless fighting to remove the influence of a biblical morality that says homosexual sex is sinful and immoral. She is attacking what she calls "heterosexism," the idea that heterosexual behavior is "normal" or in any way "better" than homosexual behavior.

However, the most striking feature in Pippin's effort to paganize Christianity is the way she is urging Christian women to adopt the evil queen Jezebel as a role model.

According to the Bible, Jezebel was responsible for paganizing the worship of God. We are told, "There was none who sold himself to do what was evil in the sight of the Lord like Ahab, whom Jezebel his wife incited. He acted very abominably in going after idols, as the Amorites had done, whom the Lord cast out before the people of Israel" (1 Kings 21:25-26). Pippin, however, adores this pagan queen who corrupted the worship of ancient Israel. Rather than fearing God's judgment of Jezebel, Pippin instead makes her a heroine of sexual independence and moral reform that young Christian women should learn to honor and should use as a model as they become feminist leaders in the church.[30]

In 1996, Pippin delivered a guest lecture at Meredith College, a Baptist college for women in Raleigh, North Carolina, and the topic of that lecture was changing the way Christian women ought to think of the ancient Jezebel. As her remarks that day drew to a close, Pippin, a *Christian* theologian lecturing at a *Christian* college, dismissed her audience of young *Christian* women by urging them to "go in the Spirit of Jezebel."[31] Instead of urging them to follow the example of Jesus Christ, this feminist *Christian* professor told them to emulate Jezebel's attitude of arrogant, pagan sexual rebellion.

Rather than teaching Christian women to follow Jesus Christ, Pippin instead prefers the wicked pagan queen Jezebel—the woman most responsible for leading ancient Israelites into sexual immorality and spiritual apostasy—the woman who corrupted God's people with pagan sexual worship—the woman who murdered faithful prophets of God (1 Kings 17:4)—the woman whose spirit was associated with another woman who in the first century led Christians at Thyatira astray, and whom the resurrected Jesus punished for "seducing my servants to practice sexual immorality" and "adultery" based on "the deep things of Satan" (Rev. 2:20-24). Amazing as it seems, Tina Pippin is paganizing Christian sexual morality by recommending young women at Christian colleges follow Jezebel as a role model.

Body Theology

While women in theology—women like Rosemary Radford Ruether, Virginia Ramey Mollenkott, and Tina Pippin—are paganizing Christian sexual morality in the interest of feminism, men are doing the same for the homosexual agenda. And of these men in theology who are paganizing Christian sexual morality, the leader has certainly been James B. Nelson, a United Church of Christ minister and professor of Christian ethics who taught at the United Theological Seminary of the Twin Cities for more than thirty years.

Nelson's lifelong mission was to "reunite" sexuality with spirituality and to attack what he labeled false "duality"—believing that pleasing God requires restricting passions of the flesh. Of course Christians have always affirmed the goodness of God's creation, including the goodness of sex. But, whereas the Bible says human nature is perverted by sin so that we cannot trust the flesh and must keep sex inside boundaries set by God, Nelson falsely accused biblical morality of rejecting the basic goodness of sex. And to fix this alleged problem, he reversed the biblical order relating sex to God.

The Bible says we must discipline the desires of the flesh, but Nelson urged Christians to reject biblical rules and change Christian theology to justify sex without limits. According to Nelson, all "Christians have inherited a disembodied notion of salvation: [the idea that] salvation means release from the lower (fleshly) into the higher (spiritual) life."[32] So he claimed:

> The time is upon us for recapturing the feeling for the bodily apprehension of God. When we do so, we will find ourselves not simply making religious pronouncements about the bodily life; we will enter theologically more deeply into this experience, letting it [sex] speak of God to us, and of us to God.[33]

While Nelson thought men and women should be united with God, he defined this connection in a thoroughly non-Christian, pagan way. Rather than becoming reconciled with God through repentance and faith in Jesus Christ, he instead claimed that people "unite" with God through sex. According to Nelson: "Sexual arousal and genital desire . . . can be bodily experiences of God's hunger" for us; "the erotic dynamic is . . . the sacred basis of our ability . . . to know God"; and "we experience our sexuality as the basic eros . . . that urges, invites, and lures us . . . into intimate communication and communion with God."[34] Nelson also paganizes the Christian doctrine of incarnation: so whereas the Bible says Jesus Christ uniquely reveals God "in the flesh," he wants Christians to believe that "in becoming flesh God is revealed through the sexual dimensions of our lives."[35]

By reversing the biblical connection between spirituality and sex, Nelson also paganizes the doctrine of salvation. So, whereas the Bible says we are saved *from* sexual sin through the cross, Nelson claims that salvation comes *from having sex.* And, whereas the Bible says sexual sin consists of indulging desires that violate God's rules, Nelson says it consists of *failing* to indulge whatever desires we have. According to Nelson, "sexual sin lies not in being too sexual, but in being not sexual enough."[36]

Based on his belief that the problem of sin consists of *restricting* sexual passion, Nelson concludes that salvation—the solution to sin—consists of getting rid of every barrier that restricts a person from indulging sexual passion. So Nelson thinks Christians should now believe that,

> Sexuality [indulging sexual passions] . . . is a pathway into the mystery of the cosmos. . . . it is a manifestation of the sacred, revealing to us what is beyond our conscious rational apprehension. True, this is a bold claim that goes against the accepted view. . . . But a holistic spirituality demands that we make this bold claim.[37]

And he also says,

> Sexual sanctification can mean growth in bodily self-acceptance, in the capacity for sensuousness, in the capacity for play, in the diffusion of the erotic throughout the body and in the embrace of the androgynous possibility.[38]

In rejecting the Bible and suggesting that Christians should take a new approach that "reunites" spirituality with sexuality on sensual terms, Nelson is aware that he is proposing something revolutionary—something completely inconsistent with scripture—something that completely upsets two thousand years of Christian teaching. And, though he does not use the term "pagan" for this "new and creative" approach, he does in fact realize it is pagan. Nelson knows he is leading Christians to abandon biblical teaching: "many specific scriptural prescriptions and proscriptions regarding sex are not the gospel's word for us today."[39] He knows he is reducing God to sex: he says accepting sex without limits is "trust[ing] in the present bodily reality of God, the Word made flesh."[40] And he knows that by doing this he is suggesting that Christians worship themselves: "yearning for . . . life-giving connectedness . . . with ourselves [through sex]. . . . means we are yearning for closer connectedness with God."[41]

But the strongest, most direct evidence showing that Nelson truly realizes he is urging Christians to *paganize* sexual morality appears in the way he explains what he means by *reuniting* sexuality with spirituality. The *reunion* Nelson has in mind is *not* one urging Christians to be faithful to scripture, and he is *not* concerned with trying to understand what God originally had in mind by designing sex in a way that unites a husband and wife in a relationship that is profoundly spiritual as well as physical. Rather than returning to scripture or trying to understand God's original plan, what Nelson means by *again* uniting sexuality and spirituality is returning to a pre-Christian *pagan* belief system that justifies promiscuous sex based on *pagan* spirituality.

Nelson divides Western history into three stages: a first, pre-Christian stage that justified unlimited sex on pagan grounds; a second stage, influenced by Christianity, in which he claims sex and religion were separated (reflecting his own overreaction to the fact that biblical morality requires discipline); and finally, an emerging third stage in which the culture is returning to the earlier pre-Christian belief system that justified unrestrained sex on pagan grounds. But Nelson goes beyond describing these three stages and argues that Christian sexual morality must change along with this new, third stage—the reuniting of sexuality with pre-Christian pagan spirituality.

Paganizing Christian sexual morality is what Nelson means by insisting that Christians need to adopt "a new and creative sexual ethics." That is what he means by blaming "heavy scriptural orientation" for perverting sexual morality in Western culture. That is what he means by claiming biblical instruction has left Christians with a sexual ethic that is "inadequately integrated into a wholistic spirituality."[42] His approach is clearly presented where he says:

> Throughout most of Christian history the vast majority of theologians who wrote about sexuality tried to approach the subject from one direction only: they began with affirmations and assertions of the faith (from the scriptures, from doctrines, from churchly teachings, and so on) and then applied those to human sexuality. Now, theologians . . . are assuming that the other [nonbiblical, pre-Christian, pagan] direction of inquiry is important as well: What does our sexual experience reveal about God? about ways we understand the gospel? about the ways we read scripture and tradition and attempt to live out the faith?[43]

James Nelson taught ethics at a United Church of Christ seminary for more than thirty years, but he did not accept biblical standards and thought Christian sexual morality had to be changed by shifting in a nonbiblical, pagan direction.

Sexual Salvation

Eugene Rogers is another male theologian who, like James Nelson, is paganizing Christian sexual morality to support the homosexual agenda. In 1999 Rogers, who teaches at the University of Virginia, published *Sexuality and the Christian Body,*[44] in which he argues that Christians can no longer be Christian if they do not accept homosexual relationships in the church. Not content with the widespread acceptance of homosexuality in business, entertainment, and politics, Rogers insists Christians must now accept homosexual behavior because, if they do not, God will deny them spiritual life.

Rogers claims to have constructed a new sexual approach to *Christian* theology:

> This book will . . . help students of Christianity to answer such questions about it as these: What is the relation of the human body to the trinitarian life of God? To the incarnate body of God's Word? To the body of the Church? To the body of Christ in the eucharist? How does human procreation relate to divine creation? How does sex relate to grace? How does nature relate to redemption and consummation?[45]

He argues that *pagan* sexual morality based on a *pagan* belief system actually makes "better sense of central claims about God, the community of the faithful, and their relationship"[46] than anything Christians have ever read in the Bible or learned in church.

So what exactly does Rogers want Christians to believe? His main focus seems to be getting Christians to accept the old pagan idea that spiritual life depends on physical sex. Whereas the Bible says intimacy with God requires that we submit to his authority and repent of sin, including sexual sin, Rogers turns this around, saying life with God depends on what human beings do for themselves through sexual experiences. According to Rogers, "erotic love" is what "joins God to human flesh." It is that by which "God takes us human beings up into the love by which God loves God [loves himself]."[47]

Rogers claims that lesbian women and gay men have much to teach Christians because they experience God through sex. He says:

> By the erotic love that joins God to human flesh, God takes us human beings up into the love by which God loves God. . . . But the love by which God brings human beings into the love by which God loves God—the love of the covenant—is primarily described in erotic terms. . . . Eros . . . is the principle description of the love by which God loves human beings. The love by which God loves human beings is eros . . . eros is a love that yearns for union with the other, yearns for the flesh of the other, is made vulnerable and passionate for the other. God's *philanthropia* is the love of a lover as well as the love of a father.[48]

From this, Rogers concludes that when homosexuals desire each other sexually they are experiencing a bodily hunger for God:

> The movement of eros [between homosexual partners] is first of all a reflection, in their very bodies, of the love God has for human beings. . . . [They feel in themselves] God's own desire for the partner . . . the Spirit gathering human beings into the love of the Father and the Son.[49]

Rogers therefore thinks that, if Christians say homosexual sex is sin, it amounts to insisting that homosexuals must reject God. He believes that if gay and lesbian people "are told their desires are sin" they will be left out of "life with God," because it will cause them to "reject the very reflex in them of the desiring God."[50] For Rogers, sexual desire always is desire for God and always embodies God's desire for us. So, if homosexuals cannot have sex exactly the way they desire, they cannot have a truly intimate spiritual relationship with God. Therefore, Rogers concludes that sin has nothing to do with breaking commands in the Bible but rather has to do with stopping people from satisfying whatever sexual desires they have.[51]

All this leads to Rogers's new version of supposedly *Christian* salvation, which really is nothing more than the ancient sexual pagan idea of salvation achieved on human terms through sex:

> Salvation . . . depends on . . . human bodies getting taken up [sexually] into God's body. For Christians, bodies are no more or less than a means by which God catches hold of and sanctifies human beings. . . . Union with God does not take place otherwise than by incorporating . . . physical bodies into God's.[52]

Note here especially how Rogers simply renames pagan salvation by changing the label to *Christian.*

With this, as noted in chapter 2, Rogers argues that homosexuals cannot be saved spiritually if told they cannot indulge their homosexual desires. Of course, in reality, denying homosexual desires does not conflict with Christian salvation as revealed in the Bible; the only conflict is between the denial of homosexual desires and the sexual *pagan* view of salvation. As Rogers himself explains:

> if there is no bodily [sexual] desire to assume, there is nothing to redeem. . . . renunciation of homosexual desires. . . . gives God nothing by which to redeem them, no hook in the flesh by which to capture them and pull them up. . . . Gay and lesbian people are left out of . . . response to God's love . . . if their bodily [sexual] desires are left out.[53]

The last step in Rogers's *pagan* approach to supposedly *Christian* moral theology is to threaten that all Christians, whether homosexual or not, will *lose their salvation* if they continue refusing to accept homosexual behavior in the life of the church. He believes that, because God is now (supposedly) uniting with homosexuals through sex,

> Failing to accept faithful, monogamous gay and lesbian marriages [in the church] may deny the work of the Spirit and put . . . Christians in danger of their salvation.[54]

So Rogers not only rejects biblical sexual morality in a most outrageous fashion, he also condemns Christians who remain faithful to scripture by saying they are no longer *Christian!*

Eugene Rogers may not worship a goddess or make Jezebel a role model, but he is paganizing Christian sexual morality as surely as Ruether, Mollenkott, Pippin, and Nelson. He may call his new sexual theology *Christian,* but just switching labels does not alter reality. It may deceive, but it does not change the fact that he is teaching something totally contrary to scripture and absolutely pagan, not Christian.

The "Sacrament" of Coming Out

Chris Glaser also has been working to paganize Christian sexual morality in order to justify homosexual relationships in the church. But unlike Nelson and Rogers, who held or hold teaching positions in moral theology, Glaser has promoted the pagan sexual agenda in local ministry.[55] Rather than creating new theological arguments, Glaser has focused instead on developing rituals affirming homosexual sex among Christians and is especially responsible for treating "coming out"—proclaiming unapologetic commitment to homosexual sex—as a new *Christian* sacrament.

In a book titled, *Coming Out as Sacrament,* Glaser openly admits to following a different "gospel" than is given in the Bible. But that is something of which he is quite proud! Glaser thinks he has found a better *sexual* gospel, based on believing that "the cosmos is . . . God's body, God's *incarnation.*"[56] He believes everything in the physical universe is part of God; and because that includes sex, he imagines that every sort of sex (no matter what) *incarnates* the presence of God, and that denying any sort of sexual desire (no matter what) amounts to denying God.

This is standard sexual paganism. But Glaser claims it is better *Christianity,* and says the liturgies in his book affirming homosexual sex are designed "so they may be used *by Christians* regardless of denomination or tradition."[57] Glaser is eager to gain acceptance for sexual paganism anywhere he can!

In redesigning *Christianity* to accommodate homosexual sex, Glaser suggests that homosexuals make "coming out" a sacrament, and he says this is needed because the act of openly affirming the spirituality of homosexual sex "reveals the sacred in our lives—our worth, our love, our lovemaking, our beloved." In fact he even says it reveals "our God"[58]—a statement that says more than he imagines, for it shows that the deity he worships certainly cannot be the God of the Bible.

What then is a sacrament? Glaser defines "sacrament" in pagan terms as something people experience in the material world that has power to affect and change things in the spirit world:

> a sacred ritual is a way that we greet God or the holy with our bodies. . . . A sacred ritual, or sacrament, is a *sensual* spiritual affair, reminding us that spirituality is not an out-of-body experience. As morning awakes us, a sacrament awakens us to the spiritual quality of life in tactile and tangible ways.[59]

No one, he claims, "not even a believer," can understand the meaning of a sacrament before experiencing it. This shows that Glaser, like other sexual pagans, believes spiritual life depends on material experience, not the other way around.

Because he thinks that coming out—declaring open, unapologetic commitment to homosexual sex—is a pagan-type sacrament, a *sensuous* physical experience producing spiritual results, Glaser concludes it is a "conversion experience" that transforms a person's spiritual life in ways that are just as valid and powerful "as an encounter with Jesus."[60] He ends up saying,

> At its best and deepest level, coming out means new [spiritual] life, fresh and refreshed [spiritual] relationships, access to a new [spiritual] community, and increased intimacy with God;[61]

> coming out . . . [is] God's self-revelation [indicating we are]. . . . harmonizing our personal integrity with God's integrity: aligning our will with the will of God, as we discern it;[62]

> Coming out as a sacrament means recognizing God's Word acting in our own life . . . promising us a new and more meaningful [spiritual] life;[63]

and he concludes,

> those of us who come out as bisexual and lesbian and gay reveal a glory larger than our self-identity: we reveal the glory of sexuality itself, a divinely created and graciously given glory . . . because we have seen in our sexuality the glory of God.[64]

As a result, Glaser's *sacrament* of coming out, his *sacrament* of commitment to homosexual sex, turns into a means (a path) by which he claims homosexuals can obtain spiritual life—may reach spiritual salvation—all on their own terms depending on themselves alone. As with others who are paganizing Christian sexual morality, *sin,* for Glaser, is nothing more than failing to accept the goodness of unlimited lust; and the only spiritual problem homosexuals have to overcome is feeling ashamed of their behavior and fearing it makes them "unworthy, unholy, [or] unredeemed."[65] Glaser's new sexual pagan and supposedly *Christian* "gospel" for practicing homosexuals is, therefore, letting them know that,

> Devising our own rituals, our own sacramental rites, may be another path toward restoring our souls. . . . [Because, after all,] Spirituality is . . . some-

> thing we do and feel, eat and drink, taste and smell. . . . spirituality is something we do with others. . . . a host of people across the globe directing their thoughts, words, and feelings toward the sacred, toward God.[66]

Like Nelson and Rogers, Glaser avoids using the term *pagan* and insists he is offering a better *Christian* gospel that produces a better *Christian* sexual morality affirming homosexual relationships in the church. But he cannot change what is true; and Glaser's thinking, like that of Nelson and Rogers, is thoroughly pagan, not Christian.

WHY EVEN PRETEND THAT PAGAN SEX IS "CHRISTIAN"?

The teachers surveyed in this chapter all claim either to be teaching or to be practicing ministry in the area of *Christian* sexual morality. But rather than conforming to scripture, or even following twenty centuries of well-established theological tradition, these teachers have each been trying to redefine Christian belief by replacing God's revelation in the Bible with a *pagan* morality justifying unlimited sex. And they are not simply mavericks doing strange things at the margins of Christian life, but are part of a large movement affecting huge sections of the church.

Mary Daly, who taught for years at a Catholic school after openly rejecting Christianity, was a unique case. To my knowledge, no other self-declared, anti-Christian pagan has been allowed to remain teaching on the faculty of a Christian school. But, while her situation was unique, many others are now teaching much the same at Christian schools. These are being allowed to stay because they have not renounced Christianity in a formal sense, and because they are insisting that what they teach is only another version of Christianity itself. While affirming that they are *Christian* and that what they teach is *Christian,* these teachers are promoting sexual paganism inside rather than outside the church.

Of these, some like Rosemary Radford Ruether openly praise pagan beliefs and practices but continue teaching at Christian schools because, however openly pagan their teaching, they still claim to be Christian themselves. Some, like Virginia Ramey Mollenkott and Eugene Rogers, do not teach at Christian schools but deceive Christian readers by endorsing pagan ideas and calling them Christian. And finally there are others, like Tina Pippin, James Nelson, and Chris Glaser, who either teach at Christian schools or lead Christian ministries and are using their positions to encourage people under their influence to accept pagan morality as simply better Christian morality.

These people are all paganizing Christianity. They are not just turning people from scripture but are teaching them to believe that what is *pagan* is *Christian*. But why? If they truly believe that the Bible is wrong and that pagans are right, why not then renounce Christianity and leave the church? Mary Daly did; why are these others not doing the same? The reason, I believe, is strategy. They are working to destroy biblical resistance at the source, not by switching it off but by switching it altogether, not by denying it but by replacing it. Instead of taking people out of church or keeping them from church, these deceivers are teaching people already in church that pagan sexual morality is no enemy but rather is a wise old friend who wants to make things better. And the result is destroying churches from top to bottom, from the inside out. Pagan sexual morality is being taught at Christian colleges and seminaries where future leaders of the church are being trained, and it is causing far more damage than could ever be accomplished by pagan enemies attacking the church from outside.

Mary Daly taught for more than thirty years at Boston College, a Jesuit Catholic school founded with a vision to produce students with outstanding moral character. Rosemary Radford Ruether taught for twenty-two years at Garrett-Evangelical Theological Seminary preparing ministers for leadership in the United Methodist Church, and now is training future leaders at the Pacific School of Religion, an independent Christian school founded by the Congregational Church. Virginia Ramey Mollenkott writes books on spirituality and sex directed especially toward Christian women. Tina Pippin teaches at Agnes Scott College, a women's college affiliated with the Presbyterian Church (USA). James Nelson taught for thirty-two years and remains emeritus professor of Christian ethics at the United Theological Seminary of the Twin Cities, a school serving the United Church of Christ. Eugene Rogers teaches moral theology at the University of Virginia, which Thomas Jefferson promised would be careful to always educate students in ways that are consistent with historic Christianity.[67] And Chris Glaser has directed a ministry in Los Angeles funded by the Presbyterian Church (USA).

With teachers telling Christians that *pagan* sexual morality is more *Christian* than the Bible, what effect is this having on Christian life in America? And especially, how is such teaching affecting the church in America? Anything this serious must have far-reaching consequences. In the next two chapters, we will see how the paganizing of Christian sexual morality is sending shockwaves through all the mainline denominations and is even producing divisions among evangelicals.

4

Mainline Denominations in Sexual Turmoil

THROUGH THE LAST DECADES of the twentieth century and now into the start of the twenty-first, mainline Christian denominations in America have been suffering turmoil relating to sex. This has been clear to people involved, but outsiders have noticed as well. One secular reporter in 1996 stated, "no issue embodies the divide between traditionalism and the changing society more than . . . the debate about sexuality, which has split churches across the nation."[1] That was not just one reporter's opinion. She was stating a fact. Moreover, evangelicals could rephrase that statement to say no issue embodies division between biblical revelation and revisionism in churches today more than battles arising over sexual behavior, sexual relationships, sexual "orientation," sexual identity, gender language, and gender roles.

Revisionist sexual morality has entered the bloodstream of the church, and factions are fighting over whether or not to replace God-centered, biblical sexual morality with self-centered morality based on satisfying the desires of the flesh. God-centered morality revealed in the Bible involves rules of behavior that never change and that apply the same to everyone however anyone feels. Biblical morality is something controlled by God, and a person is held accountable to God no matter what he or she chooses. But self-centered, desire-based morality takes the opposite approach. No standard applies the same to everyone. Nothing is fixed over time. And something true for others is irrelevant unless an individual chooses it for himself or herself. Morality is something entirely controlled by the one to whom it applies.

This makes a very big difference, of course. Trying to base *Christian* sexual morality on personal feelings rather than on God's Word changes everything, and there is absolutely no middle ground. There is no such thing as a minor step one way or the other. Any move in either direction comes with enormous implications. Basing Christian morality on anything outside the Bible (however good) always justifies some level of sin, and teaching Christians to sin shakes the church to its core.

The matter of sexual "orientation" is a case in point. Elizabeth Stuart and Adrian Thatcher are sexual revisionists. But while they reject biblical sexual morality, they also understand the enormity of the conflict:

> The invention of sexual orientation or sexuality posed particular problems for Christianity. If it is possible to say that in every era there are one or two issues which force the Churches to ask uncomfortable questions about revelation and authority, then homosexuality has been one such issue in the modern era. Of course the Churches had always known that people engaged in same-sex sexual activity, but this was regarded as a willful perversion, like lying or stealing, and the matter was relatively straightforward. But once the existence of an essential sexual orientation became accepted . . . , issues about the relative authority of the bible [*sic*], tradition and contemporary experience emerged which had to be addressed and which most Churches are still wresting with.[2]

Every mainline denomination in the United States has suffered tremendous strain from a great war that has risen between radically contrary views of sexual morality. And, whether people realize it or not, the source of this conflict is the powerful and very deadly influence of reemerging, anti-biblical paganism. The war now being fought in churches over sex is over nothing less than whether biblical revelation on sexual morality should still be the norm for Christians, and whether God's rules for sexual behavior should still be relevant for life and witness in the Christian community.

In this chapter, we will examine how every mainline Christian denomination has been seriously affected by conflict over sex. Statements issued by various denominations and other religious bodies reflecting change and division on sexual morality are provided in Appendix B, and an interdenominational statement by evangelicals is provided in Appendix A.

Anglicans Attack Anglicans

The Episcopal Church in the United States of America (ECUSA) is the mainline Anglican denomination in America, and the ECUSA has struggled with sexual moral divisions longer than any other denomination. The first real battle erupted in the 1970s over ordaining women. Conservatives were surprised and lost quickly, and sexual battles in the ECUSA have since focused on normalizing homosexual behavior—ordaining noncelibate homosexuals, blessing same-sex unions, accepting sex outside of marriage, and redefining moral opposition to homosexual behavior as "sin" punishable under church discipline.

Sexual revisionism has now permeated the Episcopal church more fully than any other American denomination, and moral war among Anglicans has risen to a more intense level than among any other body of Christians anywhere in the world. Though conservatives in the ECUSA cling to historic Anglican statements affirming biblical standards, most bishops, parishes, and seminaries in America have abandoned scripture and take a nonbiblical, self-centered view of sexual morality justifiying whatever a person desires. Sexual revisionists have ignored long-held Anglican traditions based on scripture, and are even attacking the Bible itself as inherently *corrupt* and *immoral*.

Retired Bishop John Shelby Spong, a leading advocate for the revisionist side, says traditional acceptance of the Bible as "a divine source for ethics . . . has been revealed by the ancient codes themselves to be utter nonsense." He claims the Ten Commandments are based on "nothing less than the tribal prejudices, stereotypes, and limited knowledge of the people who created them," and believes that biblical sexual standards "need to be exposed immediately as immoral and . . . removed from the ethical guidelines that any of us today would seek to follow."[3]

The heresy trial of Bishop Righter. In 1995, faithful bishops in the ECUSA tried to enforce biblical standards by charging Bishop Walter Righter with heresy. Righter served for a time with Spong in the Diocese of Newark and, with Spong's encouragement, had ordained a noncelibate homosexual in 1990. The Episcopal bishops who charged Righter with heresy were not combating something new but were taking a bold stand to resist something already widely accepted throughout their denomination. The trial almost did not take place. An Episcopal bishop cannot be tried for heresy unless at least 25 percent of bishops in the denomination support a request for trial. In Righter's case, the request for trial was supported by only one vote more than the absolute minimum—only 76 of 298 bishops eligible favored raising the issue of heresy at all.

But, since Righter's accusers did meet the required minimum, revisionists could not prevent Righter from going to trial. They could and did, however, restrict the process and manipulate the results. Rather than considering what the Bible requires, trial attorneys prosecuting Righter were required to limit their case to denominational documents alone. They could neither consider the Bible itself directly nor even appeal to twenty centuries of church tradition. The only question attorneys were allowed to debate at Righter's "heresy" trial was whether the ECUSA ever had itself (apart from scripture) officially banned ordaining noncelibate homosexuals. Righter's accusers tried to argue he had violated his ordination vow to "guard the faith, unity, and discipline of the church." But Righter's defense replied there was no official denominational document (apart from scripture) in the ECUSA that specifically prohibited ordaining practicing homosexuals.

In the end, the eight-member ecclesiastical court acquitted Righter seven to one, saying,

> There is no core doctrine prohibiting the ordination of a noncelibate homosexual person living in a faithful and committed sexual relationship with a person of the same sex. There is no discipline of the church prohibiting the ordination of a noncelibate person living in a committed relationship with a person of the same sex.[4]

As it turned out, four of the eight bishops judging Righter had themselves done the same thing of which he was accused.[5] Half of his judges had already ordained noncelibate homosexuals themselves. The sexual revisionists had packed Righter's heresy court and knew in advance that members could not convict him without convicting themselves.

International showdown at Lambeth-1998. With revisionists controlling the ECUSA, a showdown over sex was inevitable at the next worldwide meeting of Anglican bishops—an event called the Lambeth Conference—which took place in 1998. Lambeth is an international conference of Anglican bishops held in England once every ten years, with the Archbishop of Canterbury presiding. American revisionists, hoping to spread their agenda worldwide, proposed that Anglicans everywhere be instructed to revise sexual moral standards to make marriage optional before having children, to accept homosexual sex, and to treat polygamy as equal to monogamy. But conservative bishops from Western countries joined bishops from Africa and Asia to not only stop the revisionist agenda but also strongly reaffirm commitment to biblical sexual standards.

American revisionists were shocked! An overwhelming majority of bishops at Lambeth-1998 (526 to 70) voted in favor of a resolution affirming scripture. In keeping with scripture, they said, the Lambeth conference "upholds faithfulness in marriage between a man and a woman in lifelong union, and believes that abstinence is right for those who are not called to marriage." The worldwide communion of Anglican bishops also opposed the "legitimizing or blessing of same-sex unions" and "the ordination of those involved in such unions."[6] Non-Western evangelicals like Bishop Kamanyire of Uganda said the resolution was necessary because bishops from the West (especially from the United States) were "undermining the faith" and committing "evangelistic suicide." Bishop Spong, however, returned home complaining that the convention was itself "unchristian, uninformed, prejudiced and evil."[7]

Though resolutions passed at Lambeth are not enforced on national denominations like ECUSA, national denominations traditionally respect the international Anglican communion and comply. However that was not the way Anglican revisionists in America received the Lambeth resolution in 1998. They may have lost the international fight, but they still controlled the American denomination, and they were not about to let non-Western evangelicals hinder their agenda simply out of respect for Anglican tradition. When it comes to sexual morality, revisionists in the Episcopal church have no respect for tradition whether biblical or otherwise.

The year following Lambeth-1998 was filled with tremendous strife as conservatives in the ECUSA tried using the international resolution to oppose revisionist power and revisionists tried to regain the momentum they had had before Lambeth-1998. Dioceses led by revisionists rejected the Lambeth resolution, endorsing a statement offered by Spong instead, and several conservative parishes, emboldened by Lambeth, took courageous stands against the revisionist majority. One parish in Massachusetts renounced the authority of its bishop when he sided with Spong against the Lambeth resolution, others withheld funds in dioceses supporting Spong, and one parish near Seattle lost a third of its members when its rector (pastor) endorsed Spong's statement and then announced he was a practicing homosexual himself.

Biblical sexual morality declared "sin." Deep divisions rocked the ECUSA again at its triennial general convention in 2000. Participants covered much the same ground, but a new contest appeared that may someday split the denomination. Sexual revisionists offered a resolution repudiating what they called "the sin of heterosexism." The resolution did not pass, but it failed by only a slim margin, and only because some on the revisionist side thought it best to delay its passage for a few years, until a time when it would attract less controversy.

For revisionists, *heterosexism* is a term applied to any unfavorable moral distinction between heterosexual and homosexual behavior—any at all. It is not a question of civility (being polite) but refers directly to the revisionists' opposition to God's view, revealed in scripture, that homosexual behavior is always wrong—is never right for anyone, for any reason—and that moral sex takes place only between a man and a woman united in holy matrimony. Declaring *heterosexism* a *sin,* in effect, declares God to be a *sinner* and requires the church to punish people for obeying what God commands.

A declaration like this would certainly split the denomination, but other events are now forcing that as well. On August 6, 2003, bishops of the ECUSA voted 62 to 43 (59 to 41 percent) to confirm a practicing homosexual, the Reverend Gene Robinson, as Bishop of New Hampshire. With that, sexual revisionists precipitated a division in the American denomination that may rupture the Anglican communion worldwide. Bishop Kendall S. Harmon, canon theologian of the diocese of South Carolina, says it was "the most serious crisis Anglicanism has faced since its founding. You've never had a situation where half of the Anglican communion is threatening to be out of communion with the other half."[8]

Having won their goal to confirm an openly practicing, unrepentant homosexual biship, Anglican revisionists are now all for maintaining unity. But it is the sexual revisionists, not those affirming scripture and historic Christian doctrine, who are forcing division in the church. They are the ones disrupting unity by heading in a thoroughly nonbiblical—essentially pagan—direction. American Anglicans faithful to biblical sexual morality have remained in fellowship with other parts of the Anglican communion around the world. These Anglicans are not changing but simply trusting God's Word as genuine Christians always do. A statement passed by faithful Anglicans in the ECUSA, "A Place to Stand: A Call to Action," is included in Appendix B,[9] and a truly inspiring talk by Peter Jensen, Archbishop of Sydney, Australia, on the importance of remaining true to biblical moral standards on sex is included in Appendix D.

Methodists War with Methodists

The United Methodist Church (UMC) is the mainline Methodist denomination in the United States, and for three decades mainline Methodists have been rocked almost as severely by war over sex as Anglicans in the ECUSA. Trouble among Methodists began in 1972 when by a slim majority convention delegates added two sentences to their constitution, the UMC *Book of Discipline:* one saying, "We do not condone the practice of homosexuality and consider this practice incompatible with Christian teaching"; and another saying, "We do not recommend marriage between two persons of the same sex."[10] These sentences affirming historic Christian faith and practice sparked an intense war between sexual revisionists and Bible-believing Christians, one in which each side has been struggling to defeat the other.

Deepening of sexual moral divisions. In 1976, Methodist conservatives won some victories, surprising the revisionist side. They stopped a revisionist drive to approve homosexual behavior and instead won motions strengthening Methodist commitment to biblical sexual morality. They upgraded constitutional opposition to same-sex marriage, replacing, "We do not *recommend* marriage between two persons of the same sex" with "We do not *recognize* . . ." They also banned all funds "to promote the acceptance of homosexuality."[11] But conservatives did not get all they wanted, and as many ambiguities were raised as were settled. Revisionists in 1976 began asking whether acts of homosexual sex should be considered sin for everyone, whether practicing homosexuals could ever be ordained, and whether Methodist ministers who conduct same-sex unions could be disciplined under denomination rules.

In 1984, conservatives answered the largest question when delegates passed an absolute ban prohibiting Methodists from ordaining "self-avowed and practicing homosexuals."[12] In 1988, however, revisionists got the denomination to approve a four-year study on homosexuality and stacked the task force that would develop recommendations. As expected, this homosexuality task force came back in 1992 with recommendations essentially suggesting the denomination abandon the Bible and adopt a new, more sensuous approach to sexual morality. Thomas Oden of the UMC criticized the task force, saying,

> The liberated sexuality task force refused even to quote scriptures that they insisted on distorting. If they had invited the reader fairly to examine the key passages in question, it would have revealed direct and unambiguous language, such as: "Do not lie with a man as one lies with a woman; that is detestable." "The native-born and the aliens living among you must not do any of these detestable things, for all these things were done by the people who lived in the land before you, and the land became defiled. And if you defile the land, it will vomit you out as it vomited out the nations that were before you" (Lev. 18:22, 26-27, NIV).[13]

The revisionist recommendations of the homosexuality task force were defeated by UMC delegates in 1992.

Fighting over same-sex marriage. Having lost on homosexual ordination and failing to gain ground through the homosexuality task force, Methodist revisionists tried changing the definition of marriage to include same-sex unions. The denomination opposed same-sex marriage in 1972 and again in 1976, but denial was viewed by revisionists as advisory and not something enforceable. In line with this, they encouraged dissenting clergy to perform same-sex marriages in defiance of denomination policy. To counter this activism, conservatives added another sentence to their constitution, this one saying, "Ceremonies that celebrate homosexual unions shall not be conducted by our ministers and shall not be conducted in our churches." However, despite this addition, revisionists still claimed that the ban was merely advisory and could not be enforced.

As tension mounted, Jimmy Creech, a pastor in Omaha, forced the issue by uniting a lesbian couple in June 1997. He did it to test interpretation of the UMC ban, and was immediately put on suspension. A few months later, in early 1998, 1,300 UMC ministers issued a statement supporting Creech, and others threatened to follow his example. Creech was narrowly acquitted by a regional jury, but his bishop continued the case by appealing to the Judicial Council which settles matters of Methodist discipline at the national level.

Defying church authority, creating mass confusion. Sensing that discipline in the church was breaking down, the UMC Judicial Council made a quick decision settling the question by announcing that what Creech did was in fact "liable to a charge of disobedience to the order and discipline of the United Methodist Church." This required Methodist revisionists to pursue a new strategy, and they shifted from challenging the meaning of their constitution to challenging the denomination's will to enforce constitutional requirements. After the Judicial Council decision, revisionists called for acts of ecclesiastical disobedience, hoping rebellion might eventually force conservatives to relent.

In September 1998, Gregory Dell, a pastor in Chicago, blessed a union of homosexuals. His bishop, Joseph Sprague of the Northern Illinois Conference, filed a complaint but did so only to keep his job. Sprague actually sided with Dell and did what he could to help. A regional jury convicted Dell halfheartedly and did not revoke his credentials. Although the Judiciary Council had made clear that the prohibition barring same-sex marriage was mandatory (not advisory), Dell's jury left him to control his own situation.

He was allowed either to change his mind or to wait until the UMC might someday change its rules. Either way he could remain a Methodist minister.

In January 1999, sixty-seven Methodist pastors conducted an act of mass disobedience in which they officiated together at a ceremony uniting a lesbian couple in Sacramento, California. Like Sprague, Bishop Melvin Talbert of the California-Nevada Conference also sided with the violators. And like Sprague, Talbert also filed a complaint to save his job and then did what he could to stop the disciplinary process. Talbert, however, succeeded, and charges against these ministers never reached the national level.

That same year, Creech blessed a second same-sex union, and this time his credentials were revoked permanently. After his trial, Creech told reporters the denomination had judged itself, and he was simply an innocent Christian following "a vision of Jesus where all are welcomed without favor." It was a clever sound bite, but one that depended on assuming that Jesus wants disciples to now disobey God's commandments on sex.

Defiance of civil authority leads to mass arrests. The UMC convention in 2000 was the most disruptive in the history of Methodism. Delegates affirming biblical sexual morality held a majority, but revisionists came in large numbers, intent on either closing the convention down or taking it over by force. Creech, Dell, and about two hundred others were arrested by Cleveland police for disrupting a worship service. Sprague led others who tried keeping delegates from entering the meeting area. In the end, a mob of revisionists stormed the stage, trying to take the denomination over by violence. Cleveland police again intervened and revisionist bishops and pastors were dragged off to jail. They were not only challenging the authority of God and their own denomination's constitution, but civil government as well.

At the beginning of the twenty-first century, mainline Methodists are far from united. Methodist evangelicals have weathered repeated, sometimes violent attacks from sexual revisionists. But they feel encouraged and truly believe the UMC can be saved.[14] Nevertheless, sexual morality based on lust cannot coexist with Christians who honor the Bible, and so the UMC now seems headed for a split—with revisionists taking a third of its members and conservatives keeping the remaining two-thirds. The UMC began in 1968 with 11.1 million members,[15] but in 2000 membership was down to only 8.5 million. If revisionists do split the UMC, the remaining denomination will be only half what it was in 1968. Thus, even though Methodist evangelicals may be winning the sex war, it is at a tremendous price.

LUTHERANS IN SEXUAL COMMOTION

The Evangelical Lutheran Church in America (ELCA) is a third mainline denomination suffering severe turmoil over sex. Strains began in 1988 when three smaller Lutheran groups merged to form what is now the ELCA. Revisionist views became an issue while Lutherans were stressing inclusion and trying to ignore differences that could strain relations. Leaders of the new mainline Lutheran denomination tried avoiding controversy, but in working to avoid it they set off a firestorm.

Unprepared for revisionism. Lutheran troubles with sexual morality started in 1988 when three students at Pacific Lutheran Theological Seminary in Berkeley, California, announced they were noncelibate homosexuals and would seek to be ordained in the new Lutheran denomination. The three merging Lutheran groups had all assumed biblical teaching on homosexual sex being sin, no exceptions. Disobeying scripture and refusing to repent disqualified anyone from becoming ordained whatever sin it might be, so none of the merging Lutheran groups had ever thought it was necessary to have a separate ban specifically denying ordination to noncelibate homosexuals. The seminarians, however, were trying to intimidate Lutheran leaders, hoping to embarrass them into accepting a new nonbiblical view on sexual morality in an effort to avoid controversy.

Wanting to ease tensions, ELCA bishops from the western region responsible for Pacific Lutheran Seminary drafted a temporary solution to appease both sides. They accepted the revisionist claim that nothing is wrong with having homosexual desires, because they are unavoidable and natural. But they also took the traditional biblical view that homosexual behavior is sinful for everyone, so noncelibate homosexuals cannot be ordained. Of course, this meant their position was impossibly self-contradictory and pleased no one. If there is nothing wrong with homosexual desires, how could it never be right to satisfy them? But, if homosexual sex is sinful, how can desiring sin be innocent?[16] The interim measure was neither scientific nor biblical. It was strictly a political compromise to delay full-scale war until matters could be studied more carefully.

News about the homosexual seminarians and the partial ELCA accommodation angered average Lutherans, who flooded their denominational magazine, *The Lutheran,* with letters like the one from Margaret Primmer, who said,

> for over 50 years I have supported our Lord's work through the Lutheran Church. I have always been proud to say, "I am a Lutheran." I cannot tell you the embarrassment, the pain and the anguish I felt when I read the news story about certifying gay seminarians. Pacific Lutheran Seminary faculty and Western Bishops wake up—get back to the Bible and Lutheran teaching![17]

Sexuality study ignites a firestorm. To find a permanent solution, the ELCA established a task force, assigning it to study human sexuality and recommend how Lutherans should handle the brewing sexual moral crisis. But revisionists were placed in charge and naturally saw it as a chance to transform the entire denomination. The ELCA trouble over sex started with mishandling homosexual seminarians in 1988, but it literally exploded when Lutheran churches across America received copies of the sexuality task force report completed October 20, 1993.[18] Most Lutherans were either unaware of the issue or were not paying attention. So upon receiving the task force report, nearly everyone in the denomination was shocked, dismayed, and genuinely angry.[19] ELCA headquarters in Chicago received more than twenty-one thousand angry calls the first day. Those were just the calls that actually got through.

But while average Lutherans were upset about forsaking biblical standards, leaders at denomination headquarters panicked, not over scripture, not over angering God, not over failing Jesus Christ, but over losing financial support! Of course, some on the headquarters staff must have been outraged. But their official response was driven by concern over losing income, not by concern that anything might be wrong with a Lutheran task force proposing a nonbiblical approach to sex.

Herbert Chilstrom, presiding bishop of the ELCA, issued a letter praising the task force and blaming the media. He said it was all a matter of bad timing and negative spin. The task force did nothing wrong. Its work was in fact commendable. The only problem was poor public relations and terribly unfair misrepresentation in the media of what really was good work. Chilstrom's letter, however, confirmed the worst because it showed that senior denominational leaders saw nothing wrong with forsaking the Bible so long as Lutherans kept sending money. Chilstrom was not alone. Only two of sixty-seven Lutheran bishops nationwide dared criticize the task force or its report, and the only one at ELCA headquarters who did so was the editor of *The Lutheran,* Edgar Trexler.

Satisfying the flesh instead of satisfying God. While most critical reaction to the report focused on its recommendations such as changing the Lutheran definition of marriage to allow same-sex unions, accepting homosexual sex as moral, endorsing masturbation, and distributing condoms to children without telling parents, the most radical thing the task force did was propose changing the way Lutherans approach sexual morality. At its first working session, the task force decided to abandon biblical authority and create a new approach to sexual morality based on feelings, intentions, and satisfying the lusts of the flesh.

Instead of relying on scripture, they adopted a sensual approach that allowed sex in "committed relationships" (however defined) regardless of marriage, that justified sex based on feelings rather than rules of behavior, and that would never interfere with people satisfying their sexual desires on their own terms. The Lutheran sexuality task force did not ignore the Bible completely because it sometimes referred to scripture for background. But the Bible was never accepted as a source of moral authority. Instead, they feared relying on the Bible could be dangerous and warned especially that Bible passages opposing homosexual sex could not be used the way ordinary people read them.

The Lutheran sexuality task force rejected scripture from the start, and did so on purpose. And because task force members knew that most Lutherans held a high view of scripture, they also had to know it would be impossible to avoid the strong negative reaction their recommendations eventually received. We must conclude therefore the only ones truly embarrassed by the controversy were denomination leaders caught in the middle because they were trying to play both sides.

Though Chilstrom, as presiding bishop of the ELCA, tried blaming the firestorm on everything except the real cause, everyone else immediately understood what the conflict was about. It arose when faithful Lutherans finally understood what sexual revisionists were trying to do. Moving a denomination away from satisfying God toward satisfying the flesh redefines the church. It redefines Christianity. And once average Lutherans understood what truly was happening, no public relations could possibly have lessened their reaction. The denomination remains united but still seethes over sexual division. The issue is not resolved, and the opposing factions continue battling for supremacy. Membership, which began at 5.3 million in 1988, had dropped to 5 million (6 percent) by 2002.

Presbyterians Fight Presbyterians

The mainline Presbyterian denomination in America is the Presbyterian Church (USA), or PCUSA, and like mainline Anglicans, Methodists, and Lutherans, mainline Presbyterians have also suffered tremendous strife over sexual morality. In 1987, the PCUSA established a committee to evaluate sexual issues troubling Presbyterians, asking it to develop recommendations for action. The committee finished its work in 1991, and its recommendations started an uproar. Jerry Van Marter, spokesman for of the Presbyterian News Service, said he had not seen Presbyterians so upset since the denomination gave funds to Communists fighting Americans during the Vietnam War.

Sexual conflict brings division. The controversy stirred by the report came from its clearly recommending that Presbyterians should abandon scripture on matters of sex. The committee suggested the PCUSA stop restricting sex to marriage, stop treating sex between homosexuals as sin, start accepting homosexual relationships as normal, start treating same-sex unions the same as marriage, and start giving family pension benefits to homosexual partners living with church employees. John Carey, who chaired the committee, said he and most members of the committee agreed that "biblical ethics and Christian ethics for the church today are not the same thing," and for that reason the committee had ignored the Bible and tried to rethink sexual morality "in terms of the changing mores of our society."[20] A minority on the committee did not agree, and David Searfoss, who led these dissenters, called the committee's recommendations a "disastrous departure from the Reformed position on the authority of Scripture."[21]

Both sides understood that the committee report was suggesting the PCUSA forsake biblical revelation on sexual morality and shift instead toward a new flesh-based, permissive approach. The committee majority tried hiding the enormity of their proposal by using familiar Christian terms in unfamiliar ways. For example, *fidelity* in the revisionist report meant willingness to renegotiate terms of a sexual relationship "as needs and desires change" and had nothing to do with keeping vows made to God or a partner in marriage. The term sounded familiar but meant something completely different.

General Assembly in 1991. The PCUSA General Assembly in 1991 overwhelmingly rejected Carey's sexual issues committee report. But their rejection was more about quieting controversy than about opposing its revisionist agenda, and commissioners that year sent conflicting signals. While rejecting revisionist recommendations in the sexual issues committee report, they also rejected a motion to put the denomination on record declaring that marriage between a man and a woman is "the only God-ordained relationship for the expression of sexual intercourse." They also went ahead and elected a sexual revisionist, Herbert Valentine, as the next PCUSA moderator.

So, rather than quieting the controversy, the 1991 assembly left the PCUSA more divided than ever and ensured divisions over sex would evolve into protracted civil war. Later that year, Presbyterian theologian Jack Rogers said,

> The issue [for Presbyterians] is whether we can find in Scripture a norm external to ourselves, a revelation that tells us what is right and wrong. One side says "yes" to this question. The other side tends to regard individual experience as normative and to interpret Scripture accordingly.[22]

Presbyterians go to war. Through the 1990s, mainline Presbyterians were torn by denominational war over sexual morality. In 1996 they amended their constitution, the PCUSA's *Book of Order,* to say that no one could be ordained without accepting sexual "fidelity within the covenant of marriage between a man and a woman, or chastity in singleness."[23] The amendment became known as the "fidelity and chastity" clause, and after passing the assembly the new provision was ratified (and thereby made official) by a two-to-one majority of the PCUSA presbyteries (local Presbyterian governing bodies).

The fidelity and chastity clause did not mention homosexuals specifically. Rather it simply limited ordination to persons accepting biblical teaching that sex outside of marriage is wrong and never justified. The effect of the clause, however, was to ban churches from ordaining noncelibate (practicing) homosexuals, who naturally could not marry on either biblical or legal terms. It did not exclude people who experience homosexual attractions and agree to follow biblical standards by denying them. It only banned the possibility of ordaining a person who demands homosexual sex regardless of whether or not he or she is married and regardless of what God says in the Bible. The issue was biblical authority, not persecuting people who resist sexual temptation.

It could have seemed a clear victory for biblical conservatives, but that was not the case. The same assembly that added the "fidelity and chastity" clause to the PCUSA constitution also passed a revisionist proposal throwing denominational weight behind recognizing special rights for homosexual behavior supported and enforced by civil law. The agenda depended on believing that homosexual attractions are unavoidable and that therefore homosexual sex cannot be unnatural or immoral. Once again, the message to local Presbyterian churches was contradictory.

On a razor's edge. The PCUSA has been teetering on a razor's edge for nearly twenty years, and the effect is slowly dividing mainline Presbyterians into completely incompatible camps. Twice—first in 1997 and then again in 2001—PCUSA assemblies have passed revisionist motions to repeal the "fidelity and chastity" clause. And both times the attempt has failed because revisionists could not get enough local presbyteries to ratify the change. In 1998, revisionists also passed a measure instructing local churches to no longer treat homosexual behavior as sinful, to no longer insist that homosexuals stop practicing homosexual sex before being allowed to join a church, and to accept the qualifications of noncelibate (unrepentant, practicing) homosexuals ordained before the "fidelity and chastity" clause was added to the PCUSA constitution. Of course instructions like this were not consistent with the denominational constitution, but in recent years policies relating to sex in the PCUSA have been more like keeping score between opposing teams than receiving orders from a single commander.

Since 1997, evangelical Presbyterians seem to have lost majority power among commissioners attending national meetings while maintaining majority strength at the local presbytery level. For now, the opposing sides seem nearly even. But unless spiritual revival breaks out in the PCUSA, the future is more likely to favor revisionists over defenders of biblical sexual morality. Presbyterian evangelicals are not winning. They are defending one clause in the PCUSA constitution while revisionists make headway in other ways. Both sides see the other as threatening the survival of the church, and local pastors are having to choose between incompatible positions with almost no prospect of serious discipline if the national denomination says one thing and they choose to go another way instead.

Abandoning the authority of God's moral revelation to indulge the flesh always generates enormous trouble for the church, and revisionist strength in the denomination has been driving members out in droves. When mainline Presbyterians formed the PCUSA in 1983, membership was 4.2 million. But twenty years later membership was below 2.5 million and still falling almost 35,000 a year. Jack Rogers has called sexual turmoil in the PCUSA "the Presbyterian civil war,"[24] and Jerry Van Marter at denomination headquarters once complained, "there's too much defiance going on. People just aren't enforcing the [PCUSA] constitution."[25] Civil war in the church is always more destructive than any attack, however large, from opponents outside.

Baptists Battle Baptists

The Southern Baptist Convention (SBC) is the mainline Baptist denomination in the United States,[26] and like mainline Anglicans, Methodists, Lutherans, and Presbyterians, Baptists also have struggled with attacks on sexual morality in the church. However, unlike other mainline denominations, Southern Baptists have successfully resisted sexual revision and reaffirmed biblical standards. SBC battles relating to sex were part of a larger war over theological liberalism. The larger war focused on the doctrine of scripture, but sexual morality was a major issue energizing both sides.

Renewing faith in the Bible. In the early 1990s, two Southern Baptist churches in North Carolina challenged denominational resolve to maintain biblical standards opposing homosexual behavior. Pullen Memorial Baptist Church in Raleigh performed a same-sex marriage ceremony, and Binkley Memorial Baptist Church in Chapel Hill ordained a noncelibate homosexual to a position of ministry leadership. Both churches were swiftly expelled, and a member reported they knew they had "pushed the button on the mother of all issues."

For several years thereafter, Southern Baptist churches in other states left the denomination for similar reasons. However, a much larger number recommitted themselves to honoring scripture and gained courage to resist revisionist pressure. Some denomination institutions once thought lost to the revisionists were amazingly turned around. And nowhere was this more dramatic than at Southeastern Baptist Theological Seminary in Wake Forest, North Carolina—the institution at which I have served since 1993.

Before Southern Baptists began reforming, Southeastern was known for being the most theologically liberal and sexually permissive of all Southern Baptist institutions. Faculty could not be hired who affirmed the inerrancy of scripture—especially on sexual issues—and professors ridiculed students for still believing homosexual behavior was sin. My predecessor in Christian ethics taught a class on human sexuality, to which he brought homosexual advocates. These advocates would describe their lives and invite students to experiment with homosexual experiences themselves. In other words, they *recruited* seminarians to the homosexual lifestyle and did so in the very classes meant to prepare them for Christian ministry. The textbook used for this class was filled with photographs of genitalia and included a pornographic picture from *Playboy Magazine,* all supposedly to educate future Baptist ministers.

Other indications of the tone on campus included: condoms discarded after homosexual sex, that later were discovered in the attic of the single men's dorm; a huge collection of homosexual literature in the seminary library, that I helped remove; pornography that janitors told of finding in seminary trash on a regular basis; a huge collection of pornography that fell out of the ceiling in a seminary duplex during repairs; and stories of an annual event held by seminarians at which male students ogled female students showing off "bikini tan lines." Seminary life under revisionist control was more "animal house" than "God's house." But what once was a revisionist hotbed of sexual immorality, by God's grace is now one of the strongest evangelical seminaries in America.

Of course, a switch so amazing did not happen without struggle. The period of change was tense, and enrollment fell from over 1,000 to around 480. But when evangelicals did take charge, the seminary flourished. Biblical standards on sex were restored, chapel services became the center of campus life, spiritual life blossomed, academic standards were raised, and enrollment shot from around 480 in 1992 to over 2,500 in 2003. And, of course, one big change is that students preparing for ministry now learn to evaluate sex according to biblical morality, not to evaluate biblical morality according to sex.

Affirming biblical marriage and family. In 1998 Southern Baptists added an article on "The Family" to their confessional statement, *The Baptist Faith and Message.* It claimed that marriage "is the uniting of one man and one woman in covenant commitment for a lifetime," and while affirming that men and women have "equal worth before God, since both are created in God's image," it also said God assigns gender roles in marriage. It stated,

> A husband is to love his wife as Christ loved the church. He has the God-given responsibility to provide for, to protect, and to lead his family.

Correspondingly,

> A wife is to submit herself graciously to the servant leadership of her husband even as the church willingly submits to the headship of Christ. . . . [She] has the God-given responsibility to respect her husband and to serve as his helper in managing the household and nurturing the next generation.

Reaction was divided, with tremendous support from most Baptists and much opposition in the media outside the denomination. Church historian Martin Marty called it another "in-your-face conservative pronouncement"; and Jean Elshtain, professor of social and political ethics at the University of Chicago, said, "This is coming over as anti-feminist, an attack on equality between men and women."[27] Even so, Gustav Niebuhr of the *New York Times* said it was "among the most prominent statements on family life by a major religious organization in recent years."[28] One pastor claimed, "It goes against all the things that Baptists have stood for through the years."[29] But SBC president Paige Patterson countered this sort of comment, saying the new SBC article was "only hot language to someone not real familiar with the Bible."[30]

Recommitted to biblical sexual morality. In 1999, messengers to the annual SBC convention ordered a review of *The Baptist Faith and Message,* and the proposed additions were overwhelmingly approved in 2000.[31] Again sex was the big focus. Adrian Rogers, who chaired the review committee, said "Baptist ancestors of a mere generation ago could not have imagined the need to address the issues of abortion, homosexuality, euthanasia and all manner of deviant and pagan sexuality."[32] Critics focused on sexual issues as well.

Becca Gurney of Baptist Women in Ministry objected that, "In terms of God calling gays and lesbians, when we start limiting God's call we're in dangerous territory." Stan Hastey, executive director of The Alliance of Baptists, responded that, for him, "homosexuality is not necessarily sinful," so "I cannot say that God does not call gay people to ministry." And Ken Sehested of the Baptist Peace Fellowship of North America claimed SBC opposition to homosexual behavior was immoral because it interfered with civil rights.[33]

Aftereffects of winning the war. As Southern Baptists recovered their biblical bearings, revisionists began distancing themselves and leaving the SBC. In 1990, a number of churches and associations opposing renewal started a dissenting group called the Cooperative Baptist Fellowship (CBF). Members called themselves *moderates,* implying that their views were consistent with historic Christianity. But it soon was obvious the organization included a large number of revisionists who did not accept biblical sexual morality and took a sensual approach instead.

Not wanting to alienate anyone, the CBF welcomed all, including those promoting ordination for women, homosexual behavior, ordination for noncelibate homosexuals, and same-sex marriages. Except for ordaining women, the CBF never has officially endorsed revisionist issues. But neither has it opposed them. Everyone is welcome, however they stand on sex.

In 2000, criticism of CBF links to homosexual advocacy arose because prominent members were openly advocating homosexual issues. In response, CBF coordinator Dan Vestal in July 2000 claimed the organization had never "issued any statement, taken any action or spent a single dollar that was intended in any way to condone, endorse or promote the gay-lesbian lifestyle."[34] But, despite Vestal's denial, the CBF did in fact fund curriculum materials affirming same-sex marriage and denying that the Bible condemns homosexual sex. Indeed, those materials were displayed at the CBF assembly that same year.

When Southern Baptists passed *The Baptist Faith and Message 2000,* CBF leaders reacted strongly. Vestal said, "I don't know what the CBF is going to do, but I am no longer a Southern Baptist." Stan Hastey of the Alliance of Baptists, a CBF affiliated homosexual group, claimed that additions addressing sexual issues in *The Baptist Faith and Message 2000* illustrated how the Bible is no longer "an adequate basis of authority for Baptists." And leaders of Baptist Women in Ministry, a CBF-affiliated feminist group, told members it was time they renounce all remaining connections with the mainline Baptist denomination.[35]

Because the SBC has taken a clear stand reaffirming biblical authority, which includes continuing to uphold biblical standards on sexual morality, sexual revisionists have ceased to be a source of agitation. Instead they have been leaving to find accommodation elsewhere. For mainline Baptists in the SBC, the internal war over sex is over and evangelicals have won.

Catholics Shocked, Shamed, and Divided

Pedophiles in the priesthood. A scandal engulfing the American Catholic church exploded in January 2002 when the media learned that Cardinal Bernard Law of Boston was harboring priests responsible for molesting hundreds of children. The scandal grew, and Americans soon learned that Boston was not unique. There were similar problems all over the country. Accusations were uncovered in 161 of 177 (91 percent) of the dioceses in the United States. Over a thousand priests were charged with abusing children. Cases had been handled secretly. Molesters were not reported. They were not sent to jail. Instead they remained in ministry and usually were reassigned with no warning to people in the new area.[36]

In April, the Vatican called American cardinals to Rome. Revisionists like Cardinal Roger Mahoney of Los Angeles said the scandal was caused by rules on sex that were too strict and called on the church not only to let priests marry but also to ordain women and allow homosexual priests to have sex without marriage. On the other hand, conservatives said the scandal was due to failure in faith and discipline. Richard John Neuhaus, who heads the Institute on Religion and Public Life in New York, said, "It's precisely because people have failed to act in fidelity to their vows that we have this crisis."[37]

Cardinal Law offered to resign, but the pope did not accept his offer. No one was held accountable. The Americans were simply sorry and promised to act, but even that plan ran into trouble. At the end of the meeting, they announced that a priest would be fired if "he has become notorious and is guilty of the serial, predatory, sexual abuse of minors." The statement was full of loopholes that literally said molesters would *not* be fired if their actions were secret (not notorious), limited (not repeated), and well-intended (not predatory)! One commentator wondered, "How is an adult's exploitation of a minor ever anything but predatory?"[38] Observers considered the meeting a huge failure.

In June 2002, American bishops gathered in Dallas to plan a course of action. Seven hundred and fifty journalists attended, more than twice the number of bishops. Observers were again disappointed. Before the meeting, revisionists feared the bishops might link the scandal with noncelibate homosexuals, and conservatives feared they might blame something else. Instead they were silent on that issue even though everyone knew it was the most critical of all. They created a review board and proposed that priests be fired after a single allegation, guilty or not. Nothing was done about bishops mishandling pedophiles; nothing was said about noncelibate homosexuals; and the Vatican did not want bishops punishing innocent priests.

In December 2002, a grand jury ordered the Boston archdiocese to release all files on sexual misconduct, and support for Cardinal Law crumbled. Law flew to Rome and resigned. At the end of the year the courts were handling hundreds of new cases; the cost of settling these cases was astronomical; the Boston archdiocese teetered on bankruptcy; and twelve grand juries were investigating the church itself.

A problem of enormous size. The scandal rocking Catholics is huge, but most think what has come to light is only a fraction of the actual situation. So far, the best information on how big the problem is comes from a study by the

New York Times completed one year after the scandal broke. The *Times* found that, in 2002 alone, 1,205 priests were charged with molesting at least 4,268 victims.[39] That only counts known victims, and the entire number is certainly much larger. Children molested sexually rarely come forward right away, and many never do. While the size of the problem may never be fully known, what has been uncovered is staggering. When the attorney general of Massachusetts finished examining the Boston archdiocese, he announced that priests had molested more than 1,000 victims from that one diocese alone, and that still was not the entire number.

Yet more alarming than the number of molesters and victims has been to learn that two-thirds of the bishops in the American Catholic church have participated in harboring priests they knew to be guilty of molesting children. Being reluctant to address the problem, they allowed it to grow. Pedophiles not only remained in ministry but were still promoted, a fact that has been demonstrated by the number of *bishops* who have resigned after it was discovered they abused children themselves. Pedophiles have even risen to higher office than bishop, a fact brought to light in May 2002 when Archbishop Rembert Weakland of Milwaukee resigned after it was learned that he had paid over $450,000 (in church funds) trying to keep a victim of sexual molestation from revealing that the perpetrator was the archbishop himself.

The scandal behind the scandal. Tempting though it might be for Protestants and Catholic revisionists, it is not fair to blame the pedophile scandal on the celibacy vow. Priests for centuries have abstained from sex without becoming pedophiles, so it cannot be causing the problem now. And however tempting for conservatives, neither is it fair to blame the scandal on the Second Vatican Council (1962–1965). Vatican II changed much, but nothing related to sex.

The main reason for the pedophile scandal is neither the celibacy vow nor Vatican II but another still more damaging scandal, which is that American Catholics have ordained an extraordinary number of homosexuals who simply have not been committed to sexual discipline. Amazing though it seems, Catholics have known for years that they had a problem with actively homosexual priests. But until the scandal broke, Catholic leaders simply did not have the courage to address it.

Though rarely mentioned in the media, it is well known that nearly all the victims in the pedophile scandal were boys, which naturally means the abusers are all active homosexuals. The *New York Times* verified that at least 80 percent of the victims were boys. And Richard John Neuhaus thinks the true figure is higher because "other tabulations . . . indicate that as many as 90 percent involve boys."[40] In fact, the scandal is virtually 100 percent homosexual. Catholic priests almost never molest girls.

This high percentage of boy victims is exactly opposite to what happens in the general population, where victims are mostly girls molested by heterosexuals. If the sexual orientation of Catholic priests mirrored the normal population, victims would be mostly girls as well. All of which shows that the percentage of homosexuals in the priesthood must be *a lot higher* than in the general population. Michael Peterson, who treats pedophile priests at the St. Luke Institute, says, "We don't see heterosexual pedophiles at all."[41] They are all homosexuals.

In fact, American Catholics have been complaining that homosexuals now control several seminaries and are openly organized at most. Pater Ignotus warns that American bishops are ignoring the fact that "a disproportionate number of homosexuals are being recruited into our seminaries."[42] Michael Rose, former editor of the *St. Catherine Review,* reports,

> [the] "gay subculture" is so prominent at certain seminaries that these institutions have earned nicknames such as Notre Flame (for Notre Dame Seminary in New Orleans) and Theological Closet (for Theological College at the Catholic University of America in Washington, D.C.). St. Mary's Seminary in Baltimore has earned the nickname the "Pink Palace."[43]

Before the pedophile scandal broke in Boston, apprehension over gay domination of the church already had become a top concern for Catholic leaders. Bishop Wilton Gregory, president of the U. S. Conference of Catholic Bishops, admitted, "It's an ongoing struggle to make sure the Catholic priesthood is not dominated by homosexual men."[44] And Donald Cozzens, former president of St. Mary's Seminary and Graduate School of Theology in Cleveland, says,

> An NBC report on celibacy and the clergy found that "anywhere from 23 percent to 58 percent" of the Catholic clergy have a homosexual orientation. Other studies find that approximately half of American priests and seminarians are homosexually oriented. . . . Moreover, the percentage of gay men among religious congregations of priests [Catholic orders] is believed to be even higher. . . . I heard a religious order priest with long experience in both formation and leadership state publicly at a conference on AIDS and the mission of the Church that 80 percent of his large East Coast order was gay.[45]

How did this happen? One wonders how this could happen, and four reasons have been suggested by people investigating the matter: no screening, no serious sense of sin, no real celibacy, and no respect for biblical or papal authority.

First, *no screening*. For whatever reason, Catholic seminaries in the United States for years accepted anyone who asked to enter the priesthood, no questions asked. Professor Jay Dolan of Notre Dame says, "There was no screening of candidates at all. They accepted anybody."[46] And refusing to ask screening questions applied especially to a candidate's sexual orientation. One former trustee at a Catholic seminary reports hearing the rector tell the seminary board, "We don't ask our candidates about their sexual orientation or their sexual histories. It would be a violation of a man's civil rights to deny him ordination on those grounds."[47]

Second, *no serious sense of sin*. As large numbers of homosexuals entered the priesthood, officials did little to emphasize resisting homosexual as well as heterosexual temptations. Professor Dolan reports, "instructors warned students to stay away from temptations, but they never mentioned altar boys and teenagers. Their chief concerns were . . . alcohol and women." Paul Dinter, a former priest, says bishops thought, "If a priest was having sex with a boy it meant he was weak and gave in. It meant he should go to the confession and not be weak again."[48] Homosexual sex was wrong, but not that serious. Not even with boys. Not even if repeated.

Third, *no real celibacy*. The celibacy vow for priests used to mean abstaining from any sex at all. But under pressure from homosexuals it got limited to mean only abstaining from sex with women. The *New York Times* found,

> Seminarians were taught that all other sexual activity [besides sex with women] was . . . not a violation of the celibacy vow. Some priests relied on this distinction to rationalize to their victims, the authorities or church supervisors that . . . [homosexual activities], however wrong, left their celibacy vow intact.[49]

Fourth, *no respect for biblical or papal authority*. Besides no screening, not thinking homosexual sex is really that bad, and narrowing the celibacy vow, many priests after Vatican II started pushing for still more radical changes, most of which had to do with sex. They wanted to replace traditional biblical morality affirmed by the pope with a different, culturally popular approach based on satisfying the flesh. The growing number of homosexual priests naturally aligned with this faction. Jason Berry interviewed many active homosexual priests and recalls, "I asked why, if they could not practice celibacy, they didn't leave the priesthood?" And the reason they did not was, "Most saw themselves as leading the Church toward the reform of outdated moral teachings—including celibacy."[50]

In the end, the only thing that truly explains how more than a thousand priests could molest thousands and thousands of boys without serious consequences is that a large number of Catholic leaders have been trying to change sexual morality in the church. The pedophile scandal could not have occurred if a large percentage (perhaps a majority) of American bishops and cardinals were not already behaving as if biblical sexual morality had been replaced with a new sensual approach that denies the value of sexual purity and thinks priests having sex with men, or even boys, is something good, not bad.

We have looked at how reemerging sexual paganism is causing, or has caused, severe turmoil in mainline Protestant denominations and the Catholic church. But what about evangelicals? Some evangelicals are in the mainline denominations, but most are in smaller denominations or independent churches. We will now look at whether evangelicals outside mainline Christian denominations are also being affected by sexual divisions connected with rising pagan influences in the culture.

5

Is Pagan Sexuality Affecting Evangelicals?

Are Bible-loving evangelicals immune to the influence of sexual paganism? Or are we affected too? It may feel uncomfortable, but we dare not avoid the question.

The editors of *Christianity Today,* seeing how war over sexual moral standards has caused so much trouble in mainline denominations, now suggest evangelicals outside the mainline may soon face the same thing. They observe that, "evangelicals in mainline churches have confronted these issues for decades," and therefore say, "we expect all evangelical churches will struggle with them in the next few decades." In fact, they suggest that a homosexual group called Soulforce, a group which now shows up at evangelical meetings on a regular basis, is sending a message telling evangelicals: "You are next."[1]

But that concerns the future, and we are asking if pagan sexual moral influences are affecting evangelicals already. It might be coincidental that, just as sexual paganism is returning in the culture and just as mainline Protestants and Catholics are being torn between pagan and biblical views on sexual morality, suddenly some evangelicals are: changing their view of the Trinity to avoid how it supports wives submitting to husbands in marriage; redefining how Christ relates to the church because it is the model for a husband being "head" of his family; revising the doctrine of creation to fit a new vision for human sexuality; rejecting the role of gender in church leadership; allowing divorce on the grounds that it can make people happy; arguing that singles need recreational sex; saying adultery should not affect one's eligibility for church membership; suggesting that homosexuals need not be celibate; and supporting same-sex marriage. Growing division among evangelicals on such issues could be entirely coincidental and unrelated to the similar shifts in theological liberalism and the broader culture. But mere coincidence is highly unlikely.

SLIDING AWAY FROM THE BIBLE

Of course we should not exaggerate. But neither should we avoid addressing the actual situation for fear of causing offense. Sadly, I believe there is indeed a connection between the growing prevalence of sexual paganism in the culture and how some evangelicals are reinterpreting what the Bible says about sex. The emerging power of sexual paganism in American culture is affecting unwary evangelicals, and that is because a single logical thread connects the pull of sexual paganism with desire to make sexual standards among Christians more acceptable to surrounding culture.

It starts with dissatisfaction. The gradual slide toward paganism starts when a person still committed to the Bible entertains dissatisfaction with something God says about sex, and a single logic connects a series of steps that extend from sliding ever so slightly from biblical teaching at one end to full-scale attack on biblical morality at the other. Letting dissatisfaction fester sparks interest in ways to soften or remove the offending biblical teaching. At first, this is done in ways that do not challenge the authority of scripture but only try to change its meaning.

But shaping Christian morality to the culture destroys respect for the Bible, and as respect for biblical accuracy and authority collapses, biblical moral standards seem less and less relevant. Eventually the moral authority of the Bible is abandoned completely in favor of a culturally popular, indulgent approach. Sexual morality is redefined according to sexual desires, and the indulging of sexual desires is thought necessary to achieve higher levels of personal development. At this stage, biblical standards are ridiculed, sexual differences are maligned, and the boundaries God has set to keep sex pure and good are attacked as harmful or dangerous.

Ultimately, sexual indulgence is justified in *spiritual* terms, and *sensual spirituality* leads to a pagan faith in sex. Sensual pagan spirituality then becomes a driving force that not only excuses but even demands sexual indulgence, and rituals are added to celebrate the *spirituality* of sexual sin.

Dissatisfaction with something God says on sex is the first step in a progression that leads all the way to pagan sexual morality and ritual sexual worship. Those on this path do not always go all the way to the other end. But the logic linking each step to the next is continuous, and as we have seen, Virginia Ramey Mollenkott went all the way from serving as an English language consultant to translators of the New International Version of the Bible, to promoting subversion of sexual morality in the church.[2]

Considerations from real life. The continuum I describe, from dissatisfaction with the Bible to outright sexual paganism, may seem inevitable. But that is not the case. Real life is always more complex than that. First, in real life, individuals or institutions at one step in the progression from Christianity to paganism do not always move to the next step. In some cases, the force resisting such movement is stronger than the force promoting it. But while this does happen, such cases are exceptional. The power pulling from one step to the next is strong and, while some resist, most do not.

Second, in real life, some approach each step in the progression thinking they only seek truth and are not influenced by anything else. Some truly believe their decisions at each step involve nothing more than seeking better insight on what the Bible means. Should Christians not study scripture to improve their understanding of what it says, including what it says on sex? Should we not praise scholars who are trying to make the Bible more accessible to modern readers? Of course we should. But as we do, we must never confuse making the Bible *accessible* to sinners with making it *acceptable* to sinners.

If ideas about Christian sexual morality do not come from scripture and scripture alone, they must come from something outside scripture treated as if it were superior to scripture. A person may not think his or her intentions are *pagan.* That person may only want Christian morality to seem *nicer,* or more *compassionate,* or more *compatible with natural reason,* and he or she may have no intention of changing anything essential to Christian faith. But anything outside the Bible used to make it supposedly *better* inevitably revises biblical morality in a pagan direction.

Third, in real life, ignorance of danger, or refusing to admit danger, leaves a person *more* vulnerable—never *less*—to that particular danger, and evangelicals who ignore or deny the pull of sexual paganism these days are terribly vulnerable to it. Each step in the progression from Christianity to paganism has strong advocates, and moving from one step to another is never isolated from what is going on farther down the line. Anyone dabbling with reinterpreting what the Bible says on sex faces a series of ever more radical arguments urging ever more radical revisions. Each step is loaded with seemingly logical reasons to move on to the next step. Dissatisfied evangelicals can be affected by sexual paganism even if what draws them on to the next step looks nothing like paganism.

Winning a schoolyard tug-of-war depends more on the power of the anchorman at the far end of the rope than on the strength of the first person in line, and in the same way the power against which one pulls at the first step away from biblical sexual morality depends less on the strength of whatever is first in line taken by itself than on the force pulling from the far end. Interest in judging the Bible by ideas outside the Bible is the first person you see on the opposing side in this tug-of-war, and paganism is the anchorman at the far end of the rope.

TAKE HEED LEST YOU FALL

Paul warned Christians in Corinth that they were vulnerable to false teaching even while feeling morally and spiritually strong. He warned that self-confident Christians are not beyond the deceitfulness of sin. After recalling how frequently Old Testament saints fell to sexual pagan attraction (1 Cor. 10:7-8), Paul warned, "Therefore let anyone who thinks that he stands take heed lest he fall" (v. 12). He was saying that self-confident Christians—we could say *evangelicals*—must not assume that knowing God makes them immune to deceit. And it is worth noting that Paul was not dealing with sin in generic terms but with the attraction of sexual paganism. He was saying sexual paganism can catch even self-confident Christians—even evangelicals—unawares.

In some ways Paul was saying that those most vulnerable to sexual pagan attraction are those most used to thinking everything they do is *Christian*. He was not warning new believers, conscious of how radically their lives had changed, but self-confident Christians, who were in danger of lowering their guard. Familiarity breeds contempt. Routine guard duty is deadly. Safety leads to boredom, leads to drowsiness, leads to sleep. Once a watchman goes to sleep, the enemy slips in unopposed.

The Al Qaeda terrorist organization was most dangerous when Americans took national security for granted, and Al Qaeda has been less threatening since we have realized how vulnerable we are. Similarly, complacent evangelicals are more vulnerable to sexual pagan influences than those who understand how vulnerable they are. As Israel fell to sexual pagan temptation when they took God's favor for granted, and as terrorists attack when nations take security for granted, so evangelicals now must not overlook the dangerous attraction of sexual paganism pulling Christians to revise biblical interpretation on sexual morality.

As divisions arise over sexual morality, evangelicals must not lower their guard because they are distracted by issues diverting attention away from what matters most. The most important thing in church battles over sex is not whether we, like the culture, believe that sex is good. Of course, we do. But that is not where biblical sexual morality is coming under attack. The most important challenge these days is making sure that evangelicals remain convinced that *everything* the Bible says about sex is true.

Cyprian (200–258 a.d.), a third-century bishop of Carthage, faced circumstances similar to what American evangelicals face today. Christianity had withstood open persecution and risen to favor in the culture. But Cyprian was concerned that Christians might not survive pagan ideas poisoning the faith undetected. He said,

> It is not persecution alone that we ought to fear, nor those forces that in open warfare range abroad to overthrow and defeat the servants of God. It is easy enough to be on one's guard when the danger is obvious; one can stir up one's courage for the fight when the Enemy shows himself in his true colours. There is more need to fear and beware of the Enemy when he creeps up secretly, when he beguiles us by a show of peace and steals forward by those hidden approaches which have earned him the name of the "Serpent." . . . What could be more clever and cunning than the Enemy's moves after being unmasked and worsted by Christ's coming? Light had come to the gentiles and the lamp of salvation was shining for the deliverance of mankind. . . . Thereupon the Enemy, seeing his idols abandoned and his temples and haunts deserted by the ever growing numbers of the faithful, devised a fresh deceit, using the Christian name itself to mislead the unwary. He invented heresies and schisms so as to undermine the faith, to corrupt the truth, to sunder our unity. Those whom he has failed to keep in the blindness of their old [pagan] ways he beguiles, and leads them up a new road of illusion. He snatches away people from within the Church herself, and while they think that coming close to the light they have now done with the night of the world, he plunges them unexpectedly into darkness of another kind. They still call themselves Christians after abandoning the Gospel of Christ and the observance of His [moral] law; though walking in darkness they think they still enjoy the light.[3]

Cyprian's warning is still relevant today. With sexual paganism reemerging in surrounding culture, the greatest threat to evangelicals is not what comes from outright persecution, nor is it ridicule from anti-Christian pagans like Mary Daly, Monica Sjoo, or Barbara Mor. Rather it is, as Cyprian would say, the beguiling deceit of pagan faith and morality "using the Christian name itself to mislead the unwary."

The Great Evangelical Disaster

Francis Schaeffer saw up close how the 1960s sexual revolution affected young Americans, because many of the "free love" generation found their way to his home in the mountains of Switzerland. Schaeffer's ministry focused on giving biblical answers to honest questions raised by the moral-spiritual revolution shaking the culture in those years.

Initially the moral-spiritual crisis hardly seemed relevant to evangelicals. While non-evangelicals wandered in a fog of relativity, evangelicals took their bearings from the unchanging truth of God's Word. But later, in the 1980s, Schaeffer's emphasis shifted to warn evangelicals, some of whom were beginning to change *with* culture more than witnessing *to* the culture. As we have noted, Schaeffer called this new concern "the great evangelical disaster."

He was alarmed because he saw that evangelicals were being seduced by "the world spirit of this present age":

> Accommodation, accommodation. How the mindset of accommodation grows and expands. The last sixty years have given birth to a moral disaster, and what have we done? Sadly we must say that the evangelical world has been part of the disaster. More than this, the evangelical response itself has been a disaster. Where is the clear voice speaking to the crucial issues of the day with distinctively biblical, Christian answers? With tears we must say it is not there and that a large segment of the evangelical world has become seduced by the world spirit of this present age. And more than this, we can expect the future to be a further disaster if the evangelical world does not take a stand for biblical truth and morality in the full spectrum of life.[4]

The problem was not that evangelicals were engaging the culture. That is absolutely necessary if we are to be witnesses for Christ. Rather, the problem was that a growing number of evangelicals were changing with the culture more than witnessing to it. Schaeffer saw that "accommodation has constantly been in one direction. . . . [it] has constantly taken the form of giving in to the humanistic, secular consensus which is the dominant destructive force of our day."[5]

And, for Schaeffer, the most obvious way evangelicals were accommodating the culture fell in the area of sexual morality. He said,

> If we look at many of our evangelical leaders and at much of our evangelical literature we find *the same destructive views* on divorce, extreme feminism, and even homosexuality as we find in the world. . . . it is hard to imagine how far these things have gone. Evangelicalism is deeply infiltrated

> with the world spirit of our age when it comes to marriage and sexual morality.[6]

Especially, Schaeffer noticed,

> There are those who call themselves evangelicals and who are among evangelical leadership who completely deny the biblical pattern for male and female relationships in the home and church. There are many who accept the idea of equality without distinction and deliberately set aside what the Scriptures teach at this point. And there are others who call themselves evangelical and then affirm the acceptability of homosexuality and even the idea of homosexual "marriage."[7]

As it related to sexual morality, Schaeffer was concerned: (1) that "under the guise of love, much of the evangelical world has abandoned any concept of right or wrong in divorce and any pretext of dealing with divorce according to the boundaries established in the Scriptures"; (2) that some evangelicals were accepting the idea of "monolithic uniformity or 'sameness' between men and women" and denying biblical teaching that balances "*infinite equality of worth* before God" with gender roles in the home and church; and (3) that the idea of "*equality without distinction*" was erasing opposition to homosexual sex because, "if there are no significant distinctions between men and women, then certainly we cannot condemn homosexual relationships."[8]

For Schaeffer, denying divinely assigned gender roles and justifying homosexual sex are connected. Moral compromise in both areas involved accepting a nonbiblical sense of autonomous freedom and rejecting the existence of meaningful sexual difference:

> The idea of absolute, autonomous freedom from God's boundaries flows into the idea of equality without distinction, which flows into the denial of what it truly means to be male and female, which flows into abortion and homosexuality, and the destruction of the home and the family, and ultimately the destruction of our culture.[9]

For Schaeffer, *the great evangelical disaster* arose from wanting to reinterpret scripture in order to accommodate cultural opinion, and the immediate impact came most obviously in the area of sex. Applying Schaeffer's warning to evangelicals today, we might say those drawn toward accommodating the culture on sex are, in fact, accommodating the spirit of sexual paganism.

SIGNS OF GROWING CHANGE

Two decades have passed since Francis Schaeffer warned of *the great evangelical disaster.* But instead of changing course, many evangelicals have continued shifting with the culture, and nowhere has this been more obvious than with matters concerning sex. What Schaeffer saw starting in the 1980s has matured, and his view that sex would play a key role has proven prophetic. What follows is a review of real-life cases. These are not given to embarrass but to show how some evangelicals are revising sexual morality along with the culture rather than maintaining biblical standards against moral degeneration in the culture.

Our examples do not include high-profile sex scandals like the fall of television preachers Jim Bakker and Jimmy Swaggart. Nor do they include things like the high divorce rate among evangelicals, which equals and may even be higher than our national average.[10] This is because we are not addressing those who fall short of standards they affirm, but are verifying how some evangelicals are shifting sexual moral standards to *follow* rather than *resist* prevailing cultural opinion.

Spiritualizing nonbiblical divorce. Os Guinness mentions "conservative" Christians who spiritualize divorce using ideas from the culture in place of scripture. One argued, "There can be as much sin involved in trying to perpetuate a dead or meaningless relationship as in accepting the brokenness, offering it to God, and going on from there."[11] Another said,

> "I hope my wife will never divorce me, because I love her with all my heart. But if one day she feels I am minimizing her or making her feel inferior or in any way standing in the light that she needs to become the person God meant her to be, I hope she'll be free to throw me out even if she's one hundred. There is something more important than our staying married, and it has to do with integrity, personhood, and purpose."[12]

Evangelicals may have seen a "real-life" example of such thinking in 1999 when Amy Grant ended her sixteen-year marriage to Gary Chapman. She explained that she relied on advice from a counselor who told her,

> "Amy, God made marriage for people. He didn't make people for marriage. He didn't create this institution so He could just plug people into it. He provided this so that people could enjoy each other to the fullest."[13]

On that basis Grant claimed, "if two people are not thriving healthily in a situation, I say remove the marriage. Let them heal."[14] There was no question of adultery. She sued for divorce only because she did not feel as happy as she wanted to be.

Seminary teachers ease opposition to homosexual sex and adultery. Jack and Judith Balswick teach at Fuller Theological Seminary and write Christian books on family life and sex. But while teaching future evangelical leaders, the Balswicks seem to have as much regard for prevailing sentiment as for scripture. In *Authentic Human Sexuality,* they suggest that Christians may stay in homosexual relationships without repenting and still have a real rrelationship with God, and they assume that compassionate Christians will tolerate differences over whether that is acceptable.

> We acknowledge that some gay Christians may choose to commit themselves to a lifelong, monogamous homosexual union, believing this is God's best for them. . . . Even though we hold to the model of a heterosexual, lifelong, monogamous union, our compassion brings us to support all persons as they move in the direction of God's ideal for their lives.[15]

The Balswicks also argue that "the Christian community must win trust by welcoming cohabiting couples into churches" without causing them to feel their behavior is unacceptable. This includes couples who engage "in sexual intercourse without sharing a mutual covenant commitment" as well as couples who share "a mutual covenant commitment" but deny the necessity of marriage. The Balswicks fear that addressing sin hinders extending Christian fellowship and so believe that fellowship in the church should be offered without regard for sin. In their opinion, it is tragic if cohabiting couples attending church "stop coming because they feel condemned or unaccepted."[16] The Balswicks would rather avoid sinners coming under conviction than risk alienating them from church.

"Evangelical" magazine subverts biblical morality. *The Other Side* has been a main voice for what some call the *evangelical left,* but the magazine rejects biblical morality while still claiming to be evangelical. In 1982, editor John Alexander told readers he liked how radical feminism "is profoundly subversive" and "threatens to corrupt Western values and to undermine American institutions."[17] The magazine has since published many articles affirming homosexual sex, including: "Can Homosexuals Change?" by Letha Dawson Scanzoni (says active homosexuals can have radiant Christian testimonies); "A Call to Subversion" by Virginia Ramey Mollenkott (tells homosexuals to trick evangelicals by reinterpreting the Bible); and "Out of Season" by Kathy Olsen (claims that being a lesbian is a gift from God that deepens her faith).[18]

Activist promotes homosexual sex. Ralph Blair is founder of Evangelicals Concerned, a homosexual advocacy group committed to changing evangelical thinking on sexual morality. Blair joined the Evangelical Theological Society in 1982 and remains a full member as of publication of this book. But Blair claims, "Scripture does not condemn homosexual behavior between committed Christians,"[19] and says evangelical Christians must help homosexuals "live lives which include responsible homosexual behavior."[20] Blair still writes a regular newsletter, *Review: A Quarterly of Evangelicals Concerned, Inc.,* in which he decries evangelical resistance to homosexual behavior as "pathological denial, scapegoating, hypocrisy, self-righteousness, self-serving arrogance, straining at a gnat, the leaven of the Pharisees," and criticizes evangelical opposition to same-sex marriage as "crushing the spirits of gay people" and contributing "to more unworkable marriages and divorces, broken homes, and broken hearts."[21]

Author-teacher thought homosexuals need not abstain. The late Lewis Smedes, who taught Christian ethics at Fuller Theological Seminary from 1970 to 1995, influenced many evangelicals to change moral teaching on homosexual sex. In *Sex for Christians* (1994), Smedes said he believed some homosexuals "can manage neither change nor celibacy," and therefore recommended that evangelicals should not require homosexuals to abstain but simply ask them to do the best they can. Instead of denying sexual desires, homosexuals should merely pursue what Smedes called "optimum homosexual morality." Interestingly, this appeared in a section titled "accommodation."[22]

Ethics dictionary sympathetic to homosexual ideas. In 1995, InterVarsity Press published a work called the *New Dictionary of Christian Ethics and Pastoral Theology.* But the article on "Homosexuality" relies mostly on extremely revisionist sources and misleads evangelicals on one of the most critical issues of our day.[23] David Field, who wrote the article: (1) accepts the idea that people are born with "the homosexual orientation" (even though scripture makes it clear that homosexuals cannot blame God for their behavior [Lev. 20:13]); (2) assumes homosexuals cannot help having same-sex attractions (even though the Bible condemns *desiring* sexual sin [Ex. 20:17;

Prov. 6:25; Matt. 5:27-28]); (3) believes homosexuals cannot change (even though Paul says homosexuals can become former homosexuals [1 Cor. 6:11]); (4) blames the rise of separate "gay congregations" on Christian refusal to accept homosexual behavior; and (5) approves a quote from James Nelson blaming non-homosexuals for creating the homosexual "problem."

Influential couple supports greater accommodation for homosexual behavior. Tony Campolo is a popular evangelical speaker whose wife, Peggy, is a member of Ralph Blair's homosexual advocacy group, Evangelicals Concerned, and also served a term on the council of the Association of Welcoming and Affirming Baptists, a group that encourages Baptist churches to accept and affirm the behavior of noncelibate homosexuals. The Campolos hold differing views on what the Bible says about homosexual sex and same-sex marriage. Tony believes that the Bible rejects both, while Peggy believes that it accepts both.

But while they disagree on what the Bible says about homosexuality, the Campolos agree that they are both evangelicals. Tony says,

> I believe that the Bible does not allow for same-gender sexual intercourse or marriage. Peggy believes that within the framework of evangelical Christianity, monogamous gay marriages are permissible. Each of us is an evangelical with a high view of scripture. We believe in the doctrines outlined in the Apostles' Creed, and know that to be a Christian is to have a personal relationship with Jesus Christ.[24]

Tony says Peggy is wrong on the Bible's teaching about homosexuality but that she in nonetheless "an evangelical with a high view of scripture." But revising sexual morality revises sin and salvation, and revising sin and salvation changes the gospel. So how then can Tony Campolo, though disagreeing with his wife, claim that it has no effect on what it means to "be a Christian" or on what is required to have "a personal relationship with Jesus Christ"?

But there is more. Even though the Bible condemns desiring sinful sex (Ex. 20:17; Prov. 6:25; Matt. 5:27-28), Tony Campolo also charges that evangelicals are wrong to think homosexuals must change, and he sees nothing morally wrong with having "romantic feelings between members of the same sex."[25] And even though he says the Bible requires Christians to oppose same-sex marriage, he suggests that homosexuals form same-sex *covenants* in which they promise to live with, care for, and love each other in celibate relationships "til death do them part." This amounts to marriage without sex and violates the biblical warning to "flee from sexual immorality" (1 Cor. 6:18), but Tony feels this is justified because evangelicals "must do more than simply bid them be celibate. We must find ways for them to have . . . their humanity affirmed."[26]

Evangelical Division over Gender Roles

The most serious issue dividing American evangelicals these days regards what the Bible says on gender roles. The historic view of the church has been that scripture says men and women have identical worth because we equally bear the image of God, but that God has assigned different functions to men and women in church and family life. In marriage, husbands are to function as servant leaders and wives are to function as gracious helpers. With respect to the church, men and women are both gifted to serve, but governing and teaching responsibility is assigned to men and not to women. In the last twenty years a movement has risen among evangelicals denying that God assigns gender roles. These evangelicals argue that, if men and women have equal worth, gender identity has no significance beyond the mechanics of reproduction.

In August 1987, evangelicals leading this movement formed an organization called Christians for Biblical Equality (CBE). Then in December 1987, evangelicals defending the historic biblical doctrine and teaching started a competing organization called the Council on Biblical Manhood and Womanhood (CBMW). Since that time, CBE and CBMW have grown to represent a deep and growing rift dividing evangelicals into revisionists—called *egalitarians*—and defenders of the historic view—called *complementarians*. Nothing separates evangelicals more deeply now than how we interpret what the Bible teaches on gender difference.

I believe two primary things are at stake between these opposing views—between the CBMW-complementarian and the CBE-egalitarian positions on gender roles. First is faithfulness to scripture at a time when the biblical view of sex is under severe cultural attack. Second is whether a shifting interpretation on what the Bible teaches on gender difference affects other important doctrines. We will look at both of these issues, and then consider whether division over gender roles is affected by the culture.

The first issue concerns faithfulness to scripture at a time when biblical sexual morality is under attack. Egalitarian evangelicals siding with CBE say they hold a high view of scripture even though they deny the historic biblical position on gender roles. They claim they have discovered that the church has misread the Bible for more than two thousand years, and that they are only defending what the Bible actually teaches. It is hard, of course, to imagine that the church could have been so wrong for so long. What's more, the egalitarian position depends on a concept that conflicts with scripture at many points.

Egalitarian evangelicals pursue the idea of *gender sameness without distinction:* even though the Bible says God made woman to be "a helper fit" for man (Gen. 2:18; 2:20); even though the Bible says the role of husbands in marriage reflects Christ's sacrificial authority as "head of the church," and the role of wives in marriage reflects the gracious submission of the church to Christ (Eph. 5:21-33); even though the Bible says women should not have teaching authority over men in the church (1 Tim. 2:12)); and even though Christ appointed only male apostles to lead the church (Matt. 10:1-4; Luke 6:13-16).

The second issue concerns how egalitarian revision affects other doctrines. Egalitarian evangelicals believe the shift they make is worth the cost however it affects other biblical teaching. But this is not a trivial thing. Erasing the significance of gender difference in biblical sexual morality generates serious conflict with just about everything the Bible says on setting moral boundaries for sex. Either the egalitarian position is wrong, or the entire structure of biblical sexual morality must be reconstructed.

As we have noted, the main idea in the egalitarian position—the one idea that changes everything else—is that equal worth in the image of God is not sufficient and therefore sexual equality in the Bible requires a gender-erasing *sameness without distinction.* But if gender difference has no significance for sexual interaction beyond reproduction, if gender difference is not relevant in any human relationship (including the sexual relationship) except when trying to conceive, if gender difference is not profound and does not matter for other reasons, then opposing homosexual sex makes little sense. It implies that God is either incompetent or cruel, and that the people of God—both Israel and the church—have totally missed God's true view on sexual relationships since before Mount Sinai.

This leads to asking which faction—the CBE-egalitarian faction or the CBMW-complementarian faction—is accommodating cultural pressure instead of standing for what the Bible teaches. CBE members insist they are not influenced by the culture and have simply discovered what the Bible actually means. Rebecca Merrill Groothuis, who serves on the CBE Board of Reference, strongly denies that the egalitarian position among evangelicals is "imported from modern culture."[27] But that denial is hard to believe, for four reasons.

First, it is unconvincing because *egalitarians are doing exactly what Francis Schaeffer and C. S. Lewis warned evangelicals to resist.* Seeing what was ahead, Schaeffer warned,

> the world spirit of our day would have us aspire to autonomous absolute freedom in the area of male and female relationships—to throw off all form and boundaries in these relationships and especially those taught in Scripture. . . . our age aspires not to biblical equality [of worth] and complementarity [of gender roles] in expressing God's image, but a monolithic equality which can be described as *equality without distinction.*[28]

Before that, C. S. Lewis warned against removing gender qualifications for leadership in the church because,

> To say that men and women are equally eligible for a certain profession is to say that for the purposes of that profession their sex is irrelevant. . . . [But] the kind of equality which implies that the equals are interchangeable is, among human beings, a legal fiction. . . . We have no authority to take the living and semative [determining how creatures repel or attract] figures which God has painted on the canvas of our nature and shift them about as if they were mere geometric figures.[29]

Lewis went on to say priestesses leading worship would lead the church to becoming "a different religion." Though it appeals to natural reason, Lewis saw that removing gender qualification for church leadership is no minor thing. It creates a monumental shift that replaces biblical revelation with "that old wraith Natural Religion,"[30] the term he used for *paganism.*

Second, the denial that egalitarianism is imported from modern culture is unbelievable because *egalitarian revisionism among evangelicals matches the rise of the same revisionism within the larger culture.* While egalitarian evangelicals deny following the culture, it is incredible to think that Christians, having misread the Bible for two thousand years, have just now discovered the truth about gender equality, just as the larger culture is discovering the same truth.

Third, it is hard to believe because *egalitarian revisionism has risen among evangelicals after, not before, it arose in the wider culture.* Gender revolutionaries in the culture began driving the idea of *equality without distinction* well before it started among evangelicals. Social scientists logically assume that a social change starts with those who promote it first, and that those who adopt the change later must be influenced by those who changed earlier. A change taking place ahead of its surroundings is a *leading social indicator,* and one taking place after the surrounding culture changes is a *following social indicator.* Claiming egalitarian evangelicals are not affected by surrounding culture is incredible because it depends on believing a *following social indicator* is a *leading social indicator.*

The Battle Against Biblical Sexual Morality

CHARACTERISTICS OF BIBLICAL MORALITY	CHARACTERISTICS OF ALL SEXUAL MORAL COUNTERFEITS	LINES OF ATTACK	IS THE CULTURE UNDER ATTACK?	ARE MAINLINE CHURCHES UNDER ATTACK?	ARE EVANGELICALS UNDER ATTACK?
Transcendent	Mundane	Attack on perspective	Yes	Yes	Yes (some)
God-Centered	Man-Centered	Attack on basis	Yes	Yes	Yes (some)
Selfless	Selfish	Attack on focus	Yes	Yes	Yes (some)
Relational	Non-relational	Attack on relationship	Yes	Yes	Yes (some)
God's word over experience	Experience over God's word	Attack on source of truth	Yes	Yes	Yes (some)
Objective	Subjective	Attack on nature of truth	Yes	Yes	Yes (some)
Requires discipline	Permissive	Attack on control	Yes	Yes	Yes (some)
Does not trust natural desires	Trusts natural desires	Attack on trust	Yes	Yes	Yes (some)
Same for all time	Varies with time	Attack on temporal relevance	Yes	Yes	No
Same for everyone	Different for everyone	Attack on universal relevance	Yes	Yes	No
Honors Sex	Worships sex	Attack on worship	Yes	Yes	No
Honors traditional marriage	Denies traditional marriage	Attack on marriage	Yes	Yes	Yes (some)
Trusts the Bible	Rejects the Bible	Attack on biblical truth	Yes	Yes	No
		Attack on biblical authority	Yes	Yes	No
		Attack on biblical meaning	Yes	Yes	Yes (some)
Submits to the God of scripture	Rebels against the God of scripture	Attack on God	Yes	Yes (some)	No

Fourth, it is incredible because *egalitarian evangelicals deny exactly what the culture denies.* The culture and egalitarian evangelicals both deny that men and women can be of equal worth without erasing gender roles. And the culture and egalitarian evangelicals both deny that gender differences matter except when it comes to biological reproduction. However strongly egalitarian evangelicals deny accommodating the culture, no one denies that they are shifting in ways that ease tension with the culture.

ARE EVANGELICALS TAKING IT SERIOUSLY?

When it comes to accommodating the culture by redefining sexual morality among Christians in the church, many evangelicals seem to think either that the culture is right or that the difference is not that important. They are dabbling with sexual pagan influences threatening to destroy the church, but act as if it either comes from a better gospel or just is not relevant to the true gospel of Jesus Christ. It is a terrible irony, therefore, to find outspoken sexual pagans who understand the stakes involved much better than evangelicals being attracted toward the pagan drift in our culture.

Rosemary Radford Ruether says, "We underestimate the radical intent of women's studies in religion if we do not recognize that it aims at nothing less than a radical reconstruction of the normative tradition."[31] And consider, once again, Naomi Goldenberg's warning about egalitarian Christians and Jews who revise historic biblical teaching:

> The Jewish and Christian women who are reforming their traditions do not see such reforms as challenging the basic nature of Christianity and Judaism. Instead, they understand themselves to be improving the practice of their religions by encouraging women to share the responsibilities of worship equally with men. . . . I do not agree that is a minor alteration in Judeo-Christian doctrine. The reforms that Christian and Jewish women are proposing are major departures from tradition. When feminists succeed in changing the position of women in Christianity and Judaism, they will shake these religions at their roots.[32]

Goldenberg is a *sexual pagan* who supports what *egalitarian evangelicals* are doing. But she wants them to stop fooling themselves and admit that they cannot erase the importance of gender difference without revolutionizing biblical faith and practice. She wants them to be honest, to accept facts, and to acknowledge that they are making Christianity pagan. Goldenberg is saying that pagans know paganism better than most Christians, and she is right. Sexual pagan feminists do understand the difference between sexual pagan and biblical morality, and they either express amazement at the naivete of egalitarian evangelicals (Ruether, Goldenberg) or openly urge the exploiting of that naivete for the advancement of the pagan agenda (Mollenkott).

Besides thinking gender difference does not matter except biologically, another idea of which some evangelicals are not sufficiently wary is thinking that same-sex attraction is a fixed *orientation* individuals cannot change. This involves thinking: (1) that some people are *constitutional* homosexuals, born with a fixed *sexual orientation* defining who they are even before they act as homosexuals; and (2) that for them homosexual behavior is natural and heterosexual behavior is unnatural. This key idea was accepted by Lewis Smedes; it was accepted by David Field, who wrote the IVP *New Dictionary* article on homosexuality; and, despite their other differences, it is accepted by both Tony and Peggy Campolo.

Again, evangelicals going this way must be either terribly naive or subversive; and again, sexual pagans seem to understand the stakes better than evangelicals. Elizabeth Stuart and Adrian Thatcher, who want to paganize Christian sexual morality, realize how strategic this idea is to their agenda:

> once the existence of an essential sexual orientation became accepted as scientific orthodoxy, issues about the relative authority of the bible [*sic*], tradition and contemporary experience emerged which had to be addressed and which most Churches are still struggling with.[33]

Stuart and Thatcher understand that, as is true of the idea that gender difference is irrelevant, the notion of inborn sexual orientation also changes everything else. Christians who embrace the idea can no longer hold homosexuals responsible for having same-sex desires; they can no longer insist that homosexuals must change; and they can no longer say that same-sex behavior is unnatural for everyone. Once the idea of inborn orientation takes hold, Christians start thinking the Bible is out-of-date and cannot be trusted on sex. Instead, they believe the culture is more trustworthy because it understands sex better than scripture does—better even than God himself. Biblical standards condemning homosexual behavior no longer make sense, and Christians sympathetic to inborn orientation end up having to choose between abandoning biblical sexual morality or holding to those standards even though they seem arbitrary and cruel.

Evangelicals who think they can accept this idea without changing anything important are not taking it seriously. If God is responsible for creating homosexuals who cannot help having same-sex desires and cannot change, yet he also condemns having same-sex desires with no hope of same-sex marriage, he must then be unfair, cruel, and evil. But if God is fair, kind, and good, and insists that having homosexual desires is wrong and those who have them cannot blame others, then evangelicals dare not blame God by saying homosexuals are made different and therefore cannot change or help feeling the way they do.

The deepest divisions separating evangelicals in America these days are not differences over worship, or music, or church government, or free will, or divine sovereignty, or gifts of the Holy Spirit. The deepest, most controversial matters dividing evangelicals in America these days are differences over sex. They are divisions over sexual right and wrong that reflect divisions also straining the culture and ripping mainline denominations apart.

As the culture drifts farther and farther from God's view of sex, and as mainline denominations writhe from the poison of sexual pagan revisionism, it is time that evangelicals renew their faith in what God reveals in the Bible about sex, and firmly resist accommodating morally to the culture in any way at all. The future of our families is very much at stake, and perhaps even the existence of the church as well. We have seen how totally incompatible views on sexual morality are causing deep divisions in both the culture and the church; now we will look more closely at what God says is right and true regarding standards of sexual behavior.

PART TWO

THE BIBLICAL VIEW OF SEXUAL MORALITY

6

Biblical Holiness Defines Moral Sex

BEFORE LOOKING IN more detail at the counterfeit views opposing biblical sexual morality (part 3 of this book), we need to examine what is true and right. Soldiers preparing for war need to know what they are defending; medical students preparing to fight disease need to understand the healthy body; and, if we are going to oppose counterfeit versions of sexual morality, we need first to make sure we know what God says about *true sexual morality.* We must be experts on true sexual morality before criticizing other views. The better we know the truth, the better we will be able to recognize deviations.

An interdenominational statement issued by evangelicals defending biblical sexual morality can be found in Appendix A. Part 2 of this book, beginning with this chapter, provides insight and support backing up that statement.

God set the framework for true sexual morality at creation. True sexual morality is a matter of keeping one's behavior consistent with the moral character of God. And, since sexual identity is the only detail added when the Bible tells us we are made in God's image (Gen. 1:27), the way we relate to each other as sexual beings must be very important to God. God's standards for sex are relevant to us. They apply to us fairly because they come from a source that is personal and relational like we are. God is a "who," not a "what." But the fact that the standards are relevant does not mean we can change them. God transcends the space-time-material universe, and the standards he sets for sex are transcendent as well. That puts them beyond human control.

Together, this means God's standards for sex apply fairly to us (they are relevant) even though they are beyond our control (they are transcendent).

They apply, but we cannot modify them or exempt ourselves from them. They apply whether we like them or not. They apply even if we never choose to follow them. God defines true sexual morality, and we have no say in what his standards should be. As far as God is concerned, we have only two choices: obey, or face the consequences. We should then focus on what God wants and not waste time trying to renegotiate the terms.

Biblical Sexual Morality

General Characteristics

Source of Moral Authority Is:	The God of the Bible
Moral Authority Consists of:	The holiness of God
Moral Goal Is:	The glory of God
Philosophical Basis Is:	Biblical revelation
Functional Purpose Is:	Family formation (offspring and relational union)
Approach Is:	Transcendent (beyond this world)
Moral Standards Are:	Objective (beyond choice and human control)
Main Focus Is:	Loving God
Secondary Focus Is:	Loving the spouse
Tertiary Focus Is:	Loving the family (children, relatives)
Most Important Dimension of Sex Is:	The spiritual dimension
Depth Is:	Profound (as opposed to shallow)
Sex Is Considered:	A gift from God
Sexual Morality Is Considered:	A public matter
Sexual Intimacy Is Considered:	A private matter
Marriage Should Be:	Monogamous and lifelong (traditional approach)
Traditional Marriage Is Considered:	Essential for everyone
Children Are Considered:	Blessings from God
Sexual Discipline Is Considered:	A good thing
Relation of Sex to Marriage:	Marriage justifies sex (not the reverse)
Relation of Happiness to Family Duty:	Fulfilling family duty justifies happiness
Effect on the Dimensions of Sex:	Affirms the value of sex in all dimensions
Relational Nature of Sex Is:	Affirmed
Spiritual Life Is:	Affirmed
Scripture Is:	Affirmed
God's Authority over Sex Is:	Affirmed
Ultimately Worships:	The God of the Bible

Normally people spend little time thinking over why God arranged sexual morality the way he has. But that does not make it unimportant. Sexual morality matters to human thriving as much as blood flowing in our veins—perhaps more so. We also hardly think of blood as it flows in the proper channels. But if it gets outside those channels, life is threatened and then we hardly think of anything else. The same is true for true sexual morality. If we want to live well, we must keep blood flowing in our veins and keep sex flowing in the proper moral channels.

In this chapter we shall discuss important terms, the difference between good sex and pleasing sex, holiness in relation to sex, and several ways that sexual morality is related to a Christian's relationship with Jesus Christ. Then in chapters 7 through 11 we will discuss important aspects of biblical sexual morality, including principles that shape moral sex, prohibitions that guard moral sex, and promises that bless moral sex.

Chastity Includes Abstinence and Fidelity

To begin, we need to understand three very important terms: chastity, abstinence, and fidelity. The term *chastity* refers to accepting and following true sexual morality taken as a whole. Whether a person is single or married, young or old, in private or in public, we must all be *chaste* all the time. *Chastity* means keeping sex inside the proper channels set by God, and failing to be *chaste* means taking sex outside God's channels. *Chastity* has two forms. As C. S. Lewis explains, the Christian standard is, "either marriage, with complete faithfulness to your partner, or else total abstinence."[1] This is nothing new, of course; it only summarizes God's original plan. No group of religious experts advised God on what his standards should be. No panel of community representatives voted to adopt them. And they did not evolve from years of social experience. Instead, the traditional biblical approach on sexual morality goes back to the beginning—to what God intended when he made us in the first place.

For relationships not covered by marriage, *chastity* means abstaining from sex altogether. Individuals not married to each other must never have sex with each other, whether because they are single or because they are married to someone else. But for a relationship covered by marriage, *chastity* means fidelity, not abstinence. Couples who are faithful to each other in marriage are as *chaste* as unmarried virgins who have never had sex at all. Thus we have three related moral terms: *chastity* refers to what biblical sexual morality requires taken as a whole; *abstinence* is what chastity requires outside a marriage relationship; and *fidelity* is what chastity requires inside a marriage relationship.[2]

Sadly, the meaning of chastity—both abstinence outside of marriage and fidelity in marriage—has not always been understood well, and Christians have sometimes gotten things twisted by reinterpreting biblical revelation in terms of ideas from surrounding culture. We have an example of this in the teaching of Augustine, who is otherwise respected as one of the great theologians of the church.

Augustine was schooled in Platonic philosophy, which blamed evil on material existence and thought purity was a matter of removing pleasant sensations. In regard to sex, Augustine believed the Platonic idea that sexual passion (the feeling itself) corrupts the soul regardless of marriage. So, on becoming a Christian, this former teacher of Platonic philosophy decided sexual purity meant giving up sex completely. It also led him to think that warnings in scripture against *lust* referred to sexual arousal whether it occurred in marriage or not. That assumption created a dilemma, because Augustine knew God did not order Adam and Eve to sin when he told them to "be fruitful and multiply" (Gen. 1:28).

Augustine therefore struggled to explain how husbands and wives could have sex without getting passionate and how Adam and Eve could have follow God's order without feeling aroused. Augustine's attempt to resolve this unnecessary "problem" led to some of the strangest writing he ever did. In discussing the morality of sex in marriage, Augustine wrote,

> What friend of wisdom and holy joys, who, being married . . . would not prefer, if this were possible, to beget children without this lust, so that in this function of begetting offspring the members created for this purpose should not be stimulated by the heat of lust.[3]

And, when he tried to understand how Adam and Eve could have had sex without feeling aroused, he said,

> The man, then, would have sown the seed, and the woman received it, as need required, the generative organs being moved by the will, not excited by lust.[4]

Of course, Augustine meant well. But his dilemma did not come from scripture, rather it came from Greek philosophy. Yet the mistake he made influenced Christian teaching on sexual morality for centuries. Some decided, if Augustine was right, it meant that Christians could not live holy lives (be saints) without renouncing marriage, and that getting married was a lower moral state than remaining unmarried. Monks and priests took vows in which they renounced not only immoral sex but sex in marriage as well, and for centuries most Christians thought married couples could not be *chaste*—could not live lives that were totally pure in relation to sexual desire.

It all came from Augustine's mistaken view of lust, which came from Greek philosophy, not from the Bible. In the Bible, virginity before marriage is indeed an honorable state. But fidelity in marriage is honorable as well, and it is no less honorable than abstaining from sex outside of marriage. Fidelity in marriage and abstinence outside of marriage are equally *chaste*. Nonmarital virginity is not a higher moral state than marriage, and marriage is not a higher moral state than nonmarital virginity.

Good Sex Is Pleasing Sex

God-honoring sex is pleasing—it pleases God and it pleases us—which is exactly what God intends. He cared so much about making sex pleasing that he wrapped physical pleasure, emotional satisfaction, psychological fulfillment, and spiritual meaning into one complex relationship. Sheer delight in a good sexual relationship is easy to see in the Song of Solomon. Listen to Solomon's lover: "Let him kiss me with the kisses of his mouth! For your love is better than wine" (Song 1:2). "Draw me after you; let us run. The king has brought me into his chambers [his bedroom]" (v. 4). "My beloved is to me a sachet of myrrh that lies between my breasts" (v. 13). "How handsome you are, my beloved, and so pleasant! Indeed, our couch is luxuriant!" (v. 16, NASB).

But morally good sex does not only please human lovers. It pleases God as well! We may often think of how much good sex pleases us. But how often do we think of how good sex pleases God? God is pleased whenever we honor him, and scripture makes sure we understand this includes when men and women fulfill his purposes, satisfy his principles, and respect his guidelines for morally pure sex. Paul warns Christians in the Corinthian church to avoid sexual sin, and while still speaking of sex he urges them to "glorify God in your body" (1 Cor. 6:20). Meaning what? Meaning God is glorified—God is truly *pleased*—with morally good sex. God responds favorably when men and women follow his directions. He does not get angry at sexual sin and then act indifferently when we go by the rules. He is delighted—he is truly pleased—when men and women keep sex inside the proper channels!

But while God made sex pleasing and wants us to be pleased with his creation, he never meant that we should have sex any way we please. In a fallen world, it is hard to live by God's standards, and sinners are easily pleased with things God hates. Which means the mere fact that someone likes some form of sex is no way to judge whether it is moral. Enjoying fast cars does not make it right to drive fast anywhere you please, and liking to shop does not make it right to spend money as you please with no sense of responsibility. Even though God made sex pleasing and wants us to be pleased, the morality of sex is not based on how well men and women like what they experience.

This difference explains why the Bible so frequently warns against trusting feelings when it comes to sex. In Romans, Paul says men and women who follow "the lusts of their hearts" end up "dishonoring . . . their bodies among themselves" (Rom. 1:24); and he explains that "sexual immorality and sensuality" come from indulging "desires" of the "flesh" (13:13-14). In Ephesians, he condemns "sensuality" because it involves "every kind of impurity" (Eph. 4:19), and he urges Christians to put off the "old self," which is "corrupt through deceitful desires" (v. 22). To Christians in Thessalonica, Paul explains that keeping sex pure requires developing self-control, which is the opposite of indulging "the passion of lust like the Gentiles who do not know God" (1 Thess. 4:5). Finally, he exhorts Timothy to "pursue righteousness, faith, love, and peace" and to "flee youthful passions" (2 Tim. 2:22).

Other New Testament writers say the same thing. John explains that "desires of the flesh" are part of the world system, which is rebelling against God (1 John 2:15-16). Peter says we must "not be conformed to the passions of your former ignorance" (1 Pet. 1:14). And Peter and Jude warn that scoffers will arise and lead people astray by encouraging them to follow "their own sinful desires" (2 Pet. 3:3) or "their own ungodly passions" (Jude 18).

According to the Bible, moral sex does not *follow* but rather *must discipline* natural desires. Human nature was perverted at the fall, and men and women have sinned naturally ever since. Sexual sin is natural to fallen human nature, which means that keeping sexual desires subject to moral discipline goes against how we naturally feel. Since the fall, anyone who wants to follow natural desires rebels against God. Dorothy Sayers said, "it is not the business of the church to adapt Christ to men, but to adapt men to Christ."[5] Adjusting her comment to sex, it means we must not confuse *pleasing* sex with *moral* sex. There is a connection, and in a way we can even say the connection is *natural*—God made sex a naturally pleasing experience. But, since the fall, moral sex and what pleases our fallen nature do not agree, and ignoring the difference is a big mistake.

Sex is a gift of God, and we should accept it with gratitude. But rules for enjoying God's gift of sex are set by the giver. They are set by what pleases God, not by what pleases us. Without knowing God well, some people fear that keeping sex pleasing to God will reduce their chances for truly enjoying sex themselves. But God is good, and those who give up pursuing sex on a self-pleasing basis, and agree to manage sexual behavior on a God-pleasing basis, learn that God returns more in their favor than anything they ever give up. When God comes first, sex works according to plan and is a lot more rewarding than anything sinners experience insisting on sex just to please themselves. Believe it or not, sex is included in God's promise that those who "seek first the kingdom of God and his righteousness" will have "all these things . . . added to you" (Matt. 6:33).

God Alone Defines Good Sex

Unlike at some other periods in church history, it is common today to hear Christians proclaim the goodness of sex. But then, of course, everyone praises sex these days. *MTV. Sex in the City. Playboy. Penthouse. CosmoGirl.* They all scream: "Sex is wonderful!" "Sex is good!" Are Christians saying anything different? Is the Christian message identical to what the unregenerate culture screams at every turn? Of course not! But then, if not, what should Christians be saying that is different from the world as we also proclaim the goodness of sex?

It is important to recognize, first of all, that the Bible affirms sex truly is a good part of God's creation. Sex is God's idea! He made it up. He designed it. He created it. Sex was included when God looked over "everything that he had made" and declared it was "very good" (Gen. 1:31). God never makes mistakes. Everything he makes is perfect. So because God made sex, it must be very good. And that is not the only reason the Bible gives for the goodness of sex. Sex also is very good because it joins beings made in God's image in a relationship designed to be consistent with and even to reflect that image (Gen. 1:27). The sexual relationship also enables men and women to accomplish wonderful purposes. First, it enables them to connect with each other in a profound way (2:24); and second, from that connection it enables them to produce something valuable (1:28). God did not create sex for no reason, leaving us to make up anything we like. He made sex to *unite* husbands and wives in a marriage relationship out of which they are to produce *fruit,* blessing others beyond themselves.

Because God made sex, it is not inconsistent to affirm the goodness of sex and the goodness of God at the same time. The goodness of each is entirely consistent with the other. But according to the Bible, the consistency of truly good sex with the goodness of God does not mean that sex and God are identical. They are not the same thing. One must not be confused with the other. God defines the goodness of sex; sex does not define the goodness of God. The goodness of sex depends on the goodness of God; the goodness of God does not depend on the goodness of sex. The goodness of God is greater than the goodness of sex; the goodness of sex is not greater than the goodness of God. The goodness of sex is limited by the goodness of God; the goodness of God is not limited by anything else at all, including the goodness of sex.

That is why the Bible teaches, even though sex is very good, we must never treat sex as if there were nothing better. We cannot put sex in the place of God. We must not worship sex *as God,* nor should we honor sex *in the place of God,* nor can we ever use sex *as a path to God.* Markus Barth says the Bible reveals that sex,

> is neither so great a thing as to make God's blessing, protection, and judgment superfluous—e.g. by deification of the loving couple, or by dissolving all personal distinctions and problems—nor so base and secular a matter as to be beyond the care of God and the beneficial use of the saints.[6]

Because sex that is used the way God intends is such a good thing, people are sometimes tempted to include sex in worship, and indeed arguments for this can sound quite persuasive. Sex is truly spiritual and unites soul with soul. That much is true. But some then exalt sex to the point of trying to reach God through sex or even deifying the experience of sex itself. But that crosses a very critical line from affirming the spirituality of sex to sexualizing spirituality. It switches from a biblical to a pagan view of sex. It takes the goodness of sex as a gift of God and redefines it as the presence of God.

While scripture affirms the goodness of sex, it never fails to distinguish sex itself from God himself. The goodness of sex comes from God. But good sex is not God. God defines good sex. Good sex never defines God. Which is why the Bible never allows using sex in worship either as a way to reach God (sexual idolatry), or as a way to experience intimacy with God (sexual worship). Moral sex pleases God, but men and women must *never* treat sex as a way of being intimate with God. The deception of sexual spirituality takes something true and switches it around. It goes from saying "the goodness of sex depends on God" to saying "the goodness of God depends on sex."

The ancient Israelites learned this the hard way. While waiting for Moses to return from Mount Sinai, the Israelites worshiped God with the golden calf, and their worship included sex (Ex. 32:1-6).[7] Instead of pleasing God, it offended him so much he nearly destroyed the nation. God said they "corrupted themselves" (v. 7), and his wrath "burn[ed]" against them (v. 11). Moses reflected God's view when he said what they did was "a great sin" (v. 21). But where did sex come in? Paul explains that what the Israelites did not only involved idol worship but sexual worship: "We must not indulge in sexual immorality as some of them did, and twenty-three thousand fell in a single day" (1 Cor. 10:7-8).

Paul reminded Christians at Corinth how angry God was with the Israelites regarding sexual worship because he feared some of the Corinthians were compromising. Rhetorically he asked, "Do you not know that your bodies are members of Christ? Shall I then take the members of Christ and make them members of a prostitute? Never!" (1 Cor. 6:15). In those days the greatest temple in Corinth was dedicated to Aphrodite, the goddess of love, and citizens had to have sexual relations with temple prostitutes as a matter of civic duty. Paul was addressing new Christians recently saved from sexual paganism, and was insisting they stop sexual worship completely. He was making sure they knew in particular that sexual worship (not just idolatry in general, and not just false religion in general) is entirely inconsistent with biblical sexual morality.

The goodness of sex looks different from God's point of view than it does from ours. In God's eyes, morally good sex was made to go with favorable results. But, in life the way it is now, experiencing favorable results does not by itself guarantee God's definition of good sex. In a fallen world, sexual sin promises and often delivers a degree of success, and sexual purity often comes with ridicule and suffering. If that happens, it is important to remember that good sex is not good because it always assures good results in this life, and bad sex is not bad because it necessarily leads to bad results in this life. If so, Christians would say "no harm, no foul" and would change sexual moral rules every time people found new ways to get around bad results.

Because God made the world and is good himself, good sex usually does (in most cases) lead to favorable results. But in a fallen world it does not always (in every case) work out that way, and if it does not, we must realize that God's rules on good sex stay the same no matter what. So, for example, sexual sin is wrong even if a woman works for a man who gives good jobs only to female employees who have sex with him. And sexual sin is wrong even if a school teaches students how to have sinful sex while avoiding bad results like unwanted pregnancy and sexually transmitted diseases.

Christians are saying something different than the world on the goodness of sex, because we understand that it truly is good only on God's terms. And, while we agree that God wants people to enjoy good sex, we also understand that only God has the authority to define what makes good sex truly good. Now we will look at what that means.

Good Sex Is Holy Sex

God is holy, and nothing is good in a moral sense unless it fits the holiness of God. Carl F. H. Henry says Christian ethics comes from the moral image of God,[8] which is the same as saying the holiness of God (his moral character) is the standard for evaluating all we do. Holiness is the image of God put in moral terms. The fact that the Bible repeats this theme so often shows that God went to great lengths to make sure we got the point. We are commanded: "be holy, for I am holy" (Lev. 11:44); "be holy, for I am holy" (v. 45); "be holy to your God" (Num. 15:40); "present your bodies as a living sacrifice, holy and acceptable to God" (Rom. 12:1); "be holy and blameless before him" (Eph. 1:4); and there are many other passages throughout scripture conveying the same message.[9]

What then is *holiness,* and how does it apply to us? It is hard to understand why *holiness* should be that important without having some idea what it is. It is not enough to say that God expects us to be holy and then to act as if everyone knows what that means. Most of us hear so little teaching about being holy knows that we only have a vague idea about what it is, and there are pagans who speak of holiness and mean something very different from what Christians mean.

Scripture presents holiness as something extremely positive. We could list a lot of things the Bible says are *not* holy, but that would tell us nothing about holiness in the positive sense. When God refers to holiness, he usually is focusing on something defined by its presence, not on something defined by its absence. Holiness is something worth having, and we see a little of that in Paul's prayer at the beginning of his letter to the Colossians.

Paul prayed that Christians in Colossae would be able to "walk in a manner worthy of the Lord." He then gets specific, praying that they be "fully pleasing to him, bearing fruit in every good work and increasing in the knowledge of God" (Col. 1:10). He also asks that they be strengthened "with all power, according to his glorious might" (v. 11), and he knows God will grant what he asks because those for whom he prays are "qualified . . . to share in the inheritance of the saints [those who are holy]" (v. 12). Putting all of this together, we see that holiness qualifies Christians for a lot of positive things—"worthiness" before God, "pleasing God," "bearing fruit for God," "increasing knowledge of God" and "power from God"—that come from having a very close and favorable relationship with God.

Holiness in the positive sense is nothing other than *measuring up to the character of God, which qualifies us to receive wonderful benefits from an intimate relationship with God.* Holiness is not one quality God has among others, rather it defines his character as a whole. When men and women are holy, it assures benefits that flow from knowing God on intimate terms.

Holiness in human beings is not an abstract concept but a living reality that comes from salvation through Jesus Christ, which reconciles men and women with God. Holiness in God is the perfect moral character of the Master of the Universe—a powerful, personal reality overshadowing everything everywhere—a reality so real everyone must either measure up or spend eternity in hell. Becoming holy is prerequisite for knowing God on a positive basis. It is what gives people a favorable relationship with the power running the universe.

God's ultimate moral standard for human behavior is, "Be holy, for I am holy" (Lev. 11:44, 45; 1 Pet. 1:16), and God's mandate has two parts. First, he mandates holiness. God evaluates all we do by a standard called *holiness.* But he does not apply this ultimate moral standard without revealing where it comes from. So, second, God identifies the source of this ultimate moral standard, and it is nothing other than his own moral character. God is holy and expects us to conform to himself. God is the measure for holiness. He embodies holiness. We are obligated to bring our lives into harmony with him, which is exactly what Peter says: we must "not be conformed to the passions of your former ignorance, but as he who called you is holy, you also be holy in all your conduct, since it is written, 'You shall be holy, for I am holy'" (1 Pet. 1:14-16).

Because the standard or measure defining holiness is God's own character—a reality, not a concept—to better understand holiness we must draw closer to God. We must get to know him personally, and that requires getting serious about pleasing him, something the Bible calls the *fear of God.*[10] Fearing God (getting serious about pleasing him) leads to intimacy with God. Paul says, "let us cleanse ourselves from every defilement of body and spirit, bringing holiness to completion in the fear of God" (2 Cor. 7:1). Perfecting holiness in the fear of God produces good results, but the opposite is horribly bad. If men and women are not holy, they are alienated from God and eventually lose touch with everything good.

The nineteenth-century Puritan pastor Thomas Brooks studied God's view of holiness, and grew to understand it well. Brooks wrote:

> O sirs, do not deceive your own souls; holiness is of absolute necessity; without it you shall never see the Lord. (2 Thes. i. 8-10) It is not absolutely

> necessary that you should be great or rich in the world; but it is absolutely necessary that you should be holy: it is not absolutely necessary that you should enjoy health, strength, friends, liberty, life; but it is absolutely necessary that you should be holy. A man may see the Lord without worldly prosperity, but he can never see the Lord except he be holy. A man may [go] to heaven, to happiness, without honour or worldly glory, but he can never [go] to heaven, to happiness, without holiness. Without holiness here, no heaven hereafter. "And there shall in no wise enter into it anything that defileth." (Rev. xxi. 27.) God will at last shut the gates of glory against every person that is without heart-purity.[11]

How does this affect the biblical view of sexual morality? It means that true biblical sexual morality is all a matter of keeping sex holy. According to God, good sex is holy sex, and for sex to be holy it must be consistent with God plus nothing. It also means that, while sex always engages spiritual life, the automatic spirituality of sex does not guarantee that every sexual act is automatically holy. Sexual sin is spiritual but never holy. The holiness of sex is not a feeling people experience having sex. It is a standard God uses to determine if we are keeping sex consistent with who he is and what he wants. The holiness of sex is not about what pleases you or me, it is about what pleases God.

Because sexual holiness is about keeping sex in line with God, aligning sex in any other way is unholy. In Ephesians Paul says "holiness" is the "likeness of God" (Eph. 4:24) and anything else is "impure" (v. 19) or "corrupt" (v. 22). Sexual holiness has a lot to do with keeping sex exclusive to marriage, and scripture connects honoring marriage with worshiping the one true God (Ex. 20:3; 34:14; Deut. 5:7; 6:14). Holy sex and holy worship are both exclusive, and violating boundaries either way is adultery (Jer. 3:6; 4:4; Ezek. 16:23-32).

For this and other reasons, the Bible shows that God is very serious about keeping sex holy. In Hebrews we are commanded, "Let marriage be held in honor among all, and let the marriage bed [the Greek literally refers to sexual activity] be undefiled, for God will judge the sexually immoral and adulterous" (Heb. 13:4). And Paul writes to the Ephesians, "sexual immorality and all impurity . . . must not even be named . . . among saints" (Eph. 5:3). There must not even be a hint of immoral sex among holy people.

Defining biblical sexual morality by holiness is especially clear in Paul's first letter to the church in Thessalonica. He says God's overall goal for Christians is "your sanctification" (1 Thess. 4:3)—literally "your holiness"—which he goes on to say requires:

> that you abstain from sexual immorality; that each one of you know how to control his own body in holiness and honor, not in the passion of lust like the Gentiles who do not know God; that no one transgress and wrong his brother in this matter, because the Lord is an avenger in all these things, as we told you beforehand and solemnly warned you. For God has not called us for impurity, but in holiness (1 Thess. 4:3-7).

Paul says avoiding "sexual immorality," the "passion of lust" and "impurity" all depend on "holiness." And the key to sexual morality is for each to "control his own body in holiness." The word used for "body" in this passage is not the one for bodies in a general sense (*sōma*). Rather it is a more specific term (*skeuos*) referring to equipment used for some function, and because Paul is discussing sexual morality, it obviously indicates parts of the body used for sex.

Paul says that holiness requires keeping our bodies—including our sexual body parts—under control, which means using them only in ways that are consistent with the moral character of God and in no other way. Any other way alienates a person from God (v. 5). Any other way corrupts a human sexual partner who deserves love and respect (v. 6a). And those who do not keep sex holy are warned that God will someday avenge everyone who has ever been a victim of sexual sin (v. 6b).

Sex, Marriage, and Jesus Christ

Defining biblical sexual morality by holiness—something qualifying men and women for intimacy with God—has tremendous implications, the most amazing of which is how the New Testament connects the man-woman relationship in marriage to the spiritual relationship Christians have with Jesus Christ. Francis Schaeffer says this picture is one "we would not dare use if God himself did not use it."[12] But God does, which means we dare not overlook it and should try hard to understand what it means.

Linking the relationship we have with Christ to the man-woman relationship in marriage is a major theme in the New Testament. John the Baptist mentions it first:

> You yourselves bear me witness, that I said, "I am not the Christ, but I have been sent before him." The one who has the bride is the bridegroom. The friend of the bridegroom, who stands and hears him, rejoices greatly at the bridegroom's voice. Therefore this joy of mine is now complete (John 3:28-29).

John's task as a prophet was announcing that the Messiah was arriving to begin a new, more intimate relationship with God's people, a relationship much like a bridegroom arriving to claim his bride.

Paul continues this theme in Romans, saying that our duty to bear spiritual fruit only for Christ is like a wife's duty to bear children only for her husband. A wife, he says,

> will be called an adulteress if she lives [has sex] with another man while her husband is alive. But if her husband dies, she is free from that law, and if she marries [and then has sex with] another man she is not an adulteress. Likewise, my brothers, you also have died to the law through the body of Christ, so that you may belong to another, to him who has been raised from the dead, in order that we may bear fruit for God (Rom. 7:3-4).

In Semitic practice, the moral and legal obligations of marriage began at betrothal, something that took place before the wedding and before a couple started having a sexual relationship. But betrothal meant a lot more than getting *engaged.* Engaged couples are not married. They *plan* to get married but definitely are *not* married yet. By contrast, a betrothed couple in Bible times were morally and legally married. They already were husband and wife in legal and moral terms, but they were waiting to have sex until after the wedding. That was the situation when Joseph discovered that Mary was "with child." They were only "betrothed," meaning the wedding had not occurred, and therefore it was also "before they came together" (Matt. 1:18). That is, it was before they had begun the sexual aspect of their relationship. Yet Joseph and Mary were beyond just *planning* to get married. As a betrothed couple, Mary was already Joseph's "wife" (Matt. 1:24), Joseph was already Mary's "husband" (v. 19), and in order to end their relationship the distraught Joseph was planning to "divorce" her (v. 19).

Understanding Semitic marriage is necessary to understand what Paul meant when he said we must save spiritual intimacy for Christ just as a betrothed wife must save sexual intimacy for her husband during the betrothal stage of marriage. Paul says,

> I feel a divine jealousy for you, for I betrothed you to one husband, to present you as a pure virgin to Christ. But I am afraid that as the serpent deceived Eve by his cunning, your thoughts will be led astray from sincere and pure devotion to Christ (2 Cor. 11:2-3).

The same theme appears finally in Revelation 19:6-9, where John describes a future celebration called "the marriage of the Lamb" (v. 7). After Jesus Christ returns, he says, there will be a great wedding celebration in heaven at which Christ will be united forever with the church—united in a way described as a husband taking a wife. In preparation, the church as Bride of the Lamb (v. 7) is even now dressing herself in "fine linen, bright and pure," a description John says stands for "the righteous deeds of the saints" (v. 8). This is not just a picture illustrating something real. It is the reality itself. The relationship we will have with Christ will be a real marriage—one so real the bride is already getting ready. In fact, Jesus was himself already anticipating this future wedding when, at the Last Supper, he told his disciples, "I tell you I will not drink again of this fruit of the vine until that day when I drink it new with you in my Father's kingdom" (Matt. 26:29).

The common theme in all these passages highlights a very important link between sexual fidelity and spiritual fidelity—between saving sex for marriage and saving spiritual intimacy for Jesus Christ. The relationship we will have someday with Christ will not just be somewhat like what imperfect people do when they get married here on earth. Rather, it will be the ultimately true, ultimately real marriage in relation to which all earthly marriages are at best dim reflections. That amazing connection is what scripture has in mind when it says we are presently obligated to keep sexual life holy by saving sex for marriage on earth, just as we are presently obligated to keep spiritual life holy by saving spiritual intimacy for our future marriage with Christ in heaven.

Husbands and Wives Linked to Christ and the Church

So sexual fidelity is linked with spiritual fidelity. But what does that entail? The most extensive passage on this theme in the New Testament comes in Paul's letter to the Ephesians, where he says:

> Now as the church submits to Christ, so also [literally "even in the same way"] wives should submit in everything to their husbands. Husbands, love your wives, as [literally, "even as"] Christ loved the church and gave himself up for her, that he might sanctify her, having cleansed her by the washing of water with the word, so that he might present the church to himself in splendor, without spot or wrinkle or any such thing, that she might be holy and without blemish. In the same way husbands should love their wives as their own bodies. He who loves his wife loves himself. For no one ever hated his own flesh, but nourishes and cherishes it, just as Christ does the church, because we are members of his body. "Therefore a man shall leave his father and mother and hold fast to his wife, and the

> two shall become one flesh." This mystery is profound, and I am saying that it refers to Christ and the church (Eph. 5:24-32).

Paul starts on the female side of the husband-wife relationship, telling wives they must submit themselves to the leadership of their husbands even as the church submits to the leadership of Jesus Christ. It is such a radical statement we are tempted to seek ways to soften what it says. But this is the Word of God, and therefore we cannot overlook Paul's use of a Greek word (*houtōs*), indicating he truly means that the obligation wives have to accept the leadership of their husbands is in some fashion the same as the church's obligation to accept the leadership of Christ.[13]

If Paul had meant only to compare similar things and did not want readers to think those things were identical, he would have used another word (*homoios*). Because he did not, it means Paul truly meant that wives have the same (*houtōs*) obligation to accept the leadership of their husbands as the church has to accept the leadership of Christ. This is sobering, not only for wives but also for husbands. It is an awesome responsibility for either to accept.

Paul then addresses the male side of the husband-wife relationship, telling husbands they must love their wives "just as" Christ loved the church—to the point of giving his life for her purity. In linking the obligation of husbands to love their wives with Christ's love for the church, Paul uses the same Greek word (*houtōs*) he used before in telling wives to accept the leadership of their husbands. Even as wives must submit to husbands "in the same way" the church submits to Christ (v. 24), husbands must love their wives "in the same way" Christ loves the church (v. 28). Markus Barth explains that "in the same way" in verse 28 does in fact refer back to Christ's love for the church.[14] With this we see that what God requires of husbands is awful and wonderful at the same time. Husbands are expected to love their wives by guarding their purity in marriage to the same ultimate, life-sacrificing degree Christ demonstrated by giving his very life to make the church holy and worthy of union with himself. There is no room here for selfish dictators. The leadership required of husbands must be self-sacrificing—even to the point of death!

To this point Paul has already carried discussion of the link between the husband-wife relationship and the Christ-church relationship rather far. But then he says something that truly should take our breath away. As if it were not shocking enough to say wives must submit to their husbands in the same way that the church submits to Christ, and as if it were not shocking enough to say husbands must love their wives to the same self-sacrificing degree that

Christ loves the church, Paul goes on to link sex in marriage to union with Christ as well. While still discussing Christ and the church, Paul quotes the most important passage in scripture on God's plan for sex in marriage: "Therefore a man shall leave his father and mother and hold fast to his wife, and they shall become one flesh" (Gen. 2:24).[15] To make sure we understand that he knows exactly what he is doing, Paul underscores the link being made by assuring readers, even though he has just mentioned sex, that he is still considering the link between earthly marriage and union with Christ. Paul says, "I am saying that it [the Genesis reference to God's plan for sex in marriage] refers to Christ and the church" (Eph. 5:32). The link is not only to marriage in a general sense apart from sex. It includes *sexual intimacy* in marriage as well! There is a connection between holy sex and holy intimacy with Christ! The link between marriage on earth and marriage to Christ really goes that far!

We must not forget that Paul in this passage is saying the same moral standards apply in the husband-wife relationship as apply in uniting Christ with the church. We have seen that for this Paul uses language for a real connection (*houtōs*) and is not merely drawing a picture that compares similar things not actually connected in real life. The same obligation applies in the husband-wife sexual relationship as applies in the Christ-church spiritual relationship. Both involve an exclusive, intimate relationship that God says must be holy. The same moral obligation applies in two relationships. But there is only one moral category.

But how far does this connection go linking sexual purity in God's design for marriage with spiritual intimacy with Christ? And, as Christians explore the connection, how do we avoid falling into the error sexual pagans make by turning sex into a vehicle of worship? Here we must turn to another New Testament passage.

Holy Sex Affects Intimacy with Christ

In saying there is a connection between holy sex and holy intimacy with Christ and that the same moral standards apply, Paul could be saying even more. He at least places two things in one category, but could he even be saying they are in some respect one thing? We must be careful, because here we are getting very close to the sort of thing pagans say. But Paul's repeated emphasis on standards for sexual intimacy being the same, the same, the same as for intimacy with Christ demands that we take a serious look at what God says about a *real* connection affecting *real* life. We must ask if Paul is saying that sexual holiness not only *reflects* intimacy with Christ but to some extent *expresses* it as well.

We could only speculate if we had nothing else to rely on than Ephesians 5:24-32. But Paul addresses this issue again more clearly in 1 Corinthians 6:13-20. He starts by saying, "The body is not meant for sexual immorality, but for the Lord, and the Lord for the body" (v. 13), and then asks some probing questions:

> Do you not know that your bodies are members of Christ? Shall I then take the members of Christ and make them members of a prostitute? Never! Or do you not know that he who is joined to a prostitute becomes one body with her? . . . But he who is joined to the Lord becomes one spirit with him (vv. 15-17).

Paul is saying here that one way Christians demonstrate intimacy with Christ is by means of, and not just analogous to, keeping sex holy. Holy intimacy with Christ depends on obeying God's standards—including his standards for sex. Sexual holiness and intimacy with Christ not only *should* never be separated. They *can* never be separated. And, in that sense, they truly are one thing. Chastity in relation to Christ is impossible without chastity in relation to sex. Keeping sex holy actually expresses moral-spiritual intimacy with Christ!

This amazing connection between sexual holiness and intimacy with Christ is not the only reason, but it certainly is an important reason why keeping sex holy matters to God and why he considers sexual sin so terribly offensive. Unholy sex not only defiles human relationships on earth but divine relationships in heaven. Immoral sex ruins intimacy with Christ because it raises a spiritual-moral barrier alienating people from God; and it does it, not like a punishment after the fact, but right away in the act itself. Alienation is not a price we pay for causing the problem. It *is* the problem.

Because of this, Paul urges Christians to "glorify God in your body" (1 Cor. 6:20), by which he means we are called to glorify God by what we do in keeping sex holy. The connection linking sexual holiness to glorifying God is real, not symbolic. Sexual sin actually does compromise what Paul calls being "joined to the Lord" (v. 17). God's glory is actually affected, one way or the other, by the way we use our bodies in relation to sex. Moreover, Paul says that Christians who engage in sexual sin are trying something impossible. They are trying to join Christ with a prostitute, not just symbolically but in actual fact. And the impossiblity of that attempt is indeed shocking. Paul shows that union with Christ is not just a spiritual-nonmaterial thing, and that union with a prostitute is not just a physical-material thing. Sex is multidimensional and always involves both, so we are obligated to keep faith with Christ in body as well as in spirit. Unholy physical sex ruins holy intimacy with Christ at the spiritual level.

We have tried to be very careful discussing the actual connection linking sexual holiness and spiritual holiness—linking real union with a sexual partner and real union with Christ—because what the Bible says is very close and yet is exactly the reverse of what pagans say when they link sex with spiritual life. Whereas pagans reduce holiness to sex and therefore say all sex is holy, God defines holiness according to himself and therefore says no sex is holy unless it follows his rules. It is pagan to say that having sex connects people with God, but it is biblical to say that obeying God draws people closer to him, even when that involves obeying his rules for sex.

This principle of obedience being key to intimacy with God is clear throughout scripture. In the Old Testament, God says, "Obey my voice, and I will be your God" (Jer. 7:23). In the New Testament, Jesus says, "Whoever has my commandments and keeps them, he it is who loves me. And he who loves me will be loved by my Father, and I will love him and manifest myself to him" (John 14:21). It is the same message in both the Old and New Testaments. Intimacy with God (with Christ) depends on obeying God. Anyone who wants to have or to keep intimacy with God (with Christ) must follow God's rules, which is another way of saying he or she must be holy. Peter is just repeating the idea where he refers to Christians "Having purified your souls by your obedience to the truth" (1 Pet. 1:22). These passages are not suggesting that moral obedience is a way of getting to heaven. No one can ever be that perfect. But they do say that obeying God brings a person closer to God, even when obeying him has to do with sex.

So where does this lead? Forgiveness for sin and reconciliation with God are impossible except through faith in Jesus Christ, but keeping sex holy on God's terms (obeying God's rules for sex) *does affect* intimacy with Christ in several important ways. Sexual pagans are absolutely wrong to say that having sex makes you intimate with God or joins a person to God. But they are not wrong about thinking there is a real connection between sex and intimacy with divinity. There is a real connection, because it is biblical to say that sexual sin ruins spiritual intimacy with Christ. There is a real connection, because it is biblical to say that keeping sex holy pleases Christ. There is a real connection, because it is biblical to that say keeping sex holy leads to greater intimacy—not to salvation, but to a growing relationship—with Christ even in this life. And there is a real connection, because it is biblical to say that keeping sex holy is part—not the whole thing, but certainly part—of preparing the church for greater intimacy with Christ after the Wedding Supper of the Lamb.

Because God reveals that there truly is a connection between holy sex and intimacy with Christ, Christians must say that the greatest reason for keeping sex pure on God's terms is that it not only reflects, but also in part expresses, a genuinely intimate relationship with God. Unless we understand how real this connection truly is, we cannot appreciate the profound nature of biblical sexual morality, nor is it possible to explain why keeping sex pure on earth is so important to the Supreme Being running our universe. Honoring, guarding, and maintaining the integrity of sex in marriage is linked in a real and true way to honoring, guarding, and maintaining the integrity of a relational intimacy we have already started and will enjoy forever with Jesus Christ. No wonder Paul concludes what he says to the Ephesians on sex in marriage being related to intimacy with Christ by exclaiming, "This mystery is profound" (Eph. 5:32)!

7

BIBLICAL PRINCIPLES SHAPE MORAL SEX

IN THIS STUDY OF biblical sexual morality we so far have only discussed the importance of holiness. We started with holiness for two reasons; first because that is how God approaches what he has to say on sexual morality in the Bible, and second because it is necessary for understanding everything else on the subject. That is, the holiness of God provides the only true basis for sexual morality. There is more to it than holiness, just as there is more to a river than water. And in that sense, there is more to sexual morality in the Bible than the stuff from which it is made. But everything else the Bible says on sexual morality depends on holiness, comes from holiness, and would mean nothing except for holiness. Everything else is in some fashion or other a manifestation of what the holiness of God requires of us in the area of sex. So, unless we understand the holiness of God, we are going to twist, pervert, or at least misunderstand everything that comes later.

So, now that we understand the correct basis, what else does God reveal in scripture on sexual morality? Holiness is a very large thing. It applies to everything—not just to sex but to absolutely everything we say or do. But when it comes to sexual behavior we need to get more specific. What exactly should we do, or not do, to keep sex holy? How exactly does God want us to use this special gift?

Careful examination of scripture reveals there is structure in God's approach to sexual morality. There is order to it. And the better we understand that order, the better we are going to understand what keeping sex holy requires. It is one thing to study bridge-building theory, and another to study the structure, materials, and location of a bridge we actually plan to use. Like a real bridge, biblical sexual morality also has specific structure, dimensions, and parts, which are necessary to actual use.

The holiness of God tells us the basis of biblical sexual morality. It identifies the nature and source of moral authority, and gives us the substance (the stuff) of which it is made. Now we are going to look at how God wants it all to work in real life. In examining biblical revelation, we find what God requires to keep sex holy is ordered in three basic structural categories. Positive principles define the value God assigns sexual purity, negative prohibitions guard this value, and promises reward preserving the value of sexual purity. This chapter takes up the first category, and the next several chapters will cover the second and third.

People who know little else about the Bible always seem to know at least that it contains a lot of prohibitions ruling out various sorts of sexual behavior, and of course it does. From that some, including some Christians, have concluded that God must not like sex much if he likes it at all. Non-Christians who misjudge God this way at least have a reason for not knowing scripture. But when Christians make that same mistake it is tragic. Nothing could be further from the truth.

Whether they are Christian or non-Christian, people who think the Bible presents a negative view on sex are seriously wrong. But it is revealing that those who make that mistake usually do not make it because they are exaggerating the number of prohibitions. Their error usually comes from looking only at the biblical prohibitions and failing to understand that all the prohibitions are serving a positive purpose. They are set as they are to protect and support the wonderfully positive value intended for sex within God's design.

With moral standards crumbling all around, Bible-believing Christians have much to criticize. But if the message we have on sex is simply negative all the time, no one should be surprised if nonbelievers are driven away from Christian teaching because they think God hates sex. While we should never be embarrassed to preach against sin, we also must understand we are obligated to demonstrate and explain just how wonderful God's view of sex truly is. Tim Stafford in *Christianity Today* has said,

> If there is hope in our situation, it is not in clucking tongues. It must come through a counterculture—a disciplined minority that *shows* a different way by their stubborn adherence to a distinctive pattern of life. We must become a people who are consciously, undefensively different, and who experience that differentness as a blessing. The church was such a sexual counterculture in the Roman Empire, and it could be again.[1]

Francis Schaeffer also taught that Christians are unfaithful witnesses to the Word of God if we do not stress "the end to be attained in working for the purity of the visible Church is loving relationship, first to God and then to our brothers." He urged, "We must not forget that the final end is not what we are against, but what we are for."[2] We must take that warning seriously, and must make sure the message we proclaim always focuses more on promoting the value of biblical sexual morality than on denouncing sexual sin. Both are essential. But showing sinners what they are missing when they fail to follow Christ is far more important than railing against their attraction to sin. If people cannot see what we are for, what we are against makes no sense.

What then are we for? What makes biblical sexual morality so worth having that nothing else will do?

At least seven principles can be discerned within God's revelation defining the positive value of biblical sexual morality. These work as a set. Each is necessary, and none works alone without the others. They function as a unit, so that rejecting any one affects the whole thing. These principles are positive. They each define some value essential to the way God made sex to work. They tell us what biblical sexual morality is for and explain why anything less is literally worthless. In particular, scripture reveals that sex has to be personal, exclusive, intimate, fruitful, selfless, complex, and complementary, and we will now look at each of these more closely.

Sex Must Be Personal (Relational)

The first positive principle is that sex must be *personal.* God designed sex to work as a relationship between persons, not things. Sex is designed to express a truly meaningful level of human relationship. So if sex occurs in ways that deny personal value, if it makes sex mechanical or treats people like "sex objects," then something is terribly wrong not just psychologically or emotionally but morally as well.

The value of personal relationship in sex is clearly revealed in God's creation of Adam and Eve. When God first created human life, he made sexual beings (a male and a female) who together bore "the image of God" (Gen. 1:27), and after creating them he immediately issued orders about how they should relate (Gen. 1:28). There is in this an obvious link between bearing God's image and how he intended that we use the gift of sex. How we behave sexually has to be consistent with what it means to bear God's image, and because God is a person, we must not have sex in any ways that treat per-

THE STRUCTURE OF BIBLICAL SEXUAL MORALITY

7 Principles of Essential Value	16 Prohibitions Protect the Value of Sexual Purity	4 Promises Bless Keeping Sex Pure
Sex must always be: 1. Personal (relational) 2. Exclusive (unique) 3. Intimate (profound) 4. Fruitful (productive) 5. Selfless (sacrifical) 6. Complex (multidimensional) 7. Complementary (unite corresponding difference)	1. No sex outside marriage 2. No sexual worship (spiritualized prostitution) 3. No sexual commerce (economic prostitution) 4. No homosexual sex 5. No sex with animals (bestiality) 6. No sex or marriage with close relatives (incest) 7. No pedophilia 8. No sexual violence 9. No lustful desires (inner adultery) 10. No intentional gender confusion 11. No sex during a woman's period 12. Strong opposition to divorce 13. Strong opposition to spiritually mixed marriage 14. Strong opposition to indecent exposure (immodesty) 15. Opposition to polygamy 16. Opposition to fellowship with sexually immoral Christians	Obedience always results in: 1. Abiding joy 2. Genuine satisfaction 3. Exemplary honor 4. Pure allure
EVERYTHING IS BASED ON THE HOLINESS OF GOD		

sons as if they were impersonal objects. Persons are neither animals nor things, and we must never forget that, even (or especially) when it comes to sex.

This is why the Bible always treats impersonal, nonrelational sex as something terribly bad. So, for example, one reason Solomon gives to avoid prostitutes is that sex with prostitutes squanders sex on "strangers" and "foreigners" (Prov. 5:10). Such behavior squanders something relational on a person with whom there is no relationship. It treats the person as an object. The same principle is evident where Paul compares relationship with Christ to relationship between a husband and wife in marriage (Eph. 5:25-33). Both are highly personal relationships. Christ loves, cleanses, and sanctifies the church in order to "present the church to himself" (v. 27). The personal-relational nature of sex is so highly valuable it approaches the value of the highest, most personal relationship of all—the relationship that bearers of God's image are made to have with the Creator himself.

Readers may remember how President Clinton appeared on television to argue that he did nothing wrong with Monica Lewinsky because, "I did not have sexual relations with that woman, Miss Lewinsky."[3] It turned out later they did engage in sexual activity but Clinton explained he was saying it was not immoral because there was no "relationship." That is, he believed sexual activity could not be wrong if relationship is denied. That makes sense to people who want to excuse prostitution, pornography, and other forms of impersonal, nonrelational sex. But it violates biblical sexual morality because it rejects the essential value of personal relationship in sexual activity. The very excuse used to justify Clinton's behavior was in fact one of the most important reasons that made it wrong.

Because sex was designed to be a relationship uniting persons made in the image of God, it cannot be treated as a *commodity* in which people are treated as if they were impersonal *objects*. Slavery is abhorrent precisely because it treats persons as if they were not persons. It reduces people to objects that are valued only for performance. And commercialized sex does exactly the same thing.

When I was young and single and serving as an officer in the Navy, I spent many off-duty hours passing through Olongapo in the Philippines. It lay just outside the main gate of what then was the largest U.S. Naval base in the Pacific, and featured one of the largest red-light districts in the world. Brothels lined the streets for blocks, and prostitution was the biggest source of income in the local economy. This was commercialized sex at a premium, reduced to nothing but body-parts, slick images, and every imaginable sensation packaged to sell and served at industrial strength. It was sex reduced to nothing personal, sex with nothing relational. Sellers were in for the money, and buyers were nothing but targets of exploitation. Sex was just a commodity for consuming like so much candy at a fair—and was not priced much higher.

In that situation, I had to take a hard look at my moral standards. Did God's rules make sense? Was it worth saving myself for relational sex in marriage? Or should I cross what felt like a barrier stopping me from participating in all that "fun"? Thankfully I did not compromise, and that is something for which Anna, my wife, is now very grateful. But it was hard being different. It was hard turning down what attracted so many others. What helped most was, first, having a solid conviction of duty to obey God whatever I happened to feel. But second, I was strengthened by an awareness of the tremendous value of personal/relational sex established in God's design. I was convinced it was indeed much better to save myself for a relationship I would have someday with my wife, and the effect it would have someday on our children, than to squander all that on strangers only to indulge feelings isolated to myself. It was a lesson straight from the Bible—sex is meant for uniting people in relationship, no exceptions.

SEX MUST BE EXCLUSIVE (UNIQUE)

A second positive principle sustaining biblical sexual morality is that sex must be *exclusive*. God made sex special, so special in fact that he wants us to treat each sexual relationship as something that is "one of a kind." A person with whom you have sex is not someone who should be treated as if he or she were replaceable or could be exchanged. In God's plan for sex, the value of who we are as persons transcends the material value of physical performance. Inherent worth far exceeds function.

God's plan that sex be exclusive follows from the relational value of sex being worth far more than sensual pleasure. Sex should be enjoyable and should involve sensual pleasure, but only after starting a reliable relationship in marriage. A sex partner must never be treated as if he or she were simply a tool for having good experiences. If that truly were the case, then personal worth would rise or fall with every sensual encounter, and that is totally incompatible with proper Christian thinking. Nonexclusive sex is a message that tells a sex-partner, "You are nothing special to me. The relationship we have is not unique. Sex with you is merely entertainment, just a way to pass the time and little else."

Revelation of the exclusivity principle in scripture starts at creation, where God declares that a sexual relationship causes a man and woman to become "one flesh" (Gen. 2:24), and Jesus adds to it later by saying, "What therefore God has joined together, let not man separate" (Matt. 19:6). The value of saving sex for one special partner is perhaps most evident in Malachi, where God rebukes husbands for being unfaithful to "the wife of your youth" (Mal. 2:14). The phrase "wife of your youth" can only refer to one person. No one else will ever be the one partner you had when you first became "one flesh." Malachi therefore stresses that sex should be kept exclusive to one special partner for life. Once a couple becomes one sexual unit, having sex with anyone else is rather like cutting off your head and handing it off to another body. It mutilates something irreplaceable. It severs something designed for one relationship and joins it up with something else.

In Proverbs, Solomon uses some rather vivid language to underscore the value of keeping sex exclusive. "Drink water from your own cistern, flowing water from your own well. Should your springs be scattered abroad, streams of water in the street? Let them be for yourself alone, and not for strangers with you" (Prov. 5:15-17). This leads him to say, "rejoice in the wife of your youth. . . . Why should you be intoxicated, my son, with a forbidden woman and embrace the bosom of an adulteress?" (Prov. 5:18-20). The imagery is from a time before water was piped into houses by a public utility. People living in towns and cities each had to save their own water supply in large clay pots (cisterns), and this usually meant carrying it in, one or two buckets at a time, from a river or spring somewhere outside of town. Solomon makes a comparison between keeping sex exclusive and guarding the family water supply. Both are precious to the life at home, and nonexclusive sex is just as foolish as (and really is a lot more harmful than) breaking the cistern that holds your family's precious water supply. If a cistern cracks and water pours into the street, family life is devastated. What was pure and precious is trampled into mud and lost forever. In the same way, nonexclusive sex also devastates family life, something precious is trampled into moral mud, and everyone in the family loses.

The value of exclusive sex with a single, irreplaceable partner is one of the main reasons the Bible gives such emphasis to lifelong marriage. Jesus taught that marriage is for life (Matt. 19:6). And Paul said, "a married woman is bound by law to her husband while he lives, but if her husband dies she is released from the law of marriage. . . . [S]he will be called an adulteress if she lives (has sex) with another man while her husband is alive. But if her husband dies, she is free from that law, and if she marries another man she is not an adulteress" (Rom. 7:2-3).

The permanence of biblical marriage is directly tied to the value of exclusive sex. Sex outside marriage, and leaving one marriage simply to try another, both reject the tremendously positive value of sex with a single irreplaceable partner for life. Marriage is designed to be lifelong because keeping sex exclusive raises the value of the relationship—the more exclusive, the more value; and the more valueable it is, the more exclusive it must be. Exclusive sex is precious, and passing sex around cheapens the relationship. You might as well drink muddy water from puddles in the street. Neither is worth having.

Here we must take a short detour to ask why "sharing" is bad when it comes to sex, but good when it comes to other things. Under most circumstances sharing is something we encourage. Sharing overcomes selfishness. So if sharing is so often good, why should we not share sex as well? It is wrong to share sex, but why? The answer is some things are simply not designed for sharing, and it is sin if we do. Worship cannot be shared with other gods, and sex cannot be shared around either. The difference is that worship and sex each involves a unique relationship that is irreplaceable.

In biblical terms, sharing is good when it has to do with impersonal possessions, with commodities we consume for health or pleasure. Impersonal resources should be shared because that is unselfish and puts the good of others ahead of self-centered hoarding. But when it comes to worship and sex, sinful self-centeredness pursues variety. It has no interest in treating anyone else as special. The difference is that sinful self-centeredness reduces worship and sex to commodities. It regards them as delicacies for indulging, and wants to sample or consume as much as possible. Nonexclusive sex, like nonexclusive worship, has nothing to do with selfless sharing. Rather it reduces sex to acts of indulgence that treat no one as anyone special.

During the *sexual revolution* launched in the 1960s, many of that generation stopped thinking that sex should be exclusive. Instead they preached *free sex. Free sex* meant it no longer mattered with whom you had sex. Everyone was supposed to *love* everyone else, and that meant having sex with anyone who happened to come along. Sex was for *sharing,* and it was selfish to limit yourself to one person.

But *free sex* with no one special did not last long. The AIDS epidemic forced some to reevaluate, and the sexual revolution has taken other turns. But there was something else besides AIDS in the way of absolutely free sex, and that was no one deep down really cares for sex with a person who thinks they are no one special, who thinks their relationship is not unique. The flower children of the 1960s eventually gave up *free sex* and began looking for uniquely relational sex instead. It was a costly lesson that the Bible taught all along.

Sex Must Be Intimate (Profound)

A third positive principle is that human sexual relationships must be *intimate.* Besides being personal and exclusive, sex must also involve intimacy, and sex that is shallow is in some way perverted. Moral sex demands intimacy because it is a relationship designed to be deeply meaningful and profound. Sex is not trivial, and acting as if it is trivial is wrong.

If one day you were to inherit an original Rembrandt, you would not hang it in the garage or leave it exposed to the weather. If the President of the United States were to visit your home, you would not interrupt something he was saying by taking a phone call from a neighbor. Sex without intimacy trivializes something terribly profound. Without intimacy, sex is not worth much. The heart is taken out, leaving only a shell. One might as well take the motherboard out of a computer. What is left is hardly worth having.

Sex must be intimate because God made sex to join souls and not merely to join bodies. It unites a husband and wife at the deepest level of being, spiritually as well as physically. No human relationship expresses intimacy more truly than sexual union, which is why Paul says there is something the same in union with God and union in marriage (Eph. 5:22-23). Sex without intimacy is like sugar without sweetness or fire without heat. The absence not only leaves what is left incomplete, it also changes what is left. Sex without intimacy is not true sex, in the same way that a car with no engine is not a true car. The lack makes it impossible to accomplish the reason it was designed. It leaves a sham of what was intended.

Intimacy in God's plan for sex first appears in the biblical formula for marriage at creation: "Therefore a man shall leave his father and his mother and hold fast to his wife, and they shall become one flesh" (Gen. 2:24). "Hold fast" and "one flesh" together stress the beginning of a new relationship that is characterized by profound intimacy.

In the original Hebrew, "hold fast" means clinging to someone with deep, genuine affection and loyalty.[4] Ruth "clung" (she was inseparably joined) to Naomi while Orpah loved her mother-in-law, but not enough to leave everything else behind (Ruth 1:14); and the men of Judah followed David "steadfastly" (their hearts were inseparably united) while the rest of Israel rebeled (2 Sam. 20:2). In fact, this same word expresses the absolute union of heart and soul God desires to have with his people (Deut. 10:20; 11:22; 13:4; 30:20; Josh. 22:5; 23:8). So if husbands must "hold fast" to their wives, it means the sexual relationship affirmed in marriage is meant to draw a couple so close that nothing comes between them. No divisions. No competing loyalties. No separate priorities. Nothing! Now that is intimacy!

The second term for the intimacy of sex in marriage is the word "one" that we see in the phrase "one flesh." This word is the same one that is applied in reference to the Trinity, the mysterious union of three persons combined in the one being of God. "Hear, O Israel: The LORD our God, the LORD is one" (Deut. 6:4). It expresses a kind of unity that does not erase meaningful diversity within one perfectly integrated whole.[5] For example, when the many individual curtains of the tabernacle were fastened together they became "a single whole" (Ex. 26:6, 11; 36:13), and when the people of Israel affirmed their covenant with God the many individuals spoke with "one" voice (Ex. 24:3). So, when Jesus says a husband and wife become "one" flesh and enter a relationship so intimate they no longer are two but "one" (Matt. 19:6) it does not mean they cease to have individual differences or that individuality no longer matters. They remain individual persons, but they enter a sexual relationship designed to be so intimate that they function as a single, inseparable unit.

Couples these days are experimenting with many different arrangements, and one married couple I know live in different homes, in different cities, in different parts of the country in order to pursue separate careers. They do not have other sex partners, and they try to see each other on weekends and holidays. But the situation is not temporary and is not something they are doing to survive a crisis. Though married, these individuals have chosen career goals that take them in different directions, and so to accommodate these goals they are sacrificing intimacy in their married relationship. Contemporary culture would say, "That is up to them. If that's what they want, it's no one else's business." But in God's eyes, something is wrong. They may not be committing adultery, but something is not right. Within God's plan for sex in marriage, intimacy is more than a matter of personal preference. It is part of the Creator's design and has such positive value, setting that value aside is immoral.

SEX MUST BE FRUITFUL (PRODUCTIVE)

A fourth principle giving positive value to moral sex is that God made sex to be *fruitful*. Sex should be productive, and something is out of place otherwise. Sex is not an end in itself. It is not something we have for its own sake, rather it is given to us as a capacity for achieving goals greater than itself. In other words, we do not have sex for nothing.

Here is another reason scripture keeps us from treating sex like a commodity. Commodities are not relational, but sex has to be relational. Commodities are not unique, but a sexual relationship has to be treated as something unique. Now here is one more critical difference. Commodities are assets we use up, but sex must be treated as a capacity for producing something good.

When sex works the way God designed, it not only requires intimacy focusing the relationship inward but results in focusing it outward for the good of everyone else around. Sex not only connects individuals to each other, it also builds community. It starts with generating families, which then develop into tribes, societies, nations, and civilizations. The generating power of sex means it must never be dismissed as simply a private matter. To be sure, the practice of sex is private, because that part is designed to be intimate and exclusive. But what sex produces is public. It matters to everyone. So, if sex generates nothing good for others, something must be wrong with how it is practiced.

This principle can be seen in the blessing God gave Adam and Eve when he told them to "Be fruitful and multiply and fill the earth" (Gen. 1:28). Sex was a capacity for populating the earth, and while God gave it as a blessing, that did not make it just an option Adam and Eve could handle any way they chose. God expected them to use this blessing productively and would not have been pleased if they had refused to do so. Solomon celebrates the productive value of sex in poetry, associating it with ripening figs and blossoming vines (Song 2:13). And although theologians debate the reason God killed Onan (Gen. 38:9-10), it most likely had something to do with separating sexual enjoyment from productive purposes.

So if sex must be fruitful, does this mean sex is moral only when it is used to conceive children? Some early theologians like Augustine and Aquinas thought this might be the case, but most Christian teachers today do not agree, and neither do I. Of course, references in scripture to the productivity of sex say a lot about the value of having biological children. But this does not make them exactly the same thing. Children are a tremendous blessing, but are not the only blessing generated by sex that pleases God. Sex operating within God's plan generates other very good things as well.

God has sometimes used childless sex to produce faith, which is what happened for a long time in the marriage of Abraham and Sarah (Heb. 11:11-12) and for a shorter time in the marriage of Elkana and Hannah (1 Sam. 1:5-11). We also know God wants sex to produce a quality of human relationship that glorifies him (1 Cor. 11:7), that reflects the divine image (Gen. 1:27), and this surely has to be as valuable and positive as populating the earth. It is also part of God's plan that sexual relationships produce homes that are centers of community, that reach out to bless and serve others with love and hospitality (Rom. 12:13; 1 Tim. 3:2; 5:10; Titus 1:8; Heb. 13:2; 1 Pet. 4:9). These are as much "fruit" acceptable and pleasing to God as sharing in the blessing of biological offspring. If so, then sex is not necessarily wrong just because a couple does not try to have a child every time. It is only wrong if we consume sex for its own sake with no intention of generating anything good for others.

But does that allow couples to choose a sexual relationship in marriage in which they intend to avoid having children altogether? If sex can be fruitful in other ways, and we are not required to try having children every time, does that mean it makes no difference whether an otherwise fertile married couple decides intentionally to remain childless for life? Here again some theologians will differ, but I do not think the Bible allows it. Sex can be productive in God-pleasing ways without trying to conceive children every single time, but accepting the gift of sex in marriage while rejecting children completely is not consistent with accepting children as blessings from God.

This is not to say God might call a couple to serve him in ways that require not having children, and Paul even hints at this where he says, "I think that in view of the present distress it is good for a person to remain as he is" (1 Cor. 7:26). But even such a case cannot be treated other than as an exception to what is regularly expected. Without a special calling to childless marriage, lifestyle preferences alone do not justify setting aside the clear teaching in scripture that children are always blessings from God. A blessing is something always worth having and is not something we can choose to reject without special approval.

C. S. Lewis once wrote to a young couple (Sheldon and Jean) challenging a decision they had made to never have children because they did not want to share their affection with anyone else:

> Your letter is a wonderfully clear and beautiful expression of an experience often desired but not often achieved to the degree you and Jean achieved it. My reason for sending it back is my belief that if you reread it often, till you can look at it as if it were someone else's story, you will in the end think as I do (but of course far more deeply and fruitfully than I can, because it will cost you so much more) about life so wholly (at first) devoted to US. . . . [Christians] would of course agree that man and wife are "one flesh"; they would perhaps admit that this was most admirably realized by Jean and you. But surely they would add that this One Flesh must not (and in the long run cannot) "live to itself" any more than a sin-

> gle individual. It was not made any more than he, to be its Own End. It was made for God and (in Him) for its neighbors—first and foremost among them the children it ought to have produced.[6]

The fruitfulness of sex is such a positive thing that rejecting productive sex is wrong. Productivity is something grand and truly wonderful in God's design for every sexual relationship.

SEX MUST BE SELFLESS (SACRIFICIAL)

A fifth principle in the structure of biblical sexual morality is that sex must be *selfless.* God made sex enjoyable, but not for enjoying in self-centered ways. Sex is meant to satisfy, but was not made for self-satisfaction. Sex is a gift, but how we use the gift must focus on pleasing the giver and serving the partner with whom he unites us (Mal. 2:16; Matt. 19:6). True sex is God-centered, which makes selfish, self-centered sex immoral.

While sex unites in very profound ways, it was made to operate from the inside out, not from the outside in. Sex is aligned to achieve goals beyond itself and therefore should not be calibrated on self and pursued for selfish reasons. Some wonder, of course, how sex can be truly satisfying or enjoyable without focusing on yourself. The idea of enjoying selfless sex seems contradictory. Does not getting the most out of sex require putting your own desires ahead of everything else? The surprising answer is no, both on biblical terms and based on human experience as well. God has imbedded a paradox in how sexual pleasure works that helps to restrain natural human selfishness. The more a couple focuses on pleasing each other, the more enjoyment each receives in return; and the more a person focuses on demanding his or her own satisfaction, the less satisfaction is possible. Self-centeredness always destroys satisfaction, while unselfishness always makes it better.

God certainly does work for our good (Gen. 50:20; Ps. 145:9; Matt. 7:11; Rom. 8:28; Heb. 12:10) and is himself good (2 Chron. 7:3; Ps. 34:8; 100:5; 119:68; Luke 18:19; 1 Pet. 2:3), but human self-centeredness is never a good thing; and that includes sexual behavior. Paul says, "whether you eat or drink, or whatever you do, do all to the glory of God" (1 Cor. 10:31), and one reason we should "flee from sexual immorality" is because "you are not your own, for you were bought with a price" (1 Cor. 6:18, 19-20). Sexual sin is self-centered and moral sex is not, and this even applies to sex in marriage. Paul says, "The husband should give to his wife her conjugal rights, and likewise the wife to her husband. For the wife does not have authority over her own body, but the husband does. Likewise the husband does not have authority over his own body, but the wife does" (1 Cor. 7:3-4).

Amnon, David's firstborn son, sinned greatly when he raped his half-sister Tamar (2 Sam. 13:1-22). But what he did was not simply a sin of disobedience for violating God's command against adultery, it was also a sin of terrible selfishness. Tamar warned him that it would devastate her, saying, "As for me, where could I carry my shame?"—and even suggested that he "please speak to the king, for he will not withhold me from you" (v. 13). Amnon could have asked to marry her, and she would have gone along to save face. But, the text says, Amnon "would not listen to her, and being stronger than she, he violated her and lay with her" (v. 14). He cared neither for God nor for Tamar and insisted on having sex centered entirely on himself.

When Anna became my wife, she gave up a teaching job in South Carolina, where she had been recognized as Teacher of the Year and had many wonderful friends. For my sake she moved to Illinois, where she knew no one but me, everyone spoke with a Yankee accent, winters were colder than she ever imagined, and she had to take an entry-level job out of her field. What sacrifices she made to honor marriage with me!

But there were sacrifices I made as well. Meeting her needs took priority over my need (or at least my desire) to spend long hours in the library trying to earn good grades in seminary. I could no longer spend time or money as I pleased. Every choice had to serve her good. Decisions had to be made together. I was no longer independent. Money I had saved for years now belonged to her as well. My car was her car, my home was her home, my food was her food. Nothing I had was *mine* anymore. What was formerly *mine* became *ours*. We each had to learn that a real marriage—a real sexual relationship—requires putting the good of our relationship ahead of self. Everything we gained required giving everything up, and we could not have been more satisfied.

Unselfishness in all areas including sex has such value that few marriages last without it. Those that have it grow stronger and more intense over time, while those without it wither. Unselfishness in a sexual relationship is tremendously positive, and selfishness destroys a good relationship. Sex is corrupt when it has more to do with pleasing self than with pleasing God and serving the one to whom we are (or perhaps will be in the future) joined in marriage.

SEX MUST BE COMPLEX (MULTIDIMENSIONAL)

A sixth positive principle in biblical sexual morality is that sex is *complex* and must be *treated as* complex. Human beings have bodies, minds, and souls.

We are not only bodies, not only minds, and not only souls. We are all these at once, and sex is designed to unite us at all levels. When God made us in his image, he made wonderfully complex creatures capable of a wonderfully complex, multidimensional relationship; and because this multidimensional complexity is so positive, sex that rejects it is wrong.

By God's design, human beings are embodied spirits with minds capable of reason and emotion. We are enfleshed beings with eternal souls. To handle the complex nature of human life, the New Testament uses different words revealing that we have at least three dimensions—spiritual life (*pneuma*), mental or emotional life (*psychē*), and physical life (*sōma*).[7] And in order to say something that clearly applies to human life in every dimension, Paul lists all three together: "and may your whole spirit [*pneuma*] and soul [*psychē*] and body [*sōma*] be kept blameless at the coming of our Lord Jesus Christ" (1 Thess. 5:23). We exist as multidimensional beings, and when it comes to sex, the Bible makes it clear that God made it a complex, multidimensional relationship designed to connect complex, multidimensional beings. The physical cannot be separated from the psychological or the spiritual; the psychological cannot be severed from the physical and spiritual; and the spiritual cannot be detached from the psychological and physical. God made sex to unite human beings at all levels, and pretending something less is both mistaken and immoral.

The importance of sexual complexity is revealed most clearly in the way Jesus corrected what the Pharisees were teaching on sexual sin. The Pharisees taught that sexual sin could not occur unless something takes place physically, that if physical sex does not unite bodies there can be no adultery. But Jesus rebuked them, saying, "everyone who looks at a woman with lustful intent has already committed adultery with her in his heart" (Matt. 5:28). The point he made was that sex is not only physical but also psychological and spiritual, and it is wrong to think these other dimensions are irrelevant when it comes to sexual sin. Sex is irreducibly complex and has to do with more than just the physical. You can be guilty of sexual sin even if nothing happens physically.

Paul then adds something else on sexual complexity in addressing sinful behavior among the Christians at Corinth. "The body," he says, "is not meant for sexual immorality, but for the Lord, and the Lord for the body. . . . Shall I then take the members of Christ and make them members of a prostitute? Never!" (1 Cor. 6:13-15). Like what Jesus said to the Pharisees, Paul's argument depends on understanding that sex is complex and cannot be treated in just one dimension. But this time, rather than limiting sexual morality to the physical, some church members apparently thought it could be limited to the spiritual. Most likely they were thinking, "What happens in the body does not matter because the material is passing away. Only the nonmaterial matters, because only that is eternal." But Paul renounces the idea. Why? Because sex is irreducibly complex, and the physical and spiritual dimensions of sex cannot be separated. It is the same reason Paul warns these same Christians against becoming "unequally yoked" with unbelievers (2 Cor. 6:14). Spiritual life cannot be detached from physical sex.

A third view on sexual complexity comes in Paul's warning that husbands and wives be sure to "not deprive one another [sexually], except perhaps by agreement for a limited time, that you may devote yourselves to prayer; but then come together again, so that Satan may not tempt you" (1 Cor. 7:5). The point again depends on understanding that sex has inseparable dimensions, but here Paul identifies a strategic benefit. Because sex has inseparable dimensions, physical sex in marriage serves to reinforce spiritual fidelity by inoculating the mind against temptation.

Because sex is irreducibly complex, no single dimension can be denied without corrupting sex as a whole. You might as well try hanging your hat on a two-dimensional hat rack or kicking a soccer ball in just one dimension. In multidimensional reality, each dimension affects all the others, and if one is corrupted or denied it damages the whole thing. Each is essential to the whole all the time. Respecting them together is something very positive, and anything less is perverse. C. S. Lewis captured the idea:

> The monstrosity of sexual intercourse outside marriage is that those who indulge in it are trying to isolate one kind of union (the sexual) from all the other kinds of union which were intended to go along with it and make up the total union. The Christian attitude does not mean that there is anything wrong about sexual pleasure, any more than about the pleasure of eating. It means that you must not isolate that pleasure and try to get it by itself, any more than you ought to get the pleasures of taste without swallowing and digesting, by chewing things and spitting them out again.[8]

Sex education in public schools has become a regular battleground in many communities, with one side promoting "safe sex" education and the other defending "abstinence." Those who emphasize sex education argue that schools should instruct everyone on methods of birth control and disease prevention in order to reduce bad consequences for teens—who, they say, will have sex no matter what; but opponents object that this inevitably lowers resistance to at-risk behavior and increases the very irresponsibility that schools warn teens to avoid.

As a concerned parent, I once debated this issue with neighbors at a local school but was surprised that organizers on both sides pressed speakers to focus only on health issues and to avoid addressing differences over sexual morality. It was well-intended and meant only as a strategy for winning the debate. Even so, I could not agree. I supported those who wanted to keep "safe sex" education out of public schools, but not their strategy of omitting moral issues as well. Why?

The main problem with the "safe sex" approach is it teaches sexual responsibility in a way that reduces sex to only one dimension—the physical. It assumes that sexual responsibility at a physical level can be divorced from other dimensions without causing damage or changing anything important. But the assumption is horribly perverse, first, because doing so is impossible (sex never actually operates in just one dimension); and, second, because it teaches a lie (it claims that physically responsible sex is not necessarily connected with the mental, emotional, or spiritual dimensions).

The advocates of "safe sex" education now call it "comprehensive" sex education. But nothing has changed but the label, and the new term is just as counter-productive as the first. Both labels emphasizes a different weakness. "Safe sex" draws attention to how the approach actually encourages at-risk behavior, and the "comprehensive" label draws attention to how the approach actually fails to cover morality. Comprehensive "safe sex" education is neither safe nor comprehensive.

Denying sexual complexity is the most fundamental problem with "safe sex" education. Everything else is something secondary caused by this one basic flaw. It is horribly foolish, therefore, to suppose that "safe sex" education can be stopped with a strategy that agrees to avoid all dimensions except "health." Such a strategy defeats itself by presupposing the only real reason for opposing the other side. Sex is complex. It has a multitude of interrelated dimensions. Any approach that fails to account for this complexity is wrong.

Sex Must Be Complementary (Unite Corresponding Difference)

The final principle we will discuss in defining the positive value of biblical sexual morality is that sex must be *complementary.* Sex unites beings made for each another. Men and women are human and neither is more or less human than the other. But our equal humanity does not mean we are perfectly identical. As sexual creatures, men and women are different in ways that complement each other, and the value of complementary relationship in sex is so positive that any denial or attempt to erase it is immoral.

Of all the principles we have covered, this could be the most obvious and yet most despised. It might also be the most important. Differences between male and female are easily noted, but many today wonder if these differences are good and some even challenge whether they exist at all. With God there is no doubt. The complementary nature of sexual difference is both real and good. It is part of God's good design and is so important that those who deny it risk losing touch with reality and risk never being part of a real sexual relationship.

I have said sex must be complementary and have claimed that male-female differences are obvious in common experience. But that does not mean we understand it very well. The complementary nature of sex is not a regular part of daily conversation. So what are we talking about exactly?

The moral principle has to do with the fact that sexual difference is a necessary part of God's design. When it comes to sex, we are genuinely different from each other. But we are not different in ways that are foreign or unrelated. It is not like the difference between a rock and a flower, but rather is the sort of difference you see in pieces of a puzzle or pieces of a high-performance engine carefully designed to fit one with the other so that what they make up is better than simply adding up the pieces on their own. The difference is like sections of furniture that fit "tongue and grove" or like a nut designed to fit a particular bolt. The parts are different, but different in ways that correspond.

So to say that sex is complementary means that sex is designed to unite corresponding differences needed to make something greater than what you get by just adding sexual partners. Sex is not for joining identical things, or just anything at all, or nothing at all. Unless sex brings corresponding differences together, it produces nothing of value, the parts never make up something whole, and sex never advances beyond individual isolation.

After reviewing "every beast of the field and every bird of the heavens" (Gen. 2:19), Adam found that of all the other creatures God made, not a single one "fit" (v. 20) or was "suitable" (NIV) for him. This means he found no other creature that corresponded to himself. Adam was a sexual being and knew he was made for intimacy with another who corresponded. But after examining the other creatures, he realized that something was clearly missing. Something very important, something very positive, was lacking, and

God agreed that this was "not good" (v. 18). There was something good that God still needed to do.

God then made Eve to be a "helper fit for him" (vv. 18, 20) and Adam discovered in her what he had lacked before. "This at last," he said, "is bone of my bones and flesh of my flesh" (v. 23). Here was another human being. But Eve was not a carbon copy of Adam. She was not a mere duplicate. She was of his kind, but different. Her sexuality was crafted to match and fulfill his own. Adam was male, and here was a female! She fit! She was suitable! Her sexuality corresponded to Adam's! The point we must take from this is that only a complementary relationship characterized by the joining of corresponding difference fulfills the good that God said was lacking. No other kind of sexual relationship will do. Anything else is "not good."

The idea that sex must be complementary and anything else is corrupt is affirmed consistently throughout scripture. At Sinai, God told Moses that sex between members of the same gender is an "abomination" and that sex with animals is "perversion" (Lev. 18:22-23). Then, in a dissertation on sin, Paul says same-gender sex is "contrary to nature," "shameless" and an "error" or "perversion" deserving divine retribution (Rom. 1:26-27). Jude refers to same-gender sex as "unnatural desire" (Jude 7) and in fact uses a term that literally refers to "flesh" that is "strange" or "foreign." All these terms share the idea that any behavior rejecting the complementary nature of sex is not just wrong but is wrong for that very reason. Whether it is sex with animals (that are different but not of your kind) or sex between persons of the same gender (who are of the same kind as you but not different), the offense is caused by rejecting the value and necessity of corresponding difference in a sexual relationship. Extending marriage to same-sex couples does not solve the problem, because the offense has to do with something else.

This suggests that even when sex occurs in marriage, men and women should relate to each other in ways that affirm the value of gender differences. How we express masculinity and femininity varies from culture to culture, but recognizing there is a difference is not just a question of culture. The difference between masculinity and femininity is based on something real, and no matter how cultures vary, that difference can never be erased nor can it be expressed any way at all. Masculinity and femininity exist because real union in a sexual relationship is complementary. Men and woman are different, and that is something to celebrate, not eliminate.

In September 1999, Frank Buble, aged 71, attacked his 44-year-old son Philip Buble with a crowbar and later turned himself in to police, who charged him with assault. The father and son lived together in one house, and this elderly father said his son's behavior was driving him crazy. Philip, it turned out, was having sex with his dog and claiming it was perfectly fine. The son told reporters his father was wrong not to accept his sexual orientation. He called himself the first out-of-the-closet "zoo," by which he meant a person who naturally prefers sex with animals. Philip argued his behavior should be accepted because, when a person forms a deep emotional bond with an animal, it can sometimes "develop to be a sexual one."

Of course, the father should not have assaulted his son with a crowbar. But he was right to object that Philip was doing something outrageous. We live in a day when the culture is finding it increasingly difficult to say everyone simply knows that sex with animals is wrong. Philip Buble justified sex with his dog based on his desires, and that is exactly the same line used these days for justifying homosexual sex and for redefining sexual identity however people want. If a person's subjective desires can justify homosexual sex and redefining sexual identity, then why not sex with animals? Why should it matter with whom, or with what, a person desires sex? In moral terms, sex with animals is wrong for the same reason homosexual sex and gender confusion are wrong. It denies the complementary nature of sex.

Because the complementary nature of sex has such positive value in God's design for sex, any sexual behavior that despises gender difference or is based on pretending sexual identity does not matter, does not exist, or can be anything at all, is terribly immoral. Gender difference uniting a man and a woman in the pattern God designed matters so much to God that he insists we must never act as if it does not matter.

Every principle covered in this chapter identifies something positive, and while each is very valuable, they are values designed to work as a set. When all seven are combined, sex is indeed enormously positive, and that positive combination is expressed in the Song of Solomon where it says,

> love is strong as death,
>   jealousy [ardor] is fierce as the grave.
> Its flashes are flashes of fire,
>   the very flame of the Lord.
> Many waters cannot quench love,
>   neither can floods drown it.
> If a man offered for love
>   all the wealth of his house,
>   he would be utterly despised (Song 8:6-7).

Readers today must not think this passage merely expresses romantic feelings that reduce love to nothing but feeling. God, who inspired these words, was not praising the uncertain power of human sentiment but rather was affirming the trustworthy power of commitment that sustains lifelong marriages when men and women unite in a sexual relationship that follows God's design. Biblical sexual morality is about establishing a relationship so strong and positive that anything less is "utterly despised."

8

Biblical Prohibitions Guard Moral Sex (I)

As I was growing up, my mother would sometimes tell of things she learned as a girl. One I remember had to do with learning how positive things relate to negative things. My mother and her sister had enormous fun together. But all that fun so often ended in trouble, and as a girl my mother felt mystified by why it was that she and her sister seemed always to get into trouble when they were having the most fun. When most happy, they would end up sad. *Fun* led to *trouble,* and *happy* led to *sad.* Their enthusiasm for everything positive just seemed to guarantee the opposite, and that seemed so unfair. Why should we get into trouble if we just forget the negative and only focus on positive things? Why is the greatest good not achieved by simply pursuing the positive without limits?

The Bible and common experience agree that one of the most important lessons we all learn growing up is that good things come with boundaries, and ignoring those boundaries spells disaster. Why? Because what is good and positive also defines what is not good and negative. So, if we pretend that the good and positive has no boundaries, we are doomed to cross over into what is not good and negative. I am not a skydiver, but I have been told that tumbling, gliding, and simulated flying during free fall is just thrilling. Yet, however positive that might be, if a skydiver ignores his altitude and forgets to pull his ripcord soon enough, the positive thrill of free-falling will end very negatively. Positive good is protected by limits that are negative, and this is true for sexual morality just as it is for everything else.

Frogs are cold-blooded creatures that acclimate body temperature to their surroundings. Dropped into boiling water, they sense something negative and save themselves. But when allowed to acclimatize in cool water that is heated to boiling very slowly, frogs have no sense of danger. Why? Because with no fixed way to measure temperature, their surroundings always seem to be pleasantly "warm"—the difference between their own temperature and the temperature of surrounding water always seems positive, never negative—and so they boil to death. When it comes to sexual morality, we need the negative to survive as well. If sexual standards just reflect surrounding culture, with no fixed reference, alarm bells will never sound, and we will never take action to avoid moral danger.

How was Eve deceived into choosing sin and death in the Garden of Eden? Paul explains, "Adam was not deceived, but the woman was deceived and became a transgressor" (1 Tim. 2:14). How did she get into such trouble? How could she choose something as bad as separation from God, banishment from Eden, and immediate spiritual and eventual physical death? It was because our great adversary, the Devil, who entered the serpent, tricked her into ignoring the one negative boundary to the good she enjoyed.

At first, Eve gave a balanced response. She mentioned the positive and negative together, telling the serpent, "We *may* eat of the fruit of the trees in the garden," but then explaining, God said "You *shall not* eat of the fruit of the tree that is in the midst of the garden . . . lest you die" (Gen. 3:2-3, emphasis added). At that point, the serpent exaggerated the positive—"when you eat of it your eyes will be opened, and you will be like God, knowing good and evil"—and he erased the negative—"You will not surely die" (Gen. 3:4, 5). When Eve finally succumbed, she was focusing so much on the positive that negative dangers seemed distant and perhaps even totally irrelevant. "When the woman saw that the tree was good for food, and that it was a delight to the eyes, and that the tree was to be desired to make one wise, she took of its fruit and ate" (v. 6).

All the wonderful good she enjoyed was safe as long as Eve remembered God's warning. But the moment she grew enamored with another seeming positive—and focused on it so intently that she forgot to examine any negative side—she became vulnerable and made a decision that meant losing the tremendous good she'd had before it all started. Satan is not creative, and his strategy of deception has not changed. Sex is a wonderfully good and positive thing. It quite literally is a gift of God. But the minute we focus so much on the good side of sex that we forget the negative, we risk losing the good we already have and suffering the result of God's wrath as well.

In the last chapter we studied seven principles that define the positive side of biblical sexual morality. In this chapter, we will look at the negative side—what biblical sexual morality is against. We have soundly rejected the idea

Mel Blackaby's Teaching

We must remain in the covenant
to receive the blessings of the covenant.

Decisions/Actions you will take from this session:

Viewer Guide
(for use in each session)

Session 1_____ Session Title ______________________________

Henry Blackaby's Teaching

____

____

____

____

____

____

____

____

that God hates sex and have affirmed that it is a wonderfully positive element in his good design for human life. But we do not deny that the Bible has negative things to say relating to sex as well. The thing to understand is not that God says nothing negative about sex, but that everything God prohibits (everything negative that God says related to sex) is guarding something positive. God is not arbitrary or cruel, and everything he prohibits he prohibits for good reasons. In biblical sexual morality, positive principles define the value of sexual purity, and negative prohibitions protect that value.

While prohibitions limiting sex in the Bible are surely negative, each protects one or more of the positive principles covered in the last chapter. Understanding the positive side of biblical sexual morality goes a long way toward helping us appreciate the importance of biblical prohibitions relating to sex. God's sexual prohibitions do not stand alone. Every negative limitation on sexual behavior guards something tremendously positive and good. So, even though sexual temptation is deceptive and always whispers the opposite, sexual prohibitions in the Bible do not actually prevent anyone from truly enjoying God's gift of sex. Rather, they ensure that we will never lose the best by corrupting something God made to bless us.

We can find at least sixteen sexual prohibitions in scripture:

1. No sex outside of marriage
2. No sexual worship (spiritualized prostitution)
3. No sexual commerce (economic prostitution)
4. No homosexual sex
5. No sex with animals (bestiality)
6. No sex or marriage with close relatives (incest)
7. No pedophilia
8. No sexual violence
9. No lustful sexual desires (inner adultery)
10. No intentional gender confusion
11. No sex during a woman's period
12. Strong opposition to divorce
13. Strong opposition to spiritually mixed marriage
14. Strong opposition to sexual immodesty
15. Opposition to polygamy
16. Opposition to fellowship with sexually immoral Christians

The order in which we have listed these biblical prohibitions is not purely arbitrary, but neither is it meant to suggest a rigid hierarchy. On the one hand, there are differences of moral weight involved. Jesus rebuked religious teachers of his day for neglecting what he called the "weightier matters" of God's moral law, and that presupposes comparison to other relatively less "weighty" matters (Matt. 23:23). It shows that in a sense one can be more important than another, and while some allow exceptions, others allow none at all. So, for example, mixed marriage is prohibited, but if one is in a mixed marriage it is more important to remain married even to an unbeliever than to get a divorce. So also, polygamous marriages, while not true to the original plan, are nevertheless better than either sex outside of marriage or divorce.

Still, even though the Bible indicates there can be differences in moral weight, it never issues an official list and does not specify a clear method by which to arrange norms in a rigid hierarchy. So while the list we have made here reflects an assessment of relative importance—that is, we have put matters permitting no exception ahead of matters that may or may not allow exceptions—the order given should not be taken as dogmatic or official, only as suggestive. In the end, we have to follow some order, and this is the best we can do. Readers are encouraged to think for themselves, and reasons are given to support the order we have taken.

No Sex Outside of Marriage

If any sexual prohibition is more important than others, then surely the most important is God's total rejection of sex outside of marriage—what the Bible generally calls adultery. Marriage is absolutely the most important boundary in scripture defining the limits of moral sex, and adultery is sex that disregards that critical moral boundary.

In God's plan, marriage is an absolute moral boundary that permits no exception under any circumstance—regardless of feelings, regardless of finances, regardless of mutual consent, regardless of fertility, and regardless of popular opinion or culture. C. S. Lewis says, "There is no getting away from it: the old Christian rule is, 'Either marriage, with complete faithfulness to your partner, or else total abstinence.'"[1] Sex outside of marriage is always wrong no matter how it happens, whether before, during, or after marriage. Without marriage, sex is simply wrong, and God takes it so seriously he makes adultery the ultimate paradigm for breaking faith with himself.

God's prohibition of sex outside of marriage is stated so clearly and repeated so often, God seems to have taken extra steps to make sure we do not miss its importance. At Mount Sinai, God specifically orders: "You shall not commit adultery" (Ex. 20:14; Deut. 5:18). The prohibition is repeated throughout the Old Testament, and in the New Testament it is affirmed not only by Jesus (Matt. 19:17-18; Mark 10:19; Luke 18:20) but by Paul (Rom.

13:19) and James (James 2:10-11) as well. The eighteenth chapter of Leviticus especially adds details to the general and rather brief prohibition issued in the Ten Commandments, and God makes clear that he opposes all sex outside of marriage and is not just concerned with prohibiting sex with another person's wife.

If a man and woman commit adultery voluntarily, they are equally guilty and deserve equal punishment. Gender is irrelevant. So, "If a man commits adultery with the wife of his neighbor, both the adulterer and the adulteress shall surely be put to death" (Lev. 20:10). But, while gender is not relevant among the guilty, free will (choice) affected by ability to resist are both highly relevant when it comes to determining who is guilty. A victim of rape is not punished because, in this case, only the perpetrator is guilty. "Only the man who lay with her shall die. But you shall do nothing to the young woman; she has committed no offense" (Deut. 22:25-26). Although the sex occurs outside of marriage, it is considered adultery only for the perpetrator, not for the victim.

All sex outside of marriage is denied by the general prohibition against adultery, and no voluntary sex outside of marriage is ever moral. But, under this general prohibition, biblical revelation indicates some variation of moral importance depending on whether or not the infraction offends some established marriage. This variation of moral weight is evident in different levels of punishment ordered by God in the Mosaic law. Sex with another man's wife (a married woman who has been intimate with her husband) is so serious it deserves death (Lev. 20:10; Deut. 22:22), and sex with a "betrothed virgin" (a woman who is legally married but who has not yet had sex with her husband) is treated just as seriously (Deut. 22:23-24).[2] Whether sex has yet taken place does not affect the offense; all that matters is whether a marriage is established.

By comparison, if a couple has sex without getting married and neither is married at the time, then even though it is a sinful act, they are not punished as severely. Instead of death, the couple must get married and the man pays a fine (vv. 28-29). From this, it seems that the offense involved in adultery has more to do with failing to honor the promises a couple makes to God than with having sex before confirming those promises in a public manner.

Another important element helping to define God's prohibition against adultery is found in Romans, where we are told it is limited only to this life. Paul says, "do you not know . . . the law [prohibiting adultery] is binding on a person only so long as he lives? Thus a married woman is bound by law to her husband while he lives, but if her husband dies she is released from the law of marriage. Accordingly, she will be called an adulteress if she lives with another man while her husband is alive. But if her husband dies, she is free from the law, and if she marries another man she is not an adulteress" (Rom. 7:1-3).

Jesus goes on to show that the prohibition covers not only physical acts but lust as well—internal "acts" that only occur in what Jesus called "the heart." "You have heard that it was said, 'You shall not commit adultery.' But I say to you that everyone who looks at a woman with lustful intent has already committed adultery with her in his heart" (Matt. 5:27-28). According to Jesus, even external acts of sexual adultery begin in the heart, which means the inner dimension of the moral prohibition is really more, not less, important than the outer dimension. Jesus explains, "out of the heart come . . . adultery, sexual immorality. . . . These are what defile a person" (Matt. 15:19-20). The inner aspect drives the outer, not the other way around.

King Solomon warns that adultery usually leads to social and perhaps even physical tragedy. "Can one walk on hot coals and his feet not be scorched? So is he who goes in to his neighbor's wife. . . . He who commits adultery lacks sense; he who does it destroys himself" (Prov. 6:28-29, 32). But the most fearsome warning in scripture is that God is keeping track and will some day personally punish all sex that ever takes place outside of marriage. In the Old Testament, God says, "they committed adultery and trooped to the houses of whores. . . . [Therefore] shall I not punish them for these things? declares the LORD" (Jer. 5:7-9). He also promises, "I will draw near to you for judgment. I will be a swift witness against . . . the adulterers" (Mal. 3:5). Then in the New Testament we are warned to honor marriage, "for God will judge the sexually immoral and adulterous" (Heb. 13:4).

But along with emphasizing how serious God is about punishing adultery, the Bible also reveals that he is merciful to those who repent. Jesus graciously overlooked the guilt of the woman caught in adultery, saying, "Neither do I condemn you" (John 8:11). She was caught in the act, and one has to wonder what happened to the man? But whatever happened to him, the woman's own guilt was so clear that even she makes no attempt to deny it. Everyone knew she had sinned. But Jesus, rather than acknowledging what she actually deserved, instead said, "from now on sin no more." I imagine he saw her heart and knew she had truly repented. The scripture says, "If we confess our sins, he is faithful and just to forgive us our sins and to cleanse us from all unrighteousness" (1 John 1:9).

Jesus did not remove the prohibition. The woman was obviously guilty and deserved punishment. Jesus the man had not witnessed the event (and all other eyewitnesses left the scene). But Jesus the divine Son of God, Jesus the ultimate Judge of the Universe knew exactly what she had done, and yet he did not order the punishment her behavior called for. Because she looked to him for mercy and truly repented, her punishment for adultery was postponed until Jesus bore it himself by dying on the cross.

The last word on adultery in the Bible, however, is not God's willingness to forgive, but that he will not forgive so long as the guilty refuse to repent. Personal repentance is absolutely necessary; and, if we refuse to admit wrong, God must apply judgment—and his judgment is severe. Through Jeremiah, God explains that just going through the motions is not enough. Repentance must be genuine, it must be wholehearted, or God will not accept it. "Will you . . . commit adultery . . . and then come and stand before me . . . and say, 'We are delivered [from punishment]!'—only to go on doing all these abominations? . . . [Therefore] do not intercede with me, for I will not hear you" (Jer. 7:9-16). Paul later reveals that refusing to repent for adulterous sex will certainly keep one from going to heaven—from inheriting the kingdom of God (1 Cor. 6:9-10)—and people who never repent for sexual sin are specifically mentioned among those who are forever excluded from entering the new Jerusalem (Rev. 22:15) after Christ's return.

At the start of this chapter we noted that biblical sexual prohibitions are not arbitrary, and each guards one or more positive principles defining the true value of sex. God's prohibition of adultery in the broad sense—his very strong moral opposition to all sex outside of marriage—certainly does protect the integrity of marriage. But why is this so important? The positive principles at stake seem to be that sex outside of marriage erodes and ultimately destroys the precious value of exclusivity and selflessness in the sexual relationship. Adulterous sex can to some degree remain personal, intimate, fruitful, complex, and complementary. It might weaken these, but does not necessarily destroy them. But adulterous sex can never be exclusive and selfless. By its very nature, adulterous sex rejects the value of keeping sex exclusive and is driven by self-centered interests that preempt our responsibility to always do what is best for others—in this case, those depending on us in the areas of marriage and family life. But the value of exclusive, selfless sex is so good that God never allows less. He prohibits sex outside of marriage to keep us from losing what is best.

No Sexual Worship (Spiritualized Prostitution)

Another absolute that is high on the list of sexual prohibitions in the Bible covers using sex in worship. God made sex spiritual. Sex joins soul to soul in ways that go beyond mere biology, a fact to which Paul refers where he says, "Do you not know that your bodies are members of Christ? Shall I then take the members of Christ and make them members of a prostitute? Never! Or do you not know that he who is joined to a prostitute becomes one body with her? . . . But he who is joined to the Lord becomes one spirit with him" (1 Cor. 6:15-17). So, yes, sex is spiritual, but that does not mean we should treat sex as a path to God or as a door through which we reach higher dimensions of spiritual life.

Sex truly is spiritual, but *spirituality* alone says nothing about morality. True morality comes from God alone, not from just anything that happens to be *spiritual.* God defines sex—not the other way around—so if anyone tries manipulating God though sex, he or she does something wicked that stirs God's wrath.

In the law of Moses, God absolutely prohibits sexual worship. We are told, "None of the daughters of Israel shall be a [female] cult prostitute, and none of the sons of Israel shall be a [male] cult prostitute" (Deut. 23:17). Gender is simply irrelevant, and whether one is worshiping the true God or a false god makes no difference. Sexual worship of false gods is wrong, and so is using sex in worshiping the one true God.

As we saw in chapter 6, this was at least part of the reason God was so angry at Sinai. While Moses spoke with God on the mountain, the Israelites waiting below did not suddenly go after a false god. They began worshiping the true God in a wrong way, and one thing wrong about it was their worship involved sex. Thinking of what they did, Paul warns that, "We must not indulge in sexual immorality as some of them did, and twenty-three thousand fell in a single day" (1 Cor. 10:8). A lot of people died that day because mixing sex with worship really makes God mad.

Another side of the prohibition can be seen in God's judgment of Israel at Peor just before they entered the promised land. At Peor, Israel was punished for joining in sexual worship directed toward a false god. The prophet Balaam told King Balak of Moab God would destroy Israel if the men joined with Moabite women in sexual worship (Num. 25:1-18; also Rev. 2:14). The sin of Israel at Peor was not just adultery but adulterous acts of sexual worship. When "the people began to whore with the daughters of Moab," we are told, it involved "the sacrifices of their gods." By this, we are told, "Israel yoked himself to the Baal of Peor" and "the anger of the Lord was kindled against Israel" (Num. 25:1-3).

When New Testament writers later on mention "the way of Balaam" (2 Pet. 2:15) or "Balaam's error" (Jude 11), it refers to people who like

Balaam corrupt Christians by encouraging them to reject God's prohibition against mixing sex and religion. The risen Christ rebukes the church at Pergamum because it tolerated some who "hold the teaching of Balaam," something he also calls "the teaching of the Nicolaitans" (Rev. 2:14-15). Nicolaus, a first-century proselyte from Antioch, taught that sexual norms in the Old Testament were no longer relevant and so justified sexual immorality among Christians. If Christians at Pergamum do not restore sexual purity in their church, Jesus warns, "I will come to you soon and war against them with the sword of my mouth" (v. 16).

God's anger at sexual worship flares up throughout Israel's history because he is provoked every time his people are seduced by Ashtoreth worship. Ashtoreth was a Canaanite fertility goddess especially revered by the Philistines (1 Sam. 31:10) and Sidonians (1 Kings 11:5).[3] Her worshipers believed Ashtoreth was the wife of El, the original creator God (whom the Hebrews called Elohim), and claimed that by having sex with him she had created a whole pantheon of lesser deities, the most famous being Baal, a god who controlled weather. Ashtoreth worship was intensely sexual, and she was represented at worship sites by "Asherim" (Ex. 34:13; Deut. 12:3; Judg. 6:25; 1 Kings 14:23-24; 16:33) which seem to have been wooden poles (Ex. 34:13; Deut. 7:5; 12:3; 16:21; Mic. 5:13) that could also have served as phallic symbols.[4]

Solomon was punished in later life for joining his pagan wives in sexual worship of Ashtoreth (1 Kings 11:4-6, 31-33); and following Solomon's reign, kings of Judah either pleased God or angered him depending on whether they rid the land of Ashtoreth sexual worship (1 Kings 15:12-13; 22:46; 2 Kings 23:7) or led their people into it again (2 Chron. 21:11-15). One of these, King Josiah of Judah, earns special praise for throwing out cult prostitutes who were actually usurping worship in God's temple at Jerusalem (2 Kings 23:7).

The most notorious of sexual worshipers in scripture, however, are King Ahab of Israel and his pagan queen Jezebel, "daughter of Ethbaal king of the Sidonians" (1 Kings 16:31). Jezebel turned Ashtoreth sexual worship into the national religion of Israel, even to the point of feeding 400 prophets of the goddess at her own table (1 Kings 18:19). That is, she provided room and board at government expense. Therefore we are told, "Ahab did more to provoke the LORD, the God of Israel, to anger than all the kings of Israel who were before him" (1 Kings 16:33).

As a consequence, Jezebel becomes the prototype for any woman who leads God's people to reject his prohibition against mixing sex and religion.

When Christ judges a first-century woman at the church in Thyatira, he calls her *Jezebel.* Why? Because she was claiming to be a *prophetess* (someone who speaks for God) while at the same time seducing Christians to commit sexual immorality (Rev. 2:20-23) apparently justified as a higher sort of spiritual worship.

If sexual prohibitions in the Bible are not arbitrary, what does the prohibition against sexual worship protect? Most directly it protects the high value of personal relationship in God's design for sex. Sexual worship treats human sex partners simply as *vehicles* for manipulating cosmic power. They are not persons with whom you relate in their own right or lovers who are loved for their own sake. But the biblical prohibition also guards the tremendous value of intimacy, selflessness, and complexity in God's wonderful plan for sex as it should be. Using a sex partner for worship *through acts of sex* not only treats that person as a tool, it destroys sexual intimacy, practices sex in selfish or self-centered ways, and treats sex as if it concerned the *spiritual* dimension of sex in ways that essentially deny the value of other dimensions.

God's prohibition of sexual worship also helps assure that sex remains exclusive, fruitful, and complementary. While sexual worship might not always erase these values completely, it does attack them quite often. Cult prostitutes and shamans often tend to be either homosexual or bisexual. Engaging in acts of sexual worship with temple prostitutes might be excused as a matter of serving the common good but is usually motivated by selfish reasons. And, of course, God's prohibition limiting moral sex to lifelong marriage also automatically precludes sex with temple prostitutes for any reason.

No Sexual Commerce (Economic Prostitution)

The Bible addresses two different sorts of prostitution—*spiritualized* prostitution and *economic* prostitution—and God firmly opposes both. God not only rejects sexual prostitution mixed with worship and motivated for spiritual reasons, he also opposes the sort of prostitution that links sex or sexual stimulation with commerce.

In Leviticus God commands Israel, "Do not profane your daughter by making her a prostitute" (Lev. 19:29); and in Deuteronomy he adds, "You shall not bring the fee of a [female] prostitute or the wages of a dog [a male prostitute] into the house of the Lord your God . . . for both of these are an abomination to the LORD your God" (Deut. 23:18). The terms in these passages are not the ones used for cult prostitutes, which goes to show that in these passages God is addressing commercial—not religious—prostitution. In fact, we see that God so thoroughly detests sexual commerce, he even rejects the money earned from it.

By definition, sex-as-commerce means paying (or accepting payment) for sex with *strangers*—with people you most likely never met before and neither know nor ever care to know on a personal, lasting basis. So when Solomon warns against being seduced by prostitutes, it is "lest strangers take their fill of your strength, and your labors [all the money you earn] go to the house of a foreigner" (Prov. 5:10).

Solomon also says that commercialized sex reduces a person to the status of food—it treats them like a cheap commodity. "Do not desire her beauty in your heart," he says, "and do not let her capture you with her eyelashes; for the price of a prostitute is only a loaf of bread" (Prov. 6:25-26). A person is reduced to nothing more than a meal ticket.

Later, Paul explains that prostitution does not even make sense by accepted commercial standards. In commercial transactions, moral lines depend on ownership, and Paul argues that prostitution does not even make sense in the marketplace. In commerce, to buy or sell anything requires that we first own it, and Paul reminds readers, "You are not your own, for you were bought with a price. So glorify God in your body" (1 Cor. 6:19-20).

Of course commercial sex also happens to be adultery, but scripture reveals there is something worse with adultery that is for sale than with adultery that is based on some sort of personal relationship. Both violate marriage and are very seriously wrong, but adultery for profit is worse than adultery for free. The difference comes out in something God says at a point when he runs out of patience with flagrant sexual sin. At that point, he declares, "I will not [no longer] punish your daughters when they play the whore, nor your brides when they commit [normal] adultery; for the men themselves go aside with prostitutes" (Hos. 4:14). God is not changing his mind on the morality of normal adultery, rather he is saying here that tolerating prostitution is even worse than average adultery. If fathers and husbands think that adulterous sex with prostitutes is acceptable, with no relational affection at all, then why should they expect God to punish daughters and wives for adulterous sex that may at least be relational and affectionate?

When sex is commercialized—reduced to economics and sold to anyone willing to pay an asking price—what is lost in the process? What does the prohibition of economic prostitution protect? The answer is just about every single value in God's master plan for man-woman sexual relationships. When sex is commercialized, a personal relationship between sexual partners becomes irrelevant. That sort of thing just gets in the way. Rather than valuing sex as something exclusive, intimate, fruitful, selfless, and complex, commercial prostitution treats sex as if it were mechanical (not personal), common (not exclusive), shallow (not intimate), unproductive (not fruitful), self-centered (not selfless), and simple (not complex). The only positive value not necessarily destroyed is the profound value of complementary union, but even this eroded in the end. Prostitution often capitalizes on the attraction of sexual differences, men for women and women for men (it often *may* but *not always,* for even this sometimes gets erased). Commercial sex sells whatever the market demands, and if the market demands same-sex gratification then the principle of uniting corresponding difference is destroyed along with the rest. God's prohibition against sex for economic reasons is designed to help keep it wonderfully personal, exclusive, intimate, fruitful, selfless, complex, and (in some cases) complementary.

No Homosexual Sex

God also definitely prohibits sex between members of the same gender. Within God's plan, sex is meant to unite a man and a woman in such a profound way that it not only blesses themselves but blesses others as well. And this is so tremendously valuable that anything contrary is prohibited by the one who came up with that design in the first place.

The biblical prohibition is both simple and direct. The command simply states: "You shall not lie [not have sexual relations] with a male as with a woman; it is an abomination [something calling for urgent moral judgment]" (Lev. 18:22). No qualifications. No conditions. No restricted relevance or application. And, while the way the prohibition is stated in Leviticus is specific to men, Paul shows that the general moral prohibition covers lesbian relations between women as well. "For this reason God gave them up to dishonorable passions. For their women exchanged natural relations for those that are contrary to nature" (Rom. 1:26).

Some contemporary readers try limiting application of the prohibition by distinguishing *constitutional* homosexuality (the idea that people exist who have a natural homosexual orientation that is biologically fixed and never changes) from homosexual acts by non-homosexuals (assuming the idea, of course, that people exist who behave in ways that go against their natural sexual desires). Based on making this distinction, they go on to suggest that the biblical prohibition of homosexual behavior applies only to non-homosexuals and says nothing about homosexual sex being wrong for *constitutional* homosexuals.

So how should we respond? First, we are obligated to note that the biblical prohibition addresses behavior, not status. It rules out same-sex behavior for absolutely everyone *without mentioning any exception or condition.* The prohibition is stated in terms that are universal, absolute, and unconditional and that simply leave no room for restrictions based on anything at all, including speculations arising from (future) theories regarding human psychology or biology. Any such possibility is made irrelevant. "If a man lies with a male as with a woman [no exceptions], both of them have committed an abomination" (Lev. 20:13). No one is excused, no matter what.

Second, despite this unconditional language, some will still object that, when God's prohibition against homosexual sex was instituted, science did not know what it knows today, and should we not make allowances to bring the values of scripture up-to-date? To this we reply that the prohibition was not something issued by men, but God, and no scientist will ever know more about human life than our Creator. The way the prohibition is put in Leviticus (Lev. 18:22; 20:13) not only was inspired by God but was dictated to Moses by God in audible form. We therefore must assume the Levitical prohibitions are stated as clearly and completely, and with all the nuance God thinks necessary.

Third, God adds something important to the end of Leviticus 20:13 that, understood correctly, means no one may ever blame homosexual behavior on how they are made by God. After calling both sexual partners to account, God concludes by saying "their blood is upon them" (Lev. 20:13). This is a very strong blame statement, and because the speaker is God himself, he is quite literally saying, "no one can ever excuse homosexual behavior by claiming I made them in some way that excuses same-sex relationships." No matter what scientists or social engineers ever think or say, God has already denied that claim. Nothing in the way people are made makes any difference to applying of the prohibition. Homosexual sex is wrong for everyone—no matter what.

Most of what the Bible says on homosexual sex is terribly negative. It is judged by God (Lev. 18:22; 20:13; Rom. 1:26-27; 1 Tim. 1:8-10), blamed on the participants (Lev. 20:13), and made an example of the sort of thing that without repentance keeps a person from entering the kingdom of God (1 Cor. 6:9; Rev. 22:15). But in the midst of all this warning and condemnation, there is one positive message—one ray of shining hope breaking in on a sea of black.

Anyone (again, without exception) who has ever violated God's prohibition of homosexual sex can, we are told, repent, forsake their sin, be forgiven, and be totally cleansed. After including "men who practice homosexuality" in a list of those who "will not inherit the kingdom of God," Paul goes on to say, "And such were some of you. But you were washed, you were sanctified, you were justified in the name of the Lord Jesus Christ and by the Spirit of our God" (1 Cor. 6:9-11). Not only can homosexuals be forgiven, they can change. Homosexuals can become *former* homosexuals—"such were some of you." No practicing, unrepentant homosexual will be allowed to inherit the kingdom of God, but their exclusion is totally *unnecessary.* It is *self-imposed.* On the other hand, repentant, former homosexuals will be in heaven, and that is a promise straight from God.

The prohibition of homosexual sex obviously protects the tremendous value God assigns to complementary union in sexual relationships. By God's design, sex involves a relationship that brings corresponding differences together in grand union much greater than simply adding one identical thing to another. But there is more. Homosexual sex not only rejects the necessity of complementary union in a sexual relationship, it also runs against the biblical requirement that sex always should be fruitful (productive) and selfless (sacrificial). God's prohibition of homosexual sex sets up a barrier to protect these positively valuable sexual principles. Finally, even though same-sex unions are sometimes personal, intimate, complex, and perhaps even exclusive, they usually are not. Why? Because they tend to be based on a totally different set of values—such as variety, choice, entertainment, independence, and anonymity—that together make sex impersonal, common, shallow, and one-dimensional.

No Sex with Animals (Bestiality)

Although it is not mentioned as frequently as some other prohibitions, sex with animals must also be considered high on the list of sexual behaviors prohibited by God. The Creator's gift of sex is species-specific and was not given for us to link up with just anything at all. Men and women are designed for one another, and sex with animals is horribly wrong however anyone feels about it. Most people are revolted by the idea, but mainly for hygienic reasons. According to scripture, however, the important thing at stake is not so much health as morality. Sex with animals is far outside the boundaries God has put in place to protect the high value of sex in his original plan.

Ancient Egyptians practiced sex with animals, especially in connection with worshiping gods they associated with goats,[5] and their Canaanite neighbors carried on much the same thing (Lev. 18:24). So when God called the Israelites out of Egypt and gave them the land of Canaan, he made clear that sex with animals was absolutely prohibited. "And you shall not lie [give your emission] with any animal and so make yourself unclean with it, neither shall any woman give herself to an animal to lie with it [to have sexual relations with it]: it is a perversion" (Lev. 18:23).

Anyone who violated the prohibition was cursed (Deut. 27:21), which under the Levitical system meant the community must be cleansed (Lev. 18:29) and the perpetrators (both human and animal) must be put to death (Ex. 22:19). The prohibition (with its penalty) is given to men and women equally. "If a man lies with an animal, he shall surely be put to death, and you shall kill the animal. If a woman approaches any animal and lies with it, you shall kill the woman and the animal; they shall surely be put to death; their blood is upon them" (Lev. 20:15-16). As with prohibitions against adultery and prostitution, gender is irrelevant, and as with the prohibition of homosexual behavior, God says no one is to blame except the violator himself or herself.

But why should God take bestiality so seriously? The Bible answers in two ways—one going back to creation and one having to do with values God wants maintained in our sexual relationships.

After Adam finished naming the animals, he discovered that "there was not found a helper fit for him" (Gen. 2:20). He was looking for a sexual partner, and no animal could supply what he needed. Then, in direct contrast to what no animal is fit to do, God made Eve—a woman who is defined by the fact that she is the only being in all creation suitable to be a sexual partner for the man. No animal could fulfill the sexual relationship God intended for Adam. Only a human female was suitable. So the first reason God is serious about prohibiting sex with animals is because it confuses human life with animal life and attacks the very nature of human sexual identity. Humans are not animals—we bear the image of God—and sex with animals violates that fundamental identity.

But in addition to violating human sexual identity, sex with animals also destroys everything that makes sex such a positive gift of God. Sex with animals is impersonal, common, shallow, unproductive, selfish, and one-dimensional (merely physical) while God designed sex to be personal, exclusive, intimate, fruitful, selfless, and complex. Most important of all, human sex with animals can never be complementary. It may involve partners who are sexually *different,* but they do not *correspond.* No animal can ever *complement* the sexual nature of any human partner no matter what gender it happens to be.

9

Biblical Prohibitions Guard Moral Sex (II)

No Sex or Marriage with Close Relatives (Incest)

We have already noted how important it is in God's design to honor gender differences and to separate human life from animal life. To these great distinctions, God adds another critical difference without which sex is never moral. This third difference concerns how closely sexual partners are related and leads to prohibiting sex between near relatives—whether based on blood or marriage, and whether partners even try to legitimize their relationship by getting married first.[1]

Like other prohibitions having to do with essential sexual differences (gender difference and species difference), God's prohibition of sex with near relatives is unconditional. "None of you shall approach any one of his close relatives to uncover nakedness [be sexually intimate]" (Lev. 18:6). But while violating this ban is terribly wrong, we put it below others previously covered for one very important reason. While those others were established at creation, God did not ban sex with near relatives until much later.

God issued it first to Moses at Sinai; the prohibition did not exist before that. The sons of Adam and Eve married their sisters. Of course there was at that time no other option (Gen. 4:17, 26), but there was nothing wrong about it either. It was exactly what God intended, and that sort of practice continued for generations. Abraham's brother Nahor married his niece (Gen. 11:29); Abraham's wife, Sarah, was a half-sister, "the daughter of my father though not the daughter of my mother" (Gen. 20:12); and when Isaac took Rebekah to be his wife we find she was the daughter of "Bethuel the son of Milcah, the wife of Nahor, Abraham's brother" (24:15), which made her a first cousin once removed. For generations after Adam and Eve, there was nothing wrong with marrying a near relative. Up until Sinai, marrying a close relative was not immoral because there simply was no prohibition against it. But then, at Sinai, God added something new. After Sinai, sex with a close relative was disallowed and marriage could not make it right.

In Leviticus, a single general prohibition against sex or marriage with a near relative (Lev. 18:6) is supplemented by a long list of more particular prohibitions, apparently because God wanted to leave no room for misunderstanding. No sex or marriage is allowed involving: a son with his own biological mother (18:7; 20:11); a stepson with a stepmother (18:8; 20:11; also Deut. 22:30); a brother with a full sister (Lev. 18:9; 20:17); a brother with a half-sister (18:11; 20:17)[2]; a grandfather with a granddaughter (18:10); a nephew with an aunt by blood on either side of the family (18:12-13; 20:19); a nephew with an aunt by marriage (20:20); a father-in-law with a daughter-in-law (18:15; 20:12); a brother-in-law with a sister-in-law (18:16; 20:21)[3]; being sexually intimate with a mother and her daughter at the same time (18:17; 20:14); and being intimate with sisters at the same time (18:18). Some close relations are not specifically mentioned in Leviticus—for example, fathers with daughters, stepfathers with stepdaughters, uncles with nieces, grandmothers with grandsons, or mothers-in-law with sons-in-law. But the fact that marriage of these close relations is not mentioned specifically does not mean they are allowed—first, because every near family relationship (mentioned or not) is covered by the general prohibition (Lev. 18:6); and second, because it is obvious the list is not intended to be completely exhaustive. Sex between mothers-in-law and sons-in-law (not mentioned in Leviticus) is singled out and cursed in Deuteronomy 27:23.

Although sex or marriage with any near relative is ruled immoral by this one prohibition, the range of punishments given to Moses shows that God considers some of the particular violations to be more serious than others. Sex between a son and his mother, whether biological or step (Lev. 20:11), between a father-in-law and daughter-in-law (v. 12), and with a woman and her mother at the same time (v. 14) are considered most serious and call for a death penalty. Sex or marriage between a brother and sister, whether full or half, is somewhat less serious and is enforced by banishment, not death (v. 17). Sex or marriage with an aunt related by marriage (not by blood) is punished by the community in some non-specified way that probably involved public censure ("they shall bear their sin"), and is also punished separately by God, who says he will keep the couple from having children (v. 20). Sex or marriage with a sister-in-law is punished by God with childlessness but not by the community (v. 21), and sex or marriage with an aunt who is related by blood ("your mother's sister" or "your father's sister") and therefore may never have been married to anyone else is punished only by a civil sanction ("they shall bear their iniquity") and nothing is said about any additional punishment added by God (v. 19).

Because the prohibition against sex or marriage with near relatives did not exist before Sinai, one might wonder if it was ever supposed to be universal (given to others beyond the people of Israel) or permanent (to last beyond the government of Israel in the Promised Land). But Paul in the New Testament settles both questions by showing that the prohibition remains in force and applies to Gentile converts in the church at Corinth. Corinthian Christians were not Jews, and the nation of Israel itself was under Roman rule at that time, but none of that affects Paul's application. He starts by saying, "It is actually reported that there is sexual immorality among you, and of a kind that is not tolerated even among pagans, for a man has his father's wife" (1 Cor. 5:1). But then, proceeding on, Paul indicates that while the prohibition itself is universal and timeless, the punishments given in Leviticus are not. Although the Levitical code specifies death (Lev. 20:11), Paul instead orders that "you are to deliver this man to Satan for the destruction of the flesh, so that his spirit may be saved in the day of the Lord" (1 Cor. 5:5). The sanction given is severe, but it also is something short of immediate physical death.

So what does this prohibition protect? If sex with a near relative takes place outside of marriage it opposes the same values violated by all forms of adultery—it attacks exclusivity (uniqueness) and selflessness (sacrificial love), and may also to some extent undermine personal quality (relationship), intimacy (depth), fruitfulness (productivity), complexity (multiple dimensions) and complementarity (corresponding difference). But even if a couple gets married before starting sexual relations, sex with a near family relative *still* threatens the critically important qualities of complementarity and fruitfulness.

When the human race was young, God seems to have overlooked the matter for strategic reasons. But once populating the earth was off to a good start, he imposed a greater restriction that even denies marriage between near relatives. Why did he do this? Only because it threatens the tremendous value of complementarity and fruitfulness when forming truly ideal sexual relationships. So long as a couple is married, nearness of family relationship has very little to do with maintaining personal quality, exclusivity, intimacy, selflessness, and complexity in their sexual relationship with each other. But if they are near relatives, then their relationship cannot express as much complementary *difference* as God thinks we must have to fully satisfy his ideal, and it also inevitably ends up lowering either the quality or quantity (or both) of the sort of *productivity* God wants every man-woman relationship to achieve.

NO PEDOPHILIA

Pedophilia, the act of sex between adults with children, is fast emerging in our culture as the next new boundary to attack in favor of *sexual liberation.*[4] But, while sex with children is never specifically mentioned in the Bible, it is nevertheless ruled out rather clearly by combining several other well established prohibitions. If an electric fence surrounds a building with signs saying "No Trespassing," there is no special need to also add "but if you trespass anyway, then do not walk on the grass." Why? Because the first prohibition implies the second as well. So, while pedophilia is not *explicitly* prohibited in scripture, it is prohibited in a very strong *implicit* sense.

The electric fence in front of God's prohibition of pedophilia is the combination of prohibitions against sex outside of marriage, against homosexual sex, and against sex with any near relative. When these are taken together, it is impossible for adults to have unmarried sex with children under any circumstance. Pedophilia is totally prohibited.

Now, it is interesting to note the Bible never gives a fixed age limit for morally approved sex between a male and female who are married to each other. In this case the only moral boundary that matters in the absolute sense is heterosexual marriage to a person who is not a near relative. Beyond that, age differences are governed by prudence, which includes selfless concern for the lifelong health and welfare of a marriage partner.

The last word on God's prohibition of pedophilia, however, was given by Jesus, who sharply warned adults against ever corrupting children. He explained that adults dealing with children are dealing also with him (Matt. 18:5; Mark 9:37), and revealed that every child has a guardian angel who sees "the face of my Father who is in heaven" (Matt. 18:10). And the most stern warning Jesus ever gave was directed at adults who lead children into sin. To these Jesus said, "whoever causes one of these little ones who believe in me to sin, it would be better for him to have a great millstone fastened around his neck and to be drowned in the depth of the sea" (v. 6).

The Bible's indirect prohibition of pedophilia is related to the value of keeping sex exclusive, fruitful, selfless and complementary. A commitment to these biblical values serves to ensure that sexual relationships are always truly unique (are not shared around), truly productive (are not simply consumed), truly loving in a self-sacrificing way (do not merely use another person for self-gratification), and truly unite corresponding differences (do not combine partners not truly *fit* or *suitable* for one another).

No Sexual Violence

Another very important though implicit prohibition in scripture rules out combining sex with violence. *Sadism* is sexual gratification that includes inflicting pain or humiliation on a partner; *masochism* is sexual gratification that involves allowing a partner to inflict pain or humiliation on you; and *spousal abuse* is when one marriage partner either tries to harm or succeeds in harming the other. These are all forms of sexual violence, and they all are incompatible with God's design for the man-woman sexual relationship. Sexual violence is clearly prohibited in the Bible, but like the prohibition of pedophilia it is implicit rather than explicit. It also is excluded by broader moral requirements that always rule out violent sex.

When God first established marriage, at creation, he specified that "a man shall leave his father and his mother and hold fast to his wife" (Gen. 2:24). In this original marriage formula, the word translated "hold fast" carries the sense of clinging to someone with intense loyalty and affection. It calls a couple to work at maintaining a very intimate connection and leaves no room for one to later on attack the other by inflicting suffering, pain, humiliation, or abuse.

The sort of love God requires in all we do is patient and kind, never irritable or resentful (1 Cor. 13:4-5). And Paul explains that Christians must never do anything out of selfish ambition or conceit; rather, we are to always "in humility count others more significant than yourselves" (Phil. 2:3). If this is what God requires of everyone in all personal relationships, then how much more does it apply to the sexual relationship linking husbands with wives?

God orders people in the Old Testament to "put away violence and oppression" (Ezek. 45:9), and husbands in the New Testament are told to "love your wives, as Christ loved the church and gave himself up for her" (Eph. 5:25). These texts all imply that God very strongly prohibits any form of sexual violence, and the only reason it is not mentioned specifically is because he actually requires so much more.

So what does prohibiting sexual violence protect? Most of all it protects intimacy (relational depth), selflessness (sacrificial, self-giving love), and complexity (mature relationship at all levels). Sexual violence destroys all three. It makes intimacy literally impossible, it is driven by a form of selfishness so powerful that it seeks to harm a wife or husband on purpose, and it reduces sex to something rather like war. But while sexual violence destroys these valuable qualities, God's prohibition of sexual violence helps to keep them in place. The prohibition also helps ensure that sex does not lose the value of personal relationship, fruitfulness, or complementarity. While these can sometimes survive threats of sexual violence, they hardly flourish under violent conditions, and God's prohibition provides the sort of environment in which personal relationship, fruitfulness, and complementarity are able to thrive and grow.

No Lustful Sexual Desires (Inner Adultery)

God not only prohibits adultery that is expressed physically, he also prohibits inward adultery that others may never know about and that may never be expressed in any outward act. That is, God prohibits adulterous thoughts—the harboring of desires for sexual activities that stand outside boundaries marked by other moral prohibitions such as those ruling out sex outside of marriage, commercial sex, homosexual sex, pedophilia, incest, or even immodesty. We have observed that Jesus taught that adulterous thoughts already violate God's general prohibition against pursuing sex outside of marriage. "I say to you that everyone who looks at a woman with lustful intent has already committed adultery with her in his heart" (Matt. 5:28). But even though lustful thoughts are already covered in some degree by the general ban against all sex outside of marriage, we are listing God's opposition to lustful desires as a separate prohibition because the Bible itself so often focuses on the immorality of lust apart from any outward action.

In the Ten Commandments, God himself distinguishes between the seventh commandment, which prohibits adultery (Ex. 20:14; Deut. 5:18), and the tenth, which prohibits coveting your neighbor's wife (Ex. 20:17; Deut. 5:21). In most cases, coveting another man's wife means desiring to be intimate with her in a sexual sense. It is not about merely wanting to parade her around like a sort of trophy or just being interested in access to her bank account or kids. Solomon is quite direct about warning his son to never entertain any thoughts about sex with a neighbor's adulterous wife. "Do not desire her beauty in your heart, and do not let her capture you with her eyelashes. . . . Can a man carry fire next to his chest and his clothes not be burned? Or can one walk on hot coals and his feet not be scorched? So is he who goes in to his neighbor's wife; none who touches her will go unpunished" (Prov. 6:25-29).

The key to winning or losing against sexual temptation depends on what happens in the *mind*, or what scripture sometimes calls the *heart*. Solomon shows that the key is "not desir[ing] her beauty in your heart" (Prov. 6:25).

James says the same thing when he explains that "each person is tempted when he is lured and enticed by his own desire," and if wrong desire is allowed to grow, it "gives birth to sin, and sin when it is fully grown brings forth death" (James 1:14-15). Therefore, God simply commands, "So guard yourselves in your spirit, and let none of you be faithless to the wife of your youth" (Mal. 2:15).

God says we are each responsible for how we think or feel about sex. No matter how others try to excuse it, he says, each person can indeed do something about it. No one is exempt. We are all able and are therefore responsible to keep our thoughts and desires pure (Phil. 4:8). Paul tells Timothy to "flee youthful passions and [to instead] pursue righteousness, faith, love, and peace . . . from a pure heart" (2 Tim. 2:22). Christians in Rome are urged to "put on the Lord Jesus Christ, and make no provision for the flesh, to gratify its desires" (Rom. 13:14). Others may never know what is going on in your mind. But God always knows and is holding you accountable. Some day he is going to judge all those who "have eyes full of adultery" (2 Pet. 2:14).

Harboring lustful sexual desires (having "eyes full of adultery") destroys the moral qualities of personal relationship, exclusivity, intimacy, fruitfulness, selflessness, and complexity. It makes sex impersonal by gravitating toward satisfaction that occurs either before or even without any relationship with an actual person. It wanders from one sexual image or object to another, is satisfied with shallow sex, only wants to consume sex like a commodity with no interest in producing anything beyond the experience itself, focuses only on self-satisfaction, and is entirely one-dimensional. God's prohibition against harboring lustful sexual desires helps to keep sex worthwhile by guarding against losing so much positive value.

No Intentional Gender Confusion

Although it is mentioned in scripture only once and so may not carry as much weight as the greater prohibitions against adultery, sexual worship, prostitution, homosexual sex, sex with animals, or even lust, God also absolutely prohibits trying to confuse gender identity by cross-dressing. In the law he gave Moses, God stipulated that, "A woman shall not wear a man's garment, nor shall a man put on a woman's cloak," and the prohibition is underscored by saying, "for whoever does these things is an abomination to the LORD your God" (Deut. 22:5).

The ban specifically addressed cross-dressing, but the moral issue was trying to confuse gender differences and acting as if they do not really matter. But gender difference matters very much to God. He is the one who made

Adam a man and Eve a woman, he is the one who declared that Adam alone needed a relationship that only creating a woman could satisfy (Gen. 2:18), and he now is the one who still insists that honoring gender difference really matters not only biologically but morally as well.

Because a person's attitude and intentions are at the heart of this prohibition, its application depends a great deal on cultural perception. What is viewed as men's clothing as opposed to women's clothing varies from culture to culture and from time to time. So, what the prohibition really aims to restrict is wanting to confuse the importance of gender difference *however that may be expressed* in particular situations. Cultures express the value of honoring gender difference in various ways, but all cultures have recognized there is a difference, and no culture has *ever yet* pretended there is no difference at all.

Some might wonder if God's prohibition of gender confusion by cross-dressing was meant for people other than Israel. Can we be sure it was meant to apply to people in other cultures and times? I believe so. First, the prohibition is underscored by stating that anyone who disregards it "is an abomination *to the Lord your God*" (emphasis added). Since the moral character of God never changes, he must still think it matters regardless of culture or time.

Second, the word "abomination" that underscores what is wrong with cross-dressing is the same word God uses to justify driving out the Canaanites: "because of these abominations the LORD your God is driving them out before you" (Deut. 18:12). Nothing God calls "abominable" is ever mild; the word indicates sins that are especially repugnant to God and sure to bring divine wrath on those responsible.[5] The level of God's moral concern involved in this prohibition is ultimate and cosmological, not just cultural or individual.

Third, the prohibition is connected with sexual prohibitions against homosexual sex and lust. Gender confusion by cross-dressing does not necessarily involve having sex with another person, but it does stir up sexual thoughts and desires that lead in the direction of homosexual activity. And, since homosexual sex and lust are prohibited regardless of culture or time, then prohibiting intentional gender confusion has to apply broadly as well.

God's prohibition against intentional gender confusion may only appear once in the Bible, but it serves to maintain some very important sexual values including intimacy, fruitfulness, selflessness, complexity, and especially complementarity. Disregarding the importance of gender difference attacks genuine sexual intimacy. It treats sex as something shallow, transient, and superficial, and the prohibition is one more barrier to stop that from happening. It also keeps gender confusion from turning sex into something unproductive, self-centered, and merely one-dimensional. But the most obvious role served by the prohibition against intentional gender confusion is guarding the tremendous importance of maintaining corresponding difference in a relationship linking sexual partners. Cross-dressing sends a message that corresponding difference between partners does not matter, and God's prohibition says that it does matter.

No Sex During a Woman's Period

Along with other absolute prohibitions, biblical sexual morality also includes a specific ban on sex between husbands and wives during the wife's monthly cycle of menstrual bleeding. God first tells Moses that, "You shall not approach a woman to uncover her nakedness while she is in her menstrual uncleanness" (Lev. 18:19). Later he adds details: "If a man lies with a woman during her menstrual period and uncovers her nakedness, he has made naked her fountain, and she has uncovered the fountain of her blood. Both of them shall be cut off from among their people" (Lev. 20:18).

As with God's prohibitions against adultery and sex with animals, this prohibition also holds men and women both responsible. Neither can excuse his or her behavior by blaming the other. And, while the punishment (cutting violators off from their people) may have applied only to Israel, the fact that it calls for the same sanction ordered for incestuous sex between a brother and sister (Lev. 20:17) shows that God considers these offenses to be at the same level. The punishment does not call for immediate death, but it certainly is severe and probably indicates banishment or some sort of censure that the neighbors would all know about.

Along with generally prohibiting sex during menstruation, God sets a specific block of time each month during which couples must refrain from sex. "When a woman has a discharge, and the discharge in her body is blood, she shall be in her menstrual impurity for seven days, and whoever touches her shall be unclean" (Lev. 15:19). And, although menstruation ceases with pregnancy, a similar time of separation is imposed following the birth of a child (12:2-5).

We should not easily assume that these stipulations are merely ceremonial, relate only to Israel, or are limited to ancient history and not relevant for anyone today. First, when God gave the prohibition to Moses, he listed it right along with prohibitions against adultery, incest, homosexual sex, and animal sex. Since no one doubts that *these* prohibitions continue to be relevant (since they were never merely ceremonial, national, or temporary), we have no basis for treating the no-sex-during-menstruation prohibition any differently. Second, we see that God takes the prohibition very seriously because respecting it is used to mark someone who is "righteous and does what is just and right" (Ezek. 18:5). Third, violating the ban is included (with incest, adultery, murder, and extortion) among ways in which God complains that people have "forgotten me" by despising what he calls "my holy things" (22:8-12).

Nor should we dismiss this prohibition as if it only concerned hygiene and did not necessarily set up any moral boundary. The prohibition is indeed moral and not just hygienic, first because God says it is, and second because of the values it protects. First, God just claims straight out that the prohibition sets a moral standard when he says a man who respects it is "righteous and does what is just and right." Biblical righteousness always has to do with the way behavior lines up with God's moral standards, so this reference by itself is strong evidence that God treats the prohibition as a matter of moral duty. It deals with righteousness, and not just with cleanliness.

Second, the limitation involves morality because it preserves values God thinks are critical for moral sex. Sex that exposes a woman's menstrual flow is not only messy and unhygienic but also selfish and essentially impersonal. Even when it occurs within marriage, sex during menstruation treats a woman more like an object than a person. It amounts to sex regardless of what is best for her, and God's prohibition helps to ensure that sex is selfless (expresses sacrificial love) and always remains personal (is genuinely relational).

But that is not all. In the final analysis, the one moral value perhaps most strongly affected by the no-sex-during-menstruation prohibition is the value of building and maintaining a deep, profound level of sexual intimacy. Now here is a real paradox. How can anyone say that *not* having sex helps to build *intimacy* in a sexual relationship? Would it not rather be logical to assume that intimacy is a function of *more* sex, not *less*? Well, in fact, no. The paradox is that we humans are wired so that we build up respect and appreciation for things we miss, and we take for granted, grow weary of, and become disrespectful of things that appear automatic because they happen all the time. All human relationships must have freedom to *breathe,* and if relational *space* is denied then a person feels *smothered,* not *loved.* Insisting on sex all the time, even during a woman's period, destroys relational intimacy, while giving her space helps it grow even stronger.

Comments on the experience of a young Jewish woman, recounted by Wendy Shalit in *A Return to Modesty,* illustrates this point very nicely. Asked what drew her to the practice of prohibiting sex during menstruation, she explained:

> When I was growing up, my parents would have a horrible fight at least once every month. Yeah, screaming, dishes flying, and stuff. "I can't stand your father," you know. Then they would make up, and for three weeks everything would be very kissy-kissy between them. No, sometimes they'd fight more than once a month, but usually it was once a month, like clockwork.
>
> Well, so when I first heard of Jewish modesty law, and heard about the no-sex-while-the-wife-is-menstruating rule, that's what I thought of first. My parents with their once-a-month fighting. The sheer brilliance of it! Having this time of separation, to create distance so that you can be reunited, but to have the distance created in a way other than fighting? I would never have come up with that myself. I was kind of awed by the ingeniousness, you know, of all these rules.
>
> My husband and I started trying it, after four years of marriage. Early, when I was 25. I was getting worried because we were starting to be like my parents. And it's the most amazing thing what it's done for our marriage—just this one simple rule. We have the mystery and the newness of a love affair, but we don't have to have affairs, and we don't have to fight. We still quibble, but I mean, who doesn't anyway?
>
> The important point to me is that we don't fight the way we used to anymore, or the way my parents used to. You know, the kind of fighting that comes from getting bored? That we never have because we never take each other for granted. Because each month, there's this separation.
>
> I've heard people say that the no-sex-while-the-wife-is-menstruating rule is sexist, because it comes from thinking women are unclean, and I understand what they mean. But I think because they've never tried it, it's hard for them to see what's really going on. What could be sexist about having a wonderful marriage?[6]

The answer to Shalit's question is, nothing! Nothing is wrong with having a wonderful marriage! The prohibition, in fact, protects something wonderful. It protects the precious moral (not just practical) value of building up and guarding sexual intimacy in marriage. And understanding that did not begin with some smart old Hebrews who just happened to think it up on their own. It is ingenious and brilliant because the prohibition comes from the All-Wise Creator who designed sex in the first place.

This finishes our coverage of everything in God's moral revelation on sex that is absolutely prohibited—on sex that is prohibited under any circumstance whatsoever without any exceptions at all. But the Bible also includes a few prohibitions that are not quite absolute. We put these lower on the list because, although they address types of behavior God generally opposes, he also allows some flexibility under limited circumstances that either permit some sort of exception or involve some degree of personal interpretation. These are what we turn to next.

Strong Opposition to Divorce

The best-known and most important of these remaining, perhaps not entirely absolute sexual prohibitions is God's opposition to divorce. The Bible treats marriage as terribly important, something sacred, a covenant institution defined by and accountable to God. So, because God takes marriage seriously, he strongly opposes breaking up marriages once they are formed.

God's general prohibition of divorce is clear in both the Old and New Testaments. It first appears in Malachi, where the prophet reports,

> the LORD is acting as the witness between you and the wife of your youth, because you have broken faith with her, though she is your partner, the wife of your marriage covenant. Has not the LORD made them one? In flesh and spirit they are his. . . . So guard yourself in your spirit, and do not break faith with the wife of your youth. "I hate divorce," says the LORD God of Israel, "and I hate a man's covering himself with violence as well as with his garment," says the LORD Almighty. So guard yourself in your spirit, and do not break faith (Mal. 2:14-16, NIV).

Jesus repeats the general prohibition again more briefly in debate with Pharisees: "What therefore God has joined together, let not man separate" (Matt. 19:6; Mark 10:9). And Paul applies it to Christians at Corinth:

> To the married I give this charge (not I, but the Lord): the wife should not separate from her husband (but if she does, she should remain unmarried or else be reconciled to her husband), and the husband should not divorce his wife (1 Cor. 7:10).

From this record we know God opposes divorce very strongly. He truly hates divorce because he sees it as a form of violence (Mal. 2:16). We also learn that marriage is not something husbands and wives do first on their own and then ask God to bless. Rather, they are joined in marriage by God (Mal. 2:15; Matt. 19:6). And so, because it is something God does to a couple (not something couples do to themselves), it is wrong and horribly presumptuous for anyone to act as if marriage could be ended based only on the couple's own decisions or actions.

Violating the prohibition matters because it attempts to unmake something God has made. It tries to erase something for which couples must answer to God and not merely to each other or even to the church. The Bible says, "In flesh and spirit they are his" (Mal. 2:15, NIV). And because nothing we do can undo what God does, marrying someone else after getting wrongly divorced just adds one sin to another. It compounds the sin of divorce with the sin of adultery.

Mark says Jesus taught, "Whoever divorces his wife and marries another commits adultery against her, and if she divorces her husband and marries another, she commits adultery" (Mark 10:11). So no matter whether it is the husband or the wife who initiates it, Jesus says that if either one marries someone else after getting wrongly divorced it becomes a matter of adultery. And Matthew and Luke add that even a third party who marries a wrongly divorced person commits adultery as well (Matt. 5:32; Luke 16:18).

Jesus' disciples were shocked by the standard he set regarding divorce, not because it was more lenient than expected but because it was far stricter than expected: "If such is the case of a man with his wife, it is better not to marry" (Matt. 19:10). They thought it unrealistic, and Jesus did not correct them. He did indeed set a very high standard, one that most would think impossible.

But even though God's prohibition sets a high standard, it is not entirely absolute. God who joins couples in marriage also permits some level of exception under limited conditions. We see this in several places—first in the law of Moses, where God allows divorce based on "some indecency" (*ʿerwat dābār,* Deut. 24:1); second, where Jesus says that "sexual immorality [*porneia*]" is grounds for an exception (Matt. 5:32; 19:9); third, where Jesus warns that putting God first might result in losing your wife (Luke 14:26-33[7]; 18:29-30); and fourth, where Paul indicates that a Christian may accept a divorce initiated by a nonbelieving spouse (1 Cor. 7:15).

God does make some exception to his general prohibition of divorce, but that does not make it ideal. Even where God allows some grounds for divorce, it is the exception, and God's ideal remains fighting to maintain lifelong marriage. When Jesus discussed the proper way to interpret God's allowable exception (Matt. 19:3-12), he prefaced it by saying, "from the beginning it was not so." He meant that we understand God allows making that exception (whatever it is) only as a concession to the way persistent sin—what Jesus called "hardness of heart"—affects family relationships; and while teaching on divorce, Jesus put stress on keeping marriages together, not on seeing how far people could go without becoming guilty of sin.

All evangelicals agree that God strongly opposes divorce and that he also allows some sort of exception. But at that point evangelicals divide over interpreting conditions for permissible divorce and over whether God allows remarriage after permissible divorce.

Division over conditions for morally permissible divorce comes down to whether a Christian can ever *initiate* divorce without becoming guilty of sin after he or she begins to have sex in marriage. Of course, Paul teaches that a Christian may *accept* divorce initiated by an unbelieving spouse (1 Cor. 7:15). But there Paul mentions no grounds allowing a Christian husband or wife to *initiate* divorce. If an unbelieving spouse demands divorce, all that matters then is honoring God's call to peace. So, division among evangelicals over conditions justifying permissible divorce is not about whether a Christian may accept divorce initiated by an unbelieving spouse (whatever reason he or she might have), but is about whether a Christian is ever justified *initiating* divorce himself or herself.

Most evangelicals assume that the grounds God allowed through Moses (*'erwat dābār,* "some indecency") and the grounds Jesus mentioned in explaining the Mosaic grounds (*porneia,* "sexual immorality"), must apply to marriages after a couple starts their sexual relationship. And because both passages use terms that get used for many kinds of sin related to sex, they assume the grounds God allows for permitting divorce must certainly include adultery and may even include more. Furthermore, because the exception Jesus mentioned was given while explaining the grounds God gave through Moses (Matt. 19:7-9; see Deut. 24:1), and since that allowed a person to *initiate* divorce, they conclude that means Jesus allowed Christians to initiate divorce as well.

Everyone taking this majority position agrees that physical adultery gives Christians grounds to initiate divorce, but they do not all agree on whether other grounds are included as well. Some argue that permissible grounds to divorce must include even more because Moses and Jesus both used terms that usually cover more than physical adultery alone,[8] while others resist allowing more than physical adultery as grounds justifying divorce because the more the grounds are expanded the harder it is to reconcile with God's high view of marriage.

Against this majority position, other evangelicals conclude that, while Christians may accept divorce if initiated by an unbelieving spouse, God never allows Christians to initiate divorce themselves, even for adultery.

Those holding this minority position question the majority view for some or all of the following reasons.

First, because scripture says marriage is a covenant (Mal. 2:14; Prov. 2:17) in which obligation to be faithful continues no matter how the other person behaves (Ezek. 16:59-60; Hos. 3:1), they are concerned the majority position treats marriage like a contract in which faithfulness depends on the other person keeping his or her end of the bargain.

Second, because they believe Moses was addressing a stage in Semitic marriage practice called betrothal (that has no parallel in Western culture)—a stage in which couples were legally and morally married for a period before starting sexual relations.[9] In Semitic practice, ending a marriage during the betrothal stage required a divorce (for example, see Matt. 1:18-19), and the broad, rather mild, grounds Moses allowed (*ʿerwat dābār,* "some indecency") fits God's high view of marriage only if the rather mild things included justified divorce only at the betrothal stage and not after a couple began having sex. They also argue that this explains how the Mosaic law on allowing divorce is consistent with Mosaic law denying any grounds for divorce once a woman proves she was a virgin when she first had sex with her husband (Deut. 22:13-19).

Third, because the same part of the Mosaic law that gives grounds for divorce also imposes the death penalty for physical adultery (Deut. 22:22) and therefore the grounds for allowing divorce (*ʿerwat dābār,* "some indecency," Deut. 24:1) could not have included adultery after married couples started having sex without contradicting the required death penalty.

Fourth, because what Jesus said about grounds for allowing divorce was explaining the Mosaic law as it was, nothing else. He did not add to it or change it. So, if adultery was not part of the grounds God allowed through Moses, and since that grounds applied only to the betrothal stage in semitic marriage, (before the sexual relationship began), and since Jesus was not changing what that meant, then we cannot say that Jesus added adultery to allow initiating divorce after married couples start having a sexual relationship.

Fifth, because only the minority interpretation explains how Jesus' disciples could be shocked (Matt. 19:10). Not even allowing divorce for adultery does seem unrealistic to most people. But what is unrealistic about allowing divorce for adultery?

Sixth, because only the minority interpretation explains how Mark, Luke, and Paul could all summarize what Jesus taught on divorce (Mark 10:2-12; Luke 16:18; 1 Cor. 7:10-11) without mentioning grounds for allowing divorce. Why mention something that was not relevant to Gentile readers?

Seventh, because only the minority interpretation explains why Jesus used a broad term (*porneia,* "sexual immorality") rather than the exact term for adultery (*moicheia*) when referring to grounds for allowing divorce. If Jesus had meant adultery, then why would he not use the right word?

Finally, because they believe the conservative side of the majority position (divorce only for physical adultery) depends on taking a view on adultery (that it is nothing more than a physical act) that Jesus himself criticized (Matt. 5:28), while the permissive side (divorce even for unfaithful thoughts) overlooks the disciples' shock and contradicts God's high view of marriage.

Evangelicals are also divided over whether God allows remarriage after permissible divorce. Some reject remarriage even after permissible divorce because Jesus said that parties who are victims of divorce (and are therefore not guilty of getting divorced) will be guilty of adultery if they remarry (Matt. 5:32; Luke 16:18). These also argue that this was the position held by most of the early church; that a covenant joined by God cannot be undone by anything we do; that Malachi says a divorced wife still "is your partner, the wife of your marriage covenant" (Mal. 2:14, NIV); and that Paul says believers who divorce each other "should remain unmarried or else be reconciled" (1 Cor. 7:11).

But other evangelicals disagree and argue that remarriage after morally justified divorce is allowed because, if God gives permission for divorce it is logical to assume that includes permission to remarry as well. They also argue that, while marriage is a covenant, and while no one is allowed to end a covenant established with God, God can end a covenant on his terms even when we cannot; that Paul says believers permitted to accept divorce initiated by unbelieving partners are "not enslaved" or "not bound" (1 Cor. 7:15), and denying remarriage in such cases contradicts that freedom; and that Paul also says a person released from marriage does not commit sin if he or she remarries—"But if you do marry, you have not sinned" (1 Cor. 7:28).

Why then does God oppose divorce so strongly? What is at stake? Considering the positive principles of biblical sexual morality, it is clear that God is very concerned with the value of keeping sex unique to one special relationship, of deepening intimacy against whatever challenges come along, of securing marriage on the basis of self-sacrificial love and commitment, and of ensuring that sex remains living and productive instead of used up and thrown away like a sort of empty container.

Divorce destroys exclusivity by moving from one relationship to another. It allows disappointment of all sorts to interrupt the work on driving intimacy to profound levels, something that results only when couples fight to maintain what they have despite whatever obstacles life throws in their path. Divorce gives up on selfless love and shatters the productive nature of sex by ending the relationship altogether. God hates seeing this happen, and the general prohibition he imposes against divorce keeps all these things to a minimum.

10

Biblical Prohibitions Guard Moral Sex (III)

Strong Opposition to Spiritually Mixed Marriage

Another thing God generally prohibits with qualifications is marriage uniting a godly man or woman with someone who is not. God opposes spiritually mixed marriages. According to scripture, there is nothing immoral with marrying someone of a different race, nationality, or social class. But if you are joined with God, spiritually it is sin to marry someone who is not.

The prohibition against spiritually mixed marriage appears first in the Old Testament, where it is part of a larger restriction given to Israel to keep them separate from pagan neighbors. Before entering the land of Canaan, God commanded,

> [Take care], lest you make a covenant with the inhabitants of the land, and when they whore after their gods and sacrifice to their gods and you are invited, you eat of his sacrifice, and you take of their daughters for your sons, and their daughters whore after their gods and make your sons whore after their gods (Ex. 34:15-16).

The reason for this prohibition was avoiding the risk of spiritual compromise. Sexual intimacy in marriage is powerfully related to spiritual life, and mixed marriage would make the Israelites vulnerable to spiritual compromise and corruption. Later the prohibition was clarified through Ezra: "Therefore do not give your daughters to their sons, neither take their daughters for your sons" (Ezra 9:12).

But the Old Testament prohibition was only a national rule that never applied to anyone except the people of Israel. In the New Testament, God through Paul changed it to a universal standard for Christians regardless of nationality. Writing to new Christians at Corinth, Paul says,

> Do not be unequally yoked with unbelievers. For what partnership has righteousness with lawlessness? Or what fellowship has light with darkness? What accord has Christ with Belial [a name for Satan]? Or what portion does a believer share with an unbeliever? What agreement has the temple of God with idols? For we are the temple of the living God; as God said, "I will make my dwelling among them and walk among them, and I will be their God, and they shall be my people. Therefore go out from their midst, and be separate from them, says the Lord, and touch no unclean thing; then I will welcome you, and I will be a father to you, and you shall be sons and daughters to me, says the Lord Almighty" (2 Cor. 6:14-18).

The prohibition given here is far more than a rule for just one situation (maintaining the purity of Israel in the land of Canaan). It has become a general norm, keeping any believer from marrying any nonbeliever anywhere in the world. The justification for the prohibition is more complex as well. God still wants to avoid spiritual vulnerability, "be separate from them . . . , and touch no unclean thing" (v. 17), but there is more at stake than that. At a spiritual level, marriage uniting a Christian with a non-Christian tries mixing what cannot be mixed (righteousness with lawlessness, light with darkness, Christ with Satan, the temple of God with idols). That simply cannot happen. Either the marriage will fail, or one partner will have to compromise spiritually to accommodate the other.

If a believer marries a nonbeliever, the two have absolutely nothing in common at the deepest, most profound, most important level of their sexual relationship. But not only that, there is also outright enmity at the core of their marriage of the sort that divides Satan from God (v. 15). And this cosmic enmity not only threatens the strength of their marriage, it also compromises God's plan for dwelling with his people (v. 16). The Spirit of God indwells the Christian even during sex, and spiritually mixed marriage destroys the part God should have in a sexual relationship uniting Christians. The spiritual enmity at the center of a mixed marriage also compromises the family fellowship God our Heavenly Father wants with his "sons and daughters" (v. 18; also 1 John 1:6-7).

The prohibition in 2 Corinthians implies that spiritual incompatibility is never wise for any marriage. That is, it implies that marriage will be very hard to maintain even if *nonbelievers* from different religions marry each other. But while any spiritually mixed marriage is unwise, for Christians it is also immoral.

The prohibition against spiritually mixed marriage is not absolute, because Paul orders, "if any brother has a wife who is an unbeliever, and she consents to live with him, he should not divorce her. [And also] If any woman has a husband who is an unbeliever, and he consents to live with her, she should not divorce him" (1 Cor. 7:12-13). This tells us God's prohibition against spiritually mixed marriage is not as important as remaining faithful to whatever marriage we are in, and apparently this applies the same way however a mixed marriage begins. Paul says nothing about staying in a mixed marriage only if a couple was married when both were nonbelievers and one later became a Christian. Therefore, he must also be referring to couples in a mixed marriage that came about because the Christian partner was disobedient. Apparently the difference is irrelevant for what he is saying. So, even if a marriage is mixed because a Christian has violated God's prohibition, that Christian in the mixed marriage should repent but then remain married, rather than seeking a divorce. The prohibition against spiritually mixed marriage is not as important as the prohibition against divorce, and so, in cases where both prohibitions have been violated, the prohibition against mixed marriage gives way to the prohibition against divorce.

God's general prohibition against spiritually mixed marriage is consistent with his interest in guarding the positive value of complexity, intimacy, and complementarity in sexual relationships. Spiritually mixed marriage weakens the complexity of sex by trying to construct relationships that do not include the spiritual dimension. Since sex remains spiritual no matter how we try leaving it out, relationships that ignore the spiritual dimension are doomed to failure because of what couples try pretending is not there.

The prohibition guards the value of sexual intimacy as well. The spiritual dimension of sex is not just unavoidable but is the most important dimension, and spiritually mixed marriage leaves a vacuum at the deepest level of sexual intimacy. So long as that vacuum is there, sex will never reach the potential for intimacy that God intends it to have. Nothing else in a relationship goes as deep as the spiritual dimension, and nothing else can take its place.

Finally, the prohibition against spiritually mixed marriage protects the value of complementarity in God's design for sex. If a Christian marries a non-Christian, the two may be able to complement each other physically, emotionally, and psychologically, but they cannot complement each other spiritually. At the spiritual level, they will be different, but not in a way that "fits" (Gen. 2:18). Those who honor the prohibition against spiritually mixed marriage know the value of uniting corresponding difference at the deepest level of marriage, and those who reject it suffer trouble because of what they miss.

Strong Opposition to Sexual Immodesty

A third sort of behavior God opposes strongly but about which he remains somewhat flexible is sexual immodesty. In biblical sexual morality, immodesty is closely connected with lust. But, whereas lust is about *having* wrong sexual desires *yourself,* sexual immodesty is about trying to *provoke* wrong feelings or thoughts—either corrupt desires or humiliation—in *others.*

We have put immodesty on the list of sexual prohibitions several levels below lust for three reasons. The first and most important is, even though lust happens inside a person, the standard making lust wrong does not change, because it depends on God, not us. Others may not know you are lusting. But God always knows what is in your heart, and the standard by which he judges lust is objective. God judges lust the same way for everyone, however anyone feels about it.

By contrast, God's evaluation of sexual immodesty varies tremendously because it depends entirely on what people intend, or what they think is intended. Trying to provoke wrong feelings or thoughts in other people is always very wrong, but evaluating when that happens varies from person to person and place to place. In fact, the way immodesty gets expressed varies so much that something completely innocent in one culture can be shocking in another. For example, in Thailand where I grew up as a child of missionaries, there is nothing at all immodest about a woman exposing her breasts to feed a baby in public, even while riding a crowded bus or shopping at a food market. But if a woman did that on a bus or in a grocery store in the United States, everyone would think it was terribly out of place. Why? Because here we perceive that to be immodest and so if a woman does it anyway we think she is intending to be immodest.

Although ways of expressing immodesty vary widely between cultures, what makes imodesty wrong is not culture. Rather, it is a person's immoral intention linked to the way others perceive that intention. Sexual immodesty depends on whether a person *wants* to provoke wrong feelings or thoughts in other people and on whether others *think* that is what a person is trying to do. Sometimes the very same thing can be modest or immodest in the same culture, depending on how the context affects the *message* perceived. There is nothing immodest about wearing a hospital gown with the backside of your underwear exposed, even if seen by a crowd of strangers, so long as you are a patient in a hospital. But wearing the same thing at a wedding reception is terribly immodest, even if everyone there is a relative or friend of the family. The difference depends on what you *intend* and what others *think* you are trying to do, not on the action by itself. Even when it comes to how God views your actions, immodesty still depends on a person's heart—it still depends on what you mean by what you do—not on how you choose to express it.

A second reason for putting immodesty lower on the list is that, not only does it depend on something subjective (what you intend and what others think you intend), but God in scripture also puts more emphasis on avoiding other sins like lust and divorce than he does on avoiding immodesty. This says that, while immodesty is bad, God thinks other sins are worse. Of course no sin should be excused, but some are more serious than others. Murder is worse than calling someone a bad name, and in a similar way adultery and even lust are worse than sexual immodesty.

A third reason immodesty comes below lust is the way lust and immodesty are related. Although they are different sins, immodesty cannot exist unless lust is wrong in the first place. Because it is wrong to *have* lust, it therefore must be wrong to *provoke* lust. But if lust were not wrong in the first place, provoking it would not matter. That is why, before they fell into sin, the Bible says Adam and Eve "were both naked and were not ashamed" (Gen. 2:25). When there was no chance of perverting sexual desire (when there was no chance of provoking lust), immodesty was impossible.

While God's prohibition of immodesty is in the Bible, it is not expressed as a single command: "you must never be immodest." Yet, even though a command is not listed, we know it exists because we see God applying it in different ways. Sexual modesty is related to sensing moral shame in the presence of corruption, and since the sin of sexual immodesty refuses to be ashamed of things God says are shameful, the nearest the Bible gets to giving a command prohibiting immodesty is in places where it says, "the unrighteous know no shame" (Zeph. 3:5, NIV) and the ungodly "glory in their shame" (Phil. 3:19). God is not pleased with anyone who is proud of things that should make them feel guilty and ashamed, and while this covers many things, it certainly has to include failing to be modest in situations affecting how others think about sex.

Besides corrupting what others think and desire, the main idea running through all that the Bible says on sexual immodesty is that it always involves indecent exposure or revealing to others what should not be seen, touched, or even smelled. In other words, immodesty involves exposing something private. The Hebrew word for indecent exposure or revelation (*'erwāh*) appears thirty-four times in Leviticus chapters 18–21, all in reference to various acts of immoral sex. But, while the word is commonly translated "nakedness," the original Hebrew meaning has less to do with a specific amount of clothing than with decency. This is easy to see where the Levitical code says, "you shall not uncover the nakedness of your brother's wife" and then says that doing this exposes "your brother's nakedness" as well (Lev. 18:16). Of course, since the husband is not the one committing adultery, he presumably is clothed. Nevertheless, we are told that when a wife commits adultery her husband is indecently exposed. Why? Not because he is physically bare, but rather because adultery dishonors the honorable intimacy of marriage by exposing to others what should be uniquely reserved for a husband and wife alone. A faithful husband is shamed because infidelity takes something private and exposes it to someone else. In other words, it violates modesty as well as marriage.

Of course, physical adultery compromises sexual modesty in a very profound way. But many less extreme things can do that as well, and the Bible indicates the only thing required to make something immodest is using some form of indecent exposure to provoke lust or humiliation in others. Wearing clothing designed to provoke lust is therefore indecent and obviously part of what Paul means by saying, "It is good not to . . . do anything that causes your brother to stumble" (Rom. 14:21). It also is shameful if others merely see parts of the body that they think a person wants to be private (Isa. 47:3; Mic. 1:11). God therefore orders priests to wear "undergarments to cover their naked [indecently exposed] flesh" (Ex. 28:42) and forbids them to "go up by steps to my altar, that your nakedness [what should not be revealed] be not exposed on it" (Ex. 20:26). Similarly, exposing the buttocks in public is a way of shaming prisoners (Isa. 20:4). When it comes to sexual immodesty, the message sent with exposure is far more important than exactly what is seen. So pulling up a robe around the waist in order to run or work is not immodest (1 Kings 18:46; 2 Kings 4:29; 9:1; Jer. 1:17), but seeing the same bit of leg or thigh under a priest's robe is considered immodest (Ex. 20:26).

Along this same line, Paul tells Timothy that women "should adorn themselves in respectable apparel, with modesty . . . with what is proper for women who profess godliness" (1 Tim. 2:9-10). Similarly, Peter explains that modest women should adorn themselves with "respectful and pure conduct" and "a gentle and quiet spirit" rather than depending on external accoutrements like ostentatious hair styling, clothing, or jewelry (1 Pet. 3:2-4). The moral issue has to do with maintaining a modest attitude, not with issuing a permanent ban on specific forms of external adornment.

But the general prohibition of immodesty not only has to do with what you let others see of yourself, it also applies to the way you handle opportunities to look at someone who is exposed but has no idea you can see something they want kept private. In other words, it also applies to taking indecent advantage of another person when you are able to see something you have no permission to see. God's displeasure at this is shown by Noah's curse (Gen. 9:24) after Ham saw his father indecently exposed (Gen. 9:22). Even though we do not know the details, it is clear that Ham took advantage of his father in a way everyone thought was shameful. Noah is the one who lay unconscious and exposed, but Ham is blamed for immodesty. The offense had to do with Ham's response and had little to do with how much clothing Noah was actually wearing.

A third sort of immodesty related to what one sees is indicated by God's anger with facial expressions people use to communicate sinful attitudes about sex. We know God punished Sodom and Gomorrah for "indulg[ing] in sexual immorality and pursu[ing] unnatural desire" (Jude 7). But Isaiah indicates that God is also offended when people have the same brash look that the people of Sodom had on their faces. "The look on their faces bears witness against them; they proclaim their sin like Sodom; they do not hide it. Woe to them!" (Isa. 3:9). This means God judges immodest facial expressions apart from whatever else you do, however else you are dressed and whatever else you see.

God's prohibition of immodesty covers improper touching as well. This aspect is revealed in the Mosaic law which punishes a woman who grabs a man in the crotch even to help her husband in a fight (Deut. 25:11-12). The issue is sexual modesty in the area of touch, and outside of marriage someone else's "private parts" are off-limits no matter what is at stake.

Lastly, the biblical prohibition of sexual immodesty covers what you say—in addition to what you do, how you dress, what you see, and how you express yourself facially. After mentioning sexual immorality, Paul adds, "Let there be no filthiness nor foolish talk nor crude joking, which are out of place" (Eph. 5:4). Men and women can be sexually immodest just in the way they talk, without doing, seeing, or touching anything, and Paul says it is "out of place" among people made holy through faith in Jesus Christ. Instead, he says, "it is shameful even to speak of the things that they [those walking in spiritual darkness] do in secret" (Eph. 5:12). That is, modesty prevents Paul even *to speak* directly with readers about what most likely involved extremely vulgar forms of sexual sin.

What does God's prohibition of sexual immodesty protect? Those who attack biblical sexual morality often blame concern for modesty on being afraid to accept the goodness of sex. But this is completely false. The reason

Christians value modesty is not because sex embarrasses us, but because we think sex is so honorable that we are embarrassed by anything that corrupts it. We are modest, not because we think sex is bad, but because we think sex is only good when it is pure, and anything compromising the purity of good sex is therefore horribly bad.

Any act, dress, appearance, sight, look, or talk meant to provoke sexual lust or humiliation is by definition denying the value of sex as something God made personal, exclusive, intimate, selfless, and complex. It frustrates valuing sex for building relationships between persons by either inviting others to make you an *object* of lust or humiliating someone by taking indecent *advantage* of them. Immodesty also treats sex partners as if they were nothing special, treats sex as if it were shallow, encourages selfishness (not sacrificial love), and acts as if sexual thoughts were all that matter. This not only is false but also robs us of what makes sex truly good and worthwhile. Ironically, it is not the immodest who value the goodness of sex, rather it is those who know, appreciate, and accept the need for God's prohibition of immodesty.

Opposition to Polygamy

God also opposes polygamy. But while he clearly opposes having more than one wife or husband at a time, he does not ban it for everyone. And even the way he opposes the practice is not as strong as the way he opposes other kinds of undesired behavior. The reason seems to be that, even though polygamy is not as good as monogamy, it still is a lot better than any sort of sex outside of marriage. It also is much better than divorce. So, although God does not like polygamy, he never orders people in polygamous marriages to get rid of multiple wives or husbands by divorce.

Prohibitions against polygamy are given in both the Old and New Testaments, but not in ways that include everyone or that make violating the prohibition something God punishes as sin. Kings of Israel are told not to "acquire many wives" lest their hearts be turned away from devotion to God (Deut. 17:17). The reason for opposing multiple wives is that it brings greater temptation to spiritual compromise, not that polygamy is necessarily sinful by itself. And, while the advice to kings regarding polygamy sets a good example for everyone, there is no indication that it is mandatory for everyone.

The idea that God does not punish polygamy is supported by the way he handles David's marriage to Bathsheba. Besides starting with adultery and murder, their marriage was also polygamous (2 Sam. 3:2-5; 5:13-16; 1 Chron. 3:1-9). But God never tells David to repent for polygamy, and, after

David confesses adultery and murder, God blesses their polygamous marriage by making Solomon, their second son, heir to the throne (1 Chron. 22:9-10) and successor in the line of the promised Messiah (Matt. 1:6).

In the New Testament, polygamy is prohibited for people in church leadership, but again this prohibition is not directly applied to others. Overseers (1 Tim. 3:2), deacons (3:12) and elders (Titus 1:5-6) must each be "the husband of one wife," meaning that men with *polygamous* marriages must not be church officers (not that *single* men should be disqualified). The New Testament prohibition applies to women as well, because Paul says widows should not be supported at church expense unless they had been "the wife of one husband" (1 Tim. 5:9). The New Testament prohibition clearly applies regardless of gender, but like the Old Testament prohibition it seems to be identifying something hindering an ideal rather than something sinful that must be punished. In other words, it looks as if God opposes polygamy to make sure that leaders set an example that will help marriages succeed rather than because he thinks it is something automatically wicked.

But even if this is so, even if polygamy is not sinful, that does not mean having multiple wives or husbands is not a problem. The message in scripture is that it is a problem. The best is better than anything less—even if the difference is not something immoral—and there is plenty of evidence in scripture that monogamy is much better than polygamy for achieving happy marriages.

At creation, God designed marriage as a one-man-one-woman relationship. He first created Adam (Gen. 2:7) and then Eve (v. 22), each in separate acts, and then joined them—one man and one woman—in a monogamous marriage. God did not make multiple wives for Adam or multiple husbands for Eve. The original marriage formula was simply one of each: "Therefore a man shall leave his father and mother and hold fast to his wife, and they shall become one flesh" (v. 24). Notice that monogamy was not something commanded. It was just demonstrated in the act of creation. But, since God never does anything second-rate, that fact alone set an ideal. The ideal marriage formula unites one of each sex.

Now, if monogamy was ideal before there was sin, what does that say about the possibility of *sinful* men and women succeeding with polygamous marriages? Since men and women became sinners, achieving completely harmonious sexual intimacy on a lifelong basis has been nearly impossible even for two; how much more difficult then must it be for sinners in polygamous marriages? It really is unreasonable, and scripture bears that out by reporting serious problems in every polygamous marriage it describes. For example, taking Hagar as a second wife disrupted harmony between Abraham and Sarah, and she attacked him for it later even though it was her idea in the first place (Gen. 16:1-5); Rachael and Leah were bitter rivals for Jacob's affection even though they were sisters (29:31-32; 30:1); Hannah was "deeply distressed" because Elkanah's other wife, Peninnah, "provoke[d] her grievously to irritate her" (1 Sam. 1:6); and Solomon's 700 wives and 300 concubines "turned away his heart after other gods" (1 Kings 11:3-4).

Preferring monogamy over polygamy even matters in the way God treats the first spouse in a marriage that later becomes polygamous. So we see that faithfulness in marriage refers especially to remaining faithful to the "wife of your youth" (i.e., the *first* wife; Mal. 2:14-15; also Prov. 2:17; Isa. 54:6). A statement like that is redundant except in reference to what happens in polygamous or to marriage after unjustified divorce. God's blessing of marital intimacy also focuses on the *first* wife, "the wife of your youth" (Prov. 5:18)—which indicates that God's ideal remains monogamy even in cultures that may have practiced polygamy for centuries. Finally, grief over losing a wife's *first* husband is treated as worse than losing a later husband (Joel 1:8). There can be only one *first* wife or husband, and these passages show that God especially honors the one-man-one-woman formula in marriage even when other wives or husbands are added later.

In the New Testament, Jesus reminds us that God's formula for marriage is and always has been monogamy, not polygamy. Asked about divorce, he repeats the marriage formula from Genesis but adds, "So they are no longer two but one flesh" (Matt. 19:6). The additional comment stresses what Jesus considered most important, and while highlighting the importance of the one-flesh union, he did so in a way that focused attention on monogamy over polygamy.

Jesus also set a model for ideal marriage in the relationship he established with the church. Paul teaches that husbands and wives ought to take the relationship of Christ with the church as a pattern for marriage (Eph. 5:23-32), and an angel tells John the church is "the Bride, the wife of the Lamb" (Rev. 21:9). The relationship between Jesus Christ and the church is indeed a prototype for the perfect marriage, and this New Testament prototype follows the same pattern that God set at creation. It is a marriage in which the husband and wife are each one of a kind. Each one is absolutely unique to the other, no one else will do, no duplications or additions accepted. Once more we have a pattern for what the perfect marriage looks like, and it is monogamous, not polygamous.

In summary, we have seen that while God's direct prohibition of polygamy applies just to Christian leaders, monogamy is ideal for everyone.

And, although God never punishes polygamy as something sinful, he does say it disqualifies a person from being a role model for marriage. But there is more at stake behind opposing polygamy than reducing certain kinds of temptation and increasing chances for a happy marriage. It also guards moral values God considers essential for any sexual relationship in marriage.

Favoring monogamy over polygamy is important to God because having multiple wives or husbands interferes with the degree to which marriages grow to express the values of exclusivity, intimacy, and selflessness. Other values on the positive side of biblical sexual morality do not seem to be affected, or at least are not compromised. Polygamous marriages can be relational, productive, and multidimensional, and can unite corresponding differences. But polygamy makes it harder to develop marriages that are truly unique, truly profound, and truly sacrificial. Polygamy does not necessarily destroy these qualities, but it does hinder them rather seriously.

First, whereas monogamy encourages working on a sexual relationship in marriage that is so unique that competition with rivals is irrelevant, polygamy guarantees rivalry and dilutes the unique nature of sex in marriage. Sex may be exclusive *to* a marriage, but it is not exclusive to just one partner *within* a marriage. Second, whereas monogamy encourages nurturing sexual intimacy until it reaches profound levels, polygamy discourages deepening intimacy by dividing focus among rivals. Attention to one is always threatened by calls distracting attention toward someone else, and dividing attention between rivals makes it difficult to develop depth with any single one. Third, whereas monogamy favors sacrificial love, polygamy invites favoritism and rewards self-centeredness. For husbands with multiple wives, trouble with one wife usually means ignoring the reason for the difficulty. Marriage problems are solved by shifting attention to someone else, not by addressing challenges in ways that make a marriage stronger. And, for wives sharing one husband, competition with rivals encourages self-centered behavior and discourages behavior based on sacrificial love.

Opposition to Fellowship with Sexually Immoral Christians

One last prohibition remains, and that is God's requirement that Christians walking in moral fellowship with himself break off fellowship with others who may call themselves "Christian" but insist on living sexually immoral lives. It is put last on our list for several reasons. First, God himself made it the last sexual prohibition given in the Bible. It appears in the writing of Paul, but not earlier. Second, the prohibition sets a standard that applies to behavior relevant only among Christians and among no one else. Every other sexual prohibition in the Bible sets a standard that either is required or (as in the case of prohibiting polygamy) is at least good for everyone. But this last prohibition sets a standard that has nothing to do with people outside the church. Third, the prohibition of fellowship with sexually immoral Christians sets a norm that is logically secondary, not primary. It requires something that serves to uphold other sexual norms. It does not define on its own a new form of deviant sexual behavior. Fourth, although the Bible covers other sexual prohibitions in several places, this last prohibition appears in just one passage.

And yet the mere fact that it comes last does not mean we should take it lightly. Perhaps, because it is at the bottom, we should be especially careful to remember that every prohibition in scripture is given for a reason and is therefore important. If it were not important, God would not have included it in his moral revelation.

The prohibition appears in some instructions on church discipline addressed to the church in Corinth. And, while this is the only passage in scripture mentioning this prohibition, the prohibition is important enough for Paul to repeat twice, and even to recall a third time when he had mentioned it in an earlier letter:

> I wrote you in my letter [an earlier letter written before 1 Corinthians] not to associate with sexually immoral people—not at all meaning the sexually immoral of this world, or the greedy and swindlers, or idolaters, since then you would need to go out of the world. But now I am writing to you not to associate with anyone who bears the name of brother if he is guilty of sexual immorality or greed, or is an idolater, reviler, drunkard, or swindler—not even to eat with such a one. . . . "Purge the evil person from among you" (1 Cor. 5:9-13).

Paul repeats a prohibition he had given before, and is writing about it this second time to correct a misunderstanding. While telling Christians not to associate with sexually immoral people, Paul makes it clear that the ban applies only to people who *claim to be Christian* but who practice sexual immorality and refuse to repent. He also clarifies that what he orders does not put sexual sin in a separate category, adding several other types of sin (greed, swindling, idolatry, revelry, drunkenness) that should be treated the same.

The purpose for this prohibition is keeping sexual sin from contaminating the church. "Purge the evil person from among you" (v. 13). Paul here quotes a phrase from a section in the Mosaic law dealing with sexual discipline—for punishing acts of sex outside of marriage (Deut. 22:21, 22, 24). But he adapts it in a way that is interesting. Instead of applying the death penalty mandated by Moses, Paul substitutes shame caused by denying association with others in the church. When discipline is required, Paul orders that Christians must not even "eat with such a one" (v. 11). Paul's modified version, though different from the Mosaic law, is nevertheless consistent with it at a deeper level. Under Mosaic law, sexual purity in the nation of Israel was enforced by taking physical life (on a permanent basis). In the New Testament, it is enforced by interrupting life in the church (on a temporary basis)—something that is rather mild compared to physical death but that warns unrepentant sinners that sin eventually leads to permanent exclusion from everlasting life with God (1 Cor. 6:9; Rev. 21:8; 22:15).

So what positive values are this last prohibition protecting? Because it does not address a single form of sexual sin but reinforces all sexual prohibitions in general, this last prohibition guards and protects every positive value God considers necessary for biblical sexual morality. It treats the personal, exclusive, intimate, fruitful, selfless, complex, complementary nature of sex as a whole and stresses the importance of sexual purity for the entire church, not just individual believers alone. The role of this final sexual prohibition is to protect the church against letting sin in one person's life corrupt the lives of many.

In the end, this final prohibition turns out to be the sexual component of the better-known, broader principle that calls God's people to holy standards different from the world, and that warns us that no believer can afford to accommodate lesser standards of behavior. God is long-suffering and patient, but the perfect holiness of God never compromises with sin (2 Pet. 3:9). That is why God says we must "go out from their midst, and be separate from them" (2 Cor. 6:17; also Isa. 52:11); and that is why we must not associate with "the sons of disobedience" (Eph. 5:6-7). This final prohibition should also be understood as part (the sexual part) of Paul's last warning to the Romans, in which he says,

> I appeal to you, brothers, to watch out for those who cause divisions and create obstacles contrary to the doctrine that you have been taught; avoid them. For such persons do not serve our Lord Christ, but their own appetites, and by smooth talk and flattery they deceive the hearts of the naive (Rom. 16:17-18).

Accommodation to sexual immorality matters tremendously, not only to individual Christians and their marriages here on earth but also to the purity of the church and her preparation to be the Bride of Christ at the marriage of the Lamb (Eph. 5:27; Rev. 19:6-8).

A Note About Self-Stimulated Sex (Masturbation)

Readers may notice, in covering biblical prohibitions in the area of sex, that we have said nothing about any prohibition referring directly to masturbation, the practice by which a person brings himself or herself to orgasm without anyone else involved. This is because even though the Bible lists many prohibitions relating to sex, it says nothing about self-stimulated sex per se.

In the past, some Christians have tried connecting masturbation with God's anger against Onan because "whenever he went into his brother's wife he would waste the semen on the ground, so as not to give offspring to his brother" (Gen. 38:9). But Onan did not stimulate himself. Rather, he had sex with a woman and withdrew on reaching orgasm, so the reason God got angry seems to have had more to do with getting enjoyment from sex with a woman without keeping promises owed to his brother than with *how* Onan went about avoiding his duties.

Because the Bible says nothing directly about self-stimulated sex, many have decided the practice must be moral or should at least be treated as something morally neutral—neither right nor wrong but simply allowed when better forms of sex are not available. But I do not think this is correct, and I disagree mainly because the very nature of masturbation conflicts with biblical thinking on sexual morality in some very important ways.

Of course, we should not make up demands that restrict sex beyond what God requires. Jesus was terribly critical of religious teachers who "tie up heavy burdens, hard to bear, and lay them on people's shoulders, but they themselves are not willing to move them with their finger [they offer nothing helpful]" (Matt. 23:4). But, while we should respect this important warning, we must also be careful to stand and defend all that God requires. I believe that, even though there is no specific prohibition in the Bible against self-stimulated sex, we are not left to merely do as we please because God has a lot to say about resisting passions of the flesh, and all morally worthy sex has to conform with the seven positive principles addressed in chapter 7.

For example, in scripture we are told to "make no provision for the flesh, to gratify its desires" (Rom. 13:14); to "not be conformed to this world" but rather to "be transformed by the renewal of your mind" (Rom. 12:2); and "to abstain from the passions of the flesh" because they "wage war against your soul" (1 Pet. 2:11). Furthermore, those who belong to Christ "have crucified the flesh with its passions and desires" (Gal. 5:24), and are urged to "walk by the Spirit, and you will not gratify the desires of the flesh. For the desires of the flesh are against the Spirit, and the desires of the Spirit are against the flesh, for these are opposed to each other" (vv. 16-17).

Also, I believe it is quite clear that solitary, nonrelational, shallow, self-focused, nonproductive, one-dimensional, single-gender, self-stimulated sex opposes every positive moral characteristic revealed to be essential in God's design for sex.

God made sex to be *relational,* but solitary, self-stimulated sex is never relational. God made sex to be something *exclusive,* but while solitary self-stimulated sex is exclusive physically, it is not exclusive to another person and it encourages thoughts to wander in ways that are not exclusive at all. God made sex to be *profound,* but solitary self-stimulation is shallow. God made sex to be *fruitful,* but solitary self-stimulation treats sex like a commodity rather than a capacity for production. God made sex to be *selflessly* God-centered, but solitary self-stimulation is self-centered and self-satisfying. God made sex to be *multidimensional,* but solitary self-stimulation separates physical sex from everything else.

Perhaps most seriously, God made sex to be a joining of *complementary* sexual differences, but solitary, self-stimulated sex never involves corresponding sexual union. Male passions are aroused by a male himself, and female passions are aroused by a female herself. Solitary, self-stimulated sex is not only nonrelational, but is also by nature an act of same-sex arousal and same-sex fulfillment. You are always the same gender as yourself, and imagining a heterosexual relationship does not make the reality heterosexual. Of course, imagining a heterosexual relationship is better than imagining a homosexual relationship, but the reality only actually involves one gender.

Self-stimulated sex may be less seriously outside God's design for sex than, say, physical adultery, or prostitution, or even sexual immodesty. But I believe we still must conclude that it is outside the biblical pattern and is therefore wrong. It is not a sort of behavior that merely falls short of the best but is nevertheless morally acceptable. It cannot be reconciled with God's order to "make no provision for the flesh, to gratify its desires" (Rom. 13:14), and it truly conflicts with every moral essential in God's view of sex. So, even though there is nothing in the Bible directly prohibiting self-stimulated sex, I believe it is something we must avoid in order to "present your bodies as a living sacrifice, holy and acceptable to God, which is your spiritual worship" (Rom. 12:1).

11

Biblical Promises Bless Moral Sex

In the process of raising two sons, my wife and I have learned some important lessons—some from reading, but most from trial and error—on setting rules for the family and seeing that they are obeyed. Because we love our children, we want them to develop into responsible adults able to set worthy goals and to reach them the right way. To begin that process, we started when they were very young setting boundaries for their behavior. But it was apparent right off that setting good boundaries would not be enough. There also had to be meaningful consequences connected with the boundaries we set. And we learned that to get proper results the consequences we assigned had to include some that were positive as well as others that were negative.

Discipline in our family would never have worked without punishing misbehavior. But we also learned that the need for negative discipline could be much reduced by offering some reward if the boys behaved well. My mother-in-law understood this and showed us how it worked by offering our sons ten dollars for every A they had on their report cards at the close of each semester. We continued the practice, and over the years neither son has forgotten that incentive. It has often encouraged them to persevere through a long, hard semester.

There are times under pressure when negative consequences no longer seem all that bad compared to how you feel about what you face at the moment, and at such times the prospect of a good reward may be all that makes doing right seem worthwhile. At such times, the promised reward does not make what you do either right or wrong. But it does add real motivation, especially when the going is tough. Doing your best in school is right whether someone offers you money or not. But, if someone does, the prospect can certainly encourage you to work harder than perhaps you might otherwise.

As parents we understand that not all rewards are the same, and some are better than others. For example, money can motivate children to study, but it can also lead to greed and materialism. This is because money is not morally worthy in its own right. It is a means that can be used toward ends that are either good or bad. In comparison to this, the best sort of reward for doing right is the kind that promises something morally worth having for its own sake. Promising money for grades is only a step, and what I truly want my sons to seek, as they grow older, is the higher value of earning a good reputation, of knowing the satisfaction of doing a good job, and of being recognized for excellence. Unlike mere money, these are rewards that are morally worthy for their own sake, and when my boys learn that I will know they are ready for life as independent adults.

Encouraging good behavior with rewards worth having is also part of God's approach to sexual morality. Biblical sexual morality is made up not only of positive moral principles and negative prohibitions but also of rewards with which God blesses people who follow his rules. Positive principles define the moral value God assigns to sexual purity (as we saw in chapter 7), negative prohibitions guard this value (chapters 8–10), and, as we shall now explore, *promises* reward preserving it.

Scripture shows that God offers four very worthy moral rewards to people who follow his rules on sex: abiding joy, genuine satisfaction, exemplary honor, and pure allure. These four blessings serve to motivate efforts to keep sex within God's boundaries. They are not what make sex right or wrong, because that (as we saw in chapter 6) is a matter of holiness, which is defined by the character of God alone. The blessings God associates with moral sex are not what make anything right or wrong, but they do make obeying God seem worthwhile.

The four blessings we identified are not the only good results coming from moral sex. Pleasure, fun, good health, psychological stability, and protection from emotional pain also result from obeying God's rules. But these are in a category like promising money for study—they offer incentives that are morally neutral and might be used for good or bad. The four rewards we turn to now are all moral blessings worth having for their own sake. They are incentives offered at a much higher level, and that matter a lot more, than other nice results that come with following God's moral rules on sex.

The First Blessing: Abiding Joy

Edgar Guest has written a poem capturing something precious that develops when a faithful marriage produces a web of strong relationships called *home:*

> Much I've done and much I've seen,
> To many places I have been,
> But to me there's no delight
> Like the lights of home at night.
>
> Rest is here, they seem to say,
> Peace is here to close the day,
> Love is waiting to embrace
> You within this little place,
>
> Come, let loved ones stroke your cheek,
> Let them laugh to hear you speak,
> Here all selfish bickerings cease,
> Here are love and rest and peace.[1]

Home is far more than a house. Some can live together in a house and never have a *home,* while others create a *home* for each other even when they have no place to stay. A house is a building made up of materials like wood, bricks, and cement. But a *home* is a web of strong, loving, sacrificial relationships that together result in something wonderful, deep, and meaningful called joy.

The first blessing God gives people who keep sex pure is joy—abiding joy. When God brought Eve to Adam, it started the first man-woman relationship ever created, and the result for Adam was great joy (Gen 2:23). The emotion carried in Adam's response is hard to capture in English but is close to what we mean if we say, "What a hit!" The word relates to striking a blow and expresses strong approval. Adam was not just curious. He was not just mildly interested. He was thrilled! He was delighted! The relationship God made for him brought tremendous joy.

In Proverbs, God actually orders husbands to focus on accepting the joy he awards to relationships that keep sex pure, and it is such a critical matter that the order is repeated three times. "[R]ejoice in the wife of your youth." "Let her breasts fill you at all times with delight." "[B]e intoxicated always in her love" (Prov. 5:18-19). God's standards for moral sex do not limit happiness but are there to make sure we get all the blessings that go with the plan—especially joy.

Obeying God always results in joy, and disobeying always destroys it. In

Proverbs we are told, "The hope of the righteous brings joy, but the expectation of the wicked will perish" (Prov. 10:28). And Jesus taught, "If you keep my commandments, you will abide in my love" adding, "These things I have spoken to you, that my joy may be in you, and that your joy may be full" (John 15:10-11). Because this principle covers everything, it certainly must include obeying God's rules for sex. But, to make sure we get the connection, Proverbs says, "Let your fountain [your sex life] be *blessed* . . . *rejoice* in the wife of your youth. . . . Why should you be intoxicated, my son, with a forbidden woman and embrace the bosom of an adulteress?" (Prov. 5:18-20, emphasis added).

The joy with which God blesses sexual purity is a major theme in the Song of Solomon. This love poem recorded in the Bible illustrates what happens when lovers please God as well as each other. The poem overflows with joy and delight. She delights to just sit in her lover's shadow (Song 2:3) and rejoices that he is her friend (5:16). He thinks his beloved is pleasing and full of delights (7:6). She says the love he has for her is better (perhaps more intoxicating) than wine (1:2), and he says the same about the love she has for him (4:10).

But while the lovers in the Song of Solomon illustrate the joy God awards, the ultimate role model for delighting in a morally pure sexual relationship is none other than God himself. We are told God rejoices over the relationship he has with his people, and this is a pattern for the joy lovers get when a sexual relationship goes by God's rules. God promises Israel, "You shall no longer be termed Forsaken, and your land shall no more be termed Desolate, but you shall be called My Delight Is in Her, and your land Married; for the LORD delights in you, and your land shall be married. For . . . as the bridegroom rejoices over the bride, so shall your God rejoice over you" (Isa. 62:4-5).

Similarly, in the New Testament, we are told, "for the *joy* that was set before him" (Heb. 12:2, emphasis added), Christ endured the cross "that he might present the church to himself [as a bridegroom taking a bride] in splendor, without spot or wrinkle or any such thing" (Eph. 5:27). Jesus went to the cross for the joy he has in loving us, and it is just like the joy that motivates a bridegroom to give up everything for the bride he loves. What wonderful joy! And what a blessing God therefore promises couples who obey his rules. Thinking of this, Francis Schaeffer observed,

> If human marriage is meant to be a picture of that tremendous union of Christ and his Church and of the present relationship of Christ as bridegroom to the Church as bride, surely then there should be a showing forth of joy.[2]

So far, we have said that joy is tremendous! Joy is wonderful! But what is joy anyway? Are joy and pleasure different things? And, if so, what makes joy better than pleasure? To answer, we first must clarify that when it comes to love and marriage, the pleasure of sexual experience and the joy God awards with sexual purity are not the same. Not even close. And even though some get these confused, sexual pleasure and sexual joy are completely separate things. C. S. Lewis realized that, while "joy is not a substitute for sex, sex is very often a substitute for joy," and this led him to wonder "whether all pleasures are not substitutes for joy."[3]

We also need to understand that, even if some do not realize there is a difference, joy is always far better than pleasure. One reason they are confused is that, when a couple falls in love and romantic feelings run high, joy and pleasure do not seem very different. Joy starts gently while pleasure starts with a bang, but in romance they often are starting at the same time so, if a couple gets preoccupied with pleasure and loses sight of what else is happening, they can easily slide into mistaking pleasure for joy, or assuming there is no difference. But that is too bad, because once a person tastes joy, no pleasure is adequate to substitute.

If you do not know the difference already, it is hard to distinguish pleasure from joy while you are caught in the rush of romance. But, as time goes on and novelty wears off, some important differences emerge. If you were distracted by pleasure and paid no attention to joy, you will start wishing you had; and, if you saved room for joy, you will be very glad you did.

So, what differences are there between sexual pleasure and sexual joy, and why is joy so much better? First of all, pleasure is something brief and temporary; it explodes and then quickly fades. But when you have joy, it lasts a very long time and can even last forever. You never lose joy unless you decide to give it up. You can turn away from joy, but joy never turns away from you. Joy *abides* and grows over time as you add to what you have. Put differently, you can never use joy up, and it actually increases the more you give it away. Scripture says Moses did right even though it was hard because he realized that the "pleasures of sin" are "fleeting" (Heb. 11:25). In comparison, we are told "Weeping may tarry for the night, but joy comes with the morning" (Ps. 30:5). Pleasure does not last, but joy does.

Second, pleasure has physical and mental limits that end with pain, or with losing consciousness and sometimes even death. Human bodies and minds can tolerate only so much pleasure, and when they reach their natural limits they get overloaded or break. But there is no limit to how much joy you can have. Joy can grow and increase every day of your life, and it only gets better, never worse.

Third, pleasure cannot stand suffering and always flees pain, but joy lasts through suffering and transcends (rises above) pain. Married couples can have joy caring for each other even when both are sick, but a patron at a striptease club will not stay for the show if he steps on a nail, and may even go elsewhere just because the temperature is too warm or too cold for comfort. Scripture says, "He who goes out weeping, bearing the seed for sowing, shall come home with shouts of joy, bringing his sheaves with him" (Ps. 126:6). Joy outlasts pain and sorrow, but pleasure never does. For Christians, the joy of a marriage relationship even outlasts physical death, not just because survivors have fond memories, but because they anticipate seeing one another alive again and being reunited after the resurrection.

Fourth, as C. S. Lewis says, "joy is never in our power and pleasure often is."[4] Pleasure is something we can produce for ourselves—it is something we are able to stimulate, manipulate, and control—but joy is beyond our control. We relish and appreciate joy, and we can even earn it, but we can never manufacture, manipulate, or modify joy just to please ourselves. We experience joy, but its power source and steering mechanism are beyond our reach.

Fifth, pleasure is something shallow, while joy is profound in two ways. Joy is both deeper and higher than pleasure. It is deeper because joy arises from something unaffected by material things, while pleasure simply arises from physical or mental stimulation. And it is higher as well because joy is spiritual, while pleasure is nothing but physical or mental. For this reason, pleasure can be stimulated without ever affecting emotions at all, but joy permeates all levels of life and always affects emotions in a very positive way.

Sixth, pleasure is impersonal, and if pleasure is pursued for its own sake it weakens relationships and drives people apart. But joy is always personal, serving to affirm others and to deepen relationships with them. Sexual joy delights in the loved one for who he or she is, and never simply uses a lover to stimulate sensations. It relishes building a relationship and never merely uses sex as a means for indulging passions of the flesh. The woman in the Song of Solomon rejoices because her beloved is her friend (Song 5:16) and delights in knowing he is close (2:3), and of all the joys these lovers express, the greatest is simply belonging to each other (2:16; 6:3; 7:10).

Seventh, pleasure is self-centered and joy is not. C. S. Lewis says joy, unlike pleasure, "owes all its character to its object."[5] When it comes to sex, pleasure focuses on what a lover does for you, while joy focuses on appreciating the value and worth of the lover. Said another way, sexual pleasure has to do with how you feel about yourself, but joy in a sexual relationship has to do with how you feel about your lover and the relationship you are building together.

This last description of joy does not go far enough, however. In the Bible, true joy—even joy that comes with sexual purity—is never just about loving another person here on earth. Joy is not self-centered, but it is not merely other-centered either. This is because scripture tells us the source and focus of every joy is ultimately God; joy is a fruit of the Holy Spirit (Gal. 5:22). So, even when it comes to joy and sex, the joy involved is not just about loving a lover; it is about loving God as well. Joy in a sexual relationship is something God gives lovers who please him in the way they please each other, who serve him in the way they serve each other, and who love him in the way they love each other.

True joy is neither self-centered nor centered on just anyone else at all. Rather, it comes from loving another person in a way that ultimately centers on God. Francis Schaeffer explains,

> We are finite, and therefore do not expect to find final sufficiency in any human relationship, including marriage. The final sufficiency is to be found only in a relationship to God. But on the basis of the finished work of Christ, through the agency of the Holy Spirit and the instrument of faith, there can be a real and substantial healing of relationships, and thus true joy.[6]

Eighth, pleasure is morally neutral, but joy is always morally pure. Pleasure is something people experience in ways that can be either moral or immoral, and the mere fact that something gives you pleasure is no guarantee that it is moral. But since joy is given and controlled by God, there is no such thing as immoral joy. All genuine authentic joy is pure and holy. You receive it when a relationship pleases God and follows his rules, and you lose it when a relationship goes out of bounds. You can get sexual pleasure without obeying God's rules, but you can never know joy in a sexual relationship without staying inside his boundaries. The formula for joy depends on obeying God.

David understood where joy comes from, because he told God, "You make known to me the path of life; in your presence there is fullness of joy" (Ps. 16:11). But David also learned the hard way that sexual sin robs you of joy, and the only way of getting it back is getting right with God. Therefore, David repented and prayed, "Cast me not away from your presence. . . . restore to me the joy of your salvation" (Ps. 51:11-12).

This is not new. Others have discovered these truths before. Here, for example, is a wonderful poem by William Henry Davies, written more than a hundred years ago:

> Now, Joy is born of parents poor,
> And Pleasure of our richer kind;
> Though Pleasure's free, she cannot sing
> As sweet a song as Joy confined.
>
> Pleasure's a Moth, that sleeps by day
> And dances by false glare at night;
> But Joy's a Butterfly, that loves
> To spread its wings in Nature's light.
>
> Joy's like a Bee that gently sucks
> Away on blossoms its sweet hour;
> But Pleasure's like a greedy Wasp,
> That plums and cherries would devour.
>
> Joy's like a Lark that lives alone,
> Whose ties are very strong, though few;
> But Pleasure like a Cuckoo roams,
> Makes much acquaintance, no friends true.
>
> Joy from her heart doth sing at home,
> With little care if others hear;
> But Pleasure then is cold and dumb,
> And sings and laughs with strangers near.[7]

Abiding joy is a blessing God awards those who keep sex pure, but he requires obedience. You have to go by his rules, otherwise joy is impossible, and you lose even what you have.

The Second Blessing: Genuine Satisfaction

In the story of *Moby Dick*, Herman Melville mentions something wonderful that happens between happily married couples:

> How it is I know not; but there is no place like a bed for confidential disclosures between friends. Man and wife, they say, there open the very bottom of their souls to each other; and some old couples often lie and chat over old times till nearly morning.[8]

The length of time couples stay up talking may be exaggerated, but Melville touches on something true. Faithful marriages do produce results that are far more satisfying than flashes of temporary passion. Whether it is baring souls in private conversation, knowing each other well enough to relate without words, combining strengths and weaknesses in a partnership that withstands any challenge, or learning how to always encourage the best in each other, what comes out of genuine marriage is wonderfully satisfying indeed.

James Herriot, loved for his stories about animals, also knew something of love and marriage. When courting his future wife, Herriot recalls,

> it was always a relief when I got out of the house with Helen. Everything was right then; we went to the little dances in the village institutes, we walked for miles along the old grassy mine tracks among the hills, or sometimes she came on my evening calls with me. There wasn't anything spectacular to do in Darrowby but there was a complete lack of strain, a feeling of being self-sufficient in a warm existence of our own that made everything meaningful and worthwhile.[9]

When I was growing up, my father frequently told us children that he and mother were growing more *in love* each day, that every day they were more *in love* than ever before. It was no joke. He was serious. And it made me long to have that sort of marriage someday. Now that day is here, and I know exactly what he meant. He was not referring to surface sentimentality that changes all the time but to something deeper and more important. My father was describing the mutual satisfaction that grows between couples united at the deepest level of their souls. That sort of satisfaction truly does get better every day.

The second blessing God awards those who keep his rules on sex is genuine satisfaction experienced as a powerful sense of well-being, contentment, and completion, starting in the soul and affecting every other level as well—physical, emotional, and psychological, as well as spiritual. Scripture tells husbands to claim not only God's promise of joy but a promise of satisfaction as well: "Let her breasts fill you at all times with delight" (Prov. 5:19). This is both an order and a promise. Follow God's rules, and he guarantees wonderfully fulfilling sexual satisfaction. The verb used here for God's reward (*rāwāh*) means to be satisfied, saturated, filled up, intoxicated. It is about having extra, having more than necessary, having abundance. In fact, it is the same word scripture uses for describing God's superabundant generosity. "They feast [satisfy themselves] on the abundance of your house, and you give them drink from the river of your delights" (Ps. 36:8). Husbands (and wives) are promised that moral sex leads to overflowing satisfaction! The longing we human beings have for deep, intimate connection with another person who knows and loves us for who we are is filled and satisfied in exactly the way God designed it to be at creation. The thing God said it was "not good" to miss (Gen. 2:18), and for which he made Eve for Adam, is set in place "at last"! (Gen. 2:23).

It is God's nature to satisfy, and therefore David praises God, saying, "You open your hand; you satisfy the desire of every living thing" (Ps. 145:16). But, not only is it part of his nature, God also loves satisfying, and urges, "I am the Lord your God. . . . Open your mouth wide, and I will fill it" (Ps. 81:10). Again he says, "put me to the test . . . [to see] if I will not open the windows of heaven for you and pour down for you a blessing until there is no more need" (Mal. 3:10). David announces a principle when he states that God is he "who satisfies you with good so that your youth is renewed like the eagle's" (Ps. 103:5).

But God's blessing has a condition. Receiving his promised satisfaction requires respect and obedience. Scripture says, "He fulfills the desire of those who fear [respect and obey] him" (Ps. 145:19). No one gets the reward without going by the rules. Obeying the rules guarantees satisfaction, and rejecting them means no satisfaction at all. Sin is alluring, but the bait sin offers evaporates like so much cotton candy. And no matter how large a bite or how many, sin always leaves you empty.

Scripture says, "Better is a little with righteousness than great revenues with injustice" (Prov. 16:8), and it is a lesson everyone must learn one way or another. God controls all satisfaction, and nothing satisfies unless God allows it. David learned, "I have no good apart from you" (Ps. 16:2), and so asked God to "Satisfy us in the morning with your steadfast love, that we may rejoice and be glad all our days" (Ps. 90:14).

In Isaiah God stresses logic, and asks, "Why do you spend . . . your labor for that which does not satisfy?" (Isa. 55:2). Satisfaction depends on obedience, and those who do not obey instead "eat the fruit of their way, and have their fill of their own devices" (Prov. 1:31). Insisting on freedom to pursue satisfaction on your own terms rejects God's promise, and finding satisfaction that way is hopeless.

Satisfaction along with following God's rules applies in all areas, but scripture emphasizes the way it relates to moral sex not only in Proverbs 5:19 but other places as well. As with joy, the promise of satisfaction with moral sex is demonstrated in the Song of Solomon. The longing that lovers have (and should have) for each other is powerful (Song 2:5; 5:8) and leads to satisfaction when lovers unite in the proper way in marriage. Solomon's loved wife says, "I am a wall, and my breasts are like towers. Thus I have become in his eyes like one bringing contentment" (Song 8:10, NIV). Notice that the satisfaction referred to is not so much individual and biological as relational in a deeply integrated, spiritual sense. The Hebrew word for contentment (*shālōm*) indicates a state of prosperity, completeness, and well-being. In other words, it touches the sort of thing the poet Robert Browning was describing in the line, "God's in his heaven—All's right with the world!"

Another view of satisfaction is given where Solomon praises his beloved, saying, "How . . . pleasant you are, O loved one, with all your delights!" (Song 7:6). The word used here (*nāʿîm*) is one expressing how it feels to get something wonderful, and it is the opposite of bitter (*mārāʾ*), which is how you feel after losing something good. The meaning of these words is shown by Ruth's mother-in-law, Naomi, who on returning to Bethlehem said, "Do not call me Naomi [*nāʿămı,* "pleasant"]; call me Mara [*mārāʾ,* "bitter"]" because "I went away full, and the Lord has brought me back empty" (Ruth 1:20-21). *Pleasant* is the opposite of emptiness and loss. It means feeling wonderfully full and satisfied after receiving something good.

Based on this, we can see that when Solomon praises his beloved for being "pleasant," it is not a mild thing. Rather, he is describing the wonderful, full feeling he has because of her love for him. Such satisfaction can get to be so strong that the loved one seems to have "no flaw" (Song 4:7). Of course, objectively, no person on earth is *flawless.* But the satisfaction God gives with moral sex can be so strong that any non-moral imperfection seems to vanish in relative importance.

Since nothing satisfies apart from God (Ps. 16:2; 90:14), even satisfaction with sex depends on how closely life relates to him. If couples seek ultimate fulfillment in sex apart from God, it will turn destructive even if it stays within marriage. That is because God made sexual satisfaction to work as a blessing for obedience, not to be something we use to fill the place only he should have in our lives. If that happens, sexual satisfaction becomes an idol that destroys itself. Francis Schaeffer says,

> If we try to find everything in human relationships or if we forget that neither we nor they are perfect, we destroy them. The simple fact is that the bridge is not strong enough. To try to run on to the bridge of human relationships that which it cannot bear is to destroy both the relationship and ourselves. But for the Christian, who does not need to have everything in human relationships, human relationships can be beautiful.[10]

But there is more. The Bible not only warns that sexual sin never satisfies, but also says it guarantees the judgment of God. The allure of sexual sin is a sham, a lie, an illusion, a myth. It deceives, defiles, and then destroys. Solomon warns, "Can a man carry fire next to his chest and his clothes not be burned? So is he who goes in to his neighbor's wife; none who touches her will go unpunished" (Prov. 6:27-28). The logic is simple. "He who commits adultery lacks sense; he who does it destroys himself" (v. 32). It ends with regret. "[A]t the end of your life you [will] groan, when your flesh and body are consumed, and you [will] say, 'How I hated discipline, and my heart despised reproof! . . . I am at the brink of utter ruin'" (5:11-14). And, in the end, sexual sin leads to eternal spiritual death. It is not only unsatisfying and empty but leads to losing everything satisfying and good in the fires of hell (7:27; Heb. 13:4; Rev. 21:8).

By contrast, the satisfaction God promises in relation to moral sex is very much worth having. Sex is multidimensional, and the satisfaction that comes with moral sex is not only strong and deep but also affects all levels at once. It is not just profound but also complex. It is not just intense but also integrated. It leaves you full and complete because every part in God's design for sex is aligned and working according to plan.

When God said, "I will feast the soul of the priests with abundance, my people shall be satisfied with my goodness" (Jer. 31:14), he used the same verb (*rāwāh*) Solomon used for the satisfaction God promises husbands pursuing a morally pure relationship with their wives (Prov. 5:19). Is there a connection? I think so. Not only because these are both promises of God, but also because what satisfies in both cases is moral goodness itself, something God supplies those who are obedient. Both concern spiritual satisfaction that fills and transcends satisfaction of the body when life in the body conforms to God's standards.

When God says we will be satisfied with his "goodness," it is a moral statement. God's moral goodness is the power that sets everything in its rightful place and fills life with meaning, purpose, and blessing. So, when we say moral sex satisfies every level at once, it is because every piece on every level is rightly integrated and working as designed. Thirst for sexual purity was surely part of what Jesus had in mind when he said, "Blessed are those who hunger and thirst for righteousness, for they shall be satisfied" (Matt. 5:6).

The satisfaction God awards with moral sex is deep and integrating because it is spiritual and therefore affects all levels of a man-woman relationship at once. Couples who know this satisfaction feel wonderfully connected not only with each other but also, beyond themselves, with the one who made them, with the Creator who designed the way sex works and who is running the universe in which they live. Their relationship fits with who they were made to be, it fits with the true meaning and purpose of sex, and it fits with the role they were made to have in the grand order of the universe. In complementing each other the way God intends, they complement God as well, and he in turn complements their sexual relationship with satisfaction. There is no limit to such fulfillment, and nothing is more satisfying, other than new life in Christ.

Many surveys have found a remarkable connection between satisfying sex and following God's rules for sex and marriage, and of these, several have discovered an especially strong link between sexual satisfaction and strong religious (mostly Christian) faith. A survey conducted in the 1940s by professors at Stanford University discovered that women who attend church frequently are more likely to report high sexual satisfaction than women in other categories. In 1975, *Redbook* magazine surveyed 100,000 women and was surprised to find those who were "highly religious" were not only more likely to save sex for marriage but were also more likely to describe their sex life as being "very good." *Christianity Today* magazine sampled readers in 1992 and found a clear connection between premarital abstinence and sexual satisfaction in later marriage. It also found that, among Christians, those who save sex for marriage are less likely later to consider divorce.[11]

The Family Research Council and the University of Chicago conducted separate surveys in 1993 that together included more than 4,500 participants, and both found that couples who keep sex exclusive to marriage report the highest level of sexual satisfaction, while sexually active singles and couples who allow sex outside of marriage report the lowest. Lastly, a survey by the Institute for American Values, published in 2002, found that, among couples in "very unhappy" marriages, 80 percent of those who stayed married despite unhappiness reported having happy marriages five years later. But of those who divorced to find happiness, only 19 percent reported being happy five years later.[12] Linking divorce with dissatisfaction, Schaeffer says,

> Modern multiple divorce is rooted in the fact that many are seeking in human relationships what human relationships can never give. Why do they have multiple divorce, instead of merely promiscuous affairs? Because they are seeking more than merely the sexual relationship. But they can never find it, because what they are seeking does not exist in a purely finite relationship. It is like trying to quench thirst by swallowing sand.[13]

Genuine sexual satisfaction is a blessing God promises those who keep his rules. It works this way because God designed sex to fulfill something basic in human nature. It satisfies—not in the final and perfect sense that comes only from knowing God himself—but it does satisfy truly and profoundly. But, to know this blessing, sex must be moral. There is no other way. It requires obedience.

THE THIRD BLESSING: EXEMPLARY HONOR

The poet Michael Field once wrote about an elderly husband reflecting back on a life of faithful marriage. He must have countless memories—some good, some bad. But, considering everything, he focuses on one thing that for him stands higher than all. This is what he says:

> They bring me gifts, they honour me,
> Now I am growing old;
> And wondering youth crowds round my knee,
> As if I had a mystery
> And worship to unfold.
>
> To me the tender, blushing bride
> Doth come with lips that fail;
> I feel her heart beat at my side
> And cry: "Like Ares in his pride,
> Hail, noble bridegroom, hail!"[14]

The couple in the poem are near the end of their lives, and a younger generation is gathering at their knees. What is the secret of their long and happy marriage? The answer comes in the second verse. The husband still sees his wife as the "blushing bride" he married long ago, even though now she comes with "lips that fail." Their secret is something called *honor.* They have honored each other for years, and nothing now compares to the value they gain from each other. Though her body is weak, her value is stronger than ever, and feeling "her heart beat at my side" is the highest tribute anyone can give. And, in a marriage like that, you can be sure she thinks the same of him.

The third blessing God assigns sexual purity is exemplary honor—something having to do with favorable reputation—the opposite of shame and disgrace. In my training as a midshipman at the United States Naval Academy, honor was emphasized because it was "a quality which renders a man . . . incapable of any action which would bring reproach on his integrity."[15] Shakespeare believed the same and wrote, "Mine honor is my life; both grow in one. Take honor from me, and my life is done."[16] So if honor is that important, what does it mean, and how does it relate to sex and marriage?

To begin, we must see that honor has two sides. One is something others give you, and the other is something you give someone else. Either way, the key thing is connecting moral quality with reputation. Honor is a thing people must deserve and is otherwise false. We can define it as giving respect and praise for good reasons (such as character, actions, or some assigned role) to someone who deserves it, and receiving it for the same reasons from people whose character, judgment, and knowledge of us truly matter. We might add as well that, while honor shapes all human relationships, its importance varies with the level of relationship involved. Honor hardly matters at all in superficial or very impersonal situations, but is terribly important in relationships that are profound. Knowing this is critical for dealing with relationships involving sex, since sex connects human beings at one of the deepest levels possible.

In scripture, the meaning of honor is given in God's statement that "those who honor me I will honor, and those who despise me shall be lightly esteemed" (1 Sam. 2:30). Honor is something we give God as we recognize and respect his worth, and he then esteems us in return. But it works both ways, and despising God means he takes a dim view of us as well. Honoring God is more than words or sentiment. We must also obey him. Because of this, the Bible goes on to say that honor from God requires that we be "blameless," and failing in this regard results in "shame" (Ps. 37:18-19). This all has to do with honoring God and receiving honor from him. But there are other sorts of honor as well, so Paul says we should "aim at what is honorable not only in the Lord's sight but also in the sight of man" (2 Cor. 8:21).

To understand the critical link between honor and sexual purity, we must start at creation. Before sin came, we are told, Adam and Eve "were both naked and were not ashamed" (Gen. 2:25). They were sinless in every way, but the Bible underscores how it affected what they thought of sex. Without sin, there was no fear of shame. They were quite literally exposed "to God and the world." But because they were sinless, their nakedness was perfectly honorable. Purity covered dignity, and nothing else was needed. They were naked but not immorally exposed.

That all changes when sin arrives, and when Adam tries to explain why he hid he says, "I was afraid, because I was naked" (3:10). A monumental shift has taken place. The connection between sex and honor remains, but Adam sees it from a new point of view. Just as innocence assured dignity and made clothes unnecessary, so now guilt leaves them exposed—and the first thing affected was their view of sex.

But we must not draw wrong conclusions. To avoid this we need to observe two things. First is the vulnerability they sensed. The exposure causing Adam and Eve to feel ashamed was not physical but moral. They were not afraid of weather but of what God thought of them. Second, the sin which left them exposed was not itself an act of sex.[17] Sin affects sex, but sex is not sin. Corruption of human nature changed Adam and Eve's perspective on the connection between sex and honor. Without sin, they had nothing to fear, but as sinners they were understandably afraid. Moral innocence no longer covered their dignity, making them vulnerable. Honor now required covering up. When it comes to something as profound as sex, it is a shameful thing for sinners to be exposed.

As with other blessings that go with obeying God's rules on sex, honor is not only promised but also ordered. It is not left to choice but is required. We must seek God's reward of honor. Hebrews commands, "Let marriage be held in honor among all, and let the marriage bed be undefiled, for God will judge the sexually immoral and adulterous" (Heb. 13:4). Similarly, Paul says we must "abstain from sexual immorality," which means we must each "control his own body in . . . honor" (1 Thess. 4:3-4).

These passages command honor in relation to sex, first with respect to marriage and then as it affects the impression that our conduct has on others (both God and men). Honoring marriage (Heb. 13:4) will of course enhance good will toward people who save sex for marriage, and mastering personal behavior (1 Thess. 4:4) raises the dignity others see in you. We must seek God's blessing, and he rewards those who do.

Honor is worth having, not only because it protects from shame (Gen. 2:25; Ps. 37:19), but also because it adds something positive. This new thing is greater personal worth—not material worth but moral worth. Real honor has something to do with making you a better person. Exercise not only proves that you have muscles but helps them grow larger and stronger. In the same way, moral behavior not only proves what sort of character you have but makes your character grow. The Bible mentions this where Christians are told that we must "grow up in every way into him who is the head, [that is] into Christ" (Eph. 4:15), and God plans for us to be "transformed into the same image [as Christ] from one degree of glory to another" (2 Cor. 3:18). One way that we grow in Christ's image involves keeping sex morally pure, and since that is part of growing like Christ, it enhances moral worth as well.

The last verses of Proverbs describe how this works for a wife and mother, two roles that obviously depend on sexual fidelity. They start by asking, "An excellent wife who can find?" and answer that, "She is far more precious than jewels" (Prov. 31:10). Then comes a list of things making her worthy of honor. Everyone in her family benefits, but the credit reflects on her. "Her children rise up and call her blessed; her husband also, and he praises her: 'Many women have done excellently, but you surpass them all'" (vv. 28-29). These last verses end with, "Give her of the fruit of her hands, and let her works praise her in the gates" (v. 31). The formula throughout is that worthy behavior reveals worthy character, and worthy character deserves honor.

One statement needs special attention: "Strength and dignity are her clothing" (v. 25). This involves two words that are elsewhere used for the honor of God. "Splendor and majesty [*hādār*] are before him; strength [*ʿōz*] and joy are in his place" (1 Chron. 16:27). *Strength* in this case does not mean physical power but power to command respect—power to move others by respect and reputation—the sort of power claimed in the advertisement that says, "When E. F. Hutton speaks, everyone listens." The second word, translated *dignity* or *majesty*, refers to the effect generated by awe-inspiring goodness. They are two ways of saying one thing. The message is clear. A woman who is godly and responsible in all things including sex and marriage is not just worthy of honor in human terms but reflects the majesty of God. She deserves the same sort of honor. Not equal honor. Not greater honor. But honor of the same kind. The moral categories are the same.

Loss of honor caused by sexual sin is another theme in scripture, but this is simply the same thing in reverse. As honor blesses sexual purity, so dishonor comes with sexual sin. In fact, the Bible has so many warnings about dishonor, shame, disgrace, fear, and loss of reputation caused by sinning sexually that one might think God's view of dishonor nearly always involves sex. If exceptions exist, they are few. In any case, sexual sin always forfeits honor from God and usually shames a person in the eyes of others as well.

Before she was raped, Tamar rebuked Amnon, saying, "where could I carry my shame? And as for you, you would be as one of the outrageous fools in Israel" (2 Sam. 13:13). In other words, doing such a thing will not just violate *her* but will destroy *his* honor as well. He will lose all respect. Any honor he has in the eyes of others will be replaced by disdain.

Solomon later warns that sex outside of marriage is not just a path to death (Prov. 5:5) but a sure way of losing honor as well. "Keep your way far from her, and do not go near the door of her house, lest you give your honor to others" (vv. 8-9). Even with men, sexual sin usually sacrifices public opinion and respect (v. 14). The reason is that, "He who commits adultery lacks sense; he who does it destroys himself. Wounds and dishonor will he get, and his disgrace will not be wiped away" (6:32-33). In the words of Nicolas Boileau-Despreaux, a French poet who lived in the seventeenth century, "Honor is like an island, rugged and without a beach; once we have left it, we can never return."[18]

If you fail sexually but then repent, you will be forgiven by God and often by offended family members as well. Still, what happened cannot be changed and remains a mark against your character. Why? The reason is, forgiveness does not change whatever weakness led to the failure. It can set punishment aside, but character is a question of behavior whether you get punished or not. Because of this, honor is terribly hard to recover no matter how much you repent later on.

Jim Bakker and Jimmy Swaggart both headed large televised ministries and fell to sexual sin at the height of success. Both repented and were forgiven. But, for the rest of their lives, neither will have the respect and influence he had before. Solomon and Calvin Coolidge knew what they were saying, and it must be a warning to everyone who cares about honor. Losing it means disgrace that is very hard to change.

C. S. Lewis makes an important distinction about what people mean when they speak about sex and shame:

> Modern people are always saying, "Sex is nothing to be ashamed of." They may mean two things. They may mean "There is nothing to be ashamed of in the fact that the human race reproduces itself in a certain way, nor in the fact that it gives pleasure." If they mean that, they are right. Christianity says the same. It is not the thing, nor the pleasure, that is the trouble. . . . If anyone says that sex, in itself, is bad, Christianity contradicts him at once. But, of course, when people say, "Sex is nothing to be ashamed of," they may mean "the state into which the sexual instinct has now got is nothing to be ashamed of." If they mean that, I think they are wrong. . . . it is everything to be ashamed of.[19]

The point is that real honor and real shame in relation to sex are not matters of biology or psychology, and anyone who thinks so is wrong. What separates honor from shame is not physical or emotional, but moral. And the morality involved comes from God, not men. It is real morality, the sort by which God measures you, not the sort people say they can choose or make up themselves. Lewis therefore separates sexual biology (which is honorable) from the way human nature has affected how people think about sex (which is not).

This is why we must always be careful to separate honor based on what

God thinks from honor that merely reflects human opinion. What others praise *can* be true and should not be taken lightly. After all, Paul did say we should try being honorable even in the sight of man (2 Cor. 8:21). But human opinion sometimes goes horribly wrong, either because people get the wrong impression or because they start thinking in ways that rebel against God. The result is that honor from others connected with sex is not reliable, and only honor from God is correct all the time. Both matter, but only one can be trusted.

The reason we need to be cautious around honor from others where it affects sex is that sinners tend to excuse the sort of thing of which they are guilty themselves. Paul says, they "suppress the truth . . . by their unrighteousness" (Rom. 1:18). And at times the cultural situation is one in which, "On every side the wicked prowl, as vileness is exalted among the children of man" (Ps. 12:8). Whole cultures can be overrun with what God calls "dishonorable passions" (Rom. 1:26) since "those who practice such things . . . not only do them but give approval to those who practice them" (v. 32). If this gets to be extensive, honor and shame at the human level can sometimes become reversed, so that shameful things are honored and honorable things are treated as if they were shameful.

In scripture, culture-wide reversals of honor and shame are extreme situations, not the usual thing, and history is witness that most societies have tended to respect sexual fidelity even without knowing scripture. But culture-wide reversals have happened and could happen again. Jesus never trusted the honor of men (John 5:41) and neither should we. If honor from men supports God's approach on sex, marriage, and family, then it adds an extra dimension to his blessing. But if not, honor from God is enough. In the end, it is the only kind of honor that ever really matters.

The Fourth Blessing: Pure Allure

It is unusual these days to think of sexual modesty as *alluring*. How can attracting a sexual partner be consistent with restraint and discipline? Is not attracting sexual interest a matter of advertising what you have? The popular answer is, "If you've got it, flaunt it!" But the real answer is no. Sexual modesty is a powerful thing. There are different sorts of attractive power when it comes to sex, and the very best (the sort that is purest and strongest) has more to do with holding off than showing off.

People have understood this a long time, and Shakespeare gives a nice example in *Romeo and Juliet*. The romantic couple have just met and, to attract Romeo, Juliet does not flaunt herself but instead withdraws:

> Thou knowest the mask of night is on my face,
> Else would a maiden blush bepaint my cheek
> For that which thou hast heard me speak tonight. . . .
> if thou thinkest I am too quickly won,
> I'll frown, and be perverse, and say thee nay,
> So thou wilt woo; . . .
> I should have been more strange, I must confess,
> But that thou over-heard'st, ere I was 'ware,
> My true-love's passion: therefore pardon me;
> And not impute this yielding to light love, . . .
> although I joy in thee,
> I have no joy of this contract to-night:
> It is too rash, too unadvis'd, too sudden;
> Too like the lightning, which doth cease to be
> Ere one can say, It lightens. . . .
> [But] this bud of love, by summer's ripening breath,
> May prove a beauteous flower when next we meet.[20]

To attract Romeo, Juliet is modest, and that inspires him even more.

Years ago in high school, I observed that the sort of girl guys competed for were not the easy ones who threw themselves at boys or showed off all they had. Rather it was girls who had dignity, poise, and mystery because they were saving something. They were keeping themselves for the right person at the right time, and that made them special. The easy girls were made jokes of in the locker room. Not even guys who took advantage of them respected them, and to be fair I am sure those girls thought just as little of *them.*

Without modesty, no one is appealing in ways that inspire love and commitment to a lasting relationship. Whether it is Shakespeare or high school, the lesson is the same. Immodesty stirs lust that cares nothing about relationship, while modesty stirs love and commitment. It never works the other way, and that is because lust and love are totally different things.

The fourth blessing God promises with sexual purity is pure allure arising from sexual modesty—a power to attract others, especially of the opposite sex, by inspiring them to think you are worth a lot. Wendy Shalit, in *A Return to Modesty,* says,

> Certainly sexual modesty may damp down superficial allure, the kind of allure that inspires a one-night stand. But the kind of allure that lasts—that is what modesty protects and inspires. . . . Modesty dampens down crudeness, it doesn't dampen down *Eros*. In fact, it is more likely to enkindle it.[21]

It works this way because God made it to work this way. There is a connection between sexual allure and sexual morality, and those who understand this have the advantage when it comes to attracting someone worth having. We covered God's prohibition of immodesty in chapter 10. There we focused on why modesty is right and immodesty is wrong. But a blessing comes along with following God's moral rules on sex, and that is the part we are looking at now.

When Peter tells women, "let your adorning be the hidden person of the heart with the imperishable beauty of a gentle and quiet spirit," he follows by adding, "which in God's sight is very precious" (1 Pet. 3:4). Sexual modesty is attractive to God, which alone means a lot. But that is not all. Modesty attracts men in a powerful way as well, and Solomon provides an example when he tells the woman he is going to marry, "You have captivated my heart, my sister, my bride; you have captivated my heart with one glance of your eyes, with one jewel of your necklace" (Song 4:9). Solomon is captivated, not because this woman is brazen or loose, but because she is modest. With modesty it only takes a glance, it only takes a jewel, and you can capture the heart of a king!

Biblical modesty is not about avoiding something dirty but about guarding something precious. Impure sex is worthless, but pure, innocent, exclusive sex is worth a lot and very desirable. The reason goes back to God, who made sex in the first place. The most beautiful, attractive, desirable person in existence is God himself, and what makes him appealing is goodness. God's glory comes from goodness, his beauty comes from holiness, his attractiveness comes from purity. But these are all one thing. What makes God attractive is pure, holy goodness.

When Moses requests, "show me your glory," God answers, "I will make my goodness pass before you" (Ex. 33:18-19). In a song praising God, Moses sings, "Who is like you, majestic in holiness" (15:11). And, everyone must "worship the Lord in the splendor of holiness" (Ps. 29:2; 96:9; 1 Chron. 16:29). God embodies the attractiveness of goodness, and because he made sex, it applies there as well. Sexual purity is attractive because purity in God is attractive.

The attractive power in alluring sexual modesty is revealed several places in scripture, first when Rebekah meets Isaac, then in the poetry of Solomon, and last in the wisdom of Proverbs. When Rebekah sees Isaac coming to meet her on first arriving at his home, she reacts by emphasizing modesty. She is promised in marriage but he is not yet her husband. So, on dismounting from her camel, "she took her veil and covered herself." Then, after they are married, we are told Isaac truly "loved her" (Gen. 24:65-66). There is a huge difference between what Rebekah does (covering herself before a future husband) and references elsewhere to prostitutes hiding their identities (38:15; Song 1:7). Rebekah was not hiding her identity; everyone already knew who she was. Rather, it was modesty in the presence of sexual interest.

Her message to everyone (and especially Isaac) was that a sexual relationship with her was extraordinarily precious and had to be reserved for the right time. Isaac obviously got the message, because it inspired real love. Remember, this was an arranged marriage in which he had no say. It could have been very perfunctory. But her modesty made him appreciate her value, and she captured his heart. What resulted was not a marriage held together by lust or merely law, but love.

The same power to attract through the pure allure of sexual modesty appears in the Song of Solomon. Before marriage, Solomon longs for his future wife. "Let me see your face, let me hear your voice, for your voice is sweet, and your face is lovely" (Song 2:14). In that culture, rules of modesty required women to veil their faces in public and did not allow them to speak with men outside their families. So, even though they will be married, Solomon cannot see her face or hear her voice. But that inspires love, and his longing for her grows.

After they are married (3:6-11), modesty then bears some wonderful fruit. Modesty does not only say no but also yes—no to everyone else and no when the time is not right, but yes to the right person at the right time. Pure, innocent, exclusive sex in marriage is extraordinary because what was denied so long, and still is denied everyone else, is given to one special person. The Song of Solomon refers to sex as "a garden locked . . . a spring locked, a fountain sealed" that is filled with "all choicest fruits" and "all chief spices." Outside of marriage it is locked, hidden, and sealed. But when the couple marries, the wife tells her husband, "Awake, O north wind, and come, O south wind! Blow upon my garden, let its spices flow. Let my beloved come to his garden and eat its choicest fruits" (4:12-16).

Here is something extraordinary! She takes the key locking everyone out, and gives it to him! She has kept everyone out, and that made her special; but now she gives him the key, allowing him in, and that makes *him* special. That is why modesty is alluring! It does not keep the garden locked forever, but saves it for the right person at the right time.

Incidentally, this is what the traditional wedding veil signifies. It stands for modesty's amazing turn from denial to access—from locking others out to letting a special person in. Until they are man and wife, the bride's face is veiled. There is a barrier. But, when they are married, the minister says, "You may kiss the bride." The barrier is lifted, and they kiss. It stands for the sexual intimacy she has saved, and when they are married, she allows him inside the barrier. Many brides now go through the wedding ceremony with faces uncovered the whole time, and some have stopped wearing veils at all. In an age that is forgetting modesty, it is enough to make you wonder if the bride has any barrier to remove. Lifting the wedding veil stands for something we should not forsake.

There is a final lesson on the pure allure of modesty in the Song of Solomon which has to do with how a wife stays attractive to her husband in marriage. Even after Solomon and his wife are married (Song 3:6-11) and are sexually active (4:16; 6:2-3), the wife still says, "Turn away your eyes from me, for they overwhelm me" (6:5). What is she doing? She obviously loves him (2:16; 6:3; 7:10) and desires him very much (8:1). But easy access taken for granted cheapens the seeming value of sex even in marriage. A wife is a person, not a machine, and she needs to be wooed even after she is married. If sex becomes automatic and common, it no longer seems special, and a wife loses her appeal. Modesty is an engine that drives pure allure even within marriage. In this case, modesty is not about stopping sex but about keeping it special. Solomon's wife retains some mystery, and acting modestly is the way she stays alluring to her husband.

We have learned something from Genesis and the Song of Solomon, but the attractive power of alluring sexual modesty is nowhere explained more clearly than where Proverbs discusses an excellent wife. We have looked at this passage for what it says about honor, but it explains the allure of modesty as well. We have seen how modesty attracts, including the way that withholding sex makes it special; and we have noticed as well that what is attractive comes from purity. But what exactly is there in sexual purity that makes it magnetic? What about it is desirable? The details are given in Proverbs 31:10-31. Remember that God's attractiveness (his glory, splendor, and beauty) is all a matter of character (goodness, holiness, and purity). Now from Proverbs 31:10-31 we find that God made the allure in sexual relationships on the same design. The power of modesty to allure comes from character as well. So what makes an excellent (truly modest) wife appealing?

First, she has the allure of unique value. "She is far more precious than jewels" (v. 10). "Many women have done excellently, but you surpass them all" (v. 29). No one else compares. She stands far above the rest.

Second, she has the allure of reliability. "The heart of her husband trusts in her" (v. 11). "Her lamp does not go out at night" (v. 18). "She is not afraid of snow for her household, for all her household are clothed in scarlet" (v. 21). "She looks well to the ways of her household and does not eat the bread of idleness" (v. 27). She can be counted on no matter what.

Third, she has the allure of someone wonderful to be around. "She opens her hand to the poor and reaches out her hands to the needy" (v. 20). "The teaching of kindness is on her tongue" (v. 26). She is kind, unselfish, and generous, all of which make her the kind of friend you want when things are rough as well as when things are pleasant.

Fourth, she has the allure of success based on industry and wisdom. "She rises while it is yet night and provides food for her household" (v. 15). "With the fruit of her hands she plants a vineyard" (v. 16), and "makes linen garments and sells them" (v. 24). "She opens her mouth with wisdom" (v. 26). She is a great partner for any enterprise.

Fifth, she has the allure of someone possessing a great reputation. Because of her reputation, "Her husband is known in the gates when he sits among the elders of the land" (v. 23); her behavior is well-known and respected by leaders of their community—"let her works praise her in the gates" (v. 31).

Sixth, she has the allure of dignity. "Strength and dignity are her clothing" (v. 25). She impresses people, not because she is pushy, loud, or brash, but because everywhere she goes, people sense that she is special. Her quality is something others sense without needing to have it explained.

Put that all together, and you have an amazingly attractive woman. She is perfectly modest but is certainly no wallflower. What allures men, stirring them to love, romance, sacrifice, and commitment, is her character. This is the sort of woman who, when she is still single, men are drawn to, because her alluring purity says she is truly extraordinary. They desire a relationship with her. They want intimacy with her, including a physical relationship. But the power attracting them to her is not lust but longing for a partner who is exceptional, trustworthy, great to be with, successful, admired by others, and always impressive. Men treat her as special because she truly is special. She is not vulgar, common, or ordinary, but one-in-a-million. She is not trash, but a jewel. Modesty is how a woman tells men, "Exclusive intimacy with me is worth everything you have. It is worth lifelong commitment because it is worth your life, and to win me a man had better be extraordinary himself."

Confirmation of God's blessing even comes from the ways in which sinners try perverting it. Once, driving in an unfamiliar city, I passed a billboard advertising female "escorts" in a way that obviously meant prostitutes. What caught my attention was how this particular business claimed its prostitutes were *classy*. In other words, it was claiming that sex with these prostitutes was more appealing because these particular prostitutes were not available to just anyone at all. They were saving themselves for special customers—like anyone who happened to be driving past that billboard! It was a horrible contradiction, but it showed that even prostitutes know sex is cheapened and is therefore less appealing if available to just anyone at all. Sex is always more desirable if saved for someone special.

Child pornographers, pedophiles, and men returning from dates boasting about sex with a virgin, are drawn by the same thing. They all believe sex with innocence is appealing, that sex is better if you are the only partner someone has, and that sharing sex around makes it cheap. These perversions all confirm something true. Innocence, exclusivity, and uniqueness are indeed alluring. But, when these qualities are perverted (as in pedophilia), their perversion destroys the very thing making them attractive. Those who pervert those qualities fail to see that God never lets anyone enjoy innocence, exclusivity, and uniqueness outside his moral boundaries, and anyone who tries to do so only gets a false reflection made worse for destroying something good.

At the start of her career, Britney Spears raced up the popular music charts not only because she sang well, but also because she had the image of being a good girl worthy of being admired by her fans. She seemed better than other performers because she was pure. She was a virgin. She was modest. She had standards that set her apart and made her special. Then her image began to change.

First it was her dancing, then her clothes, then her lyrics, and finally it affected what she did in real life. Now all she offers is lust. The appeal she had of sexual purity is gone. Without modesty, her only attraction is the sort that makes her common—not special. She has traded pure allure for lust, and she has traded respect for titillation.

Starting with the allure of modesty that made her special, Spears compromised in favor of lust, so that now she has lost what made her special in the first place. Lust attracts fans at the cost of dignity and admiration. Modesty inspires fans to admire the performer, while lust reduces the performer to performance and focuses fans on themselves.

Tragically, Spears is not alone and represents a whole new generation of women who are trading the allure of sexual modesty for lust. Distracted by lust, they are losing the stronger, more worthy appeal of mystery worth pursuing and intimacy worth having. They are, in other words, losing a blessing they can have only if they follow God's rules. To this generation Wendy Shalit says,

> It is high time sexual modesty came out of the closet. Not only can you not get AIDS from it, not only is it morally right, but . . . modesty is really much more exciting than promiscuity. Without obstacles in the way of desire, what is there to desire? . . . Modesty is proof that morality is sexy. It may even be the proof of God, because it means that we have been designed in such a way that when we humans act like animals, without any sense of restraint and without any rules, we just don't have as much fun.[22]

The pure allure of sexual modesty is one of four blessings God promises with sexual purity. Sex within God's boundaries is powerfully attractive in a way that is lost once you take it out of bounds. Abiding joy, genuine satisfaction, exemplary honor, and pure allure are profoundly valuable, but they are not hard to understand. Follow God's rules and you will like the results. Obeying God is very worthwhile.

SOME FINAL REMARKS

Biblical sexual morality is not just good, it is awe-inspiring in beauty, depth, complexity, and glory. It is perfectly delightful in every detail. God made it that way for our benefit, but it honors God as well (1 Cor. 6:20). He is a benefactor who enjoys our enjoyment when we use his gift according to plan.

As with everything God created, the more we understand the excellence of his design for sex the more we must worship in gratitude. And that means obeying. Who in his right mind would think otherwise? How can we thank God for a gift worth more than we possibly deserve? The only way is by accepting and following God's directions.

But not everyone does this. We turn now to four counterfeit views of sexual morality competing against the biblical view in American life and culture. Each counterfeit opposes biblical sexual morality with a different way of defining what makes sex right or wrong. Each one is based on enough truth to deceive, but at heart each is destroying God's gift by denying that he gave it and by throwing out the directions he has given.

PART THREE

COUNTERFEIT VIEWS OF SEXUAL MORALITY

12

Romantic Sexual Morality: Sex as Affection

It is no secret that American culture is drifting far from the standards of sexual morality found in the Bible. In place of sexual standards tied by faith or tradition to what God reveals in scripture, our culture is fast embracing several other views, all of which are fundamentally opposed to biblical sexual morality.

Four counterfeit views on sexual morality have emerged to compete with the traditional influence of biblical morality in American culture, and these can be identified as *romantic, playboy, therapeutic,* and *pagan* versions of sexual morality. Each is distinct and offers a different way of understanding what makes sexual behavior right or wrong. Readers must understand that we are not simply considering exceptions to traditional standards. These are completely different ways of defining sexual morality. We are not quibbling over where to place a few boundary markers. Rather we are in a battle over who owns the property and gets to say how it should be used.

Naturally some big differences distinguish each counterfeit from the others, but all the counterfeits are competing with *biblical,* or what some call *traditional,* sexual morality and are trying to replace it with something quite contrary. None of the counterfeits can be right unless what God says in scripture is immoral. On the other hand, if the Bible is right, then all the countefeits are terribly wicked. There is no compromise position in this contest. If one side is right, the others are wrong. This does not mean we should be rude or unkind toward those we think are mistaken. Christians are bound to love everyone with the love of Christ, even those we think are wrong.

Nevertheless, we are dealing with a very serious matter. We are dealing with divisions over whether what God says in scripture is right or wrong.

It is important that Christians become familiar with sources of competition seeking to replace the traditional influence of biblical sexual morality in Western culture. We are all aware *that* challenges have arisen. But how many actually understand *what* these challenges are and *how* they are being made? Some new ways of thinking are rather beguiling, and unwary Christians may find themselves far astray before realizing they have actually taken another path.

In this chapter we will evaluate romantic sexual morality, and in later chapters we will go on to review the playboy, therapeutic, and pagan approaches to sexual morality. In each case we will first identify characteristic features of that approach and will then consider how it fails God's approach to sexual morality as revealed in the Bible.

In February 2001, superstar movie celebrities Tom Cruise and Nicole Kidman shocked friends and fans by announcing they were getting divorced after ten years of marriage. Both were highly successful professionals. Money was no problem, and neither questioned the actual fidelity of the other. For years their affection for one another had been praised throughout the world of entertainment. Hollywood friends called them "the ultimate A-list couple," meaning their love represented a romantic ideal that inspired those who knew them. So, when Cruise and Kidman announced their divorce, many seemed caught off-guard. All that *People* magazine could say was they just "ran out of steam,"[1] and reporters suggested busy careers had demanded so much time and energy that the couple just could not keep romantic feelings high enough to justify marriage.

Interestingly, those who were most shocked seemed to be Hollywood friends who knew them best. Actors and actresses, familar with the typical brevity of Hollywood relationships, could not believe their marriage was over because they said Tom and Nicole were such a "close couple," were "so much in love," were a "perfect match," and "just adored each other." They did not think it wrong or unusual, however, that people should get divorced after feelings changed. They were only stunned because feelings between Cruise and Kidman had grown cold after having once been so strong.

Sadly, this faith in ideal romance had not seemed nearly as trustworthy to Nicole. She had wanted to remain married to Tom for life, and yet she admitted having feared what would happen if their feelings cooled. In an interview a few months before, Nicole had said, "All I can say is I hope we are together when we are 80. I can't say we will be, but I will be so devastated if we are not." She had sensed earlier the insecurity of marriage based on feelings, and their divorce proved her right—her marriage did fall apart and she was devastated.

But why did Cruise, Kidman, and their friends all assume that marriage is over once affection cools? How could Cruise walk away from a wife and two children after ten years of marriage just because he felt differently? And why were their friends so amazed that strong romantic feelings did not last? It all depends on understanding romantic sexual morality and how it falls short of true sexual morality given in the Bible.

Description of Romantic Sexual Morality

What we are calling *romantic* sexual morality could also be called *sentimental* sexual morality, and others have called it the *ethic of intimacy* or the *affectional view.*[2] All these terms refer to an approach to sexual morality constructed on the basis of romantic feelings. Anyone listening to secular music, watching soap operas, or reading romantic fiction will recognize this approach. Romantic sexual morality so glorifies the importance of sentimental affection in sexual relationships that sex is justified based on feelings alone. It says couples have only to decide if they are *in love,* and if they are, then sex is moral whatever else might be the case.

The characteristics of romantic sexual morality are especially evident in the lyrics of secular love songs, such as, "You Light Up My Life," which Debby Boone made the number one hit song for 1977. Boone concluded, "it can't be wrong when it feels so right."[3] And while she claimed in interviews that the song was about spiritual life, music fans generally interpreted her words as justifying sex based on feelings. Other singers and song lyrics have been more direct. Gina G, in "Fresh," sings, "I wanna do all the things that turn you on," and justifies it by saying, "if it feels so right, how can it be wrong tonight?"[4] Diana Ross, in "Love Makes It Right," repeats, "love will make it right, love will choose the night."[5] And, in "I Honestly Love You," Olivia Newton-John claims honest love means ending the moment with sex instead of "just a kiss."[6]

Romantic sexual morality believes that affectionate feelings are irresistible and reason is irrelevant because being "in love" is so overwhelming. In "Hooked on a Feeling," B. J. Thomas denies personal responsibility because "I can't stop this feelin' deep inside of me."[7] If feelings justify actions, then of course sex cannot be stopped either, and that is exactly what Faith Hill says in "Go the Distance." Singing about justifying sex, Hill claims she simply "can't resist" because "our hearts lead us on" and "the feelin's way too strong."[8] Sometimes romantic sexual morality goes beyond just *allowing* sex to suggesting that sex may even be *mandated* by very strong affection. This seems to be what Linda Ronstadt says when she urges, "don't pass up the chance" because "this time it's true romance,"[9] and Olivia Newton-John says the same to a lover, explaining, "this feeling doesn't come along every day" so "you shouldn't blow the chance."[10]

ROMANTIC SEXUAL MORALITY

General Characteristics

Source of Moral Authority Is:	Self
Moral Authority Consists of:	Sensing Affection
Moral Goal Is:	Mutual sentimentality
Philosophical Basis Is:	Modernism
Functional Purpose Is:	Producing happiness
Approach Is:	Mundane (of this world)
Moral Standards Are:	Subjective (depends on choice and human control)
Main Focus Is:	Love of feeling "in love"
Secondary Focus Is:	Loving a lover
Tertiary Focus Is:	(Nothing else)
Most Important Dimension of Sex Is:	The emotional dimension
Depth Is:	Hopes for depth but ends up shallow (not profound)
Sex Is Considered:	A spontaneous act
Sexual Morality Is Considered:	A private matter (no one else's business)
Sexual Intimacy Is Considered:	Either public or private matter (depending on choice)
Marriage Should Be:	Monogamous and lifelong (if possible)
Traditional Marriage Is Considered:	Ideal but not necessary for everyone
Children Are Considered:	Competition
Sexual Discipline Is Considered:	A bad thing
Relation of Sex to Marriage:	Sex justifies marriage
Relation of Happiness to Family Duty:	Emotional happiness justifies fulfilling family duty
Effect on the Dimensions of Sex:	Reduces sex to emotion
Relational Nature of Sex Is:	Affirmed
Spiritual Life Is:	Ignored or denied
Scripture Is:	Ignored or denied
God's Authority over Sex Is:	Ignored or denied
Ultimately Worships:	The emotional-sexual self

But if affection is what makes sex right, how strong must the affection be? Here romantics go two ways, with some moving toward idealism and others toward realism. Romantic idealists believe "true love" will last forever if feelings are strong enough. They say sex is right when feelings become strong enough to assure lasting love. Thus Suzanne Glass represents romantic idealism in, "Is It Gonna Last?" where she sings, "I'm gonna take the chance now baby 'cause I think it's gonna last."[11]

But deciding when feelings have reached the right level is not easy, and any uncertainty is excruciating because so much depends on guessing correctly. So, for example, Jimi Jamison of the group Survivor wants "a love that's everlasting" but wonders "if the feeling's strong enough?"[12] Carole King complains she cannot tell if the "light of love" in her lover's eyes is "a lasting treasure, or just a moment's pleasure."[13] And Jennifer Lopez hopes for love that "lasts a lifetime" but does not know if it is "love knocking at my door or just the sound of my beating heart."[14]

Suffering heartache from several bad guesses turns many idealists into romantic realists hoping they can protect their feelings by lowering expectations. Realists still believe feelings justify sex, but they no longer expect feelings to last or even be strong. Genuine affection at the moment takes the place of lasting love. Jennifer Lopez illustrates romantic realism in songs where she decides a pang of feeling means "you and me were meant to be" even though "I barely know you," and where she keeps a lover from promising "forever" because she only wants "honest" feelings on a day-to-day basis.[15] Romantic realism knows that feelings change, but adds that once the feelings go, they will never return. Renewing lost love is hopeless, and someone who "hangs on" must be either selfish or immature. Losing love cannot be helped, and no one is responsible. The Righteous Brothers announced that once "you've lost that lovin' feelin'," then it's "gone, gone, gone"[16]; Gordon Lightfoot said "the feeling's gone and I just can't get it back"[17]; and Carole King explained "it's too late, baby, now" because "something inside has died."[18]

The shift from hope in "lasting love" to expecting nothing more than "love at the moment" can be wrenching, because those who accept less often do so reluctantly. In "Angel of the Morning," which could be one of the saddest songs ever recorded, Merrilee Rush sings of accepting sex in the night even though abandoned by her lover in the morning. They were "victims of the night," but it was justified by "love" and "it was what I wanted now." Romantic realists end up thinking any infatuation justifies sex so long as it is *real,* and brief infatuation can be *real* even if it does not last the night. Consistent with that logic, Rush says there is "no need to take me home" because she is "old enough to face the dawn."[19] But her words rasp on her emotions and are poignant precisely because listeners get the idea she really does not want to give up hoping for a love that will take her home and last forever.

While the idealist side in romantic sexual morality holds that strong affection will guarantee lifelong relationships, the realist side either denies that ever happens or treats the occurrence as something so rare it cannot be expected in most cases. So, instead of one-lover-for-life, romantic realists justify and expect a series of lovers who will come and go as feelings come and go. A sexual relationship is exclusive, but only while feelings last. Fidelity in romantic sexual morality is not to a particular lover but to a particular feeling, so fidelity in a relationship applies only so long as a lover is loved and shifts when affection shifts.

Unlike other counterfeit approaches to sexual morality, the romantic view takes a fairly positive view of marriage and generally prefers it to couples simply *living together* without having any obligation to each other. But while romantic morality regards marriage as something good, it does not believe marriage is required to have sex. In romantic morality, marriage does not legitimize expressing romantic affection with sex; rather, expressing romantic affection with sex legitimizes marriage. Romantics think marriage is a good way to express feelings; but if feelings fade, then sex is bad and the marriage is over.

The same logic that justifies sex without marriage also kills marriage when the level of shared affection drops. Killing *dead* marriages is treated as a duty. The idea of holding marriage together in hope that feelings might return is dismissed as naive, and trying to keep someone in a marriage against his or her feelings is criticized as cruel. Faith Hill, in "Life's Too Short to Love Like That," cuts off a relationship because her feelings have changed so that what was *right* now is *wrong*. If affection evaporates, any sexual relationship is immoral whether partners are married or not.

In romantic sexual morality, forsaken lovers must let unfaithful lovers go no matter how bad it makes them feel. Merrilee Rush sings, "there'll be no strings to bind your hands, not if my love can't bind your heart."[20] And Bonnie Tyler, in "Don't Turn Around," believes she has a duty to let her lover go even though "it's tearing me up" and she really wants to "scream out loud that I love you" and to plead, "don't go! don't go! don't go!"[21] Instead of blaming heartache on the faithless, romantic morality blames the faithful. Breaking hearts is moral, but having your heart broken is not. If the forsaken have hurt feelings, it is their own fault. So, in "Just Walk Away," Celine Dion explains, "I've got to take the blame and find the strength I need to let you go."[22] The pain of loving someone whose feelings have changed is all her fault.

Taken as a whole, romantic sexual morality makes a duty of following romantic affection into sex because feeling *in love* is irresistible—but it also requires lovers to stifle affection if forsaken. Romantic sexual morality praises lasting love—but it also expects that most lovers are going to come and go as feelings shift. Romantic sexual morality tells lovers to trust feelings—but not enough to be burned by a lover who might leave at any moment, and never for a second longer than your love-of-the-moment happens to love you in return.

EVALUATION OF ROMANTIC SEXUAL MORALITY

Even though standards based on romantic sexual morality obviously clash with biblical sexual morality, Christians should recognize what the romantic approach gets right before criticizing how it goes wrong. In fact, what makes romantic sexual morality tempting are exactly those aspects that are nearest to biblical truth. Romantic morality is right to think that love is a good thing in sexual relationships. It is right to understand that sex is a relationship and not a commodity. And it is right to believe that sex should be saved for a loved one, and that good sexual relationships involve strong feelings. Christian criticism of romantic sexual morality is not about whether love is essential in sex and marriage, rather we differ over what real love has to do with feelings, and whether feelings make sex moral.

However else we disagree at other points, we can acknowledge that sex based on affection is at least better than sex based on lust; and couples having sex because they love each other is certainly better than strangers using each other as sex *objects*. But saying that sex with love is better than sex without love is like saying cars run better on gas than on sand. Just putting gas in the tank does not give me permission to drive without a license, and neither does adding affection give couples permission to have sex without marriage.

God designed sex to engage powerful feelings, but strong romantic feelings cannot be the blessings God wants them to be unless those feelings are kept in proper channels. Romantic sexual morality is right to appreciate the importance of feelings in sex and marriage, but it is wrong about the channels. So, having recognized what the romantic approach gets right, here are seven important ways in which romantic sexual morality goes wrong.

1. It Misunderstands True Love

While this might sound odd, the first problem with romantic sexual morality is that it really does not understand true love. Jesus says we must love each other with the same sort of selfless love that sent him to the cross (John 13:34; 15:12), and that sort of love involves far more than feelings, because it endures excruciating pain and transcends even the fear of death itself. And, lest we think true love in sexual relationships is something else, Paul tells husbands they must love their wives "as Christ loved the church and gave himself up for her" (Eph. 5:25).

True love in the Bible is a decision of the mind and will, with feelings riding on top or following behind. True love is something secure on which feelings hang, but which lasts unchanged whether feelings are there or not. C. S. Lewis explains the difference:

> Love as distinct from "being in love" is not merely a feeling. It is a deep unity, maintained by the will and deliberately strengthened by habit; reinforced by (in Christian marriages) the grace which both . . . [partners] ask, and receive from God. They can have this love for each other even at those moments when they do not like each other; as you love yourself even when you do not like yourself. They can retain this love even when each would easily, if they allowed themselves, be "in love" with someone else. "Being in love" first moved them to promise fidelity: this quieter love enables them to keep the promise. It is on this love that the engine of marriage is run: being in love was the explosion that started it.[23]

Romantic sexual morality sees no difference between real love and its ornaments. So it mistakes romantic feelings for the real thing and then expects decorations to serve in place of the foundation. If the stakes were not so great, the error would be as comical as riding a saddle without a horse or making a cake of nothing but frosting.

Romantic sexual morality celebrates feelings and expects them to be as reliable as real love. And because feelings change, romantic morality always dashes expectations, not because there is anything wrong with the goal but because it mistakes the goal for something else. Paul Brady approaches the truth in the song, "The Long Goodbye," in which he wonders, "just what kind of love keeps breaking a heart, no matter how hard we try?"[24] Real love does not break hearts, but mistaking affection for real love does so every time.

2. *It Offers False Hope*

The second problem with romantic sexual morality is that it turns true love into false hope. Romantic morality not only misunderstands the goal, it also blocks off the only true way of reaching it. Because the romantic approach is wrong about real love, it does not understand that real love is complex and works on many levels at once. Without realizing this, romantic morality tries to separate the emotional dimension from other vital parts, and the result is much like picking a flower. I may enjoy its beauty for a while, but a flower starts dying the moment I cut it from its roots.

God made sex a complex relationship that joins human partners physically, psychologically, and spiritually as well as emotionally, and every sexual relationship affects all dimensions whether we acknowledge it or not. Because romantic sexual morality tries to separate emotions from the rest, it generates trouble for other dimensions of sexual union, especially the spiritual part. Whenever a man and a woman have sex, a transcendental relation is set up between them which must be eternally enjoyed or eternally endured whether they like it or not. Sex outside God's moral boundaries often faces problems caused by human rivalry and jealousy, but its most serious result is corruption of the spiritual relationship without which lovers cannot know true love. True love is completely impossible without union on the spiritual level, and romantic sexual morality blocks the possibility of finding it by ignoring how it works in several dimensions at once and corrupting spiritual union with sexual impurity.

By blocking the way to real love, romantic sexual morality prevents couples from reaching the stage in a relationship where the benefits of lasting love become evident. With anything involving feelings, the initial thrill of fresh feelings must die to make way for lasting satisfaction, and this applies as much to love and romance as anything else. C. S. Lewis made this clear:

> It is simply no good trying to keep any thrill: that is the very worst thing you can do. Let the thrill go—let it die away—go on through that period of death into the quiet interest and happiness that follow—and you will find you are living in a world of new thrills all the time. But if you decide to make thrills your regular diet and try to prolong them artificially, they will get weaker and weaker, and fewer and fewer.[25]

Feeling *in love* is a good thing—it is the explosion that moves lovers toward marriage. But it is not the best thing, and if you think you must always start over when the initial emotional explosion dies down you will never reach the better satisfaction of real love which is the engine on which lifelong marriages are run.

3. *It Turns Promises into Lies*

The third problem with romantic sexual morality is that it turns promises into lies. Romantic idealists are always promising "undying" love. But they do not really expect lovers to keep such promises, and if some do trust a lover's promise, they suffer heartache along with a large dose of blame for being "naive." In one song, Diana Ross simply claims, "Love lies 'cause it doesn't last forever. . . . You give and it just takes and leaves your heart to ache. Love lies."[26]

Romantic sexual morality makes promises that are either irrelevant or false. If feelings really are everything, then a promise makes no difference; and, if promises are given with no intention of being kept, then lovers must be liars. Feelings always change, and no one can guarantee how they will feel in the future, so the idea of promising anything based on feelings is utter nonsense. This leaves two ironies regarding romantic morality and promises. First, because it believes feelings should be more reliable the stronger they get, romantic morality suggests that promises are more trustworthy the less they are needed and are completely trustworthy only when not needed at all. Second, because romantic morality does not distinguish between love and passion, it leaves lovers wondering if promises are most reliable exactly when they are least reliable.

4. It Rejects Responsibility

The fourth problem with romantic sexual morality is that it really is much too weak to handle sexual passion. When it comes to feelings, romantic morality is all about giving in and not being responsible, and it is most permissive exactly at the points where discipline is needed most—when teens are alone in the back seat of a car, when a husband sees more of a business partner than his wife, when the burdens of family life seem less fun than entertaining undemanding friends, or when illness denies all chance of romance. Those looking for love go astray when searching for it the hardest, those trying to keep sex for one true love are deceived when most vulnerable, those depending on love lasting are abandoned when weakest, and those responsible for families are tempted to leave exactly when most needed.

Because romantic morality depends on feelings, it has no way to hold feelings accountable. No morality is more reliable than the foundation on which it builds, so whatever depends on romantic sexual morality is never more secure than the feelings on which romantic morality is built. Jesus warned of building lives on anything resembling sand (Matt. 7:24-27), and nothing resembles shifting, unstable sand more than the shifting, unstable feelings of romantic affection. Romantic sexual morality denies responsibility for the future and resigns the security of marriage to fate—a very one-sided sort of fate because good results depend on an impossible ideal. Lasting marriage is a sucker's jackpot that depends on never-changing romantic sentiments, which is about like offering a prize for keeping a cloud fixed in the sky. In the end, the weakness of romantic sexual morality endangers everyone and everything that depends on lasting marriages. The security and welfare of children, the economic interdependence of families, and eventually the social stability of society itself, all become victims of passing personal emotion.

5. *It Reverses the Connection Between Affection and Morality*

A fifth problem with romantic morality is that it reverses the way feelings of affection relate to sex and marriage. The mind-directed sort of love that shapes sexual morality in the Bible requires couples to enter a covenant commitment in which each accepts a moral obligation to be faithful to the other in marriage for life before they are allowed to have sex. In scripture, love that governs personal relationships is something that comes from God, not from emotions (1 John 4:7). And God's love is "unfailing" and "righteous," which means it never changes and always agrees with his standards of morality (Ps. 33:5; Prov. 15:9). As a result, affectionate feelings may precede, accompany, or follow the time a couple accepts the moral obligations of marriage. But the timing of romantic feelings never justifies having sex before a couple accepts these lasting moral obligations.

Romantic sexual morality takes the unconditional promise of lifelong fidelity that justifies sex in biblical morality and replaces it with feelings, while assuming that nothing else should be affected. But, of course, it changes everything. For, whereas God says sexual morality must define and guide the way couples express affectionate feelings, romantics instead say that feelings of sexual affection are what should shape and define sexual morality. So, while biblical morality justifies sex based on a promise of lifelong fidelity and therefore protects marriage with something that should never change, romantic sexual morality legitimizes sex based on affection and therefore leaves marriage vulnerable to something that never stops changing.

6. *It Worships Feelings*

The sixth problem with romantic morality is that it depends on pride and encourages couples to idolize feelings. Francis Schaeffer once pointed out,

> One does not have to have had much pastoral experience to have met married couples who refuse to have what they can have, because they have set themselves a false standard of superiority. . . . [I]f their marriage

> does not measure up to their own standards of superiority, they smash everything to the ground. They must have the ideal love affair of the century just because they are who they are! . . . You suddenly see a marriage smashed—everything gone to bits, people walking away from each other, destroying something really possible and beautiful—simply because they have set a proud standard and refuse to have the good marriage they can have.[27]

Romantic sexual morality may not produce self-centered individuals but it often does produce self-centered couples. Romantic idealists believe perfect love is something they can achieve by putting their own shared feelings over everything in life. In their minds, the more *us-centered* they get the closer they are to perfection. But in reality, their quest for perfect *us-centeredness* amounts to nothing more than us-centered, two-person pride.

In the Bible true love is God-centered, and anything else is perverted by some sort of pride. Paul explains that real love does "*nothing* out of selfish ambition or vain conceit" but instead, "Each of you should look not only to your own interests, but also to the interests of others" (Phil. 2:3-4, NIV, emphasis added). Because it covers everything, Paul's exhortation certainly includes sexual relationships. And what Jesus said must have shocked hearers when he announced that anyone who "does not *hate* [even] his . . . wife . . . cannot be my disciple" (Luke 14:26, emphasis added; also Luke 18:29). These words still shock many today, but his message is not difficult to understand once we realize that Jesus was using *hate* to indicate priority with respect to the role God should play in our lives. Jesus was warning that relationships with people who are closest to us in life—most particularly within marriage and family relationships—are going to be idols competing with loyalty to Christ, unless we learn to love every *loved one* in a way that places love and loyalty to Christ over absolutely everything else—even sexual loyalty within marriage.

Loving a wife or husband in marriage is something very good, but it can become something bad if self-centered, two-person pride ("just us over everything else") makes it an idol limiting how we are willing to love and obey Jesus Christ. If I really love a spouse, I will want the best for him or her as defined by loyalty to Christ, and loving that person any other way is less than what is truly best for the *loved one*. Romantic sexual morality is idolatrous because it puts romantic affection between lovers here on earth in a role God reserves for himself alone.

7. It Destroys the Affection It Promises

The seventh problem with romantic sexual morality is not just ironic but tragic. It is that taking the romantic approach destroys the very affection it promises. God designed sex to create a total union between persons at all levels at once, but romantic morality tells individuals to avoid unconditional commitments and hinders partners from pursuing total union. Partners share only what they feel at the moment, and each has to restrain expectations to keep them from growing beyond the feelings of the other. But when expectations are constantly denied and longings are constantly restricted, emotions get poisoned and wither. It is impossible for any reasonable person to invest significant emotions in a relationship that might end at any moment.

It is not romantic sexual morality, but biblical morality, that truly assures the growth of affection in sexual relationships. While biblical morality protects loving emotions, romantic sexual morality exposes them to danger and eventually crushes whatever develops. Feelings in a sexual relationship flourish only when free of fear, and they are free of fear only if protected by a commitment of will that hangs nothing on the feelings themselves. They flourish when committed, will-directed love sustains the security of a sexual relationship in marriage. But they die if they must carry the weight of maintaining the security of any sexual relationship on their own.

Affection in a sexual relationship cannot reach its maximum potential without maximum protection, and it only has sufficient protection when sex is guarded by unconditional, covenant commitment to be faithful in marriage. Rather than hindering affection between lovers, saving sex for marriage as required by biblical morality is the only real way to free affections long enough to reach full maturity.

So what of the questions we asked about Tom Cruise and Nicole Kidman at the start of this chapter? First, from the fact that reporters, friends quoted in the media, and Cruise and Kidman themselves all apparently assumed that marriage is over if affection fades, it would appear that the romantic approach to sex and marriage is simply accepted without question in the world of secular entertainment. Second, Tom Cruise apparently felt justified leaving a ten-year marriage because romantic morality says it is wrong to stay married after feelings fade away. And third, Hollywood friends were shocked even though other romances come and go daily, because romantic idealists really think feelings will remain if strong enough, and those who knew Cruise and Kidman were sure their affection had reached the unchanging stage.

But while we should be saddened by divorce, should anyone really be surprised that feelings fluctuate even after they have become very strong? Feelings rise and fall all the time, and no one can possibly guarantee that their feelings will stay unchanged over time. If we are honest about feelings, then the promises of romantic sexual morality ring hollow because they hang some of life's greatest treasures—love, sex, and marriage—on the weakest of all safeguards. The better we understand true love and affection, the more we should also respect biblical sexual morality.

Sheldon and Davy (Jean) Vanauken, whom we met in chapter 7, were young American newlyweds who met C. S. Lewis while they were students at Oxford University in England. Before becoming Christians, the Vanaukens were romantic idealists who lived for love and tried to make sure the affection they felt for each other would last by putting it over everything else in life. But even while attempting this, they worried that it might not be enough.

Seeing other romantic relationships failing all around, the Vanaukens realized that *inloveness* does not last without having the right sort of protection. But what can truly protect love? Being romantics, they thought there could be nothing stronger than love itself. So they placed hope in the ideal that, "it's love that keeps a love secure, and only by love of love can love endure."[28] Even so, they feared something could be missing and wondered if they were just hoping that the untrustworthy might somehow make itself trustworthy.

Their dilemma was solved when C. S. Lewis led the Vanaukens to faith in Jesus Christ and challenged them to rethink how they thought about love, sex, and marriage. Becoming Christians changed their love for each other by anchoring it in the greater, more enduring love of Christ. But loving God first was hard for Sheldon, and only when Davy died of a mysterious illness did he truly begin to see that God always returns far more than we ever give to him. Because it took losing his wife, he called what he learned God's *severe mercy*. But the lesson with which Sheldon Vanauken struggled was really far less severe than the heartaches and broken dreams that litter the path of romantic sexual morality.

Do you actually want to find love so true and strong it lasts for life? Do you want romantic feelings that flourish without fear? Do you want a marriage so dependable it endures no matter what life throws at you? Do you want a lover who will never leave no matter how either of you feels? Do you want sexual intimacy that grows richer and deeper year after year because you and your lover can afford the risk of sharing your true feelings—the bad with the good? Do you want to avoid heartbreak and heartache without giving up on love? Then reject romantic sexual morality and try biblical sexual morality instead.

13

Playboy Sexual Morality: Sex as Pleasure

Hugh Hefner's Playboy publishing empire has always been about more than just business. From the start, it also has been a crusade to justify the morality of pursuing sexual pleasure for its own sake regardless of marriage or anything else. While Hefner's business certainly has made money, it has also played a key role in the moral turnover now called the *sexual revolution.* The ultimate impact on American life and culture has been far greater than first imagined, but the idea of changing social opinion was always part of the plan.

Hefner set out to reshape the way Americans think about sexual morality, and *Playboy* magazine, the Playboy clubs, Playboy entertainment products, and the Playboy mansion were all (and still are) vehicles to this end. In an interview with Fox News in 2003, Hefner said,

> "Well, I think I've lived long enough to see the world change, and I do believe in a real way that we live in a *Playboy* world now. I think you see that reflected certainly in all of the men's magazines, but you see it in the world in general, in terms of fashions and pop culture. . . . when I started *Playboy,* I really wasn't trying to start a sex magazine, I was trying to incorporate sex in a total lifestyle package. I was the guy that tried to give sex a good name. Everybody talked about sex, but I was trying to give it a good name."[1]

No person of our time better exemplifies unrestrained pursuit of sexual pleasure than Hugh Hefner. No one has tried harder to live life according to playboy morality than Mr. Playboy himself. But nearing the age of 72 in January 1998, Hugh Hefner was feeling crushed and miserable. With a personal fortune of almost $400 million, the king of sex American-style was heartbroken over rejection by the one woman he loved most.

Over a lifetime of seeking sexual pleasure, Hugh Hefner has had a series of female companions. He found each one desirable in her own way. But every single one—except for his first wife, Millie, whom he divorced in 1959—eventually rejected him. Each one tried, but failed, to keep him to herself alone. After a string of live-in relationships lasting through the sixties, seventies, and eighties, Hefner fell hard for Kimberley Conrad, and she became the second Mrs. Hefner in 1989. He planned to make Conrad his "Playmate for a lifetime," and the prospect of marrying her made him giddy.

But just ten years later, it was over. Kimberley Hefner moved out and filed for divorce. Hugh Hefner wanted it to last, and once said, "I don't think I will ever love anyone again as much as I love her." But the woman Hefner really loved, the one he endearingly called his "Kimberella," the one he wanted to be his for life rejected him too. Why? Because, like all the rest, she too became angry about not being able to have him to herself. She also became terribly bored with Hefner's shallow lifestyle, explaining: "It was the same thing every night . . . I was lonely. . . . He goes out on these dates with eighteen-year-old girls, then he comes home and tells me, 'The whole time I'm with them all I could think of was you.' You know what? . . . I'm happy with my boys. They're all the men I need."[2]

When she left, Hugh Hefner said it felt like being punched in the guts. His personal physician, Dr. Mark Saginor, said when Kimberley walked out the leader of the sexual revolution was "squashed like a June bug." Saginor reported that Hefner "couldn't move. He was in the bushes. And the minute she comes back, he'll be right back in the bushes. He runs like a whipped puppy whenever she crooks a finger or bats an eyelash."[3]

The following story, paraphrased from a journalistic account by Bill Zehme, provides a poignant description of what life must have been like for Hefner after Kimberly left:

> It was a Friday movie night at the Playboy mansion in January 1998. Hugh Hefner was hosting as usual. But he was feeling low—just managing to cover a broken heart with the bustle of guests and entertainment. Dinner was over. But then, as his guests settled down for a private screening of John Huston's movie version of *Moby Dick,* Kimberley breezed in from next door where she had been living since filing for divorce. These are her friends too.

> "Hi" she said, tapping Hefner lightly on the shoulder. "Kimber!" he said, exploding from his seat. Suddenly Hefner was alive. More engaged than he had been all evening. But she wasn't there for him. She didn't stay. As the movie started, Hefner sank into the plush leather which covered his seat. But his hands were trembling. No one sat next to him either. This was January 1998, and no one had sat next to Hugh Hefner on movie night for nearly eight years. It was not for any lack of sexual playmates. The ultimate Playboy sat alone by himself that evening simply because his heart was aching, and he sat alone for all those years just because he was lonely.[4]

Hugh Marston Hefner grew up in a Midwestern Methodist family that many believe was partly responsible for his turn against biblical morality, which he criticized for being *rigid* and *puritanical.* But in fact Hefner's home environment was not unusual, and his parents, Glenn and Grace Hefner, may even have been more lenient than most. Hugh Hefner's family background was certainly conservative by Playboy standards, but it never was *fundamentalist* or *puritanical.* Neither was it *rigid.* So allegations sometimes made that Hugh Hefner as a boy was driven to playboy morality by repressive parents have no basis in fact. Rather, it appears Hefner's frequent attacks on *puritanism* are rooted more in caricature than experience.

The Hefner family attended church, but Hefner's father once told an interviewer neither he nor his sons ever had what evangelicals call a *conversion* experience. Glenn Hefner said he believed the Bible was inspired, but he was a quiet man who only spoke about beliefs when asked, and that does not seem to have been very often. Hefner's mother was the disciplinarian of the family, but she also held rather liberal views on everything from theology to sex. Grace Hefner did not think the Bible could be taken literally, and she seems to have accepted her son's rejection of Christianity and refusal to continue attending church after becoming a teenager.[5]

Like many parents of their generation, Hugh Hefner's parents were embarrassed to talk about sex, but that did not make them restrictive on the subject. When Hugh entered his teens, his mother bought him the most *progressive* book she could find on the subject of sex, and what she got did not come from a Christian bookstore. When young Hugh began showing his mother's sex book to friends, other mothers in the neighborhood called Mrs. Hefner to complain and demanded she keep Hugh from showing it to their sons.[6]

As we have noted, Hugh Hefner himself and the Playboy enterprise have always been about something more than business or entertainment. The man and his publishing empire have been dedicated to changing what people in the culture think and believe about sexual morality. Now we will look more closely at the playboy view of sexual morality and how it compares to biblical standards.

Description of Playboy Sexual Morality

"Playboy," the name Hugh Hefner chose for his magazine, refers to someone who lives for pleasure and who believes that acts of physical sex are justified for no other reason than their ability to entertain. As a result, some have said Hefner's playboy message is, "Go out and play, and don't worry about it." For a playboy, the recreational pleasure associated with sexual experience is not just one among other important aspects. Instead, according to the playboy view, recreational pleasure is what sex is all about. Play is the way sex is used, and pleasure is its goal. In this sense "playboy" refers to a value system used to justify the way someone like Hugh Hefner prefers to live. The playboy lifestyle is justified by a moral philosophy, and that philosophy includes a morality of sexual behavior.

Jon Davies and Gerard Loughlin have tried to describe a new idea to which many in our culture are turning, and what they capture lies at the heart of playboy sexual morality. It is that, "Sex is about pleasure not love; passing the time—excitedly—with a friend, acquaintance or stranger, without commitment or hurt. . . . Its goal is not procreation . . . but . . . the glow of successful performance. Sex is like food, a commodity, and the culture in which it is bought and sold a veritable pornotopia."[7]

Playboy sexual morality begins with the physical pleasure associated with sexual experience and proceeds to construct an entire framework of moral thinking based on it. The experience of physical pleasure is treated as a self-justifying ultimate good that determines the morality of everything else in life. Nothing is higher than the sensation of physical pleasure, and the value of everything else depends on it. By this criterion, sex that produces physical pleasure is always right, and no sexual act is wrong unless it fails to produce sensual pleasure.

In playboy morality, sexual pleasure is pursued for its own sake, so Hugh Hefner says he thinks "sex can sometimes, quite properly, be an end in itself."[8] In the playboy pursuit of sexual pleasure, nothing is ruled out except sex that is nonconsensual or that threatens to harm health or physical well-being. But the playboy respect for mutual consent and avoiding harm is not based on anything higher than pleasure itself. It simply assumes that the pursuit of pleasure requires it and will be compromised if these principles are violated.

PLAYBOY SEXUAL MORALITY

General Characteristics

Source of Moral Authority Is:	Self
Moral Authority Consists of:	Sensing physical pleasure
Moral Goal Is:	Entertainment (having fun)
Philosophical Basis Is:	Modernism
Functional Purpose Is:	Producing physical pleasure
Approach Is:	Mundane (of this world)
Moral Standards Are:	Subjective (depends on choices and human control)
Main Focus Is:	Love of self
Secondary Focus Is:	(Nothing else)
Tertiary Focus Is:	(Nothing else)
Most Important Dimension of Sex Is:	The physical dimension
Depth Is:	Shallow (not profound)
Sex Is Considered:	A commodity to spend or consume
Sexual Morality Is Considered:	A private matter (no one else's business)
Sexual Intimacy Is Considered:	More public than private matter (depending on taste)
Marriage Should Be:	Whatever individuals choose
Traditional Marriage Is Considered:	Optional but not ideal
Children Are Considered:	Burdens
Sexual Discipline Is Considered:	A bad thing
Relation of Sex to Marriage:	Morally unrelated
Relation of Happiness to Family Duty:	Physical happiness justifies fulfilling family duty
Effect on the Dimensions of Sex:	Reduces sex to biology (natural impulse)
Relational Nature of Sex Is:	Denied
Spiritual Life Is:	Ignored or denied
Scripture Is:	Ignored or denied
God's Authority over Sex Is:	Ignored or denied
Ultimately Worships:	The biological-sexual self

Playboy advocates usually defend their view of sexual morality by arguing that the human sex drive is a natural impulse. They say anything that goes against a natural impulse is by definition *unnatural* and must therefore be immoral, and conclude that feelings of natural pleasure are all that is needed to justify indulging our biological drive for sexual satisfaction. In practice this makes the playboy value system very self-centered, and Hefner even says one reason he prefers playboy morality is "because you're not living your life through other people."[9] Self-centeredness is also evident in Hefner's fondness for a line from Shakespeare's *Hamlet:* "to thine own self be true, and it must follow, as the night the day, thou canst not then be false to any man" (I, iii, 78). While Shakespeare intended the comment to reveal a flaw of moral character, Hefner has taken it as good moral advice.

The fact is playboy sexual morality requires neither commitment, nor permanence, nor affection. Sexual partners can be strangers who do not even know each other's names. Hefner once said, "sex without love is not nearly so destructive as the sexual conservatives would have us believe, and in fact, for a great many people sex without love is obviously preferable to no sex at all."[10] He admits that sex may be more rewarding in the context of a lasting relationship. But since neither acquaintance nor affection are needed to experience the physical pleasure of sex, he does not think they have anything to do with deciding whether a potential sexual encounter is right or wrong.

Obviously this affects what one thinks about the institution of marriage. From the playboy point of view, marriage has nothing to do with the morality of sexual actions. Looking back over his life, Hefner once told an interviewer his legacy could be summarized by saying he had shown that "there's another ethical way of living your life without being married."[11] Playboy proponents can say that marriage, personal commitment, and feelings of affection are rewarding for some. But in playboy morality these are only supplemental—things to be tried if you like. They are not morally necessary if you do not happen to prefer them. So, if a one-night stand with a stranger is all you expect, then playboy morality justifies the encounter for whatever physical pleasure can be gotten from it.

Evangelical Christians should be disappointed but not surprised when secular commerce and entertainment promote playboy sexual morality. But the influence of playboy morality goes beyond secular culture and has appeared in publications aimed at Christian readers as well. For example, Marvin M. Ellison, writing for *Christianity in Crisis,* says he believes the traditional Christian ethic is woefully inadequate because, "it denies the rich diversity of sexual experiences" and does not help people to "give and receive sexual pleasure freely." In its place he recommends a new "more earthy, sensuous" sexual morality in which marriage and heterosexuality are no longer moral norms. Ellison finally urges Christians to pursue "sexual pleasure" as "an open-ended sexual and spiritual project, full of surprises and challenge."[12]

Aiming to influence Christians with playboy sexual morality is not new. It has been part of Hefner's strategy all along. He frequently says the whole idea behind playboy is opposing *puritanism,* which for him means rejecting biblical standards that interfere with pursuing sexual pleasure for its own sake. But while playboy morality opposes biblical teaching on sexual morality, this does not mean Hefner has ignored Christians. To the contrary, he has worked hard over the years to influence Christian thinking about sexual morality by cultivating ties with influential theologians and offering cut-rate magazine subscriptions to clergy and ministerial students. Hefner once even sent an executive from *Playboy* magazine to attend courses in theology, thinking it would prepare him to better promote playboy sexual morality to readers who were Christians.[13]

Playboy sexual morality is all around us in commerce and entertainment, and its influence has even permeated some publications written for Christians. If its influence cannot be ignored, how should evangelicals respond?

Evaluation of Playboy Sexual Morality

While playboy morality is set against biblical teaching on sexual morality, Christians can and should affirm that God is not anti-pleasure. Sex is God's idea, and that includes its physical pleasure. The enjoyment of physical sensations produced by sexual intimacy is something God intends, and if it does not embarrass God then neither should it embarrass us. Christians understand that sexual pleasure is a gift from God, and they should be the first to accept what God has given with gratitude and appreciation.

This means Christians should agree when advocates for playboy morality say sexual pleasure is something good. And we can agree that there is nothing necessarily wrong with enjoying sexual pleasure, or even with giving it a place of honor in the way we think about sexual morality. Biblical opposition to playboy sexual morality is not about the goodness of sexual pleasure itself. Rather it has to do with how pleasure relates to deciding the difference between right and wrong. If biblical teaching on sexual morality affirms the essential goodness of sexual pleasure, what then is so wrong with playboy sexual morality?

1. It Deifies Sensual Pleasure

The first problem with playboy sexual morality is that it deifies physical pleasure by making it the self-justifying center of moral judgment. In the playboy system, everything is subordinate to the satisfaction of sensual pleasure. Nothing is more important. Nothing has higher value. By contrast, the Bible shows that while sexual pleasure is designed to be good, it is not self-justifying. Pleasure itself does not define the difference between right or wrong behavior. Sexual pleasure is meant to be moral, but nothing is moral just because it is pleasurable. For this reason no pleasure, sexual or otherwise, can be pursued simply for its own sake.

In scripture God is the only self-justifying moral good, so only God himself defines the difference between moral right and moral wrong. God has made sexual pleasure to be good, but it is in fact good only when realized within the moral boundaries set for it by God. Scripture honors the experience of sexual pleasure when it is moral. But it is moral only as it stays in line with the holiness of God. Referring to pleasure seekers in the first century, Paul said,

> They have become callous and have given themselves up to sensuality, greedy to practice every kind of impurity. But that is not the way you learned Christ! . . . you have heard about him and were taught in him . . . to put off your old self, which belongs to your former manner of life and is corrupt through deceitful desires, and to be renewed in the spirit of your minds, and to put on the new self, created after the likeness of God in true righteousness and holiness (Eph. 4:19-24).

So the first and most important reason for opposing playboy sexual morality is that it substitutes physical pleasure for God at the center of moral thinking. And by making a god of sexual pleasure, it not only offends the true God but perverts moral judgment about everything else as well.

2. *It Substitutes Pleasure for Joy*

The second problem with playboy sexual morality is that it fails to acknowledge any difference between pleasure and joy and therefore settles for temporary physical or mental sensations rather than trying to assure deep, abiding joy in a sexual relationship. C. S. Lewis once said, "I doubt whether anyone who has ever tasted it [joy] would ever, if both were in his power, exchange it for all the pleasures in the world. But then joy is never in our power and pleasure often is."[14]

The playboy approach to sexual morality encourages people to work at pleasure, hoping it will make them truly happy. But those who follow this path never find happiness. This is because true happiness comes from joy, not from pleasure. Pleasure and joy are entirely different things, and joy is always far better than pleasure. Happiness depends on joy because it simply is how you feel when you experience joy in your life. But pleasure does nothing more than stimulate physical and mental sensations and has nothing to do with happiness at all.

Using pleasure to make yourself happy is like trying to find gold by climbing up a tree. You might get a view of others who are finding what you want, but to find some yourself you have go down, not up. The playboy approach takes you in the wrong direction by pretending to offer something different than what you actually get.

Christians cannot afford to ignore the very important differences that distinguish joy from pleasure, nor can we forget what makes joy better. We discussed this at length in chapter 11, but the main points again are as follows.

First, whereas pleasure is temporary, joy is eternal[15]; so playboy morality substitutes what you cannot keep for what you are allowed to keep forever.

Second, whereas pleasure has physical and mental limits, joy has no limits; so playboy morality substitutes something that gets no better for something that gets better all the time.

Third, whereas pleasure cannot tolerate pain, joy endures regardless of sensation; so playboy morality offers something weaker than pain in place of something stronger.

Fourth, whereas pleasure is something we produce for ourselves, joy is from God; so playboy morality substitutes something we do for something God does.

Fifth, whereas pleasure is shallow, joy is profound; so playboy morality gives you something that has no effect on emotions for something that affects everything, especially emotions.

Sixth, whereas pleasure is impersonal, joy is personal; so playboy morality gives you something that pursued for its own sake weakens relationships, in place of something that always builds them up.

Seventh, whereas pleasure is about taking and getting, joy is about giving and serving; so playboy morality involves using other people in ways that eventually leaves everyone feeling unloved, used, and disappointed.

Finally, whereas pleasure can be either good or bad, joy is always good and never bad; so playboy morality exchanges something wonderful in favor of something that often gets you in trouble.

Because the playboy approach sees no difference between pleasure and joy, it persuades people to settle for momentary sensations at the cost of happiness that grows ever better with time. But by knowing the difference and favoring joy over pleasure, biblical morality actually enhances both.

3. It Denies Fallen Human Nature

The third problem with playboy sexual morality is that it does not understand how human nature relates to our natural desire for sex. C. S. Lewis observed that biblical morality on sexual behavior "is so difficult and so contrary to our instincts, that obviously either Christianity is wrong or our sexual instinct, as it now is, has gone wrong."[16] While playboy morality assumes that the human sexual instinct is correct as it is, the Bible tells us human nature is perverted, and this includes the human appetite for sex. Our natural passions are so warped by sin that they never line up automatically with their natural functions. Animals do not have sex except to produce offspring, but human beings pursue it at a rate far beyond the number of children they could ever care for. As a rule, animals do not have a passion for sex except when a female is ready to conceive, but the human desire for sex has no time switch, and many pursue it constantly.

Christians understand that the greatest problem with the human sexual appetite is not lack of physical gratification. Rather there is something wrong with the instinct itself. We have in our souls a hunger for relational intimacy that, while partially satisfied by physical sex, goes deeper than biological sensation. The difference is, in fact, so real and important that one can interfere with the other. Sensual passions can hinder satisfaction of soul hunger, and soul hunger sometimes fights against satisfaction of sensual passion. This is exactly what Peter warns about when he says, "Beloved, I urge you as sojourners and exiles to abstain from the passions of the flesh, which wage war against your soul" (1 Pet. 2:11). When it comes to understanding our natural instincts, playboy morality goes astray because it refuses to see the abnormality of our "normal" sexual desires, and ends up hanging morality on something that was bent out of shape when the human race fell into sin.

4. It Glorifies Self-Centeredness

The fourth problem with playboy sexual morality is that it is self-centered and glorifies selfishness. Arnold Morton, after being fired from an executive position at Playboy Enterprises, said, "Hugh Hefner? He's the sweetest, most selfish man I've ever known."[17] Morton should not have been surprised. The playboy value system glorifies the free pursuit of individual pleasure, and moral right and wrong depends on what each individual thinks will most satisfy himself. By definition, others serve only as means for satisfying yourself, sexually or otherwise, and there really is no place for treating others as centers of dignity who are worthy of respect in their own right.

By contrast, Jesus taught that true morality requires self-denial. Genuine love is other-regarding, God-honoring, and sacrificial, never self-centered, self-serving, and self-indulgent. According to Jesus, "Greater love has no one than this, that someone lays down his life for his friends" (John 15:13). He also said, "If anyone would come after me, let him deny himself and take up his cross daily and follow me. For whoever would save his life will lose it, but whoever loses his life for my sake will save it" (Luke 9:23-24). Harvard theologian Harvey Cox, who accommodates revisionist sexual morality in many ways, nevertheless got it right in 1965 when he criticized Hefner's approach, saying,

"For *Playboy*'s man, others—especially women—are *for* him. They are his leisure accessories, his playthings. For the Bible, man only becomes man by being *for* the other. . . . If Christians bear the name of one who was truly man because He was totally for the other, and if it is in Him that we know what God is and we know what life is for, then we must see in *Playboy* the latest and slickest episode in man's continuing refusal to be fully human."[18]

5. *It Reduces Sex to Sensation*

The fifth problem with playboy sexual morality is that it reduces the value of sex. While claiming to glorify sex, playboy morality reduces sex to sensation plus nothing. And by focusing on nothing except physical experience, playboy morality diminishes and eventually threatens the emotional, relational, psychological, and spiritual dimensions of human sexual union. Sexual experience is shallowed to a single dimension, and all life becomes a shell with nothing to live for except the shell itself. Anson Mount, another Playboy executive who was fired after serving Hefner many years, said, "I really still like Hef. He actually kissed me goodbye after I was fired. I feel sorry for him though. His life is an empty one."[19]

As designed by God, sex is a personal relationship that is so very special it must be exclusive. But playboy morality makes sex impersonal, nonrelational, and nonexclusive. Sex is treated as a commodity or mechanical skill to be rated by performance or productive capacity, which is exactly what Solomon means in a warning delivered against prostitutes: "Do not lust in your heart after her beauty or let her captivate you with her eyes, for the prostitute reduces you to a loaf of bread" (Prov. 6:25-26, NIV). For the playboy, bodies are everything, and the more the better. People are not valued for who they are apart from the external, physical appeal of their bodies. Persons end up being regarded as little more than accessories to bodies, and anyone can be replaced if a more appealing body comes along.

What God desires for sexual relationships is, of course, very different. In the Bible we learn that each man and woman is a personal being made in God's image. We all dwell in bodies, but we are also far more than bodies. Each human life is a unique center of transcendent worth, and for this reason all by nature crave to be valued and loved uniquely—to be irreplaceably valued for who one is regardless of his or her body. This is so much a part of human nature that we bristle if treated any other way, and we react in this way whether we know and understand the Bible or not.

Bill Davidson, writing for *The Saturday Evening Post,* once reported:

> Another possible difficulty for Hefner is . . . revulsion among womankind—and among some non-puritan males too—against the entire *Playboy* concept. A Chicago newspaperwoman told me, "I like Hef, but I resent his philosophy that a woman is merely a decoration. In the *Playboy* world, a female goes into the discard when she is not the show-girl type, when she has a bust of less than thirty-nine inches, when she reaches the age of twenty-five, and when she exhibits any intelligence."[20]

In the same article, Davidson described how one Playboy bunny lost her job for admitting that she resented how she was treated at Hefner's mansion:

> One bunny recently had the temerity to express more or less the same thoughts on the *PM East* television show, saying, "I don't really like the picture of the female being only an accessory of a man." She was summarily fired. I questioned Victor Lownes III, a chief Hefner lieutenant, about this heresy. He said, "I guess . . . we might be somewhat in error in not giving the exceptional woman full credit. But we firmly believe that women are *not* equal to men."[21]

The fact is no one likes being treated as a decoration. No one appreciates having his or her own personal worth dismissed as something that is only an *accessory.* Indeed, many who at first thought Hefner's playboy message appealing—people like Playboy bunny turned feminist leader Gloria Steinem—have ended up rejecting or even attacking it upon realizing how the playboy approach depersonalizes sex and reduces women to sex *objects.*

6. It Cannot Justify Responsibility Toward Others

The sixth problem with playboy sexual morality is that it offers no basis for the responsible treatment of others. This is the hidden side of pleasure seeking. Because the playboy approach is completely self-centered, nothing requires one person to sense any obligation toward another. Advocates for playboy sexual morality might talk about mutual consent and not causing harm to a sex partner. But these principles do not always square with every individual's view of pleasure, and if a conflict arises, self-gratification always trumps the field.

The problem cannot be dismissed lightly, because playboy morality only justifies mutual consent and avoiding harm to others by assuming these principles will always agree with the way an individual determines his own sense of pleasure. But what if an individual decides that in his case there is more pleasure to be had out of sex that is nonconsensual? What if avoiding risk to a sex partner requires self-denial? Or what if someone decides he enjoys combining sex with violence and is stimulated by causing others to suffer? If sexual morality is defined by the individual pursuit of pleasure plus nothing else, and if sexual pleasure is measured by no one other than the one who pursues it, then mutual consent and avoiding harm will not always restrain it.

Playboy morality will not prevent the powerful from seeking pleasure at the expense of the weak. Neither will it interfere with the beautiful seeking pleasure at the expense of the less beautiful, or with the rich seeking it at the expense of the poor. In the end everyone is left to watch out for himself, and no one really cares how his or her own pursuit of pleasure affects anyone else.

7. It Destroys the Pleasure It Promises

The seventh and most tragic problem with playboy sexual morality is that it too is self-defeating. It starts by exalting sexual pleasure, but it ends by reducing the enjoyment of sexual pleasure and destroying genuine sexual satisfaction. In other words, the reward promised by playboy sexual morality is a sham. This is because the playboy approach fails to realize that the more one pursues any pleasure for its own sake, the more elusive actual enjoyment of that pleasure becomes.

Whether it is sex or something else, the more intently one works at using others for selfish reasons, the harder it becomes to find anyone willing to be used. The less relational, less personal, or less unique sex becomes, the less enjoyable or truly satisfying it becomes as well. In reality, sex is difficult to enjoy when it becomes nothing special, and there is nothing at all special about sex after it is reduced to mechanical experiences of impersonal physical stimulation.

We have already noted the irony in Hugh Hefner's misery over losing his marriage to Kimberley Conrad. It was not simply ironic but terribly tragic. The man who set out to release sexual pleasure from all restrictions instead discovered that true satisfaction in a sexual relationship and even his ability to enjoy the physical pleasure of sex were both destroyed by pursuing pleasure as a goal for its own sake alone. Basketball superstar Wilt "The Stilt" Chamberlain also lived by playboy sexual morality and learned to regret it. Chamberlain once boasted of having taken more than twenty thousand women to bed. But he never married, and died lonely and dissatisfied, saying he would have traded all twenty thousand sexual encounters for a relationship with the one woman he wanted to stay with for keeps.[22]

In the final analysis, playboy morality does nothing to increase the quality of sexual pleasure, nor does it necessarily increase the *quantity* of pleasure one might expect. The number of sexual experiences outside of marriage will certainly go up, especially at the start. But any existing marriage will be threatened, and chances of forming a unique sexual relationship protected by marriage will become more remote.

Shallow sex eventually loses its appeal, and when that happens, sexual pleasure dies. The poet Robert Nichols expressed it this way:

> Come, let us sigh a requiem over love
> That we ourselves have slain in love's own bed.
> Whose hearts that had courage to drink enough
> Lacked courage to forbid the taste they bred,
> Which body captained soon, till, in disgust,
> These very hearts of bodily surfeit died,
> Poisoned by that sweet overflow of lust
> Whose past delight our substance deified.[23]

While playboy sexual morality promises sexual pleasure, it actually hinders the possibility of realizing the full degree of sexual satisfaction and pleasure which comes only when a unique sexual relationship is set free by marriage to flourish in all dimensions of its marvelous complexity. The embarrassing secret at the heart of Playboy Enterprises is how it has struggled over the years to explain statistics on sexual satisfaction that contradict its central message. Even Playboy cannot cover up the truth. A Harris poll commissioned by Playboy Enterprises and conducted in 1976–1977 found that men who followed the playboy approach on sex had less satisfying sex than any other group to which they were compared.[24]

The irony in playboy sexual morality is horribly tragic because it ends up destroying the very thing it promises. But what is tragic for the playboy approach highlights the truth of biblical sexual morality. Although pilloried by Hugh Hefner for hindering sexual pleasure, the biblical approach actually assures it. Sex God's way is selfless. Pleasure is never sought for its own sake, and sexual stimulation is restricted to a unique relationship in marriage. But couples who put God first, even in the area of sex, discover that he adds a depth and quality to sexual pleasure that far exceeds anything they can ever reach by centering on themselves.

Francis Schaeffer explains the irony this way: "Sexual love and romantic love are both equally out of place if they are extramarital and therefore outside of the proper legal [moral law] circle. Both are wrong, and equally wrong. And if either is the 'all' even within the proper legal [civil law] relationship, they must dwindle and end in an agony or a search for variety. But if the couple stand as personalities—personality facing personality—within what is the proper legal [moral law] circle, then both the romantic and the sexual has its fulfillment in the full circle of what we are, in thinking, acting, and feeling."[25]

A 1994 survey commissioned by the Family Research Council found a strong link between sexual satisfaction and those who believe sex is something that needs to be saved for marriage. In this survey, 72.3 percent of married couples in the category holding traditional moral standards answered they were "very satisfied" with their sex life. This compared to 59.3 percent of married couples who rejected traditional moral standards. The category having the lowest level of sexual satisfaction were unmarried couples who did not take a traditional approach to sexual morality. In this last group, there was only a 41.0 percent level of sexual satisfaction. The study's main finding was that amazing 31-point spread in levels of sexual satisfaction favoring those who follow norms for sexual fidelity consistent with the Bible over those who pursue more promiscuous approaches to sexual morality.[26]

Do you want sexual delight that gets better over time? Do you want to know the full measure of sexual excitement in all dimensions (physical, emotional, psychological, and spiritual) at the same time? Do you want sex to be something truly special, something truly profound? Do you want to achieve the pleasure of sex with someone who loves the real you more than your physical appearance and who believes the real you can never be replaced? Do you want to realize the lasting thrill of sex with someone so special that he or she has never been sexually intimate with anyone except you? Then reject playboy sexual morality and try biblical sexual morality instead.

14

Therapeutic Sexual Morality: Sex as Wholeness

In the seventies and eighties, along with many songs that justified sex based on love, there were some that treated sex differently. These also rejected biblical morality but for psychological rather than romantic reasons. Some claimed that sex has power to transform children into adults, and others that having sex creates self-esteem. Both notions actually came together in "Natural Woman," sung first by Carole King and then by Aretha Franklin. In that song, a woman says, "When my soul was in the lost-and-found, you came along to claim it. I didn't know just what was wrong with me, till your kiss helped me name it." From worthlessness and poor self-esteem, she sings of discovering new life through sex: "Oh, baby, what you've done to me. . . . You make me feel so alive 'cause you make me feel, you make me feel, you make me feel like a natural woman."[1]

More recent songs like "One Kiss from You" by Britney Spears, "Whole Again" by Atomic Kitten, "Pure Pleasure Seeker" by Moloko, "I Gotta Be" by Jagged Edge, and "Make Me Whole" by Amel Larrieux all associate sex with becoming "whole." And Marvin Gaye clearly justifies sex as therapy in "Sexual Healing," a song in which he announces "sexual healing is something good for me," because when "emotional stability is leaving me . . . I can get on the telephone and call you up, baby. And, honey, I know you'll be there to relieve me."[2] These songs are not just saying something about the psychological benefits of sex but are, in fact, promoting a new approach to sexual morality that justifies sex for therapeutic reasons.

In 1998, New Line Cinema released *Pleasantville,* a movie dedicated entirely to the idea that meaning and fulfillment in life come through sex. As the movie opens, two teenagers from the late nineties are pulled into a black-and-white television program meant to stand for old programs like "Leave It to Beaver" and "Father Knows Best" that idealized small-town life in the fifties. The teens are first overwhelmed by the *pleasantness* of traditional moral values as compared to the breakdown of social relationships in the contemporary world from which they came. But, rather than respect these values, the teens lead a rebellion that turns the television world from black-and-white to color as characters discover fulfillment through sex outside traditional moral lines.

Pleasantville attacks biblical sexual morality in a direct and shocking manner, but the effects of this assault are not as worthy of our attention as their cause. *Pleasantville's* attack on traditional family values comes from a belief in therapeutic sexual morality. And because this new approach is spreading rapidly through our culture, Christians must try to understand and meet this serious new challenge to biblical morality.

DESCRIPTION OF THERAPEUTIC SEXUAL MORALITY

Therapeutic sexual morality justifies sex based on ideas about human psychology. Sex is regarded as moral or immoral depending on how it relates to things such as mental health, personal development, or social success. Therapeutic sexual morality believes people *fulfill* or *actualize* themselves through sex, and everyone must have sex in order to be *whole*. No sexual behavior is right or wrong in itself because what matters is a person's inner sense of satisfaction. Homosexual sex, prostitution, and adultery are not necessarily bad, being faithful to a spouse is not necessarily good, and no one can judge sexual morality for anyone else.

The nature of therapeutic sexual morality is more radically opposed to biblical morality than either the playboy or romantic approaches. These also reject biblical standards, but only because they try to justify alternative behavior and not because they think biblical standards are actually bad for anyone. By contrast, therapeutic sexual morality not only justifies alternative behavior but attacks biblical standards as harmful, dangerous, and evil. Some who are hearing this the first time may find it hard to believe, but therapeutic morality is a very serious matter. It has been growing in our culture for years and is now so widespread it may already be the majority view.

Therapeutic morality began with ideas pioneered by the father of psychotherapy, Sigmund Freud, who defined human behavior almost entirely in terms of expressing or sublimating the sexual instinct. Freud believed the sexual instinct must always have an outlet, and if not expressed in normal ways it will come out in the form of mental illness, or neurosis, leading to acts of sexual perversion. He believed the human sex drive "behaves like a stream," and if the main channel is blocked it "proceeds to fill up collateral channels which may hitherto have been empty."[3] This way of thinking made sexual abstinence injurious to mental health and suggested that biblical morality requiring sexual discipline is harmful and should be replaced with a more permissive approach to sexual morality.[4]

THERAPEUTIC SEXUAL MORALITY

General Characteristics

Source of Moral Authority Is:	Self
Moral Authority Consists of:	Sensing psychological fulfillment (satisfaction)
Moral Goal Is:	Wholeness (self-actualization)
Philosophical Basis Is:	Modernism
Functional Purpose Is:	Producing psychological fulfillment (actualizing self)
Approach Is:	Mundane (of this world)
Moral Standards Are:	Subjective (depends on choice and human control)
Main Focus Is:	Love of self
Secondary Focus Is:	(Nothing else)
Tertiary Focus Is:	(Nothing else)
Most Important Dimension of Sex Is:	The psychological (mental) dimension
Depth Is:	Shallow (not profound)
Sex Is Considered:	The essence of personhood
Sexual Morality Is Considered:	A private matter (no one else's business)
Sexual Intimacy Is Considered:	A public matter (it declares personal identity)
Marriage Should Be:	Whatever individuals choose
Traditional Marriage Is Considered:	An obstacle (a barrier to growth)
Children Are Considered:	Burdens
Sexual Discipline Is Considered:	A bad thing
Relation of Sex to Marriage:	Totally unrelated
Relation of Happiness to Family Duty:	Psychological happiness justifies fulfilling family duty
Effect on the Dimensions of Sex:	Reduces sex to psychology
Relational Nature of Sex Is:	Denied
Spiritual Life Is:	Ignored or denied
Scripture Is:	Ignored or denied
God's Authority over Sex Is:	Denied or attacked
Ultimately Worships:	The mental-sexual self

Freud was especially concerned about the effects of limiting sex to marriage, saying that, by "glorifying monogamy," biblical sexual morality (what he called *civilized sexual morality*) "promotes modern nervousness," and prohibiting "every sexual activity other than that in legitimate matrimony" makes strong people rebel and weak people neurotic.[5] He thought "the majority of those who compose our society are constitutionally un-fit for the task of abstinence," and said,

> On the whole I have not gained the impression that sexual abstinence helps shape energetic, self-reliant men of action, nor original thinkers, bold pioneers and reformers; far more often it produces *good* weaklings who later become lost in the crowd that tends to follow painfully the initiative of strong characters.[6]

For these and other reasons Freud decided that "Marital unfaithfulness" would be the best "cure for the neurosis resulting from marriage," and "complete abstinence during youth is often not the best preparation for marriage in a young man."[7]

Carl Jung, who thought Christian theology was "a specimen of uncommon stupidity whose sole aim was to obscure the truth,"[8] pioneered the idea of *wholeness* to describe ideal inner being. In Jung's view, *wholeness* is produced by integrating natural human instincts like sex, and he thought a person's self is *split* or *stunted* if natural instincts are not integrated. Jung decided the "dark side of things" was as necessary to ideal human life as the reverse, and therefore decided Jesus Christ was not a good model for *wholeness* because "the dogmatic figure of Christ is . . . so one-sidely perfect that it demands a psychic complement to restore balance."[9] To make up for this, Jung said Christ's "Luciferian opponent," the "Antichrist," was needed to form a "balanced" whole.[10] This made sin necessary to Jung's idea of *wholeness* and made sexual immorality part of becoming a fully integrated person. Jung himself carried on adulterous affairs throughout most of his life and once wrote Freud agreeing with his idea that mental health sometimes demands sex outside of marriage. But Jung took it a step further: whereas Freud allowed it, Jung considered it necessary. Jung therefore told Freud that he believed "the license to be unfaithful" is actually "prerequisite for a good marriage."[11]

A third pioneer in psychotherapy, Erich Fromm, thought sex was "discovering myself" in the act of "penetrating" someone else, which meant no one could ever "discover" himself without having sex.[12] In fact Fromm decided self-discovery through sex was so important it did not matter who the sexual partner happened to be. He said "erotic love" shows us "We are all part of One; we are One. This being so, it should not make any difference whom we love."[13] So, while Freud said it was bad to deny sex and

Jung suggested that sexual sin is part of becoming *whole,* Fromm justified sex with anyone without regard to matters such as gender, relationship, or commitment.

Abraham Maslow and Carl Rogers carried on from Freud, Jung, and Fromm and are responsible for the form of therapeutic morality most popular in American culture today. Maslow said sex is part of the "essential core of the person" and believed everyone must have sex to become fully "human." In his view, people become "human" by "self-actualizing" themselves through sex. Thus sexual abstinence was a "failure to grow to one's potential" and something that stunts "personhood."[14] In fact, Maslow claimed the natural human capacity for sex must be used or it will "atrophy" and diminish the person.[15] This gave everyone—married or not—a moral duty to have sex, and made keeping someone from having sex as evil as withholding food from a person dying of starvation.

Like Maslow, Carl Rogers also thought everyone must have sex in order to be *whole,* but Rogers went on to separate marriage from sexual morality completely. Rogers treated marriage as a social option, but he did not think it had anything to do with deciding when sex is moral. For Rogers, sex had to do with actualizing "life-enhancing" possibilities. He believed this made sex as necessary and moral for unmarried persons as for married, and meant people could be sexually active with different partners even if they were married. He also decided that the sexual instinct demands satisfaction "in ways that enhance, rather than diminish, self-esteem,"[16] which meant he thought sexual desires should be satisfied in whatever form they arise.

Recent psycho-philosophers like Michel Foucault and James Nelson have been developing a still more radical form of therapeutic sexual morality called "queer theory." Going beyond the idea of sex for mental health or personal development, these philosophers say sex is the key to social power, and are urging that institutions like marriage, family, and work be completely reconstructed in order to allow individuals to become whatever they want to be through sex.

Michel Foucault, who died of AIDS in 1984, pioneered queer theory, saying, "sex is not a fatality" but "a possibility for creative life," and "sexuality is something that we ourselves create."[17] Foucault proclaimed that self-created sexual identity is now "more important than our soul" for defining who we are, and claimed that talk of sexuality now replaces Christian preaching as a guide for social reform.[18] Following Foucault, James Nelson (who claims to be a Christian—see chapter 3) now argues that "sexual bodyselves are subject to an enormous range of socially constructed meanings that are extraordinarily plastic and malleable," and as a result feels obligated to attack everything that treats sexuality as something that is the same "once and for all."[19]

The queer theory version of therapeutic morality represented by Foucault and Nelson assumes a *constructionist* view of sexuality—the idea that sexual identity is something we can take apart, change, and reassemble any way we choose. Constructionism rebels against the view in biblical sexual morality, called *essentialism,* that regards sexual identity as something given by God and beyond change. In biblical morality, men are not just male but *masculine,* and women are not just female but *feminine,* and it is wrong to behave in ways that go against the sexual identity each is given by God. By rejecting essentialism, queer theory denies all sexual norms, whether mental or moral. For, if sexual identity is totally self-created and yet defines what is good and normal, then any sex can be moral, sexual *wholeness* means anything, and no one can criticize the way others *act out* whatever sexuality they choose.

Therapeutic sexual morality already has strong advocates in the culture, and in one generation it has risen to become the dominant view among liberal reformers in mainline Christian denominations. For example, the Social Justice Committee of the Minnesota Council of Churches issued a statement in 1982 based on Maslow and Rogers instead of scripture. In part, that statement read:

> God's intended wholeness includes human sexuality as a gift for the expression of love and the generation of life. . . . There may be creative and whole expressions of one's sexuality at various levels in relationships between men and women, between men and other men, and between women and other women. We seek to enable persons to understand and to act out their sexuality in ways which are life-giving to themselves and to other persons with whom they are in relationship.[20]

In chapter 4, we saw how a Lutheran task force launched a firestorm in 1993 by recommending sexual standards based on psycho-philosophy, and Bishop Spong of the Episcopal Church is announcing that the church will die if Christians do not find a new basis for ethics.[21] Spong claims, "There is no credible deity existing today on whose perceived will, spelled out in an ancient text, we can base our ethical decision making"; he believes we should "loathe rather than . . . worship a deity who required the sacrifice of his son"; and he says biblical moral standards should all be exposed as horribly immoral.[22] Instead, he says, the church must "build a new basis for ethics, . . . not [looking] outside of life for some external and objective authenticating authority, but rather at the very center and core of our humanity," and this new ethic should not start with "God questions but human questions, such as: What gives us life? What lifts us into wholeness?"[23]

So, if therapeutic sexual morality is spreading through the culture and even roaring into churches, how should faithful Christians respond?

Evaluation of Therapeutic Sexual Morality

As Christians faithful to scripture and historic Christian teaching face up to the challenge of therapeutic sexual morality, we should start by agreeing that sex is indeed far more than physical and emotional. We should also agree that sex is made to satisfy a deep human need for interpersonal connection and thus affects our sense of personal well-being. And finally, we should agree that sex touches the core of human identity and that, when men and women are sexually intimate, it expresses something vital about who we are, the meaning of life, and the purpose for which we have been placed here on earth. Nevertheless, Bible-believing Christians also have serious objections about approaching sexual morality in a way that elevates psycho-philosophy over scripture and makes a person's sense of private sexual satisfaction the measure of moral good for everyone in every way.

Bible-believing Christians do not oppose therapeutic sexual morality for recognizing the importance of psychology in sex but because it uses psycho-philosophy to upset biblical sexual standards. In a general sense, Christians oppose taking a therapeutic approach to sexual morality because it denies biblical revelation. But we also find there are many other more specific ways it goes wrong.

1. It Reverses the Relation Between Satisfaction and Morality

The first problem with therapeutic morality is that it misunderstands the way sexual satisfaction relates to morality. There is indeed a connection between sexual satisfaction and morality. But, whereas God promises satisfaction to those who act morally, therapeutic morality reverses the connection by claiming that whatever is satisfying must therefore be moral. In other words, biblical morality promises satisfaction as a reward for moral behavior, while therapeutic morality treats satisfaction as a cause that makes sex moral.

By treating sexual satisfaction as a cause rather than as a result, therapeutic thinking produces a version of sexual morality that is far too weak to sustain social responsibilities. Therapeutic morality only indulges the wants of individuals and has no way of evaluating what *ought to be.* Talk of normal sexual behavior is impossible, and no one ever needs to change. When personal satisfaction is everything, responsibility for others degenerates into competition. Self-discipline is despised, and no one has any reason to care for anyone else.

But biblical morality affects social responsibilities in quite the opposite manner. Satisfaction is promised by God to those who accept and obey his standards (Ps. 103:5). Husbands who guard the purity of sex in marriage are assured delight and satisfaction (Prov. 5:19); and healing, well-being, and inner wholeness are blessings that come when people turn from wickedness to live in ways that please and honor God (Ex. 15:26; John 5:14; 1 Thess. 5:23). As a result, sexual satisfaction under biblical morality adds strength and support to social responsibilities, and never competes with doing what is right and good for others.

2. *It Takes a Developmental View of Personhood*

A second problem with therapeutic sexual morality is that it relies on the same developmental view of personhood used to justify destroying innocent human life by abortion, infanticide, or euthanasia. When proponents of therapeutic morality say persons must have sex in order to be *whole,* they are not saying something about satisfying godly purposes for human life but are claiming something about degrees of personal worth. According to therapeutic thinking, personhood grows with sexual activity and diminishes for lack of it. Those who have sex become full persons, while those who do not have sex fail to rise to the level of full personhood. If I refrain from having sex for any reason—if I am a child, or abstain from sex because I am not married, or have taken a vow of chastity, or am on a journey away from my spouse—then I am not a complete person and do not have all the value and dignity of full personhood.

In the Bible, the value of a person's life is not measured by the use of natural functions like sex; rather, it comes from bearing God's image (Gen. 1:27; 9:6; Rom. 8:29; 2 Cor. 3:18). This is evident in the way God treats us as persons from conception (Ps. 139:13-16; Jer. 1:5), and is why harming a person in the womb is as bad as harming a mature adult (Ex. 21:22-25). By measuring personhood according to sexual activity, therapeutic morality not only devalues human life but also blasphemes Christ and belittles heroes of the faith. If one must have sex in order to become totally *human,* then the Son of God never was fully incarnate and the spotless Lamb of God is mocked for sacrificing a life worth even less than the lives of those he came to save. Similarly, John the Baptist, of whom Jesus said, "among those born of women there has arisen no one greater" (Matt. 11:11), as well as the apostle Paul, must be classified as *stunted* or *diminished* persons, because as single men neither one was sexually active. According to the view of personhood adopted in therapeutic sexual morality, Jesus, John the Baptist, and Paul were all less complete and therefore less valuable persons than either Hugh Hefner or the Marquis de Sade.

3. It Is Totally Self-Centered

A third problem with therapeutic morality is that it is totally *self*-centered. Therapeutic sexual morality is all about *self*-actualization, *self*-fulfillment, and *self*-esteem. Sex is treated only as an investment in *self,* with no reason to satisfy anyone else unless as a strategy for getting something in return. Therapeutic sexual morality makes *self* an idol, and leaves individuals no sense of moral direction other than following themselves—because they refuse to acknowledge anything greater than themselves. Morally speaking, the result is much like a dog chasing its tail. By turning inward, your inner *self* loses reference to anything higher than itself, and it ceases to improve. And the more intently self focuses on itself, the more it also risks collapsing in upon itself.

The Bible explains that fulfillment in life centers on Christ, not self, and personal development comes from serving objectives set by God (Phil. 3:12-14), not from self-centered sex. All we do in the body—including sex—must be for Christ, not for self (Gal. 2:20). Jesus rebukes the Pharisees for being "full of . . . self-indulgence" (Matt. 23:25). And Paul later explains that our natural self-centered way of thinking must be "transformed by the renewal of your mind." Psychological thinking in all areas—including sex—is pure only so long as we seek God's "good and acceptable and perfect" will over and against our own self-centered passions (Rom. 12:2).

So, while therapeutic sexual morality expects your inner *self* to satisfy itself, through itself, by focusing only upon itself, the Bible orders us to "put off your old self" in order "to be renewed in the spirit of your minds" and to "put on the new self, created after the likeness of God in true righteousness and holiness" (Eph. 4:22-24). Therapeutic morality assumes that the natural, self-centered self is sufficient to define and meet all its personal needs, but the Bible teaches that the source of true satisfaction always lies outside self, and that honest self-knowledge should lead us to humbly acknowledge that we are not "sufficient in ourselves to claim anything as coming from us, but our sufficiency is from God" (2 Cor. 3:5).

4. It Is Totally Nonrelational

The fourth problem with therapeutic morality is that it makes sex nonrelational. Starting with sexuality as an empty idea with no fixed purpose,[24] therapeutic morality approaches sex in a way that disregards the importance of relationships in sexual behavior. By placing exclusive attention on individual selves, therapeutic sexual morality hinders couples from working on relational goals that go beyond individual wants and desires. If sex is all about self-satisfaction, then building a relationship with one person in particular does not matter; and if a partner fails to satisfy, there is no relational purpose to justify staying around to work out common problems or reach common goals.

In the Bible, God at creation revealed two main purposes for sex, both of which are relational. First, he made sex for reproduction, commanding Adam and Eve to, "Be fruitful and multiply and fill the earth" (Gen. 1:28). Second, he designed sex to unite a man and a woman in a personal relationship within marriage (2:24). Both reproduction and union are parts of a complex relationship that requires cooperation between sex partners on a personal level. And because God designed sex to be a relationship uniting persons, sex is never moral when it is treated as something that is nonrelational. Without relational purposes to lift sex above self-centered competition, therapeutic morality reduces sex to little more than a ride in bumper cars at an amusement park. But those who follow biblical morality will find that sex becomes more like a glue that joins parts into a whole that surpasses the value and potential of the parts.

Francis Schaeffer offers Sigmund Freud as an example of the nonrelational emptiness of therapeutic sexual morality:

> There is no better illustration of this than the example of Freud and his fiancee. Freud, not really believing in love—saying that the end of all things is sex, but yet needing real love—writes to his fiancee, "When you come to me, little Princess, love me *irrationally.*" I have often said that no sadder word could be written, coming from such a man as Freud. Freud himself at this particular place comes to what I would call a shuddering standstill. He is damned by what he is, by the emotions of *real* love in himself, because he has been made in the image of God.[25]

In imagining how sex might work with no relational purpose, therapeutic sexual morality cannot change reality. But ignoring true reality and acting on the basis of something only imaginary is very dangerous. The danger faced in taking a therapeutic approach to sexual morality is a lot like someone becoming absorbed in a book while actually driving a car at high speed down the interstate. The change in mental orientation does not change reality, but acting as if it did will put you in very real danger no matter how strongly you imagine otherwise.

5. *It Disintegrates Sexuality*

A fifth problem with therapeutic morality is that it empties sexuality of meaning and leaves it falling apart with no idea how the pieces fit together. Like Humpty Dumpty in the nursery rhyme, who broke into so many pieces that "all the King's horses and all the King's men couldn't put Humpty together again," therapeutic morality leaves sexuality in a heap with no particular shape or purpose.

Integration has to do with fitting pieces together in a way that forms something harmonious and whole. It assumes a master plan that assigns each piece a place and requires something to hold them together once the pieces are properly assembled. By comparison, *disintegration* is when pieces meant to go together instead fall apart, either because what should be holding them together is removed or because someone lost the master plan and no one knows how to put the pieces together. It is ironic therefore that, despite stressing the value of *wholeness* in everything including sexuality, therapeutic sexual morality ends up *disintegrating* sexuality by removing the only real key to integration and denying that a master plan even exists.

We have already mentioned that sex has relational purposes, but the true meaning of sex involves something even more. God retains sovereign authority over everything he creates. He is the one in whom we all "live and move and have our being" (Acts 17:28). He is the "head over all things by means of the church" (Eph. 1:22, my translation).[26] He is the one "from whom the whole body [is] joined and held together by every joint with which it is equipped" (Eph. 4:16). Because it is part of God's created order, human sexuality is not simply a pile of blocks in some cosmic nursery that we can pick up and arrange just any way we choose. Rather, it is something that fits and holds together only when we accept it the way God made it and then use it in ways that stay within his original plan.

In scripture, sex is spiritual, emotional, and physical as well as psychological. And while the psychological dimension is very important, it is not the most important aspect of sex. Nor is it the key to integrating the rest of life. The source of real integration in life is spiritual, not psychological. And it comes from Jesus Christ, not from trying to define sexuality for ourselves. Real integration is something we attain by growing "until we all attain to the unity of the faith and of the knowledge of the Son of God, to *mature* manhood, to the measure of the stature of the *fullness* of Christ" (Eph. 4:13, emphasis added); and by separating sexual identity from the source of true integration, therapeutic sexual morality leaves sexuality disintegrated and meaningless.

6. It Denies the Value of Corresponding Difference

A sixth problem with therapeutic morality is that it rejects the need for corresponding difference in God's design for sexual union. When God created human beings, he began with a solitary male. Adam was a real man with all that comes with *manhood* at all levels of his being. Manhood defined him physically, but it shaped him emotionally, psychologically, and spiritually as well. Thus, after naming all the creatures and realizing none of them corresponded to himself, Adam became aware of a sense in which he was "alone" (Gen. 2:18).

This sense of being *alone* can seem rather odd unless we pay attention to what God was doing. Adam was not alone for lack of companions, because he was surrounded by animal friends; and he was not alone for lack of intelligent communication with some other person, because he surely had that with God. Rather, Adam was *alone* only because there was no one else of his kind to complete his manhood. And only after Adam realized this truth—that manhood does not complete itself, that manhood is meant for something greater than itself that cannot be reached by manhood alone, and that manhood therefore needed something corresponding—only after Adam realized this did God then make Eve to fit, complete, and help to achieve that for which Adam's manhood was intended all along. Eve was of his kind, but her sexuality was different. But, even though her sexual identity was not the same, neither was it foreign. Rather, it corresponded. Thus in presenting Eve as a solution to Adam's lack, God demonstrated that *womanhood* is designed to complement *manhood* in order to satisfy something greater than either. Her sexuality fit Adam's, but it was not a mere duplication of something Adam already had.

In God's plan, this joining of different yet corresponding sexual identities—manhood with womanhood—is so critical that sex is never moral without it. But that is exactly what therapeutic sexual morality denies. If human sexuality has no fixed meaning, then corresponding difference in sexual union does not matter. So, if one feels like having sex with others of his or her same gender, or if someone else wants sex with animals, then it is all justified as a quest for self-fulfillment. God has a definite plan for how sex should be used, but individual desires can wander all over.

7. It Destroys the Wholeness It Promises

The seventh problem with therapeutic sexual morality is that again it also destroys the very thing promised in the first place. Therapeutic morality promises *wholeness* while in fact keeping people from finding completion in Christ and from knowing the satisfaction of relational wholeness that comes from uniting real manhood and womanhood. The irony here is truly immense because, while biblical morality leads to real satisfaction in all areas of life including sex, therapeutic morality leads to emptiness and only intensifies dissatisfaction. In fact, Francis Schaeffer got to the crux of the matter, explaining that,

> If man tries to find *everything* in a man-woman or a friend-to-friend relationship, he destroys the very thing he wants and destroys the ones he loves. He sucks them dry, he eats them up, and they as well as the relationship are destroyed. But as Christians we do not have to do that. Our sufficiency of relationship is in that which God made it to be, in the infinite-personal God, on the basis of the work of Christ in communication and love.[27]

God designed sex in a way that rewards men and women for fulfilling purposes that no individual and no group of individuals of the same sex can achieve alone. God designed the union of manhood and womanhood to be satisfying. But it truly satisfies only when we learn to respect God's standards, and it generates as much tragedy when we ignore those standards as it does rewards when we respect them. Those who justify sex for psychological effects alone are like children reaching for flames in a fire just because they are fascinated by movement and color. Under these circumstances, grasping effects for their own sake causes pain and sorrow, while leaving them to serve their purpose brings great joy and satisfaction.

Sex should indeed be satisfying. But it was never meant to satisfy completely, never meant to satisfy everything, never meant to satisfy by itself alone, and never meant to satisfy the deepest need of all, which is the need for union with our Creator. Ultimately God and God alone satisfies completely at the deepest level of all.

It is God, not sex, of whom David says, "You open your hand; you satisfy the desire of every living thing" (Ps. 145:16). It is God, not sex, who "satisfies the longing soul, and the hungry soul he fills with good things" (107:9; also 63:5). It is God, not sex, who "heals the brokenhearted" (147:3) and "saves the crushed in spirit" (34:18). It is God, not sex, who "strengthen[s] with power through his Spirit in your inner being" (Eph. 3:16). It is God's incarnation in Christ, not sex, who gives abundant life (John 10:10). And it is God's Spirit indwelling us, not sex, who enables us to "grow up in every way" in order to reach "mature manhood" and "the fullness of Christ" (Eph. 4:13, 15).

By expecting sex to satisfy everything completely all by itself, therapeutic sexual morality destroys true human wholeness; and by respecting the role God designed sex to have in human relationships, biblical morality supports and assures the human wholeness of which advocates of therapeutic morality can only dream.

Some years ago, I knew a Christian family who seemed to have everything. The parents both enjoyed successful careers, and their children were well-adjusted and actively involved at school and church. But everything they had fell apart when the wife sought counseling with a minister serving on the staff of a neighborhood church. She went because she did not feel completely satisfied, and this counseling minister advised her to seek fulfillment in a sexual relationship with someone outside her marriage. She did, and it led to having an affair—with the counseling minister himself.

One step led to another, and the wife soon divorced her husband, abandoned her children, and ultimately denied she had ever been a Christian. Shocking? Of course! But only if you accept biblical sexual standards. It all made perfect sense coming from therapeutic sexual morality. Therapeutic sexual morality offered by a counseling minister in the church led this wife to believe that sex, not God, is the way to wholeness, growth, and abundant life. And when that happened, her family fell apart.

Do you want a sexual relationship that completes your being? Do you want to know the joy that comes with sex that fully satisfies the purpose for which it is designed? Do you want sexual identity with profound meaning and value? Do you want sex that fully integrates the real you at every level? Then turn from therapeutic sexual morality and try biblical sexual morality instead.

15

PAGAN SEXUAL MORALITY: SEX AS SPIRITUAL LIFE

"OUR MAKER, SOPHIA, we are women in your image. With the hot blood of our wombs we give form to new life. . . . With the nectar between our thighs we invite a lover, . . . with our warm body fluids we remind the world of its pleasures and sensations." So began a prayer recited by more than two thousand women attending the Re-Imagining Conference held in the Minneapolis Convention Center in November 1993. This ecumenical women's conference, sponsored by the World Council of Churches and several mainline denominations,[1] urged delegates to change their view of deity and to worship a goddess named "Sophia" using rituals based on sensual experiences unique to women.

Speaker after speaker recommended taking a sexualized approach to spiritual life. So, for example, in addition to rejecting the biblical view of God, conferees were told to "sexualize" spiritual life, to base theology on sexual experience, to share sex with friends and not limit sex to marriage, and to sexualize worship by celebrating sensual body functions. Conference speaker Rita Nakashima Brock, who has written a book claiming that the goddess Sophia raised Jesus from the dead by erotic power, told conferees to incarnate the goddess using their erotic powers.[2] Melanie Morrison, cofounder of Christian Lesbians Out Together, called women to revise the Bible because the Bible we have now, "does not reconcile me with the earth and . . . does not reconcile me with my sexual self."[3] And lesbian theologian Mary Hunt advocated taking "sex among friends as the norm," and valuing "genital sexual interaction in terms of whether and how it fosters friendship" instead of how it functions in relation to marriages or families.[4]

In the 1980s, feminists and homosexuals in the United States began turning to religion to improve their moral standing in the culture. And this eagerness to sexualize religion fired growing popular interest in sexual paganism available from multiple sources both ancient (Greek, Egyptian, and pre-Christian European religions) and contemporary (Buddhist Tantrism, Hindu Kundalini, Wicca, and neo-gnostic, neo-Celtic, or Druidic sexual worship).

Contemporary interest in sexualized religion became evident in a rather dramatic way at the 1993 RE-Imagining Conference, but its spread through American culture is well documented by a flood of new books such as: *Pure Lust,* by Mary Daly (1984); *Journeys of the Heart: A Christology of Erotic Power,* by Rita Nakashima Brock (1988); *Touching Our Strength: The Erotic as Power and the Love of God,* by Carter Hayward (1989); *Sacred Orgasms,* by Kenneth Ray Stubbs (1992); *Sensuous Spirituality,* by Virginia Ramey Mollenkott (1993); *Sexuality and the Sacred,* edited by James Nelson and Sandra Longfellow (1994); *Passionate Enlightenment,* by Miranda Shaw (1994); *Sacred Sexuality,* by A. T. Mann (1995); *Sacred Pleasure,* by Riane Eisler (1996); *Sacred Sex,* by Robert Adkinson (1997); *The Soul of Sex,* by Thomas Moore (1998); *Sexuality and the Christian Body,* by Eugene Rogers (2000); *Erotic Worship in American Tantra,* by Ramana Das Silbey and Marilena Silbey (2000); and *A Sacred Sex Devotional,* edited by Rafael Lorenzo (2000).[5]

Besides recent books, the spreading interest in sexual paganism is also demonstrated by the growing popularity of: new workshops on *erotic worship* and *sacred sex* like those offered by Ramana Das and Marilena Silbey; vacation trips like those offered by Transformational Adventures, which takes participants to exotic locations for training in *sacred loving;* new religious groups like the Universal Life Church Neberdjer Society, which is reintroducing erotic gnosticism from ancient Egypt; and of Aphrodite shrines appearing at Wiccan fairs.

Evangelicals must understand that sexual paganism has now become a serious challenge to the life and witness of the church in America. No longer ancient or foreign, pagan religious sexuality is spreading through the culture at conferences and fairs, universities and seminaries, workshops and seminars. Indeed, modern Americans now seem to be more interested than primitive tribesmen in Africa or Asia in pursuing the allure of sexual pagan religious faith and practice. And because it is now so relevant, American Christians must try to understand how sexual pagans think.

Description of Pagan Sexual Morality

Pagan sexual morality is truly the diabolical opposite of biblical sexual morality. But what may not be obvious is that, while sexual paganism opposes biblical standards, it does so in ways that match biblical categories more nearly than any other alternative. In other words, there is an ironic sense in which pagan sexual morality is "closer" to biblical thinking than playboy, romantic, or therapeutic approaches to sexual morality. This is because sexual pagans and Christians both stress the spiritual dimension of sex and place spirituality at the center of sexual morality. But while the Bible evaluates sexual behavior in terms of God's holiness, sexual pagans evaluate spiritual behavior in terms of sex, and pagan sexual morality is all about gaining spiritual life through sex.

Pagan Sexual Morality

General Characteristics

Source of Moral Authority Is:	Self
Moral Authority Consists of:	Sensing spiritual power (defined in material terms)
Moral Goal Is:	Spiritual empowerment (deification)
Philosophical Basis Is:	Postmodernism
Functional Purpose Is:	Controlling the cosmos (achieving salvation)
Approach Is:	Mundane (reduces spiritual life to material experience)
Moral Standards Are:	Subjective (depends on choice and human control)
Main Focus Is:	Love of self
Secondary Focus Is:	(Nothing else)
Tertiary Focus Is:	(Nothing else)
Most Important Dimension of Sex Is:	The spiritual dimension
Depth Is:	Profound (as opposed to shallow)
Sex Is Considered:	Key to running the universe (to spiritual life)
Sexual Morality Is Considered:	A public matter
Sexual Intimacy Is Considered:	A public matter (the more public the better)
Marriage Should Be:	Abandoned or destroyed
Traditional Marriage Is Considered:	An evil thing (an oppressive thing)
Children Are Considered:	Burdens, tools, or sacrifices
Sexual Discipline Is Considered:	A bad thing
Relation of Sex to Marriage:	Totally unrelated
Relation of Happiness to Family Duty:	Spiritual happiness justifies fulfilling family duty
Effect on the Dimensions of Sex:	Reduces sex to manipulating spiritual power(s)
Relational Nature of Sex Is:	Denied
Spiritual Life Is:	Affirmed
Scripture Is:	Attacked
God's Authority over Sex Is:	Attacked
Ultimately Worships:	The spiritual-sexual self (deifies self through sex)

We can see this reversal in Hindu Kundalini, which believes sexual energy can be used to reach increasing levels of spiritual enlightenment until one arrives at a *new reality* where all opposites join in *the bliss of abiding love.* We see it in Tantric teaching on sex being a door through which individuals try to become *absorbed into the unlimited boundless cosmic experience.* We see it in the Great Rite practiced by Wiccans and neo-Celtic Druids, who think ritual sexual worship is *a powerful force for "magick"* that aligns the *energies of universal creation.* We see it in the neo-gnostic Universal Life Church Neberdjer Society, which claims that sex is *a spiritual path* that leads to union with *the Universal Soul.* And we see it in *Pure Lust,* a book by feminist theologian Mary Daly, in which she says there is no such thing as sexual *sin* because all sex is part of the life force uniting the cosmos.[6]

Sexual paganism comes in many forms, but this is not the place to survey its variations. We only plan here to deal with characteristic features, and for that we will use *The Soul of Sex,* by Thomas Moore,[7] to illustrate contemporary promotion of the view. Other sources will be used to supplement Moore, but only where needed to ensure clarity. Moore approaches sexual paganism as an advocate, not a critic. He is a former Catholic monk who gave up religious orders to follow a different religious path, one that has led him to address spirituality and sex on pagan terms. Because Moore defends sexual paganism himself, we can assume that he presents that view as favorably as possible.

According to Moore, pagan sexual morality centers on the value pagans place on the spirituality of sex. For Moore and others taking this approach, "the highest levels of spirituality are made accessible through sex" and the soul either is not *alive,* or is not *awake,* until it encounters divine power through sex. He explains that, "wherever eros stirs, the soul comes to life" and "whenever we put a lid on eros, the soul feels deprived of breath and life."[8]

Sexual pagans have a monistic worldview, which is to say they believe that everything is ultimately *one,* and that *separations* are all just illusions. This means pagans tend to think there is no real difference between the natural and the supernatural, between deity and humanity, or between male and female. As a result, the problem of sexual morality has less to do with justifying kinds of sexual behavior than it does with overcoming the *illusion of separation.* Separation causes everything wrong and union solves the problem. Indulging sexual desires is therefore good no matter what form it takes. Like a pilot enters a cockpit to fly a plane, sexual pagans think of sex as being a sort of cockpit men and women enter to overcome separation and *fly* (control) the spiritual forces running the universe.

Because they are monists, sexual pagans believe spirituality, morality, and sexuality are all basically one. Sexual passion itself is what generates the morality of sex. They also believe that *spirituality* and *holiness* are one and the same. That makes *unholy* sex impossible to imagine and turns discussing sexual *sin* into nonsense. Moore says, "the deepest secret of sex" is coming to understand that sex (all sex) is holy. Sex, he explains, is "life precisely in its holiness," and this leads him to recommend what he calls *erotic morality.* According to Moore, erotic morality "transgresses"—intentionally violates—what he considers the less spiritual dimension of *accepted morality* and frees men and women to soar in higher spiritual regions beyond the level of ordinary life.[9] All sexual pagans therefore justify sex outside of marriage, and some go beyond merely excusing extramarital sex to argue that nonmarital sex is actually better than—is morally superior to—sex in marriage. The Neberdjer Society, for example, teaches that *nonmonogamous sexual sharing* is better than keeping sex restricted to marriage; and Mary Hunt at the 1993 Re-Imagining Conference claimed that limiting sex to marriage is selfish compared to sharing sex between friends.[10]

Along with making sex the key for linking the supernatural and natural realms, sexual pagans believe sexual passion brings a goddess or god to indwell human flesh. On this Moore says that sex is "a ritual that invites the goddess of sex to be present"; that the purpose of sex is "to incarnate" deity in human flesh; that sexual passion is the craving of our souls for the sex goddess "who inhabits and transcends the known partner"; and that the "flesh-and-blood lover . . . offers a positive route to the eternal and spiritual realm."[11] But, because sexual pagans believe that sex turns sex partners into vehicles for uniting with deity, pagan sexual morality has little room for loving a human partner for his or her own sake. Human partners become means not ends, and it does not really matter which vehicle gets you to your destination.

Because they sexualize spirituality, sexual pagans also take an erotic view of salvation. Moore believes that uniting with pagan goddesses like Aphrodite, Artemis, and Diana through sex allows people to "break through the limits of the human condition to touch upon another level of reality." According to Moore, "Aphrodite rises in the swelling of passions and organs in sex."[12] This means for pagans spiritual salvation is a work of man (something we produce by our own initiative), not a gift of God (something God produces and gives to us by grace apart from anything we do for ourselves). In sexual paganism, salvation is something that comes by using sex like a sort of lever for directing spiritual powers to accomplish what men or women decide they should do. It is quite the opposite of submitting human will and passion to conform with standards set by a sovereign God who wants our behavior to fit his character.

By reducing spirituality to sexuality, pagans assume that the amount of divine life men and women have depends on the level of passion they arouse through sex. And when carried through, such logic produces mass orgies like the Great Rite practiced by Wiccans and neo-Celtic Druids, and mass copulation rituals like the *left hand path* in Tantrism, which tries to concentrate spiritual energy by having dozens—and sometimes even hundreds—of couples reach orgasm together. Such logic also leads pagans to worship sex organs, either as *incarnations* of deity or as *temples* in which the power of deity resides.[13]

In pagan sexual morality, the only truly *immoral* sex is limiting sex to biblical standards, the only real *sin* is saying that any sort of sexual behavior is sin, and the great *enemy* of human souls is not Satan but the God who defines biblical sexual morality. Thomas Moore therefore criticizes any religion or philosophy that "defines itself against the values of paganism."[14] The neo-gnostic Neberdjer Society therefore defends the *spirituality* of sex by calling people who believe the Bible "body-hating zealots." And goddess worshipers Monica Sjoo and Barbara Mor believe they are fighting to uphold a positive view of sex by attacking "the Bible God" for producing "a violent asexual, or antisexual morality never before seen on earth."[15]

Evaluation of Pagan Sexual Morality

Pagan sexual morality so completely rejects "the Bible God" and biblical morality, it seems odd to think there might be ways in which Christians agree with pagans about sex. But strange as it seems, biblical and pagan thinking on sexual morality do indeed come together at important points, and it is hard to appreciate how seriously they oppose one another unless we first understand what they both have in common.

Bible-believing Christians should be eager to agree when sexual pagans say that men and women affect matters of great spiritual importance when they have sex. We agree that the spiritual dimension of sex is central to sexual morality and is more important than any of its other dimensions. We agree that sex is holy. We agree that sex affects the life of the soul. We agree that sex matters to God and affects access to God. And we agree that no one inherits spiritual life from others but experiences spiritual generation and growth only when deity comes to indwell our souls in a direct, personal way.

And finally, we agree when sexual pagans say that sexual morality is something that comes from the spiritual power that runs the universe and that decides the destiny of human souls. So, if Bible-believing Christians agree that pagans are right in these important ways, what makes pagan sexual morality so completely incompatible with God's moral revelation in the Bible?

1. It Rejects Every Positive Principle of Moral Sex

The first problem with pagan sexual morality is that it rejects every positive moral principle God designed for sex that is truly honorable, pure, and holy. Because each of these principles was presented and discussed at length in chapter 7, we will not repeat that discussion here. But a summary of how they compare to pagan thinking on sex is in order.

Readers will remember that true sexual morality revealed in the Bible includes at least seven principles that together define the positive value of moral sex. In particular, we said God made sex to be something that is personal (relational), exclusive (unique), intimate (profound), fruitful (productive), selfless (sacrificial), complex (multidimensional), and complementary (must unite corresponding difference); and we also said that the absence of any of these positive values perverts sex from what it was designed to be and therefore makes it immoral. But when we look at how the pagan approach treats sex, it is immediately clear that pagan sexual morality opposes every one of these principles defining what is positive about sex.

Whereas God reveals that truly good sex must be personal (relational), exclusive (unique and special), and intimate (profound and especially valuable), pagan sexual morality denies these values by treating sex as if it were impersonal (the identity of a sex partner hardly matters), common (sexual sharing is better than having just one partner), and shallow (sexual partners are just vehicles for some other agenda). And, whereas God says good sex must be fruitful (productive), selfless (serving and sacrificial), and complementary (must unite corresponding difference), pagan sexual morality tends to treat sex as if it were something unproductive (the goal is ultimately to combine all things into one thing) and self-centered (sex partners are used to reach selfish goals), and it denies that sexual differences matter (all is one).

On one principle—the one saying good sex must be complex (multidimensional)—it might seem that the pagan approach accepts what God requires. But we should not be fooled. Paganism also rejects this principle by changing what it means. When God made sex, he made it something with physical, emotional, psychological, and spiritual dimensions all meant to work together in a pattern he designed. So sexual relationships naturally disintegrate (or fail ever to be integrated) when partners approach sex in ways that separate one dimension from the rest or that mix up the way they work together. Like Christians, pagans also understand that sex has several dimensions. But while pagans usually accept the fact that sex has various levels, they scramble the pattern for how they work together by confusing sensual arousal with divine power, and by confusing passions of the flesh with spiritual life.

2. *It Sexualizes Spirituality*

The second problem with pagan sexual morality is that, instead of evaluating the spirituality of sex according to God, sexual pagans evaluate God according to the spirituality of sex. In other words, while biblical Christians define sexual things spiritually, sexual pagans define spiritual things sexually.

At this point, some might wonder if *sexual spirituality* is not just another way of saying that *sex is spiritual*. But these are not identical terms, and they actually express totally contrary points of view. Virginia Ramey Mollenkott has written a book, *Sensuous Spirituality*, in which she constructs a whole new view of theology and ethics arising out of sexual experiences she has had as a practicing lesbian.[16] This is what sexual pagans mean by *sexual spirituality*, and it is quite the opposite of going to scripture in order to understand how we must conform sexual behavior to God's moral standards.

Christians do believe that sex is spiritual. Sex truly is a gift of God, and pure intimacy with Christ is the best reason we have for wanting to flee sexual immorality (1 Cor. 6:15-17). But when Christians say that sex is spiritual, we mean that men and women are spiritual creatures even when it comes to sex, that sexual purity pleases God and sexual sin has spiritual consequences—not that spiritual life is always about sex. And, while Bible-believing Christians agree with pagans when they say that sex is always spiritual, we do not agree that the concept of spirituality by itself says anything about whether something is moral. Some spiritual things (the Devil and hell) are as wicked as others (Jesus Christ and heaven) are pure and righteous. So, because the concept of spirituality covers good and bad, and is about much more than just sex, Christians must say that pagan thinking is wrong about defining spirituality according to human sexual experience.

3. *It Reduces Holiness to Sex*

The third problem with pagan sexual morality is that instead of requiring that moral standards conform with the holy character of God, it reduces *holiness* to nothing but sex. Moore says the "deepest secret of sex" is that sex is life "precisely in its holiness rather than its secularity."[17] Rather than treating holiness as a standard for measuring sexual morality, pagan morality uses sex as the way to measure holiness. And, when *holiness* becomes nothing but sex, then by definition no sexual experience can ever be *unholy.*

As Bible-believing Christians, we know that sexual behavior is enormously important to God; and because it is so important to him, God demands that we always keep sex holy. But unlike pagans, God does not treat holiness as if it depended on sex or were based on sex. Rather God's view of holiness comes from something far higher and greater than human sexuality. In scripture, true holiness is defined by God's own moral character plus nothing else at all. That is why, throughout the Bible, God repeatedly commands, "You shall be holy, because I am holy" (1 Pet. 1:16; also note Lev. 11:44-45; 19:2; and 20:7).

Christians do not deny the pagan idea of sexual holiness because we think that anything is wrong with sex itself. Sex certainly must be holy, but that is not the same as saying that sex can never be unholy. According to the Bible, holiness comes from God himself, not from sex itself. So, while pagans say that sex defines holiness and therefore sex always *is* holy no matter what, Christians say that holiness defines what sex always *should be,* and sex is therefore holy if and only if it conforms to the holy character of God. Sexual pagans say men and women experience something holy whenever they have sex no matter what, whereas the Bible says sex is holy only when practiced inside boundaries that conform to God's holy moral character.

4. It Honors the Shameful and Shames the Honorable

The fourth problem with pagan sexual morality is that it reverses honor and shame. The pagan value system honors and glorifies behavior God calls shameful (like sexual worship, homosexual behavior, and adultery) and heaps shame and reproach on behavior God considers honorable and worthy of respect (like limiting sex to marriage and keeping it separate from worship). By denying any difference between spirituality and fleshly desires and then claiming that nothing spiritual can ever be unholy, sexual pagans conclude that arousing sexual passion is always a good thing and that any way of expressing it is automatically honorable.

Because sexual pagans think spiritual and material experiences are the same thing, they end up switching the way morality connects with sex. While God says we must learn to control the sexual appetite in order to keep it inside moral boundaries fixed by the holiness of his character, sexual pagans instead think moral standards come from sexual passion and therefore they go along wherever their passion leads. So, where biblical standards of holiness transcend (come from above) and therefore limit the flesh, pagan holiness, being of the flesh, never controls it at all. And since honor and shame have to do with respecting what is worthy and despising what is not, this leads sexual pagans to treat honor and shame completely opposite to what God reveals in scripture.

Thus, while God says, "Let marriage be held in honor among all, and let the marriage bed be undefiled" (Heb. 13:4), Mary Hunt despises married sex as "idolatrous," not even respecting it as an option for others. And, while scripture warns us to "flee youthful passions and pursue righteousness, faith, love, and peace, along with those who call on the Lord from a pure heart" (2 Tim. 2:22), Thomas Moore is eagerly promoting a day when no one will feel any shame about seeing "graphic erotic imagery" displayed in public.[18]

It is the same graphic contrast that Paul describes when he says that, when God gives men up "to dishonorable passions," they become so twisted that they not only refuse to admit they are doing something wrong but make a huge effort to "give approval to those who practice them" (Rom. 1:26,32). Nevertheless, God responds, "Woe to those who call evil good and good evil, who put darkness for light and light for darkness, who put bitter for sweet and sweet for bitter!" (Isa. 5:20). And Paul reminds us that, however men try to reverse sexual moral standards, "they [still] know God's decree that those who practice such things deserve to die" (Rom. 1:32).

No matter what anyone does or says, true sexual morality never changes. It is not something *we* make up, but is something by which God evaluates *us*. So no matter how public opinion is affected by honoring shameful sex and shaming honorable sex, true standards are unaffected. What is truly honorable and what is truly shameful always stays the same.

5. *It Sexualizes the Incarnation of Divinity*

The fifth problem with pagan sexual morality is that, even though sexual paganism believes in divine incarnation, it corrupts the whole idea by turning it into a means by which men and women manipulate deity through sex. Perhaps the greatest mystery of the gospel is how the life of one man, Jesus of Nazareth, could ever be worth enough to save every sinner who comes to God in repentance. And this mystery is explained only when we understand that Jesus was not just a man like us but was also God himself come in the flesh. Jesus was God incarnate. In Jesus Christ, God became a man to save sinners by dying in our place (John 12:27; 2 Cor. 5:21; Heb. 9:28; 1 Pet.

2:24). Jesus was able to suffer death only because he became a man; but his death paid for the sins of the world (John 3:16) only because he was God.[19] On this basis, and this basis alone, God offers forgiveness and everlasting life to all sinners who repent and have faith in Christ's atoning work on the cross.

Sexual pagans also believe in a form of divine incarnation, and they also say the embodiment of God in human flesh is necessary for uniting human beings with the life and power of deity. But the pagan view of incarnation is not something deity does for us but is something men and women control and force upon deity. In sexual paganism, divine incarnation is a work of man, not of God, and the grace of God's true incarnation in Jesus Christ is replaced with the worst sort of blasphemy—the claim that sexual arousal (or even sex organs) incarnates God *in the flesh*. Sexual pagans say we experience God by having sex, whereas the Bible says we please God when we obey him—and one way we do that is by keeping sex holy.

Of course, sexual pagans are saying that there is no such thing as sexual sin, and that satisfying lust is the same as obeying God. According to the Bible, this sort of thing exhausts God's patience: "God gave them up to a debased mind to do what ought not to be done" (Rom. 1:28). Very likely this also is exactly what Paul was thinking about when he wrote, "it is shameful even to speak of the things that they do in secret" (Eph. 5:12).

6. It Offers Salvation by Means of Sexual Sin

The sixth problem with pagan sexual morality is that instead of salvation by faith in Jesus Christ, sexual paganism offers salvation by sexual sin, and makes rebelling against God's standards of sexual purity a path to spiritual *enlightenment*. Whereas spiritual life in the Bible comes from God's indwelling Holy Spirit after forgiveness, cleansing, and reconciliation with God (on his terms), paganism denies that we have any need for forgiveness and perverts salvation by sexualizing human union with divine life (on human terms).

Like pagans, the Bible also teaches that sex affects access to God. But unlike pagans, the Bible says that God, through the sacrifice of Jesus on the cross, has already opened a "new and living way" (Heb. 10:20) for us to approach him through Jesus Christ (not through sex), and favorable communion with God is preserved by moral purity as we obey his word (not by sexual immorality). The citizens of first-century Corinth worshiped Aphrodite, the goddess of sex, and the men of Corinth believed they could unite with the goddess and access divine favor by having sex with temple prostitutes. So Paul warned the Christian men in Corinth, who had just been saved from sexual paganism:

> The body is not meant for sexual immorality, but for the Lord, and the Lord for the body. . . . Do you not know that your bodies are members of Christ? Shall I then take the members of Christ and make them members of a [temple] prostitute? Never! . . . he who is joined to a [temple] prostitute becomes one body with her. . . . But he who is joined to the Lord becomes one spirit with him. . . . Or do you not know that your body is a temple of the Holy Spirit within you, whom you have from God? . . . So glorify God in your body (1 Cor. 6:13-20).

As Christians, we must not overreact by saying that sex has no effect on access to God at all, because it does—at least negatively. Sexual holiness matters to God, and sexual behavior in the body affects spiritual union with Christ. The difference between Christian and pagan thinking on sex and salvation is not about whether or not there is any sort of link between sex and having a favorable relationship with God. It has to do with understanding that we are obligated to remain united with Christ *even during* acts of sex, which is entirely different from the pagan idea of manipulating divine powers *by means of* sex.

So, while moral sex pleases God, it is not a pathway to God; and, while immoral sex does indeed affect access to God, the effect is not favorable but unfavorable. Favorable access to God comes only through Jesus Christ (John 14:6). Whereas sexual pagans say reaching God on favorable terms depends on sexual sin, the Bible says maintaining a favorable relationship with God depends on being cleansed from all sin, including sexual sin. Whereas sexual pagans say that salvation depends on indulging sexual desires on human terms, the Bible says salvation depends on confessing that God is right about not indulging sexual desires on human terms. Whereas sexual pagans say sex is a path to God, the Bible says that holiness is the only path to God, and that no one can ever be holy enough to reach God on his or her own—the only way to become holy enough is to have all your sins forgiven through the work of Jesus Christ on the cross.

7. It Destroys the Spiritual Life It Promises

The seventh and final problem with pagan sexual morality is that, like other counterfeit approaches, it also destroys the very thing it promises. Pagan sexual morality promises spiritual life but leads to spiritual death instead. It promises a self-indulgent way to celebrate the spiritual dimension of sex, but it actually prevents men and women from finding genuine spiritual life by alienating them from the only true Master of the Universe. Whereas sexual pagans say that sexual passion by itself guarantees spiritual life, the Bible says sexual passion by itself cannot assure spiritual life. Rather, sexual sin like all sin will, in the absence of repentance and forgiveness, only assure eternal damnation.

Jesus said, "I am the way, and the truth, and the life" (John 14:6), and promised, "whoever hears my word and believes him who sent me has eternal life" (5:24). And scripture makes clear that life with Christ demands sexual purity. "But sexual immorality and all impurity . . . must not even be named [hinted at] among you, as is proper among saints" (Eph. 5:3). "Flee from sexual immorality" (1 Cor. 6:18). So rather than leading sinners to eternal life in union with God, pagan sexual morality drives sinners away from the only way they can truly be reconciled and united with God. The spiritual effect of pagan sexual morality only leaves sinners vulnerable and exposed to the coming wrath of God (Col. 3:5-6).

Sex is indeed spiritual, and sexual immorality does affect spiritual life. But sex is not a path to spiritual life just because it is spiritual, and sexual sin calls for God's judgment precisely because it corrupts something that is spiritual and not just material. Sexual paganism is a path to spiritual death, not spiritual life, because true spiritual life depends on moral reconciliation with a holy God who says we must "be holy, for I am holy" (Lev. 11:44, 45; also Lev. 19:2; 20:7; 1 Pet. 1:15).

During James Levine's long tenure as lead conductor and music director for the New York Metropolitan Opera, he changed it from a rough-and-barely-ready operation to acclaim as the finest opera house in the world. The Met usually focuses on performing classical works from composers such as Mozart, Verdi, Stravinsky, and Gershwin. But in the 1990s Levine decided to add something innovative to the Met's classical repertoire and commissioned the writing of two new compositions: *The Ghosts of Versailles,* by John Corigliano, and *The Voyage,* by Philip Glass. Both of these works were certainly *innovative,* because they both stressed sex with goddess figures leading to astonishing imaginary results.

In *Ghosts,* which premiered in 1991, the ghost of a playwright named Beaumarchais sets out to win the affections a goddess-like Marie Antoinette (a sort of Queen of Heaven) even though the audience knows she has a husband, Louis. And the relationship between Beaumarchais and Antoinette is finally consummated in a passionate, adulterous embrace that transports them to heaven, a sort of paradise by orgasm. In the first act of *The Voyage,* which Levine introduced in 1992, another goddess figure, this time as a woman spaceship commander dressed in blue and white with a veil (to appear like Mary, Queen of Heaven) has sex with ancient humans; and this ritual copulation gives them intelligence and culture and brings about the beginning of civilization. And in the second act, Queen Isabella appears to Columbus as a goddess while he is facing monsters at sea. This goddess commands the admiral to worship her as his "one true god," which he does by having sex with her. As a result, his voyage is saved, the sea monsters disappear, and he suddenly makes landfall in America.

These works were indeed *innovative,* but more for favoring sexual paganism than for their music. Both were stunning mainly because they featured blessing and spiritual development—passage to paradise, the birth of civilization and culture, successful voyages of discovery—by goddess worship through acts of *sacred sex*. They were also milestones because, in 1991 and 1992, these two works premiered by the New York Metropolitan Opera took sexual paganism from the fringes of American life and put it into the mainstream of high musical culture.

Do you want sex that pleases the divine power running the universe? Do you want sex that truly is holy? Do you want the spirituality of uniting your soul with a sexual partner who embodies the image of God? Do you want sex that delights your soul and the Creator at the same time? Do you want the sort of sex that inspires spiritual blessing? Do you want to avoid handling sex in ways that destroy your soul and alienate you from eternal spiritual life? Then reject the false allure of pagan sexual morality and try biblical sexual morality instead.

PART FOUR:

ASSESSING THE STATE OF SEXUAL MORALITY

16

WHAT IS GOING ON?

WE HAVE COVERED A LOT OF GROUND, and having reached the end of the journey we should take time to reflect on the whole thing. Like hikers climbing a mountain, we have reached a summit from which we have a better perspective. Looking back on the way we have come, we are better equipped to consider some truly large issues regarding the way biblical sexual morality fits together, the reason for all the counterfeits, and why things are happening now as they are. Each of the following topics will require looking at everything as a whole, and to address them we will need to use some things we have learned along the way.

In this chapter we will try to gain a better understanding of why there has always been so much controversy over sex, why different views have arisen challenging God's standards, and how they all seem to cooperate in opposing God's standards. In the next chapter we will look at the overall nature of the conflict we are in, and then in the last chapter we will consider the future and evaluate where current trends may be taking us.

WHY IS GOOD SEX SO HARD TO GET RIGHT?

It may sound odd, but one very large "big picture" issue has to do with why good sex has always been so hard to get right. Putting it this way invites debate over what makes sex good and who says so. But we covered that in chapter 6. The question now is not what makes moral sex moral, but what makes moral sex so hard to keep in the right channels even when you are trying. It is a question for people who accept God's authority and want to please him but still find it difficult to do so. Since God (as Creator) made sex in the first place, and since he (as Moral Ruler) made the rules, and since he (as Judge) expects us to obey them perfectly, why did he make it so hard to keep sex under control? We will consider two answers, one that we know for sure but that is incomplete, and one that involves guessing but that tries to go beyond the first.

The answer we know for sure is that the trouble we have with sex because of sin is our fault, not God's. He made sex perfect and gave it to us perfect. And, for our part, managing it was not difficult until after Adam and Eve sinned. Sin did not change sex, but it did change our ability to handle it correctly. Sin perverted human nature by corrupting human character, and the corruption of human character is what makes moral sex hard to get right. But, of course, getting that way is our fault, and God had nothing to do with it.

C. S. Lewis once said that obeying God's rules for moral sex is

> so difficult and so contrary to our instincts, that obviously either Christianity is wrong or our sexual instinct, as it is now, has gone wrong. One or the other. Of course, being a Christian, I think it is the instinct which has gone wrong.[1]

He was right, of course. But blaming ourselves for sin does not explain why God made sex so powerful in the first place. Yes, we have only ourselves to blame for falling into sin. But why did God make our sex drive so much stronger than is needed to ensure reproduction? And, why did he do it knowing all along that we would become sinners and that giving it extra power would make it that much harder for us to obey his rules? Standing a loaded gun in the hall is no problem if you just expect adults who are all trained in using firearms safely. But why would someone do that just before expecting children to visit?

Lewis noticed that all other human appetites are more or less in proportion with their natural functions. We sometimes eat too much or sleep too much, but rarely do these appetites go enormously beyond natural needs. But when it comes to sex, he said, the average person's appetite "is in ludicrous and preposterous excess of its function."[2] If men had babies every time they thought about sex, the human race would have populated several galaxies by now. It therefore makes sense to ask why God gave sex so much extra power, and why he did it knowing that we would need to manage it as sinners. Controlling natural appetites is hard enough when they are proportional, so why did God make the human sex drive so much stronger than is biologically necessary?

The Bible does not address the question, so we can only guess. Of course, we know God makes no mistakes and has good reasons for everything (Rom. 8:28; Eph. 1:11). So even though the Bible does not explain something, we should still have faith that God knows what he is doing and has good reasons for doing it. But, that said, what good reasons might he have?

One guess is that it could have been to make sure that, to join his side, sinners would need to make a hard choice against something very strong pulling the other way. In other words, it may have been a way to make sure no one ends up on God's side by mistake. Saving faith in God requires dying to self, and choosing to do so on purpose. So perhaps God gave Satan a special advantage to make sure no one comes to God except on the basis of unconditional, selfless, sacrificial faith—something we know is very important to God (Matt. 10:38-39; Luke 9:23-24; Rom. 6:1-3; 8:12-13; Gal. 2:19; Heb. 11:6; 1 Pet. 2:24). If so, then God may have created an especially strong desire that must be restrained before we can accept his authority, and there is no stronger natural desire than our human passion for sex. No one restricts his or her own sexual desires by mistake, and demanding sexual discipline makes it obvious that no one reaches God on his or her own terms. No one can approach God without giving up control over his or her natural passion for sex.

It may also be that God gave sex extra power because he was making it easier for us to agree that we cannot live holy lives without depending on him completely. God's moral standards are impossible for us to keep on our own, and nowhere is that more obvious than when it comes to controlling our sexual desires. Keeping sex pure requires superhuman strength, and trusting God over ourselves develops superhuman character. So, along with insisting that we must die to ourselves, God may also have been arranging things to help us depend on him more than we might otherwise.

Why did God make our sexual appetites so strong, so that it is so hard to get it right? The Bible does not tell us why. But the question is interesting, and the guesses we have made are consistent with what the Bible does say.

Why Such Conflict over Sex?

Another question related to the first is why there has always been so much conflict over sex. It is related to the first question because it also comes from what Lewis called the "preposterous excess" of power connected with sex. Throughout history, no other area of human behavior has been so deeply fractured by moral conflict. Even religious divisions, frequently blamed for causing more trouble than anything, turn out quite often to involve sex. It is common to say a person's religion determines his morality, but it often is the other way when it comes to sex. People quite regularly choose religious beliefs in order to excuse or justify whatever sexual practices they want to pursue.

Some of the bloodiest wars in scripture were driven by sexual divisions. For example, sexual perversion was the last straw justifying God's annihilation of Sodom and Gomorrah (Gen. 18:16–19:29; Jude 7); the war of vengeance Moses led against the Midianites was punishment for their corrupting God's people with immoral sex (Num. 31:1-54); and a civil war that almost destroyed the entire tribe of Benjamin arose from conflict over sex (Judg. 20:1–21:25). In classical history, the great battle of Troy was caused by sex. Helen, the beautiful wife of king Menelaus of Sparta, who either ran off with or was abducted by Paris of Troy, is called "the face that launched a thousand ships." And today's war on terrorism, in the view of radical Muslims, has a lot to do with preventing Western culture from polluting Muslim lands with a flood of sexual immorality.

It has been like this since the beginning of history. But why? Just understanding that sexual controversy is perpetual and always deeply divisive suggests that perhaps more is at stake in conflicts over sex than in other areas of human behavior. But if more is at stake in conflict over sex than in conflicts over wealth and poverty, racial discrimination, or destroying innocent human life, what might it be?

Paul says something about this while discussing how the human race is separated from God. In writing to Christians in Rome, Paul lists a series of steps by which people turn from God's true morality and choose the opposite (Rom. 1:18-32). Beginning with just failing to be thankful (v. 21), Paul says people move step by step farther and farther away from God's morality, until eventually they end up "full of envy, murder, strife, deceit, [and] maliciousness." They become "haters of God, insolent, haughty, boastful, inventors of evil, disobedient to parents, foolish, faithless, heartless, [and] ruthless" (vv. 29-31). Quite a list! But in the progression of steps that Paul gives, it is important to notice the pivotal role served by division over sexual morality. Notice the sexual theme running through the passage: "God gave them up in the lusts of their hearts . . . to the dishonoring of their bodies. . . . women exchanged natural relations for those that are contrary to nature . . . men [committed] shameless acts with men" (vv. 24-27).

Remember here that Paul is not explaining the fall. He is not recounting how people got to be sinners in the first place; rather, he is addressing the way Satan leads people ever deeper into sin and then keeps them in sin forever separated from God. What he shows is that Satan's most powerful weapon for accomplishing this—for turning people from God and keeping them away from turning to God for help—is perverted sexual desire. Combined with fallen human nature, the extra power God gave sex is Satan's greatest single advantage against us. It is the easiest way he has for turning people away from God because it is the one temptation people can least resist. Once you let sexual passions loose, they will land you on Satan's side every time.

But there is more in this passage. In order to release sex from moral restrictions, it takes more than a few minor exceptions to God's general view of morality. You cannot say God is generally right, except when it comes to sex. That cannot be done because there is absolutely no ground between the opposing sides. When it comes to sexual morality, people must either choose restraining sex with God or indulging sex without him. God is either totally right about sex, or he is wrong about sex and about everything else as well.

This means that perverted sexual desire is the most strategic weapon in Satan's arsenal, as well as the strongest. And what makes it so strategic is that justifying sexual sin changes a person's whole approach to morality and is the only category of sin that forces a person to do that all by itself. Other kinds of sin obviously violate God's rules, but people can rationalize exceptions and still say that God is morally good. A murderer can say God is right to prohibit killing innocent people, but then rationalize murdering his victims as exceptions who (in his eyes) *deserve to die.* And a thief can say God is right to prohibit stealing, and then rationalize exempting himself as a case of *special need.*

But that does not work when it comes to justifying sexual sin. If sexual passions are reliable and require no form of discipline, then the whole structure of biblical morality is wrong, not just one part or the other. Releasing sexual passion from moral discipline requires restructuring morality completely. God's approach will not do, some other approach must be found, and that new approach has to be one that either denies that God exists, or rejects him as evil, or "re-imagines" God in terms of indulging sexual desires. Releasing sex from moral discipline is pivotal, because doing so changes everything, including your view of God. Biblical morality turns from good to evil, light turns to dark, sweet turns to bitter (Isa. 5:20), and a person's view of God in the Bible turns from love to hate.

This sort of total moral revolution is discussed in scripture (Isa. 5:20; Matt. 10:22; John 3:19-20; Rom. 1:30; 2 Tim. 3:4; James 4:4), and in chapters 2, 3, 4, 14, and 15 we saw how it is happening again today among sexual revisionists and neo-pagans. To justify sexual sin, they too are attacking God and calling him evil. That is why Bishop John Spong says he "loathes" the God of scripture and thinks Christians need to expose biblical morality as terribly "immoral." That is why feminist theologian Mary Hunt says the very idea of limiting sex to marriage is "idolatrous." That is why feminist writer Naomi Goldberg says "women are going to bring an end to God." And that is why neo-pagans Monica Sjoo and Barbara Mor say the "Bible God" is "violently antisexual" and the enemy of what they say is the source of all life, pleasure, and love.

God Is at the Center of True Sexual Morality

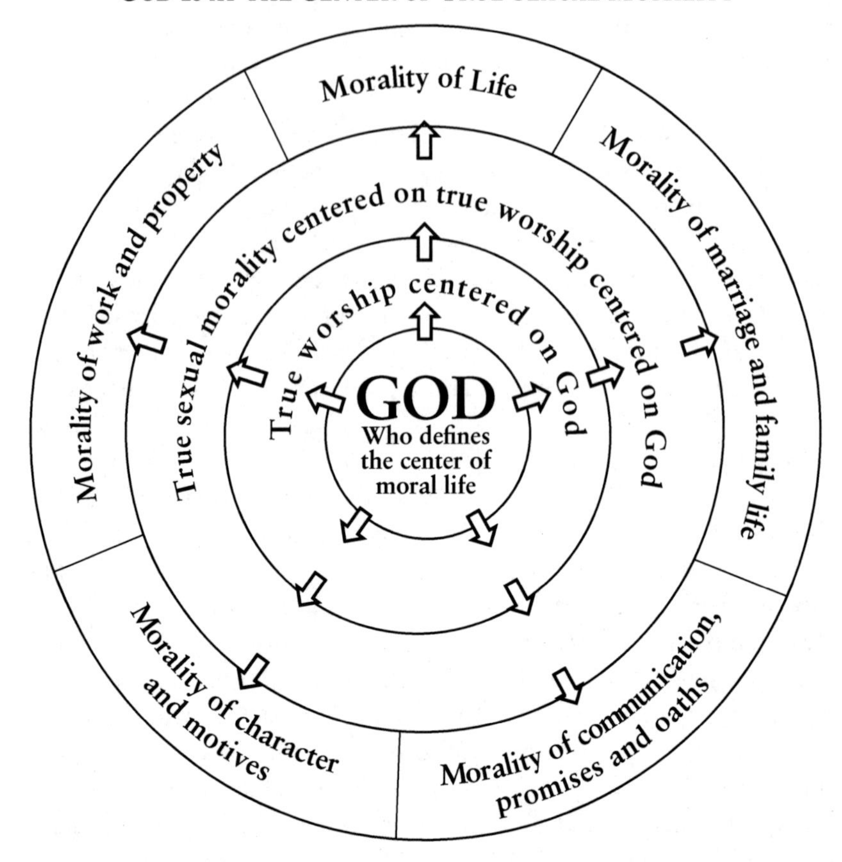

A second reason for so much conflict over sex has something to do with God's revelation that, one way or another, the way we handle sex affects intimacy with himself. The one detail God adds after saying we are made in his image is that we are sexual: "male and female he created them" (Gen. 1:27). This indicates that keeping sex pure is closely connected with respecting the image of God in humanity, and that sexual sin is a horrible violation of that image. We also find that corrupting this image had a lot to do with perverting human nature. When Adam fell into sin, he chose intimacy with Eve on immoral terms over intimacy with God on perfectly moral terms (Gen. 3:6). The sin in this case was disobedience, and it did not involve sex. But Adam most certainly realized that the decision he was making would affect his sexual relationship with Eve. In a very real sense, Adam had to choose between sex and God, and he chose sex. Obey God, no Eve, no sex. Disobey God, yes Eve, yes sex.

In chapter 6, where we explored the way God's holiness forms the basis of biblical sexual morality, we saw a profound connection between morally pure sex in the husband-wife relationship and having a morally pure spiritual relationship with God. This link between intimacy in marriage and spiritual intimacy with God, and between keeping ourselves pure for each other and keeping ourselves pure for God, indicates something even more could be at stake in sexual moral conflicts than just turning people from God. Beyond these conflicts being a strategy for keeping people in bondage to sin, there is a hint that in some way sexual purity is part of God's plan for eternity, and Satan is working very hard to ruin it.

Sexual pagans are terribly wrong about using sex in worship, terribly wrong about reaching God through sex, terribly wrong about sex being a path to spiritual life, and terribly wrong about sex running the universe. But they are not wrong about sex being spiritual and about that being its most important aspect. Keeping sex morally pure does in fact concern the core of humanity where the soul and body connect, and it does in fact affect (it does not cause, but it does affect) intimacy with God (1 Cor. 6:13, 20; Eph. 5:23, 31-32) and what he requires of us to be united with him through all eternity (1 Cor. 6:14-15; 2 Cor. 6:14-15).

More than this we dare not say. But Satan is after something. He hates sexual purity with a passion and must have a very good reason for that hatred. Satan is terribly evil, but he is not stupid. So, even though the Bible does not explain what drives him to hate sexual purity so much, just noticing how hard Satan works at ruining sexual purity is all the evidence we need to conclude that what he hates so very badly must be worth a lot.

Progression Between Counterfeit Views (Dynamic Links)

One advantage we have looking back on everything at once is being able to see characteristics linking parts together. Considering all the counterfeit views on sexual morality, we need to ask two important questions: Do differences between them reveal some order? And how are they alike? Answering the first question will identify "dynamic links," connections telling us how the counterfeits relate to one another. They show what direction the counterfeits are going, how they influence or affect each other, and how they cooperate to achieve a common goal. Answering the second question will identify "static links," the sort that show what the counterfeits share in common as opposed to biblical sexual morality; we will see that these commonalities are in a sense variations of one basic plan for leading people away from God. This section will address the first question and the next section will address the second.

There is overwhelming evidence that the sexual counterfeits have many important characteristics showing an order of progression leading one to the other. In fact I have already had this in mind, and the order in which we considered them in chapters 12 through 15 was not arbitrary. All the counterfeits oppose biblical sexual morality, but in somewhat different ways and some more seriously than others. Of all the counterfeits, romantic sexual morality is the least perverted; playboy morality is more perverted than romantic; therapeutic morality is more perverted than playboy; and pagan sexual morality is more perverted than all of them. Now we will examine this order more closely.

It is fairly easy to notice at least ten dynamic (progressive) links between these views, all revealing the same order going from romantic, to playboy, to therapeutic, to pagan, always in a steady progression of increasing perversion. The order never changes, and this has to be very significant. To me it suggests an intelligent power (Satan) working behind all the counterfeits directing or coordinating their efforts. They are not related at random in the arbitrary way you expect of things that have fallen together by chance. Rather, they are arranged by an ordered plan in which one leads to the next in one direction, always heading farther and farther away from God. On a battlefield, if you notice different units heading the same way in formation, it is very strong evidence they are on the same side and are following orders from one commander.

Here then is what leads us to think the counterfeit views on sexual morality are arranged in order and are working together:

1. ***There is order in the sequence in time in which they have arisen in American culture.*** Romantic sexual morality took root with the Romantic Movement arising in France, Germany, England, and America in the late 1700s and early 1800s. Playboy sexual morality came to national prominence with the Sexual Revolution in the 1960s. Therapeutic sexual morality spread through American culture with the rise of militant feminist and homosexual movements in the 1980s. And neo-pagan sexual morality has become very popular beginning in the 1990s.

This first progression shows something different from the rest. The other nine dynamic characteristics all have to do with how the counterfeits work, but this first characteristic merely observes the order in which they have appeared and started affecting American culture in time. The interesting thing to see is how the different counterfeits have appeared over time in exactly the

Progression Between Counterfeit Views of Sexual Morality

(DYNAMIC LINKS)

DYNAMIC LINK	ROMANTIC SEXUAL MORALITY	PLAYBOY SEXUAL MORALITY	THERAPEUTIC SEXUAL MORALITY	PAGAN SEXUAL MORALITY
Sequence in time arising in American culture	Took root with the Romantic Movement in the late 1700s and early 1800s	Took off with the Sexual Revolution in the 1960s	Spread with the rise of militant feminist and homosexual movements in the 1980s	Became popular in the 1990s and 2000s
Increasing depth of attack	Affirms love while reducing it to affection	Attacks love in any form	Attacks fundamental human identity	Attacks the soul
Increasing self-centeredness	Partly self-centered — Individuals are selfless but couples are selfish	Totally self-centered but softens selfishness with desire to be thought sophisticated	Totally self-centered — Institutionalizes self-centeredness	Totally self-centered — Revolutionizes cosmology for self-deification
Increasing opposition to relationships	Threatens meaningful relationships beyond the couple	Totally non-relational — Uses others as objects for personal gratification	Totally non-relational but thinks using others is helping them grow	Totally non-relational — Uses others as stepping stones — Others may be sacrificed for spiritual life
Increasing opposition to biblical sexual morality	Respects biblical morality (for others) — Wants the same results on easier terms	Tolerates biblical morality, but thinks playboy morality is best — Celebrates diversity and choice	Hates biblical morality — Thinks it harms people	Hates biblical morality — Thinks it interferes with personal divinity and cosmic progress
Increasing opposition to marriage	Respects marriage as an ideal, but not necessary for sex and not possible for everyone	Thinks marriage is unnecessary and restrictive but should be an option for others	Thinks traditional marriage is harmful — Wants to stop or redefine it as anything you want	Hates traditional marriage as evil — Destroys marriage and family in any form
Increasing distance from God	Only a little different from God's approach — Individuals are somewhat loving, selfless, and sacrificial	God is irrelevant but not despised	Redefines the biblical God to accommodate desire — Hates God privately, not openly	Hates God openly — Urges people to reject God and follow other deities
Increasingly direct worship of sex	Worships feelings of affection — Easier sex is a consequence	Worships moral autonomy — Reduces sex to be a choice of entertainment	Worships personal wholeness achieved through sex	Worships sex openly and directly — Mocks sexual discipline as unenlightened and corrupt
Increasing effect on other areas of behavior	Affects marriage and family but little else	Affects business, art, politics, and justice but only as an option	Makes sex the key to human life on earth	Makes sex the key to running the universe
Increasing desire to change society	Weakens respect for marriage — Demands easier divorce	Demands diversity, removing laws favoring marriage and treating all sex as a matter of private choice	Wants to revolutionize social institutions to promote sexual fulfillment for everyone	Celebrates wickedness in public — Eventually requires sex worship as a civic duty

same order that we will observe in every other category. This means the counterfeits have been arising and influencing our culture in order of ever more serious depth of attack, ever more serious perversity, ever more serious opposition to biblical morality, ever more serious opposition to marriage, ever more distance from God, ever more direct veneration of sex, and ever more radical desire to change society.

Noticing this obvious order leading from one counterfeit to the next is terribly strategic. It not only shows them heading in the same direction but indicates that they have a common goal. It also tells us we are up against something far more serious than most Christians imagine and indicates that we should be doing a better job of resisting these trends. We may not win the growing war over sexual morality this side of heaven, but it would be terrible to give up just because no one was paying attention and no one raised an alarm before it was too late.

2. ***There is order in their increasing depth of attack.*** Romantic morality affirms love while changing what love means. It honors love while reducing it to nothing but affection. Playboy morality attacks love in any form, either ignoring it completely, denying its worth, or destroying what exists. Therapeutic morality aims deeper by attacking fundamental human identity. And then pagan morality aims at the deepest level by attacking the soul.

3. ***There is order in their increasing self-centeredness.*** Romantic sexual morality is the least self-centered of these counterfeits. The individuals involved in this sort of morality are selfless, but as couples they are intensely selfish, putting their own relational interests over absolutely everything including God. Romantic morality also rewards self-centeredness when a relationship gets in trouble, because it excuses unfaithful lovers and blames bad feelings on the lovers who remain faithful. Playboy morality is more self-centered but still worries about what others think. For the playboy, selfishness is softened by wanting others to think you are sophisticated. Therapeutic morality goes farther by institutionalizing self-centeredness and trying to restrict the influence of those who do not agree. And pagan morality is the most self-centered, because sexual paganism revolutionizes cosmology (what people believe about the nature of the universe) to justify self-deification (turning people into gods and goddesses through sex).

4. ***There is order in their increasing opposition to relationships.*** Romantic sexual morality threatens meaningful relationships with anyone beyond the

romantic couple. Other significant relationships (parents, friends, children) become threatening, and truly loving God is the greatest threat of all. The playboy approach is completely nonrelational. Others are treated as if they were merely objects (sexual toys) used for personal gratification, and everyone is just expected to get used to it and be careful. Therapeutic morality is so completely nonrelational that it believes using others for self-fulfillment is good for them. Using others to satisfy yourself is viewed as helping them grow. But pagan sexual morality is again the worst and is so nonrelational that sex partners are regarded simply as stepping-stones for attaining your spiritual goals. Sometimes others may even need to be sacrificed for the sake of enhancing your spiritual life—and if so, too bad for them.

5. ***There is order in their increasing opposition to biblical sexual morality.*** Romantic morality generally respects biblical morality but wants to get the same results (lasting love, ideal marriage, deep affection) on easier terms. To sexual romantics, biblical morality is neither better nor worse, just different. Playboy morality tolerates biblical morality as an option for others. But, while the playboy celebrates diversity, he truly believes his approach is better than biblical morality. Therapeutic morality hates biblical standards, saying that they harm unmarried people by forcing them to be stunted and incomplete. But again, sexual pagans hate biblical morality the most, because to them biblical standards interfere with their quest for personal divinity, cosmic salvation, and universal harmony.

6. ***There is order in their increasing opposition to marriage.*** Romantic morality treats lasting marriage as an ideal that most people cannot achieve. It says marriage is wonderful but is not necessary for sex, is hardly ever permanent, and is not even possible for everyone. Playboy morality does not believe marriage is even an ideal. To the playboy, marriage is unnecessary and terribly restrictive, but others can try it if they like. Therapeutic morality holds that the traditional (biblical) view of marriage is not only restrictive but harmful, and wants to either stop the practice or make it something people can define however they like. Finally, sexual pagans hate traditional marriage as something evil and often end up working to destroy marriage and family relationships in any form.

7. ***There is order in their increasing distance from God.*** Romantic sexual morality is only a little removed from God's approach and remains somewhat loving, somewhat selfless, and somewhat sacrificial. Playboy morality

moves farther away. God is not necessarily despised but is mostly treated as irrelevant. Therapeutic morality is farther off, still trying to redefine the revelation of God in scripture and revise interpretation of biblical standards to allow whatever people desire. If people following therapeutic morality hate the God of scripture, they tend to keep it private while pretending to respect him in public. But sexual pagans usually hate the "Bible-God" openly and urge others to reject him in favor of pagan deities who will let them indulge their sexual passions.

8. ***There is order in their increasingly direct worship of sex.*** Romantic morality worships feelings of affection that end up justifying less sexual discipline and weaker commitment to marriage. Playboy morality worships freedom from moral restrictions and reduces sex to entertainment. Therapeutic morality worships the personal *wholeness* that it seeks to achieve through sex. But sexual paganism worships sinful sex directly, and in the end leads to mocking sexual restraint as perverted and corrupt.

9. ***There is order in their effect on other areas of behavior.*** Romantic morality affects marriage and family but almost nothing else. Playboy morality influences behavior in areas like business, art, politics, and justice, but only as an option. For example, during an interview in 2003, Hugh Hefner explained that, while he thinks the playboy approach "happens to be the best way of living your life," his influence on American culture has been to give people more choices about "alternative ways of living your life."[3] Therapeutic morality makes sex the key to life, making it the ultimate reason for human existence and the basis for everything we do. Finally, sexual paganism makes sex the key to running the universe.

10. ***There is order in their desire to change society.*** Romantic morality weakens general respect for marriage and demands easier terms for divorce. Playboy morality insists on sexual diversity, on making sex a private choice with no public relevance, and on removing laws favoring sexual relationships defined by marriage over sex with no commitment to marriage at all. Therapeutic morality wants to revolutionize social institutions to make sure all citizens are free to pursue and satisfy sexual desires however they wish. But sexual paganism is still more extreme, not only celebrating wickedness in public but using the law to promote it. The most extreme form of sexual paganism coerces citizens to support sexual worship as a matter of patriotism and civil duty.

Common Ground Uniting the Opposition (Static Links)

The second question we are asking about the counterfeits is, How are they alike? With this we are looking for "static links," characteristics having to do with how they overlap and what they have in common against biblical sexual morality. Answering this question will help us to see how the four counterfeit approaches to sexual morality are far more similar to each other than different.

This suggests, of course, that the counterfeits may actually be variations on one basic design arranged by the same master-planner (Satan). They are all built the same way, working the same way, and moving in the same direction. They all use the same strategy and end up having the same effect. Finally, we can see that at every point where the counterfeits agree, they are united against God's approach to sexual morality.

It therefore looks like what makes the counterfeits different is not the sort of difference you expect in completely separate ethical systems competing with each other. Instead, they are the sort of differences a military commander uses to increase effectiveness over a large theater of operation. In other words, they look more like the Army, Navy, Marines, and Air Force taking different assignments on the same side than like enemy armies fighting each other. The counterfeits are not opposing each other so much as they are coordinating efforts in a war against the same enemy. Their one common enemy really is the God of scripture and his standards of sexual morality.

So what evidence is there for thinking the counterfeits are presenting a united front against God and his standards? Here are twelve characteristics the counterfeits have in common:

1. ***Each starts with something true.*** Romantic morality says sex should be affectionate. Playboy morality says sex should be enjoyed, and that there is nothing bad with experiencing sensations of physical pleasure. Therapeutic morality says sex should be satisfying in a way that touches the core of one's humanity. And pagan morality says sex is spiritual and should affect the soul. Biblical morality says all these things as well. The only difference is that, while the counterfeits use these truths to justify sexual sin, biblical morality does not.

2. ***Each perverts something God made good.*** Biblical sexual morality accepts and uses God's gift of sex on God's terms, while the counterfeits all use God's gift on their own terms. Romantic morality perverts the value of affection,

Common Ground Uniting Counterfeit Views of Sexual Morality
(STATIC LINKS)

STATIC LINK	ROMANTIC SEXUAL MORALITY	PLAYBOY SEXUAL MORALITY	THERAPEUTIC SEXUAL MORALITY	PAGAN SEXUAL MORALITY
Each starts with something true	Says sex should be affectionate	Says sex should be enjoyed and there is nothing wrong with experiencing pleasure	Says sex should be satisfying and affect the core of humanity	Says sex is spiritual and should affect the soul
Each perverts something God made good	Perverts the connection between sex and love	Perverts the connection between sex and enjoyment	Perverts the connection between sex and the mind	Perverts the connection between sex and the soul
Each shifts justification from God to ouselves	Shifts from God to our affections	Shifts from God to our sensations of physical pleasure	Shifts from God to our sense of psychological wholeness	Shifts from God to our sense of spirituality
Each reduces sex to feelings	Reduces sex to emotional feelings	Reduces sex to physical feelings	Reduces sex to psychological feelings	Reduces sex to spiritual feelings
Each is anthropocentric and mundane	Sees no authority beyond human emotion	Sees no authority beyond human sensation of physical pleasure	See no authority beyond human psychology	See no authority beyond human spirituality
Each is self-centered	Self-centered couples	Solitary, self-centered individuals	Solitary, self-centered individuals	Solitary, self-centered individuals
Each puts sexual experience over God's Word	Puts emotional experience over God's Word	Puts physical experience over God's Word	Puts psychological experience over God's Word	Puts spiritual experience over God's Word
Each is permissive	Desires are released by affection	Desires are released by sensations of physical pleasure	Desires are released by wanting or needing to feel whole	Desires are released by spirituality
Each is subjective	Only you can tell if you feel affection	Only you can tell if you feel sensations of physical pleasure	Only you can tell if you feel whole	Only you can tell if you feel spiritual life in your soul
Each trusts some form of sexual desire	Trusts desire for affection	Trusts desire for sensations of physical pleasure	Trusts desire for wholeness	Trusts desire for spiritual vitality
Each varies with time	Feelings of affection vary with time	Feelings of pleasure vary with time	Feelings of wholeness vary with time	Feelings of spiritual vitality vary with time
Each varies from person to person	Evaluating affection varies from person to person	Evaluating pleasure varies from person to person	Evaluating wholeness varies from person to person	Evaluating spiritual vitality varies from person to person

corrupting the connection between sex and love. Playboy morality perverts the value of physical pleasure, corrupting the connection between sex and enjoyment. Therapeutic morality perverts the value of psychological satisfaction, corrupting the connection between sex and the mind. And pagan morality perverts the value of spiritual life, corrupting the connection between sex and the soul.

3. ***Each shifts the justification of sex from God to ourselves.*** Biblical sexual morality is based on the holiness of God and is concerned with keeping sex consistent with who God is and what he says. But the counterfeits all reject God and justify sex based on something inside ourselves. Romantic morality shifts justification from God to our affections, playboy morality shifts it from God to our sensations of physical pleasure, therapeutic morality shifts it from God to our sense of psychological wholeness, and pagan morality shifts it from God to our sense of spirituality.

4. ***Each reduces sex to feelings.*** Biblical morality recognizes that God made sex complex and says we have a moral duty to keep all levels of sex connected. The Bible also says that sex has more to do with relationships and character than with desires and feelings. But the counterfeits all pretend you can reduce sex to one thing or another and act as if feelings were the whole thing. Romantic morality reduces sex to emotional feelings, playboy morality reduces it to physical feelings, therapeutic morality reduces it to psychological feelings, and pagan morality reduces it to spiritual feelings.

5. ***Each is anthropocentric and mundane.*** Biblical sexual morality is God-centered and transcendent. It comes from divine authority beyond the created universe, which makes it something we cannot control. God is over us, not the other way around. But each counterfeit is man-centered (anthropocentric) and this-worldly (mundane). All are based on human authority. All say there is no authority beyond human control, and there is no one above us to whom we must submit. Romantic morality sees no authority beyond human emotion, playboy morality sees no authority beyond human sensations of physical pleasure, therapeutic morality sees no authority beyond human psychology, and pagan morality sees no authority beyond human spirituality.

6. ***Each is self-centered.*** Biblical morality is God-centered, but all the counterfeits are terribly self-centered. The romantic approach centers on the self-centered couple, and self-centered couples are not much better than

self-centered individuals. But the playboy, therapeutic, and pagan approaches do not even care about self-centered couples and center exclusively on solitary, self-centered individuals.

7. ***Each puts sexual experience over God's Word.*** Biblical moral standards come from God through his Word and are used to measure and evaluate sexual experience, not the other way around. But the counterfeits all turn this around, giving first priority to some aspect of sexual experience and evaluating or reinterpreting God's Word based on that. Paul describes this as being controlled by "the flesh" rather than "the Spirit" (Rom. 8:5-8). Romantic sexual morality gives priority to the emotional aspect of sexual experience, playboy morality to the physical aspect, therapeutic morality to the psychological aspect, and pagan morality to the spiritual aspect. But while the counterfeits focus on different aspects, they all agree about putting sexual experience over God's Word and deciding what to think of God's Word based on that.

8. ***Each is permissive.*** Biblical morality requires us to restrain and control sexual desires, but the counterfeits all focus on releasing them from such control. Biblical morality says that while sexual desires are indeed enjoyable, they require discipline; but each alternative view assumes that, because sexual desires are enjoyable, we should not allow anything to interfere with them. Romantic morality says sexual desires are released by affection, playboy morality by sensations of physical pleasure, therapeutic morality by wanting or needing to feel whole, and pagan morality by spirituality.

9. ***Each is subjective.*** Biblical standards are objective, meaning they are real no matter what anyone thinks, says, or does. But all the counterfeits are subjective, meaning they depend on things that you interpret however you like, that only you can understand, and that no one can ever use to hold you accountable. Only you can tell if you feel affection (romantic), only you can tell if you feel sensual pleasure (playboy), only you can tell if you feel whole (therapeutic), and only you can tell if you feel spiritual life in your soul (pagan).

10. ***Each trusts some form of sexual desire.*** Biblical morality teaches that desires of the flesh are unreliable and deceptive, but the counterfeits not only release fleshly desires from control but say they are trustworthy and should be followed as moral guides. According to biblical morality, sexual desires are natural but are not trustworthy because human nature is fallen from its nat-

ural state and is therefore corrupted by sin. But all the opposing views hold that because sexual desires are natural they must be morally pure. They all assume that human nature is unchanged—human nature never was corrupted and natural desires for sex are morally reliable without further justification. Therefore, romantic morality trusts the natural desire for affection, playboy morality trusts the natural desire for physical pleasure, therapeutic morality trusts the natural desire for psychological wholeness, and pagan morality trusts the natural desire for spiritual vitality.

11. ***Each varies with time.*** Biblical sexual standards are fixed and do not change, but the counterfeits all depend on things that change all the time. Romantic morality changes with feelings of affection, playboy morality changes with feelings of physical pleasure, therapeutic morality changes with feelings of wholeness, and pagan morality changes with feelings of spiritual vitality.

12. ***Each varies from person to person.*** Biblical standards not only stay the same over time, but apply the same to everyone. In other words, they are not just timeless but universal. By contrast, the counterfeits not only change with time but also from place to place, culture to culture, and person to person. There is no fixed standard for evaluating the validity of inner feelings of affection (romantic), or of physical pleasure (playboy), or of wholeness (therapeutic), or of spiritual vitality (pagan). Each person judges for himself however he likes, and others cannot know if a person's standard is valid or not.

To summarize, the counterfeits share so much in common that they look more like variations on one design than like systems organized along completely different designs. All follow the same general plan and serve the same general purpose, which is to lead people away from God, to keep them from God, and to remove reasons they may have for loving God and respecting his rules. Of course, this means they also keep men and women from salvation from sin and the blessings that go with morally pure sex. They keep people from finding eternal life through Jesus Christ and knowing sex filled with abiding joy, genuine satisfaction, exemplary honor, and pure allure.

17

Understanding the Conflict

Using Good to Pervert Good

One characteristic shared by all the counterfeits demands closer inspection. Since they oppose God's approach to sex and are seeking to keep people away from him, why do they each start with something truly good? If they think God is so wrong, why start with anything that is true in God's design? Why not just start with something completely different? If you think the enemy is terrible, why start with something from the enemy side?

Romantic morality starts by saying sex should be affectionate, playboy morality by saying sex should be enjoyed and there is nothing wrong with the fact that sex includes sensations of physical pleasure, therapeutic morality by saying sex should be satisfying, and pagan morality by saying sex is spiritual and should affect the soul. They all start with genuine good and use it to pervert good. The question is, why? Why do they not reject everything on God's side and start with something original? There are three logical answers: deception, perversion, and inoculation.

Reason One: Deception

The first answer is deception. The most obvious reason the counterfeits start with good is a matter of strategy. It gives them each a lure to ensnare people who are not paying attention. It is exactly the same thing con men and swindlers use to lure potential victims. A good counterfeit relies on something victims know is good to deceive them into wanting something fake. A lure appeals to the victim's perception of good and does not work if it looks fake. If a lure is working well, victims will fail to notice any difference between what appears good in the counterfeit and the real good they desire.

Everything depends on getting a victim to make one false decision. Until a victim is trapped, he is free to come or go as he likes. But after being trapped, he cannot simply change his mind and get out. It is important to realize, when a victim is lured, he is not interested in what he thinks is wrong. Rather, he is tempted by what he perceives to be something good. He makes a false decision to enter a trap because the good in the lure seems so worthwhile that it quiets any concern he might have about whether it is what it seems. The trick is getting victims to want something fake without realizing that it is fake. They are not tricked because they have bad desires but because they are gullible about wanting good. They want what seems good so much that they forget to exercise critical judgment.

Deception is Satan's best strategy and has been since the Garden of Eden. When Satan led Eve to sin, he did not simply challenge her to defy God and do something bad. Rather, he began with something good and used it to deceive her (Gen. 3:13; 2 Cor. 11:3; 1 Tim. 2:14). He got Eve to focus so much on wanting good on his terms that she forgot to be critical. She knew that all the fruits on all the trees God made were good, and that she and Adam were allowed to eat any they liked—except from just one tree. The fruit of the tree of the knowledge of good and evil was off-limits, but not because it had bad fruit. God makes everything good, so the fruit of that tree had to be good as well. And that perception of good was what Satan used to get Eve.

If the fruit of that tree was good, then why should it be off-limits? Eve did not know, and the more she thought about it the less sense it made. Satan got Eve's whole attention focused on how truly good the forbidden fruit must be. It was "a delight to the eyes," it was "good for food," and there was this added bonus of being "desired to make one wise" (Gen. 3:6). Eve began wanting good on Satan's terms so much that she never wondered if he was trustworthy, or whether it made sense to doubt God's word. Her desire for what seemed good got to be so strong that she never considered what a terrible risk it would be to trust someone she did not know over trusting the most trustworthy person she knew.

Satan is not called "the deceiver of the whole world" (Rev. 12:9) for nothing. It always has been his best strategy, and he is very skilled at it. It is significant therefore that all four counterfeit approaches to sexual morality deceive by using good to pervert good. It is Satan's trademark and therefore shows that he had something to do with the plan. The mere fact that something looks good does not make it truly moral or wise. It could be the lure of a counterfeit.

Reason Two: Perversion

The second answer is perversion. Besides being a matter of strategy, another reason the counterfeits start with good is that they have no other option. They have nothing else with which to begin. The devil is not a creator. He is very good at perverting things, but he never creates new material. He can only use God's material, and everything God makes is good. Augustine in the fourth century said that evil "is a name for nothing but the want of good," and claimed that, while good things can exist without evil, "there cannot be a nature [however corrupt] in which there is no good."[1] He meant that evil is not something that exists off by itself apart from good; rather, it exists only as the destruction or perversion of things that are good to begin with.

Evil is not real by itself, apart from its wrecking of good things. Of course, evil is real in the sense of harming, twisting, and perverting things. But in terms of its mere existence, evil depends on good. Evil is nothing except the damage suffered by things that were good and still should be good, and that even applies to Satan. Augustine taught that, "not even the nature of the devil himself is evil, in so far as it is nature, but it was made evil by being perverted."[2] Not even the most evil of evil things, Satan himself, can exist without having been good to begin with.

What changes something from good to evil is perversion. Evil does not replace good with something else but rather takes good and deforms it. Evil is the deformity of good things and only exists when things God made perfectly good become bent, twisted, crushed, or damaged compared to what they should be. It is like what happens if you take a perfect orchid and step on it. After doing that, you have a damaged orchid—a sad, crushed, pitiful version of what it was and should be. It remains an orchid, and, being an orchid, it remains a good thing even after being crushed. But the difference between what it was before being crushed, and what it is after being crushed, is evil.

The same applies to what the counterfeits do with sex. The reality of sex is something good no matter what anyone does with it. So even to corrupt sex, the counterfeits must start with real good. They do so because they have no other choice. You simply cannot do anything bad to sex without starting with the goodness of the real thing. What is wrong with the counterfeits has nothing to do with changing the original goodness of sex and everything to with perverting what people do with it.

Reason Three: Inoculation

The last reason the counterfeits start with good is that it inoculates victims from being able to see and desire anything better. Once they are caught, the good in the counterfeit makes it hard for them to see that they are trapped and could do much better if they got out. As the saying goes, "None are so blind as those who will not see."

The prophet Isaiah speaks of God's impatience with a person who "sees many things, but does not observe them" and whose "ears are open, but he does not hear" (Isa. 42:20). The main reason people do not see moral truth when it should be plain is that they do not want to see anything else and therefore never expect to see anything different. Their minds are closed even though their eyes and ears may work perfectly. People miss what they do not expect. The problem is not comprehension but attitude.

This sort of thing happens all the time. When the Department of Motor Vehicles installed a new traffic light near my home, those who ran through it most were not strangers who did not know the area but local residents who thought they knew it. At the new intersection, everyone saw the same thing. But when what they saw did not fit their expectations, some local residents refused to believe it and ran the light. Some even claimed they never saw what they saw. Expectations are so powerful they can actually stop you from seeing what you see.

What happens at new traffic lights happens at moral intersections as well, especially when expectations are connected with powerful passions like those driving sex. Once a person has a way to excuse what he wants, he loses objectivity and soon cannot see evidence for anything else no matter how plain it might be. In biblical terms, a person's heart is "hardened" (Ps. 95:8; Mark 3:5; 16:14; 2 Cor. 3:14; Heb. 3:13), a condition in which truth no longer matters because whatever a person uses to excuse sin prevents him from seeing the truth.

Scripture warns that justifying sexual sin hardens people's hearts this way. They become,

> darkened in their understanding, alienated from the life of God because of the [willful] ignorance that is in them, due to their hardness of heart. They have become callous and have given themselves up to sensuality, greedy to practice every kind of impurity (Eph. 4:18-19).

Clinging to sexual sin makes them blind to the amazing goodness of God. Elsewhere Paul says, "the mind that is set on the flesh is hostile to God, . . . it does not submit to God's [moral] law; indeed it cannot" (Rom. 8:7). He also says, "The natural person does not accept the things of the Spirit of God, . . . [because] they are folly to him" (1 Cor. 2:14).

How do people get to be so blind and hostile even toward what is best for them? Paul explains it when he says, "Claiming to be wise, they became fools" (Rom. 1:22). They excuse sexual sin by some new thing that they claim is *wise,* when in reality they are becoming *fools.* The new source of false *wisdom,* blinding them to what is best for them, consists of coming to think and believe that what seems good in a counterfeit morality is all they will ever want or need.

In the end, the little bit of good in the counterfeit sexual morality, which perverts the real goodness of God's design for sex, inoculates them from seeing or caring for anything better. In this way, using good to pervert good not only lures victims into the trap but keeps them trapped by closing their minds and hardening their hearts until they can no longer comprehend, much less want, the real thing.

Holiness and Morally Positive Sex

Looking back over the ground we have covered, another important thing to observe is the overwhelmingly positive way God approaches sex. He not only *says* that sex is good but treats it very positively as well. His *actions* are consistent with his *words.* We have all had the experience of talking with someone whose behavior did not match what he said, and we know if this happens that it is better to trust actions over words. But there is no such contradiction when it comes to the way God treats sex. He acts toward sex as positively as he speaks, and he speaks about sex as positively as he acts. When it comes to deciding if God believes what he says on sex, the evidence is that he does. So, if anyone is not sure about trusting what God says on sex, he should look at what God does and trust the evidence. But to get it right you must look at everything he does and not just focus on one part—like the prohibitions.

Look, for example, at how God bases the morality of sex on keeping it consistent with his holiness. In chapters 6 and 11 we looked at how the holiness of God is the most positive measure of good that exists anywhere at all. So, the fact that biblical sexual morality is based on God's holiness shows that he treats it very positively indeed. He simply could not base it on anything better than that.

If the Bible is clear on anything, it is the awesomely majestic, wonderfully splendid character of God summed up in the word *holy.* Here are some ways God's holy character is described in scripture. Nehemiah says "the joy of the Lord is your strength" (Neh. 8:10). David praises the wonderful character of God, saying: "in your presence there is fullness of joy; at your right hand are pleasures forevermore" (Ps. 16:11); "how abundant is your goodness" (31:19); "with you is the fountain of life" (36:9); and "my soul thirsts for you; my flesh faints for you, as in a dry and weary land where there is no water" (63:1; also 42:2; 143:6). From knowing God himself, David urges that everyone "taste and see that the Lord is good!" (34:8).

Another psalmist says, "a day in your courts is better than a thousand elsewhere," and one reason is that "no good thing does he withhold from those who walk uprightly" (84:10-11). And Isaiah even connects delight in God's wonderful character with the value of sexual purity celebrated in marriage:

> I will greatly rejoice in the Lord; my soul shall exult in my God, for he has clothed me with garments of salvation; he has covered me with the robe of righteousness, as a bridegroom decks himself like a priest with a beautiful headdress, and as a bride adorns herself with her jewels (Isa. 61:10).

In scripture we learn that God's holiness is positively good (Ex. 33:18-19), positively beautiful (1 Chron. 16:29; 2 Chron. 20:21; Ps. 29:2; 96:9), positively majestic (Ex. 15:11), positively loving (2 Chron. 20:21), and positively great (Ezek.36:23; 38:23). And we find that when the holiness of God is reflected in us, we become fruitful (Rom. 6:22), we have the privilege of knowing God more intimately (Matt. 5:8; Heb. 12:14; also 1 Cor. 13:12, 1 John 3:2, Rev. 22:3-4), and our souls are restored (Ps. 23:3) or revived (Ps. 19:7).

Basing sexual morality on the holiness of God is tremendously positive because it links the value of sexual purity with the value of God himself. Sex is beautiful because God is beautiful. Sex is wonderful because God is wonderful. Sex is positive because God is positive. But in realizing this we must be careful to never get it reversed. Christians *cannot* say God is beautiful, wonderful, and positive *because* sex is beautiful, wonderful, and positive. God's approach to the value of sex is wonderfully positive because it is in fact based on himself. Good sex does in fact reflect the goodness of God. But the goodness of God does *not* reflect the goodness of sex. The value of God does not depend on, nor does it come from, nor does it come through, the value of sex. It is always the other way around.

Not only does God base sexual morality on something positive (God's holiness), but the way he applies holiness to sex is very positive as well. What holiness requires in practice is defined by seven positive principles, each addressing a different aspect of sexual purity, and in chapter 7 we learned that keeping sex holy means always treating sex as something personal (relational), exclusive (special/unique), intimate (profound/valuable), fruitful (productive), selfless (sacrificial/serving), complex (multidimensional), and complementary (uniting corresponding difference).

And then, not only is God's way of approaching the value of sex based on something positive (his holiness) and applied positively (the seven principles), it also ends with positive results. In chapter 11 we saw that God promises four wonderful blessings to men and women who keep sex holy on his terms, and these are abiding joy, genuine satisfaction, exemplary honor, and pure allure. Each of these blessings is very worthwhile and positive.

Taking God's approach to sex as a whole helps us to see and appreciate the amazingly positive way he treats this important aspect of human life. Like bookends holding a line of books on a shelf, God's approach to moral sex not only stands on a positive base (his holiness) but is held up positively at both ends (the principles and promises). This means you could say biblical sexual morality is positive "from start to finish."

The only apparently "negative" part in God's whole approach is the prohibitions that come between the principles and promises. But even these are not really so negative after all. Of course, they do frustrate desires that point out of bounds. But they do it for positive reasons. They are actually protecting our own best good and are there to make sure we do not miss the best in God's design for sexual relationships. In this sense, you could say *everything* God does relating to sex is wonderfully positive. It is not just positive "from beginning to end" but is positive "through and through."

The fact is, God's rules for sex have nothing to do with keeping anyone from enjoying the best sex, and they have everything to do with making sure we do not settle for less than the best. The problem we have with this usually is that we are doubting whether we can believe that God's holiness is actually more positive than indulging our passions. In that case, the trouble is not with God failing to be positive enough on sex but with our failing to be positive enough on God's holiness.

When our sons were toddlers, my wife and I rearranged objects in our house. Fragile figurines and things remotely dangerous were either locked up or moved. We put limits on their immature desires, and from their perspective it seemed we were keeping them from having a lot of fun. Sharp knives and dangerous cleaning chemicals would have been fascinating, fragile porcelain figurines would have been terrific toys, and exposed electric sockets demanded exploration.

Measured by their desires, the precautions we took were all terribly negative. But what they could not understand at the time was that everything we did in restraining their desires had nothing to do with stopping their enjoyment of good and everything to do with protecting it. We did not restrain their desires in order to be frustrating but rather to keep them from harming themselves and others until their view of good grew more mature.

The same thing happens when we doubt the positive value of God's holiness compared to indulging desires without restraint. There is nothing wrong with the way God treats the value of sex, but there is a lot wrong with evaluating sexual goodness based on satisfying ourselves. Like toddlers fascinated with sharp knives, deadly cleaning chemicals, delicate figurines, and exposed electric sockets, indulging sexual passions without restraint is naive and dangerous whether we see it that way or not. The only reliable way to assure truly positive sex is trusting the holiness of God.

What Is So "Bad" About Being Good?

Christians think being good is good. Behaving morally is right. It just makes sense, and we assume that everyone agrees, whether Christian or not. Being good is good. Doing right is right. Therefore it sounds strange to ask, What is "bad" about being good? But asking the question highlights the irrational resistance people so often raise against God's wonderfully good standards for sexual behavior.

Of course, non-Christians immediately say that they are operating on another value system, and that Christians are crazy for restricting what (to them) seem like perfectly good desires, for what (again, to them) seems like no good reason. But that is not enough to answer what we are really asking. Something else is going on when people reject God's standards with a lot more passion than makes sense for people who just have different values. If that were the only issue, there would be some curiosity, some willingness to at least consider the evidence, and perhaps even some hunger for the blessings God gives with taking sex on his terms.

Some nonbelievers are curious about biblical teachings, of course. But in America these days, as in Western culture at large, negative reaction to God's standards is growing stronger and more explosive all the time. People in non-Western lands are far less reactionary. Even if raised with very different sexual values, non-Western people are generally willing to hear discussion on the value of biblical standards. If not convinced, they simply leave and rarely react emotionally. That is how people normally react when they simply have different values. When people explode defensively or react with rage at just hearing someone suggest that God might be right in regard to sex, something more is going on than merely the presence of opposing ideas on sexual morality.

Today, even some who claim to be Christians sometimes hesitate to accept God's approach on sex. Most of these would never say God's standards are bad, and yet they act as if they are not sure that God is right. They may agree that God is right on most things, but when it comes to sex they

The Post-Christian, Postmodern Battle to Fill the Void Left by Modernism
(With Counterfeit Views Added)

Battle at the Sexual Level	**CHRISTIANITY** Pulls one way	**SEXUAL MORALITY** ← →			**PAGANISM** Pulls the other way
Progression of Different Views	Biblical Sexual Morality	Romantic Sexual Morality	Playboy Sexual Morality	Therapeutic Sexual Morality	Pagan Sexual Morality
Battle at the Spiritual Level	Christian Spirituality* Tries filling the void in a self-disciplined, God-centered way →	Moral-Spiritual Void Created by Modernism • Cosmic alienation • No meaning or purpose beyond the material • Reduces people to machines, feelings to chemicals, and psychology to hormones			Pagan Spirituality Tries filling the void in a sensual, self-centered way ←

*The only other religions large enough to affect the culture—Judaism and Islam—are comparable to Christianity on sexual morality.

object and insist on setting their own conditions. Although they claim to agree that being good is good, the way they act says they really think that being good is sometimes bad. That is what people communicate when they are constantly looking for ways to avoid God's rules and ease differences between biblical standards and the culture.

Why then are non-Christians reacting more negatively, and why are even some people in the church becoming more hesitant to accept the basic goodness of God's wonderfully positive standards for sex? The answer has to do with three kinds of fear: fear of losing control, fear of losing something much desired, and fear of being wrong.

Fear of Losing Control

Francis Thompson's poem, "Hound of Heaven," describes the fear people very often feel about losing control of their lives to God:

> I fled Him, down the nights and down the days;
> I fled Him, down the arches of the years;
> I fled Him, down the labyrinthine ways
> Of my own mind . . .
>
> (For, though I knew His love Who followed,
> Yet was I sore adread
> Lest, having Him, I must have naught beside.)[3]

C. S. Lewis records how he felt at the turning point in his life when he finally decided to submit and truly accept God's complete authority:

> I had always wanted, above all things, not to be "interfered with." I had wanted (mad wish) "to call my soul my own." . . . You must picture me alone in that room in Magdalen, night after night, feeling, whenever my mind lifted even for a second from my work, the steady, unrelenting approach of Him whom I so earnestly desired not to meet. . . . [Then] In the Trinity Term of 1929 I gave in, and admitted that God was God, and knelt and prayed: perhaps that night, the most dejected and reluctant convert in all England. . . . a prodigal . . . brought in kicking, struggling, resentful, and darting his eyes in every direction for a chance of escape.[4]

The first main reason people recoil at accepting the goodness of God's authority over sex is simply being afraid to give up control. When we face the authority of God over any area of life, the choice is "all or nothing." Jesus made the audacious claim of divine right to control absolutely everything. He claimed that, "All authority in heaven and on earth has been given to me" (Matt. 28:18), and insisted that, "any one of you who does not renounce all that he has cannot be my disciple" (Luke 14:33). Jesus is God, and as God he claims total authority over everything, including sex. He makes no deals, allows no exceptions, accepts no compromises, and never negotiates.

A person confronting God's authority over sex either surrenders without conditions or must rebel. And of course many rebel. Since sex is so powerful, it often (and perhaps most often) turns out to be the thing over which people are forced to reveal who truly is in control of their lives. Are they in control? Or is God? At the point of settling who truly has the last say on sex, some who have been in the church for years are shown to be phonies. They are not truly Christian because they have never surrendered to God without setting conditions. They have never accepted God's terms and have always been more interested in giving God orders than in accepting orders from him.

But if people in church sometimes hesitate to accept God's authority over sex, such opposition is far greater among people who do not care about church at all. In the Bible, some of these are mentioned as people who "despise [God's moral] authority" because they want to "indulge in the lust of defiling passion" (2 Pet. 2:10), and as those who "reject [God's moral] authority, and blaspheme the glorious ones" because they would rather "defile the flesh" (Jude 8).

Fear of Losing Something Much Desired

Another reason people react negatively toward the awesome goodness of God's moral standards for sex is because they are afraid of losing something they want no matter what. The issue may be "having what I want" more than "having the last say." The first reason focuses on control, but the second is about keeping something you have and want so much that you will absolutely not let it go for anything. The first is driven by pride of independence, while the second is driven by pride of self-satisfaction. These often go together but they are not exactly the same.

Overreacting negatively toward good on God's terms for this reason is similar to how predatory animals react when they have prey. After killing a gazelle, a leopard is ferocious toward anything that comes close, and it focuses so much on keeping its prey that it will sometimes act quite irrationally. A predator with prey will not release what it has until either its appetite is fully satisfied or it is defeated, and predators tend to behave this way even when something better is offered in exchange.

I have seen my neighbor's cats act this way after they have caught some unlucky bird or squirrel in our backyard. Under any other circumstance, these cats are the friendliest pets imaginable. We often care for them when the owners are away. They know us and trust us and consider our yard part of their home turf. In an animal sense, I suppose they might even consider us part of their larger family. But if one of these cats has caught something—if it has prey—then we had better watch out! No matter how well they know me, no matter how good I have been to them, and no matter how affectionate they have been toward me in the past, if I approach, they will growl. They mean it as a serious warning, and I know that if I were to ignore it they would attack. It is a situation in which passion is more important than reason. Desire to keep what they possess overcomes reality, and there is no room to consider actual facts.

When people fear losing a favorite sin, they often react in the same way. Desire to hang on to what they have becomes absolute. Passion overwhelms reason. Truth becomes irrelevant, and considering something better is impossible. They are like predators with prey. They will not let go of what they have no matter what, and anything contrary is attacked whether it makes sense or not.

This is the reaction of people who are "lovers of pleasure rather than lovers of God" (2 Tim. 3:4), who take "pleasure in unrighteousness" (2 Thess. 2:12), and who claim to be free when they are actually "slaves of corruption" (2 Pet. 2: 18-19). Irrational defense of lust is a large part of what the Bible addresses when it refers to men who "by their unrighteousness suppress the truth" (Rom. 1:18). Sinners cannot actually reduce or change the relevance of God's moral truth. But they do work hard at clinging to favorite sins and at pretending they are exempt, however irrational that is.[5] Fearing to lose something much desired leads them to act as if good were bad and bad were good, no matter how little sense that makes.

Fear of Being Exposed as Wrong

A third reason people react negatively, sometimes even explosively, toward God's terms for sex is because they are afraid that God is right and they are wrong. Rather than it being about "having the last say" or "having what you want," the issue might be "not having to say you are sorry." The first reason concerns control and the second is about keeping something you want, but this third one has to do with admitting you are wrong. The first is driven by pride of independence and the second by pride of self-satisfaction, but the third is driven by pride of self-righteousness. Again, these reactions often work together, but not always. They are actually different reasons, and in real life people usually focus more on one than another even if they have more than one reason for rejecting God's way.

Of the reasons considered, the fear of admitting that one is wrong and that one is therefore deserving of punishment is more likely than the other two fears to explain especially violent reactions toward God's standards of real goodness. Accepting a higher authority is humbling, and losing what you dearly want is disappointing. But exposing the misguided beliefs and actions that people are trying to hide makes them very angry; and the more wrong a person thinks he could be, the more angry he will become toward anything he fears might blow his cover.

I am convinced that no real Christian ever resists God's approach on sex simply for fear of being exposed as wrong, because it is so absolutely contrary to what must happen for a person initially to become a Christian. Of course, Christians fail in many ways and sometimes even take over running their lives instead of allowing God to be in control; or they may begin trying to please themselves more than pleasing God. But no Christian ever fears admitting that God is right and he himself is wrong, because that is what God requires for salvation. Christians can struggle with temptation and sin. But no one is ever a Christian at all without confessing that he is wrong and God is right; and once a person is forgiven and cleansed through Christ, there is no reason ever to be afraid of being wrong again.

This means, therefore, that anyone who explodes with angry emotion toward God's moral standards on sex for fear of being exposed as wrong cannot possibly be a Christian. Reacting in this way and being a real Christian are completely incompatible. Both cannot exist at the same time. So, if someone fears that God is right and responds by covering that fear with anger rather than repentance, it indicates that he does not know the forgiveness of Jesus Christ, that he bears his sins alone, and that he fears admitting he is wrong because it means facing the wrath and judgment of God.

Defensive overreaction from fear of being wrong is mentioned by Paul in connection with sexual sin. He says people who exchange "the truth of God for a lie" to pursue "the lusts of their hearts" and who are thus "consumed [sexually] with passion for one another" (Rom. 1:24-27) will go to greater and greater lengths in order to hide their fear of being wrong. Paul explains, "Though they know God's decree that those who practice such things deserve to die [i.e., though they realize that God is right], they not only do them but give approval to those who practice them" (Rom. 1:32).

Displaying such exaggerated emotion is the way immature people respond to things they fear and want to avoid but cannot change. It is the reaction of someone who raises his voice while losing an argument. Arguing more loudly has no effect on the facts at issue and only shows that the one raising his voice fears that he is wrong but is trying to avoid admitting it. Raising your voice during an argument indicates that you fear losing based on the facts, and that you hope your shouting will make up the difference.

Amos speaks of people who "abhor him who speaks the truth" (Amos 5:10). The passage refers to people who know the honest truth and despise it on purpose. They know they are wrong and refuse to admit it. These are people who abhor someone who speaks the truth, not because they are ignorant or confused, but because they so fear being exposed that they cannot endure anyone who reminds them of what they know is true.

Getting into this state is by far the main reason people sometimes rage against the unchanging moral truth of God's wonderfully positive standards for sex. Although a person might fear giving up rights to control sex and might fear losing a favorite type of sexual gratification, if someone reacts violently toward the goodness of biblical standards for sex, it usually is because he is terribly afraid that God is right.

18

What About the Future?

THE LAST THING TO consider, looking at all these issues regarding biblical morality and its worldly counterfeits, is where this all leads. What does it say about the future? To me, the growing conflict and division over sexual morality suggests two things about where we may be headed, one based on social science and the other on scripture. On the one hand, there is good reason to believe, based on social science, that societies are strong when sexual standards are high and that they grow weak and die when sexual standards fall. And if that is so, then the social strength of American culture is declining and may not last past a few more generations. On the other hand, scripture says that division over sexual morality will split the church and will play a role in worldwide persecution before Jesus Christ returns, and in that case current developments could signal a beginning of the end times. These two observations involve two very different sorts of analysis. But that does not make them incompatible, and what they say of the future could be related.

The Future Based on Social Science

In the early twentieth century, the British social scientist J. D. Unwin conducted a massive study of six major civilizations and eighty lesser societies covering five thousand years of history in order to understand how sexual behavior affects the rise and fall of social groups.[1] Unwin's study included every social group on which he could find reliable information. He set out expecting to find evidence supporting Sigmund Freud's theory that civilizations are essentially neurotic and destroy themselves by restricting sex too much. But to Unwin's surprise, all the evidence he discovered pointed exactly the other way.

Freud had said,

> It is natural to suppose that under the domination of a *civilized* morality [one that restricts sex] the health and efficiency in life of [sic] the individuals may be impaired, and that ultimately this injury to the individual, caused by the sacrifices imposed upon him, may reach such a pitch that the *civilized* aim and end will itself be indirectly endangered.[2]

This led Freud to think civilization was unstable and perhaps self-defeating, so that he once wrote Albert Einstein saying he feared that, by limiting sex, civilization "may perhaps be leading to the extinction of the human race."[3] Freud especially feared total sexual abstinence outside monogamous marriage. Some restriction might be tolerable, but total sexual abstinence except within marriage was dangerous. According to Freud,

> It is now easy to predict the result which will ensue if sexual freedom is still further circumscribed, and the standard demanded by civilization is raised to the level . . . which taboos [prohibits] every sexual activity other than that in legitimate matrimony. Under these conditions the number of strong natures who openly rebel will be immensely increased, and likewise the number of weaker natures who take refuge in neurosis. . . . [When] civilization demands from both sexes abstinence until marriage, and lifelong abstinence for all who do not enter into legal matrimony, . . . We may thus well raise the question whether our *civilized* sexual morality is worth the sacrifice it imposes upon us.[4]

Freud was not a social scientist and never proved his theory. But he did think someone should try:

> If the evolution of civilization has such a far-reaching similarity with the development of an individual, and if the same methods are employed in both, would not the diagnosis be justified that many systems of civilization have become neurotic under the pressure of the civilizing trends? . . . [W]e should have to be very cautious and not forget that, after all, we are only dealing with analogies. . . . But in spite of all these difficulties, we may expect that one day someone will venture on this research into the pathology of civilized communities.[5]

Unwin accepted Freud's challenge, setting out to study how sexual morality affects civilization and especially whether Freud was right about the restricting of sex to monogamous marriage threatening the survival of societies. He did indeed find strong evidence linking "the cultural condition of any society in any geographical environment" with "its past and present methods of regulating the relations between the sexes."[6] But rather than being injured by restricting sex to marriage, Unwin found in every case that the "expansive energy" of a social group comes from restricting sex to marriage, and sexual license is always "the immediate cause of cultural decline."[7] In other words, all the evidence he discovered showed that the survival of a civilization or society depends on keeping sexual energy focused on supporting family life and not allowing individuals access to sex in ways that do not support family life.

Unwin found, without exception, that if a social group limited sex to marriage, and especially to lifelong monogamous marriage, it would always prosper. There was "no recorded case of a society adopting absolute monogamy without displaying expansive energy." He found that, when sexual standards were high, "men began to explore new lands . . . commerce expanded; foreign settlements [were] established, colonies [were] founded."[8] In contrast, if a social group lowered standards so that sex was no longer limited to marriage, it always lost social energy. And again he found absolutely no exceptions: "In human records there is no instance of a society retaining its energy after a complete new generation has inherited a tradition which does not insist on prenuptial [premarital] and post-nuptial [extramarital] continence."[9] In every verifiable case, he found that once a group became sexually permissive, "the energy of the society . . . decreased and finally disappeared."[10]

He came across the same pattern over and over. A society would begin with high standards limiting sex to one partner in marriage for life. This produced great social strength, and that society or culture would flourish. Then a new generation would arise demanding sex on easier terms and would lower moral standards. But when that happened the society would lose vitality, grow weak, and then die. He explained that,

> In the beginning, each society had the same ideas in regard to sexual regulations. Then the same strengths took place; the same sentiments were expressed; the same changes were made; the same results ensued. Each society reduced its sexual opportunity to a minimum and, displaying great social energy, flourished greatly. Then it extended its sexual opportunity [lowered standards]; its energy decreased, and faded away. The one outstanding feature of the whole story is its unrelieved monotony.[11]

Therefore, based on overwhelming evidence, Unwin decided, "Any human society is free to choose either to display great energy or to enjoy sexual freedom; [but] the evidence is that it cannot do both for more than one generation."[12] Not only was Freud wrong, he was dangerously wrong. No matter how strong, no society can ever avoid losing social strength once it lowers sexual standards, and once it does so, signs of growing weakness appear within one generation. Freud thought restricting sex to marriage threatened the survival of civilization and might even threaten the survival of the human race. But Unwin discovered the opposite: restricting sex to marriage makes societies strong, and easing sexual standards is what causes them to weaken and collapse.

If Unwin's study can be trusted, and if there is indeed no exception to the evidence he found linking sexual morality with social survival, it means the first thing declining sexual morality in America says about our future is that contemporary society is weakening and heading toward collapse rather rapidly. If trends continue the way they are, signs of obvious weakness will appear while our children are alive; and if standards keep dropping, American society may not last till the end of the twenty-first century.

The Future Based on God's Revelation

The second thing that the rising conflict and deepening division over sexual morality suggests about the future does not come from social science but from scripture. If we believe that the Bible is divinely inspired and completely trustworthy, we cannot say we have covered everything God reveals on sexual morality without taking up what he says about turmoil over sexual morality in the last days. This is not just a passing theme but is in fact a major part of end-time prophesy. According to scripture, in the last days, just before Jesus returns, conflict over sexual morality will divide the church and separate Christians from the rest of the world. Whether people are in the church or not, everyone will be forced either to recognize and accept God's moral authority or to rebel against it. The world's opposition to God's authority will test Christians as never before, and God will in turn test those who are rebellious; and a significant part of this testing will focus on sex. While sexual morality will not be the only thing contested, the Bible indicates that the way people respond to God's standards for sex will be a very significant factor determining who is on his side and who is not.

What Jesus and Paul Say to Expect

At the end of his earthly life, Jesus spoke of returning in the future, and his disciples asked for a sign to know when that would be. "What will be the sign of your coming and of the close of the age?" (Matt. 24:3). Jesus answered that one important sign will be the rise of a tremendous division in the church caused by false teachers claiming to speak for God but in fact rejecting biblical standards (Matt. 24:10-13): "[M]any will fall away and betray one another and hate one another" (v. 10), and this will happen because "many false prophets will arise and lead many astray" (v. 11). Because of this, "lawlessness will be increased" and "the love of many will grow cold" (v. 12).

This can only refer to a division among people who claim to be Christian, because only people claiming to be Christian can "fall away," only people claiming to be Christian can "betray one another," and only people claiming to be Christian can have a love for God that is able to "grow cold." Also, a *prophet* is someone who speaks for God, and therefore a *false prophet* is someone who claims to have God's authority but does not. A *false prophet* is a person who says he is teaching God's truth but instead teaches something opposed to it. And, to understand what Jesus said, it is also necessary to realize that in scripture *lawlessness* refers to opposing God's moral standards. With this in mind, the sign Jesus gave for his soon return was that teachers will arise in the church teaching a false version of Christian ethics, a version that is in fact so opposed to God's true moral authority that it replaces biblical morality with something completely different. And, according to Jesus, these false teachers coming in the last days will divide the institutional church so badly that church members will hate and even betray other church members.

The important thing for us to notice is that Jesus says this terrible division in the institutional church will come from false moral teaching that claims to be Christian while rejecting scripture. So the division this causes will most likely separate true Christians from false. Members of the institutional church will divide into those who remain faithful to biblical morality and those who agree with false teaching that replaces biblical morality with something else. From what Matthew records, Jesus did not say what this contest would be over and therefore never linked it directly with sexual behavior. But what he predicted certainly raised the possibility, not just because biblical morality includes standards for sex, but because sexual morality always is the first area of behavior affected when people shift from pleasing God to pleasing themselves and basing moral thinking on sensual experience rather than the character of God.

Paul predicted moral conflict in the last days as well, but he addressed conflict outside rather than inside the church. Writing to Timothy, he said:

> But understand this, that in the last days there will come times of difficulty. For people will be lovers of self, . . . unholy, . . . without self-con-

> trol, . . . lovers of pleasure rather than lovers of God, . . . Avoid such people. For among them are those who creep into households and capture weak women, burdened with sins and led astray by various passions (2 Tim. 3:1-6).

Whereas Jesus said conflict from false teaching in Christian ethics (from false prophets teaching lawlessness) will split the church, Paul said moral conflict will also arise between Christians and the world.

In Paul's words, the world outside the church (and not just false teachers inside the church) will be "lovers of pleasure rather than lovers of God" (v. 4) and will be "led astray by various passions" (v. 6). This will cause tension between the unbelieving world and Christians who are faithful to biblical morality and therefore do not accept the sensual approach. Thus the world outside the church will attack biblical standards and be critical of faithful Christians at the same time that false teachers will be leading many in the church astray. All this, Paul says, will create "times of difficulty" in "the last days" (v. 1).

Like Jesus, Paul does not identify the specific moral issue (or issues) sparking this great conflict. Neither Jesus nor Paul say it will actually focus on sexual morality. But Paul does say the opposing moral view will be man-centered and sensual, because he says people will be "lovers of self" (v. 2), "without self-control" (v. 3) and "lovers of pleasure" (v. 4). And he even connects trouble in the last days with exhorting Christians to avoid "those who creep into households and capture weak women, burdened with sins and led astray with various passions" (v. 6). So, even though Paul did not say what will drive the conflict, he did go beyond Jesus and very nearly (but not quite actually) say it will come from differences over sexual morality.

What Peter and Jude Say to Expect

After Jesus ascended to heaven and perhaps even after the life of Paul, Peter and Jude added more to the warning of moral conflict coming in the end times. They say it will come specifically from conflict over the teaching of sexual morality.

With Jesus, Peter warns Christians to be on guard against false teachers, saying scoffers will "come in the last days . . . following their own sinful desires" (2 Pet. 3:3). But, where Jesus only says these false teachers will lead church members to reject biblical moral standards (will lead them into lawlessness), Peter adds that they will "have eyes full of adultery" (2:14), and that "many will follow their sensuality" so that "because of them the way of truth will be blasphemed" (2:2). These false teachers will promote a version of counterfeit sexual morality based on sensual experience, and it will happen in the church—because it will destroy respect for morality based on scripture. Jude repeats what Peter says about scoffers "in the last time . . . following their own ungodly passions" (Jude 18). But Jude then adds that they will "cause divisions" in the church (19), which tells us Peter and Jude are both referring to the same false teachers Jesus said will signal his soon return (Matt. 24:11-12).

Jesus, Peter, and Jude all conclude their warnings of coming conflict by exhorting Christians who will be living in those days to resist compromise and remain faithful. Jesus says, "the one who endures to the end will be saved" (Matt. 24:13). Peter says, "You therefore, beloved, knowing this beforehand, take care that you are not carried away with the error of lawless people and lose your own stability" (2 Pet. 3:17). And Jude says,

> But you, beloved, build yourselves up in your most holy faith; pray in the Holy Spirit; keep yourselves in the love of God, waiting for the mercy of our Lord Jesus Christ that leads to eternal life. And have mercy on those who doubt; save others by snatching them out of the fire; to others show mercy with fear, hating even the garment stained by the flesh (Jude 20-23).

The combined witness of Jesus, Peter, and Jude is that a very clear sign by which we can know we are in the last days will be the rise of radically counterfeit sexual morality splitting the church. False teachers of Christian ethics will persuade a large section of the church to replace biblical sexual morality with a counterfeit sexual morality based on sensual experience. This will cause terrible turmoil, and the conflict will become so intense that church members on one side will hate and betray church members on the other side. Faith and loyalty to Jesus will be tested within the church itself, and division over sexual morality will separate members who take God at his Word from other members who will choose to follow sensual desires over God himself.

What Revelation Says to Expect

Prior to the book of Revelation, the New Testament makes it clear that severe conflict over sex will arise in the last days, dividing Christians in the church and pitting Christians against the world. Revelation addresses this same theme but adds some important new information. We cannot cover God's revelation on sexual morality without considering the book of Revelation.

But that is not done easily, because much of Revelation comes in the form of symbols requiring interpretation that is rather uncertain. So, as we examine what Revelation says on sexual morality in the last days, we will try not to confuse what is only guesswork with what we know for sure.

When it comes to sexual morality in the last days, the book of Revelation takes up Paul's message about trouble between Christians and the world (2 Tim. 3:1-6). As Peter and Jude add to what Jesus said about division in the church by saying that it will come from counterfeit sexual morality, so also Revelation adds to Paul's warning on trouble between Christians and the world by saying that counterfeit sexual morality will cause that conflict as well. In doing this, Revelation adds six important details to God's revelation concerning sexual morality.

First, we learn that in the last days all nations of the world will be intoxicated with sexual immorality, and this will especially affect world leaders. We are told there will be a center of worldwide political and economic power, a city referred to as Babylon, that will make "all nations drink the wine of the passion of her sexual immorality" (Rev. 14:8; also 18:3). Babylon's sexual immorality may stand for a range of immoral activity including more than literal sex, but it would hardly make sense if immoral sex in the literal sense were not a large part of it. Babylon will not only lead all nations into sexual sin but will especially focus on corrupting world leaders. "[T]he kings of the earth . . . committed sexual immorality and lived in luxury with her" (18:9; also v. 3).

When this happens, will everyone participate willingly or will some need to be coerced? The original language of Revelation 14:8 suggests some force may be involved. Babylon will at least seduce participants, but if some resist they will be "made" to share in her sexual immorality.[13]

Besides Babylon, the Great Prostitute associated with the beast of Revelation is described doing the exact same thing. She also is one "with whom the kings of the earth have committed sexual immorality," and also is one "with the wine of whose sexual immorality the dwellers on earth have become drunk" (Rev. 17:1-2). Again, her sexual immorality could stand for other things besides literal acts of sex but would not make sense if literal sex did not play a large role. Since Babylon and the Great Prostitute corrupt nations and leaders of the world in the same way, it seems likely that the city represents a system of worldwide power centralized at a single geographic location, and the Great Prostitute stands for the institution (the actual organization) that carries out the program by which nations and world leaders are corrupted.

No one is sure how to identify the Great Prostitute. She might symbolize the apostate church, made up of members who reject biblical morality when the church divides over sex. This might explain why she is a prostitute, a symbol the Old Testament uses to represent a faithless wife. In that case, the Great Prostitute of Revelation is a faithless version of the bride of Christ (Eph. 5:25-32; Rev. 19:7) just as faithless Israel is symbolized as a prostitute wife in Hosea (Hos. 1:2; 3:1; 9:1) and again in Ezekiel (Ezek.16:30-38).

But other interpretations are possible. The Great Prostitute might also be a cult of neo-pagan sexual worship that will arise in the last days, or could symbolize false religion in general, or may even be nothing more than another way to represent the city of Babylon (see Rev. 17:5, 18). In any case, we know Babylon (the city) and the Great Prostitute (whoever she is) will get nations and leaders of the world deeply involved in sexual sin, and in some way they will endorse it enthusiastically. After all, they will drink so much that they will become intoxicated or drunk (v. 2).

Second, we learn that worldwide persecution of Christians will arise in which conflict over sexual immorality will have a key role. Babylon and the Great Prostitute, who corrupt nations and their leaders with sexual immorality (Rev. 17:2; 18:3,9), will also kill Christians who remain faithful to Jesus and his standards. John says, "I saw the woman [the Great Prostitute], drunk with the blood of the saints, the blood of the martyrs of Jesus" (17:6); and of Babylon he says, "in her was found the blood of prophets and of saints, and of all who have been slain on earth" (18:24).

The reason these martyrs are killed has to do with corruption connected with sex, and the persecution is part of a program forcing everyone to accept and support immoral activity involving sexual sin. In the case of the Great Prostitute, martyrdom for resisting immoral sex is very clear. We know this because we are told the cup from which she makes herself "drunk with the blood of the saints" is "full of abominations and the impurities of her sexual immorality" (Rev. 17:4). The same link is there with Babylon, although it is not described so clearly. Persecution of Christians on account of their sexual purity is not expressed directly in connection with Babylon. But Babylon's corruption of the world through sexual immorality (18:3, 9) is the only other sinful action specifically mentioned besides killing prophets and saints (v. 24).

Persecuting Christians in relation to sexual corruption, in one place connected with Babylon and in another with the Great Prostitute, is almost certainly one event (not two separate events), and what Revelation describes is highly suggestive of coercion designed to force universal acceptance and participation in a form of cult prostitution. This is only a guess, but if correct it will mean that "the martyrs of Jesus" (Rev. 17:6) are faithful Christians who are killed for refusing to participate in this cult prostitution. And if the Great Prostitute is indeed the apostate church, that would explain why Jesus said the institutional church will become so divided that members will eventually "betray one another and hate one another" (Matt. 24:10).

Third, we learn that a group of saints will appear in heaven at that same time who will be honored for maintaining sexual purity. These are described as those "who have not defiled themselves with women, for they are virgins" (Rev. 14:4). As with the Great Prostitute, no one is sure who these men are, where they come from, or how they happen to receive this special recognition. Debate about who they are usually focuses on why there will be precisely 144,000 of them (vv. 1, 3). But this tends to obscure the obvious. What we know is: (1) they are faithful Christians who have died and gone to heaven; (2) they are honored for having kept themselves pure related to sex; (3) they earned this honor during their time on earth; (4) they earned it in a time when it was especially hard to maintain such purity, suggesting it was during a time of persecution; and (5) it is implied that they are Christians who were martyred precisely for maintaining sexual purity, or in other words were killed precisely for remaining faithful to God's standards for sexual morality.

This last point comes from the way these saints are three times described as sacrificial offerings. They are "redeemed from the earth" (Rev. 14:3), they are "redeemed from mankind" (v. 4), and they are "firstfruits for God and the Lamb" (v. 4). It is therefore likely that these saints are the same ones mentioned as "martyrs of Jesus" (17:6), those who are killed for refusing to go along with the sexual immorality demanded by the Great Prostitute (and Babylon).

We are still just guessing. But if these saints who we know will be martyred for sexual purity are indeed the same as those killed by the Great Prostitute (and Babylon), it adds more evidence for thinking that persecution of Christians by the Great Prostitute (and Babylon) will be driven by coercion to participate in a form of cult prostitution. If so, Revelation 14:1-5 shows how these martyrs will be treated upon arriving in heaven.

It is like putting pieces of a puzzle together. But again, if we are right so far, these saints "who have not defiled themselves with women" (Rev. 14:4), who are "firstfruits for God and the Lamb" (v. 4) and who (we think) are "the martyrs of Jesus" (17:6) killed for resisting cult prostitution—this group of saints may also be the ones Daniel says will shine in a dark time at the end of history (Dan. 12:1-4). According to Daniel, there will be a group of saints at the end of time (v. 4) who will "shine like the brightness of the sky above"

(v. 3) and "like the stars" (v. 3) and therefore will "turn many to righteousness" (v. 3) during the worst persecution in history. He says they will be a witness for God and his truth in "a time of trouble, such as never has been since there was a nation till that time" (v. 1). There is good reason to think these references all point to the same group of distinguished saints who will glorify God under severe persecution in the last days of history mainly by refusing to lower or revise biblical standards for sexual purity.

Fourth, we learn that after many saints are martyred for being faithful to God, including his teaching on sex, God will avenge their blood by punishing the Great Prostitute and destroying Babylon. After many are killed for not going along with the rest of the world when it follows the Great Prostitute into sexual immorality, God will turn world leaders against the Great Prostitute, and they will "make her desolate" (Rev. 17:16-17). These instruments of God's judgment will not be godly people, because most will be the same world leaders who joined with the Great Prostitute's sexual immorality (v. 2). So they will have their own reasons for turning against the one who so intoxicated them before. But God will use them to "aveng[e] on her the blood of his servants" (19:2). Babylon will fall as well, and for the same reason, and a voice from heaven will announce, "Rejoice over her, O heaven, and you saints and apostles and prophets, for God has given judgment for you against her!" (18:20).

Fifth, we learn that after (or perhaps along with) punishing the Great Prostitute and Babylon, God will give sinners a last chance to switch sides by testing their commitment to sin, and this will include whether they still insist on placing sex over God himself. After the ungodly world tests the loyalty of faithful Christians, God will test how much sinners are determined to oppose him. He will challenge them in all areas, including sex. This will happen at the sixth trumpet (Rev. 9:13-21), and because Jesus returns at the seventh trumpet (1 Thess. 4:16; Rev. 10:7) that means it will take place just before time runs out. It also means this final test will serve as a last very clear chance for anyone remaining on earth to come over to God's side.

The testing God plans at the sixth trumpet will inflict pain and suffering (Rev. 9:15-19), but in some ways it will express God's love more than his wrath. First, it will express God's love because it will make the reality and power of God absolutely unmistakable. It will remove all doubt about whether God exists or has the power to overcome opposition. Second, it will express God's love because when God's reality and power become obvious, it will then be obvious that everything else revealed in scripture is true as well. Biblical morality will be validated, and biblical prophesy will be proven absolutely reliable. It will remove any doubt about who is going to win the final contest. Third, it will express God's love because, by inflicting pain, God will remove the deceptive power of sin.

This last point is terribly important, because it shows the extraordinary extent of God's love for even the most hardened sinners. We should realize, when God inflicts pain at the sixth trumpet, it will not be the final judgment. Although it will be severe, it will be far less than what is coming later when God does actually punish sin completely. What will be happening is that God, at the sixth trumpet, will in effect withdraw the natural blessings he has been providing through creation—blessings such as health, strength, food, shelter, warmth, and pleasure and satisfaction in natural experiences such as eating, sleeping, and sex. And when he does this, it will destroy the deceptive power of sin, which relies on natural blessing to give people the false impression that life can be enjoyed without God.

The great irony of God's plan to inflict pain at the sixth trumpet is that it will in fact be a last attempt to show sinners that all good comes from God alone, and that rejecting him leads to nothing good at all. So, when this happens, just before time runs out, will sinners give up trusting pleasure when pleasure is gone? Will they have sense enough to choose the goodness and mercy of God when the only alternative is pain? Amazingly and sadly the answer will be no.

Revelation says, "The rest of mankind, who were not killed by these plagues, did not repent of the works of their hands nor give up worshiping demons and idols of gold and silver and bronze and stone and wood, which cannot see or hear or walk, nor did they repent of their murders or their sorceries . . . or their thefts" (Rev. 9:20-21). And it also says, "nor did they repent . . . of their sexual immorality" (v. 21). So, even when it only assures pain, many will still insist on pursuing sex over God. Hearts will be so hard that sinners remaining on earth at the time will choose pain and death without pleasure rather than trust God's mercy and agree that he is right.

Sexual immorality will not be the only thing hardening hearts in the last days, but it will be a significant factor affecting decisions. When God offers sinners a final chance, many will still demand sex without limits, sex without discipline, sex without accountability, sex without goals, sex without norms, sex over absolutely everything in heaven and earth, rather than agreeing to control sex on God's terms.

Sixth, the last important detail we learn from Revelation is that which side people choose in the religious-moral division over sex will be a deciding factor separating those who spend eternity with God from those who are ban-

ished from his presence forever. The final message in scripture on sexual morality is that demanding sex your way assures eternal damnation, and there is no exception. Either we submit on God's terms or we suffer the consequences on God's terms. Revelation says, "But as for . . . the sexually immoral, . . . their portion will be in the lake that burns with fire and sulfur, which is the second death" (Rev. 21:8). Refusing to repent for sexual sin will be one of the key reasons stopping many from entering the city of God. We are told, "Blessed are those who wash their robes, so that they may have the right to the tree of life and that they may enter the city by the gates. Outside are . . . the sexually immoral" (Rev. 22:14-15).

When Jesus Christ returns in judgment and glory, it will then be too late to switch sides. A deadline will arrive. Time will run out. The cosmic conflict involving sexual morality will end, and God will win. The stakes are high indeed. In fact, they cannot be higher. God has the last say no matter what. How strongly anyone objects cannot change the outcome. All who demand eternal separation from God will get what they choose. But they can only choose the separation and cannot set the terms. The price they will pay is eternal pain, eternal suffering, and the eternal absence of anything good. It is horribly tragic, and we should only mention it with tears. But those who insist on setting their own terms for sex, who insist on making up their own rules, who insist on putting sensual passion in the place of God, face a deadline after which they can no longer switch sides and after which they must suffer consequences.

Those who stay on the wrong side are choosing eternity without God, and without God nothing is enjoyable. The pleasures of sin luring them now will vanish, and what they will experience for eternity will be a form of living death with no romance, no pleasure, no satisfaction, and no spiritual power. They will lose even the little bit of perverted good luring them to justify sexual sin. They will have nothing except bitterness, pain, and regret, and they will learn how deceptive evil truly is. They will discover that, apart from God, evil truly is good for nothing. Counterfeit sexual morality will prove to be just that: counterfeit.

From J. D. Unwin's study of the way sexual behavior affects the rise and fall of society, current trends suggest American society is declining rapidly. We have begun losing social strength, and if sexual standards continue falling, American society will not last past a few more generations. In biblical prophesy, we see nothing on the fate of American society in particular. But the rise of radical division in the American church over sex, with one side rejecting biblical standards for a self-pleasing, sensual approach, and with a growing number of teachers in the field of Christian ethics substituting pagan sexual morality for biblical sexual morality, what we see happening in the American church could be the start of what Jesus said would signal his return.

Of course, conflict in the church is nothing to rejoice about. It should tear us apart. But turmoil over sexual morality in the church these days may also mean that Jesus Christ is coming soon. We could be witnessing the start of the end-times division of the church that Jesus said will come from false teaching of Christian ethics (Matt. 24:10-13), and that Peter and Jude said will arise from counterfeit sexual morality leading many astray (2 Pet. 2:1-2,14; Jude 4, 17-19).

A Closing Appeal

God's last word on sex is wonderful and awful at the same time. What you do with God's gift of sex not only affects life now but your eternal destiny as well. You can touch, feel, and experience the material dimension of sexual pleasure now. But sex is spiritual as well as material, and what you do with sexual morality has cosmic consequences that last for eternity because sexual morality (not sex itself) affects the relationship a person has with God.

According to scripture, there is nothing wrong with sex as created by God. But there is a lot wrong with human character and with our ability to handle sex morally. Sexual desire is Satan's most powerful and strategic weapon for separating men and women from God and keeping them away from him. Dealing with sexual passion forces us to choose sides in a moral conflict with cosmic dimensions, perhaps more surely and radically than anything else in life.

In this conflict, God gives Satan a natural advantage. All Satan must do to have you on his side is stir sexual desires and offer to let you indulge them without limits. And those who take the bait are hooked every time. For his part, God simply says we must believe that he is trustworthy and is doing the right thing. He requires faith and trust in himself, and in particular he demands unquestioned faith in his perfect moral character. If we do respond in faith and accept his terms, he promises to make it all worthwhile both now and forever. But you cannot be on God's side without accepting his discipline in the area of sex. No one can follow God and his or her own unrestrained desires at the same time. The two are totally incompatible. And accepting God's authority over sex never seems right unless you first believe that he is good and always tells the truth.

When a person is at the crossroads, deciding which way to go, he faces the same two challenges Satan presented Eve in the Garden of Eden. The first challenge, "Did God actually say?" (Gen. 3:1), questioned whether God is competent. Perhaps God makes mistakes you should correct? Perhaps God is deficient, and your way is better? The second challenge, "You will not surely die," questioned whether God is trustworthy. Perhaps he is competent but cruel? Perhaps he is evil and tells lies, and you must therefore look out for yourself? Before choosing sides in the conflict over sexual morality, a person must decide if God is truly good. Does he actually know what he is doing, and is he really trustworthy?

It comes down to deciding if biblical sexual morality is indeed *true sexual morality.* And what a person decides makes all the difference in the world, both now and forever. Remember that Paul said, "brothers, we are debtors, not to the flesh, to live according to the flesh. For if you live according to the flesh you will die, but if by the Spirit you put to death the deeds of the body, you will live" (Rom. 8:12-13). It is a tremendously important choice. God truly is competent. God truly is trustworthy. Together that means God is truly good. He knows what he is doing, he is right about sex, and his standards protect the best for us. Paul says if you accept God's terms you will live, and if not you will die. I hope you accept God's terms and live.

Do you want sex that is totally pure and consistent with the holiness of God? Do you want to master your sexual desires rather than have them master you? Do you want to know the goodness of sex that is personal, exclusive, intimate, fruitful, selfless, complex, and complementary? Do you want the blessings of abiding joy, genuine satisfaction, exemplary honor, and pure allure? Do you want love that truly lasts, relationships that are truly personal, intimacy that truly fulfills, and power in your life from the force running the universe? Do you want to be on the winning side when Jesus returns? Would you like eternal life instead of eternal death? Then choose God over your passions. Let him forgive your failures and give you the power to master sex on his terms. Choose the goodness of God with true sexual morality, and do not be led astray by counterfeits.

APPENDICES

APPENDIX A

COLORADO STATEMENT ON BIBLICAL SEXUAL MORALITY

(Full Statement)

Council on Biblical Sexual Ethics
Initiated by Focus on the Family
Issued 2002
www.family.org/cforum/fosi/abstinence/bv/a0028508.cfm

God intends sex to be a source of satisfaction, honor, and delight to those who enjoy it within the parameters of the moral standards He has established. Biblically speaking, human sexuality is both a gift and a responsibility. At creation, the gift of sex was among those things God declared to be "very good" (Gen. 1:31). What's more, the sexual relationship is invested with a profound significance in that it brings together a man and a woman within the context of the shared image of God (Gen. 1:27). Because sex is God's idea, and because it touches the image of God in human life, it is very important that the holiness of sexual behavior be diligently preserved. In fact, sexual behavior is moral only when it is holy (Eph. 1:4; 5:3; 1 Thess. 4:3-7; 1 Pet. 1:14-16).

Not only is sex good in itself; it is also given to serve good purposes. At creation God made it very clear that sex functions in two ways: it generates "fruit" (Gen. 1:28); and it enables relational "union" (Gen. 2:24). In other words, sexuality does not exist merely for its own sake. Rather, sex fosters human nurturing, both through the union of husband and wife and also through the enrichment of society through the building of families and communities. God also made sex to reflect the mysterious spiritual relationship He will one day enjoy with all redeemed humanity following the wedding supper of the Lamb (Rev. 19:7, 9).

According to God's plan, sexual intimacy is the exclusive prerogative of husband and wife within the context of marriage. Sexual morality, on the other hand, is everyone's concern. It matters to single individuals, to families, and to society. Most of all, it matters to God.

Sex that honors God's guidelines and standards is pleasurable. He designed sexual activity to be physically enjoyable, emotionally satisfying, psychologically fulfilling, and spiritually meaningful because He delights in the joys and pleasures of His creatures (Song 4:1-16). Men and women who honor God's standards for sexual behavior please Him as well as themselves (1 Cor. 6:20; also note analogy in Isa. 62:5).

But while sex is designed to be pleasing, not all sexual pleasure is ethical. Feelings are extremely unreliable as guides to the morality of sex. As a matter of fact, it is possible for sinful men and women to experience a form of physical enjoyment and degrees of emotional, psychological, and spiritual fulfillment even in sexual conduct that God considers abhorrent. For this reason, the Bible gives many solemn warnings against appealing to human passion or lust as the basis for our definition of moral sex (Rom. 1:24, 26; 13:13-14; 1 Thess. 4:5; 2 Tim. 2:22; 2 Pet. 3:3; 1 John 2:15-17; Jude 18). Our sex lives are moral only when conducted according to God's standards. When engaged in according to these guidelines, sexual activity is enriching, fulfilling, and eminently blessed.

We want to warn against deceptions that hinder or forestall this blessing of God upon our enjoyment of the wonderful gift of sex. We also want to help men and women understand God's good plan for sexual conduct, and thereby to realize all the joy, satisfaction, and honor God offers to sexual creatures made in His image.

Based on our understanding of biblical teaching, we make the following declarations. We do not claim that these declarations cover everything the Bible says on sexual morality. But we do believe they highlight standards that are critical for our time.

1. ***Desire and experience cannot be trusted as guidelines to the morality of sex*** (Rom. 8:5-8; 13:14; 1 Cor. 2:14; 1 Thess. 4:35; 2 Tim. 2:22; James 1:14; 1 John 2:15-16; Jude 19). Instead, the morality of sex is defined by God's holiness (Lev. 20:7-21, 26; 1 Cor. 6:18-19; Eph. 1:4; 5:3; 1 Thess. 4:3-7; Heb. 13:4; 1 Pet. 1:15-16).

Thus we affirm that men and women are free to enjoy sex in any way that honors God's holiness. We affirm that God made sex to be physically enjoyable, emotionally satisfying, psychologically fulfilling, and spiritually meaningful, and that only sex that honors God's holiness can fully realize the complexity of His design at every level. We affirm that concepts of sexual morality founded upon anything other than God's holiness always pervert God's standards of sexual moral purity.

2. ***God's standard is moral purity in every thought about sex, as well as in every act of sex.*** Sexual purity can be violated even in thoughts that never proceed to outward acts (Job 31:1; Matt. 5:28; Phil. 4:8; James 1:14-15). Sex must never be used to oppress, wrong or take advantage of anyone (1 Thess. 4:6). Rape, incest, sexual abuse, pedophilia, voyeurism, prostitution, and pornography always exploit and corrupt and must be condemned (Lev. 18:7-10; 19:29; 2 Sam. 13:1-22; Prov. 6:26; 23:27; Matt. 5:28; 1 Thess. 4:3-7; 1 Pet. 4:3; 2 Pet. 2:13-14).

Thus we affirm that God requires sexual moral purity in thought as well as in deed. We affirm that sexual desire must be disciplined to be moral. We affirm that thoughts of indulging sexual desire by outward acts of sexual sin are inward sins of lust. We deny that stimulating lust by images of sexual sin can be moral at any age or under any circumstances. We believe that no sexual act can be moral if driven by desires that run contrary to the best interests of another human being. We believe no sexual act can be moral that treats persons as impersonal objects of sexual lust. We reject the idea that thoughts about engaging in sexual sin are not immoral if not expressed in outward acts. We reject the idea that pedophilia, voyeurism, prostitution or pornography can ever be justified.

3. ***God's standards for sexual moral purity are meant to protect human happiness*** (Prov. 5:18-19; 6:32-33; John 15:10-11), but sex is not an entitlement, nor is it needed for personal wholeness or emotional maturity.

Thus we affirm that unmarried singles who abstain from sex can be whole, mature persons, as pleasing to God as persons who are faithful in marriage. We affirm that sexual celibacy is a worthy state for mature men and women (Matt. 19:12; 1 Cor. 7:1, 8; Rev. 14:4), and that lifelong celibacy can be a gift from God (1 Cor. 7:7). We affirm that freedom for service without obligations to spouse and children is a worthy advantage of the unmarried life (1 Cor. 7:32-35). We reject the idea that persons are not "whole" without sexual intercourse. We affirm that all persons, even unmarried teenagers, can rely on God for strength to resist sexual temptation (1 Cor. 10:13). We deny that unmarried teenagers must have sex and cannot abstain from sex before marriage.

4. ***God calls some to a life of marriage, others to lifelong celibacy,*** but His calling to either state is a divine gift worthy of honor and respect (1 Cor. 7:36-38). No one is morally compromised by following God's call to either state, and no one can justify opposing a divine call to either state by denying the moral goodness of that state.

Thus we affirm that God is pleased with those He calls to serve Him through the loving expression of sexual intimacy in marriage. We also affirm God is pleased with those He calls to special witness and service through a life of celibacy apart from marriage. We reject the idea that God's Word ever represents the loving expression of sexual intimacy in marriage as morally compromised.

5. ***Sexual behavior is moral only within the institution of heterosexual, monogamous marriage.*** Marriage is secure only when established by an unconditional, covenantal commitment to lifelong fidelity (Gen. 2:24; Mal. 2:14-15; Matt. 19:4-6; Mark 10:68; 1 Cor. 7:39; Rom. 7:2; Eph. 5:31), and we should not separate what God has joined (Mal. 2:14-15; Matt. 19:6; Mark 10:9). Christians continue to debate whether there are a limited number of situations in which divorce is justifi-

able (Deut. 24:1-4; Matt. 19:9; 1 Cor. 7:15), but all agree that divorce is never God's ideal; lifelong commitment should always be the Christian's goal.

Thus we affirm that God established the moral definition of marriage, and that it should not be changed according to the dictates of culture, tradition, or personal preference. We deny that the morality of marriage is a matter of mere custom, or that it should be allowed to shift with the tide of cultural opinion or social practice. Furthermore, we affirm that God views marriage as an unconditional, covenantal relationship that joins sexual partners for life. We oppose the reduction of the moral obligations of marriage to a business contract. We do not believe that divorce for reasons of dissatisfaction, difficulty, or disappointment is morally justified.

6. ***Marriage protects the transcendent significance of personal sexual intimacy.*** Heterosexual union in marriage expresses the same sort of holy, exclusive, permanent, complex, selfless, and complementary intimacy that will some day characterize the union of Christ with the redeemed and glorified Church (Eph. 5:28-33; 1 Cor. 6:12-20).

Thus we affirm that intimate sexual union in marriage is a reflection of the intimate moral and spiritual union Christ will some day enjoy with the redeemed and glorified Church. We do not agree that the meaning and purpose of human sexuality can be defined on the basis of personal preference or opinion. We oppose the idea that sexual morality is simply a matter of culture, tradition, or individual aspiration.

7. ***Sex in marriage should be an act of love and grace that transcends the petty sins of human selfishness,*** and should be set aside only when both partners agree to do so, and then only for a limited time of concentrated prayer (1 Cor. 7:3-5).

Thus we affirm that sex in marriage should be enjoyed without selfishness. We do not believe that sex should be withheld as a way of controlling, punishing, or manipulating the behavior of a spouse. We reject the morality of any sexual act, even in marriage, that does not express love seasoned by grace. We believe no sexual act can be moral if it is driven by selfishness or ambition for power.

8. ***Sex outside of marriage is never moral*** (Ex. 20:14; Lev. 18:7-17, 20; Deut. 5:18; Matt. 19:9, 18; Mark 10:19; Luke 18:20; Rom. 13:9; 1 Cor. 6:13, 18; Gal. 5:19; Eph. 5:3; 1 Thess. 4:3; Heb. 13:4). This includes all forms of intimate sexual stimulation (such as foreplay and oral sex) that stir up sexual passion between unmarried partners (Matt. 5:27-28; 2 Tim. 2:22). Such behavior offends God (Rom. 1:24; 1 Thess. 4:8) and often causes physical and emotional pain and loss in this life (Prov. 5:3-14). Refusal to repent of sexual sin may indicate that a person has never entered into a saving relationship with Jesus Christ (Rom. 1:32; 1 Cor. 6:9-10; Eph. 5:3-5; Jude 13; Rev. 22:15).

Thus we affirm that God's blessing rests on sexual intimacy only when it occurs within the boundaries of marriage. We deny that sex outside of marriage is justified for any reason. We reject the idea that sexual intimacy outside of marriage can be moral if partners are honest, consenting, or sufficiently committed. We oppose the portrayal of sexual sin as a way of enhancing the popular appeal of entertainment. We reject the idea that sex between unmarried teenagers is acceptable if it is "safe." And we do not believe that churches should welcome into fellowship any person who willfully refuses to turn away from the sin of living in a sexual relationship outside of marriage.

9. ***The Old and New Testaments uniformly condemn sexual contact between persons of the same sex*** (Lev. 18:22; 20:13; Rom. 1:26-27; 1 Cor. 6:9; 1 Tim. 1:10); and God has decreed that no one can ever excuse homosexual behavior by blaming his or her Creator (Gen. 2:24; Rom. 1:24-25).

Thus we affirm that moral sex is always heterosexual in nature. We affirm that God gives strength to His people when they ask Him for help in resisting immoral sexual desires, including desires for homosexual sex. We affirm that God has perfect knowledge concerning human sexual biology and made no mistake in prohibiting homosexual sex without qualification or exception. We deny the claim that science can justify the morality of homosexual behavior. We reject the idea that homosexual attraction is a gift from God (James 1:13). We deny the idea that homosexual relationships are as valid as heterosexual relationships. We do not agree with those who claim that it is sinful to make moral judgments that favor heterosexual behavior over homosexual behavior.

10. ***The moral corruption of sexual sin can be fully forgiven through repentance and faith in Christ's atoning work*** (1 Cor. 6:9-11; 1 John 1:9), but physical and psychological scars caused by sexual sin cannot always be erased in this life.

Thus we affirm that God fully forgives all who repent of sexual sin. We believe that relationships broken by sexual sin can be restored through genuine repentance and faith. We deny that there is any sort of sexual sin God cannot forgive. We oppose the idea that victims of sexual infidelity or abuse should never forgive those who have sinned against them.

11. ***Christians must grieve with and help those who suffer hardship caused by sexual immorality, even when it is caused by their own acts of sin*** (Rom. 12:15; Luke 19:10). But we must give aid in ways that do not deny moral responsibility for sexual behavior (John 8:11).

Thus we affirm that God calls Christians to love all who suffer social isolation, poverty, illness, or the burdens of unplanned pregnancy and single parenting, whether or not it was caused by their own sexual sin. We believe Christ set an example of loving ministry to those who suffer from the results of their own acts of sin. We reject the idea that our obligation to alleviate human suffering is valid only if such help is "deserved."

COLORADO STATEMENT ON BIBLICAL SEXUAL MORALITY

(Abridged Statement)

Council on Biblical Sexual Ethics
Initiated by Focus on the Family
Issued 2002
www.family.org/cforum/fosi/purity/bv/

The Bible reveals that God's character defines for us what it means to be sexually pure: God's mandate to His people is to "be holy, because I am holy."[1]

We believe that God intends for people to enjoy sex within His established limits. However, because we live in a fallen world, we also believe the following:

Desire and experience cannot be trusted to set the morality of sex.[2] The morality of sex is set by God's holiness.[3]

God's standard is purity in every thought about sex, as well as in every act of sex. Sexual purity is violated even in thoughts that never proceed to outward acts.[4] Sex must never be used to oppress, wrong or take advantage of anyone.[5] Rape, incest, sexual abuse, pedophilia, voyeurism, prostitution and pornography always exploit and corrupt.[6]

God's standards for sexual moral purity protect human happiness.[7] But sex is not an entitlement, nor is it needed for personal wholeness or emotional maturity.

God calls some to a life of marriage and others to lifelong celibacy, but His calling to either state is a divine gift worthy of honor and respect.[8] No one is morally compromised by following God's call to either state, and no one can justify opposing a divine call to either state by denying the moral goodness of that state.

Sexual behavior is moral only within the institution of heterosexual, monogamous marriage. Marriage is secure only when established by an unconditional, covenantal commitment to *lifelong fidelity*,[9] and we should not separate what God has joined.[10] Christians continue to debate whether there are a limited number of situations in which divorce is justifiable (Deut. 24:1-4; Matt. 19:9; 1 Cor. 7:15), but all agree that divorce is never God's ideal; lifelong commitment should always be the Christian's goal.[11]

Marriage protects the transcendent significance of personal sexual intimacy. Heterosexual union in marriage expresses the same sort of holy, exclusive, permanent, complex, selfless, and complementary intimacy that some day will characterize the union of Christ with the redeemed and glorified Church.[12]

Sex in marriage should be an act of love and grace that transcends the petty sins of human selfishness, and should be set aside only when both partners agree to do so, and then only for a limited time of concentrated prayer.[13]

Sex outside of marriage is never moral.[14] This includes all forms of intimate sexual stimulation that stir up sexual passion between unmarried partners.[15] Such behavior offends God,[16] and often causes physical and emotional pain and loss in this life.[17] Refusal to repent of sexual sin may indicate that a person has never entered into a saving relationship with Jesus Christ.[18]

The Old and New Testaments uniformly condemn sexual contact between persons of the same sex;[19] and God has decreed that no one can ever excuse homosexual behavior by blaming his or her Creator.[20]

The moral corruption of sexual sin can be fully forgiven through repentance and faith in Christ's atonement,[21] but physical and emotional scars caused by sexual sin cannot always be erased in this life.[22]

Christians must grieve with and help those who suffer hardship caused by sexual immorality, even when it is caused by their own acts of sin.[23] But we must give aid in ways that do not deny moral responsibility for sexual behavior.[24]

We want to help men and women understand God's good plan for sexual conduct, and thereby to realize all the joy, satisfaction and honor God offers to sexual creatures made in His image.

NOTES

1. Lev. 11:44, 45; 19:2; 20:7, 26; 1 Pet. 1:16
2. Rom. 8:5-8; 13:14; 1 Cor. 2:14; 1 Thess. 4:3-5; 2 Tim. 2:22; James 1:14; 1 John 2:15-16; Jude 1
3. Lev. 20:7-21, 26; 1 Cor. 6:18-19; Eph. 1:4; 5:3; 1 Thess. 4:3-7; Heb. 13:4; 1 Pet. 1:15-16
4. Job 31:1; Matt. 5:28; Phil. 4:8; James 1:14-15
5. 1 Thess. 4:6
6. Lev. 18:7-10; 19:29; 2 Sam. 13:1-22; Prov. 6:26; 23:27; Matt. 5:28; 1 Thess. 4:3-7; 1 Pet. 4:3; 2 Pet. 2:13-14
7. Prov. 5:18-19; 6:32-33; John 15:10-11
8. 1 Cor. 7:36-38
9. Gen. 2:24; Mal. 2:14-15; Matt. 19:4-6; Mark 10:6-8; 1 Cor. 7:39; Rom. 7:2; Eph. 5:31
10. Mal. 2:14-15; Matt. 19:6; Mark 10:9
11. Deut. 24:1-4; Matt. 19:9; 1 Cor. 7:15
12. Eph. 5:30-33; 1 Cor. 6:12-20

13. 1 Cor. 7:3-5
14. Ex. 20:14; Lev. 18:7-17, 20; Deut. 5:18; Matt. 19:9,18; Mark 10:19; Luke 18:20; Rom. 13:9; 1 Cor. 6:13, 18; Gal. 5:19; Eph. 5:3; 1 Thess. 4:3; Heb. 13:4
15. Matt. 5:27-28; 2 Tim. 2:22
16. Rom. 1:24; 1 Thess. 4:8
17. Prov. 5:3-14
18. Rom. 1:32; 1 Cor. 6:9-10; Eph. 5:3-5; Jude 13; Rev. 22:15
19. Lev. 18:22; 20:13; Rom. 1:26-27; 1 Cor. 6:9; 1 Tim. 1:10
20. Gen. 2:24; Rom. 1:24-25
21. 1 Cor. 6:9-11; 1 John 1:9
22. Gal. 6:7
23. Rom. 12:15; Luke 19:10
24. John 8:11

MEMBERS OF THE COUNCIL ON BIBLICAL SEXUAL ETHICS

Note: The Colorado Statement on Biblical Sexual Morality was drafted in 2002 by an interdenominational group of Christian scholars gathered at the invitation of Focus on the Family in Colorado Springs, Colorado. These biblical scholars and theologians working as a group to produce *The Colorado Statement on Biblical Sexual Morality* was referred to as the Council on Biblical Sexual Ethics.

Dr. Daniel Heimbach, professor of Christian ethics at Southeastern Baptist Seminary, served as lead scholar and drafted the initial text for *The Colorado Statement on Biblical Sexual Morality*.

Dr. Craig Blomberg is professor of New Testament at Denver Seminary.

Dr. Wayne Strickland is professor of theology and academic dean at Multnomah Bible College.

Dr. Peter Jones is chairman of the Biblical Studies Department at Westminster Seminary (California campus).

Dr. Daniel Juster is president of Tikkun Ministries, an organization that oversees and helps Messianic congregations throughout the United States.

Father Francis Martin is a member of Pope John Paul II's Institute for Studies on Marriage and Family.

Dr. La Verne Tolbert is an author, teacher, and former professor of Christian education at Talbot Theological Seminary.

Dr. Steven R. Tracy is professor of theology and ethics (and vice president of academic affairs) at Phoenix Seminary.

Pastor Roy A. Holmes is pastor of Greater Walters A. M. E. Zion Church in Chicago.

SIGN THE STATEMENT

You can add your name to the growing list of Christians who have already endorsed *The Colorado Statement on Biblical Sexual Morality.*

You may endorse *The Colorado Statement on Biblical Sexual Morality* online at www.family.org/cforum/fosi/purity/bv/. When you do this, please feel free to add a comment or statement of your own regarding the importance to Christians of affirming clear convictions on sexual morality. A Focus on the Family representative will call you to verify the information you send.

By endorsing *The Colorado Statement,* you give Focus on the Family permission to use your name and/or comments in publicizing the Colorado Statement and promoting its campaign to alert and educate the faith community about the need for sexual purity.

APPENDIX B

OTHER RELIGIOUS STATEMENTS ON SEXUAL MORALITY

Contents of Appendix B

STATEMENT ON HOMOSEXUALITY

Minnesota Council of Churches
Social Justice Committee
Adopted in 1982
Also appears in
FAITH STATEMENT
Wingspan Ministry
Saint Paul-Reformation Lutheran Church
Saint Paul, Minnesota
www.stpaulref.org/wingstat.htm

God's intended wholeness includes human sexuality as a gift for the expression of love and the generation of life. Human sexuality is broader than that expressed in biological sexual relations. Persons demonstrate true humanness in personal, intimate relationships, the most intimate of which are sexual. There may be creative and whole expressions of one's sexuality at various levels in relationships between men and women, between men and other men and between women and other women. We seek to enable persons to understand and to act out of their sexuality in ways which are life-giving to themselves and to other persons with whom they are in relationship.

HUMAN SEXUALITY FROM A CHRISTIAN PERSPECTIVE

Church of the Brethren

Adopted at the 1983 Annual Conference

www.brethren.org/ac/ac_statements/83HumanSexuality.htm

I. Position of the Church

Sexuality is elemental in human beings. It encompasses all that we are when we say "I am female" or "I am male." Physical attributes, including genitals, are an integral part of our sexual identity; however, sexuality is not just physical. It includes all thinking, feeling, acting and interacting that is derived from our maleness and femaleness.

This sexuality enriches human relationships in ways that are basic to God's own nature (Gen. 1:27). Furthermore, it offers human beings partnership with God in holy creation and recreation (Gen. 1:28).

In their enjoyment of these privileges concomitant with sexuality, God's people are to be responsible. The church identifies love and covenant as two guidelines for sexual responsibility. Furthermore, the church holds to the teaching that sexual intercourse, which can be the most intimate expression of sexuality and the bonding of human relationships, belongs within heterosexual marriage.

The church maintains an attitude of openness and willingness to evaluate specific issues related to sexuality. Moreover, the church recognizes that highly personal issues are best resolved in the confidentiality of a private setting with pastor, counselor, or family rather than in the open debate of conferences and council meetings. Seeking the guidance of Scripture, the Holy Spirit, and responsible contemporary research, the church continues to study and search for the mind of Christ in dealing with the complexities of responsible sexuality.

II. Biblical Perspective

The significance of sexuality is evident in scripture. In the Genesis 1 account of creation, sexuality is one of the first human attributes to be identified: Male and female God created them (Gen. 1:27). Other distinguishing characteristics—race, stature, intelligence—are omitted. The lifting up of sexuality in this concise account of human origin suggests how basic sexual identity is.

In Genesis 2, sexuality is associated with companionship and completeness. The first reference to humans in this chapter is neither masculine nor feminine. The Hebrew word *'adam* (v. 7), translated "man" in English, is a collective noun undifferentiated by gender. In this state, *'adam* was lonely. Then another type of human was made from *'adam*. Only then is one human called *ish,* a masculine noun meaning "man," and the other is called *ishshah,* a feminine noun meaning "woman." Adam's problem of loneliness was remedied by the separation of humankind into two sexes and by the intimacy they experienced together. This creation of *ish* and *ishshah* and the ensuing companionship culminates the Genesis 2 account of creation.

As revealed in Genesis 3, this dual sexuality can exacerbate the discordant, testing, rebellious nature of man and woman. Adam and Eve allowed themselves to be seduced by the serpent and its offer of forbidden fruit. The freedom they exerted in choosing evil rather than good resulted in their separation from each other and from God. Immediately they "knew" they were naked and they were ashamed. They were thrust into a world of conflict with all of creation, even with each other (Gen. 3:6-24).

Human experience substantiates and vitalizes these biblical revelations about sexuality. We rejoice in God's creation of two sexes, *ish* and *ishshah.* Despite "the fall" and the conflict we experience, we do not prefer an absence of sexuality. Brokenness can be healed. By God's grace we discover anew that femaleness and maleness enrich and complete our personhood.

Yet while sexuality is an important component of our being, it is not paramount. Paul urged his readers to keep perspective. His emphasis was on the new life in Christ, not on sexuality. He wrote: ". . . there is neither male nor female, for you are all one in Christ Jesus" (Gal. 3:28). Our oneness in Christ supersedes the old human distinctions and inequalities including race, economic status, and sex. Paul gave enough attention elsewhere to sexuality to make it clear that he did not ignore this subject. Yet, sexuality was not his foremost concern.

Likewise, sexuality was not central for Jesus. Although Jesus briefly addressed a few issues related to sexuality—adultery, marriage, divorce, and celibacy—these were not the emphases in his teaching. When asked to identify the greatest commandment, he named two: "Love God and love neighbor" (Mark 12:28-30). For Jesus, love was primary in all human relationships; sexuality was secondary.

Our society is preoccupied with sexuality. The repression of sex in earlier generations has been replaced now by an obsession with sex. One result is that increasing numbers of people expect too much of sexual intercourse. Performance is stressed over relationship, resulting in personal frustration and interpersonal strain. Christian values are ignored. Sex rather than God becomes the center of life.

Even the church loses perspective, although in a different way. To prepare and to consider a denominational statement on human sexuality creates anxiety. Such statements are called "monumental" by some and "the most controversial issues the church has faced in a generation" by others. If these appraisals are true, the church has overreacted. Alarmists fail to remember that generations come and generations go, but the Lord remains forever (Ps. 90:12). Sexual misuses and abuses are serious sins; however, they are not the only sins. There is no reason to become tense and condemnatory about sexual abuses out of proportion with numerous other sins that are equally serious. For the sake of the world, for the unity of the church, and for the benefit of our personal health, this is a timely moment in history to keep sexuality in perspective.

III. Biblical Guidelines for Sexual Morality

In order for sexual experiences to be complete and appropriate in God's sight, persons need to make choices based upon the counsel of the Scriptures and also of the church. Two key biblical words relating to the morality of sexual experiences are love and covenant.

A. Love

The English word *love* has two antecedents in the Greek language, *eros* and *agape,* which are crucial to the understanding of sexual morality.[1, 2] *Eros* is the love that grows out of one's own need to love and to be loved. It is the love that fulfills one's dreams and desires. It is the impulse toward life, union, creativity, and productivity. It is the self-actualizing drive affirmed in Genesis 1 where God created male and female and told them to be fruitful and multiply. It is the satisfying union affirmed in Genesis 2: "The two shall become one flesh."

Sexual attraction is a dynamic of *eros,* but *eros* is more than the mere sensation of physical pleasure. A preoccupation with techniques in our society strips *eros* of its tenderness and delight. The human body—its sensations, its beauty, its capability—is not to be disparaged. The whole body is a marvelously designed gift from God. It is to be enjoyed and utilized. But the body is not to be separated from the soul. Lovemaking is most fulfilling when it is a comfort to the body and the soul. This blending of physical pleasure and spiritual intimacy is *eros* at its best.

The Song of Songs affirms romantic love emphatically and delightfully. It is the unashamed, sensual, joyful poetry of two youthful lovers. The poem romantically describes the lips, eyes, and hair of the lovers. The man tells the woman he loves her because her love is sweet (4:10-11). He desires her because he finds her beauty attractive. She loves him because his body and his speech are desirable (5:11-16). They love each other because each brings to the other a gladness and a fullness of life. Very early, the book was viewed as an allegory by the Jews as Yahweh's love for Israel, and by the Christians as Christ's love for the church. This interpretation influenced the book's acceptance into the canon and has inspired Christian thought through the centuries. Still, the book itself contains no clue that it is meant to be understood allegorically. We must also be ready to read it as it stands: an appropriate celebration of the *eros* that leads to and finds its consummation within marriage. The Song of Songs affirms the *eros* that is a valued aspect of the human nature God created.

Agape is an equally significant dimension of love. *Agape* is unrestrained compassion for another. It is selfless giving. It is a generous responsiveness to another's needs beyond any gain for oneself. It is the love of 1 Corinthians 13 that is patient and kind, not jealous or boastful, nor arrogant or rude, does not insist on its own way, is not irritable or resentful, does not rejoice in the wrong but rejoices in the right (13:4-6). The ultimate expression of *agape* is to lay down one's life for the sake of another (John 15:13). The prototype of *agape* is Jesus' giving his life on the cross.

Eros is of the order of creation, a Godgiven gift to our human nature. *Agape,* on the other hand, is of the order of redeeming grace, the gift of the covenanting God to covenanting people. Even so, *eros* and *agape* are gifts of God and part of his plan for humanity. Neither is to be despised. Indeed, it is only when romantic love is constituted of both that it can be said, "Lo, it is very good."

B. Covenant

Christians need more than love to guide them in decision-making. Love is nebulous. Moreover, we are susceptible to self-deception, particularly in moments of sexual excitement and desire. At such times the claim of love is to be tested by actual commitment that gives content to the declaration of love. Such commitment disciplines, protects, and nurtures love relationships. Christians need covenant as well as love to guide them.

Covenants abound in biblical history, shaping relationships and undergirding community. These covenants take many forms. Some are written; many are spoken. Some are unilateral promises without obligations upon the recipient; others are conditional with specified terms. Some covenants are between equals; others are between a superior and a subordinate.

Since no single model exists, it is difficult to describe biblical covenants precisely. Characteristics present in some are absent in others, but despite these variations, several elements of biblical covenants can be identified.

Biblical covenants were generally *public.* They were not private agreements isolated from community. Even God's covenants with Noah, Abraham, and Moses were not merely individualistic. They were major covenants affecting and including the whole community for many generations. To acknowledge these communal ties, the covenants were generally confirmed by formal acts—a sign, a ritual, a recognizable verbal formula—visible or audible to the community. The rainbow was a sign of God's covenant with Noah (Gen. 9:12). Circumcision was a sign of God's promise to Abraham (Genesis 17). The "blood of the covenant," splashed over the altar and over the people, signified God's covenant with Moses (Ex. 24:5-8). In the New Testament, the bread and the cup symbolize the new covenant the covenants [*sic*] that are the foundation of the people's life together.

Biblical covenants are *pious,* reflecting Israel's sense that covenants are grounded in God. Sometimes God initiates the covenant as a primary participant. Other times God is only indirectly involved. For example, people make covenants between themselves but seal them with an oath. The oath implies religious sanction. Thus, being faithful to God implies being faithful to the covenant.

Biblical covenants are *permanent.* Sometimes this expectation of permanence is challenged by changing circumstances and bitter disappointments, yet the promise is not withdrawn. For example, the Davidic covenant that the throne of Israel would remain forever in the line of David's descent did not collapse with the Exile (586–538 b.c.). Instead there emerged new hope for a future king who would be the son of David. Furthermore, when terms of the covenant are violated, broken relationships and misery result. In such circumstances the old covenant may be dissolved by God and a new beginning offered (Jer. 31:31-34). Despite these vicissitudes in covenantal relationships, the common understanding is that covenants last forever.[3]

Finally, biblical covenants often *presuppose pilgrimage.* Abraham, Moses, and David were adventurers. God's covenants with these men pointed beyond their present realms of living to a destination—to a nation, a land, and a kingdom not yet fully reached. Jesus and his disciples were travelers. Initially, Jesus beckoned them to a journey, "Follow me . . . ." Later, he commissioned them to another journey, "Go into all the world. . . ." He promised them, . . . "I am with you always . . ." (Mark 1:17; Matt. 28:19-20). His promise was a covenant: He said he would be with them in their journeys. Such covenants have unfolding qualities. They foster adventure, newness, and surprise.

Pilgrims accept a code of conduct for their journey. Sometimes the code is specific and direct about behavioral expectations. (The Holiness Code in Leviticus 17–26, the Deuteronomic Code, or Zacchaeus' promise to Jesus in Luke 19:8). Covenants set limits. Yet the spirit of the covenant is to nourish relationships, not regiment them. Covenants, unlike contracts, offer fidelity that exceeds specification: "You will be my people; I will be your God" (Jer. 31:3b; Hos. 2:23).

The influence of covenants upon sexual behavior and relationships within Israel is evident. Unlike much contemporary, popular literature, the Bible is not primarily a story about lovers and their disconnected affairs. Rather, it is an account of families and marriages and continuing loyalties. To be sure, there are many lapses in covenantal faithfulness. This reality does not diminish the significance of covenant in the life of the Israelites: rather it underscores their need for a new covenant that incorporates not only law and judgment but also grace and renewal.

C. The Church's Guidance

In contemporary life we are often hesitant to make covenants. There are many reasons for that hesitancy. We make hasty, unwise commitments and find ourselves entangled in painful relationships. We say, "Never again." We are motivated by self-interest, convenience, and momentary pleasure at the expense of long-range rewards. We resist the responsibility of long-term commitment. We want to be autonomous, with little obligation to the community. For all these reasons we may resist making covenants, choosing instead agreements that are tentative.

The result is that in contemporary life we lack the sense of belonging and the covenantal structure that helps a relationship endure through periods when emotion is not a sufficient bond. We lack a sense of being part of a purpose and a people that extends far beyond our individual lives. It is time for the church to speak assertively of covenant, of belonging and loyalty.

To apply biblical covenant to sexuality in the modern world does not require the church to formulate a comprehensive code to cover all eventualities and contingencies. Ours is a complex and changing world. Differing family patterns, changing male and female roles, effective contraceptives, overpopulation, and the science dealing with human sexual behavior are among the phenomena that represent new dilemmas and choices profoundly affecting sexual relationships.

In addressing these realities the church must avoid undercutting individual discretion, eliminating personal responsibility for growth, and stifling the work of the Spirit among us. Yet within the covenant community, there is need for general guidelines, Bible study, and frank conversation.

In a society in which people are purported to "have sex more but enjoy it less," the time has come to reconsider the importance of both love and covenant. There are no easy answers about how to apply love and covenant to some of the real life situations in which people find themselves. Is the church willing to struggle with these issues even when answers are not always clear? The struggle will be unsettling and difficult, but the outcome may enhance morality, not diminish it, and contribute to a fuller, more human life for all persons.

IV. Implications for Human Sexuality

Much research on the subject of human sexuality is being done by physical and social scientists. For the church, however, scriptural guidance and biblical scholarship must be brought to bear upon that scientific information in order to come to an adequate understanding of the implications of human sexuality for our day.

Some specific concerns related to human sexuality have been dealt with in recent Annual Conferences: birth control,[4] pornography,[5] male and female roles,[6] abortion,[7] marriage,[8] artificial insemination,[9] and divorce.[10] It would be repetitious to dwell again on these issues.

Major issues that have not been dealt with by recent Annual Conferences include (1) sexuality for single persons, (2) homosexuality, and (3) marital fidelity. Sexuality for single persons is an area of rapidly changing mores in our society. Homosexuality is discussed now more openly than ever before in modern history. The difficulties of maintaining marital fidelity are compounded by current social stresses and continuing silence within the church on sexuality.

A. Single Persons and Sexuality

More than one-third of the adults in our society are single—unmarried, divorced, or widowed. Our biblical faith affirms singleness as a meaningful lifestyle. The lifestyles and teachings of both Jesus and Paul are models of singleness. Jesus placed singleness on a par with marriage (Matt. 19:12). Paul felt that in terms of an undivided allegiance to Christ, being single had some advantages (1 Cor. 7:1-9, 24-40).

Fullness of life for single persons depends upon certain conditions. Family is important but may exist in different forms in different times and places. However, the endurance of the family reflects the need of people, whether married or unmarried, for a primary relationship in which personhood is fostered, loneliness is diminished, and closeness and belonging are experienced. Jesus cherished his family of faith as much as his biological family (Matt. 10:35-37; 12:49). His example should spur the church toward being a spiritual family to one another in the fellowship.

Furthermore, every adult needs significant friends of the opposite sex. Jesus had female friends. His friendship with Mary, sister of Martha and Lazarus, was especially close. It was a friendship not just of chores, convenience, and function, but also of warm conversation and closeness (Luke 10:38-42). Priscilla (Acts 18:2, 18; 1 Cor. 16:19; Rom. 16:3) and Phoebe (Rom. 16:1-2) were especially important to Paul in his work. St. Francis of Assisi had a very close female companion, Sister Clara, whose friendship was invaluable especially in his later years. These all are helpful models of a nurturing friendship between persons of opposite sex, a friendship not involving sexual union. Such intimacy is an affirmation of maleness and femaleness and addresses basic human needs for wholeness of personhood among single people.

1. Biblical Insights

Although the Scriptures do not deal extensively with the sexual behavior of single persons, some boundaries are established. In the Old Testament, certain types of premarital sexual activity are punishable (Deut. 22:13-21, 23-29). In the New Testament, Paul teaches that union with a prostitute is immoral because that act inseparably joins two persons (1 Cor. 6:12-20). Paul also specifically addresses the unmarried and the widowed who find it difficult to control sexual passion (1 Cor. 7:2, 9, 36-38). Paul advocates marriage for such persons, implying that sexual intercourse is to be practiced within marriage.

2. The Church's Response

The requirement of celibacy for singles is a thorny issue that the church faces. Our current social circumstances heighten the difficulties. Physical maturation has accelerated three years in one generation. A girl now reaches puberty at 11 or 12 years of age and a boy at 13 or 14 years. Moreover, the median age at first marriage is later than ever before: 23 years for men and 21 years for women. The 10-year span between sexual maturity and marriage creates a difficult situation in which to preserve chastity, a situation different from the biblical era.

Premarital sexual relationships, especially among teenagers, are creating many problems in our society. Sexually active adolescents experience conflict in determining their values. Emotional and psychological development is impaired, at times irreversibly. Suicide is sometimes a factor. Teenage pregnancy, venereal disease, and permanent sterilization are occurring in epidemic proportions. Often these problems are the inevitable result of a society that is seductive and permissive, and promotes freedom and pleasure above responsibility and longterm satisfactions. This society and all too often a negligent church have failed to provide moral support to those many youth who do have values and seek to live by them.

The teen years should be used to mature socially and emotionally, to learn the skills of communication and problem solving, and to express sexual identity in nongenital ways. These experiences contribute to the maturity that is necessary in order to learn what love really is, to find a compatible partner, and to establish a covenant that is sound and lasting. The church believes that these principles are still valid in our time.

The engagement period should be a time for the couple to share about families, dreams, goals, habits, likes, dislikes, past experiences. It is the time to develop common interests and good communication patterns. Christian persons in dating relationships should resist the strong desire for full sexual expression and the pressures of the media and culture for sexual exploitation.

Also in contemporary society there are rapidly increasing numbers of previously married single adults. A higher divorce rate, an extended life expectancy, and the preponderance of women over men in the middle and upper age brackets are among the factors leading to this increase. Many of these persons have experienced sexual intercourse within marriage, but such experience is no longer available to them. Some of the problems that exist in our contemporary world when singleness is a matter of circumstances rather than choice did not exist in such proportions in the biblical world. It is incumbent on our society and the church to acknowledge these problems and to seek solutions.

The church counteracts the cultural emphasis on sexual self-indulgence by teaching the benefits of self-discipline and the positive aspects of a life of commitment and fidelity. In a time of casual lovemaking and pleasure seeking, covenants provide structure that sustains us in the fluctuating joys and pains of authentic relationships. Ongoing loyalties give continuity to our lives. The marks of covenant include mutual respect, public vows, lifetime accountability, and religious sanction. The church teaches that sexual intercourse belongs within the bonds of such love and covenant.

The church as a covenant community encourages single people, as well as married people to speak of their needs and concerns including sexuality. In the continuing interchange of ideas and feelings, the church seeks to be more evangelical and caring than condemnatory.

B. Homosexual Persons and Sexuality

The Church of the Brethren never has dealt officially with the issue of homosexuality. The time is here to examine openly this matter that profoundly affects the lives of millions of homosexual people and their families.

1. Misunderstandings About Homosexuality

Misunderstandings and unnecessary fears about homosexuality abound. Contrary to popular opinion, most homosexuals are not flagrantly promiscuous and do not engage in offensive public behavior. Male homosexuals are not identifiably "feminine" and lesbians are not characteristically "masculine." Teachers with homosexual orientation are often suspected of influencing pupils toward homosexual behavior but most sexual offenses reported between teacher and pupil are heterosexual in nature. For most practicing homosexuals, sexual activity is a proportionate part of their lives. Most of the time they engage in pursuits common to all.

2. Causes of Homosexuality

The causes of homosexuality are not definitely known. Is it inborn or learned? No one has the definitive answer. What is known is that people do not simply decide to become homosexual; it is more complex than that.

Some recent research suggests that the predisposition for homosexuality may be genetic. Other research suggests that certain types of family pathology produce a higher incidence of homosexuality. However, such research has not been sufficiently extensive or scientific to be conclusive. It is generally agreed that the homosexual orientation usually is formed early in life. From 5 to 10 percent of the population is said to be primarily homosexual in orientation.[11]

A significant percentage of people have occasional homosexual interests and/or experience but are not exclusively homosexual. Perhaps the majority of people are somewhere on the continuum between exclusive homosexuality and exclusive heterosexuality.

3. Biblical Insights

The Bible refers directly to homosexual conduct seven times. Genesis 18–19 and Judges 19 are narratives. Leviticus 18:22 and 20:13 are prohibitions in the Holiness Code. Romans 1:26ff.; 1 Corinthians 6:9-10; and 1 Timothy 1:10 are excerpts from epistles.

Genesis 18–19. The attempted homosexual assault by a mob of men is mentioned in the story about the decadence and subsequent destruction of the city of Sodom. Such offensive behavior was not the only sin of this wicked city. Isaiah, Ezekiel, and Jesus point to Sodom's self-indulgence, arrogance, inhospitality, and indifference to the poor. Thus, in its own later interpretations of the episode at Sodom, the Bible does not dwell on homosexual sins of the city in the way that more recent interpreters do. Nevertheless, sexual misconduct, particularly assault, is an important element in the story about Sodom's sin and destruction (2 Pet. 2:4-14; Jude 7).

Judges 19. The Judges 19:22-26 account of an incident at Gibeah is strikingly similar to the Genesis 19:4-8 account of the mistreatment of guests at Lot's house in Sodom. Since the stories are so similar, what one decides about the meaning of one passage would apply also to the other.

Leviticus 18:22; 20:13. Leviticus denounces male homosexual acts decisively in two almost identical texts. However, some difficulty arises in interpreting these verses because of their context. The Leviticus proscriptions against homosexual acts are intermingled with statutes that forbid the planting of two kinds of seed in one field, wearing garments made of two kinds of material, and trimming the edges of a man's beard (Lev. 19:9, 27). Another statute mandates executing children who curse their parents (Lev. 20:9). The church does not enforce all laws from this section of Leviticus (i.e., the Holiness Code, chapters 17–26). Some interpreters inquire:

"Upon what basis does the church select one law for enforcement, but ignore other laws?" The key is to examine the overarching principles of the total Bible. Does the rest of scripture, particularly the New Testament, reaffirm the laws from the Holiness Code that denounce male homosexual acts? To that question we now direct our attention.

Romans 1:26-27. The first chapter of Romans states that both lesbianism (the only mention of female homosexuality in the Bible) and male homosexuality are manifestations of the corruption that arises from idolatry (Rom. 1:23-27). The lust and unnaturalness of the homosexuality described in this passage are examples of how distorted life becomes when people worship and serve created things rather than the Creator (Rom. 1:25).

The persons described in this chapter "gave up natural relations for unnatural" (vv. 26-27). This phrase connotes that homosexual behavior is the willful acts of persons who had previously engaged in heterosexual relations. Not all homosexuality can be described this way. Some persons never experienced what Paul calls "natural relations" because their orientation (genetic or conditioned) is homosexual. This circumstance opens the question: Does Paul consider all kinds of homosexuality idolatrous, or does he mean to denounce only those kinds of homosexual behavior described in this passage? The one thing that is clear in this passage is that Paul considers the behavior of those who exchange heterosexual for homosexual relations to be "unnatural" and sinful.

1 Corinthians 6:9-11; 1 Timothy 1:9-11. 1 Corinthians and 1 Timothy list a series of sins all of which are condemned. Both of these lists include the Greek word *arsenokoitia* which is a form of sexual immorality. But, *arsenokoitia* is an obscure word. A comparison of English versions reveals that *arsenokoitia* is variously translated to mean heterosexual male prostitution, or sodomy, or cultic homosexuality, or all forms of homosexual activity. Apparently, there are overtones of lust and cultic prostitution. Again the question arises in the minds of some whether Paul in naming *arsenokoitia* means to denounce all forms of homosexual behavior.

In summary, seven passages forcefully denounce a variety of homosexual behavior: rape, adultery, cultic prostitution, and lust. These scriptures do not deal explicitly with some contemporary questions about various forms of homosexuality, about homosexuality as an orientation, about the onset of homosexuality prior to the age of moral accountability, and about genetic and/or environmental predispositions.

While the seven direct references in the Old and New Testaments are often isolated as the focal point of an interpretation of the biblical teaching about homosexuality, these texts are best understood within the larger framework from which the Bible approaches sexuality in general. This overarching framework, identified in the opening sections of this paper, upholds heterosexuality as the reflection of God's image (Gen. 1:27) and as the culmination of creation (Gen. 2:18-25). It is in union with a sexual opposite that male and female find fulfillment as persons and identity as a family. While some modern distinctions about homosexuality are missing in the Scriptures, homosexual behavior is considered contrary to the heterosexual norm that runs throughout scripture.

Jesus reinforced the unified biblical view of human sexuality. He upheld the sanctity of heterosexual marriage, reciting from scripture God's original intention in creation: "Have you not read that He who made them from the beginning made them male and female, and said, 'For this reason a man shall leave his father and mother and be joined to his wife, and the two shall become one?' So they are no longer two but one" (Matt. 19:4-8). Thus, Jesus affirms that heterosexual marriage is the pattern for sexual union God intended from the beginning.

This biblical affirmation of heterosexuality does not automatically exclude every other choice of sexual expression or nonexpression. Although Jesus is clear about the biblical norm, he is not categorical. In the same passage in which he upholds the sanctity of marriage (Matt. 19:3-12), he acknowledges, "not every one can receive this precept, only those to whom it is given." He then identifies some persons for whom heterosexual union is not possible: some because of factors of birth; others because of what has been done to them; and still others because they choose not to marry for the sake of the kingdom. Thus Jesus does not prescribe heterosexual marriage for every person.

4. The Church's Response

The Church of the Brethren upholds the biblical declaration that heterosexuality is the intention of God for creation. Nature, in the very functional compatibility of male and female genitalia, confirms this biblical revelation that males and females are meant for each other. This intimate genital contact between two persons of opposite sexes is not just a physical union; it also embodies the interlocking of persons. This intimate companionship is heterosexuality at its fullest. It is the context for the formation of family.

Some persons, for reasons not fully understood, experience a romantic attraction for persons of the same sex. Some of these persons claim Christ as Lord and are actively involved in the life of the church. They need the active support and love of the church as they struggle with God's plan for their lives.

In ministry to homosexual persons, the church must guard against oversimplifying Christian morality. Instead the church should endeavor with Christian love and with gentle evangelistic skill to offer redemptive help. Proof texts, condemnation, and a sense of guilt will not empower change. Rejection isolates homosexual persons from the church. It frequently results in a preoccupation with and intensification of the very inclinations their accusers deplore. The power of the Gospel incorporates an acceptance of persons who seek forgiveness for their sins and who strive to be disciples of Jesus Christ. It is this nonaccusatory acceptance that sets people free from guilt, depression, and fear. When we are saved it is not because we are without sin but because our sins are not held against us by God's grace. We are made whole through God's righteousness, not ours (Rom. 3:21–4:5).

In relating to homosexual persons, the church should become informed about such lifestyle options as the following.

Celibacy, refraining from sexual activities, is one alternative that homosexuals and bisexuals choose. The scriptural teaching on celibacy for heterosexuals provides a model for this lifestyle. Celibacy ought to be voluntary and not a requirement (1 Tim. 4:1-3). Those for whom celibacy is a gift and a special calling (Matt. 19:11 12; 1 Cor. 7:6-7) are to be honored and supported.

Conversion to a heterosexual orientation is another option. For many homosexual persons, however, this choice is extraordinarily difficult and complex. For some it is impossible. The church must seek to create a climate for hope, for praise of God, for renewed effort, for claiming and exploring the heterosexual dimensions of being. Thus the Good News is shared with homosexual persons who seek to convert to heterosexuality. Yet not all are set totally free of homosexual feelings and urges. For some, impulses diminish, mindsets change, the grip of homosexuality is broken, and affectional and physical attraction to the opposite sex can begin.

Covenantal relationships between homosexual persons is an additional lifestyle option but, in the church's search for a Christian understanding of human sexuality, this alternative is not acceptable.

There are special ways in which the church can extend Christ-like comfort and grace to homosexual and bisexual persons. These include:

- welcoming all inquirers who confess Jesus Christ as Lord and Savior into the fellowship of the church. This welcome and the resources of the church are made available by the grace of God who calls us as repentant sinners to be partakers of the faith. Some guidelines for the church's response and for discipleship have been delineated;
- intensifying efforts to understand how genetic makeup and childhood experiences have influenced the development of sexual orientation and behavior;
- challenging openly the widespread fear, hatred, and harassment of homosexual persons;
- engaging in open, forthright conversations with homosexuals. When we stop alienating one another and instead venture toward understanding, some fears disappear and interpersonal relationships become more honest;
- advocating the right of homosexuals to jobs, housing, and legal justice;
- stating clearly that all antisocial, sexually promiscuous acts are contrary to Christian morality;
- giving strong support to persons who seek to be faithful to their heterosexual marriage covenant, but for whom this is difficult because of struggles with homosexuality.

Fortunate are persons who learn not to be afraid of their feelings and thoughts and can accept these components of their sexuality within disciplined bounds. Discovering that God has good use for these dimensions of our lives helps to defuse unacceptable impulses. We all, whether homosexual or heterosexual, have desires and drives that need to be channeled appropriately to avoid sin and to center our sexuality in right relationships.

C. Married Persons and Sexuality

The Christian faith affirms that heterosexual marriage is the intended culmination of sexuality. Sexual intercourse, the most intimate of human relationships, belongs within heterosexual marriage. Within the covenant of lifelong fidelity, married couples learn to enjoy this full-bodied, fullspirited union. Furthermore, it is this loyal, loving partnership that is most conducive to the responsible conception of children.

Marriage fidelity is a matter of spirit and emotion as well as body (Matt. 5:28). Our sexuality, a sacred trust from our Creator, is too powerful and too elemental a force to be treated lightly or casually. Sexual activity that embraces spirit, emotion, and body is just as valid when engaged in for pleasure as for procreation. Such pleasure will be found as much in receiving as in giving. The need to care in consistent ways about the well being of one's spouse is essential. The desires and needs of each must be paramount in a mutual relationship. Demands and satisfactions designed to meet the needs of one partner to the exclusion of the satisfactions and needs of the other will only erode the act of intercourse and cause mutual trust and respect to disintegrate. True mutuality exists when the spiritual, emotional, and physical hungers of both persons are satisfied. Each has a responsibility for such mutual fulfillment.

Sexual intercourse between two persons who are bound by love and covenant can foster the most intimate and intense kinds of communication. At that moment—unlike any other—those two do truly become as one. Unfortunately, even within the context of marriage this is not always so. Sexual relationships, of every expression, become destructive of the Creator's design when used in self-centered ways. Sexual activity within the context of marriage can sometimes be as exploitative and selfish and destructive as sexual activity outside of marriage. This happens when sexual relationships are:

- used only to gratify personal desires,
- used as a weapon,
- withheld as punishment,
- proffered as reward,
- demanded unilaterally, or
- used as a cover-up for personal inadequacies.

In any such case, marital sexual activity is just as immoral as the misuse of sex outside of marriage. Sexual relationships ought to be a wholly fulfilling link between two affectionate people from which they emerge unanxious and satisfied.

When genuine communication exists between spouses, they will be able to tell each other about their needs and what brings them pleasure and satisfaction, without inhibition or embarrassment. It is destructive to a marriage relationship (at every level but especially in regard to sexual matters) to assume that one should instinctively know what the needs and desires and satisfactions of the other are. The risk is that expectations will not be met and one or both of the parties will feel rejected and unloved. Once those seeds of rejection take root they produce grudges, resentments, and hostility. Demanding that your mate automatically understand and fulfill your needs is a most unreasonable expectation. It is important to communicate those needs, desires, and satisfactions both verbally and nonverbally without embarrassment.

Compassion is also an essential component of satisfying sexual relationships. "Making love" is a term often used for sexual intercourse even though sometimes "love" is the missing ingredient. Intercourse without expressed feeling and caring is empty or worse. It is exploitative and selfish. Love that is communicated through the intimacies of sexual intercourse is a love that goes beyond words; indeed, is often verbally inexpressible and is, therefore, expressed through the act itself.

The importance of sexual fidelity is not to be underestimated (1 Thess. 4:2-8; Heb. 13:4). Unlike less easily recognized aspects of fidelity, sexual faithfulness is identifiable. Marriage partners know when they are sexually faithful, at least as far as overt behavior is concerned. Being loyal in this overt way may help couples learn to be faithful in other aspects of their lives together.

The covenant of faithfulness does not preclude meaningful relationships with persons other than the marriage partner. Indeed, such friendships are to be cherished. However, if these ties move beyond friendship and become amorous, the intimate relationship outside of marriage will need to be terminated. Adultery is one of the most serious temptations faced by married persons.

1. Biblical Insights

The old covenant forbids adultery. The seventh commandment in the Decalogue (Ex. 20:14 and Deut. 5:18) is concise: "You shall not commit adultery." The exact nature of adultery, however, is somewhat obscure in the old covenant. For men, adultery was often narrowly defined as sexual intercourse with the wife of a fellow Israelite (Lev. 18:20; 20:10; Deut. 5:21; 22:22; Ex. 20:17). Polygamy, concubinage and perhaps secular harlotry were allowed the married male but not the married female (Gen. 16:14; 30:1-13, 38; 2 Sam. 5:13). The double standard was evident. The rights of the male were paramount and the restraints against his sexual relationships were primarily to protect the rights of other Israelite men: the father, the betrothed, the husband.

In the new covenant, this double standard for adultery disappears. When a group of men caught a woman in adultery and inquired whether she should be stoned to death, Jesus appealed to the conscience of the men regarding their own sins (John 8:1-11). Jesus applied the prohibition of adultery to husbands and wives on an equal basis (Mark 10:1-12). Marriage, as understood by Jesus, was intended by God from the beginning of creation to be the indissoluble union by two persons (Mark 10:8-9).

Moreover, for Jesus, adultery was a matter of attitude as well as action (Matt. 5:28). He taught in the Sermon on the Mount that lust is adultery. Lust is not a passing fantasy but an untamed craving. Unless *eros* is infused and counterbalanced with *agape,* attitudes become adulterous.

Paul taught that sexual relationships are not just physical acts but deeply interpersonal experiences. It was Paul's view that even a sexual relationship that was intended to be highly casual involved a mystical union (1 Cor. 6:16).

Although adultery is a sin, neither Jesus nor Paul suggests that it is unforgivable. Jesus did not condemn the adulteress, though he told her, "Go, sin no more" (John 8:11). Paul wrote about believers whose former immorality had been washed away (1 Cor. 6:11). Quite clearly, adultery is perceived to be a violation of the marital union. But by God's grace, sexuality, though defiled, can become again what it was intended to be.

2. THE CHURCH'S RESPONSE

Amidst changing values and relaxed morality, the church should continue to speak out against adultery as well as other threats to the marriage covenant. Casual acceptance of sexual relationships outside of marriage is a part of our society and is reflected to us by our media. The church, however, should continue to hold up in its teachings the image of marriage as the permanent, spiritual, physical, and emotional bonding between a man and a woman, modeled upon God's everlasting covenant with his people (Genesis 12) and Christ's eternal union with the church (Ephesians 5).

D. FamilyLife Education

Quality education is needed to attain an understanding of sexuality and a competence in family relationships. This education begins in the home where parents teach their children not only by word but also by conduct and expression of feeling. This is the proper forum for teaching morality. The importance of confining sexual intercourse to marriage takes root in daily contact with nurturing, caring adults who teach and model this behavior.

However, given the severe stresses and strains of the family in our society, parents need the church's support and assistance in conveying Christian attitudes on sexual morality. The church should provide biblical and theological guidance on sexuality.

Education for family life is appropriate also within the public school. It is needed to supplement instruction in the home and church. Public school instruction should include information about the body, sex organs, and the reproductive system, but the emphasis should be on values and relationships. Teachers who are responsible for this task should be well trained and themselves be worthy models of mature and responsible sexuality. The church supports responsible family life education in the public school as long as the religious commitment of all students and residents of the community is respected.

Parents should keep themselves informed about the content of family-life education courses in which their children are influenced, and use that educational experience to foster open discussion of the topic of sexuality with their children. Parents should also be acquainted with the content of such courses for the purposes of continuing dialogue with school officials. In such dialogue parents should clarify their Christian principles to insure that their own ethical values are not undermined.

Family-life education will not solve all sex, marriage, and family problems. The task requires the coordinated efforts of home, church, and school.

V. Conclusion

Sexuality is God's good gift. It is a spoilable gift. Who among us does not regularly need God's grace to restore this gift that we have abused so that it again beautifies and deepens human relationships? These problems that arise for ourselves and our generation are to be faced and confessed, but this need not turn our attitude toward sexuality into a tangle of negatives. God's grace is real. Sexuality remains for us, as it was for *adham,* God's antidote for human loneliness and the answer to the human need to have a counterpart, to be one with someone, and to be in love.

Action of the General Board: At its March 1983 meeting the General Board voted to approve this position paper for presentation to the 1983 Annual Conference.

Curtis W. Dubble, Chairman
Robert W. Neff, General Secretary

Action of 1983 Annual Conference: The report from the General Board was presented by Guy E. Wampler, Jr., the chairperson of the General Board's study committee for the topic, HUMAN SEXUALITY FROM A CHRISTIAN PERSPECTIVE. In attendance were the other members of the Board's study committee: Doris Cline Egge, James F. Myer, Mary Sue Rosenberger, and Clyde R. Shallenberger. *The delegate body of the 1983 Annual Conference in a 2/3 majority vote adopted the paper on HUMAN SEXUALITY FROM A CHRISTIAN PERSPECTIVE as a position paper with one amendment* which is incorporated in the preceding wording of the paper.

NOTES

1. Barclay, William, *Letters to Galatians and Ephesians.* Philadelphia: Westminster Press, 1954, p. 54. In addition to *eros* and *agape,* there are two additional Greek words for love: *philia* which refers to the warm but nonromantic love we feel for those close to us and *storge* which refers especially to the love between parents and children.
2. Nygren, Anders, *Agape and Eros.* Philadelphia: Westminster Press, 1953. The separation between the words *eros* and *agape, eros* having to do with love involving the needs of self and *agape* having to do with love involving the needs of other persons, has been in vogue since the publication of this book. It is not clear that this neat, sharp distinction can in fact be sustained either in the New Testament or in Hellenistic literature. However, the perspective commonly called *eros* is definitely in the biblical tradition even if the word is not.
3. Roop, Eugene, "Two Become One Become Two," *Brethren Life and Thought,* vol. XXI, no.3, Summer 1976; pp. 133-137. An analysis of the expectation of permanence with covenants and yet the possibility of new covenants.

4. *Minutes of the Annual Conference, 1955–64,* "Family Planning and Population Growth" (1964), p. 328.
5. *Minutes of the Annual Conference, 1965–69,* "Theological Basis of Personal Ethics" (1966), p. 118.
6. *Minutes of the Annual Conference, 1975–79,* "Equality for Women in the Church of the Brethren" (1977), p. 340.
7. *Minutes of the Annual Conference, 1970–74,* "Abortion" (1972), p. 227.
8. *Minutes of the Annual Conference, 1955–64,* "Divorce and Remarriage" (1964), p. 320; and *Minutes of the Annual Conference, 1975–1979*; "Marriage and Divorce" (1977), p. 300.
9. *Minutes of the Annual Conference, 1955–64,* "Family Planning and Population Growth" (1964), p. 328.
10. *Minutes of the Annual Conference, 1955–64,* "Divorce and Remarriage" (1964), p.320; and *Minutes of the Annual Conference, 1975–1979,* "Marriage and Divorce" (1977).
11. Kinsey, Alfred C.; Pomeroy, Wardell B.; Martin, Clyde E.; and Gebhard, Paul H., *Sexual Behavior in the Human Male* and *Sexual Behavior in the Human Female.* Philadelphia: W. B. Saunders Company, 1948 and 1953.

RESOLUTION "CALLING ON UCC CONGREGATIONS TO COVENANT AS OPEN AND AFFIRMING"

United Church of Christ

Adopted at the 1985 General Synod

www.ucc.org/men/open.htm

WHEREAS, the Apostle Paul said that, as Christians, we are many members, but we are one body in Christ (Rom. 12:4), and Jesus calls us to love our neighbors as ourselves (Mark 12:31) without being judgmental (Matt. 7:1-2) nor disparaging of others (Luke 18:9-14); and

WHEREAS, recognizing that many persons of lesbian, gay and bisexual orientation are already members of the Church through baptism and confirmation and that these people have talents and gifts to offer the United Church of Christ, and that the UCC has historically affirmed a rich diversity in its theological and Biblical perspectives; and

WHEREAS, the Tenth through Fourteenth General Synods have adopted resolutions encouraging the inclusion, and affirming the human rights, of lesbian, gay and bisexual people within the UCC; and

WHEREAS, the Executive Council of the United Church of Christ adopted in 1980 "a program of Equal Employment Opportunity which does not discriminate against any employee or applicant because of . . . sexual orientation"; and

WHEREAS, many parts of the Church have remained conspicuously silent despite the continuing injustice of institutionalized discrimination, instances of senseless violence and setbacks in civil rights protection by the Supreme Court; and

WHEREAS, the Church has often perpetuated discriminatory practices and has been unwilling to affirm the full humanness of clergy, laity and staff with lesbian, gay and bisexual orientation, who experience isolation, ostracism and fear of (or actual) loss of employment; and

WHEREAS, we are called by Christ's example, to proclaim release to the captives and set at liberty the oppressed (Luke 4:18); and

WHEREAS, examples of covenant of Openness and Affirmation and Non-discrimination Policy may be found in the following:

EXAMPLE 1: COVENANT OF OPENNESS AND AFFIRMATION

We know, with Paul, that as Christians, we are many members, but are one body in Christ—members of one another, and that we all have different gifts. With Jesus, we affirm that we are called to love our neighbors as ourselves, that we are called to act as agents of reconciliation and wholeness within the world and within the Church itself.

We know that lesbian, gay and bisexual people are often scorned by the church, and devalued and discriminated against both in the Church and in society. We commit ourselves to caring and concern for lesbian, gay and bisexual sisters and brothers by affirming that:

We believe that lesbian, gay and bisexual people share with all others the worth that comes from being unique individuals,

We welcome lesbian, gay and bisexual people to join our congregation in the same spirit and manner used in the acceptance of any new members,

We recognize the presence of ignorance, fear and hatred in the Church and in our culture, and covenant to not discriminate on the basis of sexual orientation, nor any other irrelevant factor, and we seek to include and support those who, because of this fear and prejudice, find themselves in exile from a spiritual community,

We seek to address the needs and advocate the concerns of lesbian, gay and bisexual people in our Church and in society by actively encouraging churches, instrumentalities and secular governmental bodies to adopt and implement policies of non-discrimination, and further,

We join together as a covenantal community, to celebrate and share our common communion and the reassurance that we are indeed created by God, reconciled by Christ and empowered by the grace of the Holy Spirit;

EXAMPLE 2: INCLUSIVE NON-DISCRIMINATION POLICY

We do not discriminate against any person, group or organization in hiring, promotion, membership, appointment, use of facility, provision of services or funding on the basis of race, gender, age, sexual orientation, faith, nationality, ethnicity, marital status, or physical disability;

THEREFORE, the Fifteenth General Synod of the United Church of Christ encourages a policy of non-discrimination in employment, volunteer service and membership policy with regard to sexual orientation; encourages association conferences and all related organizations to adopt a similar policy; and encourages the congregations of the United Church of Christ to adopt a non-discrimination policy and a Covenant of Openness and Affirmation of persons of lesbian, gay or bisexual orientation within the community of faith.

A RESOLUTION REGARDING CHRISTIAN SEXUAL ETHICS

Reformed Episcopal Church
Adopted at the 46th General Council
May 23, 1990
rechurch.org/sex.html

RESOLVED, that we, the 46th General Council of the Reformed Episcopal Church, reaffirm the biblical standard given for the well-being of society:

1. That sexual intercourse should take place only between a man and a woman who are married to each other.

2. That fornication, adultery, and homosexual acts are sinful in all circumstances.

3. That Christian leaders are called to be exemplary in all spheres of morality, including sexual morality, as a condition of being appointed or remaining in office.

4. That the Church is called upon to show Christ-like compassion to those who have fallen into sexual sin, encouraging them to repent and receive forgiveness, and offering the ministry of healing to all who suffer physically or emotionally as a result of such sin.

EXCERPT FROM THE STATEMENT ON HUMAN SEXUALITY

National Council of the Churches of Christ in the USA
Commission on Family Ministries and Human Sexuality Ministries in Christian Education

Adopted November 8, 1991

We affirm that . . .

The churches' response to human sexuality must include pastoral, prophetic and educational efforts to achieve sexual and spiritual wholeness in collaboration with home, school, and community.

RESOLUTION CALLING FOR DIALOGUE ON HUMAN SEXUALITY

American Baptist Churches, USA
Adopted by the General Board
June 1993
96 For, 69 Against, 3 Abstentions
Modified by the Executive Committee of the General Board
September 1998
www.abc-usa.org/resources/resol/sexual.htm

Since our founding days, we American Baptists have heralded the Bible as central to our lives. Individuals have the right and responsibility to interpret Scripture under the guidance of the Holy Spirit within the community of faith. We have also come together to seek the mind of Christ on contemporary issues, knowing that none of our corporate statements claims to speak for all of us. The time has come for our churches, Regions, National Boards, and the General Board of the American Baptist Churches, USA to consider prayerfully the mind of Christ regarding human sexuality.

Therefore, we call on American Baptists to:

1. Testify that Jesus Christ is the unifying presence in our denomination.
2. Explore the biblical and theological issues of human sexuality.
3. Consider using the resources identified and gathered by the ABC Commission on Resources on Human Sexuality.
4. Acknowledge that there exists a variety of understandings throughout our denomination on issues of human sexuality such as homosexuality and engage in dialogue concerning these issues.
5. Respect and defend the individual integrity of all persons within our denomination and their Christian commitment as we engage the issue of human sexuality.
6. Pray fervently that as we honestly address these concerns we may seek unity and avoid divisiveness as we grow in our common mission for Jesus Christ.

Regional Boards recommending and adopting this resolution:
American Baptist Churches of Connecticut (February 20, 1993)
American Baptist Churches of Massachusetts (November 21, 1992)
American Baptist Churches of Rhode Island (November 15, 1992)
American Baptist Churches of Rochester/Genesee (December 2, 1992)
Philadelphia Baptist Association (November 21, 1992)

OUR OPEN AND AFFIRMING RESOLUTION

United Church of Christ in New Brighton, Minnesota

Adopted May 1, 1994

uccnbona.homestead.com/Index.html

The United Church of Christ passed a national resolution in 1985 encouraging all UCC congregations to declare themselves open and affirming of persons of lesbian, gay and bisexual orientation. This resolution is one example of many similar resolutions passed by individual UCC congregations in the 1980s and 1990s.

On May 1, 1994, the congregation overwhelmingly adopted this resolution:

We the members of the United Church of Christ in New Brighton, declare that we are an "open and affirming" congregation of the United Church of Christ. We seek to become more open and affirming of all persons without regard to their gender, race, skin color, marital status, class, national origin, age, physical condition, mental ability, or sexual orientation. We welcome to our congregation all who seek to follow a Christian way of life and want to be part of a Christian community.

We believe that all people are created in God's image and that our value as human beings is given to us by God and that God loves everyone without exclusion. We celebrate God's wonderful gift of human sexuality and the nourishing, life-enhancing place it can have for us.

We encourage and support the developing and nurturing of relationships—sexual or not—which are characterized by mutuality and honesty, fidelity and respect, commitment and stability, love and care.

We know that, in the history of the Church and our culture, Christians and others have been very rejecting of gay, lesbian, and bi-sexual people. We believe God calls us to move away from these rejecting attitudes and actions—especially in the Church's life.

We pledge to continue the struggle toward full inclusion of all God's people into the United Church of Christ and the Church universal. We very specifically welcome Christian people of all sexual orientations to share in the life and leadership, ministry and fellowship, worship and sacraments, responsibilities of our cultural and secular organizations, our state and nation.

We commit ourselves to oppose discrimination and prejudice against gay, lesbian, and bisexual people in our attitudes and relationships, our culture and secular organizations, our state and nation.

We continue to welcome all people to share in the life of our congregation—including those who have difficulty accepting all these declarations. We are a United Church of Christ, committed to being a sign of God's open and affirming love for all people.

RESOLUTION ON HOMOSEXUAL MARRIAGE

Southern Baptist Convention
Adopted June 13, 1996
New Orleans, Louisiana
Drafted by Daniel R. Heimbach

WHEREAS, In May 1993, the Hawaiian Supreme Court ruled that the state's exclusion of same-sex couples from marital status may be contrary to the Hawaiian state constitution because it amounts to invidious discrimination; and

WHEREAS, The Hawaiian Supreme Court has instructed the state of Hawaii to prove "compelling state interests" for limiting marriage to heterosexual couples; and

WHEREAS, The instructions of the Hawaiian Supreme Court shift the burden of proof from persons seeking to change existing law and places it instead on officers of the government who support norms of conduct long established in the Western legal tradition; and

WHEREAS, The "compelling state interests" standard is extraordinarily difficult to prove before a court already disposed to regard the exclusion of same-sex relationship from the definition of marriage as a matter of invidious discrimination, and therefore the state of Hawaii is soon likely to grant full legal status to the marriage of homosexual couples; and

WHEREAS, Under the "full faith and credit" clause of the Constitution of the United States, any marriage performed in the state of Hawaii will, apart from the enactment of state-by-state exceptions or the enactment of a new and comprehensive federal law, have to be legally recognized in every other state; and

WHEREAS, Homosexual couples from every state are preparing to obtain marriage licenses in Hawaii and then to challenge the courts, legislatures and institutions in their home states to treat their same-sex relationship as having identical status to the recognition of marriages between a man and a woman; and

WHEREAS, Challenging the exclusion of homosexual couples from the definition of marriage as sanctioned and protected by civil law is a strategy to appropriate the moral capital of marriage in order to enforce acceptance of homosexual conduct and homosexual desires in the public arenas of American life; and

WHEREAS, There is much scientific evidence showing that homosexual attractions are pathological, abnormal, and mostly if not entirely a matter of external influence, learned behavior, acquired taste and personal choice; and, although there have been speculations, no conclusive scientific evidence has been found to support claims that homosexual attractions are biologically fixed and irreversible; and

WHEREAS, Even should a biological link with homosexuality be discovered, it could not settle the morality of homosexual behavior, and could not serve to justify, much less require, any society to grant the status of marriage to homosexual couples; and

WHEREAS, God, who is both Moral Ruler of the Universe and the Creator of all that is, and who knows and understands the physical and psychological composition of all and every human life better than any human scientist will ever know it, has stated in Scripture that homosexual conduct is always a gross abomination for all human beings, both men and women, in all circumstances, without exception (Leviticus 18:22 and 20:13); and

WHEREAS, God makes it clear in Scripture that even desire to engage in a homosexual sexual relationship is always sinful, impure, degrading, shameful, unnatural, indecent and perverted (Romans 1:24-27), so any effort to extend the meaning of marriage in order to sanction the satisfaction of such desire must also be in every case sinful, impure, degrading, shameful, unnatural, indecent and perverted; and

WHEREAS, God by saying "their blood will be on their own heads" (Leviticus 20:13) has explicitly ruled out any effort by homosexual couples to justify their behavior, or to claim their homosexual relationship deserves protected legal status, by shifting blame or responsibility for their same-sex relationship to the Creator who made them; and

WHEREAS, Marriage is God's idea established in the order of creation to be a permanent union of one man with one woman (Genesis 1:28, and 2:24), and marriage is therefore first and foremost a divine institution (Matthew 19:6) and only secondarily a cultural and civil institution; and

WHEREAS, Jesus reaffirmed the origin of marriage in the order of creation and declared marriage to be a sacred, monogamous, and life-long institution joining one man with one woman (Matthew 19:4-6); and

WHEREAS, Any action by the government giving homosexual unions the legal status of marriage denies the fundamental immorality of homosexual behavior and causes the government of any nation so doing to jeopardize seriously the favor of Almighty God on whom the security, welfare, and stability of every nation, even Gentile nations (Leviticus 18:24-25, 28; Psalm 2; Amos 1:3, 6, 9, 11, 13; Isaiah 13–21), ultimately depends; and

WHEREAS, Separating marriage from the complementary union of male and female trivializes the concept of marriage in the laws, public policies, educational systems, and other institutions of society; and

WHEREAS, Only the marriage of male and female serves to tame the impulses of self-centered individuals by inter-generational obligations and commitments; and

WHEREAS, Failure in the courts and institutions of civil law to recognize the unique importance of heterosexual family units, by granting moral equivalence to the idea of same-sex relationships, will surely and very seriously undercut the formation of stable heterosexual family units in future generations; and

WHEREAS, The future of the United States of America will be placed at risk because no society can survive that does not recognize, protect and defend the unique importance of heterosexual marriage to its own health and stability; and

WHEREAS, The legal recognition of homosexual marriage carries the potential use of force, a force that will likely be turned against those who do not or cannot accept the moral equivalence of homosexual marriages; and

WHEREAS, The enforcement of marriage laws, standards of educational instruction in schools, and the regulation of fair business practices will be adjusted to require public recognition of homosexual marriages, and this adjustment will certainly undermine, and may even restrain, the public communication, influence, and independence of individuals, groups, and institutions who believe and teach that homosexual marriage is immoral in both concept and practice; and

WHEREAS, Legalizing homosexual marriage will force public schools to teach the acceptability of homosexual marriage and will likely lead to laws requiring that businesses remove distinctions between homosexual and heterosexual relationships in the way they treat marriage benefits for their employees; and

WHEREAS, Legalizing homosexual marriage raises the specter of new laws and policies intended to marginalize, privatize, or silence the social and moral influence of parents and churches which teach that homosexual marriage is wrong or that heterosexual marriage is morally superior.

Be it therefore **RESOLVED,** that we, the messengers of the one hundred thirty-ninth meeting of the Southern Baptist Convention, assembled in New Orleans, Louisiana, June 11-13, 1996, do clearly and steadfastly oppose the legalization of homosexual marriage by the state of Hawaii, or by any other state, or by the United States of America; and

Be it further **RESOLVED,** that we affirm the Bible's teaching that promotion of homosexual conduct and relationships by any society, including action by the governments to sanction and legitimize homosexual relationships by the legalization of homosexual marriages, is an abominable sin calling for God's swift judgment upon any such society (Leviticus 18:22, 28; Isaiah 3:9); and

Be it further **RESOLVED,** that we commit ourselves to pray faithfully against the legalization of homosexual marriages in American law; and to preach and teach the truth concerning what the Bible says about homosexuality, homosexual conduct and the institution of marriage, and against the foolishness, danger and moral wickedness of any government action to accept, sanction, approve, protect, or promote homosexual marriage; and

Be it further **RESOLVED,** that we commit ourselves to pray for, affirm, and support legislative and legal efforts and all persons involved in efforts to oppose the legalization of homosexual marriages through judicial actions, through public policy decisions, and through legislation introduced at both the state and federal levels of government; and we call upon all judges, all persons in public office, and all candidates for public office, to do all they can to resist and oppose the legalization of homosexual marriages; and

Be it finally **RESOLVED,** that because any law, or any policy or regulation supporting a law, that legalizes homosexual marriage is and must be completely and thoroughly wicked according to God's standards revealed in the Bible, we do most solemnly pledge our decision never to recognize the moral legitimacy of any such law, policy or regulation; and we affirm that, whatever the stakes (Daniel 3:17-18), we will never conform to or obey (Acts 4:19) anything required by any governing body to implement, impose, or act upon any such law, so help us God.

A MESSAGE ON SEXUALITY: SOME COMMON CONVICTIONS

Evangelical Lutheran Church in America
Division for Church and Society

Adopted by the Church Council of the
Evangelical Lutheran Church in America
November 9, 1996
www.elca.org/dcs/sexuality.html

Messages of the Evangelical Lutheran Church in America, adopted by the Church Council, are intended to focus attention and action on timely, pressing matters of concern to this church and society. They do not establish new policy for this church, but build upon previously adopted policy positions, especially from social statements.[1]

The wider context for this message is the continuing ferment in our society regarding sexuality and sexual behavior. The more specific context is the considerable amount of discussion and debate that has occurred throughout the Evangelical Lutheran Church in America during the past few years in response to three study documents on sexuality.[2] Differences and disagreements were at times sharp, especially regarding homosexuality. Plans to present a social statement on sexuality to the 1995 Churchwide Assembly were postponed. However, these discussions also indicated that on many aspects of sexuality there are widely shared convictions. In 1995, a report to the Churchwide Assembly and an action of the Church Council called for the development of a message on sexuality addressing "those areas for which there appears to be consensus within this church."

This message builds upon predecessor church statements,[3] as well as actions of the Evangelical Lutheran Church in America. It presents some convictions regarding sexuality on which there generally seems to be theologically based agreement within this church. It is not a social statement, nor should it be seen as moving toward new policy positions. Its purpose is to provide guidance for members of our church, and as a public witness in the wider society.

GOD'S CREATION AND NEW CREATION

Scripture is the source and norm of our proclamation, faith, and life as a church. In Scripture we read that God created humankind male and female and ". . . behold it was very good" (Gen. 1:27,31). Sexuality is a mysterious, life-long aspect of human relationships. Through sexuality, human beings can experience profound joy, purpose, and unity, as well as deep pain, frustration, and division.

Human sexuality was created good for the purposes of expressing love and generating life, for mutual companionship and pleasure. Yet it has been marred by sin, which alienates us from God and others. This results in expressions of sexuality that harm persons and communities.

Because human sexuality is a powerful, primal force in personal and communal life, both church and society seek to order sexual expectations and expression. God's Law serves this purpose by providing guidance and exposing sinfulness. For example, the Ten Commandments (Ex. 20:1-17) have implications for sexuality:

- sexuality is placed in perspective (First Commandment);
- family relationships are to be honored and nurtured (Fourth Commandment);
- destructive abuses of power that harm others are prohibited (Fifth Commandment);
- marriage is upheld and supported as a sacred union and social institution (Sixth Commandment);
- truth-telling is essential in all relationships (Eighth Commandment);
- sexual desire that lures one away from spouse or family is condemned (Tenth Commandment).

Christ's death and resurrection inaugurated God's new creation. Christians enter into this new creation and "die" to sin through baptism. As Christ was raised, so we walk in newness of life (Rom. 6:1-4). As sexual beings, we are called to a life of responsible freedom in God's new creation, while still struggling with how our sexuality is captive to sin. We live in the tension between the old age of sin, bondage, and death, and the new age of the Gospel's grace, promise, and freedom.

For Christians, the human body is a "temple of the Holy Spirit" (1 Cor. 6:19-20). Living in the power of the Spirit, we are called to avoid behaviors that harm or devalue ourselves and others, such as immoral sexual behavior (1 Cor. 5:9-11; Gal. 5:19-21). Through words and actions, Christians seek to build up one another and the whole Christian community. The law of love—"you shall love your neighbor as yourself" (Rom. 13:8-10; Gal. 5:14)—binds Christians together in anticipation of the fullness of God's reign.

Through baptism, we have been received into the body of Christ and welcomed into the Lord's family.[4] God's gracious embrace through Christ is at the heart of the Church's welcome to all to participate together in its life. Mindful of the sin to which all succumb, Christians are called to:

- *respect* the integrity and dignity of all persons, whatever their age, gender, sexual orientation, or marital status;
- *discern* and provide guidance for what it means to live responsibly as sexual beings;
- *support* through prayer and counsel those facing questions about their sexuality;
- *heal* those who have been abused or violated, or whose relationships are broken.

We live in various relationships, all of which are affected by the physiological, psychological, and social aspects of our sexual identity. People of all ages need information and experience to understand and responsibly live out their sexual identity in the varied relationships of their lives—as child or parent, sister or brother, spouse, friend, co-worker, neighbor, or stranger. This church affirms the importance of ordering society and educating youth and adults so that all might live in these relationships with mutual respect and responsibility.

Single Adults

Single adults vary widely in age and life circumstances. Some persons intentionally choose to remain single, which St. Paul commended as a Christian vocation (1 Cor. 7:8, 32-35). Others yearn to be married. For many adults, singleness is a temporary period prior to marriage. Still others become single again after having been married.

The church is to be a loving, supportive community for single persons. Language and practices that demean or exclude them are to be avoided. This church seeks to be a place where, as sexual beings, single adults can find guidance for their particular spiritual, ethical, psychological, and social issues. Knowing that they are loved by God can help single persons to be accepting of themselves and others. As a community of encouragement and healing, the church's acceptance and support of single persons is important as they experience growth, change, and disappointments in their relationships.

Marriage

Marriage is a lifelong covenant of faithfulness between a man and a woman. In marriage, two persons become "one flesh" (Gen. 2:24; Matt. 19:4-6; Mark 10:6-9; Eph. 5:31), a personal and sexual union that embodies God's loving purpose to create and enrich life. By the gift of marriage God "founded human community in a joy that begins now and is brought to perfection in the life to come."[5]

Marriage provides a structure of security and stability within which spouses may fully enjoy and risk sexual expression. The binding legal contract of marriage reinforces its "staying power" when it is threatened by sin. Within marriage, spouses can learn to exercise mutual, faithful love.

Christians yearn for marriages that are loving and life-giving. In the intimacy of marriage, spouses can learn to share feelings and fears, to listen deeply, and to respect the differences of the other. Being loved and accepted by God helps them to love and accept one another. Rather than one dominating the other, each spouse seeks to empower and encourage the other.

All marriages fall short of intentions. Some marriages are not safe spaces, but places where spouses or children are abused. Intimacy and sexual pleasure often are absent. A marriage grows and changes over time through experiences of humor and playfulness, brokenness and healing, failure and accomplishment, forgiveness and renewal.

In the growth, changes, and disappointments of a marriage, the counsel and support of the Church is important. Premarital instruction can help a couple to prepare for the covenant they are entering. During the first few years of a marriage, the guidance and support of the Christian community can help a couple to adjust and set healthy patterns for their relationship. Those more recently married can learn much from those whose marriages have grown and been tested through the years. Throughout a marriage, the ministry of the Church should assist the couple to discern and address their shortcomings, and to seek forgiveness, reconciliation, and new life.

The purpose of marriage goes beyond the intimacy and companionship it provides the couple. The wider community is symbolically present when a couple publicly exchanges vows. Witnesses pledge to support the marriage, and those exchanging vows are reminded that their marriage will affect the wider community. They are to extend themselves for the sake of others.

Responsible Procreation and Parenting

Conceiving, bearing, adopting, and rearing children can be wondrous and challenging ways through which a couple participates in God's creation and new creation. Sexual intercourse between a woman and a man can bring into being the mystery of a new human life. New reproductive technologies have opened further possibilities for conceiving and bearing children. Yet, such technologies also pose complex ethical questions.[6] This church seeks to be a community that provides spiritual support and assists persons in their deliberations on these matters.

When a woman and man join their bodies sexually, both should be prepared to provide for a child, should conception occur. When that is not their intention, the responsible use of safe, effective contraceptives is expected of the male and the female.[7] Respect and sensitivity should also be shown toward couples who do not feel called to conceive and/or rear children, or who are unable to do so.

As children and youth grow in their baptismal identity, it is important that they learn to love and respect one another and the power of their sexuality. Youth need the support and guidance of the church to resist cultural and peer pressures that encourage sexual intercourse prior to marriage. Open and honest discussion of sexual questions is to be encouraged, in ways that communicate God's guidance, forgiveness, and ongoing care. As a church, we affirm the importance of education about sexuality that emphasizes respect, mutuality, responsibility, and abstinence outside of marriage. Such education should begin in the home, and continue in congregations, schools, and other community settings.

Rearing children requires a stable, secure environment of emotional, social, spiritual, and material support and nurture. Good child rearing can occur in different parenting arrangements; it is most likely to occur in the context of an enduring, loving marriage with the support of extended family, congregation, and community. If a marriage ends, both parents carry continuing responsibility for the well-being of their children.

The Ending of a Marriage

Regrettably, some marriages end in divorce. Divorce is tragic, a consequence of human sinfulness. It is a serious breach in the community God intends for marriage (Mark 10:9). In some situations, however, divorce may be the better option.

Continuing some marriages may be destructive and abusive to those involved. In such cases, those involved should examine their responsibilities for the breakdown of the marriage. Confession and God's forgiveness bring healing and new life to persons who divorce.

The church is called to proclaim God's intention for the permanence of marriage and to minister compassionately to those who suffer as a result of divorce. The church should be a community of care and hope for those who divorce, rather than blaming, ostracizing, or being indifferent to their needs.

The Gospel promises healing through the Holy Spirit's presence in the Church's ministry of Word and Sacraments.

Remarriage can be an opportunity to use wisdom gained from the past to create a new relationship of loving commitment and joy. Those considering remarriage should seek counsel from pastors and other professionals that enables them to assess their previous marriage and prepare for the unique challenges facing a new marriage and family.

SOME MISUSES OF SEXUALITY

Sin violates what God intends for sexuality. It harms and demeans persons and relationships. This church opposes . . .

Adultery

In adultery, one abandons the sacred commitment made to a spouse and becomes sexually intimate with another person. Adultery is sinful because it breaks the trust between two people, disrupts their bond of marriage, and violates the partner. When it is secretive, it also can involve deceitfulness, lying, and hypocrisy. Only repentance, honest work, forgiveness, reconciliation, and the power of the Holy Spirit can heal such wounds.

Abuse

Abuse can be physical, verbal, psychological, or emotional. Sexual abuse is the sinful use of power to dominate or control another person sexually. Victims of abuse are vulnerable because of their age, status, and emotional or physical condition. All forms of abuse are sinful—whether heterosexual or homosexual, whether by a spouse, family member, person in authority, date, acquaintance, or stranger. Rape and other forms of nonconsensual sexual activity are sinful—whether this occurs in the home, on a date, at work, on the street, or in prison. Coercion, threats, intimidation, and manipulation are inappropriate responses to "no."

Trust and confidence are betrayed when a person of greater age or status manipulates one who is younger or more vulnerable to engage in sexual acts. Such acts are not mutual because of the power differences involved. This includes the sexual abuse of children and the sexual exploitation of clients by professionals or parishioners by clergy. Those who engage in such conduct sin against God and against the persons who are their victims. Sexual harassment is another way sexuality is used to hurt or control. Harassing words or behavior interfere with wholesome interaction and create an offensive, hostile, or intimidating environment in which to work, learn, live, or worship. All forms of verbal or physical harassment are sinful and must be confronted.

Promiscuity

Having casual sexual relations is sinful because this does not proceed from or contribute to respect, intimacy, and care of the other. Promiscuity is inconsistent with our identity as Christians (1 Cor. 6:12-20). Being sexually active in order to be popular or only to gratify sexual desire is morally wrong.

Prostitution

Prostitution is sinful because it involves the casual buying and selling of "sex," often in demeaning and exploitative ways. Prostitutes and their patrons endanger their own health and that of others. Prostitution usually arises from and contributes to a cycle of personal, economic, and social difficulties. This church abhors the dramatic global rise in "sex traffic" of young girls and boys, who are exploited sexually for the sake of economic gain.

Practices that Spread Sexually-Transmitted Diseases

Irresponsible, unprotected sexual contact can expose sexual partners to incurable and fatal sexually-transmitted diseases. Sexual practices that result in physical harm to another are sinful and must be countered. Education about sexuality should emphasize monogamy, abstinence, and responsible sexual behavior, as well as practices intended to prevent the transmission of disease during sexual intercourse. This church supports efforts to prevent, cure, and care for those afflicted with such diseases.[8]

Pornography

Pornography is sinful because it depicts sexuality in ways that are violent and/or demeaning. It asserts that sexual pleasure comes from humiliating, exploiting, or breaking down a person's resistance. Human beings are treated as objects of lust. Those who pose for such material, those who view it, and the general public become the victims of pornography.[9] Positive depictions of human sexuality, acceptance of one's own sexuality, and the cultivation of healthy sexual attitudes help to resist the lures of pornography.

Sexuality in Media and Advertising

Much of the media today contains explicit sexual references and behavior emphasizing sexual gratification apart from marriage. Damaging stereotypes of male and female sexuality also are perpetuated. Advertisers use the allure of sexuality to sell products. Sexuality becomes captive to the interests of money, power, and social status. Such manipulation of sexuality is sinful and opposed by this church. This church encourages the media to communicate expressions of sexuality that honor marriage and promote mutual respect, responsibility, and commitment to one another.

Although this church vigorously opposes the abuse of sexuality, not everything considered sinful should necessarily be made a civil offense.[10] This church supports policies and laws that foster justice, mercy, equality of opportunity, and the protection of basic human rights.[11]

The Sustaining Power of God's Grace

As Lutheran Christians, we seek God's will for sexual expression while also keeping the grace of God at the heart of our common life. This means undertaking all of our commitments to each other—including sexual relationships—with a sense of our life as a gift, with God's help to keep our promises, and with a deep sense of the sin that persists. The mercies of God continually sustain and undercut any simple division of the righteous from the unrighteous (Rom. 1:18–3:20).

On some matters of sexuality, there are strong and continuing differences among us. As we discuss areas where we differ, the power of the Holy Spirit can guide and unite us. Trust in the Gospel brings together people whose differences over sexuality ought not be a basis for division. We pray for the grace to avoid unfair judgment of those with whom we differ, the patience to listen to those with whom we disagree, and the love to reach out to those from whom we may be divided.

To a world obsessed with sexual self-fulfillment, divided by differences over sexuality, and weary of how sexuality is abused, the message of the grace of God lightens our burdens, lifts our spirits, renews our commitments, and reminds us of the deepest basis for mutual respect—the love of God we have in Jesus Christ.

NOTES

1. From "Messages on Social Issues," as adopted by the ELCA Church Council in 1989.
2. "Human Sexuality and the Christian Faith" [a study] (ELCA Division for Church in Society, 1991); "The Church and Human Sexuality: A Lutheran Perspective" [first draft of a social statement] (ELCA Division for Church in Society, 1993); "Human Sexuality: Working Draft" [a possible social statement] (ELCA Division for Church in Society, 1994). See also, "A Collection of Responses from ELCA Academicians and Synodical Bishops to 'The Church and Human Sexuality: A Lutheran Perspective'" (ELCA Division for Church in Society, 1994). None of the above documents has been adopted by the Evangelical Lutheran Church in America.
3. "Sex, Marriage, and Family" (Lutheran Church in America, 1970); "Human Sexuality and Sexual Behavior" (The American Lutheran Church, 1980); "Teachings and Practice on Marriage, Divorce, and Remarriage" (The American Lutheran Church, 1982).
4. "Holy Baptism," *Lutheran Book of Worship* (Minneapolis: Augsburg; Philadelphia: Board of Publication, 1978), 125.
5. "Marriage," *Lutheran Book of Worship,* 203.

6. In separate pamphlets of the *Procreation Ethics Series* (1986), individual authors raise some considerations related to artificial insemination, prenatal diagnosis, in vitro fertilization, and surrogate motherhood. (Copies are available from the Department for Studies of the ELCA Division for Church in Society.)
7. "Abortion," a social statement of the Evangelical Lutheran Church in America (1991).
8. See the *ELCA Message*, "AIDS and the Church's Ministry of Caring" (1989).
9. "Pornography," a social statement of The American Lutheran Church (1985).
10. This distinction has been made in many Lutheran documents, such as, "Abortion" (1991).
11. "Human Sexuality and Sexual Behavior," 7.

THE KUALA LUMPUR STATEMENT ON HUMAN SEXUALITY

2nd Anglican Encounter in the South
Adopted 10-15 February, 1997
www.episcopalian.org/efac/articles/kuala.htm

Note: What follows is the text of a statement adopted by the 2nd Anglican Encounter in the South which met in Kuala Lumpur, Malaysia, from February 10-15, 1997. The Encounter was led by the Most Reverend Joseph A. Adetiloye, Archbishop of Nigeria. 80 delegates, who were bishops and archbishops representing between 80 and 90 percent of all the Anglicans in the world, passed this statement unanimously.

1. God's glory and loving purposes have been revealed in the creation of humankind (Rom. 1:18; Gen. 1:26, 27). Among the multiplicity of his gifts we are blessed with our sexuality.

2. Since the Fall (Genesis 3), life has been impaired and God's purposes spoilt. Our fallen state has affected every sphere of our being, which includes our sexuality. Sexual deviation has existed in every time and in most cultures. Jesus' teaching about lust in the Sermon on the Mount (Matt. 5:27-30) makes it clear that sexual sin is a real danger and temptation to us all.

3. It is, therefore, with an awareness of our own vulnerability to sexual sin that we express our profound concern about recent developments relating to Church discipline and moral teaching in some provinces in the North—specifically, the ordination of practicing homosexuals and the blessing of same-sex unions.

4. While acknowledging the complexities of our sexual nature and the strong drives it places within us, we are quite clear about God's will in this area which is expressed in the Bible.

5. The Scripture bears witness to God's will regarding human sexuality which is to be expressed only within the lifelong union of a man and a woman in holy matrimony.

6. The Holy Scriptures are clear in teaching that all sexual promiscuity is sin. We are convinced that this includes homosexual practices between men or women, as well as heterosexual relationships outside of marriage.

7. We believe that the clear and unambiguous teaching of the Holy Scriptures about human sexuality is of great help to Christians as it provides clear boundaries.

8. We find no conflict between clear biblical teaching and sensitive pastoral care. Repentance precedes forgiveness and is part of the healing process. To heal spiritual wounds in God's name we need his wisdom and truth. We see this in the ministry of Jesus, for example his response to the adulterous woman, ". . . neither do I condemn you. Go and sin no more" (John 8:11).

9. We encourage the Church to care for all those who are trapped in their sexual brokenness and to become the channel of Christ's compassion and love towards them. We wish to stand alongside and welcome them into a process of being whole and restored within our communities of faith. We would also affirm and resource those who exercise a pastoral ministry in this area.

10. We are deeply concerned that the setting aside of biblical teaching in such actions as the ordination of practicing homosexuals and the blessing of same-sex unions calls into question the authority of the Holy Scriptures. This is totally unacceptable to us.

11. This leads us to express concern about mutual accountability and interdependence within our Anglican Communion. As provinces and dioceses, we need to learn how to seek each other's counsel and wisdom in a spirit of true unity, and to reach a common mind before embarking on radical changes to Church discipline and moral teaching.

12. We live in a global village and must be more aware that the way we act in one part of the world can radically affect the mission and witness of the Church.

RESOLUTION ON DOMESTIC PARTNER BENEFITS

Southern Baptist Convention
Adopted June 19, 1997
Dallas, Texas
Drafted by
Daniel R. Heimbach

WHEREAS, An increasing number of businesses, including corporate leaders such as IBM, AT&T, Sprint, Hewlett Packard, Xerox, Time Warner, Microsoft, Eastman Kodak, and Walt Disney, have established employee policies that recognize and extend employee benefits to a category of personal relationship called "domestic partner"; and

WHEREAS, The category called "domestic partner" is a strategy to promote acceptance of the idea that homosexual relationships are morally equivalent to heterosexual relationships involving a man and a woman bound together by the institution of marriage; and

WHEREAS, The provision of domestic partnership benefits is a way to promote the moral equivalence of homosexual relationships outside the political and legal system in states where established marriage and family laws do not recognize the legitimacy of homosexual marriage; and

WHEREAS, Providing domestic partnership benefits not only promotes the idea that homosexual relationships are morally legitimate but, at the same time, trivializes the meaning and sanctity of marriage; and

WHEREAS, God at creation made marriage a permanent union of one man with one woman (Gen. 1:28 and 2:24), and Jesus reaffirmed the origin of marriage in the order of creation and declared marriage to be a sacred, monogamous and life-long institution joining two persons of the opposite gender (Matt. 19:46); and

WHEREAS, God the Creator and Judge of all, has ruled that homosexual conduct is always a gross moral and spiritual abomination for any person, whether male or female, under any circumstance, without exception (Lev. 18:22 and 20:13); and

WHEREAS, Businesses that recognize the moral legitimacy of homosexual relationships by extending benefits to "domestic partners" are, at the same time and by the same action, rejecting God's true revelation regarding the sinfulness of homosexual conduct and the unique sanctity of heterosexual marriage;

BE IT THEREFORE RESOLVED, That we, the messengers of the Southern Baptist Convention, assembled in Dallas, Texas, June 17-19, 1997, oppose steadfastly the practice of extending employee benefits to domestic partnerships; and

BE IT FURTHER RESOLVED, That we prayerfully affirm those individual business leaders and businesses that either resist pressures to recognize the moral equivalence of domestic partnerships, or that work to reverse policies that erase fundamental and morally critical distinctions between homosexual relationships and heterosexual marriage; and

BE IT FINALLY RESOLVED, That we call upon business leaders to treat employees living in homosexual relationships in a manner commensurate with the love of Jesus Christ—who, though He recognized the value and dignity of individual sinners (Matt. 9:13), neither condoned nor excused the abnormality and immorality of their sin (John 8:11); rather He called them to repent, change and be restored (Luke 15:7, 10, 32) through the life-changing power of the indwelling Holy Spirit (Gal. 2:20; 1 Cor. 6:9-11).

A CALL TO AFFIRMATION, CONFESSION, AND COVENANT REGARDING HUMAN SEXUALITY

New York Mennonite Conference
Adopted September 27, 1997
bfn.org/~nymennon/humansex.htm

A Call to Affirmation

We affirm that sexuality is a good and beautiful gift of God, a gift of identity, and a way of being in the world as male and female. Genesis 1:26-31

We affirm that we can feel positive about our bodies and our sexuality because we are created in God's image and know our Creator. Genesis 2:25

We affirm that sexual drives are part of our lives, but that the satisfaction of those drives is not the chief good in life. 1 Corinthians 6:13

We affirm the goodness of singleness, marriage, and family in the Lord. 1 Corinthians 7:25-40; Proverbs 18:22; Genesis 2:18

We affirm that God intends marriage to be a covenant between one man and one woman for life, and that sexual relations outside this bond are sinful. Mark 10:7-9; 1 Corinthians 7:10- 11; 1 Corinthians 6:9

A Call to Confession

We confess that our sexual attitudes and practices too often fall short of the biblical standards. No one can boast of perfection in this area. Matthew 5:27-28; Colossians 3:5

We confess that sexist attitudes are among us where one gender is given more value than the other, damaging the self-esteem of people, hindering their full contribution to personal and broader relationships, allowing domestic violence, and limiting our ability to accept and affirm who we are in Christ. Acts 2:17-18; Galatians 3:26-28; Ephesians 5:21-30

We repent of attitudes toward the body, God's temple, which keep us from speaking appropriately and honestly about our bodies, including our sexual nature. Genesis 1:27; Song of Songs; 1 Corinthians 6:19-20

We repent of our self-righteous attitudes and our slowness to forgive sexual and moral failure. We confess our need of God's wisdom and grace when differences of

Biblical interpretation arise regarding questions of morality and sexual values. 2 Corinthians 2:6-8 (re: 1 Corinthians 5:1-5); Luke 17:3-4; Philippians 1:9-11

We confess our fear and repent of our absence of love and our lack of empathy toward those with a different sexual orientation. We also confess our tendency to focus on homosexuality to the neglect of more common sexual sins among us.

A Call to Covenant

We covenant with each other to study the Bible together and expand our insight into the biblical teachings relating to sexuality. We understand the Bible to teach that sexual relations are reserved for a man and a woman united in a marriage covenant. It is our understanding that this teaching does not allow premarital, extramarital, and same-gender sexual activity. We understand the Bible to teach the sanctity of the marriage covenant and that any violation of this covenant, emotional or sexual, is sin. We understand the Bible to condemn same-sex intercourse wherever it is mentioned.

We covenant with each other to mutually bear the burden of remaining in loving dialogue with each other in the body of Christ, recognizing that we are all sinners in need of God's grace and that the Holy Spirit may lead us to further truth and repentance. We promise compassion and prayer for each other that distrustful, broken, and sinful relationships may experience God's healing.

We covenant with each other to take part in the ongoing search for discernment and for openness to each other. As a part of the nurture of individuals and congregations we will promote congregational study of the complex issues of sexuality, through Bible study and other resource materials.

Finally, we covenant that as we discern God's will for our lives and our fellowship, we will seek to obey it through God's grace and strength. Our prayer is that we will allow the Holy Spirit to work within us as we relate with understanding to persons with varied needs and concerns in our church.

STATEMENT ON HUMAN SEXUALITY

Anglican Bishops of Canada
Adopted October, 1997
www.wfn.org/1997/11/msg00048.html

THE BACKGROUND

In 1976 the House of Bishops of the Anglican Church of Canada sought advice as it faced the issue of homosexuality in contemporary society and how the church ought to relate pastorally, and in terms of ordination. A task force presented a lengthy report to the bishops. By 1979 the bishops had committed themselves to further study and they requested the preparation of study materials to help further discussion at all levels of the church. These materials were published in 1985. In 1979, as an interim measure, the bishops issued a statement based on the following belief:

> We believe as Christians, that homosexual persons, as children of God, have a full and equal claim with all other persons, upon the love, acceptance, concern and pastoral care of the Church.

As well, the Bishops issued a four point pastoral guideline for themselves as they considered the admission of individual persons to the church's ordained ministry.

1. Our present and future considerations about homosexuality should be pursued within the larger study of human sexuality in its totality;
2. We accept all persons, regardless of sexual orientation, as equal before God; our acceptance of persons with homosexual orientation is not an acceptance of homosexual activity;
3. We do not accept the blessing of homosexual unions;
4. We will not call into question the ordination of a person who has shared with the bishop his/her homosexual orientation if there has been a commitment to the Bishop to abstain from sexual acts with persons of the same sex as part of the requirement for ordination.

In referring to this guideline in the press, Archbishop Scott, Primate of the Anglican Church of Canada at that time said, "Our statement is not meant to be, in any way, legislation or a final doctrinal statement. It is a pastoral statement and we intend it to assist us in the exercise of our pastoral ministry within the Church." The house held a number of study sessions on the topic of human sexuality through the 1980's. In 1991 a new task force was constituted by the Primate. At the General Synod of 1992 a major block of time was devoted to an open forum on the topic. More materials were made available for study and by 1994/1995 approximately 170 groups and 2500 people had used the study guide Hearing Diverse Voices, Seeking Common Ground.

At the 1995 General Synod, an important report was presented, following a hearing, which lead to a motion being presented and strongly supported which:

> Affirmed the presence and contributions of gay men and lesbians in the life of the church and condemned bigotry, violence and hatred directed toward any due to their sexual orientation.

This report recommended among other things, that the process of dialogue continue; that all of us should, "learn and reflect more about our sexuality as a whole," and that the dialogue should be extended so that the, "whole church family has an opportunity to be involved." The Faith Worship and Ministry Committee of the ACC was given a mandate to provide leadership to the church to ensure a continuation of the dialogue.

All of this effort has fostered a greater understanding of what it is to be a gay man or lesbian in the church and a heightened sense of pastoral concern on the part of the church. Also, as gay men and lesbians have found greater acceptance in the church, they have been enabled to share their experiences in a more public way to the benefit of the whole church which has become increasingly aware of the breadth and depth of their contribution.

At its April 1997 meeting, discussing this topic for the first time in open session, the House of Bishops continued its deliberations and requested the task force to redraft the 1979 guideline in the light of new pastoral awareness while at the same time retaining the original intent of the guideline. In undertaking this task we seek to articulate how far we have come, as well as to acknowledge those areas where continued study and dialogue is necessary. Theological reflection and pastoral action in the Church since 1979 have focused on four key areas, and it is these that shape our considerations in this statement. The church has reflected on the place of gay and lesbian persons in society; the place of gay and lesbian persons in the church; the significance of committed sexually active relationships between people of the same sex and the significance of such relationships for ordination of gay and lesbian persons.

Gay and Lesbian Persons in Society

As Christians we believe that homosexual persons are created in the image and likeness of God and have a full and equal claim with all other persons upon the love, acceptance, concern and care of the church. As an expression of this love and care, the Gospel of Jesus Christ compels Christians to oppose all forms of human injustice and to affirm that all persons are brothers and sisters for whom Christ died. It is on the basis of these theological insights, which remain pertinent irrespective of any considerations of the appropriateness or otherwise of homosexual acts, that the Anglican Church of Canada has affirmed that gay and lesbian persons are entitled to equal protection under the law with all other Canadian citizens. Thus, this House supported the passage of bill C-33 that made sexual orientation a prohibited ground for discrimination under the Canadian Charter of Rights and Freedoms. We call upon the church and all its members to continue to work to safeguard the freedom, dignity and responsibility of every person and to seek an end to discrimination.

Gay and Lesbian Persons in the Church

We are thankful to see a new sensitivity emerging towards gay and lesbian persons in the Church. No longer can we talk in the abstract. We are experiencing a growing awareness that the persons of whom we speak are here among us. They are our sons and daughters. They are our friends and relatives. This recognition has not always been present. The story of the Church's attitude to gay and lesbian people has too often been one of standing at a distance, even of prejudice, ignorance and oppression. All of us need to acknowledge this, and to repent for any part we may have had in creating it.

In our baptism we covenant to seek and serve Christ in all persons. We now call the church to reaffirm the mutuality of that covenant, a covenant that encourages and enables us to love others as Christ loves us. This covenant will no longer allow us to regard those among us whose orientation is homosexual simply as "needy objects" for pastoral care. Instead we are partners, celebrating together the dignity of every human being, and reaching out together for the wholeness offered to us in the Gospel. The church affirms its traditional teaching that only the sexual union of male and female can find appropriate expression within the covenant of Holy Matrimony. However, we recognize that some homosexuals live in committed sexual relationships for mutual support, help and comfort. We wish to continue open and respectful dialogue with those who sincerely believe that sexuality expressed within a committed homosexual relationship is God's call to them, and we affirm our common desire to seek together the fullness of life revealed in Christ.

Blessing of Covenanted Relationships

We continue to believe that committed same sex relationships should not be confused with Holy Matrimony. The house will not authorize any act that appears to promote this confusion. There is, and needs to be, ongoing discussion about how to respond appropriately to faithful and committed same sex relationships. In the context of the ongoing debate, this would necessitate respectful listening and learning about the nature of such relationships and their meaning for the persons involved in them. We recognize that relationships of mutual support, help and comfort between homosexual persons exist and are to be preferred to relationships that are anonymous and transient. We disagree among ourselves whether such relationships can be expressions of God's will and purpose.

While consensus may be unlikely in the near future, we believe that study and dialogue continue to be fruitful. As we continue to listen together to scripture, tradition, and reasoned argument based on the experience of the Church, including and especially the experience of its gay and lesbian members, we grow in our recognition that our disagreements reflect our attempts to be faithful to the Gospel in our different personal and pastoral contexts. As long as such dialogue continues to be fruitful we believe it should continue. We are not ready to authorize the blessing of relationships between persons of the same sex. However, in interpreting the Gospel, we must always reflect on the context to which it is addressed. We are, therefore, committed to ongoing study of human sexuality and of the nature and characteristics of human intimacy and family life as it exists in our society.

Ordination of Gay and Lesbian Persons

Among our clergy there are some who are gay or lesbian. Their ministries are often highly dedicated and greatly blessed. God has endowed them with many intellectual and spiritual gifts and we give thanks for their ministries. We reaffirm that sexual orientation in and of itself is not a barrier to ordination or the practice of ministry within the church. Within the wider parameters of suitability, it is the manner in which sexuality is expressed that must be considered. Our intimate relationships are an expression of the most profound possibilities for human relationships, including our relationship with God (Eph. 5:32). At ordination, candidates promise to live their lives and shape their relationships so as to provide a "wholesome example" to the people of God (BCP, 642). Exemplary behaviour for persons who are not married includes a commitment to remain chaste.

Conclusion

Our discussions over the past few years have taught us much. We do not have a common mind on all things. We see in part and we know in part. Where we disagree we need to continue to read the scriptures together and to engage in dialogue, that we might listen for what the Spirit is saying to the Church today.

RESOLUTION 1:10: HUMAN SEXUALITY

International Anglican Communion
1998 Lambeth Conference
Adopted August 5, 1998
Passed 526 Yes; 70 No; 45 Abstain
www.anglicancommunion.org/lambeth/1/sect1rpt.html

This Conference:

I. commends to the Church the subsection report on human sexuality;

II. in view of the teaching of Scripture, upholds faithfulness in marriage between a man and a woman in lifelong union, and believes that abstinence is right for those who are not called to marriage;

III. recognizes that there are among us persons who experience themselves as having a homosexual orientation. Many of these are members of the Church and are seeking the pastoral care, moral direction of the Church, and God's transforming power for the living of their lives and the ordering of relationships. We commit ourselves to listen to the experience of homosexual persons and we wish to assure them that they are loved by God and that all baptized, believing and faithful persons, regardless of sexual orientation, are full members of the Body of Christ;

IV. while rejecting homosexual practice as incompatible with Scripture, calls on all our people to minister pastorally and sensitively to all irrespective of sexual orientation and to condemn the irrational fear of homosexuals, violence within marriage and any trivialization and commercialization of sex;

V. cannot advise the legitimizing or blessing same sex unions nor ordaining those involved in same gender unions;

VI. requests the Primates and the ACC to establish a means of monitoring the work done on the subject of human sexuality in the Communion and to share statements and resources among us.

VII. notes the significance of the Kuala Lumpur Statement on Human Sexuality and the concerns expressed in Resolutions IV.26, V.l, V.lO, V.23 and V.35 on the authority of Scripture in matters of marriage and sexuality and asks the Primates and the ACC to include them in their monitoring process.

RELIGIOUS DECLARATION ON SEXUAL MORALITY, JUSTICE, AND HEALING

Sexuality Information and Education Council of the United States
Issued January 18, 2000
www.religiousinstitute.org/declaration.html

This declaration was developed by the Sexuality Information and Education Council of the United States (SIECUS) and circulated for religious endorsement. The Religious Declaration on Sexual Morality, Justice, and Healing is not copyrighted and can be duplicated without permission.

Sexuality is God's life-giving and life-fulfilling gift. We come from diverse religious communities to recognize sexuality as central to our humanity and as integral to our spirituality. We are speaking out against the pain, brokenness, oppression, and loss of meaning that many experience about their sexuality.

Our faith traditions celebrate the goodness of creation, including our bodies and our sexuality. We sin when this sacred gift is abused or exploited. However, the great promise of our traditions is love, healing, and restored relationships.

Our culture needs a sexual ethic focused on personal relationships and social justice rather than particular sexual acts. All persons have the right and responsibility to lead sexual lives that express love, justice, mutuality, commitment, consent, and pleasure. Grounded in respect for the body and for the vulnerability that intimacy brings, this ethic fosters physical, emotional, and spiritual health. It accepts no double standards and applies to all persons, without regard to sex, gender, color, age, bodily condition, marital status, or sexual orientation.

God hears the cries of those who suffer from the failure of religious communities to address sexuality. We are called today to see, hear, and respond to the suffering caused by violence against women and sexual minorities, the HIV pandemic, unsustainable population growth and over-consumption, and the commercial exploitation of sexuality.

Faith communities must therefore be truth seeking, courageous, and just.

We call for:

- Theological reflection that integrates the wisdom of excluded, often silenced peoples, and insights about sexuality from medicine, social science, the arts and humanities.

- Full inclusion of women and sexual minorities in congregational life, including their ordination and the blessing of same sex unions.
- Sexuality counseling and education throughout the life-span from trained religious leaders.
- Support for those who challenge sexual oppression and who work for justice within their congregations and denomination.

Faith communities must also advocate for sexual and spiritual wholeness in society. We call for:

- Lifelong, age appropriate sexuality education in schools, seminaries, and community settings.
- A faith-based commitment to sexual and reproductive rights, including access to voluntary contraception, abortion, and HIV/STD prevention and treatment.
- Religious leadership in movements to end sexual and social injustice.

God rejoices when we celebrate our sexuality with holiness and integrity. We, the undersigned, invite our colleagues and faith communities to join us in promoting sexual morality, justice, and healing.

CLARIFICATION REGARDING SAME-SEX BLESSINGS AND ONGOING DELIBERATION CONCERNING HOMOSEXUALITY

Evangelical Lutheran Church in America
Office of the Presiding Bishop
Issued May 2000
www.elca.org/ob/samesex.html

The Evangelical Lutheran Church in America upholds heterosexual marriage as the appropriate context for intimate sexual expression. The ELCA's 1996 message, Sexuality: Some Common Convictions, stated:

> Marriage is a lifelong covenant of faithfulness between a man and a woman. In marriage, two persons become "one flesh," a personal and sexual union that embodies God's loving purpose to create and enrich life. By the gift of marriage God "founded human community in a joy that begins now and is brought to perfection in the life to come."

In 1993, the ELCA's Conference of Bishops stated:

> We, as the Conference of Bishops of the Evangelical Lutheran Church in America, recognize that there is basis neither in Scripture nor tradition for the establishment of an official ceremony by this church for the blessing of a homosexual relationship. We, therefore, do not approve such a ceremony as an official action of this church's ministry. Nevertheless, we express trust in and will continue dialogue with those pastors and congregations who are in ministry with gay and lesbian persons, and affirm their desire to explore the best ways to provide pastoral care for all to whom they minister.

Recent synodical actions do not change the ELCA's stance upholding marriage.

In 1999, the Churchwide Assembly (this church's highest legislative authority) called upon all members and congregations to continue dialogue regarding homosexuality. The assembly voted:

> continue discerning conversations about homosexuality and the inclusion of gay and lesbian persons in our common life and mission and to encourage churchwide units, synods, congregations, and members of this church to participate in thoughtful, deliberate, and prayerful conversations

through use of such resources as "Talking about Homosexuality—A Guide for Congregations."

To reaffirm 1991 and 1995 actions of the Churchwide Assembly of the Evangelical Lutheran Church in America that "Gay and lesbian people, as individuals created by God, are welcome to participate fully in the life of the congregations of the Evangelical Lutheran Church in America." [excerpts from CA99.06.27]

ARTICLES ON "THE CHRISTIAN AND THE SOCIAL ORDER" AND ON "THE FAMILY"

THE BAPTIST FAITH AND MESSAGE
Southern Baptist Convention
Version Adopted June 14, 2000
www.sbc.net/bfm/bfm2000.asp

XV. THE CHRISTIAN AND THE SOCIAL ORDER

All Christians are under obligation to seek to make the will of Christ supreme in our own lives and in human society. Means and methods used for the improvement of society and the establishment of righteousness among men can be truly and permanently helpful only when they are rooted in the regeneration of the individual by the saving grace of God in Jesus Christ. In the spirit of Christ, Christians should oppose racism, every form of greed, selfishness, and vice, and all forms of sexual immorality, including adultery, homosexuality, and pornography. We should work to provide for the orphaned, the needy, the abused, the aged, the helpless, and the sick. We should speak on behalf of the unborn and contend for the sanctity of all human life from conception to natural death. Every Christian should seek to bring industry, government, and society as a whole under the sway of the principles of righteousness, truth, and brotherly love. In order to promote these ends Christians should be ready to work with all men of good will in any good cause, always being careful to act in the spirit of love without compromising their loyalty to Christ and His truth.

Exodus 20:3-17; Leviticus 6:2-5; Deuteronomy 10:12; 27:17; Psalm 101:5; Micah 6:8; Zechariah 8:16; Matthew 5:13-16, 43-48; 22:36-40; 25:35; Mark 1:29-34; 2:3ff.; 10:21; Luke 4:18-21; 10:27-37; 20:25; John 15:12; 17:15; Romans 12–14; 1 Corinthians 5:9-10; 6:1-7; 7:20-24; 10:23–11:1; Galatians 3:26-28; Ephesians 6:5-9; Colossians 3:12-17; 1 Thessalonians 3:12; Philemon; James 1:27; 2:8.

XVIII. THE FAMILY

God has ordained the family as the foundational institution of human society. It is composed of persons related to one another by marriage, blood, or adoption.

Marriage is the uniting of one man and one woman in covenant commitment for a lifetime. It is God's unique gift to reveal the union between Christ and His church and to provide for the man and the woman in marriage the framework for intimate companionship, the channel of sexual expression according to biblical standards, and the means for procreation of the human race.

The husband and wife are of equal worth before God, since both are created in God's image. The marriage relationship models the way God relates to His people. A husband is to love his wife as Christ loved the church. He has the God-given responsibility to provide for, to protect, and to lead his family. A wife is to submit herself graciously to the servant leadership of her husband even as the church willingly submits to the headship of Christ. She, being in the image of God as is her husband and thus equal to him, has the God-given responsibility to respect her husband and to serve as his helper in managing the household and nurturing the next generation.

Children, from the moment of conception, are a blessing and heritage from the Lord. Parents are to demonstrate to their children God's pattern for marriage. Parents are to teach their children spiritual and moral values and to lead them, through consistent lifestyle example and loving discipline, to make choices based on biblical truth. Children are to honor and obey their parents.

Genesis 1:26-28; 2:15-25; 3:1-20; Exodus 20:12; Deuteronomy 6:4-9; Joshua 24:15; 1 Samuel 1:26-28; Psalms 51:5; 78:1-8; 127; 128; 139:13-16; Proverbs 1:8; 5:15-20; 6:20-22; 12:4; 13:24; 14:1; 17:6; 18:22; 22:6, 15; 23:13-14; 24:3; 29:15, 17; 31:10-31; Ecclesiastes 4:9-12; 9:9; Malachi 2:14-16; Matthew 5:31-32; 18:2-5; 19:3-9; Mark 10:6-12; Romans 1:18-32; 1 Corinthians 7:1-16; Ephesians 5:21-33; 6:1-4; Colossians 3:18-21; 1 Timothy 5:8,14; 2 Timothy 1:3-5; Titus 2:3-5; Hebrews 13:4; 1 Peter 3:1-7.

RELIGIOUS DECLARATION ON HUMAN SEXUALITY

Mastering Life Ministries
Issued Fall 2000
www.MasteringLife.org
www.gospelcom.net/mlm/declaration/declaration.htm

Developed by Mastering Life Ministries to counter the influence of the Religious Declaration on Sexual Morality, Justice, and Healing developed and issued by the Sexuality Information and Education Council of the United States (SIECUS). Mastering Life Ministries is an interdenominational, nonprofit Christian ministry seeking to reach people caught in sexual sin.

Human sexual (genital) behavior is intended by God to be expressed solely within the confines of heterosexual, monogamous marriage. Since God is love, sexual activity can only be considered a true act of love when carried out within these parameters, clearly established by God in His Holy Word (the Bible).

Sexual intercourse is to be the same giving act that it represents—which is Jesus Christ's union with His Bride, the Church. It is two becoming one flesh—physically, spiritually and emotionally—the ultimate end of the separating of Eve from Adam's side.

It is a procreative and pleasure-giving act that may bear the fruit of children. It is a cause for the continuation of the human race and a bonding agent for the love shared between husband and wife. When done out of love by two spiritually healthy human beings, it will enhance the well-being and solidify the growing oneness of man and wife.

God purposed in creation that human sexual interaction be a reflection of that ultimate marriage to which He has called us—that between God and man / between Christ and the Church.

Just as God remains faithful, undivided and undeflected from His commitment to man, so this central act in marriage must remain equally faithful, undivided and undeflected—exemplifying the love, the trust and the commitment of a spouse to his/her marital partner.

Fidelity to God's blueprint for human sexual behavior is integral to healthy human spirituality.

The proscriptions on human sexual behavior established by God in His Holy Word (the Bible) are positive and life-giving. They are designed to bring both maximum glory to God and to be protective measures for those who might otherwise try to find life and fulfillment in alternative sexual behavior, which can only bring death and destruction. As such, they are an expression of God's perfect love and desire to protect those He has created.

Any deflection from these intended purposes of the Creator God is rebellion against the wisdom and goodness of God and sets one at enmity with Him until that person has repented of their actions and come into agreement once again with God's design. The idea that man has the right to chose his own methods of sexual expression flies in the face of everything taught in sacred Scripture.

For those who find themselves caught in an aberrant sexual lifestyle, God offers the atoning death of His Son, Jesus Christ, which brings forgiveness, cleansing, healing and transforming power. Jesus did not come to condemn mankind, but to save any and all who would come to Him for cleansing.

We Are Speaking Out

- We are speaking out against the attempts by those in secular and religious communities who seek to overturn and redefine the clear teachings of the Bible, to make it appear as though sexual behavior outside of the bounds described above is somehow normal and blessed by God. There has been a clear and unbroken Judeo-Christian, scriptural witness on these matters for over thirty-five hundred years.
- We are speaking out against the impression being given by a minority of religious and media figures that their version of sexual morality is consistent with the biblical witness and/or accepted by the Church.
- We are speaking out against the unchecked confusion and division sown in the Church by such apostles of immorality.
- We are speaking out against the death and destruction that such teachings have brought to our culture and the confusion that it has sown in our children.
- We are speaking out against any sex education program that would teach such ideas to our young people.
- We are speaking out against the impression given by some that those who support biblical definitions of morality hate those who refuse to accept or live by them.

We Stand in Opposition

- We oppose any and all efforts to normalize or sanctify homosexual behavior, to advocate or bless homosexual marriages or to ordain those who engage in homosexual behavior.
- We oppose any attempt to stigmatize or reject persons who are turning to Christ for forgiveness, healing and transformation who have been struggling with their sexual orientation.
- We oppose any suggestion that they are lesser or more sinful human beings than anyone else. They are welcome in the Church.
- We oppose any and all attempts to normalize or sanctify heterosexual immorality, including the use of pornography or prostitutes, adulterous or other nonmarital sexual relationships or any other behavior outside of healthy, heterosexual, marital monogamy.

- We oppose the taking of a human life in its mother's womb or any other form of abortion.

We Call Out

- We call for people to return to the God of the Bible, through His Son Jesus Christ.
- We call for people to return to God's design for human behavior (sexual and otherwise) as found in the Holy Bible.
- We call for people to seek and receive from God Almighty the forgiveness, the cleansing, the deliverance and the healing that they need as a result of their unnatural sexual behavior.
- We call for people to seek and receive from God the desire and the power to walk in His ways.
- We call for those in government to honor the institution of marriage as it has been held for thousands of years by keeping it restricted to heterosexual, monogamous unions.
- We call for government to resist the legitimization of alternative sexual lifestyles in creating civil unions for couples who do not qualify for marriage.
- We call for our educational system to remove sex education materials that promote promiscuity, homosexual behavior or any other sexual behavior outside of traditional marriage.
- We call for the producers and distributors of every form of media communication to resist the temptation to fatten their coffers by continuing to spread the toxic message of sexual immorality.
- We call for religious leaders to stand firm against the tide of moral relativism and to remain faithful to God's Holy Word.
- We call for religious leaders to refuse to ordain those who engage in homosexual or nonmarital heterosexual activity.
- We call for those leaders and laity in the Church who have not yet done so, to extend the same hand of love and grace to the repentant sinner that Christ has extended, and to repent from any condescending or hateful attitudes that they have held toward those who struggle with unholy sexual temptations.
- We call for religious leaders to refuse to bless what God calls sin, including homosexual unions, but to instead invite those who struggle with unholy sexual desire to the same fount of forgiveness and healing as everyone else—even Jesus Christ, the Lord.

A CHRISTIAN DECLARATION ON MARRIAGE

Signed by
Bishop Anthony O'Connell, Chairman
National Conference of Catholic Bishops
Committee on Marriage and Family Life
Dr. Richard Land, President
Ethics and Religious Liberty Commission
Southern Baptist Convention
Dr. Robert Edgar, General Secretary
National Council of Churches
(Name withdrawn 11/17/2000)
Bishop Kevin W. Mannoia, President
National Association of Evangelicals
Issued November 14, 2000
www.ncccusa.org/news/2000GA/marriagedec.html
www.smartmarriages.com/christian.declaration.html

Note: The ecumenical group of Christian leaders who produced this statement supporting the sanctity of marriage initially included Dr. Robert Edgar, General Secretary, National Council of Churches of Christ in the USA. Dr. Edgar, however, removed his name on November 17, 2000, after meeting with a caucus of gays, lesbians, bisexual and transgender people. In withdrawing his name, Dr. Edgar explained, "The fact that the declaration omits mention of same sex unions is taken by some as proof that all of the signatories disapprove of such unions," and that was something with which he could not agree.

As we celebrate the 2000th anniversary of the birth of the Lord Jesus Christ, entering the third millennium, we pledge together to honor the Lord by committing ourselves afresh to God's first institution—marriage.

We believe that marriage is a holy union of one man and one woman in which they commit, with God's help, to build a loving, life-giving, faithful relationship that will last for a lifetime. God has established the married state, in the order of creation and redemption, for spouses to grow in love of one another and for the procreation, nurture, formation and education of children.

We believe that in marriage many principles of the Kingdom of God are manifested. The interdependence of healthy Christian community is clearly exemplified in loving one another (John 13:34), forgiving one another (Ephesians 4:32), confessing to one another (James 5:16), and submitting to one another (Ephesians 5:21). These principles find unique fulfillment in marriage. Marriage is God's gift, a living image of the union between Christ and His Church.

We believe that when a marriage is true to God's loving design it brings spiritual, physical, emotional, economic, and social benefits not only to a couple and family but also to the Church and to the wider culture. Couples, churches, and the whole of society have a stake in the well being of marriages. Each, therefore, has its own obligations to prepare, strengthen, support and restore marriages.

Our nation is threatened by a high divorce rate, a rise in cohabitation, a rise in non-marital births, a decline in the marriage rate, and a diminishing interest in and readiness for marrying, especially among young people. The documented adverse impact of these trends on children, adults, and society is alarming. Therefore, as church leaders, we recognize an unprecedented need and responsibility to help couples begin, build, and sustain better marriages, and to restore those threatened by divorce.

Motivated by our common desire that God's Kingdom be manifested on earth as it is in heaven, we pledge to deepen our commitment to marriage. With three-quarters of marriages performed by clergy, churches are uniquely positioned not only to call America to a stronger commitment to this holy union but to provide practical ministries and influence for reversing the course of our culture. It is evident in cities across the nation that where churches join in common commitment to restore a priority on marriages, divorces are reduced and communities are positively influenced.

Therefore, we call on churches throughout America to do their part to strengthen marriage in our nation by providing:

- Prayer and spiritual support for stronger marriages
- Encouragement for people to marry
- Education for young people about the meaning and responsibility of marriage
- Preparation for those engaged to be married
- Pastoral care, including qualified mentor couples, for couples at all stages of their relationship
- Help for couples experiencing marital difficulty and disruption
- Influence within society and the culture to uphold the institution of marriage

Further, we urge churches in every community to join in developing policies and programs with concrete goals to reduce the divorce rate and increase the marriage rate.

By our commitment to marriage as instituted by God, the nature of His Kingdom will be more clearly revealed in our homes, our churches, and our culture. To that end we pray and labor with the guidance of the Holy Spirit.

May the grace of God, the presence of Christ, and the empowerment of the Holy Spirit be abundant to all those who so commit and be a blessing to all whose marriages we seek to strengthen.

CONSIDERATIONS REGARDING PROPOSALS TO GIVE LEGAL RECOGNITION TO UNIONS BETWEEN HOMOSEXUAL PERSONS

The Roman Catholic Church
The Vatican
Congregation for the Doctrine of the Faith

www.vatican.va/roman_curia/congregations/cfaith/documents/rc_con_cfaith_doc_20030731_homosexual-unions_en.html

The Sovereign Pontiff John Paul II, in the Audience of March 28, 2003, approved the present Considerations, adopted in the Ordinary Session of this Congregation, and ordered their publication.

Rome, from the Offices of the Congregation for the Doctrine of the Faith, June 3, 2003, Memorial of Saint Charles Lwanga and his Companions, Martyrs

INTRODUCTION

1. In recent years, various questions relating to homosexuality have been addressed with some frequency by Pope John Paul II and by the relevant Dicasteries of the Holy See.[1] Homosexuality is a troubling moral and social phenomenon, even in those countries where it does not present significant legal issues. It gives rise to greater concern in those countries that have granted—or intend to grant—legal recognition to homosexual unions, which may include the possibility of adopting children. The present Considerations do not contain new doctrinal elements; they seek rather to reiterate the essential points on this question and provide arguments drawn from reason which could be used by Bishops in preparing more specific interventions, appropriate to the different situations throughout the world, aimed at protecting and promoting the dignity of marriage, the foundation of the family, and the stability of society, of which this institution is a constitutive element. The present Considerations are also intended to give direction to Catholic politicians by indicating the approaches to proposed legislation in this area which would be consistent with Christian conscience.[2] Since this question relates to the natural moral law, the arguments that follow are addressed not only to those who believe in Christ, but to all persons committed to promoting and defending the common good of society.

I. The Nature of Marriage and Its Inalienable Characteristics

2. The Church's teaching on marriage and on the complementarity of the sexes reiterates a truth that is evident to right reason and recognized as such by all the major

cultures of the world. Marriage is not just any relationship between human beings. It was established by the Creator with its own nature, essential properties and purpose.[3] No ideology can erase from the human spirit the certainty that marriage exists solely between a man and a woman, who by mutual personal gift, proper and exclusive to themselves, tend toward the communion of their persons. In this way, they mutually perfect each other, in order to cooperate with God in the procreation and upbringing of new human lives.

3. The natural truth about marriage was confirmed by the Revelation contained in the biblical accounts of creation, an expression also of the original human wisdom, in which the voice of nature itself is heard. There are three fundamental elements of the Creator's plan for marriage, as narrated in the Book of Genesis.

In the first place, man, the image of God, was created "male and female" (Gen. 1:27). Men and women are equal as persons and complementary as male and female. Sexuality is something that pertains to the physical-biological realm and has also been raised to a new level—the personal level—where nature and spirit are united.

Marriage is instituted by the Creator as a form of life in which a communion of persons is realized involving the use of the sexual faculty. "That is why a man leaves his father and mother and clings to his wife and they become one flesh" (Gen. 2:24).

Third, God has willed to give the union of man and woman a special participation in his work of creation. Thus, he blessed the man and the woman with the words "Be fruitful and multiply" (Gen. 1:28). Therefore, in the Creator's plan, sexual complementarity and fruitfulness belong to the very nature of marriage.

Furthermore, the marital union of man and woman has been elevated by Christ to the dignity of a sacrament. The Church teaches that Christian marriage is an efficacious sign of the covenant between Christ and the Church (cf. Eph. 5:32). This Christian meaning of marriage, far from diminishing the profoundly human value of the marital union between man and woman, confirms and strengthens it (cf. Matt. 19:3-12; Mark 10:6-9).

4. There are absolutely no grounds for considering homosexual unions to be in any way similar or even remotely analogous to God's plan for marriage and family. Marriage is holy, while homosexual acts go against the natural moral law. Homosexual acts "close the sexual act to the gift of life. They do not proceed from a genuine affective and sexual complementarity. Under no circumstances can they be approved."[4]

Sacred Scripture condemns homosexual acts as a serious depravity . . . (cf. Rom. 1:24-27; 1 Cor. 6:10; 1 Tim. 1:10). This judgment of Scripture does not of course permit us to conclude that all those who suffer from this anomaly are personally responsible for it, but it does attest to the fact that homosexual acts are intrinsically disordered.[5] This same moral judgment is found in many Christian writers of the first centuries[6] and is unanimously accepted by Catholic Tradition.

Nonetheless, according to the teaching of the Church, men and women with homosexual tendencies "must be accepted with respect, compassion and sensitivity.

Every sign of unjust discrimination in their regard should be avoided."[7] They are called, like other Christians, to live the virtue of chastity.[8] The homosexual inclination is however "objectively disordered"[9] and homosexual practices are "sins gravely contrary to chastity."[10]

II. Positions on the Problem of Homosexual Unions

5. Faced with the fact of homosexual unions, civil authorities adopt different positions. At times they simply tolerate the phenomenon; at other times they advocate legal recognition of such unions, under the pretext of avoiding, with regard to certain rights, discrimination against persons who live with someone of the same sex. In other cases, they favour giving homosexual unions legal equivalence to marriage properly so-called, along with the legal possibility of adopting children.

Where the government's policy is *de facto* tolerance and there is no explicit legal recognition of homosexual unions, it is necessary to distinguish carefully the various aspects of the problem. Moral conscience requires that, in every occasion, Christians give witness to the whole moral truth, which is contradicted both by approval of homosexual acts and unjust discrimination against homosexual persons. Therefore, discreet and prudent actions can be effective; these might involve: unmasking the way in which such tolerance might be exploited or used in the service of ideology; stating clearly the immoral nature of these unions; reminding the government of the need to contain the phenomenon within certain limits so as to safeguard public morality and, above all, to avoid exposing young people to erroneous ideas about sexuality and marriage that would deprive them of their necessary defences and contribute to the spread of the phenomenon. Those who would move from tolerance to the legitimization of specific rights for cohabiting homosexual persons need to be reminded that the approval or legalization of evil is something far different from the toleration of evil.

In those situations where homosexual unions have been legally recognized or have been given the legal status and rights belonging to marriage, clear and emphatic opposition is a duty. One must refrain from any kind of formal cooperation in the enactment or application of such gravely unjust laws and, as far as possible, from material cooperation on the level of their application. In this area, everyone can exercise the right to conscientious objection.

III. Arguments from Reason Against Legal Recognition of Homosexual Unions

6. To understand why it is necessary to oppose legal recognition of homosexual unions, ethical considerations of different orders need to be taken into consideration.

From the Order of Right Reason

The scope of the civil law is certainly more limited than that of the moral law,[11] but civil law cannot contradict right reason without losing its binding force on conscience.[12] Every humanly-created law is legitimate insofar as it is consistent with the natural moral law, recognized by right reason, and insofar as it respects the inalienable rights of every person.[13] Laws in favour of homosexual unions are contrary to right reason because they confer legal guarantees, analogous to those granted to marriage, to unions between persons of the same sex. Given the values at stake in this question, the State could not grant legal standing to such unions without failing in its duty to promote and defend marriage as an institution essential to the common good.

It might be asked how a law can be contrary to the common good if it does not impose any particular kind of behaviour, but simply gives legal recognition to a *de facto* reality which does not seem to cause injustice to anyone. In this area, one needs first to reflect on the difference between homosexual behaviour as a private phenomenon and the same behaviour as a relationship in society, foreseen and approved by the law, to the point where it becomes one of the institutions in the legal structure. This second phenomenon is not only more serious, but also assumes a more wide-reaching and profound influence, and would result in changes to the entire organization of society, contrary to the common good. Civil laws are structuring principles of man's life in society, for good or for ill. They "play a very important and sometimes decisive role in influencing patterns of thought and behaviour".[14] Lifestyles and the underlying presuppositions these express not only externally shape the life of society, but also tend to modify the younger generation's perception and evaluation of forms of behaviour. Legal recognition of homosexual unions would obscure certain basic moral values and cause a devaluation of the institution of marriage.

From the Biological and Anthropological Order

7. Homosexual unions are totally lacking in the biological and anthropological elements of marriage and family which would be the basis, on the level of reason, for granting them legal recognition. Such unions are not able to contribute in a proper way to the procreation and survival of the human race. The possibility of using recently discovered methods of artificial reproduction, beyond involving a grave lack of respect for human dignity,[15] does nothing to alter this inadequacy.

Homosexual unions are also totally lacking in the conjugal dimension, which represents the human and ordered form of sexuality. Sexual relations are human when and insofar as they express and promote the mutual assistance of the sexes in marriage and are open to the transmission of new life.

As experience has shown, the absence of sexual complementarity in these unions creates obstacles in the normal development of children who would be placed in the care of such persons. They would be deprived of the experience of either fatherhood or motherhood. Allowing children to be adopted by persons living in such unions would actually mean doing violence to these children, in the sense that their condition of dependency would be used to place them in an environment that is not conducive to their full human development. This is gravely immoral and in open contradiction to the principle, recognized also in the United Nations Convention on the Rights of the Child, that the best interests of the child, as the weaker and more vulnerable party, are to be the paramount consideration in every case.

From the Social Order

8. Society owes its continued survival to the family, founded on marriage. The inevitable consequence of legal recognition of homosexual unions would be the redefinition of marriage, which would become, in its legal status, an institution devoid of essential reference to factors linked to heterosexuality; for example, procreation and raising children. If, from the legal standpoint, marriage between a man and a woman were to be considered just one possible form of marriage, the concept of marriage would undergo a radical transformation, with grave detriment to the common good. By putting homosexual unions on a legal plane analogous to that of marriage and the family, the State acts arbitrarily and in contradiction with its duties.

The principles of respect and non-discrimination cannot be invoked to support legal recognition of homosexual unions. Differentiating between persons or refusing social recognition or benefits is unacceptable only when it is contrary to justice.[16] The denial of the social and legal status of marriage to forms of cohabitation that are not and cannot be marital is not opposed to justice; on the contrary, justice requires it.

Nor can the principle of the proper autonomy of the individual be reasonably invoked. It is one thing to maintain that individual citizens may freely engage in those activities that interest them and that this falls within the common civil right to freedom; it is something quite different to hold that activities which do not represent a significant or positive contribution to the development of the human person in society can receive specific and categorical legal recognition by the State. Not even in a remote analogous sense do homosexual unions fulfill the purpose for which marriage and family deserve specific categorical recognition. On the contrary, there are good reasons for holding that such unions are harmful to the proper development of human society, especially if their impact on society were to increase.

From the Legal Order

9. Because married couples ensure the succession of generations and are therefore eminently within the public interest, civil law grants them institutional recognition. Homosexual unions, on the other hand, do not need specific attention from the legal standpoint since they do not exercise this function for the common good.

Nor is the argument valid according to which legal recognition of homosexual unions is necessary to avoid situations in which cohabiting homosexual persons, simply because they live together, might be deprived of real recognition of their rights as persons and citizens. In reality, they can always make use of the provisions of law—like all citizens from the standpoint of their private autonomy—

to protect their rights in matters of common interest. It would be gravely unjust to sacrifice the common good and just laws on the family in order to protect personal goods that can and must be guaranteed in ways that do not harm the body of society.[17]

IV. Positions of Catholic Politicians with Regard to Legislation in Favour of Homosexual Unions

10. If it is true that all Catholics are obliged to oppose the legal recognition of homosexual unions, Catholic politicians are obliged to do so in a particular way, in keeping with their responsibility as politicians. Faced with legislative proposals in favour of homosexual unions, Catholic politicians are to take account of the following ethical indications.

When legislation in favour of the recognition of homosexual unions is proposed for the first time in a legislative assembly, the Catholic law-maker has a moral duty to express his opposition clearly and publicly and to vote against it. To vote in favour of a law so harmful to the common good is gravely immoral.

When legislation in favour of the recognition of homosexual unions is already in force, the Catholic politician must oppose it in the ways that are possible for him and make his opposition known; it is his duty to witness to the truth. If it is not possible to repeal such a law completely, the Catholic politician, recalling the indications contained in the Encyclical Letter *Evangelium vitae,* "could licitly support proposals aimed at limiting the harm done by such a law and at lessening its negative consequences at the level of general opinion and public morality," on condition that his "absolute personal opposition" to such laws was clear and well known and that the danger of scandal was avoided.[18] This does not mean that a more restrictive law in this area could be considered just or even acceptable; rather, it is a question of the legitimate and dutiful attempt to obtain at least the partial repeal of an unjust law when its total abrogation is not possible at the moment.

Conclusion

11. The Church teaches that respect for homosexual persons cannot lead in any way to approval of homosexual behaviour or to legal recognition of homosexual unions. The common good requires that laws recognize, promote and protect marriage as the basis of the family, the primary unit of society. Legal recognition of homosexual unions or placing them on the same level as marriage would mean not only the approval of deviant behaviour, with the consequence of making it a model in present-day society, but would also obscure basic values which belong to the common inheritance of humanity. The Church cannot fail to defend these values, for the good of men and women and for the good of society itself.

Joseph Card. Ratzinger, *Prefect*
Angelo Amato, S.D.B., *Titular Archbishop of Sila, Secretary*

NOTES

1. Cf. John Paul II, *Angelus Messages* of February 20, 1994, and of June 19, 1994; *Address to the Plenary Meeting of the Pontifical Council for the Family* (March 24, 1999); *Catechism of the Catholic Church*, Nos. 2357-2359, 2396; Congregation for the Doctrine of the Faith, Declaration *Persona humana* (December 29, 1975), 8; *Letter on the pastoral care of homosexual persons* (October 1, 1986); *Some considerations concerning the response to legislative proposals on the non-discrimination of homosexual persons* (July 24, 1992); Pontifical Council for the Family, *Letter to the Presidents of the Bishops' Conferences of Europe on the resolution of the European Parliament regarding homosexual couples* (March 25, 1994); *Family, marriage and "de facto" unions* (July 26, 2000), 23.
2. Cf. Congregation for the Doctrine of the Faith, *Doctrinal Note on some questions regarding the participation of Catholics in political life* (November 24, 2002), 4.
3. Cf. Second Vatican Council, Pastoral Constitution *Gaudium et spes*, 48.
4. *Catechism of the Catholic Church*, No. 2357.
5. Congregation for the Doctrine of the Faith, *Declaration Persona humana* (December 29, 1975), 8.
6. Cf., for example, St. Polycarp, *Letter to the Philippians*, V, 3; St. Justin Martyr, *First Apology*, 27, 1-4; Athenagoras, *Supplication for the Christians*, 34.
7. *Catechism of the Catholic Church*, No. 2358; cf. Congregation for the Doctrine of the Faith, *Letter on the pastoral care of homosexual persons* (October 1, 1986), 10.
8. Cf. *Catechism of the Catholic Church*, No. 2359; cf. Congregation for the Doctrine of the Faith, *Letter on the pastoral care of homosexual persons* (October 1, 1986), 12.
9. *Catechism of the Catholic Church*, No. 2358.
10. *Ibid.*, No. 2396.
11. Cf. John Paul II, Encyclical Letter *Evangelium vitae* (March 25, 1995), 71.
12. Cf. *ibid.*, 72.
13. Cf. St. Thomas Aquinas, *Summa Theologiae*, I-II, q. 95, a. 2.
14. John Paul II, Encyclical Letter *Evangelium vitae* (March 25, 1995), 90.
15. Cf. Congregation for the Doctrine of the Faith, Instruction *Donum vitae* (February 22, 1987), II. A. 1-3.
16. Cf. St. Thomas Aquinas, *Summa Theologiae*, II-II, q. 63, a.1, c.
17. It should not be forgotten that there is always "a danger that legislation which would make homosexuality a basis for entitlements could actually encourage a person with a homosexual orientation to declare his homosexuality or even to seek a partner in order to exploit the provisions of the law" (Congregation for the Doctrine of the Faith, *Some considerations concerning the response to legislative proposals on the non-discrimination of homosexual persons* [July 24, 1992], 14).
18. John Paul II, Encyclical Letter *Evangelium vitae* (March 25, 1995), 73.

A PLACE TO STAND: A CALL TO ACTION

American Anglican Council

Adopted October 7-9, 2003

www.americananglican.org/petitions/Petition.cfm?petitionID=8

Note: This following statement was passed by conservative Anglicans in the United States, who met in Plano, Texas, to plan how they should respond to confirmation of Gene Robinson, a non-celibate homosexual, as a bishop in the Episcopal Church of the United States.

In the Name of the Father, and of the Son, and of the Holy Spirit.

As Anglican Christians committed to the Lordship of Jesus Christ, under the authority of Holy Scripture, and members of God's one, holy, catholic, and apostolic Church:

1. We proclaim our Lord's Great Commandment and His Great Commission to be our life's highest calling.

2. We repudiate the 74th General Convention's confirmation of a non-celibate homosexual to be a bishop of the Church, and its acceptance of same-sex blessings as part of our common life. These actions have broken fellowship with the larger body of Christ and have brought the Episcopal Church under God's judgment.

3. We repent of our part in the sins of the Episcopal Church, and we pray for all those who are being hurt and led astray by these actions.

4. We call the leadership of the Episcopal Church to repent of and reverse the unbiblical and schismatic actions of the General Convention.

5. We declare our commitment to the Lord's life-giving teaching about sexuality and marriage embraced by Christians throughout all ages, and as affirmed by the 1998 Lambeth Conference. We celebrate God's unconditional love for all people, and we proclaim God's transforming power for everyone seeking sexual purity and wholeness.

6. We redirect our financial resources, to the fullest extent possible, toward biblically orthodox mission and ministry, and away from those structures that support the unrighteous actions of the General Convention. We will support our partners in the Anglican Communion.

7. We appeal to the Primates of the Anglican Communion to intervene in the Episcopal Church to:

a. Discipline those bishops in the Episcopal Church who, by their actions, have departed from biblical faith and order;
b. Guide the realignment of Anglicanism in North America;
c. Encourage orthodox bishops as they extend Episcopal oversight, pastoral care, and apostolic mission across current diocesan boundaries; and
d. Support isolated and beleaguered congregations and individuals in their life and witness as faithful Anglican Christians.

To the glory of God. Amen.

KANSAS CITY DECLARATION ON MARRIAGE

Issued by
A Southern Baptist Forum on Marriage
Issued November 12, 2003
www.faithandfamily.com

Marriage is the union of one man and one woman for life. This has been the definition of marriage in Western culture for millennia. Recent events and trends have threatened to undermine this definition in the West. Homosexual marriages already are recognized in some European countries and parts of Canada. In the United States, the Vermont legislature created civil unions to provide a government-sanctioned quasi-marital relationship for homosexuals. The movement toward homosexual marriage in the U.S. is also evidenced by the proliferation of "domestic partner registries" and corporate benefits for same-sex couples. The U.S. Supreme Court's decision in Lawrence v. Texas prevents society from enforcing any laws discouraging homosexual sexual acts as corrupt or immoral. These current practices along with other pending judicial mandates threaten to throw wide open the door to full legal and moral affirmation of homosexual marriage.

We agree with the Baptist Faith and Message that "Marriage is the uniting of one man and one woman in covenant commitment for a lifetime. It is God's unique gift to reveal the union between Christ and His church and to provide for the man and the woman in marriage the framework for intimate companionship, the channel of sexual expression according to biblical standards, and the means for procreation of the human race."

Any weakening of the traditional, Judeo-Christian definition of marriage will undermine the foundation of Western culture and result in deep, permanent fractures that will fundamentally alter American culture, indeed all of Western civilization. The Colorado Statement on Biblical Sexual Morality reflects our rejection of demands for redefinition of marriage when it says, "We affirm that God established the moral definition of marriage, and that it should not be changed according to the dictates of culture, tradition, or personal preference. We deny that the morality of marriage is a matter of mere custom, or that it should be allowed to shift with the tide of cultural opinion or social practice."

We reject the claim that homosexual unions should be granted equivalent moral status to heterosexual monogamous marriage, regardless of the terminology used to describe those unions. We affirm the biblical model of marriage, the union of one man and one woman for life, as the only appropriate model for uniting people in marriage. We deny that this conviction is incompatible with redemptive ministry to homosexuals. Homosexuals need the Gospel of Jesus Christ and they need the ministry of the church, just like everyone else. We call on our fellow brothers and sisters in the Lord to reach out in redemptive ministry to homosexuals, while at the same time opposing the unbiblical concept of homosexual marriage.

We hold these beliefs for the following reasons:

Marriage is the foundational institution of human culture (Gen. 2:18-22; Matt. 19:3-9; Eph. 5:22-33; Eph. 6:1; 1 Thess. 2:7, 11; 1 Tim. 5:4).

The first social institution was marriage. As the foundation of the family, marriage is the foundational cultural institution. The family is a critically important institution in society because it supplies certain essential components to the bedrock upon which all other human relationships depend. In the family people learn compassion and mercy, essential elements that enable society to care for the weak among us. They learn how to cooperate with each other, an essential trait that enables individuals to combine their energies to accomplish great tasks. They learn commitment to others, an indispensable characteristic that assures unity and success. Most important, they learn to sacrifice for the needs of others, the linchpin of all healthy human relationships.

A family established on the marriage between a man and woman forces the cultivation of these characteristics in ways that other relationships do not. For heterosexual marriage demands the purest cultivation of these characteristics in order to succeed. Modern marriage counterfeits fail in significant ways to develop and model these characteristics. By their very nature cohabitation and same-sex relationships avoid some of the dynamics that a husband and wife must address. For example, those who cohabit often are reluctant to make a permanent commitment to each other; and same-sex relationships are never forced to deal with the fundamental differences between the sexes.

Marriage is a covenantal relationship (Gen. 2:23-25; Mal. 2:14-16; Matt. 19:5-9; Eph. 5:31).

The first commitment ceremony between a man and a woman involved a commitment to a relationship. Marriage is more than a legal contract between two individuals. Marriage, within Judeo-Christian teaching, is a covenant relationship. It is the beginning point for successful long-term relationships. Its basis is not performance but relationship. Marriage according to the words spoken at the first marriage ceremony involves leaving parental relationships and creating a permanent new relationship, in which the two enjoy a pure, selfless intimacy. Therefore, we reject current efforts to equate civil unions with marriage or to treat marriage as a contractual relationship.

Marriage creates one unity out of the two corresponding genders (Gen. 2:23-24; Matt. 19:4-6; Mark 10:6-9; 1 Cor. 6:16; Eph. 5:22-33).

In marriage the male and female form a single intimate union. When God created man, He created a male and a female. As the Baptist Faith and Message states, "The gift of gender is thus a part of the goodness of God's creation." Neither gender comprises the sum of all that it means to unite human beings in a sexual relationship. God chose to typify certain characteristics of humanity in the male and other characteristics in the female. By definition, homosexual marriage is incapable of achieving this "one flesh" union. Therefore, we reject the notion that homosexual marriage is equal to heterosexual marriage.

Marriage provides the best environment for the personal, social, and economic well-being of children (Eph. 5:22-33; Eph. 6:1; 1 Tim. 5:8; Titus 2:4-6).

The biblical model of marriage reveals a husband and wife working together, complementing each other, to provide a stable, successful home in which children are equipped to fulfill their greatest potential. Long-term homosexual relationships, especially among males, are extremely rare. Children who grow up in single-parent/adult homes are more likely to live in poverty all their lives. The absence of the support structures provided by marriage results too often in underperforming, emotionally distressed children who do not reach their fullest potential. The result will be an ever-expanding government that must assume more and more of the burden of taking care of the emotional, physical, and economic well-being of its citizens. Therefore, we reject the practice of adoption by homosexual couples.

Marriage encourages the development of healthy sexual identity in children (Gen. 1:27-28; Gen. 2:18; Deut. 6:4-25; Prov. 1:8-9).

God designed the family to be a learning environment for children. Children learn about sexuality by observing their parents. The absence of both sexes as role models will make it more difficult for children to be able to form a healthy understanding of their own sexuality and to appreciate the differences of the other sex. Homosexuality violates three fundamental principles of human sexuality. It violates the principle of exclusivity. The creation record acknowledges God's creation of only two sexes—male and female (Gen. 1:27). It violates the principle of fertility. The man and woman were designed to propagate their species through sexual union (Gen. 1:28). While the gift of sex is not limited only to this function, it is a fundamental expectation of sexuality that homosexual sex is incapable of fulfilling. It violates the principle of complementarity. God created a female to complete the male (Gen. 2:18-25). Therefore, we reject the notion that children can be raised as effectively in homosexual relationships as they can in heterosexual marriage.

Marriage is life-affirming (Gen. 1:27-28; Gen. 2:18; Prov. 5:18-19).

God instituted marriage as a means toward good. It was designed to improve quality of life and enable healthy reproductive behaviors. Homosexuals, especially males, do not tend to form long-term relationships; and they tend to die of causes directly attributable to their lifestyle 20-25 years earlier than heterosexual males. Therefore, we reject the notion that any homosexual relationship can be the equivalent of heterosexual marriage.

Marriage is the only appropriate context for sexual relations (Lev. 18:22; Rom. 1:18-32; Heb. 13:4).

We affirm the Colorado Statement's clear and extensive pronouncements on biblical, sexual morality, and its conviction that the biblical standard for sexual expression is heterosexual, monogamous marriage. We reiterate its claim that "sexual behavior is moral only within the institution of heterosexual, monogamous marriage." Therefore, we reject the claim that homosexual sex between consenting adults constitutes an acceptable, biblical sexual relationship.

Marriage is the ideal model for the family (Prov. 31:10-31; Eph. 5:22-33; Eph. 6:1-4; 1 Thess. 2:7, 11; 1 Tim. 3:1-7, 8-12; 1 Pet. 3:1-7).

We affirm those who have been forced for various reasons to live in single-parent families. We commend those parents who have determined to do the best they can to provide for and nurture their children in these situations. We acknowledge that children can and do thrive in these families. However, we do not believe that these represent the best environments for children to reach their fullest potential for reasons we have already stated.

Therefore, in order to cherish and protect marriage as a crucial asset to our society and in view of what we have expressed, we call for the following:

- The immediate passage of a Federal Marriage Amendment that will place in the U.S. Constitution the definition of marriage as the union of one man and one woman.
- The strengthening of marriage laws in all states that will emphasize the covenant nature of marriage.
- The restriction of marriage by every state to the union of one man and one woman, including civil unions or any other marriage-like union.
- The abolition of no-fault divorce.
- A greater determination by Christians to honor their marriage commitments and to resolve their differences in Christ-like, God-honoring ways rather than divorcing.

- Greater commitment from churches and other religious institutions to provide mentoring for married couples that will model and sustain healthy marriages.
- A commitment by church and other religious leaders to help prospective couples prepare for marriage before they marry through premarital counseling.

November 12, 2003
Midwestern Baptist Theological Seminary
Kansas City, Missouri

FORUM PARTICIPANTS:

Dr. Richard Land, President, The Ethics and Liberty Commission of the Southern Baptist Convention; Dr. Phil Roberts, President, Midwestern Baptist Theological Seminary; Dr. Alan Branch, Professor of Christian Ethics, Midwestern Baptist Theological Seminary; Dr. Barrett Duke, Vice President for Public Policy and Research, The Ethics and Religious Liberty Commission of the Southern Baptist Convention; Rev. Terry Fox, Pastor, Immanuel Baptist Church, Wichita, Kansas; Dr. Daniel Heimbach, Professor of Christian Ethics, Southeastern Baptist Theological Seminary; Mrs. Cindy Province, Assistant Director, Bioethics Center of St. Louis; Claude Rhea, Chief Development Officer, North American Mission Board

ENDORSEMENTS:

Dr. Alan Branch, Professor of Christian Ethics, Midwestern Baptist Theological Seminary

Rev. Pat Bulloch, Director of Missions, Heart of Kansas Baptist Association

Dr. Barrett Duke, Vice President for Public Policy and Research, The Ethics and Religious Liberty Commission of the Southern Baptist Convention

Rev. Terry Fox, Pastor, Immanuel Baptist Church, Wichita, Kansas

Harold Harper, Vice President for Broadcasting, The Ethics and Religious Liberty Commission of the Southern Baptist Convention

Dr. Daniel Heimbach, Professor of Christian Ethics, Southeastern Baptist Theological Seminary

Dr. Richard Land, President, The Ethics and Liberty Commission of the Southern Baptist Convention

Dr. Thor Madsen, Professor of New Testament, Midwestern Baptist Theological Seminary

Mrs. Cindy Province, Assistant Director, Bioethics Center of St. Louis

Claude Rhea, Chief Development Officer, North American Mission Board

Dr. Phil Roberts, President, Midwestern Baptist Theological Seminary

Joe Ulveling, Family Ministries Specialist, Missouri Baptist Convention

APPENDIX C

A WOLF IN SHEEP'S CLOTHING

A Special Report by Focus on the Family on the Sexuality Information and Education Council of the United States (SIECUS)

Note: This special report, originally published in 1990, was issued to alert individual Christians and churches concerning an organized effort by the Sexuality Information and Education Council of the United States (SIECUS) to undermine and change what Christians believe and teach on sexual morality in America.

> "Beware of false prophets who come disguised as harmless sheep, but are really wolves that will tear you apart"—Matthew 7:15 (NLT)

INTRODUCTION

Early in 1999 an ultra-liberal organization by the name of the Sexuality Information and Education Council of the United States (SIECUS) released a booklet entitled "A Time to Speak: Faith Communities and Sexuality Education." The booklet outlined a case and model for church involvement in the sex education of young people.

Superficially, many of the SIECUS programs for the faith community may seem reasonable. But an informed understanding of the SIECUS agenda, which is clearly promoted in the literature it publishes and in the programs it advances, makes it clear that "A Time to Speak" is simply a diversion intended to lull the religious community to sleep.

This paper is intended to alert people and communities of faith to the dangers represented by SIECUS and its beliefs and agenda.

BACKGROUND

Out of the revolution of the 1960s and 70s came a call to teach sex education in America's schools. The reasoning was that—with sex right out there in the fields of Woodstock and on university campuses—teens needed to better understand human sexuality.

Initially, sex education took the form of human biology instruction. The focus was on the physiological aspects of males and females as sexual beings. For the most part, sex education during the 1960s and early 70s separated girls and boys.

However, it did not take long for liberal educators and public health officials to demand a greater role for sex education. Spurred by the increase in teenage sexual activity, pregnancy and STDs in the late 1970s, sex education was expanded to include a discussion of contraception. Also, during this period the separation of boys and girls was discontinued in favor of co-ed instruction. This was a direct attack on the natural modesty of young people.

The discovery of the HIV/AIDS virus in the 1980s kicked sex education into high gear. The door was opened for instructors to actually demonstrate condom use. By the late 1980s condoms became available in some school districts through the school nurse or by referral to a "family planning" clinic, often without parental consent or knowledge. That trend toward ever more explicit and permissive sex education has continued through today.

Sex education has met varying degrees of opposition by parent groups throughout this period. The major objections by parents have been that sex education is often not age-appropriate, subverts parental authority and, in some cases, encourages premarital sexual activity. In many communities—even to this day—parents have been able to minimize the inclusion of condom instruction and distribution.

The entire evolution of sex education in America has been characterized by two facts.

First, operating mostly behind the scenes, an organization calling itself the Sexuality Information and Education Council of the United States (SIECUS) has been the strategic national leader for what has become known as "comprehensive sexuality education."

"Comprehensive sexuality education" is a code phrase for sexual education characterized by an explicit discussion of human sexuality beginning at kindergarten and extending through senior high school and also includes acceptance of homosexual practices as legitimate sexual expression.

"Comprehensive sexuality education" fails to link teenage sexual behavior with morality or societal values. Since it is assumed that teens will have sex, the focus is primarily on teaching students to use condoms and other contraceptive measures in order to minimize health risks once they become sexually active. Comprehensive sexuality education is also known as the "safe-sex" or "safer-sex" philosophy.

Most parents have never heard of SIECUS, yet much of the growth in comprehensive sexuality education can be directly attributed to the work of this organization.

Second, while some parents have been noble activists against comprehensive sexuality education, the church—by and large—has been absent from the debate. The church basically remained silent during the 1970s and 80s, when comprehensive sex education gained a foothold, in the public classrooms of this country.

What Is SIECUS?

Contrary to what its name might suggest, SIECUS is not a government agency. However, since its inception, it has worked very closely with like-minded liberals in government organizations, thus gaining an open door for new sex-ed organizations. And while SIECUS attempts to capitalize on its craftily chosen name by proclaiming itself an authority on sexuality education, its "moral" authority on matters of sexual behavior is self-generated. SIECUS is an independent, nonprofit organization with a radical-left agenda.

SIECUS promotes a variety of sexual behaviors that carry significantly greater risk of sexually transmitted diseases than the biblical practice of abstinence until marriage and faithfulness within marriage. For example, SIECUS celebrates homosexual behavior, despite the fact that this lifestyle carries a substantially greater risk of life-threatening STDs.[1] SIECUS also supports non-marital sex among adolescents, despite the fact that teen girls experience one million pregnancies and three million cases of STDs each year.[2]

In 1990, SIECUS published a booklet it called "Sex Education 2000." The booklet outlined SIECUS's goals for the turn of the century. Goal number four was, "By the year 2000, all religious institutions serving youth will provide sexuality education."[3]

SIECUS: Alpha Wolf in Sheep's Clothing

But SIECUS is not a lone wolf. Over the last few decades, a coalition of liberal sex-education groups—a "safe-sex alliance"—formed with the intention of teaching young people that sex—any sex as long as it's consensual and protected from unwanted pregnancies and relatively safe from STD infections—is a good thing.

This coalition's evolution began with Planned Parenthood founder Margaret Sanger and her radical views about sex. But Alfred C. Kinsey and his "studies" on human sexuality, published in the late 1940s, really ignited the fires. (In his biography "Alfred C. Kinsey: A Public/Private Life," author James H. Jones revealed Kinsey as a homosexual sadomasochist bent on fomenting a sexual revolution.)[4] After Kinsey's masochism brought about his death at age 62, his associates, including Wardell Pomeroy (who has been recorded making positive statements about adultery, homosexuality, pedophilia and bestiality), proudly carried on the tradition. Pomeroy was a SIECUS founder, and SIECUS is the "spiritual" leader—the alpha of the pack.

Now that SIECUS and friends are in firm control of sex education in schools, they have turned their sights on the church. In order to gain entry into churches, SIECUS spokespersons have had to tone down their public statements—although their goals are unchanged. SIECUS has worked hard to appear as the kind of mainstream, responsible and respectable organization that average Americans would welcome into their churches.

SIECUS and its allies, such as The National Campaign to Prevent Teen Pregnancy, have launched a major campaign to establish themselves as sources of information and resources regarding human sexuality for the religious community in America.

The purpose of this document is to alert the faith community to the very critical threat SIECUS represents.

The centerpiece of this campaign is a new SIECUS brochure titled: "A Time to Speak: Faith Communities and Sexuality Education."

The SIECUS brochure is extremely deceptive on many counts:

- Scriptural passages and references are contained throughout the brochure in order to add biblical credibility to SIECUS and its unbiblical message.
- Human sexuality is referred to as a wonderful gift from God (which it is) without being specific about SIECUS's definition of acceptable teenage sexual behavior. For example, SIECUS defines homosexuality and mutual masturbation by 15-year-olds as acceptable and healthy forms of sexual expression.[5]
- SIECUS emphasizes the need for churches to be involved in sexuality education, without specifically and honestly providing what should or should not be included in such education (read the shocking SIECUS guidelines beginning below).
- While various denomination resolutions regarding sexuality education are cited, only those portions of resolutions that supported the SIECUS agenda were quoted. SIECUS conveniently excluded other portions of resolutions that refuted its philosophy. For example, one of the resolutions SIECUS quoted went on to state, "We understand the Bible to teach that genital intercourse is reserved for a man and a woman united in a marriage covenant. . . . This teaching precludes premarital, extra-marital and homosexual genital activity."[6]
- Conservative church groups, such as the Catholic Church and Southern Baptist Convention, are mentioned in the brochure, no doubt to add legitimacy to SIECUS as a source of information.[7] However, senior Catholic Church and SBC officials we spoke with are opposed to SIECUS's philosophies.

It is important for the faith community to fully understand the background and philosophy of SIECUS and what it believes about sex education and human sexuality.

What Is SIECUS's Definition of Sexuality Education?

SIECUS has been a radically liberal group from its very inception. Consider the beliefs and statements of its founders:

- "Incest between adults and younger children can prove to be a satisfying and enriching experience."[8] Wardell Pomeroy, Ph.D., original SIECUS board member.
- "It is not that [pedophilia] is a bad thing or a wicked thing, it just simply should not be part of life in general, right out on the sidewalk."[9] Mary Calderone, SIECUS co-founder (for whom SIECUS recently named its corporate library).

SIECUS's radical commitment to outrageous and destructive ideas continues to this day. Following are just some of SIECUS's current guidelines for educating children about sex.[10]

Ages 5–8

Children in this age group should be taught about masturbation.

Ages 9–12

Children in this age group should be taught that there are many ways—such as outercourse, mutual masturbation and oral sex—to give and receive sexual pleasure.

Ages 12–15

Children in this age group should be taught that they could buy contraceptives in a drug store, grocery market or convenience store without a doctor's prescription.

Ages 16–18

Children in this age group can use erotic photographs, movies or literature to enhance their sexual fantasies when alone or with a partner.

What Else Does SIECUS Believe and Advocate?

- SIECUS believes that children should be given abortions and birth control without parental knowledge or consent.[11]
- SIECUS [former] president Debra Haffner has fantasized about a national "petting project" for teenagers.[12]
- SIECUS has been an outspoken opponent of a new federal program promoting abstinence until marriage.[13]
- SIECUS believes that homosexuality should be affirmed by schools and churches.[14]

In early 1999, SIECUS released a list of its readers' picks of "American heroes" who have been most influential at being positive role models for our children. The list included Madonna, Hugh Hefner, Magic Johnson, Gloria Steinem and Jocelyn Elders. Apparently, these are the people SIECUS wants young people to emulate.

What Does SIECUS Claim the Bible Says About Sex?

In the fall of 1996, Debra Haffner, the [former] president of SIECUS, took several theology classes at the Yale Divinity School. As the adage states, a little knowledge is a dangerous thing. Indeed! Ms. Haffner left Yale convinced that the religious community needed her enlightenment regarding sexuality education. And in an ultimate act of arrogance, Ms. Haffner [issued a SIECUS Report showing she] believes she possesses the new knowledge to correct nearly 2,000 years of serious biblical scholarship.

Some of the outrageous "insights" of Ms. Haffner's theology of sex include:[15]

- A major function of the Bible is to teach sexuality education.
- The Apostle Paul, along with Augustine and Aquinas and the Christian Coalition, have worked to deprive people of sexual freedom.
- The penis was chosen for the mark of the covenant between God and man "because it was the most holy part of the body."
- Abraham was involved in homosexual activity (Gen. 24:2).
- Jonathan and David had a homosexual encounter (1 Sam. 18:1; 2 Sam. 1:26).
- Adultery is not a sexual or moral sin but a violation of property rights.
- Boaz was the first sperm donor.
- Ruth and Naomi shared a homosexual relationship.
- Not a single patriarch in the Bible was monogamous.
- Proverbs 6:26 urges men to pay a loaf of bread for the services of a prostitute rather than be tempted by the wife of another man. (Proverbs 6:26 reads "For the prostitute reduces you to a loaf of bread, and the adulteress preys upon your very life." For centuries theologians have understood this verse to mean that sex outside of marriage, whether it be with a prostitute or adulteress, has severe consequences.)
- Celibacy is never presented positively in the Hebrew Bible.

Note: In August 1998 Focus on the Family published a paper entitled "What the Bible Really Says About Sex" in response to Ms. Haffner's claims. In this paper, four prominent theologians refute Ms. Haffner's claims with sound biblical interpretation. To obtain a copy, call (800) A-Family. The item number is FC099/21464.

THE DANGER OF THE SIECUS CAMPAIGN

SIECUS believes that the church should introduce comprehensive sexuality training to its young people for the following reasons:

- The majority of teens will become sexually active prior to marriage.
- Society must provide teens with the knowledge, skills and resources to avoid unintended pregnancies and STDs. To withhold information about contraception from teens puts them in life-threatening situations.
- Sexuality is an integral part of who we are as human beings.
- The church is an important influence in the life of many teens. Further, the church must be real with its kids, and this includes education about contraception.
- Therefore, churches should play a vastly expanded role in promoting and providing comprehensive sexuality education in their communities.[16]

Superficially, these tenets may sound reasonable, at least from a secular viewpoint. However, there are two major problems with this line of reasoning.

The *first problem* is that the basic foundational principle of comprehensive sexuality education—that condoms protect teens against pregnancy and STDs—is not true.

The federal government spends nearly $500 million per year to promote contraception.[17] Yet the nonmarital birthrate to sexually experienced teens stands close to the highest level ever.

While the rates of some STDs (such as HIV/AIDS) have moderated, other STDs (such as human papillomavirus [HPV], chlamydia and herpes) have reached epidemic levels. Condoms offer no protection against HPV[18] and little protection against chlamydia and herpes.[19]

Numerous research data show that comprehensive sex education contributes to the high rates of sexual activity, pregnancies and STDs. This is because comprehensive sex education presents adolescents with a confusing dual message that provides a license to become sexually active. Think about it. How will teens—with their hormones racing—react to a message that says "remain abstinent, but if you can't, use a condom"?

The *second problem* with the comprehensive sexuality message is that it is contrary to the clear teaching of scripture.

The church should be helping parents teach children about the importance of purity, character, principle, sacrifice, integrity and commitment, not about condoms and premarital sex. The church should do everything possible to help people live a life of abstinence before marriage and to help them be faithful within marriage. By adopting comprehensive sexuality the church is selling its soul to accommodate the fact that not all teens are virgins.

A recently published study, titled, "Promising the Future: Virginity Pledges as They Affect the Transition to First Intercourse," provides important evidence that pledging abstinence—such as is done in the "True Love Waits" movement—can have a dramatic effect in helping teens remain abstinent. And, even more important for this discussion, the pledge effort has proven to be especially effective for teens who are connected to a supportive faith community. The report stated, "The delay effect is substantial and almost impossible to erase. Taking a pledge delays intercourse for a long time."

Not surprisingly, SIECUS and company have tried to spin this "Promising the Future" report as evidence that kids need the safe-sex message.

So this new effort by SIECUS to reach the faith community represents a serious threat to scriptural integrity and the health of our young people. The Bible clearly teaches that sexuality is a wonderful gift from God. The Bible, with equal clarity, limits sex to a committed lifelong marriage relationship. Sex, like so many other gifts from God, brings blessings when used in a manner consistent with God's design and suffering when abused.

SIECUS correctly identifies sex as a gift of God. But SIECUS also places few restrictions on sex other than that it be consensual and "responsible" (using a condom).[20] Yet research clearly documents that nonmarital sex has adverse economic, psychological, spiritual and medical consequences.

Some churches are beginning to realize that their spiritual beliefs are seriously compromised by the SIECUS approach to sex education. For example, at its 1999 general assembly the Presbyterian Church (USA) struck down many liberal teachings that have been gradually phased in over the years. One assembly delegate commented that "[Teaching teens about contraceptives] lacks biblical integrity. We can teach the joys of sexual relationships, but we are called to live a life that proclaims Jesus. We cannot conform [to liberal thinking] any longer."[21]

The danger of SIECUS's efforts to reach the faith community takes three forms.

- Most individuals and churches deeply rooted in the Word of God will immediately see the SIECUS effort as the charade it is. But, searching for resources to help young people through the difficulties of adolescence, many church youth leaders without a firm biblical world-view may turn to SIECUS or a similar group for guidance. The result will be devastation in the lives of young people.
- Liberal church leaders may use the SIECUS material at church conventions and meetings in their attempt to add credibility to their radical agendas.
- Confused parents may rely on SIECUS-type material if the material is approved or recommended by their national church or synod headquarters.

WHAT MUST BE DONE

The body of Christ cannot afford to allow the SIECUS efforts to gain a foothold within the church. People of faith were largely silent when SIECUS invaded secular schools in the 1970s and 80s. The result has been an epidemic of out-of-wedlock births and STDs among an entire generation of young people.

Now SIECUS is attacking the church right through the front doors. People of faith must take a stand *now*. The very health and well-being of our children depend upon quick and decisive action.

The following are recommended action steps:

- Call your national, regional and district church offices to determine if SIECUS or SIECUS-type material has been or will be distributed, approved or recommended. Also ask your church officials if all the material they recommend unambiguously promotes abstinence-only until marriage. Note that SIECUS-based sex-ed materials may not always be clearly identified. Here are some characteristics that are common to such resources:
  - They base decision-making on "your values," rather than on God's revealed standards.
  - The word "tolerance" appears often throughout the text.
  - The terms "sexuality" and "mutual respect" are commonly used, but the term "sexual morality" is generally avoided.
  - Opinion polls are more likely to be cited than is the Bible.

   - "Rights" are referred to more often than are "responsibilities."
   - They tend to include many references to "sexual orientation" and to being "affirming."
   - "Wholeness" is more of a concern than is "holiness."
- If your national church body is connected in any way to SIECUS or a safe-sex philosophy, mobilize a group of parents, teenagers, pastors, theologians and youth leaders to educate others on the dangers of comprehensive sexuality education and the SIECUS philosophy.
- Draft and introduce a resolution at your church body's next district, regional and national conventions. The resolution should declare comprehensive sexuality education as inconsistent with the biblical standard of human sexuality.
- Draft and introduce another resolution affirming abstinence until marriage as the only biblical model for relational and sexual health.
- If your church has a sex-education program, confirm that it meets the following guidelines:
   - Curriculum and materials should be truly abstinence-centered.
   - Parents must be affirmed as the primary sex educators of their children.
   - Children involved in sexual activity should be referred to their parents rather than to outside sources.
   - No material or message should be value-neutral or moral-neutral.
   - Emphasis should be placed on dating guidelines, refusal skills and the biblical mandate for sexual purity until marriage.
   - All instruction should be age-appropriate and reflect the fact that embarrassment and modesty toward the subject of sex is normal, healthy and God-given, particularly among pre-adolescents and younger teens.
- Recommend the following organizations as the source of sex-education materials that are consistent with the biblical model or abstinence until marriage and faithfulness thereafter:
   - Focus on the Family (800) A-FAMILY
   - National Abstinence Clearing House (605) 335-3643
   - True Love Waits (800) 588-9248
   - National Network of Youth Ministries (619) 451-1111
   - Youth Specialties (800) 776-8008

ADDENDUM: THE SIECUS "SAFE-SEX" WEB

Debra Haffner [former SIECUS president] is among the board of advisors for an organization that calls itself the Center for Sexuality and Religion (CSR). In 1998, a consortium of liberal theologians, sexologists, educators, and health care professionals formed the CSR "to advance a positive relationship between sexuality and spirituality." Almost every one of CSR's directors and advisors signed the SIECUS declaration called the *Religious Declaration on Sexual Morality, Justice, and*

Healing, announced on January 18, 2000. That same year CSR joined with *The Renaissance Transgender Association* and the *International Foundation for Sexuality and Religion* to organize the *Fourth International Congress on Crossdressing, Sex and Gender.*

THE SIECUS-PAGAN CONNECTION

When SIECUS released its *Religious Declaration on Sexual Morality, Justice, and Healing* in January 2000, it claimed broad ecumenical endorsement and listed the names of 850 religious endorsers. But the vast majority of these religious endorsers were actually from one denomination—the Unitarian Universalists of America (UUA).

The Unitarian Universalists have almost uniformly rejected the authority of the Bible, and the denomination is openly aligned with the neo-pagan movement in the United States. Unitarians have even organized their own "Covenant of Unitarian Universalist Pagans" (CUUPS), and at the 2000 UUA General Assembly CUUPS presented a program titled: "Weaving Pagan Strands into UU Religious Education Curricula." CUUPS publishes an electronic magazine, *Connections Journal,* that includes a direct link to a web page called "Teens and Witchcraft" where teens are given instructions on "How to become a witch," "Starting a coven" and "Looking for spells."

SIECUS publicity on the *Religious Declaration on Sexual Morality, Justice, and Healing* implied its 850 endorsers were religious leaders representing a wide group of average American Christians. But average Christians in America are not openly pagan, and do not want their children seduced by witchcraft and sorcery.

SIECUS AND SEMINARIES

In 2000, SIECUS invited a number of seminary professors to a conference organized on sex education and the faith community. This was another effort to affect sexual morality in the church, this time by influencing those who train future pastors. It seems that SIECUS wants to turn shepherds into wolves.

NOTES

1. SIECUS Position Statements; "Setting the Record Straight: What Research Really Says About the Social Consequences of Homosexuality," Focus on the Family.
2. SIECUS Position Statements, 1991: Centers for Disease Control and Prevention.
3. Haffner, Debra W. (1990), "Sex Education 2000: A Call to Action," SIECUS.
4. James H. Jones, "Alfred C. Kinsey: A Public/Private Life," (New York: W. W. Norton & Company, 1997), see, for example, pp. 374 and 610.
5. "Guidelines for Comprehensive Sexuality Education: Kindergarten–12th Grade," SIECUS, 1991.
6. Mennonite Church, "Resolutions on Human Sexuality."
7. SIECUS, "A Time to Speak," pp. 30 and 33.
8. Wardell Pomeroy, Ph.D., original SIECUS board member, in a *Forum Variations* article, 1977.

9. Mary Calderone, SIECUS co-founder, in an interview with *Citizen* Magazine, "Pedophilia Steps into the Daylight," November 16, 1992.
10. "Guidelines for Comprehensive Sexuality Education: Kindergarten–12th Grade," SIECUS, 1991.
11. SIECUS Position Statements, 1991.
12. Debra Haffner, "Safe Sex and Teens," *SIECUS Report,* September/October, 1988.
13. SIECUS letter from Debra Haffner to all state governors, November 1997; *SIECUS Report,* April/May 1997; *SIECUS Report,* April/May 1998.
14. SIECUS Position Statements, 1991; "A Time to Speak," pp. 13.
15. Debra Haffner, "The Really Good News: What the Bible Says About Sex," *SIECUS Report,* October/November 1997; Haffner speech to Illinois Caucus for Sexual Health, December 8, 1998.
16. SIECUS, "A Time to Speak," pp. 13-19.
17. Subcommittee on Oversight and Investigations of the Committee on Commerce, U. S. House of Representatives, hearing on the Implementation of the Abstinence Education Provisions in the Welfare Reform Act, September 25, 1998, U. S. Government Printing Office, Serial No. 105-123.
18. Dr. Ronald Valdiserri, Deputy Director, Centers for Disease Control and Prevention, statement before a U. S. House of Representatives Subcommittee on Health and Environment, March 16, 1999.
19. Cates and Stone, "Family Planning and Sexually Transmitted Diseases," *Family Planning Perspectives,* March/April 1992, vol. 24, no. 2.
20. Debra W. Haffner, "A Time to Speak: Faith Communities and Sexuality Education," SIECUS, 1998, p. 11.
21. "Sex Curriculum in Church to Change," Associated Press, June 26, 1999.

APPENDIX D

A TALK ON ANGLICANS DIVIDING OVER ELECTING A NON-CELIBATE HOMOSEXUAL BISHOP

A Global and Gospel Perspective on Responding to the Episcopal Church of the United States Electing an Openly Practicing Homosexual—Gene Robinson—Bishop of New Hampshire
Given by: Peter Jensen, Archbishop of Sydney, Australia
Delivered at: The Falls Church (Episcopal)
July 23, 2003

Note: Peter Jensen, Archbishop of Sydney, Australia, and many other Anglicans leaders from around the world came to America just prior to the vote confirming Gene Robinson as a bishop in order to plan a suitable, worldwide response faithful to biblical sexual moral teaching. Archbishop Jensen's talk came just after this worldwide meeting of Anglican leaders, and just before Gene Robinson was made a bishop in the Episcopal Church of the United States in a vote that took place August 6, 2003. These remarks were given extemporaneously at a point of great crisis for the church.

Friends, I couldn't have dreamed, a week ago, that I would be standing here with you, and I don't suppose you could have dreamed that I would be meeting with you either. That, in itself, indicates the significance of what is going on. I'm so delighted that you have met to pray tonight, because what is going on is so momentous that if the people of God do not call upon the living God for help, we would be derelict in our duty. We are living, as it happens, in momentous days, and I can't think of anything better for you to be doing tonight than gathering like this. I trust, therefore, that I won't go on and on, but will give us time to supplicate to the Lord, which is what we are really here to do.

Where to start? Where to finish? In one sense, we've got to start a long way back. Let me tell you of the meeting of the last two days (called to plan how faithful Anglicans, worldwide, should respond to the American church electing a non-celibate bishop). We have issued a statement. So perhaps I could start at that point. I won't read all of it, but it says (in part):

> We, mainstream Anglican leaders from provinces all around the world, comprising a majority of the world's 75 million Anglicans, have gathered on the eve of the General Convention [of the Episcopal Church in the United States] to confirm a non-celibate homosexual as a bishop and to approve the creation of liturgies for the blessing of same-sex relationships. If that happens, it would shatter the church. Such unconstitutional actions would separate the church from the historic Christian faith and teaching, alienate it from the fellowship and accountability of the worldwide Anglican family and confuse the witness of the church to the love and joy of Christian marriage. In response to this crisis, we are to reaffirm our commitment to the teaching of the historic, Christian church, our fellowship with sisters and brothers in the global Anglican family and the joyful proclamation of Christ's love for the church as reflected in the sacrament of marriage. The proposed actions will precipitate a dramatic realignment of the church. The American bishops at this meeting [on how faithful Anglicans should respond to electing a non-celibate homosexual bishop] have prayed, planned and are prepared to respond as faithful members of the Anglican Communion. And should these events occur, the majority of the Primates [national Anglican leaders from around the world] anticipate convening an extraordinary meeting at which they, too, will respond to the actions of the [American] General Convention.

Now, you may be wondering, "Why all this worldwide attention to what is going on in an American church?" Let me say that it is inevitable that there will be this worldwide attention. It is because what you do here (and all the more in the last ten years with the internet) has profound influence on the rest of the millions and millions of people throughout the world—their bishops, their clergy, their teachers.

You say, "How's that the case?" Well, it influences me. I come from one city well known as a "leading gay city" [in Australia]. When I get up to preach the gospel, I'm now always being asked, "But your Anglican friends in America don't believe as you believe, do they?" So, I've got to distance myself from my American Episcopal friends and say, "I think they've fallen into grievous error." That's not good. But my problem is nothing compared to the problem, say, of the Africans, who are face-to-face with Muslims. And the Muslims in the world are saying, "There you are. You Christians are immoral, and Christianity is immoral." And this is being used [against the witness of the church]. The actions of the American church—absolutely repudiated by the African church—are going to be used against the African church, with evangelistic and other consequences. It is going to make life very difficult for them. So, you see, it is a global problem that we are dealing with here.

Now, you may say, "Yes, but there are a lot of things we may do that will have global implications. Why this one in particular? Aren't we always going on about sex? Why choose this one? Is it what you may call a *gospel* issue?" Well, dear friends, yes, we [Anglicans] have had many tensions and difficulties and disputes. I suppose the ordination of women to the priesthood and the consecration of women to the Episcopate [women bishops] would be the last ones that created a fairly big ripple round the world. And we've coped with that—whatever our views are. But this one is different. This one really is a gospel issue.

Let me read you what the apostle says in the first letter of Paul to the Corinthians, chapter 6. He says:

> Do you not know that wrong doers will not inherit the kingdom of God? Do not be deceived, fornicators, idolaters, adulterers, male prostitutes [passive homosexuals], sodomites [active homosexuals], thieves, the greedy, drunkards, revilers and robbers—none of these will inherit the kingdom of God.

Now, we're not dealing here with people who fall by temptation into sin from time to time, as we all do. We are talking here about those who adopt deliberately, as a pattern of life, that which is utterly opposed to the teaching of God in the holy scriptures. And explicitly, as well as fornication and greed, there is the practice of homosexual sex. As you know, the scriptures love sex in marriage—where it belongs. So, this is a matter of the future life and death and condemnation of souls. It is a matter of heaven and hell! We can't stand back and simply say, "Yes, well, that's okay—that's the teaching of your church. We don't agree with it." What you do here is going to have a big impact on my capacity to preach the gospel and to win people for Jesus and to win people from hell under God's good hand. It is going to have a tremendous ripple effect right throughout the world.

It's also a matter of disunity. When this happens, you're going to hear a lot about unity. You're going to hear that the bishops who set this statement going [about expelling the Episcopal Church in the United States from the worldwide Anglican Communion] are the people who have broken unity. Let us be ready for this, because the people who are breaking unity are the people who are giving themselves to this brand new teaching. That is why the bishops and archbishops, with the rest of the people who've gathered at this meeting, are really saying, "The church belongs to us. We are the Anglican Communion." Look at what the Primates [national Anglican leaders] say [in the statement read at the opening of this talk] as to who the orthodox Christians in this denomination are. It is the people who have not moved. It is the people who have not broken unity. That is the significance of the Primates for you. I've said that what you do impacts us. But we [bishops from other parts of the world] have a role to play in your church, as well. For, if you are trying to work out truth from error, one of the useful ways of doing it is to ask yourself, "Well, what do other Christians believe about all this?"

In your society, the gay agenda has been so powerful and so effective, as it has in my society, that it is easy for Christians to feel we must be a tiny minority here. There must be something wrong with us. But, we want to tell you that the vast majority of your fellow Anglicans throughout the world believe exactly what the scriptures have always taught, and what the church has always taught. You are in unity with them. And, we want to say too, that if you look across the Christians in all the world—the Roman Catholics, the Orthodox, the Baptists—if you look at all the Christians around the world, 99 percent still believe that the practice of homosexuality is sinful and endangering to souls.

You may say, "Why sex?" Well, I've said because it is a gospel issue. But the other reason "Why sex?" is because they keep talking about it. It is not we who have made this into a major subject. It is this sex-saturated Western culture of ours which makes it into a major subject. And I think God does too, actually. If you read the scriptures, there is a lot about sex and the proper way of conducting our sexual lives. It is an important matter—very much so. We ought not be surprised that the contest for the gospel is occurring in this area, at this moment. If we say, "I'd rather it didn't, I'd rather be contesting for the gospel somewhere else," our danger is that we will contest for the gospel where there is no actual fight going on. Easy for us. But it leaves other people in the lurch.

So, dear friends, I want to say to you tonight, that the matter before your church, at the moment, is of *momentous significance!* There has never been, in my lifetime, a matter like it. And, you can see the momentous nature of it by thinking too (and this is very strange and interesting in the Lord's providence) that the matter has come up [already] in England, where the Christians in England immediately rose up in arms against the appointment of a gay bishop. And the appointment was withdrawn [by the Archbishop of Canterbury, who presides over the worldwide Anglican Communion], as you probably read. It has occurred [also] in Canada in the diocese of New Westminster, where nine faithful parishes [local churches] out of a total of 80 or so in that diocese have withdrawn from allegiance to their bishop. They have called themselves the Anglican Communion in New Westminster because they have not changed at all, and we must recognize them as being the authentic Anglicans in that place. I do. I hope you do. It's not they who have changed. And a very brave bishop, the Bishop of the Yukon, Terence Buckle—praise God for this man!—has offered to be the bishop of those parishes. You can imagine the fuss that has caused! He's not a popular person! But I met him last weekend, and I didn't tell him this, but I was in awe of him! I stood when he came into the room because he is a great man! That's happening there. And then, of course, there is what's happening in your church.

Dear brothers and sisters, I can't see this [election of a non-celibate homosexual bishop] stopped in your church [the Episcopal Church of the United States]. The head of steam is so great. But I do think of Gideon. I think of his 300. I think of the way in which, when we don't trust in the arm of flesh but in the arm of the Spirit, great things can happen. I commend you again for meeting to pray, and I urge you to make this a matter of consistent prayer, particularly in the next two or three weeks. Pray for those bishops who have been meeting here today to plan how Anglicans around the world should respond to the Episcopal Church in the United States electing a non-celibate homosexual bishop, and pray that we will see, instead of a disaster, good things happening. Even if it goes the other way, pray that this [plans for how faithful Anglicans around the world should respond] will make clear what the gospel issues are, so that those who are faithful to the gospel and to the Lord will be able to stand. And that's going to be costly for everyone.

NOTES

PREFACE

1. "Anna Nicole Smith Says Pup Needs Prozac," *The News and Observer* (Raleigh, N.C.), November 14, 2002, 2A.
2. Philip Yancey, "Holy Sex: How It Ravishes Our Souls," *Christianity Today,* October 2003, 47.
3. John Feinberg and Paul Feinberg, *Ethics for a Brave New World* (Wheaton, Ill.: Crossway, 1993).

CHAPTER 1
SEX AT THE CENTER OF OUR MORAL CRISIS

1. Lillian Rubin writes, "We know there's a new vision of masculinity and femininity, but can't figure out how it fits each of us" (Lillian B. Rubin, *Intimate Strangers: Men and Women Together* [New York: Harper & Row, 1983], 8).
2. Figures are from the 2000 Census published by U. S. Census Bureau, May 15, 2001. For comparisons see William J. Bennett, *The Index of Leading Cultural Indicators* (Washington, D.C.: Heritage Foundation and Empower America, 1993).
3. Charles Krauthammer, "God and Sex at Yale," *The Weekly Standard,* September 29, 1997, 11-12.
4. "Students Sue Yale over Housing," *Christian Century,* November 5, 1997; "Orthodox Lawsuit Dismissed at Yale," *Christian Century,* August 26–September 2, 1998, 778-779.
5. Cited in R. Albert Mohler, "In Condoms We Trust: Jane Fonda Rides to the Rescue," *Fidelitas* (www.sbts.edu/mohler/FidelitasRead.php?article=fide1012).
6. Associated Press, "Graduate Gives Speech in the Buff," *News and Observer* (Raleigh, N.C.), June 18, 1998, 2A.
7. Roy Maynard, "Burned Out," *World,* September 18, 1999, 24-26; David Skinner, "What I Saw at Burning Man," *Weekly Standard,* September 27, 1999, 21-24.
8. R. U. Sirius, "The New Counterculture," *Time,* November 9, 1998, 89.
9. Maynard, "Burned Out," 24-25.
10. Cited in Skinner, "What I Saw at Burning Man," 23.
11. Maynard, "Burned Out," 24-25.
12. "Group Urges Same-Sex Blessings," *Tennessean* (Nashville), February 20, 2000 (www.tennessean.com).
13. This division into three broad categories—traditional, modern, and postmodern—is more general and inclusive than the four counterfeit versions of sexual morality covered in chapters 12–15. Readers should note that the romantic, playboy, and therapeutic approaches to sexual morality are all in the modernist category, whereas pagan sexual morality is in the postmodern.

14. Brochure for a conference on "The Family and Human Sexuality" (Ethics and Religious Liberty Commission, 1998).
15. For example, see: Drucilla Cornell, *Beyond Accommodation: Ethical Feminism, Deconstruction, and the Law* (Lanham, Md.: Rowman & Littlefield, 1999); Franklin E. Kameny, "Deconstructing the Traditional Family," *The World and I,* October 1993, 383-395; or Michel Foucault, *Ethics, Subjectivity, and Truth* (New York: New Press, 1997).
16. Abraham Kuyper, *Calvinism: Six Lectures Delivered at the Theological Seminary at Princeton* (New York: Revell, 1899), 273, his emphasis.
17. Ibid., 17, his emphasis.
18. Ibid., 47.
19. Ibid., 272-273.
20. C. S. Lewis, *Miracles: A Preliminary Study* (New York: Macmillan, 1947), 123-124.
21. Ibid., 85.
22. Ibid.
23. Francis A. Schaeffer, *The Church at the End of the Twentieth Century* (Downers Grove, Ill.: InterVarsity Press, 1970), 81.
24. Francis A. Schaeffer, *The Great Evangelical Disaster* (Westchester, Ill.: Crossway, 1984), 22-23.
25. Schaeffer, *Church at the End of the Twentieth Century,* 15-16.
26. Schaeffer, *Great Evangelical Disaster,* 36-37.
27. Schaeffer, *Church at the End of the Twentieth Century,* 81.
28. Schaeffer, *Great Evangelical Disaster,* 23.
29. Ibid., 36-37.
30. Ibid.
31. Carl F. H. Henry, *Twilight of a Great Civilization* (Westchester, Ill.: Crossway, 1988).
32. Ibid., 15.
33. Ibid., 27.
34. Ibid.
35. Ibid., 19.

CHAPTER 2
THE RETURN OF SEXUAL PAGANISM

1. Margot Adler, *Drawing Down the Moon: Witches, Druids, Goddess-worshipers and Other Pagans in America Today* (Boston: Beacon, 1986), 182.
2. In *The Politics of Women's Spirituality* (ed. Charlene Spretnak [New York: Doubleday, 1982]), forty-five feminist writers urge women to rediscover their sexual divinity through goddess worship. Other recent titles include: Mary Daly, *Pure Lust* (Boston: Beacon, 1984); Carter Hayward, *Touching Our Strength* (San Francisco: Harper, 1989); and Riane Eisler, *Sacred Pleasure* (Boston: Element, 1995).
3. David F. Wells, *No Place for Truth: Or Whatever Happened to Evangelical Theology?* (Grand Rapids, Mich.: Eerdmans, 1993), 266. The quoted portion is from Mircea Eliade, *Cosmos and History* (New York: Harper & Row, 1954), 28.
4. C. S. Lewis, *Miracles: A Preliminary Study* (New York: Macmillan, 1947), 86.
5. Ibid., 85.

6. Ibid., 124-125.
7. Michel Foucault, *The History of Sexuality,* vol. 1, *An Introduction,* trans. Robert Hurley (New York: Random House, 1990), 156.
8. Daly, *Pure Lust,* 3.
9. Thomas Moore, *The Soul of Sex: Cultivating Life as an Act of Love* (New York: HarperCollins, 1998), 138, 161.
10. Eugene F. Rogers, Jr., *Sexuality and the Christian Body: Their Way into the Triune God* (Oxford: Blackwell, 1999), 230-232.
11. Chris Glaser, *Coming Out as Sacrament* (Louisville: Westminster/John Knox, 1998), 7, 118.
12. Peter Jones, *Spirit Wars: Pagan Revival in Christian America* (Mukilteo, Wash.: WinePress, 1997), 227-228.
13. Monica Sjoo and Barbara Mor, *The Great Cosmic Mother: Rediscovering the Religion of the Earth* (San Francisco: Harper, 1987), 176.
14. Ibid., 178. The view of life and death in pagan religious sacrifice is not the same as the biblical view, which also involves life and death. In biblical religion, death destroys life and is the ultimate sanction by which God controls the destiny of men; whereas, in pagan religion, death generates life and is the ultimate means by which men control divine powers running the universe.
15. Roy Maynard, "Burned Out," *World,* September 18, 1999, 25.
16. See Mary A. Kassian, *The Feminist Gospel: The Movement to Unite Feminism with the Church* (Wheaton, Ill.: Crossway, 1992), 149-151.
17. Robin Morgan, *Going Too Far: The Personal Chronicle of a Feminist* (New York: Random House, 1977), 302.
18. For example, see the highly offensive way Daly and Caputi define the Christian God under the terms "godfather" and "god/rod," in Mary Daly and Jane Caputi, *Websters' First New Intergalactic Wickedary of the English Language* (Boston: Beacon, 1987), 203.
19. Sjoo and Mor, *Cosmic Mother,* 270.
20. Ginette Paris, *The Sacrament of Abortion* (Dallas: Spring, 1992), 8, 70. Other books by Paris promoting sexual paganism include: *La Renaissance d'Aphrodite* (Montreal: Boreal Express, 1985); *Pagan Meditations* (Dallas: Spring, 1986); and *Pagan Grace* (Dallas: Spring, 1990).
21. Ibid., 17.
22. Ibid., 56.
23. Moore, *Soul of Sex,* 69.
24. Ibid., 17.
25. John Shelby Spong, *Why Christianity Must Change or Die: A Bishop Speaks to Believers in Exile* (New York: HarperCollins, 1998), 5.
26. Ibid., 210.
27. Ibid., 95.
28. Naomi R. Goldenberg, *Changing of the Gods: Feminism and the End of Traditional Religions* (Boston: Beacon, 1979), 90.
29. Ibid., 3.
30. Ibid., 106, 25.
31. Daly and Caputi, *Wickedary,* 255.

32. Mary Daly, *Beyond God the Father: Toward a Philosophy of Women's Liberation* (Boston: Beacon, 1973), 29; Mary Daly, *Gyn/Ecology: The Metaethics of Radical Feminism* (Boston: Beacon, 1978), xi.
33. Daly, *Beyond God,* 19.
34. Daly, *Pure Lust,* 131.
35. Daly and Caputi, *Wickedary,* 189-190.
36. Ibid., 96.
37. Mary Daly, *Outercourse: The Be-Dazzling Voyage* (San Francisco: Harper, 1992), 137-140; Mary Daly, "Sin Big," *New Yorker,* February 26 and March 4, 1996, 82.
38. Daly, *Outercourse,* 144.
39. Ibid., 21.
40. Daly, *Beyond God,* 71-72.
41. Daly, "Sin Big," 76.
42. Daly, *Beyond God,* 13; Daly and Caputi, *Wickedary,* 76-77; Daly, *Pure Lust,* 423.
43. Daly, *Beyond God,* 29.
44. Daly, *Pure Lust,* 269.
45. See Daly, "Sin Big," 78; Daly and Caputi, *Wickedary,* 93; also note Daly, *Beyond God,* 95; Daly, *Pure Lust,* 9.
46. Daly, *Pure Lust,* 31, 151, 280.
47. Ibid., 152.
48. Ibid., 281.
49. Ibid., 248-249.
50. Ibid., 245-246.
51. Mary Daly, *The Church and the Second Sex: With the Feminist Postchristian Introduction and New Archaic Afterwords* (Boston: Beacon, 1985), xiv.
52. Daly, *Pure Lust,* 246.
53. Daly, *Second Sex,* xxvii.
54. Daly, *Pure Lust,* 3.
55. Paris, *Sacrament of Abortion,* 107.
56. Sjoo and Mor, *Cosmic Mother,* 377.
57. Ibid., 388.
58. Paris, *Sacrament of Abortion,* 93-94.
59. Sjoo and Mor, *Cosmic Mother,* 388-389, their emphasis.
60. Paris, *Sacrament of Abortion,* 57.
61. Ibid., 2.
62. Sjoo and Mor, *Cosmic Mother,* 377, their emphasis.
63. Ibid., 378, their emphasis.
64. Ibid., 388.
65. Paris, *Sacrament of Abortion,* 72-73.
66. Ibid., 34, 51.
67. Sjoo and Mor, *Cosmic Mother,* 208-209.

Chapter 3
Paganizing "Christian" Sexual Morality

1. Naomi R. Goldenberg, *Changing of the Gods: Feminism and the End of Traditional Religions* (Boston: Beacon, 1979), 4-5.

2. Ibid., 9.
3. Especially note: Rosemary Radford Ruether, *Sexism and God-Talk: Toward a Feminist Theology* (Boston: Beacon, 1983), 39; and Rosemary Radford Ruether, "Feminist Theology and Spirituality," in *Christian Feminism: Visions of a New Humanity,* ed. Judith Weidman (San Francisco: Harper & Row, 1984), 15.
4. Rosemary Radford Ruether, *Women and Redemption: A Theological History* (Minneapolis: Fortress, 1998), 222; and Rosemary Radford Ruether, "Asking the Existential Questions: How My Mind Has Changed," *Christian Century,* April 2, 1980, 375, 376.
5. Ruether, "Asking the Existential Questions," 375.
6. Rosemary Radford Ruether, *Disputed Questions: On Being a Christian* (Nashville: Abingdon, 1982), 136-137.
7. Ginette Paris, *The Sacrament of Abortion* (Dallas: Spring, 1992), 34; Monica Sjoo and Barbara Mor, *The Great Cosmic Mother: Rediscovering the Religion of the Earth* (San Francisco: Harper, 1987), 208.
8. Ruether, "Feminist Theology and Spirituality," 15.
9. Ruether, "Asking the Existential Questions," 377.
10. Ibid., 375; Ruether, *Sexism and God-Talk,* 21.
11. Ruether, "Feminist Theology and Spirituality," 16.
12. Ruether, *Women and Redemption,* 275.
13. Rosemary Radford Ruether, *Introducing Redemption in Christian Feminism* (Cleveland: Pilgrim, 1998), 103.
14. Rosemary Radford Ruether, *Woman-Church: Theology and Practice of Feminist Liturgical Communities* (San Francisco: HarperSanFrancisco, 1992), 130, 220, 223.
15. Ibid., 173-181, 188-190, 196-200.
16. Ibid., 189.
17. Virginia Ramey Mollenkott, *Sensuous Spirituality: Out from Fundamentalism* (New York: Crossroad, 1992), 18-21. Mollenkott's reliance on a "Spirit Guide" other than Christ himself revealed in scripture amounts to activity that God strongly abhors (see Deut. 18:10-12).
18. Ibid., 16.
19. Virginia Ramey Mollenkott, *Godding: Human Responsibility in the Bible* (New York: Crossroad, 1987), 6; Mollenkott, *Sensuous Spirituality,* 17.
20. Mollenkott, *Sensuous Spirituality,* 12.
21. Ibid., 16-17, her emphasis.
22. Ibid., 27.
23. Virginia Ramey Mollenkott, "An Evangelical Feminist Confronts the Goddess," *Christian Century,* October 20, 1982, 1044-1046.
24. Mollenkott, *Sensuous Spirituality,* 97.
25. "The RE-Imagining Conference," *American Family Association,* April 1994, 13.
26. Mollenkott, *Sensuous Spirituality,* 74.
27. Virginia Ramey Mollenkott, "A Call to Subversion," *The Other Side,* July-August 1999, 14-19.
28. Ibid., 16.
29. Tina Pippin and Susan Henking, eds., "Alter(ed) Sexualities: Bringing Lesbian and Gay Studies to the Religion Classroom," *Spotlight on Teaching* 4, no. 2 (November 1996): 1.

30. See Tina Pippin, "Jezebel Re-Vamped," *Semeia,* no. 69-70 (1995): 221-233.
31. Personal communication from an individual who attended the lecture.
32. James B. Nelson, "Reuniting Sexuality and Spirituality," *Christian Century,* February 25, 1987, 189.
33. James B. Nelson, *Body Theology* (Louisville: Westminster/John Knox, 1992), 53.
34. James B. Nelson, *Between Two Gardens: Reflections on Sexuality and Religious Experience* (New York: Pilgrim, 1983), 32; Nelson, *Body Theology,* 23; James B. Nelson and Sandra P. Longfellow, eds., *Sexuality and the Sacred: Sources of Theological Reflection* (Louisville: Westminster/John Knox, 1994), xiv.
35. Nelson, *Sexuality and the Sacred,* xiv.
36. Nelson, "Reuniting Sexuality and Spirituality," 188.
37. Nelson, *Sexuality and the Sacred,* 195.
38. Nelson, "Reuniting Sexuality and Spirituality," 189.
39. Nelson, *Body Theology,* 62.
40. Ibid., 52.
41. James B. Nelson, *The Intimate Connection: Male Sexuality, Masculine Spirituality* (Philadelphia: Westminster, 1988), 13-14.
42. Nelson, "Reuniting Sexuality with Spirituality," 189.
43. Ibid., xiv-xv.
44. Eugene F. Rogers, Jr., *Sexuality and the Christian Body: Their Way into the Triune God* (Oxford: Blackwell, 1999).
45. Ibid., 1.
46. Ibid., 11.
47. Ibid., 225.
48. Ibid.
49. Ibid., 232-233.
50. Ibid., 232.
51. Ibid., 251-252.
52. Ibid., 240.
53. Ibid., 230, 232-233.
54. Ibid., 52.
55. Chris Glaser graduated from Yale University Divinity School with an M.Div. in 1977 and served for at least ten years as director of the Lazarus Project, a ministry promoting gay and lesbian relationships funded by the Presbyterian Church (USA).
56. Chris Glaser, *Coming Out as Sacrament* (Louisville: Westminster/John Knox, 1998), 2.
57. Ibid., 120, emphasis added.
58. Ibid., 9.
59. Ibid., 4-5.
60. Ibid., 117.
61. Ibid., 11.
62. Ibid., 12.
63. Ibid., 82.
64. Ibid., 91.
65. Ibid., 118.
66. Ibid., 119-120.
67. Thomas Jefferson, *Report of the Commissioners Appointed to Fix the Site of the University of Virginia, August 1, 1818,* in *Thomas Jefferson and the Development*

of American Public Education, by James B. Conant (Los Angeles: University of California Press, 1963), 134.

CHAPTER 4
MAINLINE DENOMINATIONS IN SEXUAL TURMOIL

1. Susan Kauffman, "Students Say Divinity School Keeps Sexual Issues in Closet," *News and Observer* (Raleigh, N.C.), September 8, 1996, 1B.
2. Elizabeth Stuart and Adrian Thatcher, eds., *Christian Perspectives on Sexuality and Gender* (Grand Rapids, Mich.: Eerdmans, 1996), x.
3. John Shelby Spong, *Why Christianity Must Change or Die: A Bishop Speaks to Believers in Exile* (San Francisco: Harper-Collins, 1998), 151.
4. Walter C. Righter, *A Pilgrim's Way: The Personal Story of the Episcopal Bishop Charged with Heresy for Ordaining a Gay Man Who Was in a Committed Relationship* (New York: Alfred A. Knopf, 1998), 3.
5. Randy Frame, "Heresy Charges Dismissed," *Christianity Today,* June 17, 1996, 57.
6. Timothy Morgan, Robert Nowell, and David Virtue, "Anglicans Deem Homosexuality Incompatible with Scripture," *Christianity Today,* September 7, 1998, 32-33.
7. "Bishop Spong Delivers a Fiery Farewell," *Christian Century,* February 17, 1999, 178.
8. "Episcopalians Face Crisis," *News and Observer* (Raleigh, N.C.), July 19, 2003, 4A.
9. "A Place to Stand: A Call to Action," American Anglican Council (October 7-9, 2003). Available online at: www.americananglican.org/petitions/petition.cfm?petitionID=8. See also, "Kuala Lumpur Statement on Human Sexuality," 2nd Anglican Encounter of the South (February 10-15, 1997). Available online at: www.episcopalian.org/efac/articles/kuala.htm.
10. David Kucharsky, "United Methodists: Aspirin to Vitamins," *Christianity Today,* May 5, 1972, 38.
11. Edward E. Plowman, "United Methodists: The View from Portland," *Christianity Today,* June 18, 1976, 35, emphasis added.
12. Randy Frame, "In American Methodism's 200th Year, Evangelicals Are Celebrating," *Christianity Today,* June 15, 1984, 56.
13. Thomas C. Oden, *Requiem: A Lament in Three Movements* (Nashville: Abingdon, 1995), 156.
14. Tom Oden expresses this view in "Mainstreaming the Mainline," *Christianity Today,* August 7, 2000, 59, 61.
15. Three Methodist bodies joined to form the Methodist Church in 1939, and this became the United Methodist Church in 1968 with the addition of the Evangelical United Brethren (German Methodist) Church. For more, see *The Book of Discipline of the United Methodist Church* (Nashville: United Methodist Publishing House, 2000).
16. For further elaboration, please see my treatment of "No Lustful Desires" in chapter 9.
17. *The Lutheran* 20 (April 1988): 48.

18. *The Church and Human Sexuality: A Lutheran Perspective,* Evangelical Lutheran Church in America, Division for Church in Society, Department of Studies, Task Force on Human Sexuality (October 1993).
19. See Leonard Klein's account in "Lutherans in Sexual Commotion," *First Things* 43 (May 1994): 31-38.
20. "Irreconcilable Differences? Excerpts from the Majority Report of the PC(USA)'s Special Committee on Human Sexuality," *Christianity Today,* April 29, 1991, 38.
21. Randy Frame, "Sexuality Report Draws Fire," *Christianity Today,* April 29, 1991, 37.
22. Randy Frame, "Presbyterian Assembly Rejects Sexuality Report," *Christianity Today,* July 22, 1991, 37-38.
23. Gayle White, "Presbyterians Retain Ban on Homosexual Ordination," *Christianity Today,* August 12, 1996, 57.
24. Jack Rogers, "A Meditation on Lincoln's Second Inaugural," *The Presbyterian Outlook,* May 6, 2002, 6.
25. Cited in Judith Kohler, "Gay Clergy Ban Up for Debate," Associated Press, May 24, 2003.
26. I refer to the Southern Baptist Convention (SBC) as the mainline Baptist denomination because it is indeed the main, majority, and now certainly far largest Baptist denomination in the United States. The SBC emerged in 1845 from a loose association of Baptist churches called the General Missionary Convention of the Baptist Denomination in the United States for Foreign Missions. This was not as yet a fully organized national denomination. Baptists in the south formed the SBC as a national denomination in 1845, and Baptists in the north later organized to become the American Baptist Convention, now the American Baptist Churches USA (ABCUSA). As of 2002, the SBC comprised 16 million members, whereas the ABCUSA comprised 1.4 million members. Since repenting of historic racism in 1995, the SBC has also grown to become one of the largest black denominations in the United States with nearly 3,000 black congregations.
27. Cited in Cathy Lynn Grossman, "Baptists' Wife Edict Fires Up Feelings," *USA Today,* June 11, 1998, 6D.
28. Gustav Niebuhr, "Southern Baptists Declare Wife Should Submit to Her Husband," *New York Times,* June 10, 1998, A20.
29. Cited in Hamil R. Harris, "Baptist Call for Submissive Wives Criticized," *Washington Post,* June 12, 1998, C3.
30. Cited in Steve Kloehn, "Baptists Say Wives Should Submit," *Chicago Tribune,* June 10, 1998, 4A.
31. *Baptist Faith and Message 2000* (Nashville: Southern Baptist Convention, 2000).
32. Cited in Tony W. Cartledge and Steve DeVane, "Key Changes Proposed for BF&M," *Biblical Recorder,* May 27, 2000, 11.
33. Cited in Russell D. Moore, "CBF to Approve Funding for Pro-homosexual Groups," *SBC Baptist Press,* June 30, 2000.
34. Cited in Don Hinkle, "CBF Homosexual Stance Ignites Controversy Over Group's Direction," *SBC Baptist Press,* October 30, 2000.
35. Cited in Russell D. Moore, "CB Speakers Demand Divorce from SBC," *SBC Baptist Press,* June 30, 2000; Russell D. Moore, "Mohler Is Right, CB Members Say on Question of Biblical Authority," *SBC Baptist Press,* June 30, 2000;

Russell D. Moore, "CB Affiliated Group Urges Women to Leave the SBC," *SBC Baptist Press,* June 30, 2000.
36. Laurie Goodstein, "Decades of Damage," *New York Times,* January 12, 2003, 21.
37. Cited in Cathy Lynn Grossman, "What's Ahead for the Church," *USA Today,* April 22, 2002, 1D.
38. Andrew Sullivan, "They Know Not What They Do," *Time,* May 6, 2002, 31.
39. Goodstein, "Decades of Damage," 1.
40. Richard John Neuhaus, "Sexual and Related Disorders," *First Things* 131 (March 2003): 71.
41. Cited in Mary Eberstadt, "The Elephant in the Sacristy," *Weekly Standard,* June 17, 2002, 22.
42. Pater Ignotus, "What Are We Advertising?" *The Tablet,* April 24, 1999, 553.
43. Michael S. Rose, *Goodbye, Good Men* (Washington, D.C.: Regnery, 2002), 56.
44. Cited in Neuhaus, "Sexual and Related Disorders," 68.
45. Donald B. Cozzens, *The Changing Face of the Priesthood* (Collegeville, Minn.: Liturgical Press, 2000), 99.
46. Goodstein, "Decades of Damage," 21.
47. Rose, *Goodbye, Good Men,* 58.
48. Cited in Goodstein, "Decades of Damage," 21.
49. Cited in ibid.
50. Cited in Neuhaus, "Sexual and Related Disorders," 71.

CHAPTER 5
IS PAGAN SEXUALITY AFFECTING EVANGELICALS?

1. "Coming Attractions: Gay Activism Is Not Just Found in Liberal Churches," *Christianity Today,* August 2003, 33.
2. Virginia Ramey Mollenkott, *Sensuous Spirituality: Out from Fundamentalism* (New York: Crossroad, 1993); Virginia Ramey Mollenkott, "A Call to Subversion," *The Other Side,* July–August 1999, 14-19.
3. *St. Cyprian: The Lapsed; The Unity of the Catholic Church,* trans. Maurice Bevenot (Westminster, Md.: Newman, 1957), 43, 45.
4. Francis A. Schaeffer, *The Great Evangelical Disaster* (Westchester, Ill.: Crossway, 1984), 141.
5. Ibid., 150.
6. Ibid., 132, 139.
7. Ibid., 136-137.
8. Ibid., 133, 134-135, 136, his emphasis.
9. Ibid., 136.
10. Barna Research Group, "Christians Are More Likely to Experience Divorce than Are Non-Christians" (December 21, 1999); available online at: www.barna.org/cgibin/PagePressRelease.asp?PressReleaseID=39.
11. Os Guinness, *The Gravedigger File* (Downers Grove, Ill.: InterVarsity Press, 1983), 100. Cited from *Context,* December 15, 1981, 6.
12. Ibid. Cited from Peter Williamson and Kevin Perrotta, *Christianity Confronts Modernity* (Ann Arbor, Mich.: Servant, 1981), 12.

13. Cited in Gregory Rumburg, "Judging Amy," *CCM Magazine,* November 1999, 36.
14. Amy Grant, cited in ibid.
15. Judith K. Balswick and Jack O. Balswick, *Authentic Human Sexuality: An Integrated Christian Approach* (Downers Grove, Ill.: InterVarsity Press, 1999), 102.
16. Ibid., 144-145.
17. John F. Alexander, "Feminism as a Subversive Activity," *The Other Side,* July 1982, 8.
18. Letha Dawson Scanzoni, "Can Homosexuals Change?" *The Other Side,* January 1984, 12-15; Virginia Ramey Mollenkott, "A Call to Subversion," *The Other Side,* July–August 1999, 14-19; Kathy Olsen, "Out of Season," *The Other Side,* January–February 2001, 21-23.
19. Ralph Blair, *Holier-Than-Thou Hocus-Pocus and Homosexuality* (New York: Homosexual Community Counseling Center, 1977), 3.
20. Ralph Blair, *An Evangelical Look at Homosexuality* (New York: Homosexual Community Counseling Center, 1972). Cited in Roger J. Magnuson, *Are Gay Rights Right?* (Portland: Multnomah, 1990), 118.
21. Ralph Blair, *Review: A Quarterly of Evangelicals Concerned* (Summer 2003; Fall 2003; and Winter 2004).
22. Lewis B. Smedes, *Sex for Christians: The Limits and Liberties of Sexual Living* (Grand Rapids, Mich.: Eerdmans, 1976, 1994), 57.
23. David F. Field, "Homosexuality," in *New Dictionary of Christian Ethics and Pastoral Theology,* ed. David J. Atkinson, David F. Field, Arthur Holmes, and Oliver O'Donovan (Downers Grove, Ill.: InterVarsity Press, 1995), 450-454.
24. Tony and Peggy Campolo, "Holding It Together," *Sojourners* 28, no. 3 (May–June 1999): 28.
25. Tony Campolo, *Twenty Hot Potatoes Christians Are Afraid to Touch* (Dallas: Word, 1988), 117.
26. Ibid., 118-119.
27. Rebecca Merrill Groothuis, *Good News for Women: A Biblical Picture of Gender Equality* (Grand Rapids, Mich.: Baker, 1997), 14.
28. Schaeffer, *Great Evangelical Disaster,* 136.
29. C. S. Lewis, "Priestesses in the Church?" in *God in the Dock: Essays on Theology and Ethics,* ed. Walter Hooper (Grand Rapids, Mich.: Eerdmans, 1970), 237-238.
30. Ibid.
31. Rosemary Radford Ruether, *Disputed Questions: On Being a Christian* (Nashville: Abingdon, 1982), 125.
32. Naomi R. Goldenberg, *Changing of the Gods: Feminism and the End of Traditional Religions* (Boston: Beacon, 1979), 4-5.
33. Elizabeth Stuart and Adrian Thatcher, eds., *Christian Perspectives on Sexuality and Gender* (Grand Rapids, Mich.: Eerdmans, 1996), x.

CHAPTER 6
BIBLICAL HOLINESS DEFINES MORAL SEX

1. C. S. Lewis, *Mere Christianity* (New York: Simon & Schuster, 1980), 90.

2. Ed Young is only half right to say God's plan for moral sex is "fidelity for those who are married, [and] chastity for those who are single." Chastity does include abstinence outside of marriage, but the terms are not synonymous. Faithful partners in marriage are chaste without abstaining from sex with each other. See Ed Young, *Pure Sex* (Sisters, Ore.: Multnomah, 1997), 30.
3. Augustine, *City of God* XIV.16.
4. Ibid., XIV.24.
5. Dorothy L. Sayers, *Creed Or Chaos?* (London: Methuen, 1947), 24.
6. Markus Barth, *Ephesians* (Garden City, N.Y.: Doubleday, 1974), 712.
7. The Hebrew verb, לְצַחֵק, translated either *to indulge in revelry* (NIV) or *to play* (ESV) in Exodus 32:6 has strong sexual connotations. The account suggests some Israelites were engaging in some form of sexual worship.
8. Carl F. H. Henry, *Christian Personal Ethics* (Grand Rapids, Mich.: Eerdmans, 1957), 151-152.
9. See also Ex. 19:6; Lev. 19:2; 20:7, 26; 21:6, 8; Deut. 7:6; 14:2, 21; 28:9; 1 Sam. 2:2; Ps. 29:2; 96:9; Isa. 35:8; Hab. 1:13; Rom. 6:19, 22; 15:16; 1 Cor. 7:34; 2 Cor. 7:1; Eph. 2:21; 5:3, 27; 4:24; Col. 1:22; 3:12; 1 Thes 4:3-7; 2 Tim. 1:9; Titus 1:8; Heb. 3:1; 12:10; 1 Pet. 1:14-16; 2:5, 9.
10. See "The Fear of God," chapter 10 in John Murray, *Principles of Conduct: Aspects of Biblical Ethics* (Grand Rapids, Mich.: Eerdmans, 1957), 229-242.
11. Thomas Brooks, "Holiness the Only Way to Happiness," in *The Complete Works of Thomas Brooks,* ed. Alexander Balloch Grosart, vol. 4 (Edinburgh: J. Nichol, 1866), 187.
12. Francis A. Schaeffer, *The Church Before the Watching World* (Downers Grove, Ill.: InterVarsity Press, 1971), 39.
13. On the meaning of οὕτως, see Walter Bauer, William F. Arndt, and R. Wilbur Gingrich, *A Greek-English Lexicon of the New Testament and Other Early Christian Literature* (Chicago: University of Chicago Press, 1957), 570-571, 602; Johannes P. Louw and Eugene A. Nida, eds., *Introduction and Domains,* vol. 1, *Greek-English Lexicon of the New Testament Based on Semantic Domains* (New York: United Bible Societies, 1988), 611, 617; and David Alan Black, *It's Still Greek to Me* (Grand Rapids, Mich.: Baker, 1998), 128.
14. On this, Markus Barth says the word και (*kai*) which follows οὕτως (*houtōs*) in v. 28 "makes unmistakably clear that the word *houtōs* ('so,' 'in the same manner') at the beginning of vs. 28 points back to the love of Christ described in vss. 25-27, not forward to an egotistic love. Only if *kai* were placed before 'bodies' (*sōmata*), would this verse clearly affirm that husbands must love their wives as (or because) they 'love also their bodies.' Actually the position of *kai* indicates clearly that the husband is compared with Christ, and his love with Christ's (as in vs. 25), not husbandly love with a man's (natural) love of his own body. Paul does not depreciate the husband's love by measuring it with the stick of natural egotism and subjecting the wife to her husband's untamed selfishness. It is not only the position of *kai* which calls for this conclusion: after a quote (see, e.g. Rom. 11:5) *houtōs* has in addition to its comparative meaning a causal one, as if to say, 'therefore,' or 'on the strength of the event or argument just mentioned.' Both the question how and why are answered" (Markus Barth, *Ephesians,* 630).
15. It is commonly accepted that, while one-flesh union in Genesis 1:24 refers to more than sex itself, it certainly does have sexual union in view either as the source, ini-

tiation, validation, or ultimate expression of this relational union. Markus Barth says, "Certainly their sexual relationship is in mind, but not only this expression and means of union" (Markus Barth, *Ephesians,* 640). Gordon Hugenberger decides it "refers to the familial bondedness of marriage which finds its quintessential expression in sexual union" (Gordon P. Hugenberger, *Marriage as a Covenant* [Grand Rapids, Mich.: Baker, 1998], 163). Others saying the same include: N. P. Bratsiotis, בָּשָׂר, *Theological Dictionary of the Old Testament,* vol. 2 (Grand Rapids, Mich.: Eerdmans, 1975), 328; and Werner Neuer, *Man and Woman in Christian Perspective,* trans. G. J. Wenham (London: Hodder & Stoughton, 1990), 63.

CHAPTER 7
BIBLICAL PRINCIPLES SHAPE MORAL SEX

1. Tim Stafford, "The Next Sexual Revolution: It Will Be an Uphill Battle, but the Church Can and Must Create a Sexual Counterculture," *Christianity Today,* March 9, 1992, 28.
2. Francis A. Schaeffer, *True Spirituality* (Wheaton, Ill.: Tyndale, 1971), 175.
3. Cited at www.washingtonpost.com/wp-srv/politics/special/clinton/stories/deny012798.htm.
4. Earl S. Kalland, "דָּבַק" in R. Laird Harris, Gleason L. Archer, Jr., Bruce K. Waltke, ed., *Theological Wordbook of the Old Testament,* vol. 1 (Chicago: Moody, 1980), 177-178 (art. 398).
5. Ibid., 30.
6. Cited in Sheldon Vanauken, *A Severe Mercy* (New York: Harper & Row, 1977), 210-211.
7. J. B. Heard, *The Tripartite Nature of Man,* 5th ed. (Edinburgh: T & T Clark, 1882).
8. C. S. Lewis, *Mere Christianity* (New York: Simon & Schuster, 1996), 96-97.

CHAPTER 8
BIBLICAL PROHIBITIONS GUARD MORAL SEX (I)

1. C. S. Lewis, *Mere Christianity* (New York: Simon & Schuster, 1996), 90.
2. This underscores why Joseph was so offended on finding Mary "to be with child" while "betrothed to Joseph, before they came together" (Matt. 1:18). Although they had not had sex, he was already Mary's "husband" (Matt. 1:19), and she was already Joseph's "wife" (Matt. 1:20).
3. The goddess Ashtoreth, also called Ashteroth and Asherah, was worshiped widely throughout the ancient Near East. Ashtoreth of the Sidonians was the same as Ishtar of the Babylonians and Isis of the Egyptians. She may also have been linked to Aphrodite of the Greeks and Venus of the Romans. See William L. Reed, *The Asherah in the Old Testament* (Fort Worth: Texas University Press, 1949).
4. George Elder indicates that ancient pagan religions often used "phallic images . . . to evoke a divine power that lay behind the abundance of animal life." We cannot be sure, but since Ashtoreth was certainly a sensuous fertility goddess, it is reasonable to assume her worshipers may have been doing something similar to Egyptians who used wooden phallic images honoring Osiris and to Greeks who worshiped Hermes "in the image of a phallic stone" (see George Elder, "Phallus,"

in *The Encyclopedia of Religion,* ed. Mircea Eliade, vol. 11 [New York: Macmillan, 1987], 264-269).

5. C. F. Keil and F. Delitzsch, *Commentary of the Old Testament in Ten Volumes,* vol. 1, *The Pentateuch,* trans. James Martin (Grand Rapids, Mich.: Eerdmans, 1978), 418.

CHAPTER 9
BIBLICAL PROHIBITIONS GUARD MORAL SEX (II)

1. Keil and Delitzsch observe that the Hebrew verb used in this prohibition ("indecently expose," "uncover nakedness," "lay bare" [עָרָה]) does not distinguish between something wrong that occurs within marriage and something wrong that occurs outside of marriage. For the purpose of this prohibition, that particular distinction is essentially irrelevant (ibid., 412).
2. David's son Amnon violates this prohibition (and others) in raping his half-sister, Tamar, and it says something sad of David that Tamar appears so confident that David would approve of her marrying her half-brother if Amnon would simply ask (2 Sam. 13:13).
3. The law of levirate marriage (Deut. 25:5-6) seems to have been an exception. Under levirate law, if a married man died without children, a surviving brother had a duty to marry his deceased brother's widow and raise up children in his name. The Levitical prohibition must therefore apply to relations not covered by the levirate duty.
4. Thomas E. Schmidt, "Liberation and Pedophilia," in *Straight and Narrow?* (Downers Grove, Ill.: InterVarsity Press, 1995), 59-63; Mary Eberstadt, "Pedophilia Chic," *Weekly Standard,* June 17, 1996, 19-28; Jeffrey Satinover, "Intergenerational Intimacy," in *Homosexuality and the Politics of Truth* (Grand Rapids, Mich.: Baker, 1996), 62-66; Charles A. Donovan and Robert H. Knight, "APA Does Turnaround on Pedophilia," *Washington Watch* 9, no. 10 (July 1999): 1, 6; Mary Eberstadt, "Pedophilia Chic Reconsidered," *Weekly Standard,* January 1, 2001, 18-25; Judith Levine, *Harmful to Minors: The Perils of Protecting Children from Sex* (Minneapolis: University of Minnesota Press, 2002); "Mainstream Book Advocating Adult-Child Sex Draws Howls of Protest," Fox News, April 2, 2002; Steve Jordahl, "Normalization of Pedophilia Growing, Experts Say," *Family News in Focus,* July 30, 2002; Eric Felten, "The Deal with Older Guys," *Weekly Standard,* August 12, 2002, 14-16.
5. See article 2530a in R. Laird Harris, Gleason J. Archer, and Bruce K. Waltke, *Theological Wordbook of the Old Testament,* vol. 2 (Chicago: Moody, 1980), 976-977.
6. Cited in Wendy Shalit, *A Return to Modesty: Discovering the Lost Virtue* (New York: Simon & Schuster, 1999), 219-220.
7. Jesus says that serving him takes priority over "father and mother and wife and children and brothers and sisters" (Luke 14:26); and he continues that theme in verse 33: "So therefore, any one of you who does not renounce all that he has cannot be my disciple."
8. For example, see William F. Luck, *Divorce and Remarriage: Recovering the Biblical View* (San Francisco: Harper & Row, 1987).
9. On the betrothal stage of Semitic marriage, see John Piper, "Divorce and Remarriage: A Position Paper,"July 21, 1986, available online at:

www.desiringgod.org/resources/divorce/Div&rem-draft2; G. F. Moore, *Judaism in the First Centuries of the Christian Era,* vol. 2 (New York: Schocken, 1971; Joachim Jeremias, *Jerusalem at the Time of Jesus* (Philadelphia: Fortress, 1969); and Abel Isaksson, *Marriage and Ministry in the New Temple,* trans. Neil Tomkinson (Lund, Sweden: Gleerup, 1965).

Chapter 11
Biblical Promises Bless Moral Sex

1. Edgar A. Guest, "The Lights of Home," in *Harbor Lights of Home* (Chicago: Reilly & Lee, 1927), 15-16.
2. Francis A. Schaeffer, *True Spirituality* (Wheaton, Ill.: Tyndale, 1971), 161.
3. C. S. Lewis, *Surprised by Joy* (New York: Harcourt, Brace, 1955), 170.
4. Ibid., 18.
5. Ibid., 220.
6. Schaeffer, *True Spirituality,* 161.
7. William Henry Davies, "Joy and Pleasure," in W. B. Yeats, ed., *The Oxford Book of Modern Verse: 1892–1935* (Oxford: Clarendon, 1972), 128-129.
8. Herman Melville, *Moby Dick* (New York: Book League of America, 1929), 56.
9. James Herriot, *The Best of James Herriot* (New York: St. Martin's, 1982), 225.
10. Schaeffer, *True Spirituality,* 161-162.
11. Paul Wallin, "Religiosity, Sexual Gratification, and Marital Satisfaction," *American Psychological Review* 22 (1957): 300-305; Robert J. Levin and Amy Levin, "Sexual Pleasure: The Surprising Preferences of 100,000 Women," *Redbook,* September 1975, 51-58; Haddon Robinson, "CT Readers Survey: Sex, Marriage, and Divorce," *Christianity Today,* December 14, 1992, 29-32.
12. William R. Mattox, Jr., "What's Marriage Got to Do With It? Good Sex Comes to Those Who Wait," *Family Policy* 6, no. 6 (February 1994); Edward O. Laumann, John H. Gagnon, Robert T. Michael, and Stuart Michaels, *The Organization of Sexuality: Sexual Practices in the United States* (Chicago: University of Chicago Press, 1994), 363-365; Linda J. Waite, Don Browning, William J. Doherty, Maggie Gallagher, Ye Luo, and Scott M. Stanley, *Does Divorce Make People Happy? Findings from a Study of Unhappy Marriages* (New York: Institute for American Values, 2002).
13. Schaeffer, *True Spirituality,* 161.
14. Michael Field, "Their Gifts," in Yeats, ed., *Oxford Book of Modern Verse,* 71-72. The English spelling is original.
15. *Reef Points 1968–1969* (Annapolis, Md.: United States Naval Academy, 1968), 33. I graduated from the Naval Academy in 1972, and resigned my naval officer's commission in 1978.
16. William Shakespeare, *King Richard the Second,* 1.1.182.
17. The first-century gnostics used to think this, but they were wrong. See Peter Jones, *Spirit Wars* (Mukilteo, Wash.: WinePress, 1997). See also Kurt Rudolf, *Gnosis* (San Francisco: Harper & Row, 1983).
18. Nicolas Boileau-Despreaux, *Satires* X, 167, cited at www.WorldofQuotes.com.
19. C. S. Lewis, *Mere Christianity* (New York: Simon & Schuster, 1996), 92.
20. William Shakespeare, *Romeo and Juliet,* 2.2.85-122.

21. Wendy Shalit, *A Return to Modesty: Discovering the Lost Virtue* (New York: Free Press, 1999), 171-172.
22. Ibid., 191, 193.

CHAPTER 12
ROMANTIC SEXUAL MORALITY: SEX AS AFFECTION

1. Alex Tresniowski, "Hearts Wide Shut," *People,* February 19, 2001, 50.
2. John and Paul Feinberg designate this the *affection view*. See John Feinberg and Paul Feinberg, *Ethics for a Brave New World* (Wheaton, Ill.: Crossway, 1993), 156-158. Tim Stafford addresses the same moral perspective, referring to it as the *ethic of intimacy*. See, Tim Stafford, "Intimacy: Our Latest Sexual Fantasy," *Christianity Today,* January 16, 1987, 24-27.
3. "You Light Up My Life," words and music by Joseph Brooks (Big Hill Music, 1976).
4. "Fresh," words and music by Gina G. (Warner Brothers, 1997).
5. "Love Makes It Right," words by Carl Hampton and music by Homer Banks (East/Memphis Music, 1974).
6. "I Honestly Love You," words and music by Peter Allen and Jeff Barry (Irving Music, 1974).
7. "Hooked on a Feeling," words and music by Mark James (Screen Gems-EMI Music, 1968).
8. "Go the Distance," words by David Zippel and music by Alan Menken (Hal Leonard Corp., 1997).
9. In the song titled "Heat Wave," words and music by Eddie Holland, Lamont Dozier, and Brian Holland (Jobete Music, 1963).
10. In the song titled "I Honestly Love You."
11. "Is It Gonna Last?" words and music by Suzanne Glass (Glass House Productions, 1997).
12. In the song titled "Everlasting," words and music by Jim Peterik and Frankie Sullivan (EMI Virgin Music, 1984).
13. In the song titled: "Will You Still Love Me Tomorrow?" words and music by Gerry Goffin and Carole King (Screen Gems-EMI Music, 1960).
14. In the song titled "Could This Be Love?" words and music by Jennifer Lopez and Mark Anthony (Sony Music Entertainment, 1999).
15. In songs titled "Ain't It Funny" and "Promise Me You'll Try," words and music by, Jennifer Lopez and Marc Anthony (Sony Music Entertainment, 1999).
16. In the song titled: "You've Lost That Lovin' Feelin'," words and music by Barry Mann, Cynthia Weil, and Phil Spector (Screen Gems-EMI Music, 1964).
17. In the song titled: "If You Could Read My Mind," words and music by Gordon Lightfoot (Early Morning Music, 1969).
18. In the song titled: "It's Too Late," words and music by Toni Stern and Carole King (Colgems-EMI Music, 1971).
19. In the song titled "Angel of the Morning," words and music by Chip Taylor (Blackwood Music, 1967).
20. Ibid.
21. "Don't Turn Around," words and music by Diane Warren and Albert Hammond (Columbia Records, 1988).

22. "Just Walk Away," words and music by Albert Hammond and Marti Sharron (Columbia Records, 1993).
23. C. S. Lewis, *Mere Christianity* (New York: Macmillan, 1977), 100.
24. "The Long Goodbye," words and music by Paul Brady and Ronan Keating (Compass Records, 1998).
25. Lewis, *Mere Christianity,* 100.
26. From the song titled: "Love Lies," words and music by Alan Chapman and Michael Hanna (RCA, 1982).
27. Francis Schaeffer, *True Spirituality* (Wheaton, Ill.: Tyndale, 1971), 135-136.
28. Sheldon Vanauken, *A Severe Mercy* (New York: Harper & Row, 1977), 47.

Chapter 13
Playboy Sexual Morality: Sex as Pleasure

1. Cited in Rita Cosby, "Hugh Hefner on Fifty Years of *Playboy,*" Fox News (September 20, 2003), available online at: www.foxnews.com/story/0,2933, 980772,00.html (posted September 23, 2003).
2. Cited in Bill Zehme, "The Man Who Loved Women: Of Hef and Heartbreak," *Esquire* (August 1998). Available online at: www.britannica.com/bcom/magazine/article/0,5744,54003,00.html.
3. Cited in ibid.
4. This is a retelling in my own words of a story reported by Bill Zehme, ibid.
5. For a revealing interview with Hefner's parents, see Lillian Harris Dean, "A Conservative Looks at Playboy," *Christian Herald,* September 1968, 8-10, 52-53, 62-64, 66-67, 72-73.
6. Frank Brady, *Hefner* (New York: Macmillan, 1974), 31.
7. Jon Davies and Gerard Loughlin, eds., *Sex These Days: Essays on Theology, Sexuality, and Society* (Sheffield, England: Sheffield Academic Press, 1997), 8. These authors cause some confusion by conflating playboy with therapeutic sexual morality. While these approaches have similarities, they are completely different moralities, each with its own way of justifying what makes sex either right or wrong.
8. Dean, "Conservative Looks at Playboy," 10.
9. Joel Stein, "Back in the Swing," *Time,* March 22, 1999, 8.
10. Cited in Dean, "Conservative Looks at Playboy," 52.
11. Joel Stein, "Back in the Swing," 8.
12. Marvin M. Ellison, "Common Decency: A New Christian Sexual Ethic," *Christianity and Crisis,* November 12, 1990, 352-356.
13. In the summer of 1965, Hugh Hefner sent Anson Mount, who was then serving as public affairs manager for *Playboy* magazine, to take several courses at the University of the South's Summer School of Theology. After returning, Mount began to serve as the magazine's quasi "religion editor."
14. C. S. Lewis, *Surprised by Joy* (New York: Harcourt, Brace & World, 1955), 18.
15. Scripture says Moses chose "rather to be mistreated with the people of God than to enjoy the fleeting pleasures of sin" (Heb. 11:25).
16. Lewis, *Mere Christianity* (New York: Simon & Schuster, 1996), 90.
17. Brady, *Hefner,* 226.

18. Harvey Cox, *The Secular City: Secularization and Urbanization in Theological Perspective* (New York: Macmillan, 1965), 204.
19. Cited in Brady, *Hefner,* 225.
20. Bill Davidson, "Czar of the Bunny Empire," *Saturday Evening Post,* April 28, 1962, 38.
21. Ibid.
22. "Remembering the Big Dipper's Other Statistics," *Chicago Tribune,* October 17, 1999; available online at http://pqasb.pqarchiver.com/chicagotribune/.
23. Robert Nichols, "Sonnets to Aurelia," in W. B. Yeats, ed., *The Oxford Book of Modern Verse: 1892–1935* (Oxford: Clarendon, 1972), 340.
24. William Simon and Patricia Y. Miller, *The Playboy Report on American Men* (Chicago: Playboy Enterprises, 1979), 13.
25. Francis A. Schaeffer, *True Spirituality* (Wheaton, Ill.: Tyndale, 1971), 162.
26. William R. Mattox, "What's Marriage Got to Do With It?: Good Sex Comes to Those Who Wait," *Family Policy* 6, no. 6 (February 1994): 3.

Chapter 14
Therapeutic Sexual Morality: Sex as Wholeness

1. "Natural Woman," words and music by Gerry Goffin, Carole King, and Jerry Wexler (Screen Gems-EMI Music, 1967).
2. "Sexual Healing," words and music by Marvin Gaye, David Ritz, and Odell Brown (Columbia Records, 1982).
3. Sigmund Freud, *Three Essays on the Theory of Sexuality,* trans. James Strachey (New York: Basic Books, 1962), 36.
4. Sigmund Freud, "Civilized Sexual Morality and Modern Nervousness," in *Sigmund Freud: Collected Papers,* trans. Joan Riviere, vol. 2 (New York: Basic Books, 1959), 88-99.
5. Ibid., 77, 87.
6. Ibid., 88, 92.
7. Ibid., 90, 92.
8. Carl G. Jung, *Memories, Dreams, Reflections,* ed. Aniela Jaffe, trans. Richard and Clara Winston (New York: Pantheon, 1963), 59.
9. Carl G. Jung, *Aion,* in *Collected Works,* vol. 9:2, trans. R. F. C. Hull (London: Routledge & Kegan Paul, 1959), 42.
10. Jung said, "There can be no doubt that the original Christian conception of the imago Dei embodied in Christ meant an all-embracing totality that even includes the animal side of man. Nevertheless the Christ-symbol lacks *wholeness* in the modern psychological sense, since it does not include the dark side of things but specifically excludes it in the form of a Luciferian opponent" (ibid., 41). He also said the Antichrist is "the dark half of the human totality," without which the psychological self "lacks body and humanity" (ibid., 42).
11. Sigmund Freud and Carl G. Jung, *The Freud/Jung Letters: The Correspondence Between Sigmund Freud and C. G. Jung,* ed. William McGuire, trans. Ralph Manheim and R. F. C. Hull (Cambridge, Mass.: Harvard University Press, 1988), 289. Jung's extramarital sexual life is covered by John Kerr, *A Most Dangerous Method: The Story of Jung, Freud, and Sabina Spielrein* (New York: Vintage, 1993).

12. Erich Fromm, *The Art of Loving* (New York: Harper & Brothers, 1956), 31.
13. Ibid., 55.
14. Abraham H. Maslow, *Toward a Psychology of Being* (New York: D. van Nostrand, 1968), 193.
15. Ibid., 201.
16. Carl R. Rogers, *Becoming Partners: Marriage and Its Alternatives* (New York: Delacorte, 1972), 214.
17. Michel Foucault, *Ethics, Subjectivity and Truth* (New York: New Press, 1997), 163.
18. Michel Foucault, *The History of Sexuality,* vol. 1, *An Introduction,* trans. Robert Hurley (New York: Random House, 1980), 7-8, 155-156. Foucault claims that sex is "the explanation for everything" and "henceforth serves as our master key" for defining "who we are" (78). He also says it is the point through which "each individual has to pass in order to have access to his own intelligibility, to the whole of his body, to his identity" (155-156), and is therefore "more important than our soul" (156).
19. James B. Nelson, *Body Theology* (Louisville: Westminster/John Knox, 1992), 48.
20. "Statement on Homosexuality" (Minneapolis: Minnesota Council of Churches, Social Justice Committee, 1982). Quoted in Roger J. Magnuson, *Are Gay Rights Right?* (Portland: Multnomah, 1990), 117-118.
21. John Shelby Spong, *Why Christianity Must Change or Die: A Bishop Speaks to Believers in Exile.* (San Francisco: HarperSanFrancisco, 1998). This is the main message of the book, but see especially pages 149-167.
22. Ibid., 159, 95, 151.
23. Ibid., 160.
24. Michel Foucault claimed that "the deployment of sexuality" must be used to define sexual conduct because in his view "sex" has no fixed purpose (*History of Sexuality,* 154).
25. Francis A. Schaeffer, *True Spirituality* (Wheaton, Ill.: Tyndale, 1971), 127.
26. Here I have translated the Greek dative in the instrumental sense. See, A. T. Robertson, *A Grammar of the Greek New Testament in the Light of Historical Research* (Nashville: Broadman, 1934), 532-534.
27. Schaeffer, *True Spirituality,* 161.

CHAPTER 15
PAGAN SEXUAL MORALITY: SEX AS SPIRITUAL LIFE

1. Mainline denominations that either helped finance the conference or sent official representatives included: the United Methodist Church, the Presbyterian Church (USA), the Evangelical Lutheran Church in America, the American Baptist Church, and the United Church of Christ.
2. Rita Nakashima Brock, "Re-Imagining Sexuality and Family," Re-Imagining Conference (Minneapolis, 1993), audiocassettes. Her book is *Journeys by Heart: A Christology of Erotic Power* (New York: Crossroad, 1988).
3. Cited in James R. Edwards, "Earthquake in the Mainline," *Christianity Today,* November 14, 1994, 40.

4. Mary E. Hunt, "Re-Imagining Sexuality and Family," Re-Imagining Conference (Minneapolis, 1993), audiocassettes. Also cited in Edwards, "Earthquake in the Mainline," 43.
5. Mary Daly, *Pure Lust: Elemental Feminist Philosophy* (Boston: Beacon, 1984); Brock, *Journeys by Heart;* Carter Hayward, *Touching Our Strength: The Erotic as Power and the Love of God* (San Francisco: Harper, 1989); Kenneth Ray Stubbs, *Sacred Orgasms,* vol. 3, *The Secret Garden Trilogy* (Tucson: Garden, 1992); Virginia Ramey Mollenkott, *Sensuous Spirituality: Out from Fundamentalism* (New York: Crossroad, 1993); James Nelson and Sandra Longfellow, eds, *Sexuality and the Sacred* (Louisville: Westminster/John Knox, 1994); Miranda Shaw, *Passionate Enlightenment* (Princeton, N.J.: Princeton University Press, 1994); A. T. Mann, *Sacred Sexuality* (Boston: Element, 1995); Riane T. Eisler, *Sacred Pleasure: Sex, Myth, and the Politics of the Body—New Paths to Power and Love* (New York: Harper, 1996); Robert Adkinson, *Sacred Sex* (New York: Thames & Hudson, 1997); Thomas Moore, *The Soul of Sex: Cultivating Life as an Act of Love* (New York: HarperCollins, 1998); Eugene F. Rogers, *Sexuality and the Christian Body* (Oxford: Blackwell, 2000); Ramana Das Silbey and Marilena Silbey, *Erotic Worship in American Tantra* (Fairfax, Calif.: 3rd Millennium Magic, 2000); and Rafael Lorenzo, *A Sacred Sex Devotional* (Rochester, Vt.: Inner Traditions, 2000).
6. Mary Daly, *Pure Lust,* 3.
7. Thomas Moore, *The Soul of Sex: Cultivating Life as an Act of Love* (New York: HarperCollins, 1998).
8. Ibid., 138, 161.
9. Ibid., 105, 174.
10. Hunt, "Re-Imagining Sexuality and Family"; see also Edwards, "Earthquake in the Mainline," 43.
11. Ibid., 9-10.
12. Ibid., 7, 51.
13. For example, Hindu Shaktiism, Tantrism, and the neo-gnostic Universal Life Church Neberdjer Society all treat the female sex organ as a *temple* of sacred sexual worship.
14. Moore, *Soul of Sex,* 68.
15. Monica Sjoo and Barbara Mor, *The Great Cosmic Mother: Discovering the Religion of the Earth* (San Francisco: Harper, 1987), 269.
16. Mollenkott, *Sensuous Spirituality,* see esp. 11-12.
17. Moore, *Soul of Sex,* 105.
18. Ibid., 105.
19. The life of a sinner can only pay for his own sins, so a sinner cannot give his life for another man's sins. But, even if there were a sinless man and even if God allowed it, substituting one merely human life for another could never save more than just one sinner. Only the life of God incarnate is worth enough to pay for all sin, for all people, for all time (John 3:16; 12:47; Rom. 6:10; Heb. 10:12, 14). This doctrine was discussed at length by Anselm in *Cur Deus Homo* (Why God Became Man).

CHAPTER 16
WHAT IS GOING ON?

1. C. S. Lewis, *Mere Christianity* (New York: Simon & Schuster, 1996), 90.
2. Ibid.
3. Cited in Rita Cosby, "Hugh Hefner on Fifty Years of *Playboy,*" Fox News, September 20, 2003; available online at: www.foxnews.com/story/0,2933,980772,00.html (posted September 23, 2003).

CHAPTER 17
UNDERSTANDING THE CONFLICT

1. Augustine, *City of God* XI.22 and XIX.13.
2. Ibid., XIX.13.
3. Francis Thompson, "The Hound of Heaven," in W. B. Yeats, ed., *The Oxford Book of Modern Verse: 1892–1935* (Oxford: Clarendon, 1972), 54-59.
4. C. S. Lewis, *Surprised by Joy* (New York: Harcourt, Brace, 1955), 228-229.
5. Translators usually take the preposition ἐν in this phrase in a way that treats the "unrighteousness" or "wickedness" of men as a sort of tool people use to keep God's moral truth from being applied in their lives. But if God's truth never changes and applies no matter what, its relevance can only be ignored and not actually reduced. However, ἐν does sometimes indicate purpose (for) or goal (to), which to me makes more sense in the context of Romans 1:18. Sinners cannot change truth or stop it from actually applying. But they do resist it in favor of unrighteousness. See James Hope Moulton, *A Grammar of New Testament Greek,* vol. 3, *Syntax,* by Nigel Turner (Edinburgh: T & T Clark, 1963), 264. See also Robert W. Funk, *A Grammar of the New Testament* (Chicago: University of Chicago Press, 1961), 118.

CHAPTER 18
WHAT ABOUT THE FUTURE?

1. Joseph Daniel Unwin, *Sex and Culture* (London: Oxford University Press, 1934); *Sexual Regulations and Cultural Behavior* (London: Oxford University Press, 1935); and *Hopousia: Or the Sexual and Economic Foundations of a New Society* (London: George Allen & Unwin, 1940).
2. Sigmund Freud, *Collected Papers,* trans. Joan Riviere, vol. 2 (New York: Basic Books, 1959), 76.
3. Sigmund Freud, *The Standard Edition of the Complete Psychological Works of Sigmund Freud,* trans. and ed. James Strachey in collaboration with Anna Freud, vol. 22 (London: Hogarth, 1964), 214. Also note, ibid., vol. 11 (1957), 54, 215.
4. Freud, *Collected Papers,* 87-88, 99.
5. Author's translation. See Sigmund Freud, *Gesammelte Werks,* vol. 14 (London: Imago, 1940–1952), 504-505. See also, Freud, *Standard Edition,* vol. 21 (1961) 110; and Ernest Jones, *The Life and Work of Sigmund Freud,* vol. 3 (New York: Basic Books, 1957), 346. My translation follows Ernest Jones.
6. Unwin, *Sex and Culture,* 340.
7. Unwin, *Sexual Regulations,* 31; and Unwin, *Sex and Culture,* 326.
8. Unwin, *Hopousia,* 82-83; see also *Society and Culture,* 431; and *Sexual Regulations,* 20, 32.

9. Unwin, *Hopousia,* 84-85.
10. Unwin, *Sex and Culture,* 382; see also ibid., 380, 431; *Sexual Regulations,* 21, 34; *Hopousia,* 84.
11. Unwin, *Sex and Culture,* 381.
12. Ibid., 412.
13. The Greek verb, πεπότικεν, is the third-person singular, perfect, indicative, active of ποτίζω (to give someone to drink). But when the verb is followed by a double accusative it becomes causative (to make someone drink) (see Walter Bauer, *A Greek-English Lexicon of the New Testament,* trans. and ed. William F. Arndt and F. Wilbur Gingrich [Chicago: University of Chicago Press, 1957], 702). So, even though the verb is not imperative, all English translations render it "made all nations drink," suggesting that an element of coercion could be involved.

APPENDIX A

1. Scripture versions are not specified in the appendices. Abbreviations of Bible books have been standardized.

Bibliography

Abramov, Tehilla. *The Secret of Jewish Femininity: Insight into the Practice of Taharat Hamishpachah.* Southfield, Minn.: Targum, 1988.

Ackerman, Diane. *A Natural History of Love.* New York: Knopf, 1995.

Adkinson, Robert. *Sacred Sex.* New York: Thames & Hudson, 1997.

Adler, Margot. *Drawing Down the Moon: Witches, Druids, Goddess-Worshipers and Other Pagans in America Today.* Boston: Beacon, 1986.

"Adultery: A New Furor over an Old Sin." *Newsweek,* September 30, 1996, 54-60.

Akin, Daniel. *God on Sex: The Creator's Ideas About Love, Intimacy, and Marriage.* Nashville: Broadman & Holman, 2003.

Alcorn, Randy C. *Christians in the Wake of the Sexual Revolution.* Portland: Multnomah, 1985.

Alexander, John F. "Feminism as a Subversive Activity." *The Other Side,* July 1982, 8.

Ambrose of Milan. *Concerning Virgins* I.5.25-26.

Anderson, Kerby, ed. *Marriage, Family, and Sexuality.* Foreword by Dennis Rainey. Grand Rapids, Mich.: Kregel, 2000.

Anderson, Neil T. *A Way of Escape.* Eugene, Ore.: Harvest, 1998.

Arterburn, Stephen, Fred Stoeker, and Mike Yorkey. *Every Man's Battle: Every Man's Guide to Winning the War on Sexual Temptation One Victory at a Time.* Colorado Springs: WaterBrook, 2000.

_______, Fred Stoeker, and Mike Yorkey. *Every Man's Battle Guide: Weapons for the War against Sexual Temptation.* New York: Random House, 2003.

_______, and Fred Stoeker. *Every Woman's Desire: An Every Man's Guide to Winning the Heart of a Woman.* Colorado Springs: WaterBrook, 2001.

_______, Fred Stoeker, and Mike Yorkey. *Every Young Man's Battle: Strategies for Victory in the Real World of Sexual Temptation.* Colorado Springs: WaterBrook, 2002.

Ashcroft, Mary Ellen. *Temptations Women Face.* Downers Grove, Ill.: InterVarsity Press, 1991.

Augustine of Hippo. *City of God* I.16; III.3-5; VI.9; XIV.13- 26; XV.15-20; XIX.22; XX.17.

_______. *The Confessions.*

_______. *The Good of Marriage.* Vol. 27 of *The Fathers of the Church.* Translated by Charles T. Wilcox. Westminster, Md.: Christian Classics, 1948.

_______. *Post-Nicene Fathers.* Ser. 1. III, 400-407; V, 86-87, 264-297; VI, 18-20.

Bailey, Derrick Sherwin. *Common Sense About Sexual Ethics: A Christian View.* New York: Macmillan, 1962.

_______. *The Man-Woman Relation in Christian Thought.* London: Longmans, 1959.

_______. *The Mystery of Love and Marriage: A Study in the Theology of Sexual Relation.* New York: Harper & Brothers, 1952.

_______. *Sexual Relation in Christian Thought.* New York: Harper & Brothers, 1959.

Bainton, Roland H. *What Christianity Says About Sex, Love, and Marriage.* New York: Association, 1957.

Balswick, Judith K. and Jack O. Balswick. *Authentic Human Sexuality: An Integrated Christian Approach.* Downers Grove, Ill.: InterVarsity Press, 1999.

Barbanel, Josh. "How the Study of Sexual Abuse by Priests Was Conducted." *New York Times,* 12 January 2003.

Barna Research Group. "American Faith Is Diverse, as Shown Among Five Faith-Based Segments." January 29, 2002. Available online at: www.barna.org/cgibin/Page.

_______. "Christians Are More Likely to Experience Divorce than Are Non-Christians." December 21, 1999. Available online at: www.barna.org/cgibin/PagePress Release.asp?PressReleaseID=39

Barth, Markus. *Ephesians.* Garden City, N.Y. Doubleday, 1974.

Beach, Frank A., ed. *Human Sexuality in Four Perspectives.* Baltimore: Johns Hopkins University Press, 1977.

Beam, Lindy. "Teen Magazines and the New Feminism: How Glossies Look at Sex, Self-Reliance, Spirituality, and More." *Plugged In,* April 2002, 3-4.

Bennett, William J. *The Broken Hearth: Reversing the Moral Collapse of the American Family.* New York: Doubleday, 2001.

_______. "Sex." In *The Death of Outrage: Bill Clinton and the Assault on American Ideals.* New York: Free Press, 1988, 13-30.

_______. *The Index of Leading Cultural Indicators: American Society at the End of the Twentieth Century.* New York: Broadway, 1999.

Beslow, Audrey. *Sex and the Single Christian.* Nashville: Abingdon, 1987.

"Bishop Spong Delivers a Fiery Farewell." *Christian Century,* February 17, 1999, 178.

Blair, Ralph. *An Evangelical Look at Homosexuality.* New York: Homosexual Community Counseling Center, 1972.

_______. *Holier-Than-Thou Hocus-Pocus and Homosexuality.* New York: Homosexual Community Counseling Center, 1977.

Blattner, John. "UnMasking the Great Unmentionable: Pastors *Can* Fall into Sexual Sin, but Here's How to Avoid It." *Equipping the Saints,* Summer 1988, 17-21.

Bork, Robert H. *Slouching Towards Gomorrah: Modern Liberalism and American Decline.* New York: HarperTrade, 1996.

Boswell, James. *Christianity, Social Tolerance, and Homosexuality.* Chicago: University of Chicago Press, 1980.

Boteach, Shmuley. *Kosher Sex: A Recipe for Passion and Intimacy.* New York: Doubleday, 1999.

Brady, Frank. *Hefner.* New York: Macmillan, 1974.

Brock, Rita Nakashima. *Journeys by Heart: A Christology of Erotic Power.* New York: Crossroad, 1988.

Brongersma, E. "Boy-Lovers and Their Influence on Boys: Distorted Research and Anecdotal Observations." *Journal of Homosexuality* 20 (1990): 145-173.

Brooks, Thomas. "Holiness the Only Way to Happiness." In *The Complete Works of Thomas Brooks,* vol. 4. Edited by Alexander Balloch Grosart. Edinburgh: J. Nichol, 1866.

Brueggemann, Walter. *Genesis: A Bible Commentary for Teaching and Preaching.* Atlanta: John Knox, 1982.

Burns, James. *Radical Respect: A Christian Approach to Love, Sex, and Dating.* Eugene, Ore.: Harvest, 1992.

Byrne, Brendan. "Sinning Against One's Own Body: Paul's Understanding of the Sexual Relationship in 1 Corinthians 6:18." *Catholic Biblical Quarterly* 45 (1983): 608-616.

Cahill, Lisa Sowle. *Between the Sexes: Foundations for a Christian Ethics of Sexuality.* Philadelphia: Fortress, 1985.

"A Call to Affirmation, Confession, and Covenant Regarding Human Sexuality." New York Mennonite Conference, September 27, 1997. Available online at: bfn.org/~nymennon/humansex.htm.

Calvin, John. *Institutes of the Christian Religion* II.8.41-44; IV.12.22- 28; IV.13.15-21; IV.19.34-37.

Campolo, Peggy. "Let Our Light Shine on All Who Seek God." *Lancaster Intelligencer Journal* (Lancaster, Pa.). November 25, 2000.

Campolo, Tony, and Peggy Campolo. "Holding It Together." *Sojourners* 28 (May–June 1999): 28.

_______. *Twenty Hot Potatoes Christians Are Afraid to Touch.* Dallas: Word, 1988.

Carnes, Patrick. *Don't Call It Love: Recovery from Sexual Addiction.* New York: Bantam, 1992.

Cartledge, Tony W., and Steve DeVane. "Key Changes Proposed for BF&M." *Biblical Recorder.* May 27, 2000.

Chilstrom, Herbert W., and Lowell O. Erdahl. *Sexual Fulfillment: For Single and Married, Straight and Gay, Young and Old.* Minneapolis: Augsburg, 2001.

Christ, Carol P. *Rebirth of the Goddess: Finding Meaning in Feminist Spirituality.* Reading, Mass.: Addison-Wesley, 1997.

"The Christian and the Social Order." *The Baptist Faith and Message.* Southern Baptist Convention, June 14, 2000. Available online at: www.sbc.net/bfm2000.asp.

"The Christian Family." *The Baptist Faith and Message.* Southern Baptist Convention, June 14, 2000. Available online at: www.sbc.net/bfm2000.asp.

Chrysostom, John. *Post-Nicene Fathers.* Ser. 2. XIII, 149-151.

The Church and Human Sexuality: A Lutheran Perspective. Evangelical Lutheran Church in America, Division for Church in Society, Department of Studies, Task Force on Human Sexuality, 1993. Available online at: www. colorado.edu/StudentGroups/lcm/elca-sex-statement.txt

Clapp, Rodney. "Why Christians Have Lousy Sex Lives." *Re:Generation Quarterly* 1 (Summer 1995): 7-10.

"Clarification Regarding Same-Sex Blessings and Ongoing Deliberation Concerning

Homosexuality." Evangelical Lutheran Church in America, Office of the Presiding Bishop, May 2000. Available online at: www.elca.org/ob/.

Clement of Alexandria. *Ante-Nicene Fathers.* II, 262, 377-378.

Cline, Sally. *Women, Passion, and Celibacy.* New York: Crown, 1994.

Cole, W. G. *Sex and Love in the Bible.* New York: Associated Press, 1959.

Coleman, William. *Cupid Is Stupid!* Downers Grove, Ill.: InterVarsity Press, 1991.

Colorado Statement on Biblical Sexual Morality. Council on Biblical Sexual Ethics, 2002. Available online at: www.family.org/cforum/fosi/purity/by.

"Coming Attractions: Gay Activism Is Not Just Found in Liberal Churches." *Christianity Today* (August 2003): 33.

Considerations Regarding Proposals to Give Legal Recognition to Unions Between Homosexual Persons. Roman Catholic Church, the Vatican, Congregation for the Doctrine of the Faith, June 3, 2003. Available online at: www.vatican.va/roman_curia/congregations/cfaith/documents/rc_con_cfaith_doc_20030731_homosexual-unions_en.html.

Cooperman, Alan, and Pamela Ferdinand. "Cardinal Law Steps Down." *Washington Post,* December 14, 2002.

Cornell, Drucilla. *Beyond Accommodation: Ethical Feminism, Deconstruction, and the Law.* Lanham, Md.: Rowman & Littlefield, 1999.

Countryman, L. William. *Dirt, Greed, and Sex.* Philadelphia: Fortress, 1988.

Cozzens, Donald B. *The Changing Face of the Priesthood.* Collegeville, Minn.: Liturgical Press, 2002.

"Crisis Sparks Reassessment: Bishops May Call Rare Plenary Council to Address Problems." *New York Times,* June 21, 2003.

Cutrer, William R., and Sandra Glahn. *Sexual Intimacy in Marriage.* Grand Rapids, Mich.: Kregel, 2001.

Cyprian of Carthage. *St. Cyprian: The Lapsed; The Unity of the Catholic Church.* Translated by Maurice Bevenot. Westminster, Md.: Newman, 1957.

Dallas, Joe. *Desires in Conflict.* Eugene, Ore.: Harvest, 1991.

Daly, Mary. *Beyond God the Father: Toward a Philosophy of Women's Liberation.* Boston: Beacon, 1973.

_______. *The Church and the Second Sex: With the Feminist Postchristian Introduction and New Archaic Afterwords.* Boston: Beacon, 1985.

_______. *Gyn/Ecology: The Metaethics of Radical Feminism.* Boston: Beacon, 1978.

_______. *Outercourse: The Be-Dazzling Voyage.* San Francisco: Harper, 1992.

_______. *Pure Lust: Elemental Feminist Philosophy.* Boston: Beacon, 1984.

_______. "Sin Big." *The New Yorker* (February 26 and March 4, 1996): 76, 78, 80-82, 84.

_______, and Jane Caputi. *Webster's' First New Intergalactic Wickedary of the English Language.* Boston: Beacon, 1987.

Davidson, Richard M. "The Theology of Sexuality in the Beginning: Genesis 1–2." *Andrews University Seminary Studies* 26 (Spring 1988): 5-24.

_______. "The Theology of Sexuality in the Beginning: Genesis 3." *Andrews University Seminary Studies* 26 (Summer 1988): 121-131.

_______. "Theology of Sexuality in the Song of Songs: Return to Eden." *Andrews University Seminary Studies* 27 (Spring 1989): 1-19.

Davies, Bob, and Lori Rentzel. *Coming Out of Homosexuality*. Downers Grove, Ill.: InterVarsity Press, 1994.

Davies, Jon, and Gerard Loughlin, eds. *Sex These Days: Essays on Theology, Sexuality and Society*. Sheffield, England: Sheffield Academic Press, 1997.

Dawn, Marva J. *Sexual Character: Beyond Technique to Intimacy*. Grand Rapids, Mich.: Eerdmans, 1993.

Dean, Lillian Harris. "A Conservative Looks at Playboy." *Christian Herald* (September 1968): 8-10, 52-53, 62-64, 66-67, 72-73.

Dedek, John F. "Premarital Sex: The Theological Argument from Peter Lombard to Durand." *Theological Studies* 41 (December 1980): 643-667.

Demant. V. A. *Christian Sexual Ethics*. New York: Harper & Row, 1963.

D'Emilio, John, and Estelle Freedman. *Intimate Matters: A History of Sexuality in America*. New York: HarperTrade, 1988.

DeMoss, Robert. *Sex and the Single Person.* Grand Rapids, Mich.: Zondervan, 1995.

DeYoung, J. B. "The Contributions of the Septuagint to Biblical Sanctions Against Homosexuality." *Journal of the Evangelical Theological Society* 34 (June 1991): 157-177.

_______. "The Meaning of 'Nature' in Romans 1 and Its Implications for Biblical Perspectives of Homosexual Behavior." *Journal of the Evangelical Theological Society* 31 (1988): 429-447.

Diamond, Eugene, and Rosemary Diamond. *The Positive Value of Chastity.* Chicago: Franciscan Herald, 1983.

Diamond, Milton, and Arno Karlen. *Sexual Decisions*. Boston: Little, Brown, 1980.

Dillow, Joseph. *Solomon on Sex*. Nashville: Thomas Nelson, 1989.

Ditzion, Sydney. *Marriage, Morals, and Sex in America: A History of Ideas*. New York: Hippocrene, 1970.

Dobson, James C. *Love for a Lifetime: Building a Marriage That Will Go the Distance*. Sisters, Ore.: Multnomah, 1993.

_______. *Straight Talk*. Dallas: Word, 1991.

_______. *Straight Talk to Men: Recovering the Biblical Meaning of Manhood.* Nashville: Word, 1995.

_______. *Straight Talk to Men and Their Wives*. Waco, Tex.: Word, 1984.

_______. *What Wives Wish Their Husbands Knew About Women*. Wheaton, Ill.: Tyndale, 1975.

Dominian, Jack, and Hugh Montefiore. *God, Sex, and Love: An Exercise in Ecumenical Ethics*. Philadelphia: Trinity, 1989.

_______. *Passionate and Compassionate Love: A Vision for Christian Marriage.* London: Darton, Longman, & Todd, 1991.

_______. *Proposals for a New Sexual Ethic*. London: Darton, Longman, & Todd, 1977.

Donovan, Charles, and Robert Knight. "APA Does Turnaround on Pedophilia." *Washington Watch,* July 1999, 1, 6.

Dorr, Roberta Kells. *David and Bathsheba.* San Francisco: Harper & Row, 1986.

Duffy, Martin, ed. *Issues in Sexual Ethics.* Souderton, Pa.: United Church People for Biblical Witness, 1979.

Duin, Julia. *Purity Makes the Heart Grow Stronger.* Ann Arbor, Mich.: Servant, 1988.

Durfield, Richard, and Renee Durfield. *Raising Them Chaste.* Minneapolis: Bethany, 1991.

Duty, Guy. *Divorce and Remarriage.* Minneapolis: Bethany, 1967.

Dworkin, Andrea. *Woman Hating.* New York: Dutton, 1974.

Dwyer, John C. *Human Sexuality: A Christian View.* Kansas City: Sheed & Ward, 1987.

Eberstadt, Mary. "The Elephant in the Sacristy." *Weekly Standard,* June 17, 2002, 22-33.

_______. "Pedophilia Chic." *Weekly Standard,* June 17, 1996, 19-28.

_______. "'Pedophilia Chic' Reconsidered: The Taboo Against Sex with Children Continues to Erode." *Weekly Standard,* January 1–January 8, 2001, 18-25.

Eckstrom, Kevin. "Catholic Bishops Gather Under Scrutiny." Religion News Service. *News and Observer* (Raleigh, N.C.), June 20, 2003.

Eiseman, Tom L. *Temptations Men Face.* Downers Grove, Ill.: InterVarsity Press, 1990.

Eisler, Riane T. *Sacred Pleasure: Sex, Myth, and the Politics of the Body—New Paths to Power and Love.* New York: Harper, 1996.

ElHage, Alysse. "The Case for Abstinence: Why Comprehensive Sex Education Sends the Wrong Message." *Findings* (2002): 1-6.

Elliot, Elisabeth. *Passion and Purity: Learning to Bring Your Love Life Under Christ's Control.* Grand Rapids, Mich.: Revell, 1984.

_______. *Sex Is a Lot More than Fun.* Magnolia, Mass.: Elisabeth Elliot Gren, 1986.

_______. *What God Has Joined.* Wheaton, Ill.: Crossway, 1983.

Ellisen, Stanley A. *Divorce and Remarriage in the Church.* Grand Rapids, Mich.: Zondervan, 1977.

Ellison, Marvin M. "Common Decency: A New Christian Sexual Ethic." *Christianity and Crisis,* November 12, 1990, 352-356.

"Episcopalians Face Crisis." *News and Observer* (Raleigh, N.C.), July 19, 2003.

Evangelical Alliance. "Living in Sin Now OK, Say a Third of Christian Young Adults." May 1, 2001. Available online at: www.eauk.org/contentmanager/.

Evdokimov, Paul. *The Sacrament of Love.* Translated by Anthony P. Gythiel and Victoria Steadman. Crestwood, N.Y.: St. Vladimir's Seminary Press, 1995.

Feinberg, John S., and Paul D. Feinberg. "Sexual Morality." In *Ethics for a Brave New World.* Wheaton, Ill.: Crossway, 1993.

Field, David F. "Homosexuality." In *New Dictionary of Christian Ethics and Pastoral Theology.* Edited by David J. Atkinson, David F. Field, Arthur Holmes, and Oliver O'Donovan. Downers Grove, Ill.: InterVarsity Press, 1995, 450-454.

Final Report of the Attorney General's Commission on Pornography. Introduction by Michael J. McManus. Nashville: Rutledge Hill, 1986.

Ford, Jeffrey E. *Love, Marriage, and Sex in the Christian Tradition from Antiquity to Today.* San Francisco: International Scholars Publications, 1999.

Foster, David K. *Sexual Healing: God's Plan for the Sanctification of Broken Lives.* Jacksonville, Fla.: Mastering Life Ministries, 2001.

Foster, Richard. *Money, Sex, and Power: The Challenge of the Disciplined Life.* San Francisco: Harper & Row, 1985.

Foucault, Michel. *Ethics, Subjectivity, and Truth.* New York: New Press, 1997.

_______. *The History of Sexuality.* Vol. 1, *An Introduction.* Vol. 2, *The Use of Pleasure.* Translated by Robert Hurley. New York: Pantheon, 1978; Random House, 1980; Vintage, 1988, 1990.

_______. *Language, Counter-Memory, Practice.* Ithaca, N.Y.: Cornell University Press, 1977.

Fox, Robin Lane. *Pagans and Christians.* San Francisco: HarperSanFrancisco, 1988.

Frame, Randy. "Heresy Charges Dismissed." *Christianity Today* (June 17, 1996): 57.

_______. "In American Methodism's 200th Year, Evangelicals Are Celebrating." *Christianity Today,* June 15, 1984, 56.

_______. "Presbyterian Assembly Rejects Sexuality Report." *Christianity Today,* July 22, 1991, 37-38.

_______. "Sexuality Report Draws Fire." *Christianity Today,* April 29, 1991, 37.

Francoeur, Robert T., Martha Cornog, and Timothy Perper, eds. *Sex, Love and Marriage in the Twenty-first Century: The Next Sexual Revolution.* San Jose, Calif.: toExcel, 1999.

_______, Patricia Barthalow Koch, and David L. Weis, eds. *Sexuality in America: Understanding Our Sexual Values and Behavior.* New York: Continuum, 1998.

Freud, Sigmund. "Civilized Sexual Morality and Modern Nervousness." In *Sigmund Freud: Collected Papers.* Vol. 2. Translated by Joan Riviere. New York: Basic Books, 1959.

_______, and Carl G. Jung. *The Freud/Jung Letters: The Correspondence Between Sigmund Freud and C. G. Jung.* Edited by William McGuire. Translated by Ralph Manheim and R. F. C. Hull. Cambridge, Mass.: Harvard University Press, 1988.

_______. *The Standard Edition of the Complete Psychological Works of Sigmund Freud.* Translated and edited by James Strachey in collaboration with Anna Freud. Vol. 11 (1957). Vol. 21 (1961). Vol. 22 (1964). London: Hogarth.

_______. *Three Essays on the Theory of Sexuality.* Translated by James Strachey. New York: Basic Books, 1962.

Friedman, Manis. *Doesn't Anyone Blush Anymore? Love, Marriage, and the Art of Intimacy.* Minneapolis: Image, 1997.

Friedrich, Paul. *The Meaning of Aphrodite.* Chicago: University of Chicago Press, 1978.

Fromm, Erich. *The Art of Loving.* New York: Harper & Brothers, 1956.

Frye, Roland Mushat. "The Teachings of Classical Puritanism on Conjugal Love." *Studies in the Renaissance* 2 (1955): 148-159.

Frymer-Kensky, Tikva. *In the Wake of the Goddesses: Woman, Culture, and the Biblical Transformation of Pagan Myth.* New York: Free Press, 1992.

Fuchs, Eric. *Sexual Desire and Love.* New York: Seabury, 1983.

Furnish, V. P. *The Moral Teaching of Paul.* Nashville: Abingdon, 1979.

Gallagher, Maggie. *The Abolition of Marriage: How We Destroy Lasting Love.* Washington, D.C.: Regnery, 1996.

_______. *Enemies of Eros: How the Sexual Revolution Is Killing Family, Marriage, and Sex, and What We Can Do About It.* Chicago: Bonus, 1989.

Gardella, Peter. *Innocent Ecstasy: How Christianity Gave America an Ethic of Sexual Pleasure.* New York: Oxford University Press, 1985.

Gardner, Christine J. "Tangled in the Worst of the Web: What Internet Porn Did to One Pastor, His Wife, His Ministry, Their Life." *Christianity Today,* March 5, 2001, 42-49.

Gardner, Tim Alan. *Sacred Sex: A Spiritual Celebration of Oneness in Marriage.* Colorado Springs: WaterBrook, 2002.

Garland, Diana S., and David E. Garland. *Beyond Companionship: Christians in Marriage.* Eugene, Ore.: Wipf & Stock, 2003.

Gledhill, Tom. *The Message of the Song of Songs.* Downers Grove, Ill.: InterVarsity Press, 1994.

Gerber, Aaron H. *Biblical Attitudes on Human Sexuality.* Great Neck, N.Y.: Todd & Honeywell, 1982.

Giddens, Anthony. *The Transformation of Intimacy: Sexuality, Love, and Eroticism in Modern Societies.* Stanford, Calif.: Stanford University Press, 1992.

Gilder, George. *Sexual Suicide.* New York: Bantam, 1973.

Glaser, Chris. *Coming Out as Sacrament.* Louisville: Westminster/John Knox, 1998.

Glickman, S. Craig. *A Song for Lovers.* Downers Grove, Ill.: InterVarsity Press, 1976.

Goergen, Donald. *The Sexual Celibate.* New York: Doubleday, 1979.

Goldenberg, Naomi R. *Changing of the Gods: Feminism and the End of Traditional Religions.* Boston: Beacon, 1979.

Goldingay, John. "The Bible and Sexuality." *Scottish Journal of Theology* 39 (1986): 175-188.

Goodstein, Laurie. "Decades of Damage." *New York Times,* January 12, 2003.

_______. "Trail of Pain in Church Crisis Leads to Nearly Every Diocese." *New York Times,* January 12, 2003.

Gray, John. *Mars and Venus in the Bedroom: A Guide to Lasting Romance and Passion.* New York: Harper-Collins, 2001.

"Great Sex: Reclaiming a Christian Sexual Ethic." *Christianity Today,* October 2, 1987, 25-27.

Grelot, P. *Man and Wife in Scripture.* New York: Herder & Herder, 1964.

Grenz, Stanley J. *Sexual Ethics: An Evangelical Perspective.* Louisville: Westminster/John Knox, 1997.

_______. "What Is Sex For?" *Christianity Today*, June 12, 1987, 22-23.

Grossman, Cathy Lynn. "What's Ahead for the Church: American Cardinals Meet at the Vatican: Narrowly Focused Summit on Sex Abuse Scandal Raises Hopes for Greater Change." *USA Today*. April 22, 2002.

Groothuis, Rebecca Merrill. *Good News for Women: A Biblical Picture of Gender Equality*. Grand Rapids, Mich.: Baker, 1997.

Gudorf, Christine E. *Body, Sex, and Pleasure: Reconstructing Christian Sexual Ethics*. Cleveland: Pilgrim, 1994.

Guernsey, Dennis. *Thoroughly Married*. Waco, Tex.: Word, 1975.

Harris, Hamil R. "Baptist Call for Submissive Wives Criticized." *Washington Post*, June 12, 1998.

Harris, Joshua. *Boy Meets Girl: Say Hello to Courtship*. Sisters, Ore.: Multnomah, 2000.

_______. *I Kissed Dating Goodbye*. Introduction by Rebecca St. James. Sisters, Ore.: Multnomah, 1997.

Hart, Archibald D., Catherine Hart Weber, and Debra Taylor. *The Secrets of Eve: Understanding the Mystery of Female Sexuality*. Nashville: Word, 1998.

_______. *The Sexual Man: Masculinity Without Guilt*. Dallas: Word, 1994.

Hart, Thomas N. *Living Happily Ever After: Toward a Theology of Christian Marriage*. New York: Paulist, 1979.

Hays, Richard B. "Relations Natural and Unnatural: A Response to John Boswell's Exegesis of Romans 1." *Journal of Religious Ethics* 14 (Spring 1986): 184-215.

Hefling, Charles, ed. *Our Selves, Our Souls and Bodies: Sexuality and the Household of God*. Cambridge, Mass.: Cowley, 1996.

Heimbach, Daniel R. *An Assessment of Pagan Sexual Morality*. Portland: Theological Exchange Network, 2000. Available online at: www.cbmw.org/html/Heimbach%20pa.

_______. "The Bible in the Moral War over the Rejection of Homosexuality by the Military Services: A View from Inside the Pentagon." *Faith and Mission* 11 (Spring 1994): 48-63. Also in *Premise* 2 (August 27, 1995): 1-20.

_______. *The Bible in the Moral War over the Rejection of Homosexuality by the Military Services: A View from Inside the Pentagon*. Portland: Theological Exchange Network, 1994.

_______. "Biblical Considerations Relevant to Homosexuals in the Military: A View from Inside the Pentagon." In *God and Caesar*. Edited by Michael Bauman and David Hall. Camp Hill, Pa.: Christian Publications, 1994, 217-240.

_______, et al. *Colorado Statement on Biblical Sexual Morality*. Colorado Springs: Focus on the Family, 2002. Available online at: www.family.org/.

_______. *Counterfeit Sexuality: Defending Biblical Sexual Morality from Four Threats to God's Design for Biblical Sexual Behavior*. Colorado Springs: Focus on the Family, 2003.

_______. "Eternally Fixed Sexual Being for an Age of Plastic Sexuality." Council for Biblical Manhood and Womanhood. July 2000. Available online at: www.cbmw.org/.

_______. "The Gay Rights Movement: An Agenda to Deconstruct the Traditional Family." *Faith and Mission* 12 (Spring 1995): 60-71.

_______. "Intentional Design: What the Bible Says About Homosexuality." *Home Life* 50 (1997): 27.

_______. "Pagan Sexuality at the Center of the Contemporary Moral Crisis." *Faith and Mission* 17 (Spring 2000): 15-31. Available online at: www.cbmw.org/html/Heimbach%20paper.htm.

_______. *Pagan Sexuality at the Center of the Contemporary Moral Crisis.* Wake Forest, N.C.: Southeastern Baptist Theological Seminary, 2001.

_______. "Pagan Sexual Morality: A Rising New Challenge." *Tedsbridge* (Fall 2001): 14-15.

_______. "Resolution on Domestic Partner Benefits." Southern Baptist Convention, June 19, 1997.

_______. "Resolution on Homosexual Marriage." Southern Baptist Convention, June 13, 1996.

_______. "Same-Sex Marriage and the Traditional Family: Is It a Threat?" *News and Observer* (Raleigh, N.C.), April 4, 1996.

_______. "The Unchangeable Difference: Eternally Fixed Sexual Identity for an Age of Plastic Sexuality." In *Biblical Foundations for Manhood and Womanhood.* Edited by Wayne Grudem. Wheaton, Ill.: Crossway, 2002, 275-289.

Henry, Carl F. H. *Christian Personal Ethics.* Grand Rapids, Mich.: Eerdmans, 1957. See pages: 88, 158, 183, 204, 239, 243, 260, 274, 299, 305-307, 312-313, 328-330, 353, 425, 427-428, 435-436.

_______. *Twilight of a Great Civilization.* Westchester, Ill.: Crossway, 1988.

Heth, William A., and Gordon J. Wenham. *Jesus and Divorce: The Problem with the Evangelical Consensus.* Nashville: Thomas Nelson, 1985.

Heyward, Carter. *Touching Our Strength: The Erotic as Power and the Love of God.* San Francisco: Harper, 1989.

Himmelfarb, Gertrude. *The De-Moralization of Society: From Victorian Virtues to Modern Values.* New York: Knopf, 1995.

Hinkle, Don. "CBF Homosexual Stance Ignites Controversy over Group's Direction." *SBC Baptist Press.* 30 October 2000.

Holmes, Urban T. "The Sexuality of God." In *Male and Female: Christian Approaches to Sexuality.* Edited by Ruth Tiffany Barnhouse and Urban T. Holmes. New York: Seabury, 1976.

Hoque, Richard. *Sex, Satan, and Jesus.* Nashville: Broadman & Holman, 1982.

Horner, Tom. *Sex in the Bible.* Rutland, Vt.: Charles E. Tuttle, 1974.

House, Wayne H., ed. *Divorce and Remarriage: Four Christian Views.* Downers Grove, Ill.: InterVarsity Press, 1990.

Hsu, Albert Y. *Singles at the Crossroads: A Fresh Perspective on Christian Singles.* Downers Grove, Ill.: InterVarsity Press, 1997.

Huff, Deborah W. "What Price Promiscuity?" *Fundamentalist Journal,* November 1, 1982, 50-51, 62.

Hugenberger, Gordon P. *Marriage as a Covenant.* Grand Rapids, Mich.: Baker, 1998.

Hughes, R. Kent. "Discipline of Purity." In *Disciplines of a Godly Man*. Wheaton, Ill.: Crossway, 1991, 21-31.

Human Sexuality from a Christian Perspective. Church of the Brethren, 1983. Available online at: www. brethren.org/ac/ac_statements/83Human Sexuality.htm.

Hunt, Morton M. *The Natural History of Love*. New York: Doubleday, 1994.

Hurtado, Larry W., ed. *Goddess in Religion and Modern Debate*. Atlanta: Scholars Press, 1990.

Hybels, Bill, and Rob Wilkins. *Tender Love*. Chicago: Moody, 1993.

Irigaray, Luce. *An Ethics of Sexual Difference*. Translated by Carolyn Burke and Gillian C. Gill. Ithaca, N.Y. Cornell University Press, 1993.

"Irreconcilable Differences? Excerpts from the Majority Report of the PC(USA)'s Special Committee on Human Sexuality." *Christianity Today*, April 29, 1991, 38.

Jastrow, Joseph. *Freud: His Dream and Sex Theories*. New York: World, 1932.

Jenkins, Jerry. *Hedges: Loving Your Marriage Enough to Protect It*. Brentwood, Tenn.: Wolgemuth & Hyatt, 1989.

Jensen, Joseph. "Human Sexuality in the Scriptures." In *Human Sexuality and Personhood*. Chicago: Franciscan Herald, 1981.

Jerome. *Post-Nicene Fathers*. VI, 29-30. 71, 77, 345.

Jersild, Paul T. *Spirit Ethics: Scripture and the Moral Life*. Minneapolis: Fortress, 1999.

Jones, Peter. *Spirit Wars: Pagan Revival in Christian America*. Mukilteo, Wash.: WinePress, 1997.

Jones, Stanton L., and Brenna B. Jones. *How and When to Tell Your Children About Sex*. Colorado Springs: NavPress, 1993.

_______, and Don E. Workman. "Homosexuality: The Behavioral Sciences and the Church." *Journal of Psychology and Theology* 17 (1989): 213-25.

Jones, Thomas. *Sex and Love: When You're Single Again*. Nashville: Thomas Nelson, 1990.

Jung, Carl G. *Aion*. In *Collected Works*. Vol. 9:2. Translated by R. F. C. Hull. London: Routledge & Kegan Paul, 1959.

_______. *Memories, Dreams, Reflections*. Edited by Aniela Jaffe. Translated by Richard and Clara Winston. New York: Pantheon, 1963.

Jung, Patricia Beattie, and Joseph Andrew Coray, eds. *Sexual Diversity and Catholicism: Toward the Development of Moral Theology*. Collegeville, Minn.: Liturgical Press, 2001.

_______, and Ralph F. Smith. *Heterosexism: An Ethical Challenge*. Albany, N.Y. State University of New York Press, 1993.

Kameny, Franklin E. "Deconstructing the Traditional Family." *The World and I*, October 1993, 383-395.

Kansas City Declaration on Marriage. A Southern Baptist forum on marriage, November 12, 2003. Available online at: www.faithandfamily.com.

Kassian, Mary A. *The Feminist Gospel: The Movement to Unite Feminism with the Church*. Wheaton, Ill.: Crossway, 1992.

Kelsey, Morton T., and Barbara Kelsey. *Sacrament of Sexuality: The Spirituality and Psychology of Sex*. Rockport, Mass.: Element, 1986.

Kerr, John. *A Most Dangerous Method: The Story of Jung, Freud, and Sabina Spielrein*. New York: Vintage, 1993.

Kinsey, Alfred C., Wardell B. Pomeroy, Clyde E. Martin, and Paul H. Gebhard. *Sexual Behavior in the Human Female*. Philadelphia: Saunders, 1953.

_______, Wardell B. Pomeroy and Clyde E. Martin. *Sexual Behavior in the Human Male*. Philadelphia: Saunders, 1948.

Klein, Leonard. "Lutherans in Sexual Commotion." *First Things* 43 (May 1994): 31-38.

Kloehn, Steve. "Baptists Say Wives Should Submit." *Chicago Tribune*, June 10, 1998.

Kosnik, Anthony. *Human Sexuality: New Directions in American Catholic Thought*. New York: Paulist, 1977.

Krauthammer, Charles. "God and Sex at Yale." *Weekly Standard*, September 29, 1997, 11-12.

Kuala Lumpur Statement on Human Sexuality. 2nd Anglican Encounter in the South, February 10-15, 1997. Available online at: www.episcopalian.org/efac/articles/kuala.htm.

Kuyper, Abraham. *Calvinism: Six Lectures Delivered at the Theological Seminary at Princeton*. New York: Revell, 1899.

Laaser, Mark. *Faithful and True: Sexual Integrity in a Fallen World*. Grand Rapids, Mich.: Zondervan, 1996.

Labash, Matt. "Among the Pornographers." *Weekly Standard*, September 21, 1998, 20-25.

LaHaye, Tim, and Beverly LaHaye. *The Act of Marriage*. Grand Rapids, Mich.: Zondervan, 1976.

Lamm, Maurice. *The Jewish Way in Love and Marriage*. New York: HarperCollins, 1980.

Land, Richard, and John Perry. *For Faith and Family: Changing America by Strengthening the Family*. Nashville: Broadman & Holman, 2002.

Laumann, Edward O., John H. Gagnon, Robert T. Michael, and Stuart Michaels. *The Social Organization of Sexuality: Sexual Practices in the United States*. Chicago: University of Chicago Press, 1994.

Lavoie, Denise. "Boston Priests Probably Abused 1,000, Report Says." Associated Press. *News and Observer* (Raleigh, N.C.), July 24, 2003.

Lea, Henry C. *The History of Sacerdotal Celibacy in the Christian Church*. New York: Russell & Russell, 1957.

Lebacqz, Karen. "Appropriate Vulnerability: A Sexual Ethic for Singles." *Christian Century*, May 6, 1987, 435-438.

_______. "Difference or Defect: Intersexuality and the Politics of Difference." *Annual of the Society of Christian Ethics* 17 (1997): 213-229.

_______. "Love Your Enemy: Sex, Power, and Christian Ethics." *Annual of the Society of Christian Ethics* (1990): 3-23.

_______, and Deborah Blake. "Safe Sex and Lost Love." *Religious Education* 83 (Spring 1988): 201-210.

_______. "Sexual Pastoral Ethics: A Theological View." *Dialog* 32 (Winter 1993): 33-36.

Lee, Victoria. *Soulful Sex*. Berkeley, Calif.: Conari, 1996.

Leites, Edmund. *The Puritan Conscience and Modern Sexuality*. New Haven, Conn.: Yale University Press, 1986.

Leo, John. "A Gay Culture in the Church." *U.S. News and World Report* (June 3, 2002): 16.

Levin, Robert J., and Amy Levin. "Sexual Pleasure: The Surprising Preferences of 100,000 Women." *Redbook,* September 1975, 51-58.

Levine, Judith. *Harmful to Minors: The Perils of Protecting Children from Sex*. Minneapolis: University of Minnesota Press, 2002.

Lewis, C. S. *The Allegory of Love: A Study in Medieval Tradition*. New York: Oxford University Press, 1958.

_______. *The Four Loves*. New York: Harcourt Brace Jovanovich, 1961.

_______. *Miracles: A Preliminary Study*. New York: Macmillan, 1947.

_______. "Priestesses in the Church?" In *God in the Dock: Essays on Theology and Ethics*. Edited by Walter Hooper. Grand Rapids, Mich.: Eerdmans, 1970, 237-238.

_______. *Surprised by Joy: The Shape of My Early Life*. New York: Harcourt, Brace, 1955.

Lewis, Robert. *Real Family Values: Leading Your Family into the Twenty-first Century with Clarity and Conviction*. Sisters, Ore.: Multnomah, 2000.

Lindsell, Harold. *The World, the Flesh, and the Devil*. Washington, D.C.: Canon, 1974.

Lorenzo, Rafael. *A Sacred Sex Devotional*. Rochester, Vt.: Inner Traditions, 2000.

Luther, Martin. *Luther's Works*. Edited by Jaroslav Pelikan, et al. St. Louis: Concordia, 1958–1971. 1:56, 71-72, 83-84, 92, 104-105, 115-140, 163-169, 176, 198-199, 203, 237-238; 2:29-31, 356, 377; 9:200-251; 14:288; 15:130-132; 25:13; 27:67-69, 281-289; 28:5-56; 38:154-155; 52:259-273; 54:161, 324, 422.

Mack, Dana, and David Blankenhorn. *The Book of Marriage: The Wisest Answers to the Toughest Questions*. Grand Rapids, Mich.: Eerdmans, 2001.

Mackin, Theodore. *The Marital Sacrament*. New York: Paulist, 1989.

Magnuson, Roger J. *Are Gay Rights Right?* Portland: Multnomah, 1990.

Mahaney, C. J. "A Song of Joy: Sexual Intimacy in Marriage." In *Building Strong Families*. Edited by Dennis Rainey. Wheaton, Ill.: Crossway, 2002.

Mann, A. T. *Sacred Sexuality*. Boston: Element, 1995.

Mansfield, Harvey. "A Nation of Consenting Adults." *Weekly Standard,* November 16, 1998, 35-37.

Manson, Mike. *The Mystery of Marriage*. Portland: Multnomah, 1985.

Marshner, Connie. *Decent Exposure: How to Teach Your Children About Sex*. Brentwood, Tenn.: Wolgemuth & Hyatt, 1988.

Maslow, Abraham H. "Self-Esteem (Dominance-Feeling) and Sexuality in Women." In *Sexual Behavior and Personality Characteristics*. Edited by M. F. DeMartino. New York: Grove, 1966.

_______. *Toward a Psychology of Being.* New York: D. Van Nostrand, 1968.

Masters, William H., and Virginia E. Johnson. *Homosexuality in Perspective.* New York: Bantam, 1982.

_______. *The Pleasure Bond: A New Look at Sexuality and Commitment.* Boston: Little, Brown, 1970.

Mattox, William R., Jr. "What's Marriage Got to Do with It? Good Sex Comes to Those Who Wait." *Family Policy* 6, no. 6 (February 1994).

Maudlin, Michael G. "Life, Death, and Sex." *Christianity Today,* March 9, 1992, 21.

Maynard, Roy. "Burned Out." *World* (September 18, 1999): 24-26.

McArthur, John J., Jr. *On Divorce.* Chicago: Moody, 1985.

McCance, Dawne. "Understandings of 'the Goddess' in Contemporary Feminist Scholarship." In *Goddess in Religion and Modern Debate.* Edited by Larry W. Hurtado. Atlanta: Scholars Press, 1990.

McDowell, Josh, and Dick Day. "Is God a Cosmic Killjoy?" *Worldwide Challenge,* June 1987, 76-78.

_______. "Helping Your Teen Say No to Sex." *Focus on the Family,* February 1989, 2-6.

McFague, Sallie. *The Body of God.* Minneapolis: Fortress, 1993.

McMorris, Christine. "Treading Carefully: The Gay Press." *Religion in the News* 5 (Summer 2002): 12-13, 25.

A Message on Sexuality: Some Common Convictions. Evangelical Lutheran Church in America, Division for Church and Society, November 9, 1996. Available online at: www.elca.org/dcs/sexuality.html.

Michael, Robert T., John H. Gagnon, Edward O. Laumann, and Gina Bari Kolata. *Sex in America: A Definitive Survey.* Boston: Little, Brown, 1994.

Miles, Herbert J. *Sexual Happiness in Marriage.* Grand Rapids, Mich.: Zondervan, 1967.

_______. *Sexual Understanding Before Marriage.* Grand Rapids, Mich.: Zondervan, 1957.

Moberly, Elizabeth. *Homosexuality: A New Christian Ethic.* Greenwood, S.C.: Attic, 1983.

Mohler, R. Albert. "In Condoms We Trust: Jane Fonda Rides to the Rescue." *Fidelitas.* Available online at: www.sbts.edu/mohler/Fidelitas.

Mollenkott, Virginia Ramey. "A Call to Subversion." *The Other Side,* July-August 1999, 14-19.

_______. "An Evangelical Feminist Confronts the Goddess." *Christian Century,* October 20, 1982, 1043-1046.

_______. "Gender Diversity and Christian Community." *The Other Side,* May and June 2001, 24-27.

_______. *Godding: Human Responsibility in the Bible.* New York: Crossroad, 1987.

_______. *Omnigender: A Trans-Religious Approach.* Cleveland: Pilgrim, 2001.

_______. *Sensuous Spirituality: Out from Fundamentalism.* New York: Crossroad, 1992.

Monti, Joseph. *Arguing About Sex: The Rhetoric of Christian Sexual Morality.* Albany, N.Y.: State University of New York Press, 1995.

Moore, James. *Sexuality and Marriage.* Minneapolis: Augsburg, 1987.

Moore, Thomas. *The Soul of Sex: Cultivating Life as an Act of Love.* New York: HarperCollins, 1998.

Morgan, Elisa. *I'm Tired of Waiting!* Wheaton, Ill.: Victor, 1989.

Morgan, Robin. *Going Too Far: The Personal Chronicle of a Feminist.* New York: Random House, 1977.

Moynihan, Daniel Patrick. "Defining Deviancy Down." *The American Scholar* 62 (1993): 17-30.

Murray, Ian H. *Evangelicalism Divided.* Carlisle, Pa.: Banner of Truth, 2000.

Murray, John. *Principles of Conduct: Aspects of Biblical Ethics.* Grand Rapids, Mich.: Eerdmans, 1957.

Morrison, Eleanor S., and Vera Borosage. *Human Sexuality: Contemporary Perspectives.* Palo Alto, Calif.: Mayfield, 1977.

Nelson, James B. *Between Two Gardens: Reflections on Sexuality and Religious Experience.* New York: Pilgrim, 1983.

_______. *Body Theology.* Louisville: Westminster/John Knox, 1992.

_______. *Embodyment: An Approach to Sexuality and Christian Theology.* Minneapolis: Augsburg, 1978.

_______. *The Intimate Connection: Male Sexuality, Masculine Spirituality.* Philadelphia: Westminster, 1988.

_______. *Moral Nexus: Ethics of Christian Identity and Community.* Philadelphia: Westminster, 1971.

_______. "Reuniting Sexuality and Spirituality." *Christian Century,* February 25, 1987, 187-190.

_______, and Sandra P. Longfellow, eds. *Sexuality and the Sacred: Sources for Theological Reflection.* Louisville: Westminster/John Knox, 1994.

Neuer, Werner. *Man and Woman in Christian Perspective.* Translated by Gordon J. Wenham. London: Hodder & Stoughton, 1990.

Neuhaus, Richard John. "Sexual and Related Disorders." *First Things* 131 (March 2003): 768-774.

Niebuhr, Gustav. "Southern Baptists Declare Wife Should Submit to Her Husband." *New York Times,* June 10, 1998.

Nissinen, Martti. *Homoeroticism in the Biblical World: A Historical Perspective.* Minneapolis: Fortress, 1998.

No Apologies: The Truth About Life, Love and Sex. Wheaton, Ill.: Tyndale, 1999.

Northup, Leslie A. *Ritualizing Women: Patterns of Spirituality.* Cleveland: Pilgrim, 1997.

Nyren, Anders. *Agape and Eros.* Translated by Philip S. Watson. Philadelphia: Westminster, 1953.

O'Connell, Anthony, Richard Land, and Kevin Mannoia. "A Christian Declaration on Marriage." A joint statement by the National Conference of Catholic Bishops, the Southern Baptist Convention, and the National Association of Evangelicals, November 14, 2000. Available online at: www.ncccusa.org/. Also available online at: www.smartmarriages.com/christian.declaration.html.

Oden, Thomas C. "Mainstreaming the Mainline." *Christianity Today,* August 7, 2000, 59, 61.

_______. *Requiem: A Lament in Three Movements.* Nashville: Abingdon, 1995.

O'Donovan, Oliver. "Transsexualism and Christian Marriage." *Journal of Religious Ethics* 11 (Spring 1983): 135-162.

Oliver, Mary Anne McPherson. *Conjugal Spirituality: The Primacy of Mutual Love in Christian Tradition.* Kansas City: Sheed & Ward, 1994.

Olsen, Kathy. "Out of Season." *The Other Side,* January-February 2001, 21-23.

Olthuis, James H. *I Pledge You My Troth: Marriage, Family, Friendship.* San Francisco: HarperSanFrancisco, 1975.

O'Neil, Nena, and George O'Neil. *Open Marriage: A New Life Style for Couples.* New York: Avon, 1972.

Ostling, Richard N. "Keating Takes a Parting Shot: Resigns from Lay Catholic Board." Associated Press. *News and Observer* (Raleigh, N.C.), June 17, 2003.

Packard, Vance. *The Sexual Wilderness.* New York: David McKay, 1968.

Packer, J. I. "Marriage and Family in Puritan Thought." In *A Quest for Godliness: The Puritan Vision of the Christian Life.* Wheaton, Ill.: Crossway, 1990, 259-273.

Pagels, Elaine. *Adam, Eve, and the Serpent.* New York: Random House, 1988.

Pamer, Nan. *Modesty: A Fresh Look at a Biblical Principle.* Hazelwood, Mo.: Word Aflame, 1990.

Paris, Ginette. *Pagan Grace.* Dallas: Spring, 1990.

_______. *Pagan Meditations.* Dallas: Spring, 1986.

_______. *La Renaissance d'Aphrodite.* Montreal: Boreal Express, 1985.

_______. *The Sacrament of Abortion.* Dallas: Spring, 1992.

Patterson, Paige. *Song of Solomon.* Chicago: Moody, 1986.

Patton, Michael S. "Masturbation from Judaism to Victorianism." *Journal of Religion and Health* 24 (Summer 1985): 133-146.

Payne, Leanne. *The Broken Image: Restoring Personal Wholeness Through Healing Prayer.* Grand Rapids, Mich.: Baker, 1995.

_______. *Crisis in Masculinity.* Grand Rapids, Mich.: Baker, 1995.

_______. *The Healing of the Homosexual.* Wheaton, Ill.: Crossway, 1984.

Peale, Norman Vincent. *Sin, Sex and Self-Control: A Practical, Common-Sense, Inspiring Challenge to the Individual.* Carmel, N.Y.: Guideposts, 1965.

Peterson, Karen S. "Cohabitating Is Not the Same as Commitment." *USA Today.* August 7, 2002.

Phipps, William E. *Recovering Biblical Sensuousness.* Philadelphia: Westminster, 1975.

Piper, John, and Wayne Grudem, eds. *Recovering Biblical Manhood and Womanhood: A Response to Evangelical Feminism.* Wheaton, Ill.: Crossway, 1991.

_______. *What's the Difference? Manhood and Womanhood Defined According to the Bible.* Foreword by Elisabeth Elliot. Wheaton, Ill.: Crossway, 1990.

Piper, Otto A. *The Biblical View of Sex and Marriage.* New York: Scribner's, 1960.

_______. *The Christian Interpretation of Sex.* New York: Scribner's, 1941.

Pippin, Tina. "Jezebel Re-Vamped." *Semeia* 69/70 (1995): 221-233.

_______, and Susan Henking, eds. "Alter(ed) Sexualities: Bringing Lesbian and Gay Studies to the Religious Classroom." *Spotlight on Teaching* 4 (November 1996): 1.

"A Place to Stand: A Call to Action." American Anglican Council, October 7-9, 2003. Available online at: www.americananglican.org/petitions/Petition.cfm?petitionID=8.

Plowman, Edward E. "United Methodists: The View From Portland." *Christianity Today,* June 18, 1976, 35.

Popenoe, David, Jean Bethke Elshtain, and David Blankenhorn, eds. *Promises to Keep: Decline and Renewal of Marriage in America.* Lanham, Md.: Rowman & Littlefield, 1996.

Posner, Richard A. *A Guide to America's Sex Laws.* Chicago: University of Chicago Press, 1998.

_______. *Sex and Reason.* Cambridge, Mass.: Harvard University Press, 1992.

Prokes, Mary Timothy. *Toward a Theology of the Body.* Grand Rapids, Mich.: Eerdmans, 1996.

"Purity Without Modesty?" *Breakaway,* September 2001, 12.

Ramsey, Paul. "The Covenant of Marriage and Right Means." In *The Essential Paul Ramsey: A Collection.* Edited by William Werpehowski and Stephen D. Crocco. New Haven, Conn.: Yale University Press, 1995, 137-150.

_______. *One Flesh: A Christian View of Sex Within, Outside and Before Marriage.* Bramcote, England: Grove, 1975.

"The RE-Imagining Conference." *American Family Association.* April 1994.

Reisman, Judith A., and Edward W. Eichel. *Kinsey, Sex, and Fraud: The Indoctrination of a People.* Lafayette, La.: Lochinvar-Huntington, 1990.

"Religious Declaration on Human Sexuality." Mastering Life Ministries, Fall 2000. Available online at: www.MasteringLife.org; also www.gospelcom.net/mlm/declaration/declaration.htm.

"Religious Declaration on Sexual Morality, Justice, and Healing." Sexuality Information and Education Council of the United States, January 18, 2000. Available online at: www.religiousinstitute.org/declaration.html.

"Resolution 1.10: Human Sexuality." International Anglican Communion, 1998 Lambeth Conference, August 5, 1998. Available online at: www.anglicancommunion. org/lambeth/1/sect1rpt.html.

"Resolution Calling for Dialogue on Human Sexuality." American Baptist Churches, USA, June 1993. Available online at: www.abc-usa.org/resources/resol/sexual.htm.

"Resolution 'Calling on UCC Congregations to Covenant as Open and Affirming.'" United Church of Christ, 1985. Available online at: www.ucc.org/men/open.htm.

"A Resolution Regarding Christian Sexual Ethics." Reformed Episcopal Church, May 23, 1990. Available online at: rechurch.org/sex.html.

Rice, Philip F. *Human Sexuality.* Madison, Wis.: Brown & Benchmark, 1988.

Rogers, Carl R. *Becoming Partners: Marriage and Its Alternatives.* New York: Delacorte, 1972.

_______. *A Way of Being*. Boston: Houghton Mifflin, 1980.

Rosellini, Lynn. "Sexual Desire: Whether It's Dull Appetite or Ravenous Hunger, Millions of Americans Are Unhappy with Their Intimate Lives." *U.S. News and World Report* (July 6, 1992): 61-66.

Rosenau, Douglas E. *A Celebration of Sex*. Nashville: Thomas Nelson, 1994.

Rougemont, Denis de. *Love in the Western World*. Translated by Montgomery Belgion. New York: Pantheon, 1956.

Rubin, Lillian B. *Erotic Wars: What Happened to the Sexual Revolution?* New York: Farrar, Straus, & Giroux, 1990.

Ruether, Rosemary Radford. "Asking the Existential Questions: How My Mind Has Changed." *Christian Century*, April 2, 1980, 374-378.

_______. *Disputed Questions: On Being a Christian*. Nashville: Abingdon, 1982.

_______. *Gaia and God: An Ecofeminist Theology of Earth Healing*. San Francisco: HarperSanFrancisco, 1992.

_______. "Feminist Theology and Spirituality." In *Christian Feminism: Visions of a New Humanity*, edited by Judith Weidman, 9-32. San Francisco: Harper & Row, 1984.

_______. *Introducing Redemption in Christian Feminism*. Cleveland: Pilgrim, 1998.

_______. *Sexism and God-Talk: Toward a Feminist Theology*. Boston: Beacon, 1983.

_______. *Women and Redemption: A Theological History*. Minneapolis: Fortress, 1998.

_______. *Womanguides: Readings Towards a Feminist Theology*. Boston: Beacon, 1985.

_______. *Woman-Church: Theology and Practice of Feminist Liturgical Communities*. San Francisco: Harper & Row, 1985.

Russell, Bertrand. *Marriage and Morals*. New York: Bantam, 1968.

Righter, Walter C. *A Pilgrim's Way: The Personal Story of the Episcopal Bishop Charged with Heresy for Ordaining a Gay Man Who Was in a Committed Relationship*. New York: Alfred A. Knopf, 1998.

Riley, Patrick. *Civilizing Sex: On Chastity and the Common Good*. Edinburgh: T & T Clark, 2000.

Rinehart, Paula. "Losing Our Promiscuity: The Church Has an Unprecedented Chance to Reach a Generation Burned by Commitment-Free Sex." *Christianity Today*, July 10, 2000, 32-39.

Robinson, Haddon. "CT Readers Survey: Sex, Marriage, and Divorce." *Christianity Today*, December 14, 1992, 29-32.

Rogers, Eugene F. *Sexuality and the Christian Body: Their Way into the Triune God*. Oxford: Blackwell, 1999.

Roiphe, Katie. *Last Night in Paradise: Sex and Morals at the Century's End*. New York: Little, Brown, 1997.

Rose, Michael S. *Goodbye, Good Men*. Washington, D.C.: Regnery, 2002.

Rousseau, Mary. *Sex Is Holy*. Boston: Amity, 1986.

Rubin, Lillian B. *Intimate Strangers: Men and Women Together*. New York: Harper & Row, 1983.

Rumburg, Gregory. "Judging Amy." *CCM Magazine,* November 1999, 32-38.

Ryken, Leland. "Were the Puritans Right About Sex?" *Christianity Today,* April 7, 1978, 13-18.

Ryle, J. C. *Holiness.* Old Tappan, N.J.: Revell, 1979.

Sailhamer, John. *Genesis Unbound: A Provocative New Look at the Creation Account.* Sisters, Ore.: Multnomah, 1996.

Salomonsen, Jone. *Enchanted Feminism: Ritual, Gender, and Divinity Among the Reclaiming Witches of San Francisco.* New York: Routledge, 2002.

Sandfort, T. "Pedophilia and the Gay Movement." *Journal of Homosexuality* 13 (Winter 1986–Spring 1987): 89-110.

Satinover, Jeffrey. *Homosexuality and the Politics of Truth.* Grand Rapids, Mich.: Baker, 1996.

Sayers, Dorothy L. *Creed Or Chaos?* London: Methuen, 1947.

Scanzoni, Letha Dawson. "Can Homosexuals Change?" *The Other Side,* January 1984, 12-15.

Schaeffer, Francis A. *The Church at the End of the Twentieth Century.* Downers Grove, Ill.: InterVarsity Press, 1970.

_______. *The Church Before the Watching World.* Downers Grove, Ill.: InterVarsity Press, 1971.

_______. *The Great Evangelical Disaster.* Westchester, Ill.: Crossway, 1984.

_______. *True Spirituality.* Wheaton, Ill.: Tyndale, 1971.

Scharen, Christian Batalden. *Married in the Sight of God: Theology, Ethics, and Church Debates over Homosexuality.* Lanham, Md.: University Press of America, 2000.

Schaumburg, Harry W. *False Intimacy: A Biblical Understanding of Sexual Addiction.* Colorado Springs: NavPress, 1992.

Schmidt, Thomas E. *Straight and Narrow? Compassion and Clarity in the Homosexual Debate.* Downers Grove, Ill.: InterVarsity Press, 1995.

Schueler, G. F. "Why Modesty Is a Virtue." *Ethics* 107 (April 1997): 467-85.

Scroggs, Robin. *The New Testament and Homosexuality.* Philadelphia: Fortress, 1983.

Scruton, R. *Sexual Desire: A Moral Philosophy of the Erotic.* New York: Free Press, 1986.

Sears, Alan, and Craig Osten. *The Homosexual Agenda: Exposing the Principle Threat to Religious Freedom Today.* Nashville: Broadman & Holman, 2003.

See, Carolyn. "The New Chastity." *Cosmopolitan,* November 1985, 382-383.

Seidman, Steven. *Difference Troubles: Queering Social Theory and Sexual Politics.* New York: Cambridge University Press, 1997.

_______. *Embattled Eros: Sexual Politics and Ethics in Contemporary America.* New York: Routledge, 1992.

_______. *The Social Construction of Sexuality.* New York: Norton, 2003.

"Sex in America." *U.S. News and World Report,* October 17, 1994, 74-81.

Shalit, Wendy. *A Return to Modesty: Discovering the Lost Virtue.* New York: Simon & Schuster, 1999.

Shaughnessy, Paul. "The Gay Priest Problem." *Catholic World Report.* November 2000. Available online at: www.catholic.net/article/Igpress/2000-11/essay.html.

Shaw, Miranda. *Passionate Enlightenment.* Princeton, N.J.: Princeton University Press, 1994.

Shedd, Charles W. *Letters to Karen: On Keeping Love in Marriage.* Nashville: Abingdon, 1965.

_______. *Letters to Philip: On How to Treat a Woman.* Garden City, N.Y. Doubleday, 1968.

Silbey, Ramana Das, and Marilena Silbey. *Erotic Worship in American Tantra.* Fairfax, Calif.: 3rd Millennium Magic, 2000.

Simon, William, and Patricia Y. Miller. *The Playboy Report on American Men.* Chicago: Playboy Enterprises, 1979.

Simos, Miriam. "Ethics and Justice in Goddess Religion." *Animia* 7 (Fall 1980): 61-68.

Sirius, R. U. "The New Counterculture." *Time,* November 9, 1998, 89.

Sjoo, Monica, and Barbara Mor. *The Great Cosmic Mother: Rediscovering the Religion of the Earth.* San Francisco: Harper, 1987.

Skinner, David. "What I Saw at Burning Man." *Weekly Standard,* September 27, 1999, 21-24.

Small, Dwight Hervey. *Christian: Celebrate Your Sexuality.* Old Tappan, N.J.: Revell, 1974.

_______. *Design for Christian Marriage.* Old Tappan, N.J.: Spire, 1959.

Smedes, Lewis B. *Sex for Christians: The Limits and Liberties of Sexual Living.* Grand Rapids, Mich.: Eerdmans, 1976, 1994.

Sommers, Christina Hoff. *Who Stole Feminism?: How Women Have Betrayed Women.* New York: Simon & Schuster, 1994.

Sonnenberg, Roger. *Human Sexuality: A Christian Perspective.* St. Louis: Concordia, 1998.

Sorokin, Pitirim A. *The American Sex Revolution.* Boston: Porter Sargent, 1956.

Spong, John Shelby. *Living in Sin? A Bishop Rethinks Human Sexuality.* San Francisco: HarperSanFrancisco, 1988.

_______. *Why Christianity Must Change or Die: A Bishop Speaks to Believers in Exile.* New York: Harper-Collins, 1998.

Spretnak, Charlene, ed. *The Politics of Women's Spirituality.* New York: Doubleday, 1982.

Sproul, R. C. *The Intimate Marriage.* Wheaton, Ill.: Tyndale, 1986.

Stafford, Tim. "Intimacy: Our Latest Sexual Fantasy." *Christianity Today,* January 16, 1987, 24-27.

_______. "Love, Sex and the Whole Person." *Campus Life,* May 1977, 74-78.

_______. "The Next Sexual Revolution: It Will Be an Uphill Battle, but the Church Can and Must Create a Sexual Counterculture." *Christianity Today,* March 9, 1992, 28-29.

_______. *Sexual Chaos.* Downers Grove, Ill.: InterVarsity Press, 1993.

_______. *The Sexual Christian.* Wheaton, Ill.: Victor, 1989.

_______. "Teaching Teens to Say 'No.'" *Worldwide Challenge,* June 1987, 80-82.

Stanley, Scott. *The Heart of Commitment: Cultivating Lifelong Devotion in Marriage.* Nashville: Thomas Nelson, 1998.

Stanton, Glenn T. *Why Marriage Matters: Reasons to Believe in Marriage in Postmodern Society.* Colorado Springs: Pinon, 1997.

Starhawk (Miriam Simos). "Witchcraft and Women's Culture." In *Womanspirit Rising: A Feminist Reader in Religion.* Edited by Carol P. Christ and Judith Plaskow. San Francisco: Harper & Row, 1979.

"Statement on Homosexuality." Minnesota Council of Churches, Social Justice Committee, 1982.

"Statement on Human Sexuality." Anglican Bishops of Canada, October 1997. Available online at: www.wfn. org/1997/11/msg00048.html.

"Statement on Human Sexuality." National Council of the Churches of Christ in the USA, Commission on Family Ministries and Human Sexuality Ministries in Christian Education, November 8, 1991.

Stedman, Rick. *Pure Joy! The Positive Side of Single Sexuality.* Chicago: Moody, 1993.

Stoltenberg, John. *Refusing to Be a Man: Essays on Sex and Justice.* Portland: Breitenbush, 1989.

Stott, John. *Homosexual Partnerships? Why Same-Sex Relationships Are Not a Christian Option.* Downers Grove, Ill.: InterVarsity Press, 1984.

Strauch, Alexander. *Men and Women: Equal Yet Different: A Brief Study of the Biblical Passages on Gender.* Littleton, Colo.: Lewis & Roth, 1999.

Stroka, Barbara. *One Is a Whole Number.* Wheaton, Ill.: Victor, 1978.

Stuart, Elizabeth, and Adrian Thatcher, eds. *Christian Perspectives on Sexuality and Gender.* Grand Rapids, Mich.: Eerdmans, 1996.

Stubbs, Kenneth Ray. *Sacred Orgasms.* Vol. 3 of *The Secret Garden Trilogy.* Tucson: Garden, 1992.

Sumrall, Lester. *Sixty Things God Said About Sex.* Nashville: Thomas Nelson, 1981.

_______. *Ecstasy.* Nashville: Thomas Nelson, 1980.

Symons, Donald. *The Evolution of Human Sexuality.* New York: Oxford University Press, 1979.

Tannahill, Reay. *Sex in History.* New York: Madison, 1982.

Taylor, Rhena. *Single and Whole.* Downers Grove, Ill.: InterVarsity Press, 1984.

Tertullian. *Ante-Nicene Fathers.* III, 293-94, 404, 443; IV, 25, 28-35, 48, 53-58, 63-69.

Thatcher, Adrian, and Elizabeth Stuart, eds. *Christian Perspectives on Sexuality and Gender.* Grand Rapids, Mich.: Eerdmans, 1996.

_______. *Liberating Sex: A Christian Theology.* London: SPCK, 1993.

Thielicke, Helmut. *The Ethics of Sex.* Translated by John W. Doberstein. New York: Harper & Row, 1964.

_______. *Sex.* Vol. 3. of *Theological Ethics.* Translated by John W. Doberstein. Grand Rapids, Mich.: Eerdmans, 1979.

Thomas, Gary. *Sacred Marriage: What If God Designed Marriage to Make Us Holy More than to Make Us Happy?* Grand Rapids, Mich.: Zondervan, 2000.

_______. "Where True Love Waits: How One Woman Dramatically Changed the

Teen Pregnancy Rate in Rhea County, Tennessee." *Christianity Today,* March 1, 1999, 40-45.

Timmerman, Joan. *Sexuality and Spiritual Growth*. New York: Crossroad, 1992.

Trible, Phyllis. *God and the Rhetoric of Sexuality*. Philadelphia: Fortress, 1978.

Trobisch, Walter. *Essays on Love: A HIS Reader on Love and the Christian View of Marriage*. Downers Grove, Ill.: InterVarsity Press, 1968.

_______. *I Loved a Girl*. Manila: The Lutheran Center, 1963.

_______. *I Married You*. New York: Harper & Row, 1971.

_______. *Love Is a Feeling to Be Learned*. Downers Grove, Ill.: Downers Grove, 1971.

Turner, Philip, ed. *Men and Women: Sexual Ethics in Turbulent Times*. Cambridge, Mass.: Cowley, 1989.

_______. "Sex and the Single Life." *First Things* 33 (May 1993): 15-21.

_______. *Sex, Money, and Power: An Essay in Christian Social Ethics*. Cambridge, Mass.: Cowley, 1985.

_______. *Sexual Ethics and the Attack on Traditional Morality*. Cincinnati: Forward Movement, 1988.

Unwin, Joseph Daniel. *Hopousia: Or the Sexual Economic Foundations of a New Society*. London: Allen & Unwin, 1940.

_______. *Sex and Culture*. London: Oxford University Press, 1934.

_______. *Sexual Regulations and Cultural Behavior: An Address Delivered Before the Medical Section of the British Psychological Society*. London: Oxford University Press, 1935.

van Leeuwen, Mary Stewart. "Sexual Values in a Secular Age." *Radix* (November–December): 4-11.

van Leeuwen, Raymond C. "'Be Fruitful and Multiply': Is This a Command or a Blessing?" *Christianity Today,* November 12, 2001, 59-61.

Vanauken, Sheldon. *A Severe Mercy*. New York: Harper & Row, 1977.

Veith, Gene Edward. "The Christian *Cosmo* Girl: Christian Writer Creates a Stir with 'Sex and the Single Evangelical.'" *World,* February 19, 2000, 15-16.

Vincent, M. O. *God, Sex, and You*. Philadelphia: Lippincott, 1971.

Waite, Linda J., Don Browning, William J. Doherty, Maggie Gallagher, Ye Luo, and Scott M. Stanley. "Does Divorce Make People Happy? Findings from a Study of Unhappy Marriages." Institute of American Values. 11 July 2002.

_______, and Maggie Gallagher. *The Case for Marriage: Why Married People Are Happier, Healthier, and Better off Financially*. New York: Doubleday, 2000.

Wallin, Paul. "Religiosity, Sexual Gratification and Marital Satisfaction." *American Psychological Review* 22 (1957): 300-305.

Walsh, Andrew. "Bishops Up Against the Wall." *Religion in the News* 5 (Summer 2002): 8-11.

"The War Within: An Anatomy of Lust." *Leadership Journal*. Fall 1982, 30-48.

"The War Within Continues: An Update on a Christian Leader's Struggle with Lust." *Leadership Journal* (Winter 1988): 24-33.

Warfield, Benjamin B. "Love in the New Testament." *Princeton Theological Review* 16 (1918): 153.

Warren, Scott, and Michael Warren, eds. *Perspectives on Marriage: A Reader*. New York: Oxford University Press, 1993.

Watts, Alan, and Eliot Elisofon. *Erotic Spirituality*. New York: Collier, 1974.

Weber, Christine Lore. *Woman Christ*. San Francisco: Harper & Row, 1987.

Weber, Joseph. "Human Sexuality: The Biblical Witness." *Religion in Life* 49 (Fall 1980): 336-348.

Weidman, Judith, ed. *Christian Feminism: Visions of a New Humanity*. San Francisco: Harper & Row, 1984.

Wells, David F. *No Place for Truth: Or Whatever Happened to Evangelical Theology?* Grand Rapids, Mich.: Eerdmans, 1993.

Wenham, Gordon J. "The Old Testament Attitude to Homosexuality." *Expository Times* 102 (Spring 1991): 359-363.

White, Gayle. "Presbyterians Retain Ban on Homosexual Ordination." *Christianity Today*, August 12, 1996, 57.

White, John. *Eros Defiled: The Christian and Sexual Sin*. Downers Grove, Ill.: InterVarsity Press, 1977.

_______. *Eros Redeemed*. Downers Grove, Ill.: InterVarsity Press, 1993.

White, Kevin. *The First Sexual Revolution: The Emergence of Male Heterosexuality in Modern America*. New York: New York University Press, 1993.

_______. *Sexual Liberation or Sexual License? The American Revolt Against Victorianism*. Chicago: Irvan R. Dee, 2000.

Whitehead, Barbara. "The Failure of Sex Education." *Atlantic Monthly* (October 1994): 55-74.

Whitehead, Evelyn Eaton, and James D. Whitehead. *A Sense of Sexuality: Christian Love and Intimacy*. New York: Doubleday, 1989.

Wier, Terry, and Mark Carruth. *Holy Sex: God's Purpose and Plan for Our Sexuality*. New Kensington, Pa.: Whitaker, 1999.

Williamson, Peter, and Kevin Perrotta. *Christianity Confronts Modernity*. Ann Arbor, Mich.: Servant, 1981.

Wilson, Douglas. *Reforming Marriage*. Moscow, Idaho: Canon, 1995.

Yancey, Philip. "Holy Sex: How It Ravishes Our Souls." *Christianity Today*, October 2003, 46-51.

_______. "The Lost Sex Study." *Christianity Today*, December 12, 1994, 80.

Yoder, John Howard. *Singleness in Ethical and Pastoral Perspective*. Elkhart, Ind.: Associated Mennonite Biblical Seminaries, 1974.

York, Michael. *The Emerging Network: A Sociology of the New Age and the Neo-Pagan Movements*. London: Rowman & Littlefield, 1995.

Young, Ed. *Pure Sex*. Sisters, Ore.: Multnomah, 1997.

Zazas, Peter S. "Cast Out the Evil Man from Your Midst." *Journal of Biblical Literature* 103 (June 1984): 259-261.

_______. "1 Corinthians 6:9ff.: Was Homosexuality Condoned in the Corinthian Church?" *Society of Biblical Literature Seminar Papers* 17 (1979): 205-212.

Zehme, Bill. "The Man Who Loved Women: Of Hef and Heartbreak." *Esquire*. August 1998.

General Index

Scripture Index